HOOVER'S GUIDE TO THE TOP CHICAGO COMPANIES

The Reference Press
Austin, Texas

™

The Reference Press, Inc.

10   9   8   7   6   5   4   3   2   1

Publisher Cataloging-In-Publication Data

Hoover's Guide to the Top Chicago Companies.

Includes indexes.
1. Business enterprises — Directories. 2. Corporations — Directories.
HF3010   338.7

Profiles from *Hoover's Handbooks* are also available on America Online, Bloomberg Financial Network, CompuServe, Dow Jones News Retrieval, eWorld, LEXIS-NEXIS, Microsoft Network, Reuters NewMedia, SandPoint Hoover, and on the Internet at Hoover's Online (http://www.hoovers.com), Pathfinder (http://pathfinder.com), InfoSeek (http://www.infoseek.com), PAWWS Financial Network (http://www.pawws.secapl.com), and infoMarket (http://www.infomkt.ibm.com).

ISBN 1-878753-68-1 trade paper

This book was produced by The Reference Press on Apple Macintosh computers using Adobe's PageMaker software and fonts from its Clearface and Futura families. Cover design is by Daniel Pelavin. Electronic prepress and printing were done by Victor Graphics, Inc. in Baltimore, Maryland. Text paper is Postmark White 60# (manufactured by Union Camp). Cover stock is 10 point, coated one side, film laminated.

US AND WORLD DIRECT SALES
The Reference Press, Inc.
6448 Highway 290 E., Suite E-104
Austin, TX 78723
Phone: 512-454-7778
Fax: 512-454-9401
e-mail: refpress6@aol.com

US BOOKSELLERS AND JOBBERS
Little, Brown and Co.
200 West Street
Waltham, MA 02154
Phone: 800-759-0190
Fax: 617-890-0875

US WHOLESALER ORDERS
Warner Publisher Services
Book Division
9210 King Palm Drive
Tampa, FL 33619
Phone: 800-873-BOOK
Fax: 813-664-8193

EUROPE
William Snyder Publishing
5, Five Mile Drive
Oxford OX2 8HT
England
Phone & fax: +44-(01)86-551-3186
e-mail: 100072.2511@compuserve.com

THE REFERENCE PRESS

The Reference Press Mission Statement

1. To produce business information products and services of the highest quality, accuracy, and readability.

2. To make that information available whenever, wherever, and however our customers want it through mass distribution at affordable prices.

3. To continually expand our range of products and services and our markets for those products and services.

4. To reward our employees, suppliers, and shareholders based on their contributions to the success of our enterprise.

5. To hold to the highest ethical business standards, erring on the side of generosity when in doubt.

ABBREVIATIONS

AFL-CIO – American Federation of Labor and Congress of Industrial Organizations

AMA – American Medical Association

AMEX – American Stock Exchange

ARM – adjustable rate mortgage

ASIC – application-specific integrated circuit

ATM – asynchronous transfer mode

CAD/CAM – computer-aided design/computer-aided manufacturing

CASE – computer-aided software engineering

CD-ROM – compact disc – read-only memory

CEO – chief executive officer

CFO – chief financial officer

CISC – complex instruction set computer

CMOS – complementary metal oxide silicon

COO – chief operating officer

DAT – digital audio tape

DOD – Department of Defense

DOE – Department of Energy

DOS – disk operating system

DOT – Department of Transportation

DRAM – dynamic random-access memory

EPA – Environmental Protection Agency

EPROM – erasable programmable read-only memory

EPS – earnings per share

ESOP – employee stock ownership plan

EU – European Union

EVP – executive vice president

FCC – Federal Communications Commission

FDA – Food and Drug Administration

FDIC – Federal Deposit Insurance Corporation

FPGA – field programmable gate array

FSLIC – Federal Savings and Loan Insurance Corporation

FTC – Federal Trade Commission

FTP – file transfer protocol

GUI – graphical user interface

HMO – health maintenance organization

HR – human resources

HTML – hypertext markup language

IC – integrated circuit

ICC – Interstate Commerce Commission

IPO – initial public offering

IRS – Internal Revenue Service

ISDN – Integrated Services Digital Network

LAN – local-area network

LBO – leveraged buyout

LCD – liquid crystal display

LNG – liquefied natural gas

LP – limited partnership

Ltd. – limited

MIPS – million instructions per second

NAFTA – North American Free Trade Agreement

NASA – National Aeronautics and Space Administration

Nasdaq – National Association of Securities Dealers Automated Quotations

NATO – North Atlantic Treaty Organization

NYSE – New York Stock Exchange

OCR – optical character recognition

OEM – original equipment manufacturer

OPEC – Organization of Petroleum Exporting Countries

OS – operating system

OSHA – Occupational Safety and Health Administration

OTC – over-the-counter

PBX – private branch exchange

PCMCIA – Personal Computer Memory Card International Association

P/E – price-to-earnings ratio

PPO – preferred provider organization

RAM – random-access memory

R&D – research and development

RBOC – Regional Bell Operating Company

REIT – real estate investment trust

RISC – reduced instruction set computer

ROA – return on assets

ROE – return on equity

ROI – return on investment

ROM – read-only memory

S&L – savings and loan

SEC – Securities and Exchange Commission

SEVP – senior executive vice president

SIC – Standard Industrial Classification

SPARC – scalable processor architecture

SVP – senior vice president

VAR – value-added remarketer

VAT – value-added tax

VC – vice chairman

VP – vice president

WAN – wide-area network

www – world wide web

CONTENTS

ABOUT *HOOVER'S GUIDE TO THE TOP CHICAGO COMPANIES*

For a place known as the "Second City," Chicago certainly is first in many categories. Chicago boasts the world's tallest building (the Sears Tower), the busiest airport (O'Hare International), the oldest and largest commodity exchange (Chicago Board of Trade), and, believe it or not, the winningest professional sports team (the Cubs, with over 10,000 victories in franchise history). The "Hog Butcher to the World" is also the world's convention center, home to the nation's doctors and lawyers (both the American Medical Association and the American Bar Association are based there), and a leader in the retailing and insurance industries. It is also the U.S. center of general niche industries, including commercial food preparation equipment (Middleby, Premark, Scotsman, and Whitman) and mattresses (Restonic, Serta, and Spring Air).

Hoover's Guide to the Top Chicago Companies is just one of a series of regional guides produced by The Reference Press. Guides to the top San Francisco Bay area and Texas companies have already been published, and guides to New York and Southern California companies will follow shortly. These books complement our other publications, which include *Hoover's Handbook of American Companies*, *Hoover's Handbook of World Business*, *Hoover's Handbook of Emerging Companies*, *Hoover's Guide to Private Companies*, *Hoover's Guide to Computer Companies*, and *Hoover's MasterList of America's Top 2,500 Employers*, among others. Our company profiles and other information are also available electronically on diskette and CD-ROM and on online services (e.g., America Online, CompuServe, and the Microsoft Network) and the Internet (e.g., Hoover's Online at http://www.hoovers.com).

This book is the product of extensive research. Our first step was to identify the region that we would be examining. For the purposes of this book we consider the Chicago area to include all municipalities in the following 4 metropolitan statistical areas (MSAs): Aurora–Elgin, IL; Chicago, IL; Gary–Hammond, IN; and Joliet, IL. We realize that everyone will have a different concept of what makes up the "Chicago area," but this definition seemed the fairest that we could come up with.

Next, we consulted our extensive database of company information to identify public and private businesses headquartered in the region. We then turned to other sources to look for companies we may have missed, such as the *Crain's Chicago Business* list of leading private companies and other trade publication lists. We contacted all of the companies that were candidates for inclusion in the book to obtain or update our information. Most companies were helpful and cooperative; some were not. For those companies that did not cooperate, we obtained the most reliable information we could find and in some cases made estimates regarding revenue. In all such cases, the revenue figure is marked as an estimate.

Hoover's Guide to the Top Chicago Companies profiles all public companies in the region, all private companies with revenues of over $200 million, and all private companies with revenues of less than $200 million for whom we could compile accurate information. In addition to traditional for-profit companies, we have also included cooperatives (e.g., Ace Hardware), foundations (e.g., The John D. and

Catherine T. MacArthur Foundation), nonprofit organizations (Blue Cross and Blue Shield Association and Rotary International), partnerships (e.g., Arthur Andersen), and universities (e.g., The University of Chicago and Northwestern University). We have included these enterprises because we believe they are as important to driving the region's economy and creating jobs as the for-profit sector.

After determining our universe of Chicago-area businesses, we selected 130 of them for in-depth profiles. These companies range from massive Blue Cross and Blue Shield Association (1994 revenues of $71.4 billion) to tiny PC Quote (1994 revenues of $12.9 million). We profiled 77 of the largest companies in our two-page format, each with up to 10 years of financial data and a separate section on its history. We also included long profiles of a few unique Chicago enterprises with colorful histories (e.g., advertising agency Leo Burnett and brewer G. Heileman). The remainder of the profiles (mostly of interesting or fast-growing companies under $1 billion in sales) are in our one-page format, with up to 6 years of financial data and a shorter history integrated into the overview of the company. In choosing these companies we have tried to represent the full spectrum of Chicago-area businesses. All 615 of the companies in the book have capsule profiles.

This book consists of 5 components:

1. The first section, "Using the Profiles," describes the contents of the profiles and explains the ways in which we gathered and compiled our data.

2. Next we have included "A List-Lover's Compendium," which contains lists of the largest and fastest-growing companies in the book as well as selected lists from other sources to provide you with different viewpoints.

3. The third section of the book contains the 130 in-depth profiles of Chicago-area businesses. The first 77 profiles are in our long, two-page format. The next 53 are in our medium-length, one-page format. The profiles are arranged alphabetically within each section.

4. The next section provides capsule profiles of 615 companies. If an in-depth profile also exists for a company, the page number of that profile is included in the entry for easier reference.

5. The book concludes with 3 indexes: (1) the companies organized by industry groupings, (2) the companies organized by headquarters location, and (3) the main index of the book, containing all the names of brands, companies, and people mentioned in the in-depth profiles.

As always, we hope you find our books useful and informative. We invite your comments via phone (512-454-7778), fax (512-454-9401), mail (6448 Hwy. 290 East, Ste. E-104, Austin, TX 78723), or e-mail (comments@hoovers.com).

The Editors
Austin, Texas
January 1996

Using the Profiles

Organization of the Profiles

The company profiles are presented in either a one-page or two-page format. The two-page profiles contain extensive historical information, in addition to up to 10 years of financial data. The one-page profiles offer a shorter history and up to 6 years of financial data. In both formats the profiles are presented in alphabetical order. This alphabetization is generally word by word, which means that U.S. Robotics precedes USG Corporation. We have shown the full legal name of the enterprise at the top of the page, unless it is too long, in which case you will find it above the address in the Where section of the profile. If a company name is also a person's name, like Arthur Andersen or Leo Burnett, it will be alphabetized under the first name; if a company name starts with initials, like R. R. Donnelley, look for it under the initials (here, RR). All company names (past and present) used in the profiles are indexed in the last index in the book.

Each profile lists the exchange where the company's stock is traded if it is public, the ticker symbol used by the stock exchange, and the company's fiscal year-end. This data can be found at the top left of the second page for two-page profiles and in the upper left corner of the How Much chart for one-page profiles.

The annual financial information contained in most profiles is current through fiscal year-ends occurring as late as June 1995. For certain nonpublic entities, such up-to-date information was not available. In those cases, we have used the most current data we could find. We have included nonfinancial developments, such as officer changes, through December 1995.

Overview

In this section we have tried to give a thumbnail description of the company and what it does. The description will usually include information on the company's strategy, reputation, and ownership. In the one-page profiles we also provide a brief history of the company, including the year of founding and the names of the founders where possible. We recommend that you read this section first.

When

This section, which appears only in the two-page profiles, reflects our belief that every enterprise is the sum of its history, and that you have to know where you came from in order to know where you are going. While some companies have very little historical awareness and were unable to help us much, and other companies are just plain boring, we think the vast majority of the enterprises in the book have colorful backgrounds. When we could find information, we tried to focus on the people who made the enterprise what it is today. We have found these histories to be full of twists and ironies; they can make for some fascinating, quick reading.

Who

Here we list the names of the people who run the company, insofar as space allows. In the case of public companies, we have shown the ages and pay levels of key officers. In some cases the published data are for last year although the company has announced promotions or retirements since year-end. We have tried to show current officers, with their pay for the latest year available. The pay represents cash compensation, including bonuses, but excludes stock option programs. Our best advice is that officers' pay levels are clear indicators of who the board of directors thinks are the most important on the management team.

While companies are free to structure their management titles any way they please, most modern corporations follow standard practices. The ultimate power in any corporation lies with the shareholders, who elect a board of directors, usually including officers or "insiders" as well as individuals from outside the company. The chief officer, the person on whose desk the buck stops, is usually called the chief executive officer (CEO). Normally, he or she is also the chairman of the board. As corporate management has become more complex, it is common for the CEO to have a "right-hand person" who oversees the day-to-day operations of the company, allowing the CEO plenty of time to focus on strategy and long-term issues. This right-hand person is usually designated the chief operating officer (COO) and is often the president of the company. In other cases one person is both chairman and president.

A multitude of other titles exists, including chief financial officer (CFO), chief administrative officer, and vice chairman (VC). We have always tried to include the CFO, the chief legal officer, and the chief personnel or human resources officer. The people named in the profiles are indexed at the back of the book.

Where

Here we include the company's headquarters street address and phone and fax numbers as available. The back of the book includes an index of companies by headquarters locations.

We have also included as much information as we could gather and fit on the geographical distribution of the company's business, including sales and profit data. Note that these profit numbers, like those in the What section below, are usually operating or pretax profits rather than net profits. Operating profits are generally those before financing costs (interest income and payments) and before taxes, which are considered costs attributable to the whole company rather than to one division or part of the world. For this reason the net income figures (in the How Much section) are usually much lower, since they are after interest and taxes. Pretax profits are after interest but before taxes. When sales and operating profits by region were not available or were not appropriate, we have published other measures of geographic diversity. For example, for re-

gional retailers we have listed the number of stores by state.

What

This section lists as many of the company's products, services, brand names, divisions, subsidiaries, and joint ventures as we could fit. We have tried to include all its major lines and all familiar brand names. The nature of this section varies by industry, company, and the amount of information available. If the company publishes sales and profit information by type of business, we have included it. The brand, division, and subsidiary names are listed in the last index in the book.

Key Competitors

In this section we have listed those other companies that compete with the profiled company. This feature is included as a quick way to locate similar companies and compare them. The universe of key competitors includes all public companies and all private companies with sales in excess of $500 million. In a few instances we have identified smaller private companies as key competitors. All the companies in the book are listed by broad industry groups in the first index at the back of the book.

How Much

Here we have tried to present as much data about each enterprise's financial performance as we could compile in the allocated space. While the information varies somewhat from industry to industry and is less complete in the case of private companies that do not release these data (though we have always tried to provide annual sales and employment), the following information is generally present.

A 10-year table (6 years for the one-page profiles), with relevant annualized compound growth rates, covering:

• Fiscal year sales (year-end assets for most financial companies)

- Fiscal year net income (before accounting changes)

- Fiscal year net income as a percent of sales (as a percent of assets for most financial firms)

- Fiscal year earnings per share (EPS) (fully diluted unless italicized)

- Stock price high, low, and close (for the calendar year unless otherwise noted)

- High and low price/earnings ratio (P/E) (for the calendar year unless otherwise noted)

- Fiscal year dividends per share

- Fiscal year-end book value (shareholders' equity per share)

- Fiscal year-end or average number of emyees

All revenue numbers are as reported by the company in its annual report.

The 10-year information on the number of employees (6 years on the one-page profiles) is intended to aid the reader interested in knowing whether a company has a long-term trend of increasing or decreasing employment. As far as we know, we are the only company that publishes this information in print format.

The year at the top of each column in the How Much section is the year in which the company's fiscal year actually ends. Thus, data for a company with a February 28, 1995 year-end are shown in the 1995 column. Stock prices for companies with fiscal year-ends between January and April are for the prior calendar year and are so footnoted on the chart. For companies with fiscal years in May or June, the 1995 stock data are for the 5 or 6 months preceding the fiscal year-end. This fact is also footnoted on the chart.

Key year-end statistics in this section generally show the financial strength of the enterprise, including:

- Debt ratio (total debt as a percent of combined total debt and shareholders' equity)

- Return on equity (net income divided by the average of beginning and ending common shareholders' equity)

- Cash and marketable securities

- Current ratio (ratio of current assets to current liabilities)

- Total long-term debt, including capital lease obligations

- Number of shares of common stock outstanding (less treasury shares)

- Dividend yield (fiscal year dividends per share divided by the calendar year-end closing stock price)

- Dividend payout (fiscal year dividends divided by fiscal year EPS)

- Market value at calendar year-end (calendar year-end closing stock price multiplied by fiscal year-end number of shares outstanding)

- Research and development as a percent of sales, when available (one-page profiles only)

- Advertising as a percent of sales, when available (one-page profiles only)

For financial institutions and insurance companies, we have also included annual sales, equity as a percent of assets, and return on assets in this section.

Per share data have been adjusted for stock splits. The data for some public companies (and private companies with public debt) have been provided to us by Media General Financial Services, Inc. Other public company information was compiled by The Reference Press, which takes full responsibility for the content of this section.

In the case of private companies that do not publicly disclose financial information, we usually did not have access to such standardized data. We have gathered estimates of sales and other statistics from numerous sources; among the most helpful were trade publications such as *Crain's Chicago Business*, *Advertising Age*, and *Forbes*'s list of the largest private companies. ▲

Chicago Economic Outlook

OVERVIEW OF THE CHICAGO ECONOMY AND BUSINESS ENVIRONMENT

By John Schmeltzer

If Chicago-area business owners were to rely upon economic indicators, most would choose to let their businesses coast. After all, the indicators are pointing to a slowing of the Chicago economy along with the rest of the nation.

But don't tell that to area executives. They say they have little fear of inflation or higher interest rates. Even more significantly, many say they see downward trends in both labor costs and the prices of raw materials. Prices aren't going to rise much, but neither are wages.

It's the same mentality that has gripped the former Rust Belt region of the country since the late 1980s, when the rust began flaking off and the region became the engine of the nation's economic recovery.

Don't expect the Chicago economy to head south anytime soon. Like an island, it's still going to do better than most other areas of the country.

There are signs of a slowing economy: fewer than half of the area's executives expect to add workers during 1996. That's due

in part to the auto industry, upon which the Midwest, and the Chicago area, is still heavily dependent. Even though Detroit is the home of the nation's auto industry, many people don't realize that cars have been built in Illinois as far back as the Model T.

Most economists expect employment to grow about 1.8% nationally and in the midwestern region during 1996. But 3 Midwest states, one being Illinois, will likely lag. Experts say they expect job growth in those states to average only 1.4%.

More than 7.5 million people now live in the Chicago region. They make up a workforce of more than 3 million people with a total disposable income of nearly $150 billion. Only the New York and Los Angeles–Long Beach areas have a higher level of disposable income.

Many of the area's largest companies are headquartered in Chicago's suburbs — in fact, over half of the area's largest are there. Fifteen of the largest companies are located along the Tri-State Tollway between Rosemont and Lake Forest, 12 can be found

Total Employment

Area	1976	1986	1992	1993†	Percentage Change 1976–86	1986–93
Chicago	1,247,416	1,149,993	1,096,100	1,087,416	(7.8)	(5.4)
Cook County	2,020,583	2,051,227	2,138,340	2,151,545	1.5	4.9
Collar counties*	430,363	603,559	844,030	871,982	40.2	44.5
Chicago SMSA	2,450,946	2,654,786	2,982,370	3,023,527	8.3	13.9
Illinois	3,664,597	4,034,096	4,291,293	4,299,683	10.1	6.6

† Figures for 1993 are preliminary and subject to revision.
* The collar counties are DuPage, Kane, Lake, McHenry, and Will.

Sources: U. S. Census Bureau, Illinois Department of Employment Security

along the East-West Tollway corridor between Oak Brook and Naperville, while 8 can be found in the northwest suburbs.

Instead of consumer spending being the largest component of the area's economy, businesses will take a larger role as they retool factories and position their businesses for the Information Age. Leading that trend will be Naperville-based Spyglass, Inc., the computer software company that provides World Wide Web access with its Internet browser, Enhanced Mosaic.

Spyglass, along with Motorola, Inc., and U.S. Robotics Corporation, are among the high-tech companies that have become keys to the Chicago economy. While there's no Silicon Valley in the Chicago region, the area's economy is increasingly becoming technology-driven.

Nearly 20% of the 100 largest companies in the Chicago area now say their principal business lies in electronics, computers, or communications technology. That's up nearly 5% in little more than a year.

But unlike many areas of the country, businesses in the Chicago region are heavily diversified. Perhaps as a reflection of the region's roots, over 20% of earnings of Chicago-area companies are derived from manufacturing. Steel used to be a big part of that business. While still an important component of the region's economy, among the major steelmakers only Inland Steel Industries, Inc., is still headquartered in the area.

Only the earnings of the service industry are higher than the manufacturing component — constituting nearly 35% of the

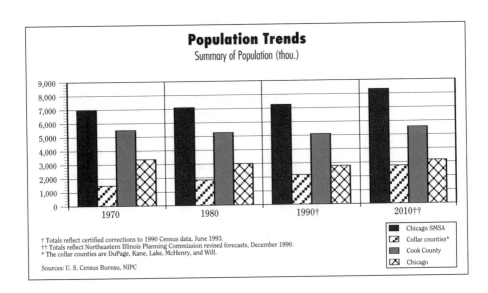

Population Trends
Summary of Population (thou.)

Legend:
- Chicago SMSA
- Collar counties*
- Cook County
- Chicago

† Totals reflect certified corrections to 1990 Census data, June 1993.
†† Totals reflect Northeastern Illinois Planning Commission revised forecasts, December 1990.
* The collar counties are DuPage, Kane, Lake, McHenry, and Will.

Sources: U. S. Census Bureau, NIPC

region's total corporate earnings. Retailing, wholesale distribution, and the transportation and communications industries account for about 25% of the area's earning power.

A list of Chicago's largest employers is a who's who of American business. In addition to Motorola, they include Ameritech Corporation, the regional Baby Bell; Sears, Roebuck and Co., the nation's 2nd largest retailer; Unicom Corporation, parent of Commonwealth Edison Co., one of the country's largest electric utilities; Walgreen Co., the nation's #1 drugstore chain (until the merger of Rite Aid and Revco is completed); First Chicago NBD Corporation, the nation's 7th largest bank; and insurance giant Allstate Corporation.

Even though some important Chicago-area companies don't have a Chicago or suburban Chicago mailing address, their impact upon the region's economy can't be dismissed. Four of the biggest located in downstate Illinois are Peoria-based Caterpillar Inc., Moline-based Deere & Company, Decatur-based Archer-Daniels-Midland Company, and Bloomington-based State Farm Insurance Company.

Food processing continues to play a large role in the region's economy. Whether it is the candy kitchens of Archibald Candy, where Fannie May chocolates are made, or the kitchens of Sara Lee Corporation, the Quaker Oats Company, or McDonald's Corporation, food is the fuel that keeps Chicago running.

Not to be outdone is the biomedical-pharmaceutical industry led by Abbott Laboratories and Baxter International Inc., both of which call the northern Chicago suburbs home. Most people outside the Chicago area are unaware that more people are employed here in the health care and bio-medical fields than anywhere else in the country.

While mergers and acquisitions have diminished Chicago's importance as a banking center, it is still the the home of some of the world's most important markets, including the Chicago Board of Trade and the Chicago Mercantile Exchange.

Mergers and acquisitions have had the same impact upon the region's rail industry. At one time, Chicago, because it was the crossroads of the nation, was home to many of the country's great railroads. Today, only the Illinois Central Corporation remains.

Business Establishments
Number of individual businesses

Area	1986	1992	% Change 1986–1992
Chicago	50,280	52,611	4.6
Cook County	98,353	114,300	16.2
Collar counties*	36,140	54,405	50.5
Chicago SMSA	134,493	168705	25.4
Illinois	214,580	235,141	9.6

* The collar counties are DuPage, Kane, Lake, McHenry, and Will.

Source: Illinois Department of Employment Security (IDES)

While the importance of the rail industry has dropped, it's been replaced by the airline industry. Suburban Elk Grove Village is the home of United Airlines, the nation's 2nd largest airline.

It's the diversity of businesses — spanning food, transportation, high tech, and manufacturing — that now serves to insulate the region from some of the more extreme swings that have occurred in recent years on the East and West Coasts.

The Chicago region has firmly left the Rust Belt days of the early 1980s behind — becoming home to an economy that would be ranked 13th in the world (right behind India and ahead of Australia) if it were a separate country.

John Schmeltzer writes about banking and economics for the Chicago Tribune.

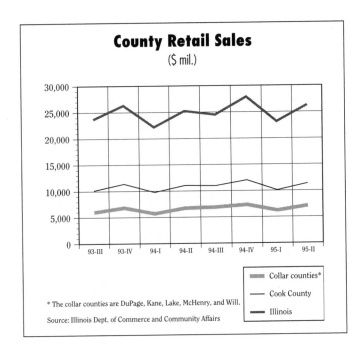

County Retail Sales
($ mil.)

Collar counties*
Cook County
Illinois

* The collar counties are DuPage, Kane, Lake, McHenry, and Will.

Source: Illinois Dept. of Commerce and Community Affairs

CHICAGO

A List-Lover's Compendium

The 50 Largest Companies by Sales in the Chicago Area

Rank	Company	City	Sales* ($ mil.)
1	Blue Cross and Blue Shield Association	Chicago	71,414
2	Sears, Roebuck and Co.	Chicago	53,920
3	Amoco Corporation	Chicago	30,362
4	Motorola, Inc.	Schaumburg	22,245
5	The Allstate Corporation	Northbrook	21,464
6	Sara Lee Corporation	Chicago	17,719
7	IGA, Inc.	Chicago	16,500
8	UAL Corporation	Elk Grove Township	13,950
9	Ameritech Corporation	Chicago	12,570
10	CNA Financial Corporation	Chicago	11,000
11	Walgreen Co.	Deerfield	10,395
12	WMX Technologies, Inc.	Oak Brook	10,097
13	Baxter International Inc.	Deerfield	9,324
14	Abbott Laboratories	Abbott Park	9,156
15	McDonald's Corporation	Oak Brook	8,321
16	Arthur Andersen & Co, SC	Chicago	8,134
17	Montgomery Ward Holding Corp.	Chicago	7,038
18	The Quaker Oats Company	Chicago	6,365
19	Navistar International Corporation	Chicago	6,342
20	Unicom Corporation	Chicago	6,278
21	Stone Container Corporation	Chicago	5,749
22	The Marmon Group	Chicago	5,301
23	First Chicago Corporation	Chicago	5,095
24	R. R. Donnelley & Sons Company	Chicago	4,889
25	Household International, Inc.	Prospect Heights	4,603
26	Inland Steel Industries, Inc.	Chicago	4,497
27	Aon Corporation	Chicago	4,157
28	Alliant Foodservice Inc.	Deerfield	4,100
29	FMC Corporation	Chicago	4,011
30	Topco Associates, Inc.	Skokie	3,700
31	The Kemper National Insurance Companies	Long Grove	3,601
32	Illinois Tool Works Inc.	Glenview	3,461
33	Premark International, Inc.	Deerfield	3,451
34	Morton International, Inc.	Chicago	3,355
35	W.W. Grainger, Inc.	Skokie	3,023
36	Spiegel, Inc.	Downers Grove	3,016
37	ServiceMaster Limited Partnership	Downers Grove	2,985
38	Jewel Food Stores, Inc.	Melrose Park	2,950
39	Brunswick Corporation	Lake Forest	2,700
40	Whitman Corporation	Rolling Meadows	2,659
41	Dean Foods Company	Franklin Park	2,630
42	Hyatt Corporation	Chicago	2,600
43	Cotter & Company	Chicago	2,575
44	Dominick's Finer Foods Inc.	Northlake	2,500
45	Caremark International Inc.	Northbrook	2,426
46	Ace Hardware Corporation	Oak Brook	2,326
47	Fruit of the Loom, Inc.	Chicago	2,298
48	USG Corporation	Chicago	2,290
49	Comdisco, Inc.	Rosemont	2,240
50	Tribune Company	Chicago	2,155

* Most recent fiscal year

The 50 Largest Employers in the Chicago Area

Rank	Company	City	Employees*
1	Sears, Roebuck and Co.	Chicago	360,570
2	McDonald's Corporation	Oak Brook	183,000
3	Sara Lee Corporation	Chicago	149,100
4	Blue Cross and Blue Shield Association	Chicago	146,352
5	Motorola, Inc.	Schaumburg	132,000
6	IGA, Inc.	Chicago	130,000
7	Borg-Warner Security Corporation	Chicago	91,698
8	Arthur Andersen & Co, SC	Chicago	82,121
9	UAL Corporation	Elk Grove Township	77,900
10	WMX Technologies, Inc.	Oak Brook	74,400
11	Walgreen Co.	Deerfield	68,000
12	Ameritech Corporation	Chicago	63,594
13	Montgomery Ward Holding Corp.	Chicago	58,600
14	Baxter International Inc.	Deerfield	53,500
15	Hyatt Corporation	Chicago	52,275
16	Abbott Laboratories	Abbott Park	49,464
17	The Allstate Corporation	Northbrook	46,300
18	Amoco Corporation	Chicago	43,205
19	R. R. Donnelley & Sons Company	Chicago	39,000
20	Fruit of the Loom, Inc.	Chicago	37,400
21	Restaurant Co.	Itasca	35,000
22	ServiceMaster Limited Partnership	Downers Grove	34,000
23	Stone Container Corporation	Chicago	29,100
24	Jewel Food Stores, Inc.	Melrose Park	29,000
25	The Marmon Group	Chicago	28,000
26	Andrew Corporation	Orland Park	26,118
27	Premark International, Inc.	Deerfield	24,000
28	Zenith Electronics Corporation	Glenview	22,500
29	FMC Corporation	Chicago	21,344
30	Brunswick Corporation	Lake Forest	20,800
31	Advocate Health Care	Oak Brook	20,400
32	Pampered Chef Ltd.	Addison	20,400
33	National Council of Young Men's Christian Associations of the United States of America	Chicago	20,000
34	Spiegel, Inc.	Downers Grove	19,700
35	Illinois Tool Works Inc.	Glenview	19,500
36	Unicom Corporation	Chicago	18,460
37	Aon Corporation	Chicago	18,000
38	Dominick's Finer Foods Inc.	Northlake	18,000
39	First Chicago Corporation	Chicago	17,630
40	The Quaker Oats Company	Chicago	17,000
41	Northwestern Healthcare	Chicago	16,427
42	CNA Financial Corporation	Chicago	15,600
43	Household International, Inc.	Prospect Heights	15,500
44	Inland Steel Industries, Inc.	Chicago	15,500
45	Whitman Corporation	Rolling Meadows	15,271
46	Navistar International Corporation	Chicago	14,910
47	CBI Industries, Inc.	Oak Brook	14,440
48	Specialty Foods Corporation	Deerfield	13,900
49	Morton International, Inc.	Chicago	13,800
50	JMB Realty Corporation	Chicago	12,500

* Most recent fiscal year

The 50 Fastest-Growing Companies by Sales in the Chicago Area

Rank	Company	City	One-Year Sales Growth % Change	Sales* ($ mil.)
1	CenterPoint Properties Corporation	Chicago	276	34
2	Spyglass, Inc.	Naperville	189	10
3	MFRI, Inc.	Niles	153	76
4	Growth Environmental, Inc.	Oak Brook	152	20
5	General Drug Company	Chicago	151	341
6	U.S. Robotics, Inc.	Skokie	135	889
7	McWhorter Technologies, Inc.	Carpentersville	129	242
8	First Merchants Acceptance Corporation	Deerfield	126	23
9	Midland Paper Company	Elk Grove Village	122	347
10	Eagle Finance Corp.	Libertyville	121	14
11	First Industrial Realty Trust, Inc.	Chicago	109	69
12	Equity Residential Properties Trust	Chicago	106	231
13	Enviropur Waste Refining & Tech Inc.	McCook	101	17
14	Amerin Corporation	Chicago	98	11
15	HA-LO Industries, Inc.	Niles	92	69
16	Telular Corporation	Buffalo Grove	86	33
17	American Classic Voyages Co.	Chicago	79	195
18	Alternative Resources Corporation	Lincolnshire	78	95
19	Prime Residential, Inc.	Chicago	76	35
20	McClier	Chicago	74	150
21	PC Wholesale	Bloomingdale	67	65
22	Manufactured Home Communities, Inc.	Chicago	64	69
23	VisionTek Inc.	Gurnee	63	302
24	Loren Buick, Inc.	Glenview	63	76
25	Scotsman Industries, Inc.	Vernon Hills	63	267
26	Fort Dearborn Lithograph Company	Niles	61	98
27	Intercargo Corporation	Schaumburg	60	81
28	Salton/Maxim Housewares, Inc.	Mount Prospect	58	77
29	First Alert, Inc.	Aurora	58	248
30	Tellabs, Inc.	Lisle	54	494
31	PLATINUM technology, inc.	Oakbrook Terrace	54	96
32	Sundance Homes, Inc.	Schaumburg	53	119
33	CDW Computer Centers, Inc.	Buffalo Grove	53	413
34	Personal Creations, Inc.	Willowbrook	51	6
35	Capitol Construction Group, Inc.	Wheeling	50	90
36	Celex Group, Inc.	Lombard	48	44
37	General Instrument Corporation	Chicago	46	2,036
38	Triangle Technologies, Inc.	Downers Grove	46	7
39	Bob O'Connor Ford	Evergreen Park	46	75
40	Ed Miniat, Inc.	Chicago	45	138
41	Lindberg Corporation	Rosemont	44	100
42	M-Wave, Inc.	Bensenville	43	28
43	Johnstown America Industries, Inc.	Chicago	42	468
44	CCC Information Services, Inc.	Chicago	41	88
45	Lincoln Park Zoo	Chicago	41	10
46	Aurora Eby-Brown Co.	Naperville	39	1,450
47	Wisconsin Central Transportation Corporation	Rosemont	39	211
48	Comark, Inc.	Bloomingdale	38	411
49	Duraco Products, Inc.	Streamwood	38	69
50	Enco Manufacturing Company	Chicago	38	51

Note: To be included on this list, companies must have sales greater than $5 million. These rates may have resulted from acquisitions or internal growth.
* Most recent fiscal year

The 50 Fastest-Growing Employers in the Chicago Area

Rank	Company	City	One-Year Employment Growth % Change	Employees*
1	Scotsman Industries, Inc.	Vernon Hills	138	2,182
2	Telular Corporation	Buffalo Grove	102	273
3	First Merchants Acceptance Corporation	Deerfield	100	200
4	PLATINUM technology, inc.	Oakbrook Terrace	95	743
5	U.S. Robotics, Inc.	Skokie	92	1,451
6	Equity Residential Properties Trust	Chicago	80	1,635
7	Graycor, Inc.	Homewood	68	900
8	WMS Industries Inc.	Chicago	63	3,381
9	Alternative Resources Corporation	Lincolnshire	60	333
10	Ben Franklin Retail Stores, Inc.	Carol Stream	58	1,974
11	CDW Computer Centers, Inc.	Buffalo Grove	58	390
12	Northwestern Healthcare	Chicago	57	16,427
13	Technology Solutions Company	Chicago	54	423
14	Spyglass, Inc.	Naperville	52	73
15	HA-LO Industries, Inc.	Niles	47	202
16	M-Wave, Inc.	Bensenville	43	200
17	SPS Transaction Services, Inc.	Riverwoods	42	3,480
18	Johnstown America Industries, Inc.	Chicago	40	2,000
19	Indeck Energy Services, Inc.	Buffalo Grove	36	171
20	The Vigoro Corporation	Chicago	36	1,900
21	TRO Learning, Inc.	Hoffman Estates	34	267
22	Celex Group, Inc.	Lombard	33	516
23	Zebra Technologies Corporation	Vernon Hills	32	501
24	The Cherry Corporation	Waukegan	31	3,986
25	SigmaTron International, Inc.	Elk Grove Village	30	917
26	Advance Ross Corporation	Chicago	29	327
27	VisionTek Inc.	Gurnee	29	180
28	U.S. Can Corporation	Oak Brook	28	3,500
29	United States Cellular Corporation	Chicago	26	2,250
30	Intercargo Corporation	Schaumburg	26	287
31	PORTEC, Inc.	Lake Forest	26	779
32	First Commonwealth, Inc.	Chicago	25	100
33	Mercury Finance Company	Northbrook	25	1,500
34	Varlen Corporation	Naperville	25	2,531
35	Telephone and Data Systems, Inc.	Chicago	23	5,322
36	General Instrument Corporation	Chicago	22	12,300
37	American Classic Voyages Co.	Chicago	22	2,248
38	R. R. Donnelley & Sons Company	Chicago	21	39,000
39	IDEX Corporation	Northbrook	20	3,000
40	Methode Electronics, Inc.	Chicago	20	3,000
41	Wisconsin Central Transportation Corporation	Rosemont	20	1,704
42	Sundance Homes, Inc.	Schaumburg	19	176
43	Sportmart, Inc.	Wheeling	19	4,512
44	Federal Signal Corporation	Oak Brook	18	5,243
45	Caremark International Inc.	Northbrook	18	9,150
46	Spiegel, Inc.	Downers Grove	18	19,700
47	Molex Incorporated	Lisle	16	9,500
48	Brunswick Corporation	Lake Forest	16	20,800
49	SPSS Inc.	Chicago	15	410
50	Pepper Cos. Inc.	Chicago	15	921

Note: To be included on this list, companies must have 50 or more employees. These rates may have resulted from acquisitions or internal growth.
* Most recent fiscal year

The 50 Largest Job Creators in the Chicago Area

Rank	Company	City	Jobs Added*	Employees*
1	McDonald's Corporation	Oak Brook	14,000	183,000
2	Motorola, Inc.	Schaumburg	12,000	132,000
3	Blue Cross and Blue Shield Association	Chicago	10,469	146,352
4	Arthur Andersen & Co, SC	Chicago	9,399	82,121
5	Montgomery Ward Holding Corp.	Chicago	7,250	58,600
6	R. R. Donnelley & Sons Company	Chicago	6,900	39,000
7	Walgreen Co.	Deerfield	6,100	68,000
8	Northwestern Healthcare	Chicago	5,982	16,427
9	Borg-Warner Security Corporation	Chicago	4,698	91,698
10	Sara Lee Corporation	Chicago	3,200	149,100
11	ServiceMaster Limited Partnership	Downers Grove	3,000	34,000
12	Spiegel, Inc.	Downers Grove	3,000	19,700
13	Brunswick Corporation	Lake Forest	2,800	20,800
14	Fruit of the Loom, Inc.	Chicago	2,400	37,400
15	General Instrument Corporation	Chicago	2,200	12,300
16	WMX Technologies, Inc.	Oak Brook	1,800	74,400
17	Sears, Roebuck and Co.	Chicago	1,570	360,570
18	Caremark International Inc.	Northbrook	1,397	9,150
19	Molex Incorporated	Lisle	1,333	9,500
20	WMS Industries Inc.	Chicago	1,301	3,381
21	Navistar International Corporation	Chicago	1,298	14,910
22	Scotsman Industries, Inc.	Vernon Hills	1,267	2,182
23	W.W. Grainger, Inc.	Skokie	1,124	11,343
24	AMSTED Industries Incorporated	Chicago	1,100	9,000
25	TNT Freightways Corporation	Rosemont	1,095	12,184
26	SPS Transaction Services, Inc.	Riverwoods	1,030	3,480
27	Telephone and Data Systems, Inc.	Chicago	979	5,322
28	The Cherry Corporation	Waukegan	938	3,986
29	Federal Signal Corporation	Oak Brook	817	5,243
30	Specialty Foods Corporation	Deerfield	800	13,900
31	U.S. Can Corporation	Oak Brook	755	3,500
32	Equity Residential Properties Trust	Chicago	728	1,635
33	Ben Franklin Retail Stores, Inc.	Carol Stream	724	1,974
34	Borg-Warner Automotive, Inc.	Chicago	720	7,330
35	Sportmart, Inc.	Wheeling	708	4,512
36	Alberto-Culver Company	Melrose Park	700	9,300
37	Morton International, Inc.	Chicago	700	13,800
38	U.S. Robotics, Inc.	Skokie	696	1,451
39	FMC Corporation	Chicago	648	21,344
40	Pittway Corporation	Chicago	600	5,400
41	Johnstown America Industries, Inc.	Chicago	575	2,000
42	Information Resources, Inc.	Chicago	560	6,360
43	CBI Industries, Inc.	Oak Brook	520	14,440
44	Varlen Corporation	Naperville	501	2,531
45	IDEX Corporation	Northbrook	500	3,000
46	Illinois Tool Works Inc.	Glenview	500	19,500
47	Methode Electronics, Inc.	Chicago	500	3,000
48	The Vigoro Corporation	Chicago	500	1,900
49	Andrew Corporation	Orland Park	496	26,118
50	DeVry Inc.	Oakbrook Terrace	495	3,770

Note: These rates may have resulted from acquisitions or internal growth.
* Most recent fiscal year

The Chicago 500: Largest Companies by Sales
in *Hoover's Guide to the Top Chicago Companies*

Rank	Company	Sales* ($ mil.)	Rank	Company	Sales ($ mil.)
1	Blue Cross and Blue Shield Association	71,414	51	General Instrument Corporation	2,036
2	Sears, Roebuck and Co.	53,920	52	Specialty Foods Corporation	1,979
3	Amoco Corporation	30,362	53	National Council of Young Men's Christian Assoc. of the USA	1,935
4	Motorola, Inc.	22,245	54	IMC Global Inc.	1,924
5	The Allstate Corporation	21,464	55	CBI Industries, Inc.	1,891
6	Sara Lee Corporation	17,719	56	Borg-Warner Security Corporation	1,793
7	IGA, Inc.	16,500	57	Anixter International, Inc.	1,733
8	UAL Corporation	13,950	58	Inflo Holdings Corporation	1,700
9	Ameritech Corporation	12,570	59	Northwestern Healthcare	1,680
10	CNA Financial Corporation	11,000	60	Old Republic International Corp.	1,679
11	Walgreen Co.	10,395	61	NIPSCO Industries, Inc.	1,676
12	WMX Technologies, Inc.	10,097	62	Wm. Wrigley Jr. Company	1,661
13	Baxter International Inc.	9,324	63	NICOR Inc.	1,609
14	Abbott Laboratories	9,156	64	Kemper Corporation	1,602
15	McDonald's Corporation	8,321	65	Rykoff-Sexton, Inc.	1,569
16	Arthur Andersen & Co, SC	8,134	66	Northern Trust Corporation	1,479
17	Montgomery Ward Holding Corp.	7,038	67	Zenith Electronics Corporation	1,469
18	The Quaker Oats Company	6,365	68	Aurora Eby-Brown Co.	1,450
19	Navistar International Corp.	6,342	69	Bankers Life Holding Corporation	1,438
20	Unicom Corporation	6,278	70	Unitrin, Inc.	1,366
21	Stone Container Corporation	5,749	71	Alberto-Culver Company	1,358
22	The Marmon Group	5,301	72	The University of Chicago	1,313
23	First Chicago Corporation	5,095	73	Helene Curtis Industries, Inc.	1,266
24	R. R. Donnelley & Sons Company	4,889	74	Hyatt Corporation	1,240
25	Household International, Inc.	4,603	75	Borg-Warner Automotive, Inc.	1,223
26	Inland Steel Industries, Inc.	4,497	76	Molex Incorporated	1,198
27	Aon Corporation	4,157	77	CF Industries, Inc.	1,183
28	Alliant Foodservice Inc.	4,100	78	Nalco Chemical Company	1,171
29	FMC Corporation	4,011	79	GATX Corporation	1,155
30	Topco Associates, Inc.	3,700	80	Advantis	1,135
31	The Kemper National Insurance Companies	3,601	81	Frank Consolidated Enterprises	1,124
32	Illinois Tool Works Inc.	3,461	82	JMB Realty Corporation	1,100
33	Premark International, Inc.	3,451	83	Tang Industries, Inc.	1,100
34	Morton International, Inc.	3,355	84	Unified HealthCare Network	1,100
35	W.W. Grainger, Inc.	3,023	85	Budget Rent a Car Corporation	1,081
36	Spiegel, Inc.	3,016	86	Outboard Marine Corporation	1,078
37	ServiceMaster Ltd. Partnership	2,985	87	Shurfine International, Inc.	1,059
38	Jewel Food Stores, Inc.	2,950	88	Gaylord Container Corporation	1,051
39	Brunswick Corporation	2,700	89	Peoples Energy Corporation	1,033
40	Whitman Corporation	2,659	90	AMSTED Industries Incorporated	1,030
41	Dean Foods Company	2,630	91	TNT Freightways Corporation	1,017
42	Cotter & Company	2,575	92	Great American Management and Investment, Inc.	1,010
43	Dominick's Finer Foods Inc.	2,500	93	Duchossois Industries, Inc.	1,000
44	Caremark International Inc.	2,426	94	Old World Industries, Inc.	1,000
45	Ace Hardware Corporation	2,326	95	Wickes Lumber Company	987
46	Fruit of the Loom, Inc.	2,298	96	United Stationers Inc.	981
47	USG Corporation	2,290	97	Bally Entertainment Corporation	942
48	Comdisco, Inc.	2,240	98	Boise Cascade Office Products	909
49	Tribune Company	2,155	99	U.S. Robotics, Inc.	889
50	The UNO-VEN Company	2,144	100	Restaurant Co.	854

* Most recent fiscal year

The Chicago 500: Largest Companies by Sales
in *Hoover's Guide to the Top Chicago Companies* (continued)

Rank	Company	Sales ($ mil.)	Rank	Company	Sales ($ mil.)
101	Sweetheart Holdings, Inc.	846	151	AAR Corp.	451
102	TTX Company	810	152	Walsh Group	450
103	Galileo International Partnership	801	153	Stepan Company	444
104	Safety-Kleen Corp.	791	154	Falcon Building Products, Inc.	441
105	BT Office Products Int'l, Inc.	790	155	Rand McNally & Company	439
106	Pittway Corporation	778	156	Field Container Company L. P.	425
107	Pioneer Financial Services, Inc.	774	157	Jordan Industries, Inc.	424
108	The Interlake Corporation	753	158	Sportmart, Inc.	424
109	Rush-Presbyterian-St. Luke's		159	General Binding Corporation	420
	Medical Center	746	160	Chicago Airport System	420
110	Chemcentral Corporation	745	161	Ivex Packaging Corporation	419
111	Telephone and Data Systems, Inc.	731	162	Quill Corporation	418
112	The Vigoro Corporation	727	163	CDW Computer Centers, Inc.	413
113	Hartmarx Corporation	725	164	Central Grocers Cooperative, Inc.	412
114	Bell & Howell Holdings Company	720	165	Comark, Inc.	411
115	Follett Corporation	713	166	Wirtz Corporation	410
116	Wallace Computer Services, Inc.	713	167	Encyclopædia Britannica, Inc.	405
117	Trustmark Insurance Company	711	168	True North Communications Inc.	404
118	Coca-Cola Bottling Co. of Chicago	705	169	Bradner Central Company	400
119	Certified Grocers MIdwest, Inc.	701	170	IDEX Corporation	400
120	Advocate Health Care	698	171	Hewitt Associates LLC	396
121	Loyola University of Chicago	697	172	Ancilla Systems	386
122	The Hub Group, Inc.	687	173	WMS Industries Inc.	385
123	Federal Signal Corporation	677	174	Ferralloy Corporation	378
124	Northwestern University	676	175	Information Resources, Inc.	377
125	Leo Burnett Company, Inc.	675	176	UNR Industries, Inc.	372
126	Washington National Corporation	657	177	Franciscan Sisters Health	
127	G. Heileman Brewing Co., Inc.	636		Care Corp.	369
128	Andrew Corporation	627	178	Fel-Pro, Inc.	365
129	Dade International, Inc.	624	179	Arthur J. Gallagher & Co.	356
130	Envirodyne Industries, Inc.	599	180	Ben Franklin Retail Stores, Inc.	355
131	Baker & McKenzie	594	181	Clark Foodservice Inc.	350
132	Illinois Central Corporation	594	182	Midland Paper Company	347
133	CCH Incorporated	579	183	Varlen Corporation	342
134	U.S. Can Corporation	563	184	General Drug Company	341
135	Antec Corporation	554	185	EESCO Inc.	340
136	Lane Industries, Inc.	553	186	The Cherry Corporation	339
137	A.M. Castle & Co.	537	187	Tempel Steel Company	336
138	The Inland Group, Inc.	532	188	United States Cellular Corporation	332
139	EVEREN Securities, Inc.	530	189	Spring Air Company	330
140	Acme Metals Incorporated	523	190	Edward Don & Company	325
141	AM International, Inc.	510	191	Chas. Levy Companies	320
142	CC Industries, Inc.	502	192	DEKALB Genetics Corporation	319
143	Tellabs, Inc.	494	193	Johnson Publishing Company, Inc.	307
144	Pepper Cos. Inc.	485	194	White Hen Pantry Inc.	307
145	A B Dick Company	480	195	ELEK-TEK, Inc.	306
146	Medline Industries, Inc.	476	196	Alexian Brothers Health System	303
147	AptarGroup, Inc.	474	197	The Florsheim Shoe Company	302
148	Serta Inc.	470	198	VisionTek Inc.	302
149	Johnstown America Industries, Inc.	468	199	Underwriters Laboratories Inc.	300
150	Martin Oil Marketing Ltd.	462	200	Tootsie Roll Industries, Inc.	297

The Chicago 500: Largest Companies by Sales
in *Hoover's Guide to the Top Chicago Companies* (continued)

Rank	Company	Sales ($ mil.)
201	System Software Associates, Inc.	294
202	Joe Rizza Enterprises Inc.	293
203	Farley Foods USA	285
204	St. Paul Bancorp, Inc.	283
205	Duplex Products, Inc.	276
206	Methode Electronics, Inc.	275
207	Euromarket Designs Inc.	274
208	Scotsman Industries, Inc.	267
209	AMCOL International Corporation	265
210	Elkay Manufacturing Company	264
211	Mayer, Brown & Platt	263
212	Sidley & Austin	255
213	Grant Thornton	254
214	International Jensen Incorporated	253
215	Mercury Finance Company	253
216	Power Contracting & Engineering Corporation	250
217	QST Industries Inc.	250
218	First Alert, Inc.	248
219	Playboy Enterprises, Inc.	247
220	SPS Transaction Services, Inc.	246
221	Binks Manufacturing Company	244
222	ABC Rail Products Corporation	243
223	Sage Enterprises Inc.	243
224	McWhorter Technologies, Inc.	242
225	Covenant Ministries of Benevolence	238
226	Tuthill Corporation	237
227	Duo-Fast Corporation	236
228	Equity Residential Properties Trust	231
229	DeVry Inc.	229
230	Material Sciences Corporation	228
231	Town and Country Homes, Inc.	225
232	The John Nuveen Company	220
233	Cambridge Homes, Inc.	220
234	Fellowes Manufacturing Company	220
235	First Midwest Bancorp, Inc.	217
236	Allied Products Corporation	216
237	Kirkland & Ellis	215
238	Lawson Products, Inc.	213
239	Wisconsin Central Transportation	211
240	John B. Sanfilippo & Son, Inc.	209
241	Schwarz Paper Company	209
242	Richardson Electronics, Ltd.	208
243	McDermott, Will & Emery	207
244	Globe Glass & Mirror Company	206
245	S&C Electric Company	202
246	ASAP Software Express, Inc.	200
247	Pampered Chef Ltd.	200
248	JG Industries, Inc.	196
249	American Classic Voyages Co.	195
250	Littelfuse, Inc.	195

Rank	Company	Sales ($ mil.)
251	Metra	193
252	DoAll Company	192
253	Lawter International, Inc.	191
254	Hostmark Management Group, Inc.	188
255	American Medical Association	187
256	HealthCare COMPARE Corporation	187
257	Schawk, Inc.	186
258	Quixote Corporation	185
259	Chicago Corporation	185
260	MMI Companies, Inc.	177
261	Farley, Inc.	176
262	MacLean-Fogg Company	175
263	Patrick Dealer Group	173
264	Crain Communications Inc	171
265	Safeway Insurance Company	170
266	Bliss & Laughlin Industries Inc.	169
267	DePaul University	168
268	Rymer Foods Inc.	167
269	GLS Corporation	166
270	DSC Logistics	162
271	Forsythe McArthur Associates, Inc.	160
272	Donlen Corporation	156
273	Intermatic, Incorporated	154
274	Oil-Dri Corporation of America	153
275	Artra Group Incorporated	152
276	Seigle's Home & Building Centers	151
277	The John D. and Catherine T. MacArthur Foundation	150
278	McClier	150
279	William Blair & Company	150
280	J. H. Roberts Industries	149
281	Winston & Strawn	146
282	A. J. Gerrard & Company	145
283	Turtle Wax, Inc.	145
284	Cole Taylor Financial Group, Inc.	144
285	Libertyville Classic Group	143
286	Celozzi-Ettleson Chevrolet, Inc.	142
287	Paul H. Schwendener, Inc.	141
288	Newly Weds Foods, Inc.	140
289	Graycor, Inc.	140
290	Ed Miniat, Inc.	138
291	World's Finest Chocolate, Inc.	138
292	Humphreys, Inc.	135
293	Rittenhouse, Inc.	135
294	Butera Finer Foods, Inc.	133
295	Continental Motors Group	133
296	Indeck Energy Services, Inc.	132
297	MAF Bancorp, Inc.	132
298	Jenner & Block	131
299	Furnas Electric Company	130
300	Middleby Corporation	130

Rank	Company	Sales ($ mil.)	Rank	Company	Sales ($ mil.)
301	Restonic Corporation	130	351	Levy Restaurants	99
302	Weber-Stephen Products Company	130	352	Fort Dearborn Lithograph Company	98
303	River Forest Bancorp, Inc.	128	353	PORTEC, Inc.	98
304	Juno Lighting, Inc.	127	354	Motor Works of Barrington, Inc.	96
305	Ero, Inc.	127	355	PLATINUM technology, inc.	96
306	RHC/Spacemaster Corporation	127	356	Champion Parts, Inc.	95
307	Steve Foley Auto Group	127	357	Kreher Steel Company	95
308	Bagcraft Corporation of America	125	358	Lyon Metal Products, Inc.	95
309	Ferrara Pan Candy Company	125	359	Northwestern Golf Company	95
310	Lettuce Entertain You Enterprises	125	360	Alternative Resources Corporation	95
311	Katten Muchin & Zavis	124	361	Soft Sheen Products Inc.	94
312	McCain Manufacturing Corp.	120	362	Seko-Air Freight, Inc.	93
313	Harpo Entertainment Group	120	363	Houston Foods Company	92
314	Woodhead Industries, Inc.	120	364	Vienna Sausage Manufacturing Co.	90
315	Jacobs Twin	120	365	Bruss Company	90
316	Sundance Homes, Inc.	119	366	Capitol Construction Group, Inc.	90
317	Warrior Insurance Group Inc.	118	367	Charles Industries Ltd.	90
318	Wilton Industries, Inc.	118	368	Fansteel Inc.	89
319	Garvey International, Inc.	118	369	Office Electronics Incorporated	89
320	Bell Bancorp, Inc.	118	370	Hammacher Schlemmer & Co.	89
321	Sonnenschein Nath & Rosenthal	118	371	CCC Information Services, Inc.	88
322	Velsicol Chemical Corporation	116	372	Cummins-American Corporation	88
323	Archibald Candy Corporation	116	373	DeSoto, Inc.	87
324	ICM Industries, Inc.	115	374	Jernberg Industries	87
325	Paterno Imports Ltd.	115	375	Keck, Mahin & Cate	87
326	Mazzetta Company	114	376	Lord, Bissell & Brook	87
327	American Bar Association	113	377	Evans, Inc.	87
328	Capsure Holdings Corporation	113	378	L. E. Myers Co. Group	87
329	Harza Engineering Company	113	379	Baird & Warner, Inc.	86
330	Vitalink Pharmacy Services, Inc.	112	380	Precision Twist Drill Company	86
331	Klein Tools, Inc.	112	381	Faul Chevrolet & Geo	86
332	Loeber Motors, Inc.	111	382	Miner Enterprises, Inc.	84
333	Daubert Industries, Inc.	110	383	Mesirow Financial Holdings Inc.	83
334	Volvo Sales & Service Center, Inc.	110	384	Cobra Electronics, Inc.	82
335	North American Processing Co.	109	385	Torco Holdings, Inc.	82
336	Zebra Technologies Corporation	107	386	Al Baskin Company	82
337	FlorStar Sales, Inc.	107	387	Axia, Inc.	81
338	Arrow Chevrolet, Inc.	106	388	Lynch Group	81
339	Seyfarth, Shaw, Fairweather & Geraldson	106	389	Intercargo Corporation	81
340	The Art Institute of Chicago	105	390	Dukane Corporation	80
341	Berlin Packaging Corporation	105	391	Berlin Industries, Inc.	80
342	Jel Sert Company	105	392	Chernin's Shoes, Inc.	80
343	Steiner Electric Company	105	393	Lakewood Engineering & Manufacturing Company	80
344	Standard Financial, Inc.	105	394	Skidmore, Owings & Merrill	79
345	Gerber Plumbing Fixtures Corp.	104	395	NSBancorp, Inc.	78
346	Amity Packing Company	101	396	Continental Web Press, Inc.	78
347	C. P. Hall Company	100	397	Hoffer Plastics Corporation	78
348	Nelsen Steel & Wire Company	100	398	T. C. Manufacturing Company	78
349	Rose Packing Company	100	399	Urban Shopping Centers, Inc.	78
350	Lindberg Corporation	100	400	Rodman & Renshaw Capital Group	77

The Chicago 500: Largest Companies by Sales
in *Hoover's Guide to the Top Chicago Companies* (continued)

Rank	Company	Sales ($ mil.)	Rank	Company	Sales ($ mil.)
401	Hill Mechanical Group	77	451	Chicago Bulls	58
402	Salton/Maxim Housewares, Inc.	77	452	Schumacher Electric Corporation	57
403	Burnham Broadcasting Company	77	453	Sleepeck Printing Company	57
404	Loren Buick, Inc.	76	454	Stimsonite Corporation	56
405	Sipi Metals Corporation	76	455	Market Facts, Inc.	56
406	MFRI, Inc.	76	456	A. Epstein & Sons International, Inc.	55
407	Continental Materials Corporation	75	457	Industrial Coatings Group, Inc.	55
408	Bob O'Connor Ford	75	458	Strombecker Corporation	54
409	Segerdahl Corporation	75	459	Atlas Lift Truck Rentals & Sales	54
410	AGI, Inc.	75	460	Chicago National League Ball Club	54
411	Woodfield Ford Sales, Inc.	74	461	Bodine Electric Company	53
412	Edelman Public Relations	74	462	Delphi Information Systems, Inc.	53
413	Fluid Management L.P.	73	463	Sayers Computer Source	53
414	J. W. Allen & Company	73	464	Dietzgen Corporation	52
415	George S. May International Company	73	465	May & Speh, Inc.	52
416	Folger Adam Company	72	466	Nelson Westerberg, Inc.	52
417	Paddock Publications, Inc.	71	467	SPSS Inc.	52
418	Treasure Island Foodmart, Inc.	70	468	F&B Manufacturing Company	52
419	Columbia Pipe & Supply Company	70	469	American HealthCare Providers	51
420	Stock Yards Packing Company	70	470	Illinois Auto Electric Company	51
421	Wozniak Industries, Inc.	70	471	Enco Manufacturing Company	51
422	Emkay, Inc.	70	472	Bigsby & Kruthers, Inc./Knot Shops	50
423	First Industrial Realty Trust, Inc.	69	473	Chicago Natural Gas, Inc.	50
424	Duraco Products, Inc.	69	474	E&D Web, Inc.	50
425	Manufactured Home Communities	69	475	Environetx	50
426	HA-LO Industries, Inc.	69	476	Parkview Metal Products, Inc.	50
427	Northeastern Illinois University	68	477	Superior Graphite Company	50
428	A. Finkil & Sons Company	67	478	Old Second Bancorp Inc.	49
429	Heritage Financial Services, Inc.	67	479	Southside Ford Truck Sales, Inc.	49
430	Advance Ross Corporation	67	480	C. J. Vitner Company	48
431	Amli Residential Properties Trust	66	481	Brookfield Farms, Inc.	48
432	Beco Group	66	482	FCL Graphics, Inc.	48
433	Phoenix Duff & Phelps Corporation	66	483	Indiana Federal Corporation	48
434	Technology Solutions Company	66	484	Lombard Lincoln Mercury, Inc.	47
435	Chicago Bears Football Club, Inc.	65	485	Advance Mechanical Systems, Inc.	47
436	Lind-Waldock & Company	65	486	U. S. Precision Glass Company	47
437	Chicago Heights Steel Company	65	487	Bresler's Industries, Inc.	46
438	G. K. Enterprises, Inc.	65	488	United Homes, Inc.	46
439	PC Wholesale	65	489	Long Company	46
440	Zoll Foods Corporation	65	490	Chicago White Sox	46
441	Nightingale-Conant Corporation	64	491	First Oak Brook Bancshares, Inc.	45
442	Solar Press, Inc.	63	492	SigmaTron International, Inc.	45
443	Teltrend Inc.	62	493	Brook Furniture Rental, Inc.	45
444	Richco Plastic Company	60	494	O'Bryan Brothers, Inc.	45
445	Hexacomb Corporation	60	495	STS Holdings, Inc.	45
446	Oxford International Ltd.	60	496	Celex Group, Inc.	44
447	Circuit Systems, Inc.	60	497	Rauland-Borg Corporation	44
448	Option Care, Inc.	59	498	Pinnacle Banc Group, Inc.	44
449	Allscrips Pharmaceuticals, Inc.	59	499	Amerihost Properties, Inc.	43
450	Rotary International	59	500	Premier Financial Services, Inc.	43

The Chicago 500: Largest Companies by Employees
in *Hoover's Guide to the Top Chicago Companies*

Rank	Company	Employees*	Rank	Company	Employees
1	Sears, Roebuck and Co.	360,570	51	General Instrument Corp.	12,300
2	McDonald's Corporation	183,000	52	USG Corporation	12,300
3	Sara Lee Corporation	149,100	53	TNT Freightways Corporation	12,184
4	Blue Cross and Blue Shield		54	Dean Foods Company	11,800
	Association	146,352	55	W.W. Grainger, Inc.	11,343
5	Motorola, Inc.	132,000	56	Bally Entertainment Corp.	11,200
6	IGA, Inc.	130,000	57	Hartmarx Corporation	11,000
7	Borg-Warner Security Corp.	91,698	58	The University of Chicago	10,954
8	Arthur Andersen & Co, SC	82,121	59	Tribune Company	9,900
9	UAL Corporation	77,900	60	Loyola University of Chicago	9,556
10	WMX Technologies, Inc.	74,400	61	Molex Incorporated	9,500
11	Walgreen Co.	68,000	62	Alberto-Culver Company	9,300
12	Ameritech Corporation	63,594	63	Caremark International Inc.	9,150
13	Montgomery Ward Holding		64	AMSTED Industries Inc.	9,000
	Corp.	58,600	65	Inflo Holdings Corporation	9,000
14	Baxter International Inc.	53,500	66	Alliant Foodservice Inc.	8,800
15	Abbott Laboratories	49,464	67	Budget Rent a Car Corporation	8,700
16	Hyatt Corporation	47,000	68	Sweetheart Holdings, Inc.	8,600
17	The Allstate Corporation	46,300	69	Rush-Presbyterian-St. Luke's	
18	Amoco Corporation	43,205		Medical Center	8,511
19	R. R. Donnelley & Sons Co.	39,000	70	Outboard Marine Corporation	8,500
20	Fruit of the Loom, Inc.	37,400	71	The Kemper National Insurance	
21	Restaurant Co.	35,000		Companies	8,295
22	ServiceMaster Ltd. Partnership	34,000	72	Duchossois Industries, Inc.	8,000
23	Stone Container Corporation	29,100	73	Borg-Warner Automotive, Inc.	7,330
24	Jewel Food Stores, Inc.	29,000	74	Unitrin, Inc.	7,289
25	The Marmon Group	28,000	75	Follett Corporation	7,200
26	Andrew Corporation	26,118	76	Great American Management and	
27	Premark International, Inc.	24,000		Investment, Inc.	7,000
28	Zenith Electronics Corporation	22,500	77	Lane Industries, Inc.	7,000
29	FMC Corporation	21,344	78	Wm. Wrigley Jr. Company	7,000
30	Brunswick Corporation	20,800	79	IMC Global Inc.	6,800
31	Advocate Health Care	20,400	80	Northern Trust Corporation	6,608
32	Pampered Chef Ltd.	20,400	81	Safety-Kleen Corp.	6,600
33	National Council of Young Men's		82	Information Resources, Inc.	6,360
	Christian Assoc. of the USA	20,000	83	Leo Burnett Company, Inc.	6,308
34	Spiegel, Inc.	19,700	84	Hostmark Management Group,	6,100
35	Illinois Tool Works Inc.	19,500	85	Kemper Corporation	6,000
36	Unicom Corporation	18,460	86	GATX Corporation	5,800
37	Aon Corporation	18,000	87	Bell & Howell Holdings Company	5,791
38	Dominick's Finer Foods Inc.	18,000	88	Franciscan Sisters Health Care	5,750
39	First Chicago Corporation	17,630	89	Northwestern University	5,650
40	The Quaker Oats Company	17,000	90	Nalco Chemical Company	5,601
41	Northwestern Healthcare	16,427	91	CC Industries, Inc.	5,449
42	CNA Financial Corporation	15,600	92	Old Republic International Corp.	5,400
43	Household International, Inc.	15,500	93	Pittway Corporation	5,400
44	Inland Steel Industries, Inc.	15,500	94	Rykoff-Sexton, Inc.	5,330
45	Whitman Corporation	15,271	95	Telephone and Data Systems, Inc.	5,322
46	Navistar International Corp.	14,910	96	CCH Incorporated	5,290
47	CBI Industries, Inc.	14,440	97	Baker & McKenzie	5,248
48	Specialty Foods Corporation	13,900	98	Federal Signal Corporation	5,243
49	Morton International, Inc.	13,800	99	Envirodyne Industries, Inc.	4,900
50	JMB Realty Corporation	12,500	100	Manufactured Home Communities	4,600

* Most recent fiscal year

The Chicago 500: Largest Companies by Employees in *Hoover's Guide to the Top Chicago Companies* (continued)

Rank	Company	Employees	Rank	Company	Employees
101	The Interlake Corporation	4,536	151	Acme Metals Incorporated	2,750
102	Wickes Lumber Company	4,523	152	Johnson Publishing Company	2,662
103	Sportmart, Inc.	4,512	153	Chicago Airport System	2,614
104	Ancilla Systems	4,500	154	Tellabs, Inc.	2,585
105	Hewitt Associates LLC	4,493	155	Varlen Corporation	2,531
106	NIPSCO Industries, Inc.	4,391	156	Fel-Pro, Inc.	2,510
107	Anixter International, Inc.	4,200	157	Ivex Packaging Corporation	2,500
108	Coca-Cola Bottling of Chicago	4,200	158	Urban Shopping Centers, Inc.	2,455
109	Cotter & Company	4,200	159	Farley Foods USA	2,400
110	Rand McNally & Company	4,200	160	Metra	2,400
111	Gaylord Container Corporation	4,100	161	Elkay Manufacturing Company	2,375
112	BT Office Products International	4,000	162	Alexian Brothers Health System	2,300
113	Dade International, Inc.	4,000	163	Encyclopædia Britannica, Inc.	2,300
114	Walsh Group	4,000	164	Littelfuse, Inc.	2,270
115	The Cherry Corporation	3,986	165	United States Cellular Corporation	2,250
116	True North Communications	3,929			
117	Jordan Industries, Inc.	3,900	166	American Classic Voyages Co.	2,248
118	Underwriters Laboratories Inc.	3,900	167	Field Container Company L. P.	2,232
119	DeVry Inc.	3,770	168	DSC Logistics	2,200
120	Wallace Computer Services, Inc.	3,765	169	G. Heileman Brewing Company	2,200
			170	UNR Industries, Inc.	2,200
121	Ace Hardware Corporation	3,664			
122	Lettuce Entertain You Enterprises, Inc.	3,600	171	Scotsman Industries, Inc.	2,182
123	Northern Illinois University	3,600	172	Admiral Maintenance Service L.P.	2,100
124	United Stationers Inc.	3,600	173	First Alert, Inc.	2,095
125	Covenant Ministries of Benevolence	3,500	174	Frank Consolidated Enterprises	2,020
			175	Northeastern Illinois University	2,004
126	Levy Restaurants	3,500	176	Chas. Levy Companies	2,000
127	Tang Industries, Inc.	3,500	177	Comdisco, Inc.	2,000
128	U.S. Can Corporation	3,500	178	Galileo International Partnership	2,000
129	SPS Transaction Services, Inc.	3,480	179	Johnstown America Industries	2,000
130	AM International, Inc.	3,400	180	Medline Industries, Inc.	2,000
131	Falcon Building Products, Inc.	3,400	181	Serta Inc.	2,000
132	Helene Curtis Industries, Inc.	3,400	182	TTX Company	2,000
133	NICOR Inc.	3,400	183	Tuthill Corporation	2,000
134	WMS Industries Inc.	3,381	184	Ben Franklin Retail Stores, Inc.	1,974
135	Archibald Candy Corporation	3,354	185	Bankers Life Holding Corp.	1,950
136	AptarGroup, Inc.	3,300	186	AAR Corp.	1,940
137	Arthur J. Gallagher & Co.	3,300	187	Schawk, Inc.	1,902
138	Peoples Energy Corporation	3,278	188	Amerihost Properties, Inc.	1,900
139	Illinois Central Corporation	3,250	189	The Art Institute of Chicago	1,900
140	The Florsheim Shoe Company	3,248	190	The Vigoro Corporation	1,900
141	General Binding Corporation	3,226	191	Duplex Products, Inc.	1,852
142	Boise Cascade Office Products Corporation	3,120	192	DEKALB Genetics Corporation	1,800
143	A B Dick Company	3,000	193	DoAll Company	1,800
144	Advantis	3,000	194	Farley, Inc.	1,800
145	Grant Thornton	3,000	195	International Jensen Incorporated	1,800
146	IDEX Corporation	3,000	196	System Software Associates, Inc.	1,790
147	Methode Electronics, Inc.	3,000	197	Wirtz Corporation	1,780
148	DePaul University	2,950	198	S&C Electric Company	1,719
149	EVEREN Securities, Inc.	2,840	199	Wisconsin Central Transportation Corporation	1,704
150	Duo-Fast Corporation	2,800	200	Tootsie Roll Industries, Inc.	1,700

The Chicago 500: Largest Companies by Employees
in *Hoover's Guide to the Top Chicago Companies* (continued)

Rank	Company	Employees	Rank	Company	Employees
201	Binks Manufacturing Company	1,682	251	L. E. Myers Co. Group	1,000
202	Equity Residential Properties		252	Middleby Corporation	994
	Trust	1,635	253	Charles Industries Ltd.	975
203	Sidley & Austin	1,606	254	Intermatic, Incorporated	965
204	Allied Products Corporation	1,600	255	Jenner & Block	945
205	Artra Group Incorporated	1,600	256	Crain Communications Inc	939
206	HealthCare COMPARE Corp.	1,600	257	Winston & Strawn	926
207	Quixote Corporation	1,599	258	Material Sciences Corporation	925
208	JG Industries, Inc.	1,597	259	Klein Tools, Inc.	923
209	Pioneer Financial Services, Inc.	1,570	260	Pepper Cos. Inc.	921
210	Furnas Electric Company	1,500	261	SigmaTron International, Inc.	917
211	Henry Crown and Co.	1,500	262	Juno Lighting, Inc.	915
212	Mercury Finance Company	1,500	263	Chicago Corporation	908
213	Spring Air Company	1,500	264	Market Facts, Inc.	903
214	Tempel Steel Company	1,500	265	Gerber Plumbing Fixtures	
215	CF Industries, Inc.	1,471		Corporation	900
216	Champion Parts, Inc.	1,470	266	Graycor, Inc.	900
217	Precision Twist Drill Company	1,470	267	Humphreys, Inc.	900
218	U.S. Robotics, Inc.	1,451	268	Axia, Inc.	889
219	Baird & Warner, Inc.	1,445	269	ELEK-TEK, Inc.	882
220	Trustmark Insurance Company	1,419	270	Fansteel Inc.	867
221	ABC Rail Products Corporation	1,402	271	Solar Press, Inc.	853
222	Euromarket Designs Inc.	1,400	272	Turtle Wax, Inc.	850
223	RHC/Spacemaster Corporation	1,350	273	World's Finest Chocolate, Inc.	850
224	AMCOL International Corp.	1,328	274	CCC Information Services, Inc.	846
225	Aurora Eby-Brown Co.	1,327	275	Chemcentral Corporation	834
226	First Midwest Bancorp, Inc.	1,293	276	Evans, Inc.	825
227	John B. Sanfilippo & Son, Inc.	1,274	277	Lawson Products, Inc.	810
228	Stepan Company	1,265	278	Harza Engineering Company	807
229	Fellowes Manufacturing Co.	1,258	279	Clark Foodservice Inc.	800
230	Globe Glass & Mirror Company	1,250	280	Edelman Public Relations	
231	Quill Corporation	1,248		Worldwide	800
232	A.M. Castle & Co.	1,200	281	The Inland Group, Inc.	800
233	Kirkland & Ellis	1,200	282	Lloyd Creative Temporaries	800
234	MacLean-Fogg Company	1,200	283	Lyon Metal Products, Inc.	800
235	McDermott, Will & Emery	1,190	284	Seko-Air Freight, Inc.	800
236	Restonic Corporation	1,115	285	Schumacher Electric	
237	St. Paul Bancorp, Inc.	1,103		Corporation	790
238	American Medical Association	1,100	286	EESCO Inc.	785
239	The UNO-VEN Company	1,100	287	PORTEC, Inc.	779
240	Bagcraft Corporation of America	1,088	288	Vitalink Pharmacy Services, Inc.	775
241	Washington National Corp.	1,088	289	Cole Taylor Financial Group, Inc.	760
242	Woodhead Industries, Inc.	1,079	290	Seigle's Home & Building Centers	760
243	Lyric Opera of Chicago	1,077	291	American Bar Association	750
244	Edward Don & Company	1,062	292	ICM Industries, Inc.	750
245	Preferred Staffing	1,061	293	Newly Weds Foods, Inc.	750
246	Katten Muchin & Zavis	1,015	294	Oxford International Ltd.	750
247	Al Baskin Company	1,000	295	Rittenhouse, Inc.	750
248	Butera Finer Foods, Inc.	1,000	296	PLATINUM technology, inc.	743
249	Chicago National League		297	Skidmore, Owings & Merrill	733
	Ball Club Inc.	1,000	298	J. H. Roberts Industries	730
250	George S. May International		299	Dukane Corporation	725
	Company	1,000	300	Continental Materials Corporation	713

Rank	Company	Employees	Rank	Company	Employees
301	Certified Grocers Midwest, Inc.	700	351	Joe Rizza Enterprises Inc.	500
302	Richco Plastic Company	698	352	Miner Enterprises, Inc.	500
303	Antec Corporation	695	353	Northwestern Golf Company	500
304	Hoffer Plastics Corporation	675	354	Weber-Stephen Products Co.	500
305	Oil-Dri Corporation of America	665	355	Wozniak Industries, Inc.	500
306	Lind-Waldock & Company	650	356	Ero, Inc.	499
307	Treasure Island Foodmart, Inc.	650	357	Rodman & Renshaw Capital	
308	The Hub Group, Inc.	633		Group Inc.	490
309	Heinemann's Bakeries, Inc.	630	358	O'Bryan Brothers, Inc.	480
310	Cummins-American Corporation	626	359	Comark, Inc.	472
			360	Daubert Industries, Inc.	472
311	Lindberg Corporation	610			
312	Warrior Insurance Group Inc.	609	361	Ferrara Pan Candy Company	450
313	A. Epstein & Sons International	600	362	Jel Sert Company	450
314	A. J. Gerrard & Company	600	363	Peapod, Inc.	450
315	Capsure Holdings Corporation	600	364	Rotary International	450
			365	Strombecker Corporation	450
316	Keck, Mahin & Cate	600			
317	Rose Packing Company	600	366	STS Holdings, Inc.	450
318	Velsicol Chemical Corporation	600	367	MFRI, Inc.	442
319	Playboy Enterprises, Inc.	593	368	Heritage Financial Services, Inc.	440
320	U. S. Precision Glass Company	590	369	Bliss & Laughlin Industries Inc.	437
			370	Hill Mechanical Group	431
321	Corcom, Inc.	588			
322	River Forest Bancorp, Inc.	581	371	F&B Manufacturing Company	430
323	Lawter International, Inc.	577	372	Jernberg Industries	428
324	Paddock Publications, Inc.	575	373	Continental Web Press, Inc.	425
325	Standard Financial, Inc.	575	374	Office Electronics Incorporated	423
			375	Technology Solutions Company	423
326	Folger Adam Company	566			
327	Feralloy Corporation	560	376	Delphi Information Systems, Inc.	419
328	Fluid Management L.P.	560	377	Soft Sheen Products Inc.	419
329	Lord, Bissell & Brook	560	378	DeSoto, Inc.	417
330	William Blair & Company	555	379	The Field Museum	411
			380	Nelson Westerberg, Inc.	410
331	Fort Dearborn Lithograph				
	Company	550	381	SPSS Inc.	410
332	Lakewood Engineering &		382	Rymer Foods Inc.	408
	Manufacturing Company	550	383	NSBancorp, Inc.	402
333	McWhorter Technologies, Inc.	550	384	A. Finkil & Sons Company	400
334	Vienna Sausage Manufacturing		385	AGI, Inc.	400
	Company	550	386	Amli Residential Properties	
335	Circuit Systems, Inc.	540		Trust	400
			387	Berlin Industries, Inc.	400
336	Richardson Electronics, Ltd.	540	388	Brook Furniture Rental, Inc.	400
337	The John Nuveen Company	537	389	McClier	400
338	Mayer, Brown & Platt	533	390	MMI Companies, Inc.	400
339	Wilton Industries, Inc.	530			
340	Museum of Science & Industry	528	391	QST Industries Inc.	400
			392	Seyfarth, Shaw, Fairweather &	
341	Bodine Electric Company	525		Geraldson	400
342	Schwarz Paper Company	520	393	Sleepeck Printing Company	400
343	T. C. Manufacturing Company	520	394	Safeway Insurance Company	392
344	MAF Bancorp, Inc.	519	395	CDW Computer Centers, Inc.	390
345	Celex Group, Inc.	516			
			396	Selfix, Inc.	385
346	Mesirow Financial Holdings Inc.	505	397	Parkview Metal Products, Inc.	383
347	Zebra Technologies Corporation	501	398	C. J. Vitner Company	380
348	Burnham Broadcasting Company	500	399	Option Care, Inc.	379
349	Henry Valve Company	500	400	Topco Associates, Inc.	375
350	Hexacomb Corporation	500			

The Chicago 500: Largest Companies by Employees
in *Hoover's Guide to the Top Chicago Companies* (continued)

Rank	Company	Employees
401	G. K. Enterprises, Inc.	370
402	Chicago Faucet Company	365
403	Bell Bancorp, Inc.	364
404	Airways Transportation Group of Companies	360
405	Dyna Group International, Inc.	360
406	J. W. Allen & Company	360
407	K & R Express Systems, Inc.	360
408	Paterno Imports Ltd.	357
409	Morningstar, Inc.	350
410	Sage Enterprises Inc.	350
411	Superior Graphite Company	350
412	Volvo Sales & Service Center	350
413	Chicago Heights Steel Company	345
414	Industrial Coatings Group, Inc.	343
415	Old Second Bancorp Inc.	340
416	Premier Financial Services, Inc.	338
417	Alternative Resources Corp.	333
418	Advance Ross Corporation	327
419	Chernin's Shoes, Inc.	325
420	Cambridge Homes, Inc.	320
421	Steiner Electric Company	320
422	Vance Publishing Corporation	317
423	Indiana Federal Corporation	311
424	Dietzgen Corporation	310
425	Gonnella Baking Company	305
426	American Labelmark Company	300
427	Continental Motors Group	300
428	General American Door Company	300
429	General Employment Enterprises, Inc.	300
430	May & Speh, Inc.	300
431	Jacobs Twin	293
432	Teltrend Inc.	293
433	Duraco Products, Inc.	292
434	Phoenix Duff & Phelps Corporation	290
435	Intercargo Corporation	287
436	Medicus Systems Corporation	285
437	Rauland-Borg Corporation	285
438	Pinnacle Banc Group, Inc.	282
439	First Oak Brook Bancshares, Inc.	277
440	Kelso-Burnett Company	276
441	White Hen Pantry Inc.	276
442	Growth Environmental, Inc.	275
443	Patrick Dealer Group	275
444	Telular Corporation	273
445	Enco Manufacturing Company	270
446	FlorStar Sales, Inc.	267
447	TRO Learning, Inc.	267
448	Bruss Company	265
449	Faul Chevrolet & Geo	265
450	Merchants Bancorp, Inc.	265
451	Stimsonite Corporation	265
452	Chicago Rivet & Machine Co.	261
453	Central Grocers Cooperative, Inc.	260
454	Educational Publishing Corp.	260
455	Landauer, Inc.	260
456	Magneco/Metrel, Inc.	260
457	Hinsdale Financial Corporation	257
458	Jack Carl/312-Futures, Inc.	251
459	Zenith Controls, Inc.	251
460	C. P. Hall Company	250
461	CFI Industries, Inc.	250
462	Hammacher Schlemmer & Company	250
463	John G. Shedd Aquarium	250
464	Nightingale-Conant Corporation	250
465	Paul H. Schwendener, Inc.	250
466	Prime Residential, Inc.	240
467	Steve Foley Auto Group	238
468	Segerdahl Corporation	235
469	GLS Corporation	229
470	Advance Mechanical Systems	225
471	Celozzi-Ettleson Chevrolet, Inc.	221
472	Minuteman International, Inc.	221
473	Carqueville/TCR Graphics, Inc.	217
474	Sommer & Maca Industries, Inc.	216
475	Columbia Pipe & Supply Co.	215
476	Ed Miniat, Inc.	213
477	Loeber Motors, Inc.	210
478	Garvey International, Inc.	208
479	McCain Manufacturing Corp.	206
480	Midland Paper Company	205
481	HA-LO Industries, Inc.	202
482	Quality Screw & Nut Company	202
483	Amity Packing Company	200
484	First Merchants Acceptance Corp.	200
485	Kukla Press, Inc.	200
486	Libertyville Classic Group	200
487	M-Wave, Inc.	200
488	Nelsen Steel & Wire Company	200
489	The John D. and Catherine T. MacArthur Foundation	195
490	Bigsby & Kruthers, Inc./ Knot Shops	194
491	Arrow Chevrolet, Inc.	190
492	Bradner Central Company	187
493	Bob O'Connor Ford	185
494	Duff & Phelps Credit Rating Co.	183
495	CFC International, Inc.	182
496	Berlin Packaging Corporation	180
497	General Drug Company	180
498	Motor Works of Barrington, Inc.	180
499	VisionTek Inc.	180
500	Zoll Foods Corporation	180

Chicago-Area Companies on the *FORTUNE* 500 List of Largest U.S. Corporations

Rank	Company	City	1994 Sales ($ mil.)	Employees
9	Sears, Roebuck	Chicago	54,559	360,000
21	Amoco	Chicago	26,953	43,205
28	Motorola	Schaumburg	22,245	132,000
56	Sara Lee	Chicago	15,536	145,900
62	UAL	Elk Grove Township	13,950	77,900
76	Ameritech	Chicago	12,570	63,594
107	WMX Technologies	Oak Brook	10,097	74,400
119	Baxter International	Deerfield	9,324	53,500
120	Walgreen	Deerfield	9,235	61,900
124	Abbott Laboratories	Abbott Park	9,156	49,464
140	McDonald's	Oak Brook	8,321	183,000
185	Unicom	Chicago	6,278	18,460
201	Quaker Oats	Chicago	5,955	20,000
204	Stone Container	Chicago	5,749	29,100
217	Navistar International	Chicago	5,337	14,910
226	First Chicago Corp.	Chicago	5,095	17,630
235	R.R. Donnelley & Sons	Chicago	4,889	39,000
251	Household International	Prospect Heights	4,603	15,500
261	Inland Steel Industries	Chicago	4,497	15,479
277	Aon	Chicago	4,157	27,000
281	FMC	Chicago	4,051	21,344
331	Illinois Tool Works	Glenview	3,461	19,500
333	Premark International	Deerfield	3,451	23,900
369	W. W. Grainger	Skokie	3,023	11,343
371	Spiegel	Downers Grove	3,016	16,700
376	ServiceMaster	Downers Grove	2,985	34,000
386	Santa Fe Pacific	Schaumburg	2,955	15,768
394	Morton International	Chicago	2,850	13,100
395	Brunswick	Lake Forest	2,836	20,800
425	Whitman	Rolling Meadows	2,659	15,271
438	Cotter	Chicago	2,574	4,000
460	Dean Foods	Franklin Park	2,432	12,100
461	Caremark International	Northbrook	2,426	9,150
478	Ace Hardware	Oak Brook	2,326	3,664
483	Fruit of the Loom	Chicago	2,298	37,400
487	USG	Chicago	2,290	12,300

Source: *FORTUNE*; May 15, 1995

Chicago-Area Companies on the *Business Week* 1000 List of America's Most Valuable Companies

Rank	Company	City	1995 Market Value ($ mil.)
14	Motorola	Schaumburg	33,810
22	Amoco	Chicago	29,473
25	Abbott Laboratories	Abbott Park	28,680
31	Ameritech	Chicago	23,644
33	McDonald's	Oak Brook	23,066
46	Sears, Roebuck	Chicago	17,323
65	WMX Technologies	Oak Brook	13,091
68	Sara Lee	Chicago	12,631
69	Allstate	Northbrook	12,357
100	Baxter International	Deerfield	8,787
169	Walgreen	Deerfield	5,815
177	Unicom	Chicago	5,439
183	Wm. Wrigley Jr.	Chicago	5,244
185	R.R. Donnelley	Chicago	5,213
192	Illinois Tool Works	Glenview	5,107
217	CNA Financial	Chicago	4,565
220	First Chicago	Chicago	4,549
223	Quaker Oats	Chicago	4,328
225	Morton International	Chicago	4,324
234	Household International	Prospect Heights	4,226
257	General Instrument	Chicago	3,880
272	Newell	Freeport	3,769
277	Tribune	Chicago	3,727
284	Aon	Chicago	3,549
323	W. W. Grainger	Skokie	3,102
356	Premark International	Deerfield	2,754
362	Molex	Lisle	2,687
368	U. S. Cellular	Chicago	2,623
394	Telephone & Data Systems	Chicago	2,476
405	Nalco Chemical	Naperville	2,334
410	Unitrin	Chicago	2,306
414	Tellabs	Lisle	2,269
422	Andrew	Orland Park	2,227
433	FMC	Chicago	2,153
436	New York Times	Oak Brook	2,141
446	Stone Container	Chicago	2,113
473	Whitman	Rolling Meadows	1,982
493	Brunswick	Lake Forest	1,897
501	ServiceMaster	Downers Grove	1,864
502	Mercury Finance	Northbrook	1,857
507	Northern Trust	Chicago	1,839
520	Fruit of the Loom	Chicago	1,777

Chicago-Area Companies on the *Business Week* 1000 List of America's Most Valuable Companies (continued)

Rank	Company	City	1995 Market Value ($ mil.)
595	Illinois Central	Chicago	1,443
614	IMC Global	Northbrook	1,378
615	Kemper	Long Grove	1,375
653	Inland Steel Industries	Chicago	1,281
654	NICOR	Naperville	1,276
655	Old Republic International	Chicago	1,276
667	Caremark International	Northbrook	1,253
673	Dean Foods	Franklin Park	1,238
705	UAL	Elk Grove Township	1,179
731	Spiegel	Downers Grove	1,109
734	Bankers Life Holding	Chicago	1,105
751	USG	Chicago	1,082
753	HealthCare Compare	Downers Grove	1,079
754	Navistar International	Chicago	1,079
758	Itel	Chicago	1,074
825	Safety-Kleen	Elgin	953
835	Comdisco	Rosemont	936
841	Federal Signal	Oak Brook	930
849	CBI Industries	Oak Brook	919
852	Peoples Energy	Chicago	916
868	GATX	Chicago	888
882	John Nuveen	Chicago	865
887	SPS Transaction Services	Riverwoods	863
895	Equity Residential Properties Trust	Chicago	846
949	Alberto-Culver	Melrose Park	781
966	Wisconsin Central Transportation	Rosemont	757
988	Tootsie Roll Industries	Chicago	727

Source: *Business Week*; March 27, 1995; market value calculated as of February 28, 1995

Chicago-Area Companies on the *Forbes* List of the 500 Largest Private Companies in the U.S.

Rank	Company	City	Revenues ($ mil.)	Employees
11	Montgomery Ward & Co	Chicago	7,038	58,750
20	Marmon Group	Chicago	5,300	28,000
27	Alliant Foodservice	Deerfield	4,200	8,000
45	Dominick's Finer Foods	Northlake	2,470*	7,500
62	Specialty Foods	Deerfield	1,979	13,900
95	Eby-Brown	Naperville	1,530	1,411
119	H Group Holding	Chicago	1,240*	47,000
130	Amsted Industries	Chicago	1,165	9,300
136	Duchossois Industries	Elmhurst	1,126*	8,000
145	Budget Rent a Car	Lisle	1,081	8,700
150	Frank Consolidated Enterprises	Des Plaines	1,045	675
185	Tang Industries	Mt. Prospect	920*	2,000
187	Moorman Manufacturing	Quincy	914	2,900
194	Sweetheart Holdings	Chicago	888*	8,600
205	Restaurant Company	Itasca	854	12,000
217	Coca-Cola Bottling Co of Chicago	Niles	810*	4,200
226	Wirtz	Chicago	800*	1,800
243	Chemcentral	Bedford Park	753	834
249	Follett	River Grove	728	6,800
272	Hub Group	Lombard	687	681
275	Leo Burnett	Chicago	678	6,382
278	Everen Capital	Chicago	674	570
328	Baker & McKenzie	Chicago	594	5,226
332	Boler	Itasca	586*	3,000
411	Medline Industries	Mundelein	476	2,000
418	Jordan Industries	Deerfield	465	5,248
422	Pepper Cos	Chicago	460	908
432	Field Container	Elk Grove Village	450	2,400
437	Walsh Group	Chicago	450	350
445	Rand McNally & Co	Skokie	439	3,800
475	Comark	Bloomingdale	411	461
478	Encyclopædia Britannica	Chicago	405	2,800
485	Inland Group	Oak Brook	400*	753
498	Ivex Packaging	Lincolnshire	391	2,504

*Estimated
Source: *Forbes*; December 4, 1995

Chicago-Area Companies on the *Inc.* 500 List of Fastest-Growing Private Companies

Rank	Company	City	Sales Growth 1990–94 (% increase)	1994 Sales ($ mil.)
26	Hub Group Distribution Services	Arlington Heights	4,927	11,612
31	Health Tech Industries	South Holland	4,112	18,994
43	Sendai Media Group	Lombard	2,906	27,325
124	Country Peddlers & Co. of America	Alsip	1,531	13,634
149	Fitigues	Chicago	1,329	13,022
154	Everyday Learning	Evanston	1,295	7,211
172	Morningstar	Chicago	1,212	30,856
187	Personal Creations	Willowbrook	1,165	5,591
231	Magnum Technologies	Belleville	996	3,958
238	Platinum Entertainment	Downers Grove	958	10,357
248	Linderlake	Alsip	918	3,768
335	VisionTek	Gurnee	705	300,417
346	HBS Computers	Lisle	694	1,595
389	Metamor Technologies	Chicago	635	7,934
427	Original American Scones	Oak Park	581	5,322
438	Preferred Staffing	Rolling Meadows	563	10,933
497	Lloyd Creative Temporaries	Des Plaines	517	8,160

Source: *Inc.*; October 17, 1995

Chicago-Area Companies on *Black Enterprise*'s Top 100 Black-Owned Industrial/Service Companies

Rank	Company	City	1994 Sales ($ mil.)
2	Johnson Publishing Co. Inc.	Chicago	306.6
11	Soft Sheen Products Inc.	Chicago	97.2
16	Burrell Communications Group	Chicago	80.8
27	Sayers Computer Source	Mt. Prospect	55.1
35	Luster Products Co.	Chicago	46.0
38	Capsonic Group Inc.	Elgin	43.0
65	Edge Systems Inc.	Aurora	27.3
91	Crown Energy Inc.	Chicago	19.0
96	UBM Inc.	Chicago	18.2

Source: *Black Enterprise*, June 1995

Top Chicago Companies

CITY OF CHICAGO

OVERVIEW

A lot of business has been blowing the Windy City's way. After years of watching jobs move to neighboring suburbs and other states, Chicago (the nation's 3rd largest city, after New York and Los Angeles) has a growing industrial base, is filling downtown office buildings, and was awarded the 1996 Democratic Convention (expected to bring in $100 million).

Mayor Richard Daley II takes much of the credit for this wave of success. In 1994 Chicago began a $220 million infrastructure program intended to improve life and work within the city limits. Daley's office also initiated a Business Express program, which cuts administrative red tape for local companies.

Chicago's residents enjoy vibrant arts, music, sports, and social scenes. The city is fa-mous as a jazz capital, and Chicago Cubs baseball fans are known for undying loyalty to a team that last won the World Series in 1908. The University of Chicago and Northwestern University are world-renowned.

Highways, railroads, and shipping lanes radiate like spokes from the city, underscoring Chicago's important role as a hub for Midwest manufacturing and trade. The Chicago Board of Trade is the world's largest and oldest futures market.

While striving to improve Chicago's living and business climate, Democrat Daley has developed an antagonistic relationship with the Republican-led Illinois legislature and the suburbs surrounding Chicago, battling over growth, resources, and spending priorities.

WHEN

The area that became Chicago was visited by French explorers Louis Joliet and Father Jacques Marquette as early as 1673. The British won Canada from the French in 1763 and claimed what is now northeastern Illinois as well. In 1804 the US completed Fort Dearborn near the mouth of the Chicago River, establishing a competing claim to the area that was not resolved until the War of 1812.

Chicago's first 48 blocks were platted in 1830. Within 3 years, a modicum of civilization was achieved when William Lill established the first brewery (backed by Mayor William Ogden). Chicago was incorporated in 1837 with 4,170 residents and quickly became an important Great Lakes port. By 1857 more than 4,000 miles of rail lines radiated from it.

Chicago grew quickly during the Civil War. But in 1871 the Great Chicago Fire devastated the largest city in the Midwest, destroying 17,450 buildings in a day. Chicago rebounded in 3 years, and its vast rail connections and large port spurred heavy industrial development. Job growth attracted immigrants, and by 1880 the city counted 500,000 citizens.

Labor battles including the Haymarket Riot of 1886 wracked Chicago in the 1880s and 1890s and formed the seed from which organized labor developed. Amid this unrest, the city flaunted its newfound cosmopolitan standing by hosting the Columbian Exposition in 1892–93. The development of the refrigerator railcar helped make Chicago a meatpacking center. By the early 20th century, the city also had become home to great architects Daniel Burnham, Louis Sullivan, and Frank Lloyd Wright.

Gangsters like Al Capone and John Dillinger fought for control of a lucrative bootlegging trade during Prohibition. Meanwhile, European immigrants and southern blacks pushed the city's population to 3.4 million by 1945.

After WWII urban decay weakened the city. However, Chicago's fortunes changed after Richard Daley was elected mayor in 1955. Daley's 21-year rule constituted the last big-city political machine. The mayor not only ensured that snow was plowed from the streets but built a power base capable of legendary feats (such as the alleged delivery of Illinois's electoral votes in favor of the Kennedy presidential campaign in 1960).

Daley's star waned after the 1968 Democratic Convention, in which Chicago police violently attacked reporters and antiwar protesters, causing a national uproar. He hung on tenuously until his death in 1976. With businesses and jobs fleeing the city, Chicago was passed in population by Los Angeles in 1984.

Daley's son Richard II became mayor in 1990. His first major crisis occurred in 1992 when a pile driver punctured a tunnel under the Chicago River. Water rushed in, filling basements throughout the business district and causing millions of dollars in damage.

In 1995 Daley's administration was castigated for its slow response to a heat wave that killed more than 700 residents. That same year Chicago agreed to pay $36 million to settle some lawsuits stemming from the 1992 flood. Nevertheless, Daley has scored political points by putting police back on neighborhood beats, running a tight fiscal ship, and using Washington ties to deliver scarce federal money.

Form of government: Mayor/council
Fiscal year ends: December 31
Motto: *Urbs in Horto* (City in a Garden)

WHO

Mayor: Richard M. Daley II, age 53, $170,000 pay
City Clerk: James Lanski
City Comptroller: Walter K. Knorr
Commissioner, Mayor's Office of Budget and Management: Diane Aigotti
Commissioner Fire: Ray Orozco
Commissioner Health: Sheila Lyne
Commissioner Management Information Systems: Sal Lato
Commissioner Planning and Development: Jeff Boyle
Commissioner Police: Matt Rodriguez
Commissioner Purchasing: Al Gryze
Commissioner Streets and Sanitation: Eileen Carey
Commissioner Transportation: Tom Walker
Commissioner Finance: Barbara Lumpkin
Commissioner Revenue: Ernie Wish
Commissioner Personnel: Glen Carr
Auditors: Deloitte & Touche LLP

WHERE

HQ: 121 N. LaSalle St., Chicago, IL 60602
Phone: 312-744-4000
Fax: 312-744-9538 (Mayor's Office)
County: Cook
Elevation: 623 feet above sea level

The City of Chicago encompasses 228 square miles on the southwestern shore of Lake Michigan in northeastern Illinois.

WHAT

Selected Performing Arts Organizations/Events
Allied Arts Concerts
Chicago International Film Festival
Chicago International Theater Festival
Chicago String Ensemble
Chicago Symphony Orchestra
Hubbard Street Dance Chicago
League of Chicago Theaters (116 members)
Lyric Opera of Chicago
Ravinia Festival

Selected Colleges and Universities
Art Institute of Chicago
Chicago State University
DePaul University
DeVry Institute of Technology
Loyola University of Chicago
Northwestern University
St. Xavier University
University of Chicago
University of Illinois at Chicago

Major Professional Sports Teams
Chicago Bears (National Football League)
Chicago Blackhawks (National Hockey League)
Chicago Bulls (National Basketball Association)
Chicago Cubs (National League baseball)
Chicago White Sox (American League baseball)

Selected Cultural Attractions
Balzckas Museum of Lithuanian Culture
Bicycle Museum of America
Chicago Academy of Sciences
Chicago Architecture Foundation
Chicago Historical Society
DuSable Museum of African-American History
Jane Addams Hull House
Lincoln Park Zoo
Morton Arboretum
Museum of Contemporary Art
Museum of Science and Industry
Navy Pier
Newberry Library
Smart Museum of Art

	1994 Revenues	
	$ mil.	% of total
Property tax	637	20
Federal/state grants	589	18
Utility tax	368	11
Sales tax	334	10
Transportation tax	247	8
State income tax	214	7
Internal service	205	7
Service charges	93	3
Fines	88	3
Interest	54	2
Licenses/permits	45	1
Other	355	10
Total	**3,229**	**100**

HOW MUCH

	Annual Growth	1985	1986	1987	1988	1989	1990	1991	1992	1993	1994
Population (mil.)	(1.1%)	3.01	3.01	3.02	3.02	3.03	2.78	2.78	2.77	2.75	2.73
Employment (mil.)	(0.3%)	1.25	1.27	1.29	1.30	1.34	1.33	1.30	1.24	1.26	1.22
Per capita income ($)	3.5%	11,046	11,620	12,548	11,619	12,379	13,058	13,941	14,850	14,930	15,070
Market value of real estate ($ bil.)	—	51	58	60	67	69	82	91	94	94	—
Retail sales ($ bil.)	(1.0%)	15.2	15.3	15.7	15.6	16.4	17.6	18.2	15.9	14.5	13.9
City revenue ($ mil.)	5.0%	2,076	2,126	2,388	2,366	2,662	2,768	2,844	2,882	3,022	3,229

Per Capita Income ($) 1985–94

Top Chicago Companies

ABBOTT LABORATORIES

Based in a northern suburb of Chicago, Abbott Labs is a diversified health care company that develops, manufactures, and sells diagnostic, therapeutic, and nutritional products. The company is the world leader in the production of the antibiotic erythromycin, and its baby formula Similac commands the #1 position in the US baby-formula market. Abbott is a worldwide leader in in-vitro diagnostic products such as thyroid tests, cancer monitoring tests, and tests for detecting hepatitis and AIDS antibodies, among others.

Abbott has 2 divisions: pharmaceutical and nutritional products (including chemical and agricultural products), and hospital and laboratory products (anesthetics, drug delivery systems, diagnostic systems). The traditionally lean and efficient company's R&D department is adept at developing niche products (such as nutritional supplements) and finding new uses for already developed drugs. Its pipeline has many products in all stages of investigation.

Abbott is committed to expanding its growing overseas markets. It sells products in about 130 countries, and almost 40% of its sales take place outside the US. The company has manufacturing plants in North America, Europe, and Japan. Abbott is carefully adapting its products for the developing markets in Latin America and Asia.

Family physician Wallace Abbott founded the Abbott Alkaloidal Company in a Chicago suburb in 1888 to sell his improved form of the dosimetric granule (a pill that supplied uniform quantities of drugs). By 1900 sales were $125,000. The AMA criticized Dr. Abbott for his aggressive marketing, but the doctor successfully defended himself, receiving support from much of the medical profession.

During WWI Abbott scientists discovered techniques for synthesizing anesthetics and sedatives previously available only from some German companies. In 1922 the company improved its research capacity by buying Dermatological Research Laboratories. In 1928 Abbott acquired John T. Milliken of St. Louis, which brought Abbott well-trained salesmen.

Abbott went public in 1929. Flamboyant salesman DeWitt Clough became president in 1933; the Abbott magazine *What's New*, prepared by Clough's promotional staff, was a significant new corporate marketing tool. The company began to operate internationally in the mid-1930s, opening branches in Argentina, Brazil, Cuba, Mexico, and the UK.

Abbott was one of several drug companies that increased penicillin production during WWII. After the war, the company introduced new forms of penicillin. Research toward other antibiotics yielded Erythrocin (1952), Abbott's form of the antibiotic erythromycin. In the 1960s the company added consumer products (Selsun shampoo, Murine) and infant and nutritional formulas (such as Similac), but drugs and hospital products remained its mainstay. The FDA banned artificial sweetener Sucaryl (introduced in 1950) in 1970 after tests indicated it might be carcinogenic. In 1971 mil-

lions of intravenous solutions were recalled following contamination reports.

In 1981 Abbott introduced a hospital nutritional support service. In the early 1980s the company was licensed to sell Japanese-developed pharmaceuticals in the US. Profits increased steadily after 1979, when Robert Schoellhorn became CEO. Schoellhorn cut R&D and fired several top managers; in 1990 he was laid off.

In 1990 Abbott received FDA approval to market ProSom (an insomnia drug). The company came under legal fire from children of women who, in the 1950s, took DES, a synthetic hormone that may cause cancer. In 1992 Abbott exchanged rights to its controversial HIVIG (HIV immune globulin) product, which may fight AIDS, to North American Biologicals for 16% of the company.

The FTC brought suit for price fixing against Abbott, Bristol-Myers Squibb, and American Home Products in 1992. The other 2 settled out of court, but Abbott fought the allegations. By the end of 1992, Abbott had paid about $140 million in settlements.

In 1993 Hytrin, a hypertension drug, received FDA approval for the treatment of enlarged prostates. Also in 1993 the company strengthened its lead in the US anesthesia market by introducing generic inhalation agents isoflurane and enflurane.

In late 1994 the company purchased the nutritional business of the Spanish concern Puleva. In 1995 the FDA approved Abbott's new ulcer treatment, Prevacid, and expanded treatment uses for 2 drugs: Depakote (an anticonvulsant) for manic depression, and Lupron (a prostate cancer treatment) for anemia due to fibroid tumors.

NYSE symbol: ABT
Fiscal year ends: December 31

WHO

Chairman and CEO: Duane L. Burnham, age 53,
$1,594,269 pay
President and COO: Thomas R. Hodgson, age 53,
$1,219,438 pay
SVP Finance and CFO: Gary P. Coughlan, age 50,
$786,923 pay
SVP Strategic Improvement Processes: David A.
Thompson, age 53, $752,692 pay
SVP Pharmaceutical Operations: Paul N. Clark, age 48,
$732,692 pay
SVP Hospital Products: John G. Kringel, age 55
SVP, Secretary, and General Counsel: Jose M. de Lasa,
age 53
SVP Chemical and Agricultural Products: Robert L.
Parkinson Jr., age 44
SVP Chief Scientific Officer: David V. Milligan, age 54
SVP Diagnostic Operations: Miles D. White, age 39
SVP Human Resources: Ellen M. Walvoord
Auditors: Arthur Andersen & Co, SC

WHERE

HQ: 100 Abbott Park Rd., Abbott Park, IL 60064-3500
Phone: 708-937-6100
Fax: 708-937-1511

	1994 Sales		1994 Operating Income	
	$ mil.	% of total	$ mil.	% of total
US	5,758	63	1,558	70
Europe, Africa & Middle East	1,662	18	352	6
Pacific, Far East & Canada	1,246	14	182	16
Latin America	490	5	131	8
Adjustments	—	—	(20)	—
Total	**9,156**	**100**	**2,203**	**100**

WHAT

	1994 Sales		1994 Operating Income	
	$ mil.	% of total	$ mil.	% of total
Pharmaceutical & nutritional prods.	4,951	54	1,385	63
Hospital & lab prods.	4,205	46	818	37
Total	**9,156**	**100**	**2,203**	**100**

Selected Brand Names

Agricultural Products
ProGibb (plant growth
regulator)
VectoBac (larvacide)
XenTari (insecticide)

Consumer Products
Murine (eye and ear drops)
Selsun Blue (dandruff
shampoo)

Hospital Products
ADD-Vantage (IV system)
ADx (drug testing
equipment)
IMx (immunoassay testing
system)
LifeShield (needleless
IV system)
Opticath (monitor)

Transpac (blood pressure
monitor)

Nutritional Supplements
Advera (nutrition for
AIDS patients)
Ensure (adult nutrition)
PediaSure (infant formula)

Prescription Drugs
Abbokinase (blood clot
dissolver)
Biaxin (antibiotic)
Depakote (anticonvulsant)
Hytrin (hypertension and
prostate treatment)
Lupron (cancer drug)
Survanta (treatment for
premature infant
respiratory distress)

KEY COMPETITORS

American Home Products	Diagnostic Products	Merck Nellcor
Bausch & Lomb	DuPont	Nestlé
Baxter	Genentech	Purepac
Becton, Dickinson	Genzyme	Rhône-
Biogen	Glaxo Wellcome	Poulenc
Bristol-Myers Squibb	Hoechst	Roche
Chiron Corp.	Johnson & Johnson	St. Jude Medical
C. R. Bard	Medtronic	Unilever

HOW MUCH

	Annual Growth	1985	1986	1987	1988	1989	1990	1991	1992	1993	1994
Sales ($ mil.)	11.8%	3,360	3,808	4,388	4,937	5,380	6,159	6,877	7,852	8,408	9,156
Net income ($ mil.)	14.0%	465	541	633	752	860	966	1,089	1,239	1,399	1,517
Income as % of sales	—	13.8%	14.2%	14.4%	15.2%	16.0%	15.7%	15.8%	15.8%	16.6%	16.6%
Earnings per share ($)	16.0%	0.49	0.58	0.70	0.84	0.97	1.11	1.28	1.47	1.69	1.87
Stock price – high ($)	—	9.00	13.75	16.75	13.09	17.59	23.19	34.88	34.19	30.88	34.00
Stock price – low ($)	—	4.98	7.92	10.00	10.72	11.56	15.63	19.63	26.13	22.63	25.38
Stock price – close ($)	16.0%	8.55	11.41	12.06	12.03	17.00	22.50	34.44	30.38	29.63	32.63
P/E – high	—	18	24	24	16	18	21	27	23	18	18
P/E – low	—	10	14	14	13	12	14	15	18	13	14
Dividends per share ($)	17.8%	0.17	0.21	0.24	0.29	0.34	0.40	0.48	0.58	0.66	0.74
Book value per share ($)	11.1%	1.96	1.94	2.31	2.74	3.08	3.30	3.77	4.00	4.48	5.04
Employees	4.0%	34,742	35,754	37,828	38,751	40,249	43,770	45,694	48,118	49,659	49,464

1994 Year-end:
Debt ratio: 20.7%
Return on equity: 39.3%
Cash (mil.): $315
Current ratio: 1.12
Long-term debt (mil.): $287
No. of shares (mil.): 803
Dividends
  Yield: 2.3%
  Payout: 39.6%
Market value (mil.): $26,211

**Stock Price History
High/Low 1985–94**

ACE HARDWARE CORPORATION

OVERVIEW

Oak Brook, Illinois–based Ace Hardware is a leading US dealer-owned hardware wholesaler cooperative with more than 5,300 dealer-owners who operate Ace Hardware stores in the US, Europe, the Middle East, and Central and South America. Ace acts as middleman between manufacturers and dealers, distributing products through 14 Retail Support Centers. It also makes its own brand-name paint. Its dealers own 100% of the company and receive dividends from Ace's net profits as well as from Ace Paint.

Ace is hoping to trump its rivals Cotter & Co. (True Value Hardware) and Servistar Corp.

with its New Age of Ace strategy, designed to boost annual revenues to $5 billion by the year 2000. Key elements are rapid international expansion and Ace's adoption of new technology to reduce costs and speed up inventory delivery times. Outside the US, sales were up 50% in 1994, and 36 new stores were opened. New markets served include Germany, Indonesia, Nicaragua, and the Philippines.

Faced with stiff competition from its warehouse-style rivals, Ace is imposing a limited range of standard store formats to help dealers optimize their sales. Ace is also weeding out its noncompetitive mom-and-pop dealers.

WHEN

Ace traces its roots to a group of Chicago-area hardware dealers — Frank Burke, Richard Hesse, E. Gunnard Lindquist, and Oscar Fisher — who joined together in 1924 to pool their hardware buying and their promotional costs. In 1928 the group incorporated as Ace Stores, Inc., and began operations as a wholesaler, with Burke as president. Burke stepped down a year later and was replaced by Hesse, who would remain president of the company for the next 44 years.

The company opened its first warehouse in 1929, and by 1933 Ace had 38 dealers. That same year the company held its first convention so that dealers could review and purchase merchandise. The company continued to grow during the next 2 decades, and by 1949 it had 133 dealers in 7 states.

In 1953 Ace began to allow dealers to buy stock in the company through the Ace Perpetuation Plan. In the 1960s Ace began to expand into the South and the West, and in 1969 it opened distribution centers in Benicia, California, and in Atlanta, its first such facilities outside of Chicago.

In the early 1970s the do-it-yourself market began to surge as inflation pushed up the fees for plumbers and electricians. As the market grew, large home-center chains began to gobble up market share from independent dealers like those franchised through Ace. In response Ace and its dealers became a part of a growing trend in the hardware industry — cooperatives.

In 1973 Hesse sold Ace to its dealers for $6 million (less than half its book value), and in 1974 Ace began operating as a cooperative. Hesse stepped down, and Arthur Krausman became head of the company. Three years later the dealers took full control when the

company's first Board of Dealer-Directors was elected.

Ace continued to expand in 1975 when it began exporting products, and in 1978 Ace signed up a number of dealers in the eastern US. By 1979 it had dealers in all 50 states. Ace began an aggressive building program in 1980 to add distribution centers to serve its growing network of dealers.

In 1984 Ace began manufacturing its own paint when it opened a paint plant in Matteson, Illinois. By 1985 Ace had reached $1 billion in sales. That same year the company initiated its Store of the Future Program, allowing dealers to borrow up to $200,000 to upgrade their stores and conduct market analyses.

In 1989 the company began to test a computer network, called ACENET, that allowed Ace dealers to check inventory, send and receive electronic mail, make special purchase requests, and keep up with prices on commodity items such as lumber. Also in 1989 Ace added a Lumber & Building Materials convention to its list of annual meetings.

Ace established an International Division in 1990 to handle its overseas stores. In 1992, 4 Ace dealers in Florida sued the company for allegedly signing up a wholesaler as a dealer. According to Ace's membership requirements, owner-dealers must be retailers.

In 1993 Ace opened a Retail Support Center in Princeton, Illinois, and in 1994 it began expansion programs at its Little Rock, Arkansas, and Hartford, Connecticut, centers. The company also plans to open a Retail Support Center in Colorado Springs, Colorado.

In 1995 Ace announced plans to develop 3 to 5 prototype stores to act as a laboratory for new operations and merchandising ideas.

Dealer-owned cooperative
Fiscal year ends: December 31

WHO

Chairman: Richard E. Laskowski, age 53
CEO: Roger E. Peterson, age 57, $925,000 pay
President and COO: David F. Hodnik, age 47,
$411,250 pay
SVP Retail Operations and Marketing: William A.
Loftus, age 56, $305,500 pay
VP Corporate Strategy and International Business: Paul
M. Ingevaldson, age 49, $273,760 pay
VP Retail Support and New Business: David F. Myer,
age 49, $198,050 pay
VP Merchandising: Michael C. Bodzewski, age 45
VP Finance: Rita D. Kahle, age 38
VP, General Counsel, and Secretary: David W. League,
age 55
VP Information Systems: Donald L. Schuman, age 56
VP Human Resources: Fred J. Neer, age 55
Auditors: KPMG Peat Marwick LLP

WHERE

HQ: 2200 Kensington Ct., Oak Brook, IL 60521
Phone: 708-990-6600
Fax: 708-573-4894

Ace serves dealers with retail operations in all 50 states
and in 55 countries.

Retail Support Centers
Baltimore, MD
Charlotte, NC
Dallas, TX
Gainesville, GA
Hartford, CT
La Crosse, WI
Lincoln, NE
Little Rock, AR
Prescott Valley, AZ
Princeton, IL
Sacramento, CA
Tampa, FL
Toledo, OH
Yakima, WA

WHAT

	1994 Sales
	% of total
Warehouse sales	62
Direct shipment	36
Bulletin sales	2
Total	**100**

	1994 Warehouse Sales
	% of total
Paint, cleaning & related supplies	19
Plumbing & heating supplies	16
Hand & power tools	14
General hardware	13
Electrical supplies	12
Garden, rural equipment & related supplies	11
Sundries	9
Housewares & appliances	6
Total	**100**

Dealer Services
Advertising
Fixtures and equipment
In-store displays
Insurance
Retail computer services
Store planning and development
Training

KEY COMPETITORS

84 Lumber
Ames
Benjamin Moore
Cotter & Co.
D.I.Y. Home Warehouse
Eagle Hardware &
Garden
Grossman's
Hardware Wholesalers
Hechinger
Home Depot
Imperial Chemical
Kmart
Lowe's
McCoy
Menard
Montgomery Ward
National Home Centers
Our Own Hardware
Payless Cashways
Pratt and Lambert
Price/Costco
Sears
Servistar
Sherwin-Williams
United Hardware
Distributing
Venture Stores
Wal-Mart
Wickes Lumber
Wolohan Lumber

HOW MUCH

	Annual Growth	1985	1986	1987	1988	1989	1990	1991	1992	1993	1994
Sales ($ mil.)	9.7%	1,009	1,061	1,198	1,382	1,546	1,625	1,704	1,871	2,018	2,326
Net income ($ mil.)	8.0%	32	37	42	54	51	60	59	61	57	64
Income as % of sales	—	3.2%	3.4%	3.5%	3.9%	3.3%	3.7%	3.5%	3.2%	2.8%	2.8%
Dividends ($ mil.)	8.4%	31	37	44	50	53	58	58	63	59	64
Employees	6.4%	2,096	2,253	2,477	2,741	2,875	2,931	3,110	3,256	3,405	3,664

1994 Year-end:
Debt ratio: 33.7%
Return on equity: 33.4%
Long-term debt (mil.): $64.3

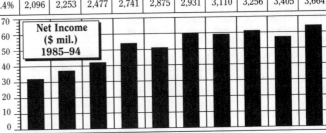

Net Income
($ mil.)
1985–94

ALBERTO-CULVER COMPANY

OVERVIEW

Alberto-Culver has regained some of its shimmer and sheen with the improved performance of its core beauty and household products. Based outside Chicago, Alberto-Culver markets health and beauty and household products (Alberto VO5 shampoos and hair treatments, SugarTwin sweetener, Mrs. Dash seasonings, and Kleen Guard furniture polish) and operates the world's largest chain of beauty supply stores, Sally Beauty Supply.

The expansion of Sally Beauty Supply has been responsible for much of the company's earnings growth over the past several years. However, after the failed introduction of a line of poultry seasonings called Village Saucerie in 1994, earnings from the household, grocery,

and toiletries divisions of Alberto-Culver rebounded sharply in 1995.

The management of Alberto-Culver has largely been assumed by Howard and Carol Bernick, the son-in-law and daughter of Leonard and Bernice Lavin, the company's founders. In 1994 Howard Bernick, president, was named CEO, succeeding Leonard Lavin. Carol Bernick became president of the Alberto-Culver USA unit.

The company generates 1/4 of its sales from foreign markets. Under a joint venture announced in 1994, C&C Cash & Carry Beauty Supply of Japan will operate its stores as Sally units. In 1995 Alberto-Culver bought Swedish-based Molnlycke Toiletries for $50 million.

WHEN

Alberto VO5 Conditioning Hairdressing was developed by a chemist (named Alberto) to rejuvenate the coiffures of Hollywood's movie stars from the damage of harsh studio lights. In 1955, 36-year-old Leonard Lavin and his wife, Bernice, bought the Los Angeles–based beauty supply firm that manufactured VO5 from Blaine Culver for $400,000 and relocated it to Chicago. That same year the company began a key component of its corporate strategy — aggressive marketing — by running the first television commercial for VO5. Within 3 years Alberto VO5 Conditioning Hairdressing had earned the top spot in its category, with sales of more than $5 million. In 1959 the company expanded its product line by buying TRESemme Hair Color.

In 1960 Alberto-Culver built a new plant and headquarters in Melrose, Illinois, and it went public in 1961. That same year the company formed an international division to market its products in Australia, Canada, England, Guatemala, Honduras, Jamaica, Mexico, and Puerto Rico. During the 1960s Alberto-Culver introduced a series of product innovations. These included Alberto VO5 shampoo (1962), New Dawn Hair Color (the first shampoo-in permanent hair color, 1963), and FDS (the first feminine deodorant body spray, 1966). Sales grew from $25 million in 1961 to over $100 million in 1964 with these product introductions.

Alberto-Culver bought 3 companies in 1969 — SugarTwin, maker of a low-calorie sugar substitute; Milani Foods, a marketer of food products for the restaurant and institutional markets; and Sally Beauty Company, a retailer of products for hairstylists and barbers. After

its acquisition Sally Beauty expanded rapidly (it now has more than 1,400 outlets offering salon products and appliances to professional and retail customers).

Alberto-Culver changed advertising in 1972 by putting two 30-second television ads — the industry's first — in a 60-second spot. The company launched TCB (an ethnic hair care line) in 1975 and Alberto VO5 Hot Oil Treatment (its first 60-second hot oil deep conditioner) in 1976. Also introduced in 1976, Static Guard became the country's best-seller. These products gave Alberto-Culver a reputation as an innovator, and the company backed up its innovations with generous spending on promotions.

Alberto-Culver bought John A. Frye Shoe Company in 1977 and Phillippe of California, which made handbags, in 1980. Although initially successful, these companies were sold in 1986 after raking up $16 million in losses over a 3-year period. Alberto-Culver shook off these losses and successfully developed a series of healthy food products, including Mrs. Dash (a salt alternative, 1983) and Molly McButter (a nonfat butter flavoring, 1987). In 1988 Howard Bernick succeeded Leonard Lavin (his father-in-law) as president and COO.

Alberto-Culver bought Cederroth International AB, a producer of health and hygiene goods, in 1991. In 1993 the company broadened its product lines by introducing Alberto VO5 Hot Oil Therapy (2 shampoos and 2 conditioners), and TRESemme Gold (4 conditioning treatments). In 1995 Alberto-Culver introduced Alberto VO5 Naturals, a natural shampoo line. In fiscal 1995 the company earned $53 million on sales of $1.4 billion.

NYSE symbol: ACV
Fiscal year ends: September 30

WHO

Chairman: Leonard H. Lavin, age 75, $1,632,796 pay
VC, Secretary, and Treasurer: Bernice E. Lavin, age 69, $557,000 pay
President and CEO: Howard B. Bernick, age 42, $892,654 pay
EVP; President, Alberto-Culver USA: Carol L. Bernick, age 42, $662,800 pay
President, Sally Beauty Company: Michael H. Renzulli, age 54, $900,000 pay
President, Alberto-Culver International: John G. Horsman Jr., age 56
SVP Finance and Controller: William J. Cernugel, age 52
VP Research and Development: Thomas J. Palione, age 49
VP and General Counsel: Raymond W. Gass, age 57
VP Human Resources, Alberto-Culver USA: Douglas E. Meneely, age 47
Auditors: KPMG Peat Marwick LLP

WHERE

HQ: 2525 Armitage Ave., Melrose Park, IL 60160
Phone: 708-450-3000
Fax: 708-450-3354

Alberto-Culver sells its personal use products in more than 100 countries.

	1994 Sales		1994 Operating Profit	
	$ mil.	% of total	$ mil.	% of total
US	919	75	74	87
Other countries	301	25	11	13
Adjustments	(4)	—	—	—
Total	**1,216**	**100**	**85**	**100**

WHAT

	1994 Sales	
	$ mil.	% of total
Sally Beauty & other	633	52
Mass-marketed personal use products	488	40
Institutional products	105	8
Adjustments	(10)	—
Total	**1,216**	**100**

Selected Brands and Products

Personal Use Products	Mrs. Dash
Alberto	Smithers
Alberto Balsam	Static Guard
Alberto One Step	SugarTwin
Alberto VO5	
Beyond (fragrance)	**Health and Hygiene Products**
Bold Hold	Lactacyd (liquid soap)
Command (aftershave)	Salve (adhesive bandages)
Consort	Samarin (antacids)
TCB	Savett (wet wipes)
TRESemme	Seltin (salt substitute)
	Topz (cotton buds)

Household and Grocery Products	**Institutional Products**
Baker's Joy	Hair care products
Diafoods Thick-it	Indola
Kleen Guard	TRESemme
Milani	TCB
Molly McButter	

KEY COMPETITORS

Allou	Johnson Publishing
Amway	Mary Kay
Avon	McCormick
Dep	Monsanto
Estée Lauder	Philip Morris
Gillette	Procter & Gamble
Helene Curtis	Rhône-Poulenc
Johnson & Johnson	Wella

HOW MUCH

	Annual Growth	1985	1986	1987	1988	1989	1990	1991	1992	1993	1994
Sales ($ mil.)	14.2%	369	435	515	605	717	796	874	1,091	1,148	1,216
Net income ($ mil.)	40.3%	2	9	18	27	29	35	30	39	41	44
Income as % of sales	—	0.6%	2.0%	3.5%	4.4%	4.1%	4.4%	3.4%	3.5%	3.6%	3.6%
Earnings per share ($)	37.4%	0.09	0.34	0.64	1.00	1.13	1.30	1.06	1.36	1.44	1.57
Stock price – high ($)	—	7.59	12.50	14.13	19.13	26.69	33.25	34.25	32.00	28.25	27.38
Stock price – low ($)	—	3.13	6.75	7.38	9.69	16.38	19.13	20.50	21.25	20.13	19.38
Stock price – close ($)	15.7%	7.34	9.75	10.38	18.38	22.31	33.25	31.63	25.50	23.13	27.25
P/E – high	—	84	37	22	19	24	26	32	24	20	17
P/E – low	—	35	20	12	10	15	15	19	16	14	12
Dividends per share ($)	12.1%	0.10	0.10	0.12	0.14	0.17	0.20	0.22	0.24	0.28	0.28
Book value per share ($)	16.4%	3.00	4.19	4.77	5.16	6.11	8.10	8.83	10.03	10.47	11.81
Employees	11.5%	3,500	4,200	4,600	4,900	5,600	5,900	7,300	7,600	8,600	9,300

1994 Year-end:
Debt ratio: 18.8%
Return on equity: 14.1%
Cash (mil.): $50
Current ratio: 1.86
Long-term debt (mil.): $43
No. of shares (mil.): 28
Dividends
  Yield: 1.0%
  Payout: 17.8%
Market value (mil.): $754

Stock Price History
High/Low 1985–94

ALLIANT FOODSERVICE INC.

OVERVIEW

Alliant Foodservice used to be spelled K-R-A-F-T. Formerly Kraft Foodservices and part of the Kraft General Foods business owned by Philip Morris, it was bought in 1995 by Clayton, Dubilier & Rice, a New York–based investment partnership specializing in LBOs. Alliant is based in Deerfield, Illinois, and is the 2nd largest US distributor of high-volume foods to hospitals, hotels, restaurants, schools, and other nonretail outlets. Alliant holds an estimated 3% market share in the $120 billion US food service distribution business. (SYSCO Corp. is the largest, with 10%.)

The company distributes more than 160,000 products, such as industrial-size packages of cheese and mayonnaise. Alliant has a 5-year deal to remain the exclusive distributor of Kraft-brand food service products, which include Bull's-Eye barbecue sauce, Miracle Whip salad dressing, and Philadelphia Brand cream cheese. Alliant also has an alliance with Baxter International for distribution to health care markets. The company operates 39 distribution centers throughout the US.

Although profit margins in the food service industry are extremely thin (Alliant's earnings are estimated at $60 million, from sales of $4 billion), the company's management insists there is ample room for improvement. Receivables and payables processing has been consolidated in a highly automated facility in Phoenix, for example. In addition, Alliant is continuing efforts started at Kraft to differentiate itself with better service through a quality management program known as Service So Good.

James Miller, who had been president of the division at Kraft since 1991, is Alliant's CEO.

WHEN

In 1903 James L. Kraft, son of a Canadian farmer, started a wholesale cheese business in Chicago. He was soon joined by his 4 brothers, and in 1909 the J. L. Kraft & Bros. Co. was incorporated.

The company pioneered major developments in cheese, the first being a blended, pasteurized cheese that was packaged in tins and would not spoil. Kraft received a patent in 1916 on what became known as process cheese. The company went public as Kraft Cheese Company in 1924 and over the years significantly altered American eating habits with the development of Velveeta (1928), Miracle Whip (1933), Kraft caramels (1933), Kraft macaroni and cheese dinner (1937), Parkay margarine (1940), sliced process cheese (1950), and Cheez Whiz (1952). In 1953 J. L. Kraft died.

The company, by then a division of National Dairy Products Corp., continued to diversify its product lines and to expand internationally. In 1969 National Dairy renamed itself Kraftco, and in 1976 the name was changed again to Kraft Inc. to reflect a renewed focus on food products and to align the entire company with what was by then an internationally recognized trademark.

In 1980 Kraft merged with Dart Industries, a Los Angeles–based conglomerate that included Duracell batteries, Tupperware, and West Bend appliances. The new company, Dart & Kraft, never became the consumer products giant envisioned by its architects, and the companies parted ways in 1986.

In 1988 Kraft was purchased by Philip Morris for $12.9 billion. Three years earlier Philip Morris had bought General Foods for $5.6 billion in an effort to reduce its dependence on tobacco sales and apply its considerable marketing skills to food products. General Foods was created in 1929 when the Postum Cereal Company acquired General Foods Company, the frozen foods company started by Clarence Birdseye. By 1985 General Foods included major American staples such as Jell-O, Kool-Aid, Maxwell House, Oscar Mayer, and Tang.

Philip Morris combined its 2 food businesses into one subsidiary called Kraft General Foods. The Kraft Foodservice Division was developed to sell the company's products in high volume to institutional and other nonretail outlets such as schools and hospitals.

In 1994 new management at Philip Morris decided to sell the low-margin Foodservice Division to Clayton, Dubilier & Rice, an investment firm started in 1978 that specializes in buying divisions of large companies. Previously the firm had bought units from General Motors, IBM, and Westinghouse.

Clayton paid $700 million for Kraft Foodservice in early 1995. The deal included an agreement for the new company to retain exclusive rights to distribute more than 700 Kraft products (which accounted for $650 million of its sales) for 5 years as well as a requirement that the name Kraft Foodservice be changed within one year. In late 1995 the company rechristened itself Alliant Foodservice Inc.

Private company
Fiscal year ends: Saturday nearest December 31

WHO

Chairman: Andrall E. Pearson
President and CEO: James A. Miller
EVP National Sales and Operations: William E. Beedie
EVP Marketing/Procurement/Logistics: Daryl D. Boddicker
EVP and CFO: Jack A. Peterson
SVP Human Resources: George E. Arseneau
VP and Treasurer: Don Civgin
VP Information Systems: Robert P. Doyle
VP Operations Finance: Frieda E. Ireland
VP Marketing and Public Relations: Gary Karp
VP Procurement and Logistics: Donald T. Polacheck
VP National Sales and Operations: Gregory Schaffner
VP Major Accounts: Harry B. Smith
VP Corporate Controller: Joseph P. Tomczak
VP Tax: William G. Wolfe
VP, General Counsel, and Secretary: Cathy C. Anderson

WHERE

HQ: One Parkway Dr. North, Deerfield, IL 60015
Phone: 847-405-8500
Fax: 847-405-8980

Alliant Foodservice distributes food products throughout the US.

WHAT

Selected Products
Cleaning supplies
Disposables
Fresh produce
Grocery products
Meat
Poultry
Refrigerated and frozen foods
Seafood
Tabletop items

Selected Exclusive Brand Products
Esplendido (Mexican food)
Glenview Farms
Kraft Brands
  Bull's-Eye barbecue sauce
  Mayonnaise
  Miracle Whip salad dressing
  Philadelphia Brand cream cheese
  Prepared Salad Dressings
  Velveeta pasteurized process cheese spread
Luzzati (Italian food)
Monogram (nonfood items)
Natural Resource (fresh produce)

Joint Venture
Dietary Products, Inc. (with Baxter Healthcare; foodservice for health care industries)

KEY COMPETITORS

Alex Lee
AmeriServ Food
Cagle's
Gordon Food Service
Heinz
JP Foodservice
Performance Food
Rykoff-Sexton
Services Group
SYSCO
US Foodservice

HOW MUCH

	Annual Growth	1985	1986	1987	1988	1989	1990	1991	1992	1993	1994
Sales ($ mil.)	7.9%	—	—	—	—	—	—	—	—	3,800	4,100
Employees	—	—	—	—	—	—	—	—	—	—	8,800

4,500										
4,000										
3,500										
3,000										
2,500			Sales ($ mil.)							
2,000			1993–94							
1,500										
1,000										
500										
0										

THE ALLSTATE CORPORATION

OVERVIEW

Allstate's fate is in its own good hands now. In 1995 Sears won approval to spin off its 80% share of the insurance company that has been a part of the retailer since 1931.

Allstate is the 2nd largest home and auto insurer in the US (after State Farm), with about a 12% market share. It also offers life insurance and annuity and pension products and sells property/liability insurance to small businesses. The company operates in Canada, Japan, and South Korea and is a worldwide reinsurer through its Allstate Reinsurance Co., based in London.

The move to independence is changing the way the company does business. It is moving to strengthen its nonproperty lines, especially its life, annuity, and pension products. Allstate has traditionally sold its products through its own network of 14,500 agents in the US and Canada. The company also accepts business from over 2,000 independent agents, primarily in rural areas, where they wouldn't compete with Allstate's own agencies.

To facilitate its sales plans, Allstate uses its database to target existing customers for additional sales. It also concentrates on areas that are less vulnerable to natural disasters than California and other coastal areas.

Allstate started out on the heels of one of its worst earnings years ever, mainly because of losses (over $1 billion) attributable to the Northridge earthquake in California.

WHEN

Allstate, the "good hands" company, had its origins in a friendly game of bridge played in 1930 on a Chicago-area commuter train between Sears president Robert Wood and a friend, insurance broker Carl Odell. Odell suggested that Sears sell auto insurance through the mail. Woods liked the idea, financed the company, and in 1931 put Odell in charge (making that hand of bridge a very good one for Odell). The company was named Allstate, after one of Sears's brands of tires.

Allstate was born just as Sears was beginning its push into retailing, and Allstate went with it, selling insurance out of all the new Sears stores.

Growth was slow during the Great Depression and World War II, but the postwar boom was a gold mine for Sears and for Allstate. The growth of suburban developments made it necessary to have a car, 1950s prudence made it necessary to insure the car, and Sears made it easy to buy the insurance, at their stores and, increasingly, at free-standing agencies. In the late 1950s Allstate added home and other property/casualty insurance lines as well as life insurance. Allstate's life insurance in force zoomed from zero to $1 billion in 6 years, the fastest growth ever in the life insurance industry.

In 1960 Sears formed Allstate Enterprises as an umbrella for all its noninsurance operations. In 1970 Allstate Enterprises bought its first S&L. The insurance company continued to acquire other S&Ls and to add subsidiaries throughout the 1970s and 1980s.

This strategy dovetailed neatly with Sears's own plan, which was to become a diversified financial services company. In 1985 Sears introduced the Discover Card through Allstate's Greenwood Trust Company.

In the late 1980s it was obvious that Sears would never be a financial services giant. Moreover, it was losing so much in retailing that by 1987 Allstate was the major contributor to corporate net income. Sears began to dismantle its financial empire in the 1990s.

Allstate had its own problems to contend with. Beginning in 1989 it changed its relations with its sales force, including the imposition of de facto sales quotas (said to have hurt underwriting standards).

Allstate suffered from a backlash against high insurance rates. When Massachusetts instituted no-fault insurance in 1989, Allstate stopped writing new auto insurance there. Later Allstate settled a suit with California over rate rollbacks called for under 1988's Proposition 103 by agreeing to refund $110 million to affected customers.

Some of Allstate's underwriting practices have brought regulatory investigations and fines. Georgia fined the company $3.5 million for failing to tell people why their auto policies were canceled (while at the same time offering them more expensive policies). Texas assessed an $850,000 fine against Allstate for discriminating against unmarried drivers or those who did not buy other Allstate insurance products by refusing to insure them or by placing them in high-risk, high-rate categories. In Washington, state regulators investigated the company's practice of using credit history as an underwriting criterion.

In 1995 the company sold 70% of PMI, its mortgage insurance unit, to the public. The IPO raised over $93 million for Allstate.

NYSE symbol: ALL
Fiscal year ends: December 31

WHO

Chairman and CEO: Jerry D. Choate, age 56,
$528,421 pay (prior to promotion)
President and COO: Edward M. Liddy, age 49,
$200,000 pay (prior to promotion)
President, Business Insurance Unit: John D. Callahan,
$416,258 pay
President, Allstate Life Insurance: Louis G. Lower II,
age 49, $416,000 pay
SVP and Treasurer: Myron J. Resnick, age 63,
$313,500 pay
SVP and CFO: Thomas J. Wilson, age 37
SVP and Chief Information Officer: Frank W. Pollard
SVP, Secretary, and General Counsel: Robert W. Pike
SVP Human Resources: Joan M. Crockett, age 44
Auditors: Deloitte & Touche LLP

WHERE

HQ: Allstate Plaza, Northbrook, IL 60062
Phone: 847-402-5000
Fax: 847-402-0045

Allstate sells life and property/casualty insurance in the
US, Puerto Rico, and Canada; it also operates in Japan
and Korea and sells reinsurance worldwide.

WHAT

	1994 Assets	
	$ mil.	% of total
Treasury & agency securities	2,091	3
Mortgage-backed securities	6,220	10
Municipal bonds	16,294	27
Corporate bonds	12,905	21
Mortgage loans	3,234	5
Other investments	7,434	12
Cash & other assets	13,191	22
Total	**61,369**	**100**

	1994 Sales		1994 Net Income	
	$ mil.	% of total	$ mil.	% of total
Personal property/ casualty ins.	16,462	77	(172)	—
Business ins.	1,687	8	145	28
Life insurance	2,857	13	312	59
Mortgage guaranty insurance	387	2	70	13
Corporate	1	0	(61)	—
Other	70	0	(67)	—
Total	**21,464**	**100**	**227**	**100**

Selected Subsidiaries
Allstate Life Insurance Co.
Forestview Mortgage Insurance Co.
Glenbrook Life and Annuity Co.
Glenbrook Life Insurance Co.
Lincoln Benefit Life Company
Northbrook Indemnity Company
Northbrook Life Insurance Co.
Northbrook National Insurance Co.
Northbrook Property and Casualty Insurance Co.
Surety Life Insurance Company
Tech-Cor, Inc. (auto safety testing)

KEY COMPETITORS

20th Century Industries
Allmerica Property
American Financial
American General
Berkshire Hathaway
Chubb
CIGNA
Cincinnati Financial
CNA Financial
Home Holdings
ITT Hartford
Kemper National Insurance
Liberty Mutual
Lincoln National
Loews
Mutual of Omaha
Nationwide Insurance
Ohio Casualty
Old Republic
Progressive Corp.
Prudential
SAFECO
St. Paul Cos.
State Farm
Travelers
USF&G

HOW MUCH

	Annual Growth	1985	1986	1987	1988	1989	1990	1991	1992	1993	1994
Assets ($ mil.)	14.8%	17,740	21,417	25,608	31,030	35,583	41,478	43,378	52,098	59,358	61,369
Net income ($ mil.)	(2.3%)	596	738	946	768	815	701	723	(500)	1,302	484
Income as % of assets	—	3.4%	3.4%	3.7%	2.5%	2.7%	1.7%	1.5%	—	2.2%	0.8%
Earnings per share ($)	(63.9%)	—	—	—	—	—	—	—	—	2.99	1.08
Stock price – high ($)	—	—	—	—	—	—	—	—	—	34.25	29.88
Stock price – low ($)	—	—	—	—	—	—	—	—	—	27.13	22.63
Stock price – close ($)	(19.5%)	—	—	—	—	—	—	—	—	29.50	23.75
P/E – high	—	—	—	—	—	—	—	—	—	11	28
P/E – low	—	—	—	—	—	—	—	—	—	9	21
Dividends per share ($)	100.0%	—	—	—	—	—	—	—	—	0.36	0.72
Book value per share ($)	(18.0%)	—	—	—	—	—	—	—	—	22.89	18.78
Employees	(2.8%)	—	—	—	55,003	55,789	57,232	54,144	51,515	49,000	46,300

1994 Year-end:
Equity as % of assets: 13.7%
Return on assets: 0.8%
Return on equity: 5.2%
Long-term debt (mil.): $869
No. of shares (mil.): 449
Dividends
  Yield: 3.0%
  Payout: 66.7%
Market value (mil.): $10,657
Sales (mil.): $21,464

Stock Price History
High/Low 1993–94

AMERITECH CORPORATION

OVERVIEW

Ameritech has stayed out of the merger mania among telephone and cable companies and has passed up offers to form national wireless communications networks. Instead, the Chicago–based company is focusing on core telecommunications services in its own 5-state Great Lakes region.

CEO Richard Notebaert continues to promote opening its local telecommunications market to competition in exchange for entering the long distance and cable television markets. Major competitors, including AT&T and Teleport Communications, have already begun to offer some forms of local telecommunications services.

In transforming itself into a full-service communications company, Ameritech reorganized its operations along customer groups, including consumer and business customers and pay phone, cellular, advertising, and leasing customers. The company is also developing for its customers such new services as long distance and interactive services. Ameritech has investments in foreign telecommunications companies, including Telecom Corp. of New Zealand and Centertel of Poland.

With the recommendation of the Justice Department, Ameritech has requested permission from a federal judge to enter the long distance market on a trial basis in Chicago and in Grand Rapids, Michigan, in 1996. In exchange, AT&T would be allowed to compete in the local telephone markets in these areas.

WHEN

Ameritech began as an arm of AT&T. From 1880 to 1885 the Bell System consolidated small, individual telephone companies into larger companies that, under franchise agreements, could construct long distance lines to other Bell exchanges. Gradually the long distance lines became AT&T Long Lines; local operations were retained by the Bell Operating Companies. Illinois Bell, now Ameritech's largest operating company, was originally known as Chicago Telephone and operated between 1881 and 1920.

In the late 1870s E. T. Gilliland Company of Indianapolis, long part of Ameritech's Indiana Bell company, was considered Bell's most innovative manufacturer. In 1881 Gilliland sold 61% of its operations to Western Electric, at that time controlled by Bell's chief rival, Western Union. The purchase could have destroyed Bell and changed the history of US telephony, but Bell regained Gilliland through an outside investor named Jay Gould, who bought shares quietly.

A century later, in 1984, AT&T spun off its local operating subsidiaries as part of its antitrust settlement. Ameritech, which began operations that same year, received 5 of AT&T's 22 telephone subsidiaries, Ameritech Mobile Communications (cellular service provider), and a share in Bell Communications Research (Bellcore, the R&D arm shared by the Bell companies).

Since divestiture Ameritech has expanded its paging services by purchasing existing operations. It also began offering electronic mail and information services by starting iNet (1987) with Bell Canada and Telenet. In 1990

Ameritech was chosen, along with Bell Atlantic, to acquire an interest in New Zealand's public phone system for $2.5 billion. The following year it joined France Telecom and the Polish government to create a national cellular phone system in Poland.

Back in the US, in 1991 Ameritech bought CyberTel, one of the 2 cellular firms in St. Louis (the other is Southwestern Bell); Knowledge Data Systems (data processing systems); and NOTIS (library information software systems). In 1992 then-CEO William Weiss held a fateful meeting in which he asked each top executive to write a "profile" of Ameritech as envisioned in 1995. Afterward only 4 executives who shared Weiss's enthusiasm for radical corporate change (current CEO Notebaert among them) joined him in planning the company's future in video, long distance, and wireless services. In the same year Ameritech and Singapore Telecom acquired a 49.9% interest in Norway's NetCom GSM (cellular services). In 1993 Ameritech bought 15% of MATAV, Hungary's telephone company.

In 1994 Ameritech signed a memorandum of understanding with Walt Disney, BellSouth, and SBC Communications to develop and deliver video programming to consumers. Ameritech also made an investment in General Electric Information Services, which links companies with customers and other groups to provide such electronic business services as invoicing, e-mail, and inventory management. In 1995 Ameritech, along with the other 6 Bell companies, announced plans to sell Bellcore, their jointly owned R&D unit.

NYSE symbol: AIT
Fiscal year ends: December 31

WHO

Chairman, President, and CEO: Richard C. Notebaert, age 47, $1,463,783 pay
EVP Corporate Strategy and Business Development: W. Patrick Campbell, age 48, $722,092 pay
EVP and General Counsel: Thomas P. Hester, age 57, $662,700 pay
EVP International: Walter S. Catlow, age 50
EVP and CFO: Oren G. Shaffer, age 52
SVP Corporate Communications: Rita P. Wilson, age 48
SVP State and Government Affairs: Thomas J. Reiman, age 45
SVP Human Resources: Walter M. Oliver, age 49
Auditors: Arthur Andersen & Co, SC

WHERE

HQ: 30 S. Wacker Dr., Chicago, IL 60606
Phone: 312-750-5000
Fax: 312-207-1601

WHAT

	1994 Sales	
	$ mil.	% of total
Local service	5,337	42
Interstate access	2,218	18
Long distance	1,456	12
Intrastate access	612	5
Directory, cellular & other	2,947	23
Total	**12,570**	**100**

Selected Affiliates
Centertel (24.5%, cellular services, Poland)
MATÁV (15%, long distance and cellular services, Hungary)
NetCom (25%, cellular services, Norway)
Telecom Corporation of New Zealand, Ltd. (24.8%)
Worldview Systems Corp. (40%, electronic travel information)

Selected Services
Advertising services
Cellular and other wireless services
Billing and collection services
Interactive services
Leasing services
Local and toll services
Long distance services
Network access services
Paging services

Telephone Companies
Illinois Bell Telephone Co.
Indiana Bell Telephone Co., Inc.
Michigan Bell Telephone Co.
The Ohio Bell Telephone Co.
Wisconsin Bell, Inc.

KEY COMPETITORS

AirTouch	MCI
ALLTELL Corp.	MFS Communications
American Business Information	NYNEX
	Pacific Telesis
AT&T Corp.	SBC Communications
Bell Atlantic	Sprint
BellSouth	TCI
BT	Telephone and Data Systems
Cable & Wireless	Teleport Communications
Century Telephone	Time Warner
Contel Cellular	U.S. Long Distance
Cowles	U.S. Signal
Frontier Corp.	U S WEST
GTE	Worldcom

HOW MUCH

	Annual Growth	1985	1986	1987	1988	1989	1990	1991	1992	1993	1994
Sales ($ mil.)	3.8%	9,021	9,362	9,536	9,903	10,211	10,663	10,818	11,153	11,710	12,570
Net income ($ mil.)	0.9%	1,078	1,138	1,188	1,237	1,238	1,254	1,166	1,346	1,513	1,170
Income as % of sales	—	11.9%	12.2%	12.5%	12.5%	12.1%	11.8%	10.8%	12.1%	12.9%	9.3%
Earnings per share ($)	1.6%	1.84	1.97	2.12	2.28	2.30	2.37	2.20	2.51	2.78	2.13
Stock price – high ($)	—	17.77	25.39	24.97	24.47	48.06	34.88	34.88	37.25	45.56	43.13
Stock price – low ($)	—	12.42	16.34	18.50	20.50	24.00	26.25	27.88	28.13	35.00	36.25
Stock price – close ($)	9.5%	17.77	22.09	21.16	23.94	34.00	33.38	31.75	35.63	38.38	40.38
P/E – high	—	10	13	12	11	21	15	16	15	33	20
P/E – low	—	7	8	9	9	10	11	13	11	25	17
Dividends per share ($)	6.6%	1.08	1.16	1.25	1.35	1.46	1.58	1.70	1.76	1.86	1.92
Book value per share ($)	(1.7%)	12.76	13.33	13.86	14.57	14.25	14.63	15.18	12.94	14.41	10.98
Employees	(1.8%)	74,885	77,538	78,510	77,334	77,326	75,780	73,967	71,300	67,192	63,594

1994 Year-end:
Debt ratio: 51.2%
Return on equity: 16.8%
Cash (mil.): $74
Current ratio: 0.56
Long-term debt (mil.): $4,448
No. of shares (mil.): 551
Dividends
 Yield: 4.8%
 Payout: 90.1%
Market value (mil.): $22,268

Stock Price History
High/Low 1985–94

AMOCO CORPORATION

OVERVIEW

The 3rd largest enterprise in Chicago (after Blue Cross and Sears), Amoco is North America's #1 natural gas producer and one of the world's largest oil and chemical companies, with confirmed oil reserves of 2.2 billion barrels and gas reserves of 18.2 trillion cubic feet. Its 3 main businesses are refining and marketing (Amoco Oil), oil and gas exploration and production (Amoco Production), and chemical production (Amoco Chemical). A 1994 restructuring split the duties of those 3 units among 17 business groups.

Since 1991 Amoco has shed weak product lines (including its oil well chemicals business) and has invested $1.7 billion to beef up its faster-growing and profitable businesses. One such profit center Amoco has developed is its polyester chemical business. It holds 40% of the world market in paraxylene and purified terephthalic acid, both used in the production of polyester. To support the booming demand for polyester in the growing economies in Asia, Amoco and its partners in Indonesia, Singapore, and Taiwan are investing $2 billion to expand the manufacturing capacity for these chemicals.

In 1995 Amoco and Shell Oil announced the creation of a limited partnership to handle much of their US operations. Amoco will own 65% of the venture.

WHEN

John D. Rockefeller organized the Standard Oil Trust in 1882. In 1886 he risked buying and storing Lima (Ohio) oil, a high-sulphur crude. Rockefeller anticipated the discovery of a sulphur-removing process, which, indeed, was patented in 1887 by chemist Herman Frasch. Certain that his copper oxide process would work on a commercial scale, Frasch persuaded the company to try it on the Lima crude. Its success assured the company a continued oil supply.

In 1889 Standard Oil organized Standard Oil of Indiana as its upper midwestern subsidiary, complete with a new refinery in Whiting, Indiana. The subsidiary built a strong retail marketing organization, including company-owned service stations and a research laboratory at the refinery — innovations at the time.

In 1911 the Supreme Court ordered Standard Oil to split up because of antitrust violations; the split-up created 33 new independent oil companies. The decision left Standard (Indiana) with 2 operations, oil refining and domestic marketing, and its exclusive right to the Standard name in the Midwest. The company purchased its crude oil and transportation from former Standard sisters Prairie Oil & Gas and Prairie Pipe Line.

In 1917 Standard (Indiana) began buying crude oil production companies; in 1925 it purchased controlling interest (81% by 1929) in Pan American Petroleum and Transport, one of the world's largest crude producers, with production facilities in Mexico and Venezuela. In 1923 Pan American bought a 50% interest in American Oil, founded in 1922 by Louis Blaustein. He had introduced antiknock gasoline, marketed under the Amoco name. Standard (Indiana), recognizing the additional value of oil converted to chemicals, began Amoco Chemicals in 1945. The company purchased Utah Oil Refining (1956), along with other refineries in the 1950s and 1960s.

In 1978 the supertanker *Amoco Cadiz* ran aground, dumping 120,000 tons of oil (6 times more than the 1989 *Exxon Valdez* spill) off the French coast, resulting in a $128 million judgment against Amoco in 1990.

Standard (Indiana) bought Cyprus Mines (copper and industrial minerals) in 1979, but in 1985 it spun off its industrial minerals business as Cyprus Minerals (now Cyprus Amax).

Standard (Indiana) changed its name to Amoco in 1985. In 1988 Amoco bought debt-ridden but resource-rich Dome Petroleum of Canada, making Amoco the largest private owner of North American natural gas reserves.

In 1992 a consortium led by Amoco finished laying a 255-mile natural gas pipeline in the North Sea. Also in 1992 the company signed agreements for drilling exploration wells in Romania and for exploration rights in China, making Amoco the first foreign oil company to explore the Chinese mainland.

In 1994 Amoco and Norsk Hydro agreed to jointly evaluate oil and gas exploration opportunities off the Russian coast. The company made 2 significant natural gas discoveries off Trinidad in 1994 as well as major oil discoveries in the Gulf of Mexico, the North Sea, and Colombia.

After a profitable year in polypropylene production in Europe in 1994, Amoco announced plans to build a 440 million pounds-per-year polymer plant in Geel, Belgium, due to begin operations in 1996.

In 1995 Amoco teamed up with Shell and Exxon to develop a deep-water oil platform.

NYSE symbol: AN
Fiscal year ends: December 31

WHO

Chairman and CEO: H. Laurance Fuller, age 56, $1,678,865 pay
President: William G. Lowrie, age 51, $724,053 pay (prior to promotion)
SEVP Strategic Planning and International Business Development: James E. Fligg, age 59, $657,504 pay (prior to promotion)
EVP Chemical Sector: Enrique J. Sosa, age 55
EVP Exploration and Production Sector: L. Richard Flury, age 48
EVP Petroleum Products Sector: W. Douglas Ford, age 51
EVP and CFO: John L. Carl, age 47
SVP and General Counsel: George S. Spindler, age 57
SVP Human Resources: R. Wayne Anderson, age 53
Auditors: Price Waterhouse LLP

WHERE

HQ: 200 E. Randolph Dr., Chicago, IL 60601
Phone: 312-856-6111
Fax: 312-856-2460

Amoco conducts operations in approximately 40 countries. Foreign exploration activities are carried out primarily in the Arabian Peninsula, Argentina, Australia, Canada, China, Colombia, the Gulf of Suez, New Zealand, the Nile Delta (Egypt), the North Sea, Poland, Romania, Trinidad, Venezuela, and West Africa.

	1994 Sales		1994 Operating Income	
	$ mil.	% of total	$ mil.	% of total
US	24,003	80	1,836	70
Canada	2,555	9	349	13
Europe	1,403	5	47	2
Other regions	1,899	6	380	15
Adjustments	502	—	—	—
Total	**30,362**	**100**	**2,612**	**100**

WHAT

	1994 Sales		1994 Operating Income	
	$ mil.	% of total	$ mil.	% of total
Refining, mktg. & transportation	23,531	68	1,585	55
Exploration & production	6,460	19	591	21
Chemicals	4,662	13	684	24
Other	144	—	(248)	—
Adjustments	(4,435)	—	—	—
Total	**30,362**	**100**	**2,612**	**100**

Lines of Business
Chemical manufacturing
Marketing of refined products and chemicals
Oil and gas exploration and production
Petroleum refining

Other Operations
Amoco Technology Co. (lasers, solar power, biotechnology)
AmProp, Inc. (real estate)
Ecova Corporation (hazardous waste disposal)

KEY COMPETITORS

Amerada Hess	DuPont	PDVSA
Ashland, Inc.	Elf Aquitaine	PEMEX
Atlantic Richfield	Enron	Pennzoil
	Exxon	Petrobrás
BASF	Hercules	Petrofina
Bayer	Hoechst	Phillips
British Gas	Imperial Oil	Petroleum
British Petroleum	Koch	Repsol
	Lyondell	Sinclair Oil
Broken Hill	Petrochemical	Sun Company
Chevron	Mobil	Tenneco
Coastal	Norsk Hydro	Texaco
Columbia Gas	Occidental	TOTAL
Diamond Shamrock	Oryx	Union Carbide
	Panhandle	Unocal
Dow Chemical	Eastern	USX–Marathon

HOW MUCH

	Annual Growth	1985	1986	1987	1988	1989	1990	1991	1992	1993	1994
Sales ($ mil.)	0.6%	28,873	20,231	22,388	23,919	26,760	31,581	28,296	26,219	28,617	30,362
Net income ($ mil.)	(1.0%)	1,953	747	1,360	2,063	1,610	1,913	1,173	850	1,820	1,789
Income as % of sales	—	6.7%	3.7%	6.1%	9.4%	8.6%	6.6%	6.1%	3.2%	6.4%	5.9%
Earnings per share ($)	(0.3%)	3.71	1.46	2.66	4.00	3.12	3.77	2.36	1.71	3.66	3.60
Stock price – high ($)	—	35.13	36.06	45.13	40.13	55.75	60.38	55.00	53.75	59.25	64.13
Stock price – low ($)	—	25.13	26.56	28.50	33.81	36.81	49.25	45.63	41.75	48.13	50.88
Stock price – close ($)	7.5%	30.94	32.63	34.50	37.50	54.63	52.38	49.13	48.75	52.88	59.13
P/E – high	—	10	25	17	10	18	16	23	31	16	18
P/E – low	—	7	18	11	9	12	13	19	24	13	14
Dividends per share ($)	3.2%	1.65	1.65	1.65	1.75	1.90	2.04	2.20	2.20	2.20	2.20
Book value per share ($)	2.9%	22.39	22.14	23.50	25.80	26.75	28.03	28.52	26.11	27.53	28.97
Employees	(1.5%)	49,545	46,775	46,774	53,423	53,653	54,524	54,120	46,994	46,317	43,205

1994 Year-end:
Debt ratio: 24.4%
Return on equity: 12.8%
Cash (mil.): $1,789
Current ratio: 1.32
Long-term debt (mil.): $4,387
No. of shares (mil.): 496
Dividends
  Yield: 3.7%
  Payout: 61.1%
Market value (mil.): $29,352

Stock Price History
High/Low 1985–94

AON CORPORATION

OVERVIEW

Aon — the name means oneness in Gaelic — unites a wide variety of insurance and insurance brokering and consulting companies that operate throughout the US and worldwide.

The Chicago-based company's primary operation (developed by self-improvement advocate W. Clement Stone) is Combined Insurance, the leader of Aon's Accident and Health group. This group also includes Union Fidelity, Globe Life Insurance, and Ryan Insurance Group (the insurance company founded by chairman and CEO Patrick Ryan; it merged with Combined in 1982). The group offers old-fashioned indemnity insurance for accident- and sickness-only policies, often for terms as short as 6 months. It also offers cancer insurance, Medicare supplement, and disability coverage to individuals, businesses, and affinity groups. Combined Insurance sells through a network of 9,000 career agents.

Aon's life insurance group comprises Combined Insurance's life insurance operations, Globe Life Insurance, Union Fidelity Life, and Life Insurance Co. of Virginia, the segment's primary operating company. In addition to its commissioned sales force, the company sells through regional stock brokerage houses and banks and other financial institutions.

The newest and fastest-growing of Aon's segments is insurance brokerage and consulting. Built up by Ryan, the group is anchored by the Rollins Hudig Hall Group, one of the largest insurance brokers in the world. During the first half of the 1990s this group expanded primarily through acquisitions. The spree continued in 1995 with the acquisition by its Godwins International consulting firm of HRStrategies, a human resources consulting firm that has offices in the US as well as in Lithuania and Russia.

WHEN

Combined Insurance was founded in 1947 by W. Clement Stone, who started his working life in 1908 as a 6-year-old paperboy in Chicago, helping supplement the earnings of his seamstress mother. As a child he read and absorbed the optimistic messages of the 19th century Horatio Alger novels, which detailed the successes of plucky, enterprising heroes.

Mrs. Stone never made a go of the dress business, so when her son was in high school she bought a small Detroit insurance agency. She had better luck there and in 1918 brought her son into the business. Young Stone sold low-cost, low-benefit accident insurance, issuing the policies on the spot (in essence, underwriting the policy himself for the issuing company).

In 1922 Stone opened his own agency, the Combined Registry Co. While selling policies himself (up to 122 per day), he recruited a nationwide force of agents. But many of them were unproductive, and when the Depression descended, Stone reduced his force while improving training, offering agents the benefit of his experience and positive mental attitude.

Forced by his son's respiratory illness to winter in the South, Stone followed the sun to Arkansas and Texas. In 1939 he bought American Casualty Insurance Co. of Dallas. Other acquisitions were consolidated as the Combined Insurance Co. of America in 1947.

The company grew through the 1950s and 1960s, continuing to sell its old-fashioned health and accident policies. In the 1970s

Combined expanded overseas despite being hit hard by the recession.

In 1982, after 10 years of stagnant growth under Clement Stone Jr., the elder Stone (then 79) reassumed control until the completion of a merger with Ryan Insurance Co. allowed him to transfer power to Patrick Ryan.

Ryan, the son of a Wisconsin Ford dealer, had started his company as an auto credit insurer in 1964 at the age of 26. In 1976 the company acquired the insurance brokerage units of the Esmark conglomerate. Ryan's less personal management style differed radically from Stone's rah-rah boosterism, which gave Stone some early 2nd thoughts. But these were overcome (in part by Ryan's interest in philanthropy, a major concern of Stone's), and Stone turned the reins over to Ryan (who owns 12% of the company; Stone owns 1%).

Although life, health, and accident segments remained key components of the company's revenues, Ryan increased the company's emphasis on insurance brokering and added more upscale insurance products. He also trimmed staff and took other cost-cutting measures. Combined's name was changed to Aon in 1987. In 1991 the company bought Hudig Langeveldt, Europe's largest insurance brokerage (dating back to 1688). Since then Aon has added more brokering and consulting businesses. In 1995 Aon sold Union Fidelity Life to GE Capital and agreed to sell insurance subsidiary Life Insurance Co. of Virginia to GE Capital for $960 million.

NYSE symbol: AOC
Fiscal year ends: December 31

WHO

Chairman, President, and CEO: Patrick G. Ryan, age 57,
$951,925 pay
EVP and Chief Counsel: Raymond I. Skilling, age 55,
$685,904 pay
EVP, CFO, and Treasurer: Harvey N. Medvin, age 58,
$677,201 pay
EVP: Daniel T. Cox, age 49, $606,847 pay
SVP and Senior Investment Officer: Michael A.
Conway, age 48, $465,200 pay
SVP: Richard F. Ferruci
SVP and Secretary: Arthur F. Quern
VP Professional Development (HR): Stephen C. Taylor
VP Compensation and Benefits: John A. Reschke
VP Financial Relations: Joan E. Steel
VP and Controller: James D. White
VP and Internal Auditor: Thomas A. Curatolo
Auditors: Ernst & Young LLP

WHERE

HQ: 123 N. Wacker Dr., Chicago, IL 60606
Phone: 312-701-3000
Fax: 312-701-3100

Aon operates worldwide, offering consumer insurance in
Australia, Belgium, Canada, France, Germany, Ireland,
the Netherlands, New Zealand, Spain, the UK, and the
US and commercial insurance in those and 31 other
countries.

	1994 Sales		1994 Pretax Income	
	$ mil.	% of total	$ mil.	% of total
US	3,324	80	419	78
Other countries	833	20	118	22
Total	**4,157**	**100**	**537**	**100**

WHAT

	1994 Assets	
	$ mil.	% of total
Cash & equivalents	509	3
Government instruments	1,625	9
Stocks	939	5
Bonds	3,684	21
Mortgage-backed securities	3,464	19
Mortgage loans	568	3
Policy loans	215	1
Other	6,918	39
Total	**17,922**	**100**

	1994 Sales		1994 Pretax Income	
	$ mil.	% of total	$ mil.	% of total
Insurance brokering & consulting	1,422	34	159	30
Accident & health	1,297	31	178	33
Life insurance	947	23	113	21
Specialty property & casualty	316	8	54	10
Corporate & other	175	4	34	6
Total	**4,157**	**100**	**538**	**100**

Selected Subsidiaries

Aon Risk Services, Inc.   Nicholson Leslie Group Ltd.
Aon Specialty Group, Inc.   Rollins Hudig Hall
Combined Insurance   Group, Inc.
   Co. of America   Ryan Insurance Group
Godwins International, Inc.   Union Fidelity Life
The Life Insurance   Insurance Co.
   Co. of Virginia   Virginia Surety Co., Inc.

KEY COMPETITORS

AIG   Frank B. Hall   Torchmark
Alexander &   General Re   Transamerica
   Alexander   Hilb, Rogal   Travelers
American General   Johnson & Higgins   UNUM
Arthur Gallagher   Marsh &   Willis Corroon
Chubb   McLennan

HOW MUCH

	Annual Growth	1985	1986	1987	1988	1989	1990	1991	1992	1993	1994
Assets ($ mil.)	21.1%	3,196	5,905	7,084	8,266	9,156	10,432	11,633	14,290	16,279	17,922
Net income ($ mil.)	9.4%	161	184	185	180	232	239	242	206	324	360
Income as % of assets	—	5.0%	3.1%	2.6%	2.2%	2.5%	2.3%	2.1%	1.4%	2.0%	2.0%
Earnings per share ($)	7.7%	1.61	1.84	1.87	1.86	2.36	2.41	2.47	1.93	2.81	3.14
Stock price – high ($)	—	17.51	21.84	21.01	19.18	28.85	28.43	27.85	36.02	39.02	35.75
Stock price – low ($)	—	12.59	17.01	13.67	14.59	18.01	17.84	19.84	26.10	30.85	29.25
Stock price – close ($)	7.1%	17.26	17.59	15.26	18.68	28.18	23.18	26.43	36.02	32.27	32.00
P/E – high	—	11	12	11	10	12	12	11	19	14	11
P/E – low	—	8	9	7	8	8	7	8	14	11	9
Dividends per share ($)	6.6%	0.71	0.74	0.79	0.84	0.91	0.99	1.05	1.11	1.18	1.26
Book value per share ($)	8.9%	9.99	11.57	11.66	13.19	14.57	14.92	18.10	21.73	22.40	21.43
Employees	12.8%	6,086	8,700	9,200	8,500	9,000	9,000	11,000	15,000	18,000	18,000

1994 Year-end:
Equity as % of assets: 12.6%
Return on equity: 15.9%
Return on assets: 2.1%
Long-term debt (mil.): $496
No. of shares (mil.): 105
Dividends
   Yield: 3.9%
   Payout: 40.1%
Market value (mil.): $3,354
Sales (mil.): $4,157

**Stock Price History
High/Low 1985–94**

(chart scale: 40, 35, 30, 25, 20, 15, 10, 5, 0)

ARTHUR ANDERSEN & CO, SC

OVERVIEW

Chicago-based Arthur Andersen is the biggest and most diversified of the Big 6 accounting firms. Andersen's consulting business, which accounts for about half of sales, is the largest and most developed of the Big 6's consulting businesses. The firm is known for strict adherence to procedures and rules and conformity among its professional staff, which has earned them the sobriquet "Arthur Androids."

Arthur Andersen is composed of 2 distinct units: Arthur Andersen & Co., which provides auditing, business advisory services, tax services, and specialty consulting services; and Andersen Consulting, which provides strategic services and technology consulting. The name of the coordinating company, Arthur Andersen & Co, SC, will be changed to Andersen Worldwide to eliminate confusion.

Andersen, along with the rest of the Big 6, has been stung in recent years by litigation arising from disappointing performances of IPOs and from wrongdoing by the management of companies it has audited. As a result, the firm has begun to shy away from doing audits for IPO companies and to drop clients.

Arthur Andersen's computer technology expertise is an important part of its consulting practice. In 1995 the firm made a pact with PeopleSoft to develop client/server software for manufacturing companies.

WHEN

Arthur Andersen, an orphan of Norwegian parents, worked in the Chicago office of Price Waterhouse in 1907. In 1908 at 23, after becoming the youngest CPA in Illinois, he began teaching accounting at Northwestern University. Following a brief period in 1911 as controller at Schlitz Brewing, Andersen became head of the accounting department at Northwestern. In 1913 at age 28, he formed a public accounting firm, Andersen, DeLany & Company, with Clarence DeLany.

Establishment of the Federal Reserve and implementation of the federal income tax in 1913 aided the firm's early growth by increasing the demand for accounting services. The company gained large clients, including ITT, Briggs & Stratton, Colgate-Palmolive, and Parker Pen, during the period between 1913 and 1920. In 1915 it opened a branch office in Milwaukee. After DeLany's departure in 1918, the firm adopted its present name.

Andersen grew rapidly during the 1920s and added to its list of services financial investigations, which formed the basis for its future strength in management consulting. The firm opened 6 offices in the 1920s, including ones in New York (1921), Kansas City (1923), and Los Angeles (1926).

When Samuel Insull's utility empire collapsed in 1932, Andersen was appointed the bankers' representative and guarded the assets during the refinancing. Andersen opened additional offices in Boston and Houston (1937) and in Atlanta and Minneapolis (1940).

Andersen's presence dominated the firm during his life. Upon his death in 1947, it found new leadership in Leonard Spacek. During Spacek's tenure, which continued until 1963, the firm opened 18 new US offices and began a period of foreign expansion with the establishment of a Mexico City office, followed by 25 more in other countries.

Andersen has been an innovator among the major accounting firms. The company opened Andersen University, its Center for Professional Education, in the early 1970s on a campus in St. Charles, Illinois, and provided the first worldwide annual report in 1973. To broaden its scope, it transferred its headquarters to Geneva in 1977.

During the 1970s Andersen increased its consulting business, which accounted for 21% of revenues by 1979; by 1988 consulting fees made up 40% of revenues, making Andersen the world's largest consulting firm. Tension between the consultants and the auditors eventually forced a 1989 restructuring, which established Arthur Andersen and Andersen Consulting as distinct entities.

A rash of megamergers among the then–Big 8 accounting firms led Andersen and Price Waterhouse to flirt briefly with a merger (1989), but discussions broke down.

In 1992 the RTC sued Arthur Andersen for $400 million, alleging negligence in auditing failed Benjamin Franklin Savings. The firm paid the RTC $65 million in 1993 to settle the case as part of a "global" settlement, exempting it from future government charges for its role as auditor of failed US S&Ls.

In 1994 Arthur Andersen and Deloitte & Touche were named in a $1.1 billion suit brought by investors who claim the firms and Prudential Securities inflated the prices of several limited partnerships. Also that year the #8 UK accounting firm, Binder Hamlyn, was merged into Arthur Andersen. In fiscal 1995 the firm's revenues topped $8 billion.

International partnership
Fiscal year ends: August 31

WHO

Chairman, Managing Partner, and CEO: Lawrence A.
Weinbach
Managing Partner, Arthur Andersen: Richard L.
Measelle
Managing Partner, Andersen Consulting: George T.
Shaheen
CFO: John D. Lewis
General Counsel: Jon N. Ekdahl
Manager Human Resources: Peter Pesce
CEO, Arthur Andersen & Co. (US): James Kackley

WHERE

HQ: 18, quai Général-Guisan, 1211 Geneva 3,
Switzerland
Phone: +41-22-214444
Fax: +41-22-214418
US HQ: Arthur Andersen & Co., SC, 69 W. Washington
St., Chicago, IL 60602-3094
US Phone: 312-580-0069
US Fax: 312-507-2548

Arthur Andersen & Co, SC, maintains over 350 offices in
74 countries.

	1994 Sales	
	$ mil.	% of total
Arthur Andersen		
Americas	1,919	29
Europe, India, Africa &		
Middle East	1,110	16
Asia/Pacific	489	7
Subtotal	**3,518**	**52**
Andersen Consulting		
Americas	1,801	27
Europe, India, Africa &		
Middle East	1,113	16
Asia/Pacific	306	5
Subtotal	**3,220**	**48**
Total	**6,738**	**100**

1994 Worldwide Personnel		
	No.	% of total
Americas	37,382	51
Europe, India, Africa &		
Middle East	23,676	33
Asia/Pacific	11,664	16
Total	**72,722**	**100**

WHAT

Operating Units

Arthur Andersen
Auditing
Business advisory and corporate specialty services
Tax services

Andersen Consulting
Application software products
Business process management
Change management services
Client/server–based solutions
Object-oriented technology
Strategic services
Systems integration services
Technology services

Selected Representative Clients

American Express
Cadbury Schweppes
Chemical Bank
First Chicago
Inland Steel
KLM
New South Wales Police Service
NYNEX
Pacific Bell

KEY COMPETITORS

Bain & Co.
Booz, Allen
Boston Consulting
 Group
Control Data Systems
Coopers & Lybrand
DEC
Deloitte & Touche
EDS

Ernst & Young
H&R Block
IBM
KPMG
Marsh & McLennan
Perot Systems
Price Waterhouse
SHL Systemhouse

HOW MUCH

	Annual Growth	1985	1986	1987	1988	1989	1990	1991	1992	1993	1994
Sales ($ mil.)	17.5%	1,574	1,924	2,316	2,820	3,382	4,160	4,948	5,577	6,017	6,738
Offices	5.8%	215	219	226	231	243	299	307	318	324	358
Partners	4.9%	1,630	1,847	1,957	2,016	2,134	2,292	2,393	2,454	2,487	2,517
Employees	11.1%	28,172	36,117	39,645	45,918	51,414	56,801	59,797	62,134	66,478	72,722

1994 Year-end:
Sales per partner:
 $2,676,996

ARTHUR ANDERSEN & CO.

Sales ($ mil.)
1985–94

7,000
6,000
5,000
4,000
3,000
2,000
1,000
0

BAKER & MCKENZIE

OVERVIEW

Baker & McKenzie, based in Chicago, is the world's largest law firm. With more than 50 offices housing over 1,700 lawyers in more than 30 countries, the "megafirm" offers a complete range of legal services, with particular expertise in international issues.

One key to the firm's success in crossing borders has been its attention to local customs, made possible by staffing overseas offices with native lawyers. Critics have compared this method of expansion to franchising (earning it the nickname McFirm). While it offers a full menu of services, Baker & McKenzie has struggled to establish consistent quality throughout its global operations.

Another key factor is Baker & McKenzie's policy of allowing local offices to keep most of their revenues (a practice known as "eat what you kill") instead of sending profits to the home office.

As formerly state-run economies adopt free-market practices, multinationals are rushing in for a piece of the action. To guide them through the often rough legal waters, Baker & McKenzie has established offices in places such as Beijing in 1993 (it is the international firm with the largest presence in China), Vietnam in 1994, and Almaty, Kazakhstan, the largest of the former Soviet Union's Central Asia republics, in 1995.

WHEN

Russell Baker came to Chicago from his native New Mexico on a railroad freight car to attend law school. Upon graduation in 1925 he started practicing law with his classmate Dana Simpson under the name Simpson & Baker. Inspired by Chicago's role as a manufacturing and agricultural center for the world and influenced by the international focus of his alma mater, the University of Chicago, Baker dreamed of developing an international law practice based in Chicago.

In his first cases Baker represented members of Chicago's growing Mexican-American community in a variety of minor criminal and civil matters. Since he frequently dealt with Mexican lawyers and issues involving multiple jurisdictions and legal systems, Baker developed an expertise in international law, which brought in other clients. In 1934 Abbott Laboratories retained him to handle its worldwide legal affairs, and Baker was on his way to fulfilling his dream.

In 1949 Baker joined forces with Chicago litigator John McKenzie, forming Baker & McKenzie. In 1955 the firm opened its first foreign office in Caracas to meet the needs of its expanding US client base, and over the next 10 years it opened offices in Amsterdam, Brussels, Zurich, São Paulo, Mexico City, London, Frankfurt, Milan, Tokyo, Toronto, Paris, Manila, Sydney, and Madrid. Another 23 offices were added in the Americas, Europe, and Asia between 1965 and 1990. Baker's death in 1979 did not slow the firm's growth or change its international character.

To manage the sprawling law firm, Baker & McKenzie created the position of chairman of the executive committee (1984). Australian John McGuigan, former managing partner of

the firm's Hong Kong office, was elected by his partners for a 5-year term as chairman starting in 1992. McGuigan cited the need to break down trade and commerce barriers between countries as one of the significant challenges facing the international financial and legal community in the 1990s.

In late 1991 the firm dropped the Church of Scientology as a client, losing an estimated $2 million in business. It was speculated that pressure from client Eli Lilly (which makes the drug Prozac, which Scientologists actively oppose) influenced the decision.

In 1992 Baker & McKenzie was ordered to pay $1 million for wrongfully firing an employee who later died of AIDS. The firm fought the verdict and finally settled for an undisclosed amount in 1995.

In 1994 Baker & McKenzie closed its Los Angeles office (the former MacDonald, Halsted & Laybourne, acquired in 1988) amid considerable rancor. That year a former secretary at the firm received a $7.1 million judgment for sexual harassment by a partner. In late 1994 a San Francisco Superior Court judge reduced the amount awarded to $3.5 million.

In 1995 McGuigan stepped down as chairman. He was replaced by John Klotsche, a senior partner from the firm's Palo Alto, California, office.

As the electronic age evolves, the firm is putting new information technology to use with an in-house computer network called BakerNet II connecting 48 of the firm's worldwide offices. (BakerNet I was a financial information network.) This gives its attorneys access to up-to-date rule changes (resulting from NAFTA, for example) and other legal information anywhere there is a telephone hookup.

International partnership
Fiscal year ends: June 30

WHO

Chairman of the Executive Committee: John C.
Klotsche, age 51
COO: Frank M. Wheeler
CFO: Robert S. Spencer
Director, Human Resources: Mary Weis
Auditors: Arthur Andersen & Co, SC

WHERE

International Executive Offices: One Prudential Plaza,
130 E. Randolph Dr., Chicago, IL 60601
Phone: 312-861-8800
Fax: 312-861-8823

Offices

Almaty, Kazakhstan	Miami, US
Amsterdam, The Netherlands	Milan, Italy
Bangkok, Thailand	Monterrey, Mexico
Barcelona, Spain	Moscow, Russia
Beijing, China	New York, US
Berlin, Germany	Palo Alto, US
Bogotá, Colombia	Paris, France
Brasília, Brazil	Prague, Czech Republic
Brussels, Belgium	Rio de Janeiro, Brazil
Budapest, Hungary	Riyadh, Saudi Arabia
Buenos Aires, Argentina	Rome, Italy
Cairo, Egypt	St. Petersburg, Russia
Caracas, Venezuela	San Diego, US
Chicago, US	San Francisco, US
Dallas, US	Santiago, Chile
Frankfurt, Germany	São Paulo, Brazil
Geneva, Switzerland	Singapore
Hanoi, Vietnam	Stockholm, Sweden
Ho Chi Minh City, Vietnam	Sydney, Australia
Hong Kong	Taipei, Taiwan
Juárez, Mexico	Tijuana, Mexico
Kiev, Ukraine	Tokyo, Japan
London, UK	Toronto, Canada
Madrid, Spain	Valencia, Spain
Manila, Philippines	Warsaw, Poland
Melbourne, Australia	Washington, DC, US
Mexico City, Mexico	Zurich, Switzerland

WHAT

	1994 Revenue	
	$ mil.	% of total
North America	187	34
Europe & Middle East	169	31
Asia & Australia	141	26
Latin America	49	9
Total	**546**	**100**

Areas of Practice	Selected Publications
Antitrust	*Asia Pacific Legal*
Banking/commercial	*Development Bulletin*
lending/consumer finance	*Canadian Legal Report*
Bankruptcy	*China Law Quarterly*
Corporate financings	*Computer & Software*
Criminal law	*Update*
Employee benefits	*EEC Competition Law*
Environmental/land	*Newsletter*
use/natural resources	*Employee Benefits Update*
Estate planning	*European Benefits Update*
Foreign trade	*European Legal*
General corporate law	*Developments Bulletin*
Government relations	*International Executive*
Health and hospital law	*Transfers Update*
Immigration	*Latin American Legal*
Insurance	*Development Bulletin*
Intellectual property	*US Employment Law*
Labor/management relations	*Update*
Maritime/shipping	
Mergers and acquisitions	
Oil and gas/mining	
Real estate	
Taxation	

KEY COMPETITORS

Cleary, Gottlieb	Pillsbury Madison
Cravath, Swaine	Shearman & Sterling
Jenner & Block	Sidley & Austin
Jones, Day	Skadden, Arps
Kirkland & Ellis	Sullivan & Cromwell
Mayer, Brown & Platt	Weil, Gotshal
McDermott, Will	White & Case
Milbank, Tweed	Winston & Strawn

HOW MUCH

	Annual Growth	1986	1987	1988	1989	1990	1991	1992	1993	1994	1995
Revenue ($ mil.)	14.9%	—	196	261	341	404	478	504	512	546	594
Total lawyers	7.7%	908	946	1,179	1,339	1,522	1,580	1,604	1,662	1,642	1,776
Partners	4.7%	333	338	404	432	478	479	497	537	500	505
Associates	9.2%	575	608	775	907	1,044	1,101	989	1,125	1,142	1,271
Associates per partner	4.2%	1.73	1.80	1.92	2.10	2.18	2.30	1.99	2.09	2.28	2.50
Number of offices	6.6%	31	35	41	48	49	45	49	54	52	55
Employees	2.1%	—	—	—	—	4,736	4,887	4,919	5,054	5,114	5,248

**Starting Salaries for
First-Year Associates:**[1]
1980 — $32,000
1984 — $47,000
1986 — $65,000
1990 — $70,000
1992 — $70,000
1993 — $70,000
1994 — $70,000
1995 — $75,000

BAKER & MᶜKENZIE

Total Number
of Lawyers
1986–95

[1] Chicago office

BALLY ENTERTAINMENT CORPORATION

OVERVIEW

Sure, you could go to the gym and sweat for an hour, but wouldn't you rather belly up to a blackjack table? Casting its lot with more sedentary pleasures, Bally Entertainment announced that it would spin off Bally's Health & Tennis Corporation, the nation's #1 fitness club operator, and concentrate on its casino business. The Chicago-based company operates 2 casino hotels in Atlantic City, one casino hotel in Las Vegas, a dockside gaming facility in Robinsonville, Mississippi (near Memphis), and a riverboat casino in New Orleans (which opened in 1995). Bally's Health &

Tennis operates 332 fitness centers, primarily located in major metropolitan areas.

The 1990s have been a busy time for Bally. Led by CEO Arthur Goldberg, who owns 4.9% of the company, Bally has been reorganizing itself, trying to cut costs and unload the massive debt incurred in the 1980s.

The company continues to expand its gambling operations. In 1995 it announced plans to build a $420 million Parisian-theme casino-resort in Las Vegas that will include 2,500 hotel rooms, an 80,000-square-foot casino, and a replica of the Eiffel Tower.

WHEN

Bally's predecessor, Lion Manufacturing of Chicago, was founded in 1931 by Roy Moloney, Joel Linehan, and Charles Weldt. Lion produced the Ballyhoo, the first pinball machine, in 1932 and its first slot machine in 1938. During WWII Lion made detonator fuses and gun sights for bombers but after the war went back to making games. Lion produced soft drink and coffee dispensers in the 1950s; it sold the coffee machine business in 1960.

The death of Moloney in 1957 sent the company into chaos until 1963, when sales manager William O'Donnell and his partners bought Lion. The global market for slot machines grew during the 1960s, and Lion, with its new Money Honey slot machine and computerized control system (Slot Data System), became the industry leader. The company was renamed Bally in 1968 in honor of its first pinball game and went public in 1969.

Throughout the 1970s O'Donnell led the company through a series of acquisitions, including Midway Manufacturing (arcade games, 1969), Gunter Wulff Appartebau (amusement games, Germany, 1972), and American Amusements (amusement arcades, renamed Aladdin's Castle, 1974). The company launched its first casino hotel in 1977. But before the New Jersey Gaming Commission would issue a license to Bally, it required O'Donnell to resign and place his company stock in a blind trust. Apparently, part of the money he had used to buy the company in 1963 had come from persons connected with organized crime. O'Donnell admitted that accepting the money had been a mistake but asserted that Bally had no connection with organized crime. Robert Mullane replaced him as chairman.

Business boomed at Aladdin's Castle in the early 1980s when Bally introduced a new gen-

eration of video arcade games, including Space Invaders (1979) and Pac-Man (1980). Bally continued to diversify, buying Six Flags Corporation (1982), Health & Tennis Corporation of America (1983), Great America Theme Park (from Marriott, 1984), Lifecycle (fitness equipment, 1984), MGM Grand Hotels in Las Vegas and Reno (1986), and the Golden Nugget Casino in Atlantic City (1987). Bally successfully fended off a takeover attempt by Donald Trump in 1987, funding the battle by selling its theme parks. Bally sold most of its amusement game manufacturing business in 1988 and Aladdin's Castle in 1989.

In 1990 the company missed an $18.4 million interest payment on its Nevada casinos and pulled out of a deal to buy London's Clermont casino. It spun off its gaming equipment manufacturing operations as Bally Gaming International in 1991. Robert Brennan became Bally's largest shareholder by buying a 6.8% stake in 1992. Later that year, however, he sold most of the shares after Bally CEO Arthur Goldberg declined to meet with him.

In 1993 Bally opened a saloon and gambling hall near Memphis on the Mississippi River. Because it no longer made gambling equipment, the company changed its name from Bally Manufacturing Corporation to Bally Entertainment Corporation in 1994.

In 1995 Bally signed a joint venture with Lady Luck Gaming and moved its Bally's Saloon and Gambling Hall about 15 miles closer to Memphis, to a site owned by Lady Luck, which owns a 240-room hotel there. Also in 1995 Alpha Hospitality agreed to develop and manage a casino and resort in the city of Rising Sun, Indiana (near Cincinnati). The project includes a riverboat casino that will dock on the Ohio River, a hotel, a showroom pavilion, 3 restaurants, and shopping facilities.

NYSE symbol: BLY
Fiscal year ends: December 31

WHO

Chairman, President, and CEO: Arthur M. Goldberg, age 53, $2,200,000 pay
EVP and COO, Casino Holdings; President and COO, Bally's Park Place, Inc.; President and COO, GNAC CORP.: Wallace R. Barr, age 49, $1,150,000 pay
EVP, CFO, and Treasurer: Lee S. Hillman, age 39, $650,000 pay
SVP and COO, Bally's Grand: Darrell A. Luery, age 54, $810,000 pay
SVP and General Counsel: James Montana
VP Management Information Systems and Chief Information Officer: Robert G. Conover, age 49
VP Corporate Affairs and Governmental Relations: Bernard J. Murphy, age 48
VP and Corporate Controller: John W. Dwyer, age 42
VP Audit: Jerry W. Thornburg, age 51
VP Human Resources: Harold Morgan, age 38
Secretary: Carol Stone DePaul, age 38
Auditors: Ernst & Young LLP

WHERE

HQ: 8700 W. Bryn Mawr Ave., Chicago, IL 60631
Phone: 312-399-1300
Fax: 312-693-2982

Casinos/Hotels
Bally's Casino Lakeshore Resort (New Orleans; riverboat with 30,000-sq.-ft. casino)
Bally's Las Vegas (56,000-sq.-ft. casino and more than 2,800 hotel rooms)
Bally's Park Place (Atlantic City; 71,400-sq.-ft. casino and more than 1,250 hotel rooms)
Bally's Saloon & Gambling Hall (Robinsonville, MS; riverboat with 40,000-sq.-ft. casino adjacent to 240-room Lady Luck Hotel)
The Grand (Atlantic City; 46,300-sq.-ft. casino and more than 500 hotel rooms)

WHAT

	1994 Sales	
	$ mil.	% of total
Casinos	723	77
Rooms	89	9
Food & beverage	67	7
Other	63	7
Total	**942**	**100**

	1994 Sales		1994 Operating Income	
	$ mil.	% of total	$ mil.	% of total
Bally's Park Place	377	40	88	58
Bally's Las Vegas	272	29	40	26
The Grand	250	27	24	16
Bally's Mississippi	39	4	(14)	—
Adjustments	4	—	(13)	—
Total	**942**	**100**	**125**	**100**

Subsidiaries
Bally's Grand, Inc. (80%, operates Bally's Las Vegas)
Bally's Louisiana, Inc. (operates Bally's Casino Lakeshore Resort riverboat casino)
Bally's Park Place, Inc. (operates Bally's Park Place casino hotel resort)
Bally's Tunica, Inc. ("Bally's Mississippi," operates Bally's Saloon and Gambling Hall)
GNAC, CORP. (operates The Grand casino hotel resort)

KEY COMPETITORS

Argosy Gaming	Hilton	Pratt Hotel
Aztar	Hollywood	Primadonna Resorts
Boyd Gaming	Casino	Resorts International
Carlson	ITT Corp.	Sahara Gaming
Circus Circus	Mashantucket	Showboat
Grand Casinos	Pequot	Station Casinos
Griffin Gaming	Gaming	Trump
Harrah's	MGM Grand	Trump Hotels &
Entertainment	Mirage Resorts	Casinos

HOW MUCH

	Annual Growth	1985	1986	1987	1988	1989	1990	1991	1992	1993	1994
Sales ($ mil.)	(3.5%)	1,295	1,593	1,676	1,867	1,990	1,997	1,413	1,297	1,320	942
Net income ($ mil.)	—	26	24	57	38	26	(292)	(35)	22	(18)	(68)
Income as % of sales	—	2.0%	1.5%	3.4%	2.0%	1.3%	—	—	0.9%	—	—
Earnings per share ($)	—	0.95	0.81	1.62	1.12	0.66	(10.57)	(1.10)	(0.05)	(0.27)	(1.08)
Stock price – high ($)	—	18.63	24.13	27.75	25.25	29.75	15.63	6.50	8.25	12.75	9.63
Stock price – low ($)	—	11.13	14.63	10.50	12.88	13.50	2.13	1.88	4.13	6.00	5.25
Stock price – close ($)	(10.4%)	16.50	19.75	12.88	22.13	15.13	2.13	5.25	7.88	8.50	6.13
P/E – high	—	20	30	17	23	45	—	—	—	—	—
P/E – low	—	12	18	7	12	21	—	—	—	—	—
Dividends per share ($)	(100.0%)	0.20	0.20	0.20	0.22	0.29	0.23	0.00	0.00	0.00	0.00
Book value per share ($)	(9.4%)	15.16	15.91	21.40	21.64	21.25	10.68	9.99	8.90	7.75	6.23
Employees	(12.6%)	37,800	46,500	29,600	32,875	32,900	26,200	30,000	31,000	19,200	11,200

1994 Year-end:
Debt ratio: 81.2%
Return on equity: —
Cash (mil.): $184
Current ratio: 1.40
Long-term debt (mil.): $1,259
No. of shares (mil.): 47
Dividends
  Yield: —
  Payout: —
Market value (mil.): $288

**Stock Price History
High/Low 1985–94**

BAXTER INTERNATIONAL INC.

OVERVIEW

Baxter International's 2 main product segments are medical specialties (products for blood processing, dialysis systems, and cardiovascular devices) and medical/laboratory products and distribution (anesthetics, surgery supplies and products, intravenous systems, and sales and distribution services). Baxter distributes its 200,000 health care–related products in 100 countries.

Baxter, based in Deerfield, Illinois, is concentrating more on its medical specialties segment — 2/3 of its capital and R&D budgets are going toward improving and expanding that segment because of worldwide growth potential. In late 1995 the company announced that it would spin off most of its medical laboratory products and distribution services businesses, effectively dividing the company

in 2. The remaining company will keep cardiovascular, kidney dialysis, biotech, and international operations.

The company is creating alliances with foreign firms to fuel international growth. It has alliances in Brazil, Hungary, Mexico, the Philippines, Taiwan, Thailand, and Turkey. Product lines in these markets are IV solutions and nutritional and disposable medical products. In China the company, in conjunction with a local alliance, is building a renal products manufacturing plant and planning another.

Baxter is becoming a player in the transplant niche of the biotech industry. Nextran, a company created by Baxter and DNX in 1994, has on the market its first product, a monitoring kit to test organ donor and recipient compatibility.

WHEN

Idaho surgeon Ralph Falk, his brother Harry, and California physician Donald Baxter formed the Don Baxter Intravenous Products Corporation in 1931 to distribute the intravenous (IV) solutions Baxter made in Los Angeles. Two years later the company opened its first manufacturing plant in Glenview, Illinois. Ralph Falk bought Baxter's interest in 1935 and began R&D efforts leading to the first sterilized vacuum-type blood collection device (1939), which could store blood for 21 days instead of a few hours. Demand for Baxter's products during WWII spurred sales above $1.5 million by 1945.

In 1949 the company created Travenol Laboratories to make and sell drugs. Baxter went public in 1951 and began an acquisition program the following year. Failing health caused both Falks in 1953 to give company control to William Graham, a manager since 1945. Graham continued the acquisition program, absorbing 5 US companies: Hyland Labs (1952), Wallerstein Company (1957), Fenwal Labs (1959), Flint, Eaton (1959), and Dayton Flexible Products (1967).

In 1975 Baxter moved its headquarters to Deerfield, Illinois. The company had $1 billion in sales in 1978, the same year it introduced the first portable dialysis machine. In 1985 Baxter acquired American Hospital Supply, a Baxter distributor from 1932 until 1962. American's sales were 65% higher than Baxter's, but American distributed more lower-margin products than Baxter, which manufactured most of its own items. The

merger made Baxter the world's largest hospital supply company.

Offering more than 120,000 products and an electronic order-entry system that connected customers with over 1,500 vendors, Baxter captured nearly 25% of the US hospital supply market in 1988. That same year the company changed its name to Baxter International.

In 1992 Baxter spun off Caremark (home infusion therapy and mail-order drugs), which was competing directly with hospitals, Baxter's main source of revenues. Baxter retained Caremark's renal division, which had a 75% world market share in dialysis machines.

Baxter pleaded guilty in 1993 to paying Syria a bribe (in the form of deeply discounted medical supplies) in an effort to be removed from an Arab blacklist of companies doing business in Israel and apologized for the "unintentional violation." A 4-month suspension from doing business with the Veterans Administration followed. Also in 1993 the company centralized its gene therapy research. President James Tobin's sudden departure in December 1993 (he had been appointed in March 1992) capped a difficult year for Baxter.

In 1994 Baxter signed an 8-year agreement with giant Columbia/HCA Healthcare to supply intravenous products and services and some diagnostic products to its 195 hospitals and 100 surgery centers throughout the US. Also in 1994 Baxter sold its medical diagnostic test businesses to Bain Capital.

In 1995 Bio-Plexus, maker of patented self-blunting blood collection needles, announced Baxter would begin distributing its needles.

NYSE symbol: BAX
Fiscal year ends: December 31

WHO

Chairman Emeritus: William B. Graham, age 83
Chairman and CEO: Vernon R. Loucks Jr., age 60,
$1,380,100 pay
SVP and CFO: Harry M. Jansen Kraemer Jr., age 40,
$474,615 pay
SVP, Secretary, and General Counsel: Arthur F.
Staubitz, age 55
SVP Human Resources: Herbert E. Walker, age 60
Group VP Baxter World Trade Corporation: Manuel A.
Baez, age 53, $478,007 pay
Group VP Corporate Research and Development: Dale
A. Smith, age 63
VP Government Affairs: David J. Aho, age 45
VP Corporate Development and Strategy: John F.
Gaither Jr., age 45
VP Manufacturing, Operations, and Strategy: James H.
Taylor Jr., age 56
Auditors: Price Waterhouse LLP

WHERE

HQ: One Baxter Pkwy., Deerfield, IL 60015
Phone: 847-948-2000
Fax: 847-948-2887

Baxter sells products in about 100 countries. Baxter has
71 manufacturing plants in 21 countries, 149 distribution centers, and 25 research facilities worldwide.

	1994 Sales		1994 Pretax Income	
	$ mil.	% of total	$ mil.	% of total
US	6,831	74	453	41
Europe	1,245	13	251	23
Other regions	1,248	13	393	36
Adjustments	—	—	(296)	—
Total	**9,324**	**100**	**801**	**100**

WHAT

	1994 Sales		1994 Pretax Income	
	$ mil.	% of total	$ mil.	% of total
Medical/lab prods. & distribution	5,767	62	474	43
Medical specialties	3,557	38	621	57
Adjustments	—	—	(294)	—
Total	**9,324**	**100**	**801**	**100**

Selected Products
Artificial heart valves
Blood-handling equipment
Cardiac catheters
Cardiac monitoring and bypass systems
Dialysis products and services
Electromechanical heart assist systems
Gammagard S/D (immune system disorder treatment)
Intravenous therapy products
Laboratory apparatus and supplies
Nutritional supplies
Peritoneal dialysis products (home dialysis)
Surgical instruments and supplies

KEY COMPETITORS

Abbott Labs
American Home
  Products
Amgen
Ballard Medical
Bayer
Bergen Brunswig
Ciba-Geigy
C. R. Bard
Diagnostic Products
Genentech
Hoechst
Johnson & Johnson

Medtronic
Merck
Mitek Surgical
Northfield Labs
Novo Nordisk
Pfizer
Roche
St. Jude Medical
Somatogen
Thermo Electron
U.S. Surgical
Vital Signs

HOW MUCH

	Annual Growth	1985	1986	1987	1988	1989	1990	1991	1992	1993	1994
Sales ($ mil.)	16.5%	2,355	5,543	6,223	6,861	7,399	8,100	8,921	8,471	8,879	9,324
Net income ($ mil.)	17.7%	137	219	323	388	446	40	591	606	(268)	596
Income as % of sales	—	5.8%	4.0%	5.2%	5.7%	6.0%	0.5%	6.6%	7.2%	—	6.4%
Earnings per share ($)	11.0%	0.83	0.79	1.09	1.30	1.49	(0.05)	2.00	2.13	(0.97)	2.13
Stock price – high ($)	—	16.88	21.25	29.25	26.13	25.88	29.50	40.88	40.50	32.75	28.88
Stock price – low ($)	—	12.38	15.13	15.50	16.25	17.50	20.50	25.63	30.50	20.00	21.63
Stock price – close ($)	6.7%	15.75	19.25	22.75	17.63	25.00	27.88	40.00	32.38	24.38	28.25
P/E – high	—	20	27	27	20	17	—	20	19	—	14
P/E – low	—	15	19	14	13	12	—	13	14	—	10
Dividends per share ($)	12.1%	0.36	0.39	0.43	0.49	0.55	0.62	0.72	0.83	0.97	1.01
Book value per share ($)	3.3%	9.86	11.57	11.79	12.61	13.49	13.45	14.45	13.59	11.52	13.18
Employees	(1.3%)	60,000	60,000	60,000	61,500	61,000	60,600	60,400	61,300	60,400	53,500

1994 Year-end:
Debt ratio: 43.6%
Return on equity: 17.3%
Cash (mil.): $471
Current ratio: 1.57
Long-term debt (mil.): $2,341
No. of shares (mil.): 282
Dividends
  Yield: 3.6%
  Payout: 47.4%
Market value (mil.): $7,975

**Stock Price History
High/Low 1985–94**

BELL & HOWELL HOLDINGS

OVERVIEW

Although many of the movies made in this country (both in Hollywood and at home) were once filmed with Bell & Howell cameras and shown through its projectors, the Skokie, Illinois–based company has developed a more modern image. It now focuses on information access and mail-processing systems through 4 separate business units.

Bell & Howell's UMI Company is an information gatherer, maintaining a database that includes more than 18,000 periodicals, 7,000 newspapers, 1.2 million dissertations, 130,000 out-of-print books, 200 research collections, and 11 million abstracts. Access to the electronic vaults is provided through the UMI InfoStore, which offers reprints of documents electronically (CD-ROM, online, and magnetic tape), through microfilm and microfiche, and on paper. The Bell & Howell Publication Sys-

tems Company provides information storage and retrieval systems for such image-intensive technical reference information as parts catalogs for car dealerships. Another subsidiary, Information Management, designs and supplies a full range of electronic filing systems for documents, including microfilm readers and cameras and desktop scanners.

Bell & Howell's Mail-Processing Systems division is a leading maker of high-volume systems sold to financial institutions, insurance and credit card companies, and the US Postal Service.

After being privately held by a group of investors headed by Texas billionaire Robert Bass since a 1988 LBO, Bell & Howell was taken public in 1995 to raise cash to reduce the company's significant debt. Bass still controls 24% of the company's stock.

WHEN

At the turn of the century, when Chicago was the US motion picture capital, Donald Bell worked as a movie projectionist in theaters around northern Illinois. He met Albert Howell, a mechanical expert who had patented an improvement to film projectors, and in 1907 they formed the Bell & Howell Company to manufacture, lease, and repair movie equipment.

Starting out mainly as a repair shop, Bell & Howell rose to prominence in the movie industry by establishing 35mm as the standard film width. The company manufactured machines using 35mm film and refused to repair machines that used any other width.

In 1912 the company developed its first all-metal camera (after one of their wood-and-leather models was eaten by termites). The 2709 camera, as it was known, was produced until 1958.

In 1916 Bell fired Howell and bookkeeper Joseph McNabb for changing the company's operations while Bell was away on a sales trip. The following day Howell and McNabb, with financial backing from Rufus Kittredge and Charles Ziebarth, bought out Bell's interest for $183,895 and ran the company themselves. By 1919 nearly all of the movie equipment used in rapidly growing Hollywood was made by Bell & Howell.

In the 1920s the company made a 16mm camera for nonprofessionals (based on film developed by Eastman Kodak), which achieved widespread success. In 1932 Bell & Howell unveiled the 16mm sound-on-film projector.

In 1945 the company went public. It appointed 29-year-old Charles Percy as CEO, the youngest ever of a large company, in 1949 after McNabb's death. In 1951 Howell died. Three years later Bell & Howell was awarded its first Oscar for technical contributions to the film industry. The company would go on to win 3 more Oscars (1962, 1975, and 1981).

Through acquisitions after WWII, the company diversified into many different fields, including microfilm equipment (Pathe Manufacturing, 1946), mail-order form equipment (the Inserting and Mailing Machine Co., 1958), a training school for electronics and media (DeVry Technical Institute, 1966), and publishing (Merrill Publishing, 1967).

In the 1970s the company sold off its camera business (including the popular Super 8mm camera) to concentrate on mail sorting and microimagery. Restructuring (which included the 1987 sale of Devry Institute) continued unabated until 1988, when Robert Bass took the by-then sluggish company private in an LBO. The Bass-led management team focused on the information management technologies and sold off noncore assets. However, the company's performance didn't meet expectations, and in 1989 Bass sold Merrill Publishing for $260 million.

In 1993 Bell & Howell restructured its massive debt load and wrote off $174 million in goodwill. By 1994 its database and mail-processing businesses were performing strongly. In late 1995 it again went public in an offering that raised more than $60 million.

NYSE symbol: BHW
Fiscal year ends: Saturday nearest December 31

Chairman and CEO: William J. White, age 57,
$1,180,450 pay
President and COO: James P. Roemer, age 48,
$338,679 pay
EVP and CFO: Nils A. Johansson, age 47, $448,957 pay
President, UMI: Henry G. Riner, age 44
VP: Robert T. Stirling, age 51, $318,288 pay
VP: Robert A. Nero, age 49, $258,504 pay
VP: Richard S. Austin, age 57
VP: Dieter E. A. Tannenberg, age 62
VP, Controller, and Chief Accounting Officer: Stuart T.
Lieberman, age 43
VP and Treasurer: Patrick J. Graver, age 49
VP Human Resources: Maria T. Rubly, age 40
Secretary and Corporate Counsel: Gary S. Salit, age 51
Auditors: KPMG Peat Marwick LLP

WHERE

HQ: Bell & Howell Holdings Company,
5215 Old Orchard Rd., Skokie, IL 60077-1076
Phone: 847-470-7100
Fax: 847-470-9825

Bell & Howell designs, manufactures, and markets
information access systems and mail-processing systems
in Europe, North America, and Asia.

	1994 Sales		1994 Operating Income	
	$ mil.	% of total	$ mil.	% of total
US	578	80	43	88
Europe	132	18	5	10
Other regions	10	2	1	2
Total	**720**	**100**	**49**	**100**

WHAT

	1994 Sales		1994 Net Income	
	$ mil.	% of total	$. mil.	% of total
Information access	404	56	47	—
Mail-processing systems	316	44	2	—
Interest expense	—	—	(49)	—
Other expenses	—	—	(10)	—
Total	**720**	**100**	**(10)**	**—**

Business Units
Bell & Howell Publication Systems Company
Information Management
Mail-Processing Systems
UMI Company

Selected Trademarks

Article Clearinghouse	Mailmobile
Copiscan II	MicroSeal
DataQuest	PowerPages
FlexiMailer	ProQuest
Image Search for Windows	ProQuest Direct
The Information Store	Simplefiler
InfoStore	StraightShot
Lightspeed	Synergy 9000

KEY COMPETITORS

ADP	Minolta
Anacomp	NewsBank
Canon	On-Line Computer Library
Dow Jones	Center
Dun & Bradstreet	Pitney Bowes
Eastman Kodak	Reed Elsevier
EDS	Ricoh
ElectroCom Automation	SilverPlatter Information
Fujitsu	Thomson Corp.
Hewlett-Packard	Wang
IBM	Xerox
Knight-Ridder	

HOW MUCH

	Annual Growth	1985	1986	1987	1988	1989	1990	1991	1992	1993	1994
Sales ($ mil.)	3.1%	548	602	584	589	630	612	625	670	676	720
Net income ($ mil.)	—	32	33	61	(34)	26	(31)	(24)	(22)	(183)	(10)
Income as % of sales	—	5.9%	5.5%	10.5%	—	4.1%	—	—	—	—	—
Employees	(3.3%)	7,853	7,373	7,158	6,733	6,733	5,966	6,000	5,770	5,771	5,791

1994 Year-end:
Debt ratio: 100.0%
Return on equity: 10.5%
Cash (mil.): $16
Current ratio: 0.80
Long-term debt (mil.): $519

Net Income
($ mil.) 1985–94

BLUE CROSS AND BLUE SHIELD

OVERVIEW

For over 60 years the Blue Cross name (and that of the younger Blue Shield) has stood for accessible health care for otherwise uninsurable people. In most states this mission has been recognized and rewarded by the granting of quasi-charitable status (and tax breaks) for the autonomous Blue Cross and Blue Shield organizations that belong to the Blue Cross and Blue Shield Association. But the future status of the "Blues," as they are called, seems sure to be radically different from the past.

The financial situations of the individual Blues range from the perpetually troubled and scandal-ridden Empire Blue Cross (New York) to the prosperous Blue Cross and Blue Shield of Ohio, but most are following a path that may turn the Blue Cross name into little more than a familiar trademark.

In 10 years the number of organizations has fallen from 78 to 67 as the Blues have gone out of business, consolidated, or converted to for-profit status. The #1 enterprise in Chicago (based on revenues) recognized this trend in 1994 when it allowed members to continue using its name and logos after going for-profit. Many of the remaining associations are also flirting with for-profit status through alliances with HMOs and other caregivers, which are intended to bring the uninsured into the private medical sector while cutting costs.

WHEN

Blue Cross's history began in 1929, when an official at Baylor University began offering schoolteachers 21 days of hospital care for $6 a year. The idea spread through Texas and into Iowa and Illinois. Fundamental to the plans was a community rating system, which based premiums on the community's claims experience rather than subscribers' conditions.

The Blue Cross symbol was devised by an executive of the Minnesota plan in 1933. By 1935 there were 15 plans in 11 states, and many of them began using the Blue Cross symbol as well. In the 1930s many states ratified the plans' nonprofit status. In 1936 the American Hospital Association formed the Committee on Hospital Service (renamed the Blue Cross Association in 1948) to coordinate the plans.

As Blue Cross grew, state medical societies began sponsoring prepaid medical plans to cover physicians' fees. In 1946 they banded together under the aegis of the AMA as the Associated Medical Care Plans (which became the Association of Blue Shield Plans).

In 1948 the Blues tried to merge but were thwarted by the AMA. Nevertheless, the Blues cooperated on public policy matters (i.e., lobbying) while competing for members, and each Blue formed a nonprofit stock corporation to coordinate the activities of its plans.

Enrollment grew in the late 1940s and 1950s. In 1960 Blue Cross insured almost 1/3 of the US population. The Blues began administering Medicare and other government health plans in the 1960s. By 1970 half of Blue Cross's premiums came from government entities.

Rapidly rising medical costs in the 1970s forced the Blues to adopt such cost control measures as utilization review of hospital admissions to stem increasing premiums; many plans even abandoned the community rating system. Most began emphasizing preventive care in HMO or PPO environments.

The Blues joined forces in 1982, but this had little effect on the associations' bottom lines, as losses continued to grow.

By the 1990s the Blues had become big business, and some of the state associations had begun offering their officers the high salaries and perks enjoyed by private-sector executives, while still insisting on special regulatory treatment. In 1992 this sparked a federal investigation.

In 1993 it was discovered that Empire Blue Cross of New York (which had received more than $100 million in state aid because of a $250 million loss) had overstated the amount of its losses attributable to its small-group and individual policyholders, who had been subject to repeated rate increases. In 1995 Empire began a reorganization that will funnel many of its members into managed care plans and reduce its traditional indemnity coverage.

Blue Cross of California has been a pioneer in converting to for-profit status. In 1993 it bundled most of its health care operations into a for-profit company, Wellpoint Health Networks, and sold 20% to the public. In 1995 Blue Cross of California established 2 charitable foundations with endowments equal to its total assets ($3.2 billion) to compensate for decades of tax breaks. A proposed merger between Wellpoint and Health Systems International would have completed the conversion to for-profit status, but in late 1995 the deal fell apart. Blue Cross of California is still expected to fund the foundations.

Nonprofit association
Fiscal year ends: December 31

President and CEO: Patrick A. Hays, age 52
EVP and COO: Thomas Kinser
EVP Business Alliances: Harry P. Cain II
EVP Franchise Operations and CFO: David Murdoch
General Counsel and Corporate Secretary: Roger G. Wilson
SVP Policy, Representation, and Membership Services: Mary Nell Lehnhard
VP Chief Administrative Officer: Kris Kurschner
Auditors: Coopers & Lybrand L.L.P.

WHERE

HQ: Blue Cross and Blue Shield Association,
676 N. St. Clair St., Chicago, IL 60611
Phone: 312-440-6000
Fax: 312-440-6609

The association has offices in Chicago and Washington, DC; 67 licensees operating in all 50 states, the District of Columbia, and Puerto Rico, Australia, Canada, Jamaica, and the UK; and 96 million private and Medicare subscribers.

	1994 Plans
	No.
Washington	7
New York	6
Pennsylvania	5
Idaho	2
Missouri	2
Ohio	2
Tennessee	2
Puerto Rico	2
Other locations	39
Total	**67**

WHAT

	1994 Enrollment	
	No. of subscribers (mil.)	% of total
Private	65	68
Medicare	31	32
Total	**96**	**100**

Policies and Programs
Group major medical insurance
Health maintenance programs (HMO–USA)
Individual major medical insurance
Medicare administration
Preferred-provider organizations

KEY COMPETITORS

Aetna
Chubb
CIGNA
Employee Benefit Plans
Equitable Cos.
Family Health Plan
FHP International
Foundation Health
Gencare Health
Group Health Cooperative
Harvard Community
Health Systems
Healthsource
Healthwise
Humana
John Hancock
Kaiser Foundation Health Plan
MassMutual
MetLife
New York Life
Northwestern Healthcare Network
Oxford Health Plans
PacificCare
Physician Corp. of America
Prudential
Sierra Health Services
Summit Care
UniHealth America
United HealthCare
U.S. Healthcare
Value Health

HOW MUCH

	Annual Growth	1985	1986	1987	1988	1989	1990	1991	1992	1993	1994
Net subscriptions revenue ($ mil.)	6.2%	41,508	43,526	46,345	51,249	56,040	62,566	67,068	70,913	71,161	71,414
Pvt. subscribers (mil.)	(2.0%)	78	77	76	74	73	70	68	68	66	65
Employees	4.6%	98,000	110,000	118,000	125,000	129,000	133,000	138,000	143,000	135,883	146,352

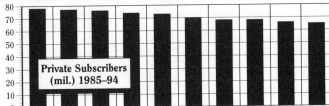

Private Subscribers (mil.) 1985–94

Blue Cross Blue Shield

BORG-WARNER AUTOMOTIVE, INC.

OVERVIEW

What's good for General Motors is good for Borg-Warner Automotive (BWA). The Chicago-based company earned 27% of its 1994 sales from GM; Ford is another major customer (39%). BWA supplies auto parts to every major automaker in the world; it makes highly engineered powertrain components for cars, light trucks, and RVs. Its products include automatic and manual transmissions, transfer cases, emission-control systems, clutches, friction plates, and timing chain systems.

BWA, which has manufacturing plants in 10 countries, is the world's leading independent maker of 4-wheel-drive transfer cases (installed in popular sport-utility vehicles) and automatic transmission components. BWA was spun off from Borg-Warner Security in 1993; subsidiaries of Merrill Lynch own about 40% of the company.

BWA wants to double its revenues by the year 2000. It had a very good year in 1994 — sales grew 24% — and the company plans to expand quickly into new geographic markets and acquire related companies. BWA has formed joint ventures in Asia and Europe to produce some of its parts.

John Fiedler, named president and COO in mid-1994, was named CEO in January 1995.

WHEN

Borg-Warner Automotive traces its roots back to the 1928 merger of 4 major Chicago auto parts companies (Borg & Beck, clutches; Warner Gear, transmissions; Mechanics Universal Joint; and Marvel Carburetor). The newly named Borg-Warner Corporation quickly began to diversify, acquiring numerous other companies, including Ingersoll Steel & Disc (agricultural blades and discs) and Norge (refrigerators).

The Great Depression struck shortly after Borg-Warner's formation, but the company weathered the crisis largely through the contributions of its Norge and Ingersoll divisions. In the late 1930s Borg-Warner purchased several companies, including Calumet Steel (1935) and US Pressed Steel (1937).

In the early 1940s Borg-Warner geared up for wartime production and manufactured parts for planes, trucks, and tanks; in 1941 it received a navy contract to build amphibious tanks for use in the Pacific. Between 1942 and 1945 Borg-Warner produced more than 1.6 million automotive transmissions, leaving the company in a good position to manufacture transmissions for the growing automobile industry at the end of WWII. Its 1948 contract with Ford to build half its transmissions resulted in massive growth.

In 1950 Roy Ingersoll, president of the Ingersoll Steel & Disc division, assumed leadership of Borg-Warner and embarked on a major diversification program. In 1956 Borg-Warner purchased several companies, including York (air conditioning and refrigeration), Humphreys Manufacturing, Industrial Crane & Hoist, Dittmer Gear, and the Chemical Process Company.

In 1968 James Beré became president and continued to expand the company away from its core businesses. Key acquisitions during this time included Recold Corporation (refrigeration, 1966), Precision Automotive Components (1966), H. Robert Industries (institutional products and furniture, 1970), and Unit Parts (auto parts, 1972).

Norge was sold to Fedders Corporation for $20 million in 1968, and in 1980 Borg-Warner sold its Ingersoll Products division to a group of investors led by Jack Maxwell. The company entered the security business in 1978 when it bought Baker Industries (which provided armored transport under the Wells Fargo name). In 1982 it acquired Burns International Security Services. Borg-Warner spun off York to its shareholders in 1986.

In 1987 Borg-Warner was threatened by a takeover from Irwin Jacobs and Samuel Heyman until Merrill Lynch Capital Partners organized an LBO and took the company private, assuming $4.5 billion in debt. To help pay the debt, Borg-Warner sold off everything but its automotive and security units, including its chemical group to General Electric for $2.3 billion (1988) and its credit unit, Chilton, to TRW for $330 million (1989).

In 1993 the company went public again as Borg-Warner Security. It then spun off Borg-Warner Automotive to its shareholders. That same year Mercedes-Benz picked Borg-Warner Automotive to supply transfer cases for a 4-wheel drive vehicle it plans to begin building in the US in 1997.

In 1995 the company formed a joint venture in India (Divgi-Warner) to make and sell transmission assemblies, bought out the remainder of its Italian joint venture (Regina-Warner), and purchased the precision-forged products division of US-based Federal-Mogul for $28 million.

NYSE symbol: BWA
Fiscal year ends: December 31

WHO

Chairman: J. Gordon Amedee, age 69, $750,000 pay
President and CEO: John F. Fiedler, $421,282 pay
EVP: Ronald M. Ruzic, age 56, $447,812 pay
EVP: Gary P. Fukayama, age 47, $416,366 pay
EVP: Fred M. Kovalik, age 57, $415,800 pay
EVP: Terry A. Schroeder
VP and Treasurer: Robin J. Adams, age 41
VP, Secretary, and General Counsel: Laurene H.
  Horiszny, age 39
VP Human Resources: Geraldine Kinsella, age 47
Auditors: Deloitte & Touche LLP

WHERE

HQ: 200 S. Michigan Ave., Chicago, IL 60604
Phone: 312-322-8500
Fax: 312-322-8849

The company operates 18 manufacturing facilities.

	1994 Sales		1994 Operating Income	
	$ mil.	% of total	$ mil.	% of total
US	1,048	86	104	77
Europe	105	9	8	6
Other regions	70	5	22	17
Total	**1,223**	**100**	**134**	**100**

WHAT

	1994 Sales	
	$ mil.	% of total
Powertrain systems	555	43
Automatic transmission systems	401	31
Morse TEC	244	19
Control systems	97	7
Adjustments	(74)	—
Total	**1,223**	**100**

Powertrain Systems
4-wheel drive and all-wheel drive transfer cases
Industrial transmissions
Manual transmissions

Automatic Transmission Systems
Brake plates
Friction plates
One-way clutches
Synchronizer rings
Torque converters
Transmission bands

Morse TEC
Chain tensioners and snubbers
Crankshaft and camshaft sprockets
CVT chain belts
Front-wheel and 4-wheel drive chain and timing chain
  systems
Timing chain systems

Control Systems
Engine and emission-control components and systems
Fuel- and vapor-management components and systems
Transmissions and steering suspension systems

Subsidiaries and Affiliates
Beijing Warner Gear Co., Ltd. (39%, manual
  transmissions, China)
Borg-Warner Automotive Korea Inc. (60%, friction
  products, Korea)
Divgi-Warner Private, Ltd. (60%; transfer cases, locking
  hubs, and manual transmissions; India)
Korea Powertrain, Ltd. (20%, torque converters, Korea)
NSK-Warner K.K. (50%, friction products, Japan)
Regina Warner S.p.A. (chain, Italy)
Warner-Ishi Corp. (50%, turbochargers, US)

KEY COMPETITORS

AlliedSignal	Dana	SPX
A. O. Smith	Danaher	Superior Industries
Arvin Industries	Eaton	Tecumseh
Caterpillar	PACCAR	Products
Cummins Engine	Siemens	TRW

HOW MUCH

	Annual Growth	1985	1986	1987	1988	1989	1990	1991	1992	1993	1994
Sales ($ mil.)	4.9%	—	—	—	—	965	926	820	926	985	1,223
Net income ($ mil.)	26.6%	—	—	—	—	20	(13)	(36)	(12)	33	64
Income as % of sales	—	—	—	—	—	2.1%	—	—	—	3.3%	5.3%
Earnings per share ($)	95.0%	—	—	—	—	—	—	—	—	1.41	2.75
Stock price – high ($)	—	—	—	—	—	—	—	—	—	28.00	34.00
Stock price – low ($)	—	—	—	—	—	—	—	—	—	20.50	21.63
Stock price – close ($)	(10.3%)	—	—	—	—	—	—	—	—	28.00	25.13
P/E – high	—	—	—	—	—	—	—	—	—	20	12
P/E – low	—	—	—	—	—	—	—	—	—	15	8
Dividends per share ($)	20.0%	—	—	—	—	—	—	—	—	0.13	0.15
Book value per share ($)	9.6%	—	—	—	—	—	—	—	—	20.14	22.08
Employees	10.9%	—	—	—	—	—	—	—	—	6,610	7,330

1994 Year-end:
Debt ratio: 16.7%
Return on equity: 13.0%
Cash (mil.): $15
Current ratio: 0.87
Long-term debt (mil.): $87
No. of shares (mil.): 24
Dividends
  Yield: 0.6%
  Payout: 5.5%
Market value (mil.): $609

Stock Price History
High/Low 1993–94

(chart axis values: 35, 30, 25, 20, 15, 10, 5, 0)

BORG-WARNER SECURITY

OVERVIEW

Borg-Warner Security, the largest and broadest supplier of security services in the US, provides guard, alarm, armored transportation, and courier services under such well-known brand names as Burns, Pony Express, and Wells Fargo. But the growing number of armored car heists, skyrocketing insurance costs, heavy debt, and labor unrest at subsidiary Pony Express Courier Corp. have investors feeling less than secure.

The company's hopes that the national preoccupation with crime would be reflected in an increased use of the company's services have proven unfounded. Competition from lower-cost, smaller security operations has cut into the market share of Borg-Warner's security guard business (the company has about 73,000 guards). Borg-Warner also missed a business opportunity by failing to make a concerted push into the fast-growing residential alarm business.

The company has begun to gear itself up competitively by reorganizing its US guard services operations into 10 business units to improve its ability to compete regionally and serve multilocation customers. It also secured a major contract to provide security services for the 1996 Olympic Games in Atlanta.

WHEN

While Borg-Warner's current operations are all in the security industry, its origins can be traced to a 1928 merger of 4 major Chicago auto parts companies. The merger produced Borg-Warner Corporation, which diversified into other fields over the next 50 years, acquiring numerous other companies in areas including agricultural equipment, steel, air-conditioning and refrigeration, and furniture.

The company entered the security business in 1978 when it bought Baker Industries, which provided armored car and security services under the Wells Fargo and Pony Express brands, for $118 million. Wells Fargo had been established in 1852 when Henry Wells and William Fargo (both executives of American Express) formed a company to transport freight and deliver mail between the East Coast and the pioneer settlements in California. The completion of the transcontinental railroad in 1869 brought about the demise of its short-lived stagecoach empire. In 1904 Wells Fargo moved its headquarters to New York, and in 1905 it separated its banking and express operations. Wartime regulations during WWI forced Wells Fargo to consolidate its domestic services with other major express companies, although Wells Fargo continued some overseas operations until the 1960s.

Borg-Warner's other leading brand-name security service, Pony Express, traces its roots to 1858, when William Russell and a number of horseback riders established an overland mail route between St. Joseph, Missouri, and Sacramento, California. Wells Fargo operated the westernmost leg of the Pony Express (Salt Lake City to San Francisco) in 1861. The Pony Express ended when transcontinental telegraph lines were completed later that same year. Both the Pony Express and Wells Fargo trademarks subsequently reverted to the control of American Express until 1967, when Baker Industries acquired them.

Between 1977 and 1991 Borg-Warner acquired 72 protective services companies. In 1982 the company acquired Burns International Security Services, one of the largest providers of security guards for plants, offices, and other buildings, for $82 million. Burns International was founded in 1910 by William Burns, a leading investigator and the first head of the agency that became the FBI.

In 1987 Borg-Warner was threatened with a takeover by Irwin Jacobs and Samuel Heyman until Merrill Lynch Capital Partners organized an LBO and took the company private, assuming $4.5 billion in debt. To help pay the debt, Borg-Warner sold its chemical group and everything else but its automotive, security, and credit units to General Electric for $2.3 billion (1988); it sold its credit unit, Chilton, to TRW for $330 million (1989).

In 1992 the company acquired Security Bureau Inc., a provider of contract security guard services, for $26.9 million.

In 1993 the company went public again as Borg-Warner Security. It then spun off Borg-Warner Automotive to its shareholders.

Borg-Warner Security's earnings were hurt by theft in 1994, with armored cars singled out as the most popular target. Losses from external theft rose to $16 million, as compared to $2 million a year earlier. Five employees were killed in the line of duty in 1994.

In 1995 former Emerson Electric president Joe Adorjan was named to succeed Donald Trauscht as CEO at the year's end. That year the Borg-Warner Protective Services subsidiary won a $20 million contract to provide security at 2 Consumers Power Co. nuclear plants.

NYSE symbol: BOR
Fiscal year ends: December 31

WHO

Chairman, President, and CEO: Donald C. Trauscht,
age 61, $650,000 pay
EVP; President, Wells Fargo Alarm Services: Neal F.
Farrell, age 60, $400,000 pay
**SVP (HR); President, Borg-Warner Protective Services
Corp.:** John D. O'Brien, age 52, $325,000 pay
VP Finance: Timothy M. Wood, age 47, $275,000 pay
VP Law and Corporate Secretary: Edwin L. Lewis,
age 49
President, Pony Express Courier Corp.: Bob E. Moree
Assistant Secretary: Diana W. Bligh
Assistant Treasurer: Scott R. Veldman
Auditors: Deloitte & Touche LLP

WHERE

HQ: Borg-Warner Security Corporation,
200 S. Michigan Ave., Chicago, IL 60604
Phone: 312-322-8500
Fax: 312-322-8849

The company serves more than 160,000 customers from
600 offices located throughout the United States and in
Canada, Colombia, and the UK.

WHAT

	1994 Sales		1994 Operating Income	
	$ mil.	% of total	$ mil.	% of total
Guard services	1,210	68	54	71
Armored services	211	12	7	9
Alarm services	206	11	15	19
Courier services	166	9	1	1
Total	**1,793**	**100**	**77**	**100**

Guard Services
Contract guard and related security services (Burns,
Globe, Wells Fargo)

Armored Transport Services (Wells Fargo)
Armored transport for cash and valuables
ATM services
Cash management services

Alarm Services
Electronic security services (Pony Express, Wells Fargo)
Integrated guard, patrol, and alarm services for high-end
Los Angeles neighborhoods (Bel-Air Patrol)

Courier Services (Pony Express)
Non-negotiable financial document transportation
Time-sensitive package transportation

Selected Subsidiaries and Affiliates
Bel-Air Patrol
Borg-Warner Protective Services Corp.
International Air Courier
Pony Express Courier Corp.
Pyro Chem, Inc.
Wells Fargo Alarm Services
Wells Fargo Armored Service Corp.
Wells Fargo Security Products

KEY COMPETITORS

ADT
American Protective
Am-Pro
Command Security
Honeywell
Loomis Armored
National Guardian
Pinkerton's
Pittston Services
Sensormatic

HOW MUCH

	Annual Growth	1985	1986	1987	1988	1989	1990	1991	1992	1993	1994
Sales ($ mil.)	(6.6%)	3,330	3,379	2,957	2,145	2,216	2,340	2,376	1,621	1,765	1,793
Net income ($ mil.)	(25.3%)	180	155	2	(3)	36	12	(6)	39	(226)	13
Income as % of sales	—	5.4%	4.6%	0.1%	—	1.6%	0.5%	—	2.4%	—	0.7%
Earnings per share ($)	(46.5%)	—	—	—	—	—	—	—	1.96	(9.88)	0.56
Stock price – high ($)	—	—	—	—	—	—	—	—	—	22.88	22.00
Stock price – low ($)	—	—	—	—	—	—	—	—	—	18.00	8.25
Stock price – close ($)	(52.4%)	—	—	—	—	—	—	—	—	20.50	9.75
P/E – high	—	—	—	—	—	—	—	—	—	—	39
P/E – low	—	—	—	—	—	—	—	—	—	—	15
Dividends per share ($)	—	—	—	—	—	—	—	—	—	0.00	0.00
Book value per share ($)	57.9%	—	—	—	—	—	—	—	—	1.24	1.95
Employees	1.2%	82,000	78,000	72,800	70,200	75,300	86,800	84,500	78,350	87,000	91,698

1994 Year-end:
Debt ratio: 91.5%
Return on equity: 36.7%
Cash (mil.): $16
Current ratio: 0.81
Long-term debt (mil.): $454
No. of shares (mil.): 22
Dividends
  Yield: —
  Payout: —
Market value (mil.): $219

**Stock Price History
High/Low 1993–94**

BRUNSWICK CORPORATION

OVERVIEW

Brunswick's business is leisure. The 150-year-old Illinois-based company is the leading US maker of recreation and leisure products as well as the world's leading manufacturer of pleasure boats and equipment. It operates one of North America's largest bowling chains (Brunswick Recreation Centers) as well as restaurants (Circus World Pizza) and manufactures bowling equipment (Brunswick), fishing rods and reels (Zebco and Browning), golf equipment, and billiard tables (Brunswick). Almost 3/4 of the company's revenues comes from its marine operations, which include a variety of outboard motors (for example, Mercury, Mariner, and Force); boats designed for sport fishing (Robalo), pleasure (Bayliner),

performance (Astro), and yachting (Sea Ray), among others; and trailers and accessories.

Despite a surge in profits, Brunswick has been in choppy waters of late. Earnings in 1994 were up 240%, but the company's prospects were clouded by federal investigations into its defense business and personal conflicts among executives (causing president John Reilly to jump ship after 9 months on the job). The government dropped its case, and the company sold most of its military operations in 1995.

In May 1995 former Johnson & Johnson executive Peter Larson was brought on board to succeed chairman Jack Reichert, who retired in 1995.

WHEN

Swiss immigrant woodworker John Brunswick built his first billiard table in 1845 in Cincinnati. In 1874 he formed a partnership with Julius Balke, and in 1884 they teamed with H. W. Collender, forming the Brunswick-Balke-Collender Company.

Following Brunswick's death, son-in-law Moses Bensinger became president and diversified into bowling equipment in the 1880s. His son B. E. followed as president (1904) and led the company into wood and rubber products, phonographs, and records. (Al Jolson recorded "Sonny Boy" on a Brunswick label.) Brunswick went public after WWI.

By 1930 Brunswick had sold many businesses to concentrate on bowling and billiards, sports that had acquired bad reputations during the 1920s and 1930s. When B. E. died in 1935, his son Bob became CEO and launched a massive promotional campaign to make the sports more respectable.

Bob Bensinger moved to chairman in 1954, and his brother Ted succeeded him as CEO. Rival A.M.F. introduced the first automatic pinsetter in 1952, and Brunswick followed in 1956. By 1958 Brunswick had captured the industry lead, as bowling equipment sales rose 650% between 1956 and 1961. Under Ted, Brunswick diversified, adding MacGregor (sporting goods, 1958), Aloe (medical supplies, 1959), Mercury (marine products, 1961), and Zebco (fishing equipment, 1961). The company adopted its present name in 1960.

By 1963 bowling sales had plummeted, and in 1965 Brunswick lost $76.9 million. The company sold many unprofitable enterprises, intensified research on an automatic scorer

and metal fiber technology (for industrial and defense applications), and emphasized health products through subsidiary Sherwood Medical Industries. In 1978 Brunswick added Oxford Laboratories (medical diagnostics) and the Vapor Corporation (energy and transportation products). To foil a takeover by Whittaker Corporation in 1982, Brunswick sold Sherwood to American Home Products. CEO Jack Reichert, a former pin boy who became chairman in 1983, cut corporate staff 59% and promoted the marine business.

In 1986 Brunswick sparked an industry-wide consolidation trend by spending $774 million to buy boat builders Bayliner and Ray Industries.

A marine industry slump led to a $71 million loss in 1989. The company restructured and cut costs, which enabled it to post a profit in 1990. Brunswick bought Kiekhaefer Aeromarine (marine propulsion engines, 1990) and Martin Reel Company (fly reels, 1991). In 1992 Brunswick and Tracker Marine (Missouri-based boat manufacturer) agreed to form a partnership to manufacture boats and marine equipment.

That same year the company acquired the Browning line of rods and reels. In 1993 the company announced plans to sell its Technical Group (aerospace, defense, electronics, machinery, automotive, aircraft, and oil and gas products); the sale went through once the federal investigation was closed.

In 1995 Brunswick's Mercury division formed a joint venture with Orbital Engine (Australia) to design and make fuel systems for small, 2-cycle engines to meet stricter EPA emission standards.

NYSE symbol: BC
Fiscal year ends: December 31

WHO

Chairman, President and CEO: Peter N. Larson, age 55
EVP; Group President, Brunswick Marine: John M. Charvat, age 64, $684,197 pay
SVP and CFO: Peter B. Hamilton
VP; President, Mercury Marine Division: David D. Jones, age 52, $588,384 pay (prior to promotion)
VP; President, Brunswick Division: Frederick J. Florjancic Jr., age 48, $476,301 pay
VP; President, Zebco Division: Jim W. Dawson, age 60
VP and Chief of Human Relations: Kenneth B. Zeigler
President, US Marine Division: Robert C. Steinway, age 43
President, Sea Ray Division: William J. Barrington, age 44
Controller: Thomas K. Erwin, age 45
General Counsel: Robert T. McNaney, age 60
Auditors: Arthur Andersen & Co, SC

WHERE

HQ: One N. Field Ct., Lake Forest, IL 60045-4811
Phone: 847-735-4700
Fax: 847-735-4765

Brunswick operates approximately 35 US plants, 5 foreign plants, and 7 pizza restaurants. Of its 126 bowling centers, 117 are in North America and 9 in Germany and Austria.

	1994 Sales		1994 Operating Income	
	$ mil.	% of total	$ mil.	% of total
US	2,213	82	205	79
Other countries	487	18	53	21
Total	**2,700**	**100**	**258**	**100**

WHAT

	1994 Sales		1994 Operating Income	
	$ mil.	% of total	$ mil.	% of total
Marine	1,991	74	175	68
Recreation	709	26	83	32
Total	**2,700**	**100**	**258**	**100**

Selected Brand Names

Boats

Astro	Fisher	Procraft	Ski Ray
Bayliner	Jazz	Quantum	Spectrum
Ciera	Laguna	Robalo	Starcraft
Cobra	Maxum	Sea Ray	Trophy
Escort (trailers)	MonArk	Sea Rayder	US Marine

Boat Motors

Force	MotorGuide	Stealth
Mariner	Quicksilver Marine	Thruster
MerCruiser	(parts/accessories)	
Mercury Marine		

Recreation Centers/Restaurants
Brunswick Recreation Centers
Circus World Pizza

Sporting Goods
Bowling (Anvilane, Armor Plate 3000, AS-90, BallWall, BowlerVision, Brunswick, Colorvision, GS-10, Guardian, Leiserv, Perry-Austen, Rhino, Systems 2000)
Billiards (Brunswick)
Golf (Brunswick Golf, Precision FCM)
Fishing (Classic, Martin, Pro Staff, Quantum, Zebco)

KEY COMPETITORS

AMF	Genmar	Outboard Marine
Anthony	Harley-Davidson	ShowBiz Pizza
Industries	Honda	Time
Callaway Golf	Johnson Worldwide	Suzuki
Fountain	MacAndrews	Volvo
Powerboat	& Forbes	Yamaha

HOW MUCH

	Annual Growth	1985	1986	1987	1988	1989	1990	1991	1992	1993	1994
Sales ($ mil.)	6.4%	1,539	1,717	3,086	3,282	2,826	2,478	2,088	2,059	2,207	2,700
Net income ($ mil.)	2.9%	100	110	169	193	(71)	71	(24)	38	38	129
Income as % of sales	—	6.5%	6.4%	5.5%	5.9%	—	2.9%	—	1.8%	1.7%	4.8%
Earnings per share ($)	1.6%	1.17	1.32	1.90	2.20	(0.81)	0.80	(0.27)	0.41	0.39	1.35
Stock price – high ($)	—	11.38	19.69	30.25	24.13	21.50	16.13	16.38	17.75	18.50	25.38
Stock price – low ($)	—	7.75	10.81	6.75	14.50	13.00	6.38	8.00	12.13	12.50	17.00
Stock price – close ($)	6.3%	10.91	16.94	14.75	16.88	14.13	9.00	13.88	16.25	18.00	18.88
P/E – high	—	10	15	16	11	—	20	—	43	47	19
P/E – low	—	7	8	4	7	—	8	—	30	32	13
Dividends per share ($)	6.5%	0.25	0.28	0.30	0.40	0.44	0.44	0.44	0.44	0.44	0.44
Book value per share ($)	4.8%	6.23	7.80	9.52	10.97	8.82	9.33	8.79	8.65	8.44	9.54
Employees	1.2%	18,700	26,800	28,400	28,500	25,700	20,500	19,500	17,000	18,000	20,800

1994 Year-end:
Debt ratio: 26.4%
Return on equity: 15.0%
Cash (mil.): $203
Current ratio: 1.70
Long-term debt (mil.): $319
No. of shares (mil.): 95
Dividends
  Yield: 2.3%
  Payout: 32.6%
Market value (mil.): $1,802

Stock Price History High/Low 1985–94

BUDGET RENT A CAR CORPORATION

OVERVIEW

Budget is turning blue in an effort to rake in more green. The Lisle, Illinois–based rental car company is the nation's 5th largest in sales (after Hertz, Enterprise, Avis, and Alamo) and is striving to change its image from cut-rate to business (or even luxury) class. To underscore the shift, Budget changed its corporate color from orange (associated with "cheap" service quality) to blue. The company is owned by Beech Holdings Corp., which in turn is controlled by Fulcrum II Ltd. Partnership, the general partner of the investment banking firm Gibbons, Green, van Amerongen. Ford Motor Co. (which owns Hertz) has invested several hundred million dollars in Budget and holds nonvoting stock in Beech.

In an effort to win more leisure travelers (who account for a fast-growing 45% of the rental market), CEO William Plamondon has implemented a new strategy that stresses customer service and value over price.

Budget hopes customers will begin to see rental vehicles as part of the vacation reverie — adding Audis, BMWs, Humvees, and Jaguar convertibles to its fleet of Fords and Lincolns. Its "World Class Drives" program includes maps with local history notes and coupons for restaurants, hotels, and entertainment.

Budget also hopes its strategy will help customers overlook a $5-a-day rate hike (the first of many Budget and its rivals say they need). Industry costs more than doubled from 1993 to 1995 because of changing contracts with automakers. Competition (and customers reluctant to give up features like unlimited mileage) have made it difficult for car rental companies to maintain their windshield-thin profit margins.

WHEN

In 1958 Morris Mirkin and Jules Lederer established an auto rental company in Los Angeles. Starting with 10 cars, they charged customers $4 a day and 4¢ a mile. Two years later they formed Budget Rent a Car Corporation of America. The firm grew fast, primarily through franchising and by concentrating on the leisure travel market. Budget moved its headquarters to Chicago in 1967.

Transamerica Corporation bought Budget for more than $5 million in 1968. The firm began to develop small-business accounts and national corporate accounts. In 1976 Budget dropped the "of America" portion of its name.

By the 1980s Budget had altered its growth strategy and begun acquiring its franchisees in an effort to establish systemwide standards. In 1985 a bitter price war broke out in the rental car industry, hurting earnings. The following year tax reform legislation repealed the investment tax credit the companies enjoyed. As a result, the large corporations that owned the 4 major rental firms (Hertz, Avis, Budget, and National) were looking to unburden themselves. Concurrently, the rental companies' high cash flows attracted the interest of investment firms specializing in LBOs. In 1986 Gibbons, Green, van Amerongen bought Budget for $460 million and took it private. The new owners offered 30% of Budget's stock to the public the following year and used the entire $40 million in proceeds to pay its debt.

The rental companies' voracious appetite for new cars had attracted Detroit's attention. The Big 3 had begun to invest in the firms in order to lock in car purchase agreements, thus ensuring demand during a recession.

In 1988 Budget's management decided to buy back its public stock. Gibbons's partner, Fulcrum II Limited Partnership, formed Beech Holdings Corp., which became the new parent of Budget. Budget's management chipped in about $33 million and Ford Motor Co. plunked down $300 million to finance the deal. In return, Ford got nonvoting stock in Beech, and it signed a 10-year auto purchase agreement with Budget. Manufacturers like Ford offered rental companies large rebates and began buying cars back after just 4 months. As operating costs declined, so did rental rates.

Budget began opening corporate-owned outlets in Europe by 1989. The following year the firm capped its domestic acquisition campaign with the purchase of Diversified Services, its biggest franchisee. The buyout gave Budget direct access to Florida and Los Angeles, the 2 largest US car rental markets.

When auto sales began to improve in 1992, Detroit began to slash the high rebates and buy-back deals the rental companies enjoyed. In 1993 Budget lost money as smaller competitors and customers alike resisted rental rate hikes. That same year William Plamondon capped a 14-year career with Budget by becoming president and CEO.

In 1994 Budget claimed a profitable year as the airlines' price war fueled increased travel. In 1995 Budget (along with several rivals) canceled its unlimited mileage program, then reinstated it after customers protested.

Private company
Fiscal year ends: December 31

WHO

Chairman: Jack A. Frazee
President and CEO: William N. Plamondon, age 47
SVP and General Counsel: Robert Aprati
Acting CFO: Ollie Thorp
VP Information Systems: Don Savlic
VP Human Resources: David Finley

WHERE

HQ: 4225 Naperville Rd., Lisle, IL 60532
Phone: 708-955-1900
Fax: 708-955-7799
Reservations: 800-527-0700

Budget has operations at 1,000 US locations and 2,200 locations in 117 other countries.

WHAT

Selected Rental Fleet (159,000 vehicles worldwide)

Economy
Ford Aspire
Ford Fiesta

Compact
Ford Escort

Midsize
Ford Contour
Mercury Mystique

Full-size
Ford Taurus
Mercury Sable

Premium
Ford Crown Victoria
Mercury Grand Marquis

Luxury
Lincoln Continental
Lincoln Mark VIII
Lincoln Town Car
Jaguar XJ6
Jaguar XJS convertible

Minivans and Sport Utility
Ford Aerostar
Ford Explorer
Ford Windstar
Humvee

Motorcycle
Harley-Davidson FXDS
  Dyna Convertible (UK
  only)

Selected Subsidiaries
BRAC Credit Corp. (financial services)
Budget Car Sales (new and used car dealers)

KEY COMPETITORS

Accor
Agency Rent-a-Car
Alamo Rent A Car
AMERCO
Avis
Chrysler
Enterprise Rent-A-Car
Ford
National Car Rental
Ryder

HOW MUCH

	Annual Growth	1985	1986	1987	1988	1989	1990	1991	1992	1993	1994
Sales ($ mil.)	9.4%	—	—	—	512	673	983	1,088	1,145	1,018	1,081
Net income ($ mil.)	—	—	—	—	—	—	—	—	—	—	7
Income as % of sales	—	—	—	—	—	—	—	—	—	—	0.6%
Employees	(8.5%)	—	—	—	—	—	—	—	10,400	10,400	8,700

Budget
car and
truck rental

Sales ($ mil.)
1988–94

(Bar chart y-axis: 1,200 / 1,000 / 800 / 600 / 400 / 200 / 0)

CAREMARK INTERNATIONAL INC.

OVERVIEW

Caremark International, based in Northbrook, Illinois, has carved itself lucrative territories in several segments of the health care industry. As one of the largest managers of prescription drug benefit programs for corporations, insurance companies, government employee groups, and managed care organizations in the US, Caremark dispenses more than 40,000 prescriptions daily from 4 mail-order facilities. The company uses a database to prevent overmedication or potentially harmful combinations of drugs and works to develop new drug therapy approaches.

Caremark's Disease State Management division offers orthopedic and oncological services and also provides specialized care to patients suffering from high-cost, chronic disorders such as hemophilia, HIV/AIDS, and kidney failure. By providing all of the services needed

for a particular disease, the company is able to reduce the overall cost of treatment as well as research ways to improve the effectiveness of the treatment.

Caremark is moving rapidly into physician practice management, whereby it provides management services to clinics while freeing the physicians to focus on medical services. By linking the clinics together, Caremark is building an integrated health care delivery network to supply all of an individual's health care needs. Since 1992 the company has agreed to provide its services to 6 multispecialty medical group practices with a total of nearly 1,000 physicians.

Caremark's international division offers out-of-hospital care services (e.g., nutritional therapy and HIV/AIDS care) in Canada, Europe, Japan, and Puerto Rico.

WHEN

Caremark was founded in 1979 as Home Health Care of America by James Sweeney, a former Baxter executive, who realized the benefits of caring for seriously ill patients outside of expensive hospitals. Not only did patients (especially the elderly) appreciate receiving treatment at home, but the services were less costly. As insurers and Medicare and Medicaid began to cover the costs of home treatment (as a reasonable alternative to hospital care), the home care market took off, growing in the early 1980s by 20% per year.

By 1985 the company had 33 home care centers and $70 million in revenues. With plans for expansion into new businesses, the name was changed to Caremark. That year it acquired Federal Prescription Service, a $7.5 million mail-order prescription business. It also purchased the Health Data Institute, which sold software and management services to insurers and large corporations, thus connecting Caremark with this important market segment and providing the company with a database on 25 million Americans.

In 1987 Caremark sold its prescription drug unit, then named America's Pharmacy, to Newport Pharmaceuticals. Shortly after, Caremark was bought by Baxter, a leading medical equipment maker, for $528 million.

Sweeney left the company in 1988 to pursue other start-up ventures (he eventually became CEO of Coram Healthcare), but his creation continued to grow. With Baxter supplying the equipment, Caremark was able to significantly increase its home care business.

The company was also able to use its experience in the pharmaceuticals business to help Baxter build a mail-order pharmacy.

Caremark's 1991 sales topped $1 billion. However, the home care provider's success didn't please Baxter's main customers — hospitals. Partly because of pressure from these competitors, Baxter spun off Caremark in 1992. At the time, Caremark's operations included the 2nd largest mail-order drug service (behind Medco Containment Services), the home-infusion division, and the home care centers. The company, based now in Illinois, was headed by Lance Piccolo, an ambitious protégé of Baxter's chairman, Vernon Loucks.

Piccolo steered Caremark toward physician practice management, believing that was where industry growth would occur. In 1993 it acquired a physician's group in Houston and another large clinic in Oklahoma City. That year it also expanded into the kidney dialysis markets with the acquisition of a network of clinics in Minnesota, Wisconsin, and South Dakota.

In 1995 Caremark pleaded guilty to charges of paying kickbacks to physicians for referrals to its home health care services and paid $159 million in fines. The company sold the tarnished home-infusion unit that year to Coram Healthcare (Sweeney's company) to help fund its move into physician networks. In late 1995 Caremark purchased CIGNA's managed care business assets in Southern California, adding to a clinic network in Los Angeles purchased earlier that year.

NYSE symbol: CK
Fiscal year ends: December 31

WHO

Chairman and CEO: C. A. Lance Piccolo, age 54,
$866,106 pay
President and COO: James G. Connelly III, age 49,
$506,826 pay
SVP and CFO: Thomas W. Hodson, age 48, $471,926 pay
SVP, Integrated Services: Donna C. E. Williamson,
age 42, $372,144 pay
VP, Pharmaceutical Services: Kristen E. Gibney, age 46,
$360,644 pay
VP, Secretary, and General Counsel: Thomas R.
Schuman, age 53
VP and Controller: John M. Pellettiere Jr., age 44
VP Human Resources: Kent J. De Lucenay, age 46
Auditors: Price Waterhouse LLP

WHERE

HQ: 2215 Sanders Rd., Northbrook, IL 60062
Phone: 847-559-4700
Fax: 847-559-4792

Caremark provides health care services in Canada,
France, Germany, Japan, the Netherlands, Puerto Rico,
the UK, and the US.

WHAT

	1994 Sales	
	$ mil.	% of total
Pharmaceutical services	1,097	45
Disease state management	631	26
Home infusion	442	18
Physician practice management	190	8
International	66	3
Total	**2,426**	**100**

Pharmaceutical Services
Medical data management
Prescription services division

Disease State Management Services
Growth hormone distribution
Nephrology
    Chabot Clinic (San Francisco)
    Regional Kidney Disease Program (Minneapolis)
Oncology
Orthopedics
Therapeutic services
    Hemophilia
    Immune deficiencies

Selected Physician Practice Management Clients
Atlanta Medical Associates
Friendly Hills HealthCare Network (La Habra, CA)
Kelsey-Seybold Clinic (Houston)
North Suburban Clinic (Skokie, IL)
Oklahoma City Clinic
Strategic HealthCare Management

KEY COMPETITORS

American Oncology
Apria Healthcare
Beverly Enterprises
Blue Cross
Eli Lilly
Express Scripts
Foundation Health
Genesis Health
  Ventures
Merck

National HealthCare
OccuSystems
PhyCor
Physician Reliance
Physicians Resource
  Group
SmithKline Beecham
Systemed
Value Health

HOW MUCH

	Annual Growth	1985	1986	1987	1988	1989	1990	1991	1992	1993	1994
Sales ($ mil.)	28.7%	—	—	—	535	708	928	1,194	1,461	1,783	2,426
Net income ($ mil.)	18.9%	—	—	—	28	34	52	69	27	78	80
Income as % of sales		—	—	—	5.3%	4.8%	5.6%	5.8%	1.9%	4.4%	3.3%
Earnings per share ($)	66.4%	—	—	—	—	—	—	—	0.39	1.04	1.08
Stock prices – high ($)		—	—	—	—	—	—	—	15.00	20.75	26.75
Stock prices – low ($)		—	—	—	—	—	—	—	12.00	11.88	15.75
Stock prices – close ($)	7.3%	—	—	—	—	—	—	—	14.88	19.75	17.13
P/E – high		—	—	—	—	—	—	—	38	20	25
P/E – low		—	—	—	—	—	—	—	31	11	15
Dividends per share ($)		—	—	—	—	—	—	—	0.00	0.00	0.00
Book value per share($)	(36.6%)	—	—	—	—	—	—	—	4.67	5.70	1.88
Employees	21.2%	—	—	—	2,880	3,470	4,240	5,340	6,270	7,753	9,150

1994 Year-end:
Debt ratio: 42.2%
Return on equity: 17.9%
Cash (mil.): $32
Current ratio: 1.45
Long-term debt (mil.): $237
No. of shares (mil.): 259
Dividends
  Yield: —
  Payout: —
Market value (mil.): $4,441

Stock Price History
High/Low 1992–94

CBI INDUSTRIES, INC.

OVERVIEW

CBI Industries is pumping up profits with industrial gases. The company's Liquid Carbonic subsidiary is the world's largest supplier of carbon dioxide, which is used for refrigeration, carbonated beverages, chemical production, and water treatment. The subsidiary also produces, processes, and markets other industrial/medical gases such as argon, liquefied natural gas (LNG), and nitrous oxide.

CBI's other major business is Chicago Bridge & Iron, which is a leading manufacturer of vessels for oil, gas, and water storage. Its contract services division provides design and construction project management services for a wide variety of industrial projects, including wastewater treatment plants, defense-related facilities, and refineries.

CBI also owns Statia Terminals, a provider of transshipment, storage, and blending services for hydrocarbons and other liquid products. This subsidiary is part of CBI's investments segment, which owns real estate and financial interests in noncore companies.

CBI is in the process of expanding its gases division (which accounted for 48% of total 1994 revenues), using cash generated by its construction businesses. Investments in 1994 included expansion of carbon dioxide facilities in Brazil, Thailand, and the US and interests in industrial gas companies in emerging markets, such as Colombia, Paraguay, and Turkey.

Liquid Carbonic is also benefiting from the growing hydrogen and liquefied natural gas markets in the US. In 1994 the Willis, Texas, LNG plant went online, supplying fuel for bus fleets in Austin, El Paso, and Houston. In early 1995 a hydrogen/carbon monoxide plant in Lake Charles, Louisiana, was completed.

WHEN

The origins of CBI Industries date back to 1867, when Horace Horton designed and built his first wooden bridge over the Zumbro River in Minnesota. He went on to build more bridges, including 11 across the Mississippi. In 1889 he merged his business with the Kansas City Bridge and Iron Company (which was started in 1881 by George Wheelock, C. E. Moss, and A. M. Blodgett) and moved the enterprise to Chicago to become the Chicago Bridge & Iron Company (CB&I).

As the railroads expanded across the US in the early 1900s, CB&I prospered as an expert bridge builder. This experience with iron structures was used to develop and build water tanks and other municipal works required by the new towns created by the railroads.

During WWI, CB&I built 150 barges, each with a capacity of 5,000 tons. Following the war, the company was enlisted by the booming American oil industry to build storage tanks for the oil being found in the Southwest.

The company's success was partly the result of innovative designs and techniques for building iron structures. The Chibridge Spacer, for example, accurately punched 12 holes at a time in steel plates without the use of a huge template, saving time and improving the fit. Other innovations included floating roof storage tanks and the Hortonsphere vessel, a pressurized liquid and gas storage facility.

WWII found the company again helping the navy by building landing ships and huge, floating drydocks on which to repair damaged ships. CB&I did more business during the 4

years of the war than during all of the company's first 52 years.

Postwar growth at CB&I tracked the demand for public works and industrial projects around the world, such as cryogenics, hydroelectric and nuclear power, and even projects for the US space program. In 1963 the company won a contract to help build the Mangla Dam in Pakistan. That year CB&I went public.

After experiencing a boom in demand for storage facilities during the oil embargo of the early 1970s, the company developed a cheaper way of extracting carbon dioxide from liquefied natural gas (a process patented as Cryex). In 1979 CB&I was reorganized as a holding company and renamed CBI Industries.

During the 1980s CBI looked to diversification in order to avoid the unpredictable shocks of the energy business, and in 1984 it purchased Liquid Carbonic, the world's leading supplier of carbon dioxide. (Liquid Carbonic had been founded in 1888 to provide gas to soda fountains and soft drink bottlers.) The subsequent crash of oil prices and the energy business in the late 1980s was partially offset by CBI's new industrial gas division.

The company helped rebuild war-torn Kuwait in the early 1990s. A high debt load combined with lower earnings in the construction division resulted in an unsuccessful takeover attempt in 1994 by Airgas, which wanted the highly profitable Liquid Carbonic division. In late 1995 rival Praxair announced that it would pay $1.5 billion for CBI. After a 2-month battle, CBI agreed to terms with Praxair.

NYSE symbol: CBI
Fiscal year ends: December 31

WHO

Chairman, President, and CEO: John E. Jones, age 60,
$607,000 pay
EVP Finance and CFO: George L. Schueppert, age 56,
$340,000 pay
EVP; President, Chicago Bridge & Iron Co.: Lewis E.
Akin, age 57, $325,000 pay
EVP; President, Liquid Carbonic Industries Corp.:
Robert J. Daniels, age 61, $308,515 pay
SVP and General Counsel: Charles O. Ziemer, age 55,
$220,000 pay
President, Statia Terminals, Inc.: James G. Cameron
VP and Treasurer: Buel T. Adams, age 62
VP and Controller: Alan J. Schneider, age 49
VP Human Resources: Stephen M. Duffy, age 45
Auditors: Arthur Andersen & Co, SC

WHERE

HQ: 800 Jorie Blvd., Oak Brook, IL 60521-2268
Phone: 708-572-7000
Fax: 708-572-7405

CBI Industries has operations in more than 25 countries
around the world, including Argentina, Australia, Brazil,
Canada, Chile, Japan, Malaysia, Mexico, Poland, Spain,
Saudi Arabia, Thailand, and the US.

	1994 Sales	
	$ mil.	% of total
US	882	47
Other Western Hemisphere	727	38
Eastern Hemisphere	282	15
Total	**1,891**	**100**

WHAT

	1994 Sales	
	$ mil.	% of total
Industrial gases	907	48
Contracting services	832	44
Investments	152	8
Total	**1,891**	**100**

Selected Subsidiaries

Chicago Bridge & Iron Company (contracting services)
CBI Na-Con, Inc. (construction-related services)
CBI Walker, Inc. (water and wastewater equipment)
Chicago Bridge & Iron Technical Services Co.
  (engineering and research services)
Cooperheat, Inc. (post-weld heat treatment services)
Ershigs, Inc. (fiberglass vessel construction)
MQS Inspection, Inc. (examination and testing services)

Liquid Carbonic Industries Corp. (industrial gases)

Statia Terminals, Inc. (oil storage and blending
  facilities)

Gases

Acetylene	Liquefied natural gas
Argon	Nitrogen
Carbon dioxide	Nitrous oxide
Carbon monoxide	Oxygen
Hydrogen	

KEY COMPETITORS

ABB	Halliburton
ADM	L'Air Liquide
Air Products and	Morrison Knudsen
Chemicals	Offshore Logistics
Airgas	Parsons Corp.
Bechtel	Perini
Black and Veatch	Peter Kiewit Sons'
Crowley Maritime	Praxair
Dillingham Construction	Textainer Capital
Duke Power	Trans Ocean

HOW MUCH

	Annual Growth	1985	1986	1987	1988	1989	1990	1991	1992	1993	1994
Sales ($ mil.)	2.1%	1,572	1,155	1,160	1,376	1,495	1,576	1,615	1,673	1,672	1,891
Net income ($ mil.)	1.1%	41	16	8	17	27	48	53	66	(40)	45
Income as % of sales	—	2.6%	1.4%	0.7%	1.3%	1.8%	3.0%	3.3%	3.9%	—	2.4%
Earnings per share ($)	(1.6%)	1.27	0.47	0.25	0.58	0.86	1.41	1.38	1.62	(0.89)	1.10
Stock price – high ($)	—	19.33	21.25	22.00	21.25	22.58	29.58	37.13	37.50	32.00	35.88
Stock price – low ($)	—	12.17	12.83	10.67	12.92	12.92	16.83	23.50	25.75	21.75	20.00
Stock price – close ($)	7.6%	13.25	19.25	13.25	16.92	21.63	26.83	32.38	29.63	30.38	25.63
P/E – high	—	15	45	89	37	26	21	27	23	—	33
P/E – low	—	10	27	43	22	15	12	17	16	—	18
Dividends per share ($)	(5.5%)	0.80	0.40	0.40	0.40	0.40	0.40	0.40	0.44	0.48	0.48
Book value per share ($)	1.5%	15.55	15.67	15.84	12.61	13.38	15.22	18.36	17.98	17.19	17.79
Employees	1.8%	12,263	12,161	12,000	11,400	11,900	12,100	12,480	14,300	13,920	14,440

1994 Year-end:
Debt ratio: 51.4%
Return on equity: 6.9%
Cash (mil.): $51.0
Current ratio: 1.37
Long-term debt (mil.):$666.7
No. of shares (mil.): 38
Dividends
  Yield: 1.9%
  Payout: 43.6%
Market value (mil.): $976

Stock Price History
High/Low 1985–94

CCH INCORPORATED

OVERVIEW

"A very friendly, very big fish" is the way Wolters Kluwer chairman Cor Brakel described CCH after the Dutch publisher landed the Riverwoods, Illinois–based company. Wolters Kluwer, one of Europe's largest legal and tax publishers, agreed to pay $1.9 billion for the company. CCH had been controlled by the Thorne family, whose 57% stake goes to the fishing Dutchmen.

Formerly Commerce Clearing House, Inc., CCH adopted its new moniker as part of a makeover the company had been giving itself, evolving from a mainframe computer–based and loose-leaf–format tax information publish-

ing firm to a distributor of "knowledge products" such as CCH ACCESS Online (an online computer service), CD-ROMs, and tax return software.

CCH is a leading publisher of loose-leaf reports and books on tax and business law for accountants and lawyers. The company also offers legal information services to corporations and software for tax processing. Its computer services business has switched from processing returns on mainframe computers to a do-it-yourself orientation, offering tax return software for its clients to use on their own PCs.

WHEN

The Corporation Trust Company was formed in 1892 and began providing state-required legal representation to such early customers as U.S. Steel, AT&T, and Prudential. When the Tariff Act of 1913 was introduced, the company began publishing the *Income Tax Reporter*, providing information on this first federal income tax law, including the law's text, related administrative decisions, and other documents. The company began publications covering the new Federal Trade Commission and Federal Reserve Board in 1914, and subscriptions to the *Reporter* grew as tax laws were amended in 1916 and 1917.

William KixMiller had started publishing import/export and income tax guides as Commerce Clearing House (CCH) in Chicago in 1892, and banker Oakleigh Thorne bought into CCH in 1907. Both Corporation Trust and Commerce Clearing House grew in the 1920s, reporting on the myriad new state, local, corporate, and inheritance tax laws. In 1927 the 2 companies merged as Commerce Clearing House, based in Chicago.

CCH began buying independent state tax publications and utility and industrial indices and digests. In 1933 KixMiller sold his interest, and in the 1930s the company started new publications covering New Deal regulations and agencies. In 1945 CCH created a Canadian subsidiary.

In the late 1950s the company published the *Corporation Law Guide* and the *New York Stock Exchange Guide*. CCH went public in 1961. In 1965 CCH bought a Mexican tax and business law publisher and Facts on File (both sold in 1993) and formed Computax. CCH bought more companies in the 1970s and 1980s, including the Washington Service Bureau (1979), a software operation (1980), and

Trademark Research Corporation (1983). CCH became so well versed in tax law that its largest customer was the US Internal Revenue Service. In 1986 the company moved its headquarters from Chicago to Riverwoods, Illinois. CCH acquired 4 companies involved in tax processing in 1988 and 1989 and 2 microcomputer software companies in 1990. CCH ACCESS, an electronic research system, was introduced in 1990.

In 1991 Oakleigh Thorne, the patriarch's great-great-grandson, took on the responsibility of revitalizing the company. He cut 1,200 jobs and started the transition from mainframe computers to PCs. The company bought software developer Optima Technologies in 1991 (sold in 1993) and launched Standard Federal Tax Reporter on CD-ROM in 1992.

In 1993 CCH bought most of the tax services of Matthew Bender & Co. and sold National Quotation Bureau (securities information). Also in 1993 the company introduced HR Assistant human resource software to enable human resources professionals to make policy decisions in compliance with labor law.

Deciding to forego short-term profits for long-term goals, CCH restructured internally in 1993 and 1994, indicating a change in hierarchy by streamlining senior management (dropping the job titles of most senior managers). The company also consolidated printing operations, moving all printing to a Florida location, and cut jobs.

In 1994 the company introduced Tax Assistant software, which provides research, analysis, and compliance tools for tax preparers.

CCH introduced an online service for small businesses, called CCH Business Owner's Toolkit, in 1995.

Nasdaq symbol: CCHIA
Fiscal year ends: December 31

WHO

Chairman: Oakleigh B. Thorne, age 62, $290,000 pay
President, CEO, and Member Executive Committee:
Oakleigh Thorne, age 37, $334,477 pay (prior to promotion)
Member Executive Committee: Ralph C. Whitley, age 51, $363,662 pay
Senior Officer Product/Customer Management:
Jonathan Copulsky, age 40, $289,879 pay
Senior Officer Finance and CFO: John I. Abernethy, age 37
Senior Officer Strategy: Christopher Ainsley, age 36
Senior Officer Administration: JoAnn Augustine, age 47
Senior Officer Operations: Thomas N. Taylor, age 54
Senior Officer Service Products: John J. Lynch Jr., age 36
Senior Officer Knowledge: Hugh J. Yarrington, age 52
Director Human Resources: Judith Kohn
Auditors: Deloitte & Touche LLP

WHERE

HQ: 2700 Lake Cook Rd., Riverwoods, IL 60015
Phone: 847-267-7000
Fax: 847-267-2873

CCH operates in Australia, Canada, Japan, New Zealand, Singapore, the UK, and the US.

	1994 Sales		1994 Operating Income	
	$ mil.	% of total	$ mil.	% of total
US	474	82	7	28
Other countries	105	18	18	72
Total	**579**	**100**	**25**	**100**

WHAT

	1994 Sales		1994 Operating Income	
	$ mil.	% of total	$ mil.	% of total
Publishing	385	66	(9)	—
Legal info. svcs.	117	13	13	38
Computer svcs.	77	21	21	62
Total	**579**	**100**	**25**	**100**

Publishing
Books
CD-ROMs
Loose-leaf news reports

Legal Information Services
Corporate name registration
Government documents
Legal filings services
Public records searches
Statutory representation
Trademark searches

Computer Processing Software
Tax return processing
Tax return software

KEY COMPETITORS

Arthur Andersen
Bureau of National Affairs
Computer Language Research
Corporation Service
Dow Jones
Dun & Bradstreet
H&R Block
Intuit
Knight-Ridder
Lacerte Software
McGraw-Hill
Primark
Price Waterhouse
Reed Elsevier
SCS Computer
Thomson Corp.
Times Mirror
Viacom
Washington Post
West Publishing

HOW MUCH

	Annual Growth	1985	1986	1987	1988	1989	1990	1991	1992	1993	1994
Sales ($ mil.)	2.7%	454	505	552	612	677	716	704	659	578	579
Net income ($ mil.)	(9.1%)	45	48	53	50	34	41	34	(14)	6	19
Income as % of sales	—	9.9%	9.4%	9.6%	8.1%	5.1%	5.7%	4.4%	—	1.0%	3.3%
Earnings per share ($)	(8.7%)	1.25	1.32	1.47	1.38	0.96	1.15	0.89	(0.39)	0.19	0.55
Stock price – high ($)	—	25.38	32.75	35.50	32.50	32.75	26.75	27.00	23.75	20.25	21.00
Stock price – low ($)	—	16.63	23.75	24.19	23.25	21.25	21.25	19.00	15.75	14.25	15.00
Stock price – close ($)	(4.0%)	24.63	30.50	30.75	23.75	21.50	22.25	20.50	18.25	18.25	17.00
P/E – high	—	20	25	24	24	34	23	30	—	—	38
P/E – low	—	13	18	17	17	22	17	18	—	—	27
Dividends per share ($)	3.1%	0.53	0.60	0.48	0.86	0.70	0.70	0.70	0.70	0.70	0.70
Book value per share ($)	1.6%	3.73	4.44	5.24	6.00	6.05	6.30	6.30	3.63	2.85	4.30
Employees	(6.5%)	9,733	9,997	10,105	10,307	7,782	7,613	7,027	6,600	5,728	5,290

1994 Year-end:
Debt ratio: 1.1%
Return on equity: 19.9%
Cash (mil.): $83
Current ratio: 0.98
Long-term debt (mil.): $0
No. of shares (mil.): 21
Dividends
 Yield: 4.1%
 Payout: 127.3%
Market value (mil.): $363

**Stock Price History
High/Low 1985–94**

CNA FINANCIAL CORPORATION

OVERVIEW

CNA Financial is part of Loews Corp. (which owns 84% of CNA), the wide-ranging empire of the Tisch family that also includes Bulova Corp. (watches), CBS, Loews Hotels, and Lorillard (cigarettes). The company is the umbrella organization for a wide range of insurance companies, including Continental Casualty Co. and Continental Assurance.

In May 1995, after receiving shareholder approval, CNA welcomed another Continental to its family: Continental Corp. (CNA already owned 16% of that company). As part of the transaction, Continental Corp. merged with CNA's Chicago Acquisition Corp. and became a wholly owned subsidiary of CNA Financial. The merger cost approximately $1.1 billion (at $20 per share) and brought CNA into the top 10 of US insurance companies. The business lines of the 2 companies are primarily prop-

erty/casualty insurance. Continental Corp. will bring investment management operations to CNA, which also has significant group life operations.

Both CNA and Continental Corp. have been hard hit in the 1990s by natural and man-made disasters such as hurricanes, storms, floods, and riots. However, CNA has withstood them better because financial support and, more important, investment skills provided by Loews helped CNA survive its underwriting losses. Both companies were hit by rising interest rates in 1994.

After the 1995 merger, CNA began consolidating operations to produce significant cost savings. About 5,000 of the combined 20,000 jobs were to be eliminated in the year after the merger, many of them at Continental Corp.'s metropolitan New York–area offices.

WHEN

CNA merged with its elder, if not its better, in 1995. Continental Corp. was founded in 1852 as the Continental Insurance Co. because merchant Henry Bowen could not find a company offering the type of fire insurance he wanted. Bowen assembled a group of investors and started out with about $500,000 in capital. The company grew westward with the railroads.

In 1882 Continental added marine insurance and tornado insurance. In 1889 the company made Francis Moore, developer of the Universal Mercantile Schedule (a system of assessing fire hazards in buildings), president.

About the time Continental was writing the book on fire insurance, several midwestern investors were having trouble assessing risk in their own insurance field — disability. In 1897, after 2 earlier attempts had failed for lack of adequate capitalization, this group founded the Continental Casualty Co. in Hammond, Indiana. In the early years its primary clients were railroads providing disability insurance to their employees (railroading being a fairly hazardous profession then). Continental Casualty soon merged with other companies in the field. By 1904 the company was writing business in 41 states and territories, and by the next year it had branch offices in 9 states and Hawaii.

Both Continentals added new insurance lines in 1911: Continental Insurance went into personal auto, and Continental Casualty formed Continental Assurance, a subsidiary, to sell life insurance. Continental Insurance continued growing, partly through acquisi-

tions. By 1915 it had 4 primary companies, which — spurred by the growing patriotism of the immediate prewar era — it called the America Fore Group.

Both companies rose to the challenges presented by the world wars and the Depression, and they entered the 1950s ready for new growth. Both made new acquisitions in insurance, and in the 1960s they began to diversify into other fields as well.

Continental Insurance added interests in Diners Club and Capital Financial Services, and in 1968 it formed a holding company, Continental Corp. Continental Assurance (which formed CNA Financial, its own holding company) went even farther afield, adding mutual funds companies, consumer finance companies, nursing homes, and a home builder.

By the early 1970s, setbacks in the housing business and the recession had CNA on the ropes. After merger negotiations with Gulf Oil failed, Robert and Laurence Tisch bought most of CNA in 1974 and cut costs ruthlessly. Continental Corp. had its own problems in the 1970s, including an Iranian joint venture that got caught up in the revolution.

Both companies suffered losses arising from Hurricane Andrew in 1992, but CNA, having gone through its housecleaning in the 1970s, was better able to deal with the blow than Continental, which came out of the 1980s in need of restructuring. Although the company had been streamlining itself, in 1994 it threw in the towel and took the CNA merger offer.

NYSE symbol: CNA
Fiscal year ends: December 31

WHO

Chairman: Edward J. Noha, age 67
CEO: Laurence A. Tisch, age 72
SVP and CFO: Peter E. Jokiel
SVP, General Counsel, and Secretary: Donald M. Lowry
Chairman and CEO, CNA Insurance Cos.: Dennis H. Chookaszian, age 51, $1,242,091 pay
President, CNA Insurance Cos.: Philip L. Engel, age 54, $825,539 pay
SVP, CNA Insurance Cos.: Carolyn L. Murphy, $558,333 pay
SVP, CNA Insurance Cos.: Jae L. Wittlich, $464,842 pay
SVP Human Resources: Floyd E. Brady
Auditors: Deloitte & Touche LLP

WHERE

HQ: CNA Plaza, Chicago, IL 60685
Phone: 312-822-5000
Fax: 312-822-6419

WHAT

	1994 Assets	
	$ mil.	% of total
Cash & equivalents	5,184	12
Treasury & agency securities	10,782	24
State & municipal bonds	3,769	9
Corporate & other bonds	3,284	7
Asset-backed securities	2,563	6
Stocks	1,184	3
Receivables & recoverables	7,274	16
Separate account assets	6,080	14
Other	4,200	9
Total	**44,320**	**100**

	1994 Sales	
	$ mil.	% of total
Commercial property/casualty	6,562	58
Group life	2,443	22
Other property/casualty	1,687	15
Individual life	596	5
Other & adjustments	(288)	—
Total	**11,000**	**100**

Selected Subsidiaries
1897 Corp.
1911 Corp.
Agency Management Services, Inc.
American Casualty Co.
Cinema Completions International, Inc. (50%)
CNA Automation, Inc.
CNA (Bermuda) Services, Ltd.
CNA Management Co. Ltd. (UK)
CNA Management (International) Ltd. (Jersey Channel Islands)
Continental Assurance Co.
Continental Casualty Co.
Galway Insurance Co.
Larwin Developments, Inc.
National Fire Insurance Co. of Hartford
Transcontinental Insurance Co.
Transcontinental Technical Services, Inc.
Transportation Insurance Co.
Valley Forge Insurance Co.
Viaticus, Inc.

KEY COMPETITORS

20th Century Industries	GEICO	Nationwide Insurance
AARP	Guardian Life Insurance	New York Life
Aetna	ITT Hartford	Pacific Mutual Life
Allstate	John Hancock	Prudential
American Financial	Liberty Mutual	State Farm
Chubb	MassMutual	Travelers
CIGNA	MetLife	USAA
	Mutual of Omaha	USF&G

HOW MUCH

	Annual Growth	1985	1986	1987	1988	1989	1990	1991	1992	1993	1994
Assets ($ mil.)	13.6%	14,116	16,678	19,563	22,941	28,682	31,089	35,673	36,680	41,912	44,320
Net income ($ mil.)	(20.9%)	305	404	393	546	614	367	613	(267)	268	37
Income as % of assets	—	2.2%	2.4%	2.0%	2.4%	2.1%	1.25	1.7%	—	0.6%	0.1%
Earnings per share ($)	(22.6%)	5.11	6.25	6.96	8.59	9.73	5.77	9.80	(10.79)	4.26	0.51
Stock price – high ($)	—	65.13	75.00	66.50	66.13	108.75	100.00	99.25	104.50	101.00	82.25
Stock price – low ($)	—	31.50	47.25	47.00	51.00	57.63	49.63	62.75	78.50	74.25	60.00
Stock price – close ($)	0.1%	64.50	53.75	55.63	60.50	98.00	68.63	98.00	98.00	77.50	64.88
P/E – high	—	13	12	11	8	11	17	10	—	24	161
P/E – low	—	6	8	8	6	6	9	6	—	17	118
Dividends per share ($)	—	0.00	0.00	0.00	0.00	0.00	0.00	0.00	0.00	0.00	0.00
Book value per share ($)	8.8%	33.24	40.37	46.40	65.87	64.74	70.23	80.24	75.07	84.59	71.08
Employees	2.2%	12,800	14,000	15,000	15,900	16,700	17,200	17,800	17,200	16,800	15,600

1994 Year-end:
Equity as % of assets: 9.9%
Return on assets: 0.1%
Return on equity: 0.8%
Long-term debt (mil.): $912
No. of shares (mil.): 62
Dividends
Yield: —
Payout: —
Market value (mil.): $4,012
Sales ($ mil.): $11,000

Stock Price History
High/Low 1985–94

COMDISCO, INC.

OVERVIEW

Comdisco isn't a 1970s dance revival, but it is hustling new life out of old computers. Based in Rosemont, Illinois, the company buys, sells, and leases new and used computer equipment and peripherals to major corporations. It also leases medical equipment (Comdisco Medical Equipment Group) and semiconductor capital equipment (Comdisco Electronics Group). Another division, Comdisco Disaster Recovery Services, provides emergency backup computer support to customers whose systems have failed as a result of fire, flood, power failure, or other calamities.

Comdisco takes advantage of its presence in the high-tech industry through its Venture Lease Division, which leases equipment to start-up companies in the biotechnology, communications, semiconductor, and software industries. Part of the financing includes the right for Comdisco to acquire a small percentage of the company's stock. Young companies are thus able to meet their computing needs more cheaply, and Comdisco has picked up the potential for stock profits and bigger equipment customers. Clients have included Cyrix and Sybase, and the current portfolio has more than 265 companies.

Comdisco has had some recent troubles. In 1994 the company's founder, Kenneth Pontikes, died at age 54. He was replaced by Jack Slevin. The change in leaders has occurred amid competition from manufacturers leasing their own equipment and from many customers' conversion to networked PCs. The lower profits from the less expensive PCs mean lower commissions for Comdisco's sales force, and many salespeople have waltzed over to higher-paying rivals.

One Slevin initiative is to move into systems integration consulting. In 1995 Comdisco hired at least 80 consultants, but competitors like EDS and Andersen Consulting have filled the dance cards of many potential customers.

WHEN

In 1969, at age 29, former IBM salesman Kenneth Pontikes borrowed $5,000 from his father to set up Computer Discount Corporation. He saw a market niche in the increasing dependence of large corporations on mainframes. Gambling that companies would rather lease than pay outright for expensive equipment that might soon become obsolete, Pontikes built his company by leasing IBM mainframes. It grew quickly, recording sales of $1 million during its first year. In 1971 the company reincorporated as Comdisco and went public.

The company grew rapidly until 1974, when Intel put $250 million worth of used IBM System 360 computers up for sale just after Comdisco had agreed to purchase hundreds of the same computer. The drop in prices for the 360 eliminated Comdisco's opportunity for profits, and it lost nearly $1 million that year.

In 1976 Comdisco Financial Services was created to help customers finance leases of equipment from Comdisco and help them dispose of their old equipment. Four years later Comdisco Disaster Recovery Services (CDRS) was formed to help businesses whose computer systems were down or damaged because of flood, fire, or other misfortune. The company also began expanding overseas. Offices were set up in West Germany and Switzerland (1979), the UK (1983), and Japan (1985).

With the company's operations generating plenty of cash and the staff gaining specialized knowledge of the computer industry, Pontikes formed Comdisco Equities in 1984 to engage in stock arbitrage of potential takeover targets. However, the subsidiary was shut down after the stock market crash of 1987 produced a net loss of $80 million. Comdisco was still able to participate in high-risk computer stocks through its Venture Lease Division, which leased equipment to high-tech start-ups for a price that included the right to purchase a stake in the company.

As its revenues passed the $1 billion mark (1985), the company looked for ways to further diversify its leasing business. Telephone equipment was added in 1985, and in 1988 the Comdisco Medical Equipment Group was created to refurbish and lease MRIs and other medical systems. In 1992 the Comdisco Electronics Group was formed to supply used semiconductor capital equipment.

Despite the company's attempts to diversify out of mainframes, the widespread switch to PCs, combined with the 1990–91 recession, cut its profits. Compounding those problems was a suit launched by IBM that accused Comdisco of using older IBM parts to produce computer mainframes to compete with newer IBM models. Comdisco finally settled the suit in 1994, paying IBM $70 million while denying any wrongdoing. Also that year company founder Pontikes died of cancer. His brother William and son Nicholas are still part of Comdisco's top management. In 1995 the company earned $96 million on sales of $2.2 billion.

NYSE symbol: CDO
Fiscal year end: September 30

WHO

President and CEO: Jack Slevin, age 58, $800,000 pay
EVP; President, Leasing Products Division; President, Comdisco International Division: Robert A. Bardagy, age 55, $859,000 pay
EVP; President, Disaster Recovery Services Division: Nicholas K. Pontikes, age 30, $585,000 pay
EVP Operations: William N. Pontikes, age 53, $501,000 pay
EVP, CFO, and Treasurer: John J. Vosicky, age 46, $501,000 pay
EVP: Alan J. Andreini, age 48
VP; EVP, Systems Integration Services Division: William O. Bray
President, Comdisco Venture Lease Division: James P. Labe
VP and General Counsel: Jeremiah M. Fitzgerald
VP Human Resources: Lucie A. Buford
Auditors: KPMG Peat Marwick LLP

WHERE

HQ: 6111 N. River Rd., Rosemont, IL 60018
Phone: 847-698-3000
Fax: 847-518-5440

	1994 Sales		1994 Operating Income	
	$ mil.	% of total	$ mil.	% of total
US	1,717	79	76	84
Europe	293	14	1	1
Canada	84	4	13	14
Pacific Rim	60	3	1	1
Adjustments	(56)	—	(2)	—
Total	**2,098**	**100**	**89**	**100**

WHAT

	1994 Sales	
	$ mil.	% of total
Leasing	1,538	73
Sales	271	13
Disaster recovery	242	12
Other	47	2
Total	**2,098**	**100**

Selected Divisions
Comdisco Canada Ltd.
Comdisco Direct
Comdisco Electronics Group
Comdisco Federal Marketing Group
Comdisco International
Comdisco Investment Group
Comdisco Medical Equipment Group
Comdisco Medical Exchange (equipment refurbishing)
Comdisco Parts
Comdisco Portfolio Asset Management
Comdisco Professional Services
Comdisco State and Local Government Marketing
Comdisco Technical Services
Comdisco Venture Lease
Disaster Recovery Services
High-Technology Trade Center Group
Leasing Products
North American Sales
Systems Integration Services

KEY COMPETITORS

Amdahl	Hitachi
Amplicon	IBM
AT&T Capital	Leasing Solutions
Forsythe McArthur	Machines Bull
Fujitsu	Portfolio Acquisition
General Electric	Winthrop Resources

HOW MUCH

	Annual Growth	1985	1986	1987	1988	1989	1990	1991	1992	1993	1994
Sales ($ mil.)	7.8%	1,066	1,601	2,001	2,228	1,678	1,935	2,174	2,205	2,153	2,098
Net income ($ mil.)	(0.9%)	58	79	94	17	108	85	69	20	67	53
Income as % of sales	—	5.4%	4.9%	4.7%	0.8%	6.4%	4.4%	3.2%	0.9%	3.1%	2.5%
Earnings per share ($)	(1.6%)	1.34	1.82	2.15	0.39	2.45	1.99	1.70	0.49	1.47	1.16
Stock price – high ($)	—	18.89	23.80	34.75	23.68	32.37	27.13	27.01	23.21	21.00	24.25
Stock price – low ($)	—	7.29	11.42	11.42	16.18	19.87	13.92	17.26	12.50	13.13	17.75
Stock price – close ($)	2.7%	18.18	14.99	17.73	19.99	23.56	17.49	20.83	14.38	19.25	23.13
P/E – high	—	14	13	16	61	13	14	16	47	14	21
P/E – low	—	5	6	5	42	8	7	10	26	9	15
Dividends per share ($)	12.6%	0.12	0.14	0.18	0.22	0.23	0.26	0.27	0.27	0.29	0.35
Book value per share ($)	11.7%	6.44	8.24	10.70	10.36	12.56	14.37	15.63	15.38	16.55	17.47
Employees	11.4%	760	930	1,050	1,471	1,875	1,960	2,179	2,087	2,000	2,000

1994 Year-end:
Debt ratio: 72.5%
Return on equity: 8.3%
Cash (mil.): $51.0
Current ratio: 4.79
Long-term debt (mil.): $1,957
No. of shares (mil.): 37
Dividends
  Yield: 1.5%
  Payout: 30.2%
Market value (mil.): $849

Stock Price History
High/Low 1985–94

COTTER & COMPANY

OVERVIEW

Cotter has shut the door on manufacturing lawn mowers and hopes it improved the true value of its operations by chiseling costs. The Chicago-based, member-owned cooperative is the largest hardware wholesaler in the US, serving about 6,200 True Value Hardware Stores in the US. A subsidiary serves 391 True Value and V&S Variety Stores in Canada. Cotter also manufactures paint and paint applicators under the Tru-Test name.

Cotter & Company serves member stores by buying hardware in large quantities at a discount, then selling it to members in smaller lots and passing the savings to them through low prices and annual dividends based upon the amount purchased. Cotter also holds trade conventions for its members and helps coordinate advertising. Almost all of its stock is held by member retailers.

Since 1990 CEO Daniel Cotter (son of founder John Cotter) has stressed internal sales growth over simply signing up new members. In 1994 sales racheted up over 6% because of increased shipments to existing members. Lumber, other building materials, and farm and garden supplies led the way.

In an effort to unhinge the onslaught of competitors like Builders Square and Home Depot, Cotter & Company is cutting operating costs and refocusing. The cooperative shed its outdoor power equipment manufacturing division (Lawn Chief and Snow Chief) and ended its domestic V&S Variety (five-and-dime) Stores affiliation in 1995. The company also discontinued its supply service to 150 hardware stores and outlined a new standards program for company-backed financing of store renovations, expansions, and construction.

WHEN

In 1916, 12-year-old John Cotter started working part-time in a St. Paul, Minnesota, hardware store. At the time, small neighborhood hardware stores began to feel the pinch from big catalogers such as Sears and chain stores like Woolworth's. Both drove down prices through their wholesale buying power. In response, some hardware retailers formed wholesale cooperatives to help lower costs while maintaining their independence. Cotter was introduced to the concept on his first day as a traveling hardware salesman in 1928.

In 1947 Cotter and associate Ed Lanctot began pitching the wholesale cooperative idea to small-town and suburban hardware retailers (avoiding ensconced, big city competitors). By early 1948 the 2 men had enrolled 25 merchants for $1,500 each, and Cotter was elected chairman of the new firm. Cotter & Company introduced a direct-mail consumer catalog that same year. By 1949 the firm had 84 member retailers and sales of $385,000.

John Cotter created the Value & Service store trademark in 1951 to emphasize the advantages of an independent hardware store. By 1956 sales hit $1 million a month and 700,000 customers were reading his catalogs.

In 1963 Cotter netted 400 new members by acquiring Chicago-based Hibbard, Spencer, Bartlett (founded in 1855), one of the leading US hardware wholesalers. He paid just $2,500 for its well-known True Value trademark, which soon replaced V&S signs.

Cotter & Company acquired Dallas-based Walter H. Allen Co. in 1965 and topped $100 million in annual sales the following year. The company began using its own trucking fleet to streamline operations. In 1967 Cotter broadened its focus by purchasing the General Paint & Chemical Company (Tru-Test paint).

In 1970 the company opened its own lawn and garden equipment factory (General Power and Equipment Co., which made power mowers and Snow Chief snowblowers). Two years later the company revived the V&S name for a new five-and-dime store division known as V&S Variety Stores. Cotter's son Daniel became president in 1978. The following year the firm bought the Warner Hardware Company and sales passed $1 billion.

In 1983 Cotter acquired Atlas Tool Company and introduced its own charge card. By the end of the decade, Cotter's 7,000 member stores had pushed sales to almost $2 billion. Founder John Cotter died in 1989. Several veteran executives retired that same year.

In 1992 Cotter acquired distributor and retail store operator Macleod-Stedman (Canada), which had more than 275 outlets. The next year Cotter introduced Build America, a detailed marketing program for lumber and building materials retailers.

In 1995 Cotter sold its General Power division and the domestic V&S Variety Stores inventory. That same year the company began construction of a warehouse in Georgia that will be home to the company's True Value International division. Cotter also decided to move from its original headquarters to new digs near O'Hare Airport in early 1996.

Member-owned cooperative
Fiscal year ends: December 31

WHO

Chairman: Jerrald T. Kabelin, age 57
President and CEO: Daniel A. Cotter, age 60,
$875,000 pay
EVP and COO: Stephen J. Porter, age 42, $495,625 pay
VP and Treasurer: Kerry J. Kirby, age 48, $326,250 pay
VP and Secretary: Daniel T. Burns, age 44, $253,750 pay
VP Merchandising: David W. Christmas, age 46
VP Distribution and Transportation: John P. Semkus,
age 48
VP Marketing: Chuck Kremers
Human Resources Manager: Pat Kelley
Auditors: Ernst & Young LLP

WHERE

HQ: 8600 W. Bryn Mawr Ave., Chicago, IL 60631
Phone: 312-695-5000
Fax: 312-695-6558

Cotter has 6,200 member True Value Hardware Stores in
the US and 140 members in 40 other countries. Cotter
also has about 391 member True Value and V&S Variety
Stores in Canada.

	1994 Office and Warehouse Facilities
	Sq. ft. (thou.)
Chicago, IL	980
Harvard, IL	640
Fogelsville, PA	600
Manchester, NH	525
Corsicana, TX	450
Winnipeg, Manitoba	432
Indianapolis, IN	420
Kansas City, MO	415
Portland, OR	405
Westlake, OH	405
Kingman, AZ	375
Ocala, FL	375
Denver, CO	360
Jonesboro, GA	360
Woodland, CA	350
Mankato, MN	320
Henderson, NC	300
Total	**7,712**

	1994 True Value Hardware Stores
	% of total
California	7
Illinois	6
New York	6
Texas	6
Pennsylvania	5
Michigan	4
Ohio	4
Other US states	58
Canada	4
Total	**100**

WHAT

	1994 Sales
	% of total
Hardware goods	20
Electrical & plumbing supplies	16
Painting & cleaning supplies	14
Variety & related goods	14
Farm & garden supplies	13
Lumber & building materials	13
Appliances & housewares	10
Total	**100**

Selected Subsidiaries
Baltimore Brush & Roller Co., Inc. (paint brushes and
rollers)
Cotter Acceptance Co., Inc. (short-term business credit)
Cotter Canada Hardware and Variety Cooperative, Inc.
Cotter Insurance Agency, Inc.
Cotter Real Estate Agency, Inc. (nonresidential building
operators)
Cotter Trucking, Inc.

KEY COMPETITORS

84 Lumber	McCoy
Ace Hardware	Menard
BMC West	Orchard Supply Hardware
Eagle Hardware & Garden	Payless Cashways
Ernst Home Center	Sears
Grossman's	Servistar
Hardware Wholesalers	Sherwin-Williams
Hechinger	Waban
Home Depot	Wal-Mart
Kmart	Wickes Lumber
Lowe's	Wolohan Lumber

HOW MUCH

	Annual Growth	1985	1986	1987	1988	1989	1990	1991	1992	1993	1994
Sales ($ mil.)	4.6%	—	—	—	—	2,059	2,135	2,140	2,356	2,421	2,574
Net income ($ mil.)	0.5%	—	—	—	—	—	—	59	61	57	60
Income as % of sales	—	—	—	—	—	—	—	2.8%	2.6%	2.4%	2.3%
Employees	0.0%	—	—	—	—	4,200	4,200	4,200	4,400	4,400	4,200

1994 Year-end:
Debt ratio: 30.9%
Return on equity: 18.2%
Cash (mil.): $2
Current ratio: 1.47
Long-term debt (mil.): $76

Net Income
($ mil.)
1991–94

DEAN FOODS COMPANY

OVERVIEW

Drink your milk and eat your vegetables, and you may help Dean Foods, a diversified dairy and specialty food processor and distributor, grow bigger and stronger. The Franklin Park–based company's network of 28 regional dairies in 13 states and the Virgin Islands turns out milk (homogenized whole, low-fat, skim, chocolate, and buttermilk), ice cream (regular, light, reduced-fat, and nonfat), yogurt, cottage cheese, sour cream, and ultra-high temperature (UHT) specialty dairy products (half-and-half, cooking and whipping creams, flavored milks, and aerosol toppings). Dean's dairy products are sold to grocery, club, and convenience store chains and to institutional customers in selected markets in the US, the Caribbean, and Mexico. A sizable portion of the company's dairy products and UHT products are sold under private-label brands.

Dean's Specialty Food Products segment includes frozen and canned vegetables, green olives, peppers, relishes, pickles, syrups, assorted powdered products, sauces, puddings, and dips. The company is the national leader in the frozen and canned vegetable category. Its products are sold to retail and food service markets in Canada, Europe, Japan, Mexico, Puerto Rico, and the US under private labels as well as under the company's own brand names, including the well-known Bird's Eye brand. It is also a leader in the sale of private-label pickles and claims to be the largest producer of powdered nondairy coffee creamers in North America. Dean operates a trucking subsidiary, DFC Transportation, and it also gets revenue from the government through bid contracts on canned meat products.

Traditionally, Dean's growth has been driven by acquisitions (at least 12 since 1990), though in response to changing diet trends the company has focused more recently on expansion through the release of new products, including nonfat dips and dairy items.

WHEN

Dean Foods was founded in 1925 by Sam Dean, a Chicago evaporated milk broker, as the Pecatonica, Illinois–based Dean Evaporated Milk Company. By the mid-1930s the company had moved into the fresh milk industry. Dean began making ice cream in 1947, about the same time that geographic expansion became the company's priority. It purchased a number of established regional dairies outside of the Midwest throughout the late 1940s and 1950s. In 1952 Dean's R&D lab developed the first powdered, nondairy coffee creamer, the bedrock of its specialty foods division. The company went public in 1961. That same year Dean acquired the Green Bay Food Co. and entered the pickle business. The company changed its name to Dean Foods in 1963.

CEO Howard Dean, grandson of founder Sam, joined Dean Foods in 1965. The company pursued its acquisition strategy throughout the 1960s, though it ran into trouble with the Federal Trade Commission in the late 1960s. It later had problems with the Teamsters Union when it attempted to close its unprofitable operations. In 1969 Dean acquired the Amboy aseptic business.

Howard Dean became company president in 1970. In 1976 Dean acquired Gandy's Dairy of Texas and in 1978 further expanded its dairy operations into the Southwest with the purchase of Bell Dairy and Creamland Dairy.

Acquisitions in the 1980s allowed Dean to expand into Florida, Kentucky, Pennsylvania, and Ohio. By 1985 the company's southern and southwestern dairies had become its most profitable. In 1985, the same year the company reached $1 billion in sales, Dean acquired the Ryan Milk Company of Kentucky, establishing itself in the UHT processed products market.

Dean diversified into vegetables with the 1986 acquisition of the Larsen Company, a leading processor of branded and private-label canned and frozen vegetables. By 1987 the company had become the nation's 3rd largest canned and frozen vegetable purveyor. Dean increased its stake in this growing market with the 1988 purchase of Richard A. Shaw, Inc., a California-based frozen vegetable company; the 1989 purchase of Big Stone Inc., a canned vegetable processor; and the 1990 purchase of Bellingham Frozen Foods. In 1993 the company acquired Bird's Eye, the 2nd largest national frozen vegetable brand, and in 1995 Dean added Rio Grande Foods, a southern producer of frozen vegetables, to its group.

Recent growth in the company's dairy and specialty foods divisions has been driven by the introduction of new products. In 1995 Dean introduced its Guilt-Free line of nonfat ice cream and dairy products, unveiled 3 new Bird's Eye brand vegetable dips, and spent a record $83.3 million on plant expansions.

NYSE symbol: DF
Fiscal year ends: Last Sunday in May

WHO

Chairman and CEO: Howard M. Dean Jr., $859,921 pay
President and COO: Thomas L. Rose, $588,034 pay
SVP and President, Dairy Division: Thomas A. Ravencroft, $379,996 pay
Group VP and President, Dean Foods Vegetable: Jeffrey P. Shaw, age 38, $340,165 pay
Group VP and President, Dean Pickle and Specialty Products: James R. Greisinger, age 54
Group VP, International Sales: Roger A. Ragland, age 61
Group VP, Specialty Dairy Division: Daniel E. Green, age 50
VP Sales and Marketing, Milk and Ice Cream: Douglas A. Parr, age 53, $245,812 pay
VP, General Counsel, and Secretary: Eric A. Blanchard, age 39
Treasurer: Dale I. Hecox, age 63
Director Human Resources: Jerry Berger
Auditors: Price Waterhouse LLP

WHERE

HQ: 3600 N. River Rd., Franklin Park, IL 60131
Phone: 312-625-6200
Fax: 708-928-8621

Dean Foods Company's Dairy Division operates 28 dairies in 13 states and the Virgin Islands. The company's Specialty Food Products Division has operations in 14 states and Mexico.

WHAT

	1995 Sales	
	$ mil.	% of total
Fluid milk	1,081	41
Frozen & canned vegetables	534	20
Pickles, relishes & specialty items	367	14
Ice cream	220	9
Specialty dairy	213	8
Powdered products	110	4
Sauces, puddings & dips	74	3
Other	31	1
Total	**2,630**	**100**

Selected Companies

Amboy Specialty Foods	The Larsen Co.
Aunt Jane Foods	Liberty Dairy
Bell Dairy Products	Longlife Dairy Products
Bellingham Frozen Foods	Mayfield Dairy Farms
Big Stone	McArthur Dairy
Bird's Eye	Meadow Brook Dairy Co.
Charles F. Cates & Sons	Pilgrim Farms
Cream o'Weber Dairy	Price's Creameries
Creamland Dairies	Ready Foods Products
Dean Dairy Products Co.	Reiter Dairy
Dean Milk Company	Richard A. Shaw, Inc.
DFC Transportation	Rio Grande Foods Inc.
E.B.I. Foods Ltd.	Ryan Milk Co.
Fairmont Products	St. Thomas Dairies
Frio Foods	T.G. Lee Foods
Gandy's Dairies	Verifine Dairy Products
Green Bay Food Co.	W.B. Roddenbery Co.

KEY COMPETITORS

Agway	Del Monte	Pillsbury
Associated	Dreyer's	RJR Nabisco
Milk Producers	Grand Metropolitan	Specialty
Borden	Land O'Lakes	Foods
Campbell Soup	Mid-America Dairymen	Unilever
Dairymen	Nestlé	Wessanen
Danone	Philip Morris	

HOW MUCH

	Annual Growth	1986	1987	1988	1989	1990	1991	1992	1993	1994	1995[1]
Sales ($ mil.)	8.4%	1,269	1,435	1,552	1,684	1,988	2,158	2,289	2,274	2,431	2,630
Net income ($ mil.)	7.8%	41	41	43	60	61	73	62	68	71	80
Income as % of sales	—	3.2%	2.9%	2.8%	3.6%	3.1%	3.4%	2.7%	3.0%	2.9%	3.0%
Earnings per share ($)	7.8%	1.02	1.03	1.07	1.52	1.53	1.79	1.53	1.73	1.78	2.01
Stock price – high ($)	—	22.47	25.68	21.26	25.26	27.26	33.50	31.50	32.88	33.50	31.75
Stock price – low ($)	—	16.76	15.17	16.01	19.26	20.18	24.85	22.75	23.13	25.25	27.13
Stock price – close ($)	4.9%	18.51	16.42	19.93	22.18	26.76	30.50	28.13	32.63	29.00	28.38
P/E – high	—	22	25	20	17	18	19	21	19	19	16
P/E – low	—	16	15	15	13	13	14	15	13	14	13
Dividends per share ($)	20.0%	0.13	0.31	0.36	0.39	0.43	0.48	0.54	0.59	0.63	0.67
Book value per share ($)	12.2%	5.18	5.89	6.60	7.43	8.94	10.24	10.87	12.00	13.19	14.58
Employees	7.6%	6,100	6,900	7,100	7,500	8,900	9,600	10,100	10,500	12,100	11,800

1995 Year-end:
Debt ratio: 31.3%
Return on equity: 14.4%
Cash (mil.): $5
Current ratio: 1.71
Long-term debt (mil.): $225
No. of shares (mil.): 40
Dividends
  Yield: 2.4%
  Payout: 33.3%
Market value (mil.): $1,137

Stock Price History[1]
High/Low 1986–95

[1] 1995 stock prices are through fiscal year-end (May 28).

FIRST CHICAGO NBD CORPORATION

OVERVIEW

In the rust belt union of the year, First Chicago Corp. merged with Detroit's NBD in 1995. The $5.1 billion transaction created the US's 7th largest banking company and took First Chicago off the list of possible takeover candidates. The new company, First Chicago NBD, has operations in Illinois, Indiana, Michigan, and Ohio as well as in Florida.

The merger news took some of the public attention from First Chicago Corporation's First National Bank of Chicago, which imposed a $3 fee for using a teller at the same time it began a "Customer First" program. But

some customers are more equal than others. "Customer First" applies to corporate and institutional customers. The fee applies to customers without minimum balances but, amid consumer advocate protests, does not include patrons truly in need of help.

First National Bank is the dominant bank in the Chicago market, with more than 80 branches (thanks to a program of acquiring neighborhood banks and their small personal accounts). It is one of the US's largest credit card issuers and also owns American National Bank, which caters mainly to businesses.

WHEN

In 1863 the US Comptroller of the Currency granted Charter #8 to the First National Bank of Chicago. First National, from its first office on LaSalle Street, grew rapidly. When the Chicago Fire of 1871 leveled much of the city, the bank's "fireproof" building burned too. A cashier named Lyman Gage, who later became the bank's president and William McKinley's secretary of the treasury, found that the bank's documents and money had survived in a vault, and First National resumed operations quickly as the city rebuilt.

The bank bought the Union National Bank in 1900 and Metropolitan National Bank in 1902, almost doubling in size. It then founded a subsidiary called First Trust and Savings Bank, renamed First Union Trust and Savings Bank after a 1929 merger with Union Trust.

As the Depression settled in, First National took over Foreman State Banks (1931), weathered a run on the bank for $50 million (1933), and folded First Union Trust back into First National (1933). WWII spurred the bank's growth. In 1959 it entered the international marketplace with the opening of a London office. A Tokyo office opened in 1962. A 1969 reorganization created First Chicago as the bank's holding corporation.

First Chicago grew rapidly in the early 1970s under chairman Gaylord Freeman. By the end of Freeman's tenure, sloppy underwriting practices had produced a mountain of nonperforming loans, particularly in real estate. Deputy chairman Robert Abboud took over in 1975 to deal with the $2 billion problem and with the threat of a shutdown by federal regulators. Abboud tightened underwriting standards but alienated employees and clients and slowed the bank's growth.

Barry Sullivan, who replaced Abboud, restructured the company and resumed the

bank's growth. First Chicago bought enough credit card accounts from other banks to make it the 3rd largest card issuer in the US. Under Sullivan, however, the bank tilted strongly toward energy and commercial real estate.

First Chicago took advantage of the near failure of Continental in 1984 to acquire that bank's $3 billion American National Corp., a holding company for American National Bank and Trust, which concentrates on middle market business clients.

In 1987 First Chicago plunged into the red when several Latin American countries defaulted on their loans. Yet growth continued, and First Chicago added several Chicago-area banks and failed S&Ls in the late 1980s and early 1990s. It bought Continental's personal and small business accounts when that bank discontinued consumer banking operations.

By the early 1990s the company had overinvested in commercial real estate loans, and when the bottom fell out of the market First National found itself with over $2 billion in nonperforming loans and real estate.

Sullivan, under a cloud for his lending policies, was replaced by president Richard Thomas. He focused on reducing the nonperforming loan portfolio. He also began reducing overseas operations (though the bank still has a presence in 10 non-US cities).

First Chicago's forays into other financial services have had spotty results. The company's 1994 earnings decline was largely attributable to its trading, venture capital, and equities operations, which were areas affected by interest rates and the bond market decline of early in the year.

In 1994 First Chicago won a contract from the Treasury Department to develop and install an electronic tax payment system for nationwide use.

NYSE symbol: FNB
Fiscal year ends: December 31

WHO

Chairman and CEO: Richard L. Thomas, age 64, $1,760,057 pay
VC: David J. Vitale, age 48, $846,437 pay
President and COO: Leo F. Mullin, age 52, $914,636 pay
EVP: Scott P. Marks Jr., age 48, $820,659 pay
EVP: W. G. Jurgensen, age 43, $754,770 pay
EVP and CFO: Robert A. Rosholt, age 44
EVP Corporate and Institutional Banking: John W. Ballantine, age 48
EVP Corporate and Institutional Banking: Thomas H. Hodges, age 49
EVP Corporate and Institutional Banking: Donald R. Hollis, age 59
EVP, General Counsel, and Secretary: Sherman I. Goldberg, age 52
EVP Human Resources: Marvin James Alef Jr., age 50
Auditors: Arthur Andersen & Co, SC

WHERE

HQ: One First National Plaza, Chicago, IL 60670
Phone: 312-732-4000
Fax: 312-732-5976

First Chicago operates in Australia, the Cayman Islands, China, Hong Kong, Japan, Singapore, South Korea, Taiwan, the UK, and the US.

	1994 Sales		1994 Pretax Income	
	$ mil.	% of total	$ mil.	% of total
US	4,445	87	1,034	96
Europe, Middle East & Africa	387	8	11	1
Asia/Pacific	122	2	(13)	—
Other regions	141	3	31	3
Total	**5,095**	**100**	**1,063**	**100**

WHAT

	1994 Assets	
	$ mil.	% of total
Cash & equivalents	25,633	39
Trading account	4,967	8
Unrealized derivatives gains	4,389	6
Net loans	25,224	38
Other assets	5,687	9
Total	**65,900**	**100**

	1994 Sales	
	$ mil.	% of total
Interest & fees on loans	1,897	38
Other interest	1,323	26
Credit card fees	832	16
Fees, service charges & commissions	621	12
Capital markets income	296	6
Other	126	2
Total	**5,095**	**100**

Selected Services
Credit cards
Debt trading
Leasing
Mortgage servicing
Retail and commercial banking
Trust services

Selected Subsidiaries
American National Corp.
FCC National Bank
First Chicago Capital Markets, Inc.
First Chicago International
First Chicago National Processing Corp.
First National Bank of Chicago

KEY COMPETITORS

ADVANTA
American Express
Banc One
Bank of Montreal
Bank of New York
BankAmerica
Barclays
Bell Bancorp
Canadian Imperial
Chase Manhattan
Citicorp
CoreStates Financial
CS Holding
Dai-Ichi Kangyo
First USA
H.F. Ahmanson
KeyCorp
LaSalle/Talman
MBNA
MNB
NationsBank
Northern Trust
Travelers

HOW MUCH

	Annual Growth	1985	1986	1987	1988	1989	1990	1991	1992	1993	1994
Assets ($ mil.)	6.0%	38,893	39,148	44,209	44,432	47,907	50,779	48,963	49,281	52,560	65,900
Net income ($ mil.)	16.9%	169	276	(571)	513	359	249	116	(115)	805	690
Income as % of assets	—	0.4%	0.7%	—	1.2%	0.7%	0.5%	0.2%	—	1.5%	1.0%
Earnings per share ($)	10.3%	2.84	4.70	(10.71)	7.92	4.99	3.32	1.15	(2.08)	8.43	6.88
Stock price – high ($)	—	30.13	34.88	34.00	35.25	49.63	38.25	28.75	37.75	50.63	55.50
Stock price – low ($)	—	20.13	18.88	16.63	18.75	29.25	13.13	15.63	22.88	35.50	41.13
Stock price – close ($)	5.5%	29.50	28.63	18.88	29.63	37.13	16.50	24.63	36.75	43.25	47.75
P/E – high	—	11	7	—	5	10	12	25	—	6	8
P/E – low	—	7	4	—	2	6	4	14	—	4	6
Dividends per share ($)	3.5%	1.32	1.32	1.46	1.50	1.73	1.95	2.00	1.40	1.30	1.80
Book value per share ($)	2.4%	34.10	36.91	19.18	38.32	35.05	36.25	34.90	33.19	43.25	42.14
Employees	2.4%	14,276	13,884	15,108	16,069	18,158	19,068	18,549	16,998	17,355	17,630

1994 Year-end:
Equity as % of assets: 6.9%
Return on assets: 1.2%
Return on equity: 18.9%
Long-term debt (mil.): $9,936
No. of shares (mil.): 90
Dividends
  Yield: 3.8%
  Payout: 26.2%
Market value (mil.): $4,291
Sales (mil.): $5,095

**Stock Price History
High/Low 1985–94**

THE FLORSHEIM SHOE COMPANY

OVERVIEW

One of the oldest and most prestigious shoe brands in the US, Florsheim got its feet back on the ground as an independent company in 1994 after 41 years as a unit of shoe and furnishings giant INTERCO. Leon Black's Apollo Investment Fund, the architect of INTERCO's restructuring in the early 1990s, holds 67.3% of Florsheim.

The Chicago-based company makes a range of men's shoes aimed at the mid- to upper-price quality footwear market. Famous for its dress shoes, Florsheim also makes casual, dress casual, and work shoes. Its brands include America's Tradesman by Florsheim, Barletta, Comfortech, Dri-Treds, Hy-Test, and Outsdoorsman. In 1994 Sears was the company's largest wholesale account.

With 6,000 department and specialty stores selling its shoes worldwide and a network of 368 company-operated stores, Florsheim is the leading specialty retailer of men's nonathletic, quality shoes in the US.

The company is expanding its work shoe line with a selection of steel-toed shoes. The #1 marketer of quality shoes in Australia, Canada, and Mexico, Florsheim opened its first European company-operated store in Milan in 1994, and it is planning to establish a stronger presence in Europe, Central and South America, and East Asia.

Florsheim is also building on the growing consumer preference for casual and dress casual footwear. In 1994 it introduced Dri-Treds (dress and dress casual) and Barletta, a line of Italian-made fashion footwear. In 1995 it introduced an extension of its Comfortech dress shoe line, Comfortech Maintenance Free shoes, which do not require polishing.

WHEN

The company was founded in 1892 by 24-year-old Milton Florsheim, whose father, Sigmund Florsheim, had operated a shoe shop in Chicago since 1856. Making use of new technology (the shoe-lasting machine was invented in 1882), Florsheim produced 150 pairs of shoes in 1894. In the early 1900s Florsheim became one of the first shoe companies to advertise nationally through magazines. It also pioneered manufacturer-owned retail stores in major cities and introduced low-cut shoes for men, which quickly became a fashion standard. Among other innovations, Florsheim was the first company to put shoes on display so that customers could view a selection of styles. Traditionally, shoes salesmen brought out one pair at a time from a back room.

Early in its history Florsheim established a national distribution system, supporting entrepreneurs in small towns who wished to set up retail stores to sell Florsheim shoes.

The company moved into the women's shoe market in 1929. The Wall Street crash that year and the subsequent Depression greatly hurt retail companies like Florsheim. In 1936 Milton died, and his son Irving took over. Irving became chairman in 1946, and his brother Harold succeeded him as president.

By 1949 Florsheim had recovered from the limitations imposed by wartime conditions. That year it had sales of $25 million and had 82 company-operated outlets as well as 4,500 unaffiliated stores selling its shoes.

In 1953 the Florsheim family sold the company to International Shoe (later INTERCO).

Allowed to operate as an autonomous division from 1956 on, the company quickly became International Shoe's most profitable unit. From 1953 to 1963 Florsheim's sales doubled, and by 1963 it controlled over 70% of the US high-priced shoe market.

During the 1970s cheaper imported shoes made serious inroads into the US shoe market. Florsheim exited the women's shoe business in the late 1970s and in the early 1980s shifted more of its production offshore to take advantage of cheaper labor costs. By 1989 less than 50% of the company's shoes were being made in the US.

Starved for cash since staving off a 1988 takeover attempt by the Rales brothers' private investment firm (which saddled it with $1.9 billion of debt), INTERCO filed for bankruptcy in 1991. It emerged from Chapter 11 in 1992. Florsheim spiced up its image in the 1990s, bringing in heavy-hitting NFL commentator John Madden (now a company director) as a pitchman for its shoes. It offered several new styles in 1993, expanding its casual footwear and hiking and hunting boot lines, and began upgrading its retail outlets.

As part of INTERCO's financial reorganization, in 1994 it spun off both of its prominent shoe companies: Florsheim (with Ronald Mueller as its CEO) and athletic shoes and casual shoes manufacturer Converse.

In 1995 Mueller, a Florsheim executive since 1965, retired as chairman and CEO and was replaced by Charles Campbell, a former chairman of Crystal Brands.

Nasdaq symbol: FLSC
Fiscal year ends: Saturday nearest December 31

WHO

Chairman, President, and CEO: Charles J. Campbell, age 50
VP Finance, CFO, and Secretary: Larry J. Svoboda, age 46, $189,923 pay
VP Marketing: Gregory J. Van Gasse, age 44, $181,191 pay
VP Product Development and Sourcing: Roy J. Saurer, age 60, $158,576 pay
VP Occupational Footwear: Harry S. Bock, age 56, $157,243 pay
VP Outlet Stores: George M. Chrislu, age 59
VP Retail Shops: Thomas W. Joseph, age 44
VP Wholesale Sales: Steve L. Bick, age 44
VP International Sales: Jonathan B. Howell, age 57
VP Manufacturing/Operations: Henry W. Wachholz, age 57
VP Customer Service: James J. Tunney, age 63
VP and Manager Wholesale Sales: Bruce Polcek, age 57
Director Human Resources: John Diebold
Auditors: KPMG Peat Marwick LLP

WHERE

HQ: 130 S. Canal St., Chicago, IL 60606-3999
Phone: 312-559-2500
Fax: 312-559-7408

The company markets its products in 6,000 department and specialty stores worldwide and in 368 company-operated specialty stores in Australia, Canada, Italy, and the US.

	1994 Sales % of total
US	84
Other countries	16
Total	**100**

WHAT

	1994 US Sales % of total
Wholesale	67
Retail	33
Total	**100**

Selected Shoe Products
America's Tradesman by Florsheim (work shoes)
Barletta (dress and dress casual shoes)
Comfortech (dress, dress casual, and casual shoes)
Dri-Treds (dress and dress casual shoes)
Florsheim (dress, dress casual, and casual shoes)
Hy-Test (work shoes)
Imperial (dress shoes)
Outsdoorsman (casual shoes)
Royal Imperial (dress shoes)

KEY COMPETITORS

Brown Group
Daniel Green
Dexter Shoe
Genesco
Kenneth Cole
La Crosse Footwear
NIKE
Phillips-Van Heusen
R. Griggs
Reebok
Rocky Shoes & Boots
Timberland
US Shoe
Vans
Weyco
Wolverine World Wide

HOW MUCH

	Annual Growth	1985	1986	1987	1988	1989	1990	1991	1992[1]	1993	1994
Sales ($ mil.)	(3.8%)	—	—	—	—	—	—	339	249	300	302
Net income ($ mil.)	—	—	—	—	—	—	—	(2)	(2)	12	6
Income as % of sales	—	—	—	—	—	—	—	—	—	4.1%	2.1%
Earnings per share ($)	—	—	—	—	—	—	—	—	—	—	0.78
Stock price – high ($)	—	—	—	—	—	—	—	—	—	—	9.25
Stock price – low ($)	—	—	—	—	—	—	—	—	—	—	5.50
Stock price – close ($)	—	—	—	—	—	—	—	—	—	—	5.63
P/E – high	—	—	—	—	—	—	—	—	—	—	12
P/E – low	—	—	—	—	—	—	—	—	—	—	7
Dividends per share ($)	—	—	—	—	—	—	—	—	—	—	0.00
Book value per share ($)	—	—	—	—	—	—	—	—	—	—	7.21
Employees	—	—	—	—	—	—	—	—	—	—	3,248

1994 Year-end:
Debt ratio: 63.7%
Return on equity: —
Cash (mil.): $5
Current ratio: 6.11
Long-term debt (mil.): $106
No. of shares (mil.): 8
Dividends
  Yield: —
  Payout: —
Market value (mil.): $47

**Stock Price History
High/Low 1994**

[1] 10-month fiscal year

FMC CORPORATION

OVERVIEW

Chemicals have been the catalyst for FMC's recent record revenues. The Chicago-based conglomerate manufactures chemicals for the agriculture, food, and pharmaceutical markets. It also makes machinery for the defense, energy, food processing, and transportation industries. The company's defense unit makes the Bradley fighting vehicle and its FMC Gold subsidiary develops gold and silver mines.

Once considered a stodgy old conglomerate, FMC has completed a recent restructuring that cut costs by $70 million in 1994. Since 1992 FMC has spent over $275 million to grow its business by acquiring complementary companies and establishing strategic partnerships. In 1995 it bought Moorco, a Houston-based

manufacturer of measurement products for the energy industry.

FMC, the world's top producer of natural soda ash (used in glassmaking), formed a soda ash–mining joint venture in 1995 with Nippon Sheet Glass and Sumitomo Corp., which together paid $150 million for 20% of the project. FMC will spend $45 million to boost capacity at its Green River, Wyoming, soda ash plant by 700,000 tons by 1997.

Agricultural chemicals continue to grow as a source of revenues for FMC. In 1994 the company announced it would build an $88 million plant to manufacture a new herbicide used in soybean and sugarcane farming.

Employees own nearly 22% of FMC.

WHEN

After retiring to California, inventor John Bean developed a pump to deliver a continuous spray of insecticide (1884). This invention led to the Bean Spray Pump Company (1904). In 1928 Bean Spray Pump went public and bought Anderson-Barngrover (food growing and processing equipment). The new company name, John Bean Manufacturing, gave way to Food Machinery Corporation in 1929. The company bought Peerless Pump (agricultural and industrial pumps) in 1933.

During WWII the company started making military equipment. It entered the agricultural chemical field when it purchased Niagara Sprayer & Chemical (1943). After the war it added Westvaco Chemical (1948) and changed its name to Food Machinery & Chemical.

The Bean family ran the company until 1956, when John Bean's grandson, John Crummey, retired as chairman. The company extended its product line, buying such companies as Oil Center Tool (wellhead equipment, 1957), Sunland Industries (fertilizer and insecticides, 1959), and Barrett Equipment (automotive brake equipment, 1961).

In light of its growing diversification, the company changed its name to FMC in 1961. Major purchases in the 1960s included American Viscose (rayon and cellophane, 1963) and Link-Belt (equipment for power transmission and for bulk-material handling, 1967).

To be centrally located FMC moved its headquarters from San Jose to Chicago in 1972. In 1976 it sold its pump and fiber divisions and its 50% interest in Ketchikan Pulp (part of the American Viscose purchase). FMC continued to sell its slow-growing businesses, including the semiconductor division (1979),

the industrial packaging division (1980), the Niagara Seed Operation (1980), and the Power Transmission Group (1981).

In 1979 FMC entered mining in a joint venture with Freeport Minerals for a gold mine in Jerritt Canyon, Nevada (discovered 1973). In the 1980s FMC found more gold near Gabbs, Nevada, and entered the lithium business by buying Lithium Corp. of America (1985). In a 1986 antitakeover move, FMC financed a $2 billion recapitalization, paying shareholders $80 per share and giving employees a larger stake in the company. In 1989 FMC bought the French company Mather et Platt (harvesters, food processing equipment). The next year FMC Gold bought Meridian Gold from Burlington Resources.

In 1992 FMC bought Ciba-Geigy's flame retardants and water treatment businesses and combined its defense operations with Harsco as United Defense (60% FMC-owned). In 1993 the company announced a restructuring plan that cut 1,200 jobs and included a $123 million write-off. FMC also announced that FMC Gold would take a $60 million charge to write down assets at an Idaho gold mine.

FMC's 1994 acquisitions included Abex's Jetway Systems Division, a leading designer of aircraft support systems, Caterpillar's Automated Vehicle Systems group, and the Fluid Control Systems products of National-Oilwell.

Also in 1994 FMC acquired the remaining shares of United Defense. In 1994 and 1995 United Defense won contracts worth nearly $100 million for tank recovery and Command and Control vehicles. It was also awarded a TRW subcontract for computerized battlefield communications.

WHO

Chairman and CEO: Robert N. Burt, age 57,
$1,167,831 pay
President: Larry D. Brady, age 52, $742,550 pay
EVP: William F. Beck, age 56, $553,478 pay
EVP and CFO: Michael J. Callahan, age 55
SVP: William J. Kirby, age 57, $520,790 pay
VP; General Manager, Agricultural Products Group:
William H. Schumann III, age 44
VP; General Manager, Food Machinery Group: Charles
H. Cannon, age 42
VP; General Manager, Chemical Products Group:
Robert I. Harries, age 51
**VP; General Manager, Energy and Transportation
Equipment Group:** Joseph H. Netherland, age 48
VP; President and CEO, United Defense, L.P.: Thomas
W. Rabaut, age 46
VP and General Counsel: Patrick J. Head, age 62
VP Communications: William R. Jenkins
VP Human Resources: William W. Murray
Auditors: KPMG Peat Marwick LLP

WHERE

HQ: 200 E. Randolph Dr., Chicago, IL 60601
Phone: 312-861-6000
Fax: 312-861-6176

FMC operates 100 manufacturing facilities and mines in
the US and 20 other countries.

	1994 Sales		1994 Operating Income	
	$ mil.	% of total	$ mil.	% of total
US	3,085	77	341	75
Europe	693	17	100	22
Other Americas	160	4	14	3
Other regions	73	2	2	0
Total	**4,011**	**1005**	**457**	**100**

WHAT

	1994 Sales		1994 Operating Income	
	$ mil.	% of total	$ mil.	% of total
Defense systems	1,081	27	160	34
Performance chem.	1,060	26	154	33
Machinery & equip.	973	24	33	7
Industrial chem.	867	21	119	26
Precious metals	61	2	(9)	—
Adjustments	(31)	—	—	—
Total	**4,011**	**100**	**57**	**100**

Business Units

Defense Systems	Machinery
Armament Systems	Energy and Transportation
Ground Systems	Equipment Group
International	Food Machinery Group
Steel Products	
United Defense, L.P.	**Industrial Chemicals**
	Alkali Chemicals Division
Performance Chemicals	FMC Foret, S.A.
Agricultural Products	Peroxygen Chemicals
Group	Division
BioProducts	Phosphorus Chemicals
Food Ingredients Division	Division
Lithium Division	
Pharmaceutical Division	**Precious Metals**
Process Additives Division	FMC Gold

KEY COMPETITORS

AGCO	Cyprus Amax	Hoechst
Anglo American	Dow Chemical	Homestake
ASARCO	Dresser	Mining
Baker Hughes	DuPont	Ingersoll-Rand
BASF	Freeport-McMoRan	Kerr-McGee
Berwind	Copper & Gold	Monsanto
British Aerospace	GenCorp	Morton
Broken Hill	General Dynamics	Olin
Cambrex	Halliburton	Pearson
Caterpillar	Hanson	Phelps Dodge
Ciba-Geigy	Hercules	Schlumberger

HOW MUCH

	Annual Growth	1985	1986	1987	1988	1989	1990	1991	1992	1993	1994
Sales ($ mil.)	2.3%	3,261	3,003	3,139	3,287	3,415	3,722	3,899	3,974	3,754	4,011
Net income ($ mil.)	(1.4%)	197	153	191	129	157	155	173	119	36	173
Income as % of sales	—	5.1%	6.1%	3.9%	4.6%	4.2%	4.4%	3.0%	1.0%	4.3%	4.3%
Earnings per share ($)	15.2%	1.30	1.62	4.52	3.60	4.34	4.30	4.68	3.20	0.98	4.65
Stock price – high ($)	—	12.75	26.38	60.38	39.13	49.00	38.75	51.63	53.25	54.00	65.13
Stock price – low ($)	—	9.50	15.50	24.00	24.38	31.63	25.38	29.50	42.50	41.50	45.50
Stock price – close ($)	19.6%	11.50	25.75	33.75	32.00	35.25	31.88	47.88	49.50	47.13	57.75
P/E – high	—	—	16	13	11	11	9	11	17	55	14
P/E – low	—	—	10	5	7	7	6	6	13	42	10
Dividends per share ($)	(100%)	0.33	0.10	0.00	0.00	0.00	0.00	0.00	0.00	0.00	0.00
Book value per share ($)	4.7%	7.54	(11.25)	(7.60)	(6.53)	(2.05)	4.30	8.78	6.10	5.99	11.41
Employees	(3.0%)	28,064	24,966	24,797	24,342	24,110	23,882	23,150	22,097	20,696	21,344

1994 Year-end:
Debt ratio: 70.8%
Return on equity: 54.8%
Cash (mil.): $98
Current ratio: 1.08
Long-term debt (mil.): $901
No. of shares (mil.): 37
Dividends
  Yield: —
  Payout: —
Market value (mil.): $2,109

Stock Price History
High/Low 1985–94

FRUIT OF THE LOOM, INC.

OVERVIEW

Fruit of the Loom did not enjoy the fruits of its labors in 1994. Sales were up 22%, but its net income unraveled, falling sharply. Based in Chicago, the company is the US's #1 maker of underwear and a leading manufacturer of activewear for imprints.

A number of factors took a bite out of Fruit of the Loom's profits, including higher cotton prices (it is the nation's #1 cotton buyer) and charges related to acquisitions. Its 1994 acquisitions reflect its strategy of expanding its product lines. To boost its line of women's apparel, it bought jeans maker Gitano, and to build its growing line of licensed sports apparel, it bought Artex and Pro Player.

Besides having licensing agreements with all the major US sports leagues and many universities, the company also has agreements with entertainment companies such as Walt Disney and Time Warner. In 1995 the company expects strong growth from the licensing of characters from the movies *Batman Forever*, *Mighty Morphin Power Rangers*, and *Pocahontas*.

To cut costs, Fruit of the Loom plans to move more of its production outside the US, although it does not plan to close any major US plants. The company also plans to raise prices between 4% and 7%. CEO William Farley owns 33.1% of the company.

WHEN

Jacob Goldfarb, a Polish immigrant, learned the underwear business from the bottom up. He founded his own company, Union Underwear, in 1926. By the mid-1950s Union was the biggest maker of men's briefs in the US. In 1955 Goldfarb, then 60 and worried Union might be liquidated after he died, accepted a cash offer for his company from Philadelphia & Reading Corporation.

In 1955 Philadelphia & Reading was a money-losing coal railroad operating in eastern Pennsylvania. It had started out in 1871 as the coal mining subsidiary of the Philadelphia & Reading Railroad. It remained a producer of anthracite coal until the mid-1950s, when a group of investors led by Howard Newman transformed it into a holding company (Philadelphia & Reading). Newman went on to buy Acme Boot Company (1956), Fruit of the Loom (1961), and Lone Star Steel (1965). In 1968 Philadelphia & Reading was bought by Ben Heineman's Northwest Industries.

Like Newman, Heineman had begun with a railroad — the Chicago-based North Western — in 1956. He wound up selling the railroad to its employees in 1972 and building a conglomerate that included Velsicol Chemical (acquired in 1965) and the assets of Philadelphia & Reading. Then in 1985 Heineman sold Northwest Industries to William Farley for $1.4 billion. Farley, who had already built a reputation as a deal maker, got most of the money from junk bond specialists Drexel Burnham Lambert.

That year Farley spun off Lone Star Steel to offset acquisition debt and changed Northwest's name to Farley/Northwest Industries. In 1987 he changed its name to Fruit of the Loom. That year Farley's own holding company (Farley, Inc.) made a 27-million-share public offering of its Fruit of the Loom stock but kept control of the company.

Under Farley's ownership Fruit of the Loom began to diversify, manufacturing socks (1986), branching into sweatshirts, and increasing production of women's underwear (which it began selling in 1984). But Farley, Inc., ran into trouble in 1989 when it tried to buy West Point–Pepperell through yet another Drexel-financed LBO. The junk bond market collapsed in the middle of the deal, and, trying to keep ahead of debt and interest payments, Farley shed businesses. Its voting stake in Fruit of the Loom dwindled to 33%. In September 1991, after defaulting on $20 million in payments to its bondholders, Farley, Inc., agreed to reorganize. Farley, Inc.'s voting power is now at less than 16%, but Farley himself holds 33% of the Fruit of the Loom vote and the right to appoint 25% of its board.

In 1991 Fruit of the Loom introduced a new line of infants' and toddlers' apparel and agreed to let Warnaco manufacture and sell bras under the Fruit of the Loom name.

In 1993 the company struck a licensing deal with Wilson Sporting Goods to produce and market Wilson athletic wear in the US. Also in 1993 it acquired sports clothing licensee Salem Sportswear. It bought Artex Manufacturing in 1994, which, besides sports leagues, also licenses many popular cartoon characters from Disney, Peanuts, and Looney Tunes.

In 1995 the company announced a stepped-up TV advertising campaign that included the return of "the fruits," a group of men dressed as grapes and apples, who starred in the company's TV ads for more than 10 years before being dropped in 1990.

NYSE symbol: FTL
Fiscal year ends: December 31

WHO

Chairman and CEO: William Farley, age 52,
$1,360,000 pay
VC: Richard C. Lappin, age 50, $700,000 pay
President and COO: John B. Holland, age 62,
$797,500 pay
SEVP Corporate Development: Richard M. Cion, age 51,
$572,438 pay
EVP and CFO: Larry K. Switzer, age 51
EVP Operations: John Wigodsky
EVP Manufacturing: Stan W. Vinson
SVP, General Counsel, and Assistant Secretary: Joyce
M. Russell
SVP Finance: G. William Newton
VP and Treasurer: Earl C. Shanks, age 38, $332,967 pay
VP and Controller: Michael F. Bogacki, age 40
VP Administration (HR): Burgess D. Ridge, age 50
Auditors: Ernst & Young LLP

WHERE

HQ: 5000 Sears Tower, 233 S. Wacker Dr., Chicago, IL
60606
Phone: 312-876-1724
Fax: 312-993-1749

Fruit of the Loom has 61 manufacturing facilities in
Canada, El Salvador, Honduras, Ireland, Jamaica,
Mexico, the UK, and the US.

	1994 Sales		1994 Operating Income	
	$ mil.	% of total	$ mil.	% of total
US	1,972	86	234	91
Other countries	326	14	22	9
Adjustments	—	—	(21)	—
Total	**2,298**	**100**	**235**	**100**

WHAT

Brand Names
Best
Botany 500
BVD
Fruit of the Loom
Funpals
Gitano
John Henry
Kangaroo
Lofteez
Munsingwear
Official Fan
Pro Player
Salem
Salem Sportswear
Screen Stars
Wilson (license)

Casual wear
Childrens wear
Hosiery
Sports-licensed apparel
Underwear
  Men and boys
  Women and girls

Licensing Partners
Major League Baseball
National Basketball
  Association
National Football League
National Hockey League
Time Warner
The Walt Disney Company
Warnaco Inc.
Wilson Sporting
  Goods Co.

Products
Active wear
Athletic sportswear

KEY COMPETITORS

Benetton
Bugle Boy
Calvin Klein
Esprit
The Gap
Guess
Gymboree
J. Crew
Lands' End
Levi Strauss
L.L. Bean
Movie Star

Nautica
NIKE
Oshkosh B'Gosh
Reebok
Russell Corporation
Sara Lee
Spiegel
Stage II
Starter
Tultex
VF Corp.

HOW MUCH

	Annual Growth	1985	1986	1987	1988	1989	1990	1991	1992	1993	1994
Sales ($ mil.)	16.2%	—	693	870	1,005	1,321	1,427	1,628	1,855	1,884	2,298
Net income ($ mil.)	22.3%	—	12	43	73	72	77	111	189	213	60
Income as % of sales	—	—	1.7%	4.9%	7.3%	5.5%	5.4%	6.8%	10.2%	11.3%	2.6%
Earnings per share ($)	—	—	(0.79)	0.61	1.13	1.11	1.18	1.55	2.48	2.80	0.79
Stock price – high ($)	—	—	—	9.75	7.63	16.00	15.38	28.00	49.63	49.25	33.00
Stock price – low ($)	—	—	—	3.88	4.25	6.13	6.13	7.63	26.50	22.88	23.00
Stock price – close ($)	27.2%	—	—	5.00	6.38	14.88	8.88	27.63	48.63	24.13	27.00
P/E – high	—	—	—	16	7	14	13	18	20	18	42
P/E – low	—	—	—	6	4	6	5	5	11	8	29
Dividends per share ($)	—	—	—	0.00	0.00	0.00	0.00	0.00	0.00	0.00	0.00
Book value per share ($)	24.8%	—	—	3.14	4.19	5.30	6.77	9.21	11.32	13.83	14.84
Employees	10.5%	—	16,800	19,600	23,400	26,000	27,700	26,700	31,100	35,000	37,400

1994 Year-end:
Debt ratio: 56.5%
Return on equity: 5.6%
Cash (mil.): $49
Current ratio: 3.24
Long-term debt (mil.): $1,440
No. of shares (mil.): 76
Dividends
  Yield: 0.0%
  Payout: 0.0%
Market value (mil.): $2,048

**Stock Price History
High/Low 1987–94**

G. HEILEMAN BREWING COMPANY, INC.

OVERVIEW

The G. Heileman Brewing Company is certainly not living its happiest hour. Though the Rosemont, Illinois–based company is the nation's 5th largest brewer, making and marketing such national and regional brands as Colt 45, Lone Star, Rainier, and Old Style, it has recorded steadily declining market share and profits. In fact, its current financial troubles may translate into the sale of the company's assets, and debt refinancing has become the company's primary concern.

Perhaps the only good thing happening at Heileman, which is owned by Dallas-based LBO firm Hicks, Muse, Tate & Furst, is a booming contract brewing business that accounts for an estimated 24% of the company's production volume. Heileman manufactures the popular AriZona Iced Tea for the New York–based company Ferolito, Vultaggio &

Sons, and rumors of a possible merger with or acquisition by Ferolito, Vultaggio abound.

In an effort to reposition itself in an increasingly competitive beer market, Heileman handed over its direction to a new management team (the 3rd in a year) in January 1995. New president and CEO Lou Lowenkron and his sales and marketing chief Joe Martino (a former Anheuser-Busch executive) have pledged to tread slowly, nurturing the company's existing brands and patching up relations with estranged wholesalers. This marked a radical shift from the company's strategy of less than a year before that included the rollout of 150 new brands and line extensions and the force-feeding of independent distributors. Heileman will, however, continue the nationwide promotion of its leading Pacific Northwest beer, Henry Weinhard's.

WHEN

G. Heileman was founded as the City Brewery in La Crosse, Wisconsin, in 1853 by German immigrant Gottlieb Heileman and local brewer John Gund. Gund left the company in 1872, and Heileman renamed the brewery for himself.

Upon Heileman's death in 1878, his widow, Johanna, assumed the company's direction. She placed emphasis on quality over quantity. An early ad boasted, "We don't aim to make the most beer, only the best." Heileman's beer, including its Old Style Lager, enjoyed growing popularity with the post-WWI arrival of German immigrants. Johanna died in 1917, and the company weathered Prohibition with the production of "near beer" and the sale of malt to home brewers.

With the end of Prohibition, Heileman moved into a period of rapid management turnover. New president Harry Dahl curtailed the company's malt sales, and Heileman began making brews catering to varying regional tastes. In 1941 the company, then run by Albert Bates, altered its beer recipe and shifted its focus to pricing over quality. The move was poorly received and ultimately cost Heileman consumers. By 1945, sales were at a 20-year low. In 1951 Ralph Johansen became president, but his efforts to turn the company around proved ineffective. Change came again in 1956, when Heileman treasurer Roy Kumm was named president.

Kumm, who led Heileman until 1970, returned the company's focus to quality brewing and in 1959 launched a strategy of growth

through the acquisition of regional breweries. Sales and profits soared throughout the 1960s. By 1968 Heileman had secured its place among America's top 20 brewers, and in 1969 the company bought Blatz, a nationally recognized brewer.

In 1971 Kumm turned control over to his son-in-law, Russell Cleary, who continued pursuing acquisitions. By 1980 Heileman had snatched up 5 more breweries and was the 7th largest brewer in the US. In 1983 Heileman bought Pabst (later sold), assuring the company a share of the booming national market, and in 1984 Lone Star Brewing was acquired.

The tables turned in 1987, when Heileman — then the nation's 5th largest brewer — was bought by Australian venture capitalist (and America's Cup victor) Alan Bond for $1.3 billion. By 1991 Heileman was bankrupt and saddled with $800 million in debt. On top of that, the once-flourishing US beer market was flat, with consumers showing a preference for specialty beers.

In 1994 the Dallas-based LBO firm of Hicks, Muse, Tate & Furst came to Heileman's rescue, buying the brewer for $390 million. However, by year's end Heileman had posted a net loss of $37.4 million, and sales of the company's brands were down 7.7%. Clearly dissatisfied with the results, Hicks, Muse shuffled company executives twice and in January 1995 invested an additional $25 million in the company. Hicks, Muse also announced that it was considering selling the company's assets.

Private company
Fiscal year ends: December 31

WHO

Chairman: Thomas O. Hicks
President and CEO: M. Lou. Lowenkron, age 63
EVP Finance: Daniel J. Schmid Jr.
Senior Executive Sales and Brand Marketing: Joe Martino, age 42
SVP Fin Sales: Thomas Koehler
VP Marketing: Jack Hanzlovic
VP Marketing: Davis Morris
VP Brewery Operations: Jeff Malcolm
VP and Corporate Counsel: Randy Smith
VP International Operations: Randy Hall
VP Human Resources: Jeff Scheel

WHERE

HQ: 9399 W. Higgins Rd., Ste. 700, Rosemont, IL 60018
Phone: 847-292-2100
Fax: 847-292-6870

G. Heileman brews more than 30 regional beer brands and makes nonalcoholic beverages under contract. The company operates 5 breweries in Baltimore; La Crosse, Wisconsin; Portland, Oregon; San Antonio; and Seattle.

WHAT

	1994 Estimated Sales
	% of total
Company brands	76
Contract brewing	24
Total	**100**

Selected Beer Brands
Black Label
Blatz
Champale
Colt 45
Grenadier
Henry Weinhard's
Kingsbury NA
Lone Star
Mickey's
Old Style
Rainier
Sabinas
Schmidt's
Special Export
Yakima

Contract Brands
AriZona Iced Tea
Mucho Mango juice drinks

KEY COMPETITORS

Adolph Coors
Anchor Brewing
Anheuser-Busch
Bass
Becks
Boston Beer
Carlsberg
Chicago Brewing
Danone
Foster's Brewing
Gambrinus
Genesee
Guinness
Hart Brewing
Heineken
John Labatt
Kirin
Molson
Pete's Brewing
Philip Morris
Redhook Ale Brewery
San Miguel
S&P Co.
Sierra Nevada Brewing
Stroh

HOW MUCH

	Annual Growth	1985	1986	1987	1988	1989	1990	1991	1992	1993	1994
Estimated sales ($ mil.)	(4.4%)	—	—	—	—	—	—	728	721	700	636
Employees	0.0%	—	—	—	—	—	—	—	2,150	2,200	2,150

HOUSE OF HEILEMAN

Estimated Sales
($ mil.)
1991–94

| 800 |
| 700 |
| 600 |
| 500 |
| 400 |
| 300 |
| 200 |
| 100 |
| 0 |

GATX CORPORATION

OVERVIEW

GATX makes its bucks in bulk. The Chicago-based holding company owns 5 subsidiaries that specialize in moving and storing bulk products and providing capital asset financing.

GATX's General American Transportation Corporation is the largest lessor of railway tank cars in the US, with a fleet of 59,800 railcars. GATX estimates that it provides about 25% of all US tank cars.

As the largest US independent bulk liquid storage company, GATX Terminals Corporation (Terminals) stores, handles, and transfers products for oil and chemical companies and other clients. It has 25 terminals in 11 states, 2 pipeline systems, and 8 terminals in the UK. Terminals also has 13 overseas joint ventures.

GATX Financial Services provides asset-based financing of industrial and transportation equipment through capital and operating leases and secured equipment loans. It also manages lease portfolios.

With the largest carrying capacity of any domestic fleet on the Great Lakes, the 11 vessels of GATX's American Steamship Company carried 26.3 million tons of cargo in 1994, including iron ore, coal, and limestone.

GATX Logistics, Inc., is a major provider of distribution and logistics support services in the US, with 113 warehousing facilities.

Some analysts believe that GATX will benefit from the trend in corporate America to outsource some functions, such as delivery. This trend is notable among chemical firms, GATX's major transportation clients.

In 1995 GATX formed an alliance with Rand McNally Book Services to help publishers lower transportation costs and improve their order and return logistics.

WHEN

GATX Corporation was founded as the Atlantic Seaboard Dispatch in 1898 by Max Epstein, a worker in the Chicago Stockyards. Epstein used the $1,000 commission he received for arranging the sale of 20 old railway freight cars as a down payment to purchase 28 cars for himself. He incorporated the firm as the German-American Car Company in 1902. Epstein became the first to lease specialty railcars on a long-term basis.

By 1907 Epstein had 433 railway cars and specialized in building customized freight cars. In 1916 the firm offered stock under the name General American Tank Car Company (GATC). (GATC's railcars carried the initials "GATX;" the "X" meant that a car belonged to a private line.) In 1925 GATC began a bulk liquid storage business, which later became GATX Terminals Corporation.

Epstein purchased 13 firms between 1926 and 1931. The Great Depression was good to GATC: Epstein declared he could "make better deals" at the time. The petroleum and food hauled in GATC cars were always in demand, despite economic pressures. By the 1940s GATC was the US's largest freight car lessor, with 60,000 cars including refrigerator and tank cars. Its liquid bulk storage system was the largest public liquid storage terminal facility in the US. GATC also began operating cargo ships on the Great Lakes at that time.

By 1952 GATC was the US's 4th largest maker of freight cars. In 1954 GATC acquired Fuller Co., a builder of cement plants, which produced steady profits until its 1986 sale.

In 1968 GATC formed GATX Leasing, an airplane lessor, which became GATX Capital Corporation (a principal subsidiary of GATX Financial Services). In 1968 the demand for railcars plummeted; GATC reduced manufacturing and began to refocus.

In 1973 GATC acquired the American Steamship Company, which greatly expanded GATC's role in Great Lakes shipping. In 1975 the company changed its name to GATX Corporation.

In the 1980s GATX sold or shut down its manufacturing operations and became more service-oriented, expanding its railcar and aircraft fleets and its bulk liquid storage operations. It narrowly escaped takeover attempts by Leucadia National (finance and insurance) and 2 other investment firms. GATX Terminals expanded rapidly in the late 1980s. In 1989 GATX purchased Associated Unit Companies, which became the Unit Companies, Inc., the following year, then GATX Logistics Inc. in 1993. GATX also acquired Sealand Oil Services Ltd. (Scotland) in 1993.

By the early 1990s GATC's shipping fleet had become the largest self-unloading dry bulk carrier plying the Great Lakes. In 1994 GATX continued to expand overseas and formed a joint venture with EnviroLease, Inc., to provide equipment for moving wastes and recyclables. The following year GATX added more than 5,300 new and used railcars to its fleet. Chairman James Glasser announced plans to turn over the reins to Ronald Zech in 1996.

NYSE symbol: GMT
Fiscal year ends: December 31

WHO

Chairman: James J. Glasser, age 60, $1,053,697 pay
President and CEO: Ronald H. Zech, age 51,
$629,730 pay (prior to promotion)
President, GATX Terminals Corporation: John F.
Chlebowski Jr., $391,643 pay
**VP Corporate Development, General Counsel, and
Secretary:** David B. Anderson, age 52
VP Finance, CFO, and Secretary: David M. Edwards,
age 43, $326,143 pay
VP Human Resources: William L. Chambers, age 57,
$318,010 pay
Auditors: Ernst & Young LLP

WHERE

HQ: 500 W. Monroe St., Chicago, IL 60661-3676
Phone: 312-621-6200
Fax: 312-621-6646

GATX Corporation has operations worldwide.

WHAT

	1994 Sales	
	$ mil.	% of total
Railcar leasing & management	322	28
Terminals & pipelines	303	26
Logistics & warehousing	244	21
Financial services	207	18
Great Lakes shipping	83	7
Corporate & other	(4)	—
Total	**1,155**	**100**

Selected Subsidiaries

American Steamship Company Vessels
M/V *Adam E. Cornelius*   M/V *Indiana Harbor*
M/V *American Mariner*   M/V *St. Clair*
M/V *American Republic*   M/V *Sam Laud*
M/V *Buffalo*   M/V *Walter J. McCarthy, Jr.*
M/V *Charles E. Wilson*   Str. *John J. Boland*
M/V *H. Lee White*

GATX Financial Services
Arrangement of investment lease transactions
Capital leases
Lease portfolio management
Operating leases
Secured equipment loans

GATX Logistics Services
Distribution and logistics   Packaging
  support   Real estate services
Information systems   Returns management
Just-in-time delivery   Subassembly
  systems   Warehousing space

GATX Terminals Corporation Services
Blending of liquid commodities
Bulk petroleum and chemical storage
Pipeline connections and distribution

General American Transportation Corporation
Railway tank car leasing
Specialized railway freight car leasing

KEY COMPETITORS

ACF   General Motors
Alexander & Baldwin   Interlake Steamship
American President   International-Matex Tank
BankAmerica   Terminals
Citicorp   Marmon Group
Columbia Transportation   Paktank NV
Conrail   Ryder
Consolidated Freightways   Union Pacific
CSX   USS Great Lakes Fleet
General Electric   Van Ommeren NV

HOW MUCH

	Annual Growth	1985	1986	1987	1988	1989	1990	1991	1992	1993	1994
Sales ($ mil.)	5.8%	694	512	528	572	702	870	989	1,019	1,087	1,155
Net income ($ mil.)	—	(46)	29	35	47	66	83	83	29	73	92
Income as % of sales	—	—	5.6%	6.6%	8.2%	9.4%	9.5%	8.4%	2.9%	6.7%	7.9%
Earnings per share ($)	—	(1.90)	1.21	1.82	2.52	3.17	3.54	3.51	0.82	2.99	3.78
Stock price – high ($)	—	18.75	21.00	25.38	28.25	37.88	35.75	40.25	33.75	42.25	44.63
Stock price – low ($)	—	13.88	15.00	16.69	18.50	26.75	17.63	21.50	24.25	31.38	38.25
Stock price – close ($)	11.1%	17.00	16.81	19.25	28.25	34.00	25.88	28.75	33.13	40.75	44.00
P/E – high	—	—	17	14	11	12	10	12	41	14	12
P/E – low	—	—	12	9	7	8	5	6	30	11	10
Dividends per share ($)	11.0%	0.60	0.68	0.75	0.90	1.50	1.10	1.20	1.30	1.40	1.53
Book value per share ($)	9.5%	14.69	11.65	11.06	14.83	26.37	28.96	31.42	28.42	29.32	33.12
Employees	1.9%	4,900	1,900	2,000	2,100	3,500	4,200	5,100	5,100	5,500	5,800

1994 Year-end:
Debt ratio: 75.8%
Return on equity: 14.7%
Cash (mil.): $27
Current ratio: 1.37
Long-term debt (mil.): $1,805
No. of shares (mil.): 20
Dividends
  Yield: 3.5%
  Payout: 40.5%
Market value (mil.): $876

**Stock Price History
High/Low 1985–94**

GENERAL INSTRUMENT CORPORATION

OVERVIEW

General Instrument (GI) chairman Daniel Akerson thinks "the square foot on top of your TV may be the most valuable real estate" in the electronic information industry. GI — a leading developer of products that deliver interactive data, video, and voice — pioneered the digital compression technology that will make 500-channel cable systems and interactive multimedia systems possible.

GI Communications, the division that is the source of 80% of GI's revenues, is the world's top provider of cable TV systems and subscriber terminals as well as satellite television technology. Its VideoCipher is the industry standard for encoding satellite transmissions, and in 1994 it delivered more than 4.7 million set-top decoders.

CommScope, another division, is a leading supplier of coaxial and fiber-optic cable for the cable TV industry. In 1994 CommScope delivered more than 580,000 miles of cable. GI's Power Semiconductor division makes electrical power-handling equipment used in telecommunications and automotive and consumer electronics. More than 2/3 of the division's sales are to foreign companies.

GI is securing its place in the cable TV market by licensing its digital cable technology to such manufacturers as Hewlett-Packard and Zenith for use in cable decoder boxes. In 1995 GI formed a new business unit to help companies establish interactive services such as multimedia home shopping and service guides. It is also marketing to both major segments of the nascent industry: soon after it was chosen as a supplier for GTE's video network, GI unveiled a new technology that lets cable TV companies transmit telephone signals.

Investment firm Forstmann Little owns 30% of GI.

WHEN

General Instrument was founded in New York in 1923 by Abraham Blumenkrantz, an Austrian orphan who, at age 15, came to New York, where his brother was foreman of a machine shop. Soon Blumenkrantz landed a job sweeping floors for $4 a week. He became a US citizen in 1923, at age 25, and that year started his own machine shop to manufacture variable condensers (the part that allows radios to tune in stations). Soon that company, which became General Instrument, was also making earphone jacks and tube sockets. It went public in 1939.

During WWII GI (sometimes called "Genius Incorporated" for its amazing innovations) supplied parts for bombs. In the 1940s it added phonograph record changers and television components to its growing product line. In the early 1950s it manufactured over a thousand different items, including its first end product, a converter box for the recently introduced UHF (ultrahigh-frequency) TV channels.

Blumenkrantz retired in 1955 but remained chairman of GI's finance committee. Before his death in 1961, the orphan-immigrant resided on 5th Avenue.

In 1967 GI entered the cable TV industry with its acquisition of Jerrold Communications Corp., a supplier of CATV (community antenna television) equipment. That same year GI bought American Totalisator, the world's top maker of pari-mutuel betting machines.

During the 1970s GI continued making acquisitions, buying an eclectic collection of electronics companies. Frank Hickey, who became president in 1975, began to sell noncore assets and to encourage the company's 2 most successful components, cable TV and gaming. By the late 1970s GI supplied a large portion of North America's betting and lottery machines. Also the new video game industry boosted GI's computer chip sales.

In 1983 the company acquired Tocom, a maker of cable TV converters. In 1986 it bought M/A-COM's cable TV equipment operations, which included the industry standard encryption system, VideoCipher.

In 1990 GI was acquired in a leveraged buyout by Forstmann Little & Co. Donald Rumsfeld, former secretary of defense and White House chief of staff, was named CEO. Forstmann Little took GI public again in 1992.

In 1993 Jerrold Communications and VideoCipher were joined to create the company's GI Communications division. That year former MCI president Daniel Akerson replaced Rumsfeld as CEO, while telecommunications veteran Richard Friedland became GI's president. In 1994 Bell Atlantic chose GI to supply equipment for its multimedia network.

GI's international sales boomed in 1995 with contracts for cable and telecommunications equipment in Australia, China, Mexico, and Saudi Arabia. That same year GI agreed to acquire Next Level Communications, a maker of digital telephone equipment. Also in 1995 Friedland became the company's CEO.

NYSE symbol: GIC
Fiscal year ends: December 31

WHO

Chairman: Daniel F. Akerson, age 46, $1,566,367 pay
Chairman, President, and CEO: Richard S. Friedland, age 44, $747,600 pay (prior to promotion)
Chairman, President, and CEO, CommScope: Frank M. Drendel, age 50, $562,565 pay
VP, General Counsel, and Secretary: Thomas A. Dumit, age 52, $445,752 pay
VP; President Power Semiconductor Division: Ronald A. Ostertag, age 54
VP; President GI Communications Division: Laurence L. Osterwise, age 47
VP and CFO: Charles T. Dickson, age 40
VP and Controller: Paul J. Berzenski, age 42
VP Taxes and Treasurer: Richard C. Smith, age 50
VP Human Resources: Clark E. Tucker
Auditors: Deloitte & Touche LLP

WHERE

HQ: 181 W. Madison St., Chicago, IL 60602
Phone: 312-541-5000
Fax: 312-541-8038

General Instrument is a worldwide supplier of broadband communications systems and equipment and power semiconductor products.

	1994 Sales		1994 Operating Income	
	$ mil.	% total	$ mil.	% of total
US	1,822	90	301	88
Europe	152	7	17	5
Far East	33	2	20	6
Other regions	29	1	4	1
Total	**2,036**	**100**	**342**	**100**

WHAT

	1994 Sales	
	$ mil.	% of total
Broadband communications	1,720	84
Power semiconductor	316	16
Total	**2,036**	**100**

	1994 Sales
	% of total
Analog terrestrial products	39
Analog & digital satellite products	23
Coaxial cable	22
Power semiconductor products	16
Total	**100**

Operations

Broadband Communications
CommScope (coaxial cable for cable TV applications)
GI Communications
 Analog and digital terrestrial products (allow cable TV operators to control subscribers' cable service from a central computer and to increase channel capacity, upgrade signal quality, and improve security)
 Analog and digital satellite products (scrambling and descrambling products for satellite-based distribution of television programming)

Power Semiconductors
Power Semiconductor Division (power rectifying and transient voltage suppressing components for the automotive, electronics, and telecommunications industries)

KEY COMPETITORS

ADC Telecommunications
American Power Conversion
Antec
Belden
Cable Design Technologies

Motorola
Oak Industries
Scientific-Atlanta
SGS-Thomson
Siemens
Stanford Telecommunications

HOW MUCH

	Annual Growth	1985	1986	1987	1988	1989	1990	1991	1992	1993	1994
Sales ($ mil.)	8.1%	—	—	—	—	1,377	916	929	1,075	1,393	2,036
Net income ($ mil.)	20.3%	—	—	—	—	99	(237)	(111)	(53)	90	248
Income as % of sales	—	—	—	—	—	7.2%	—	—	—	6.5%	12.2%
Earnings per share ($)	—	—	—	—	—	—	(3.43)	(1.52)	(0.54)	0.74	2.01
Stock price – high ($)	—	—	—	—	—	—	—	—	12.94	30.13	34.63
Stock price – low ($)	—	—	—	—	—	—	—	—	5.75	11.63	21.25
Stock price – close ($)	53.4%	—	—	—	—	—	—	—	12.75	28.25	30.00
P/E – high	—	—	—	—	—	—	—	—	—	41	17
P/E – low	—	—	—	—	—	—	—	—	—	16	11
Dividends per share ($)	—	—	—	—	—	—	—	—	0.00	0.00	0.00
Book value per share ($)	49.6%	—	—	—	—	—	—	—	2.48	3.24	5.54
Employees	15.6%	—	—	—	—	—	—	—	9,200	10,100	12,300

1994 Year-end:
Debt ratio: 54.1%
Return on equity: 46.6%
Cash (mil.): $5
Current ratio: 1.50
Long-term debt (mil.): $795
No. of shares (mil.): 122
Dividends
 Yield: —
 Payout: —
Market value (mil.): $3,667

Stock Price History High/Low 1992–94

HARTMARX CORPORATION

OVERVIEW

After almost losing its shirt in the early 1990s, Chicago-based Hartmarx has rolled up its sleeves and exited the retail business. With a strong hand at the controls, Hartmarx, the US's #1 maker of men's suits, sportscoats, and slacks, has pulled itself into the black after hemorrhaging cash for 3 consecutive years. The maker of such men's and women's clothing brands as Pierre Cardin, Austin Reed, and Hickey-Freeman has suffered from the trend toward casual workplace attire.

Led by Elbert Hand (CEO since 1992), the company has restructured to focus its operations on its strongest markets (men's apparel represented 79% of 1994 sales). Hartmarx sold off its Specialty Stores retail unit, discontinued the Country Miss retail and manufacturing

operations, and closed 54 Kuppenheimer men's retail units (and their supplying factories); in July 1995 Hartmarx sold its Kuppenheimer Men's Clothiers to Kupp Acquisition for $12 million.

In 1994 it introduced new lines of men's golfwear and men's sportswear (Jack Nicklaus Signature) and launched a new manufacturing and marketing division, Novapparel. Dillard Department Stores was Hartmarx's largest customer in 1994, accounting for 13% of total sales. Saudi Arabian–owned Traco International holds 21% of the company.

Although Hartmarx is looking for new marketing opportunities, tailored suits accounted for 45% of 1994 sales. Losses in the women's apparel division widened to $4 million in 1994.

WHEN

Harry Hart, 21, and his brother Max, 18, of Chicago, opened a men's clothing store, Harry Hart and Brother, in 1872. In 1887, after Marcus Marx and Joseph Schaffner joined the company, the enterprise was renamed Hart Schaffner & Marx.

The young clothiers contracted with independent tailors to produce suits for their new store. Recognizing the potential of the wholesale garment industry, they began selling to other merchants. In 1897 Hart Schaffner & Marx launched a national ad campaign in leading magazines and newspapers.

In 1910 a walkout by 17 young women protesting low wages and poor working conditions in one of the company's 48 tailoring shops sparked a citywide garment workers' strike. Schaffner and Harry Hart negotiated a settlement (not honored by the other major Chicago companies) in January 1911, and their employees returned to work.

In 1935 Hart Schaffner & Marx began adding to its domain with the purchase of Wallach Brothers, a New York men's clothing chain. Other purchases, including Hastings (a California clothier, 1952), Hanny's (Arizona, 1962), Hickey-Freeman (with stores in Chicago, New York, and Detroit; 1964), and Field Brothers (New York, 1968), led to a 1970 antitrust decree ordering Hart Schaffner & Marx to sell 30 of its 238 men's clothing stores and, for 10 years, refrain from further purchases without court approval. Among the company's subsequent approved purchases was 49% of Roberts SA, a Mexican clothing-store chain (sold in 1990). In 1982 it bought Kuppenheimer's, founded in 1876.

In 1983 Hart Schaffner & Marx became Hartmarx Corporation. A costly 1986 reorganization of the retail stores to automate, centralize buying, and consolidate credit, accounting, and distribution resulted in the loss of 800 jobs. Earnings that year fell 42%. Later acquisitions included the Raleigh clothing stores (Washington, DC; 1988) and Biltwell, a Missouri-based clothing manufacturer, in 1989 from ailing Interco.

After a brief recovery in 1987 and 1988, earnings declined to $17 million in 1989, largely because of a dramatic increase in wool prices. Hartmarx undertook further restructuring (costing $51 million) in 1990 to close unprofitable stores and other operations, reorganize its women's lines into a new marketing concept under the name Barrie Pace, and experiment with placing Kuppenheimer stores in Sears stores.

Board unhappiness with the slow pace of the downsizing of Hartmarx's retail operation led CEO Harvey Weinberg to resign in July 1992. The ultimate selling, closing, and liquidation of the company's stores put 7,000 employees out of work that year. The company also liquidated its Old Mill stores and started closing nonperforming Kuppenheimer units.

In 1994 Hartmarx expanded its marketing operations, agreeing to market shirts and ties with the Hickey-Freeman label, the company's top brand, under an exclusive licensing arrangement with Nordstrom stores.

In 1995 Hartmarx announced plans to acquire a plant in Mexico, its first manufacturing location outside the US, as part of a plan to reduce manufacturing costs.

NYSE symbol: HMX
Fiscal year ends: November 30

WHO

Chairman and CEO: Elbert O. Hand, age 55,
$756,974 pay
President and COO: Homi B. Patel, age 45,
$556,239 pay
EVP and CFO: Glenn R. Morgan, age 47, $205,390 pay
(prior to promotion)
EVP and General Counsel: Mary D. Allen, age 49
VP Marketing Services: Frank A. Brenner, age 66,
$180,295 pay
VP Long-term Planning and Investor Realtions: James
E. Condon
VP Compensation and Benefits: Linda J. Valentine
Manager, Employee Relations: Lorraine Dickson
Auditors: Price Waterhouse LLP

WHERE

HQ: 101 N. Wacker Dr., Chicago, IL 60606
Phone: 312-372-6300
Fax: 312-444-2710

Hartmarx operates manufacturing and distribution
facilities in 10 states across the US. The company also
licenses its products for sale in 17 foreign countries.

WHAT

	1994 Sales		1994 Pretax Income	
	$ mil.	% of total	$ mil.	% of total
Men's apparel	570	79	46	96
Kuppenheimer	96	13	2	4
Women's apparel	52	7	(4)	—
Licensing and other	7	1	(12)	—
Total	**725**	**100**	**32**	**100**

1994 Product Mix	
	% of total
Suits	45
Slacks	19
Sportscoats	16
Sportwear	12
Women's apparel	8
Total	**100**

Menswear
Allyn St. George
Austin Reed
Bobby Jones
Confezióni Risèrva
Fumagalli's
Gieves & Hawkes
Hart Schaffner & Marx
Henry Grethel
Hickey-Freeman
J. G. Hook
John Alexander
Karl Lagerfeld
KM by Krizia
Nicklaus
Nino Cerruti
Pierre Cardin
Racquet Club
   Wimbledon

Sansabelt
Society Brand, Ltd.
Tommy Hilfiger

Womenswear
Austin Reed
Barrie Pace
KM by Krizia
Nicklaus for Women
Suburbans

Trademark Licensing
Fumagalli's
Gieves & Hawkes
Henry Grethel
Karl Lagerfeld
KM by Krizia
Nino Cerruti
Pierre Cardin

KEY COMPETITORS

Anne Klein
AnnTaylor
Benetton
Burlington Industries
Donna Karan
Drew Pearson
Esprit
Farah
Haggar
Koret
Lands' End
Levi Strauss

Liz Claiborne
Nautica Enterprises
Oak Hill Sportswear
Oxford Industries
Phillips-Van Heusen
Polo/Ralph Lauren
Russell Corp.
Supreme
   International
VF Corp.
Warnaco Group

HOW MUCH

	Annual Growth	1985	1986	1987	1988	1989	1990	1991	1992	1993	1994
Sales ($ mil.)	(4.6%)	1,110	1,063	1,080	1,174	1,297	1,296	1,226	1,064	738	725
Net income ($ mil.)	(10.4%)	43	25	41	38	17	(62)	(38)	(220)	6	16
Income as % of sales	—	3.8%	2.3%	3.8%	3.2%	1.3%	—	—	—	0.8%	2.2%
Earnings per share ($)	(13.3%)	2.25	1.20	2.01	2.03	0.89	(3.11)	(1.74)	(8.59)	0.20	0.50
Stock price – high ($)	—	26.44	32.00	34.75	29.75	28.13	19.88	13.25	8.63	8.25	7.38
Stock price – low ($)	—	18.69	23.50	18.25	20.75	18.75	5.50	6.88	3.00	5.13	5.00
Stock price – close ($)	(15.3%)	26.34	27.00	23.50	24.25	19.75	8.75	8.00	6.38	7.00	5.88
P/E – high	—	12	27	17	15	32	—	—	—	41	15
P/E – low	—	8	20	9	10	21	—	—	—	26	10
Dividends per share ($)	(100.0%)	0.85	0.90	0.98	1.08	1.18	0.90	0.60	0.00	0.00	0.00
Book value per share ($)	(15.3%)	17.61	17.59	18.26	19.21	18.37	14.92	11.32	2.73	3.41	3.95
Employees	(8.7%)	25,000	22,000	22,000	22,500	23,500	22,000	20,000	13,000	11,200	11,000

1994 Year-end:
Debt ratio: 59.4%
Return on equity: 13.6%
Cash (mil.): $3
Current ratio: 3.23
Long-term debt (mil.): $167
No. of shares (mil.): 32
Dividends
   Yield: —
   Payout: —
Market value (mil.): $191

**Stock Price History
High/Low 1985–94**

HELENE CURTIS INDUSTRIES, INC.

OVERVIEW

Helene Curtis products make people look and feel (and even smell) better. The Chicago-based personal care products manufacturer ranks 4th in US sales (after Procter & Gamble, Unilever, and Colgate-Palmolive). It primarily makes and markets antiperspirants and deodorants, shampoos and conditioners, and body lotions. Its Suave shampoo line is #1 in the country. Other leading brands include Degree (antiperspirant/deodorant), Finesse (conditioners and shampoos), Salon Selectives (conditioners and shampoos; the 3rd largest brand in the US), and Vibrance (conditioners and shampoos).

The company markets its products to consumers through supermarkets, mass merchandisers, and drugstores. It also makes and markets professional hair care products for use and resale by cosmetologists. The

company's Quantum brand is the leading permanent wave brand sold to licensed US cosmetologists.

Helene Curtis sells its products in over 100 countries and has wholly owned subsidiaries in Australia, Canada, Italy, Japan, New Zealand, Sweden, and the UK. The company has put an emphasis on international sales. Helene Curtis is the #2 personal care manufacturer in New Zealand and Scandinavia. In 1995 its sales outside the US accounted for 36% of total revenues.

In 1994 Helene Curtis moved into the fast-growing baby care products market, launching the Suave Baby Care line of baby oil, lotion, powders, shampoos, and wipes.

Octogenarian cofounder Gerald Gidwitz is the firm's chairman. His elder brother Joseph is VC, and son Ronald is president and CEO.

WHEN

The company was founded in 1927 by Gerald Gidwitz and Louis Stein as the National Mineral Company. The firm originally made just one product, the Peach Bloom Facial Mask — a facial mud pack made of special clay mined in Arkansas — which was sold to beauty salons around the country.

As hair fashions shifted from the straight hair of the 1920s to the wavy hair of the 1930s, Gidwitz moved the company into hair care, introducing affordable permanent wave products for use in hair salons. In another innovation, the company introduced Lanolin Creme Shampoo, one of the first shampoos to use a detergent-based formula. Before this, most people washed their hair with plain soap. The popularity of the shampoo led the company to introduce a 2nd line, Suave Hairdressing, a hair tonic, in 1938.

During WWII the company (which changed its name to National Industries), while maintaining its hair care lines, also made aircraft gun turrets, radar equipment, and other materiel for the Allied war effort. The company introduced a nontoxic chemical perm solution to be used with wooden wrapping rods. By the late 1940s this cold wave method had become the most popular permanent wave technology.

Moving back to its hair care focus after WWII, the company changed its name to the more consumer-friendly Helene Curtis, after Louis Stein's wife and son. It also moved into retail sales and national advertising (with ads appearing on TV shows).

In 1950 the company introduced one of the first hair sprays with its aerosol product Spray Net. Other successful introductions included the deodorant Stopette and the dandruff shampoo Enden. When the company went public in 1956, its products were being manufactured in 25 countries.

The company expanded its range of hair care products in the 1960s with the introduction of hair conditioning products Quik Care and Sure Thing.

During the 1970s Helene Curtis introduced the first compact permanent wave machine and Everynight, a shampoo aimed at teens. In 1977 Suave became the highest-selling shampoo in the US. By 1980 the company had distributors in 110 countries.

In the 1980s Helene Curtis entered the skin care lotion market, and in 1982 it launched Finesse conditioner, which was based on a time-activated formula. The product proved so successful that the company expanded the line to include shampoos and hair sprays. Ronald Gidwitz took over as CEO in 1985.

In the early 1990s the company introduced Degree, a heat-activated antiperspirant/deodorant, capturing a notable share of the market. In 1994 the company expanded into the baby care market with the launch of Suave Baby Care products. Japan, where it had sold goods since the 1950s, accounted for more than 20% of annual sales by the mid-1990s.

In 1995 Helene Curtis moved its R&D facilities to Rolling Meadows, Illinois, to allow its main manufacturing facility to expand.

NYSE symbol: HC
Fiscal year ends: Last day in February

WHO

Chairman: Gerald S. Gidwitz, age 88
VC: Joseph L. Gidwitz, age 90
President and CEO: Ronald J. Gidwitz, age 50,
$1,071,500 pay
EVP and COO: Michael Goldman, age 58, $640,200 pay
EVP; President, Helene Curtis North America: Gilbert
P. Smith, age 58, $587,600 pay
SVP; President, Helene Curtis U.S.A.: Eugene Zeffren,
age 53, $396,400 pay
SVP: Charles G. Cooper, age 67
**SVP Human Resources; President, Helene Curtis
International:** Robert K. Niles, age 50
VP and CFO: Lawrence A. Gyenes, age 44
VP and Corporate Controller: Mary J. Oyer, age 46
VP and Chief Information Officer: Thomas J. Gildea,
age 51
VP, Secretary, and General Counsel: Roy A. Wentz,
age 45
VP: V. James Marino, age 45
VP: Robert Sack, age 58
Auditors: Coopers & Lybrand L.L.P.

WHERE

HQ: 325 N. Wells St., Chicago, IL 60610
Phone: 312-661-0222
Fax: 312-836-0125

Helene Curtis sells its products under license in over
100 countries.

	1995 Sales		1995 Operating Income	
	$ mil.	% of total	$ mil.	% of total
US	809	64	60	83
Japan	277	22	12	17
Other countries	180	14	(6)	—
Total	**1,266**	**100**	**66**	**100**

WHAT

Selected Products
Antiperspirants
Baby oil
Baby wipes
Conditioners and shampoos
Deodorants
Facial care products
Hair styling products
Lotions
Powders

Selected Brands
Degree (antiperspirant/deodorant)
Finesse (conditioners and shampoos)
ISO (hair styling products)
Quantum (hair styling products)
Salon Selectives (conditioners and shampoos)
Suave (conditioners and shampoos)
Suave Baby Care (baby oil, lotion, powders, shampoos,
and wipes)
Suave Skin Therapy (body lotion)
Vibrance (conditioners and shampoos)

Selected Subsidiaries
Helene Curtis Australia Pty. Ltd.
Helene Curtis (Europa) BV (Holland)
Helene Curtis, Inc.
Helene Curtis International Italia, S.p.A
Helene Curtis Japan, Inc.
Helene Curtis, Ltd./LTEE (Canada)
Helene Curtis New Zealand

KEY COMPETITORS

Alberto-Culver	Dep	MacAndrews
Avon	Estée Lauder	& Forbes
Body Shop	Gillette	Mary Kay
Bristol-Myers	Helen of Troy	Perrigo
Squibb	Johnson & Johnson	Procter &
Chattem	Johnson Publishing	Gamble
Colgate-Palmolive	Kimberly Clark	Shiseido
Del Labs	L'Oreal	Unilever

HOW MUCH

	Annual Growth	1986	1987	1988	1989	1990	1991	1992	1993	1994	1995
Sales ($ mil.)	15.0%	361	400	489	629	691	867	1,020	1,168	1,187	1,266
Net income ($ mil.)	6.4%	11	10	11	14	17	2	19	22	14	19
Income as % of sales	—	3.0%	2.6%	2.2%	2.3%	2.4%	0.2%	1.9%	1.9%	1.2%	1.5%
Earnings per share ($)	3.3%	1.51	1.40	1.47	1.72	1.81	0.18	2.04	2.33	1.51	2.02
Stock price – high ($)[1]	—	12.69	19.13	20.63	21.25	35.13	28.00	43.75	45.50	47.38	36.38
Stock price – low ($)[1]	—	6.63	10.00	10.38	12.00	19.31	17.50	23.88	30.25	24.88	22.75
Stock price – close ($)[1]	12.5%	11.56	14.44	12.75	19.50	24.88	25.63	40.00	41.88	29.00	33.38
P/E – high	—	8	14	14	12	19	156	21	20	31	18
P/E – low	—	4	7	7	7	11	97	12	13	17	11
Dividends per share ($)	—	0.00	0.08	0.15	0.23	0.18	0.20	0.20	0.24	0.24	0.24
Book value per share ($)	11.3%	8.59	9.90	11.28	13.75	15.22	15.36	17.02	18.95	20.18	22.54
Employees	3.9%	2,400	2,700	2,900	2,900	3,100	3,000	3,500	3,500	3,500	3,400

1995 Year-end:
Debt ratio: 39.5%
Return on equity: 9.1%
Cash (mil.): $5
Current ratio: 1.60
Long-term debt (mil.): $137
No. of shares (mil.): 10
Dividends
  Yield: 0.7%
  Payout: 11.9%
Market value (mil.): $326

**Stock Price History[1]
High/Low 1986–95**

[1] Stock prices are for the prior calendar year.

HOUSEHOLD INTERNATIONAL, INC.

OVERVIEW

Household International is cleaning house, sweeping out more of the operations it added in the 1980s in order to return to its original business: consumer loans (and their modern manifestation, credit cards). Prospect Heights, Illinois–based Household's brokerage operations and first mortgage origination business have been left at the curb, along with its chronically unproductive Australian operations and most of its branch banks outside the Midwest. This is a major change of emphasis from 2 years ago, when it aimed to be a national banking powerhouse.

In addition to making secured (home equity) and unsecured consumer loans through its primary subsidiary, Household Finance, the company is one of the top issuers of credit cards in the US. Its credit card business in recent years has blossomed on the strength of private label and affinity cards (like the GM Card, which allows users to earn points toward buying a car). The company also offers life and credit insurance, commercial vehicle and equipment leasing, and commercial loans (a new joint venture with Dominion Resources will provide loans to middle-market companies).

In 1994 Household's UK business improved greatly, but the company decided to discontinue its Australian operations and to consolidate many of its Canadian functions into US operations.

WHEN

Household Finance was founded in Minneapolis in 1878, when Frank Mackey opened a finance company to loan cash to workers between paychecks. In 1894, when the company had 14 offices throughout the Midwest, Mackey moved the headquarters to Chicago (they are now located in a suburb). The company introduced installment payments on loans in 1905.

In 1925 more than 30 such companies across the country, controlled by Mackey and operating under a variety of names, consolidated as Household Finance Corporation (HFC), a public company. That year the company paid its first quarterly dividend (it has never missed a dividend since).

In 1930 HFC set up the Money Management Institute to teach people how to handle credit. One pamphlet showed a family of 5 how to live on $150 a month. In 1931 HFC's banks froze the company's credit, stopping lending, but the freeze was lifted in 1932 and the company weathered the Depression. It made its first non-US purchase in 1933, buying Central Finance, a Canadian company. After WWII the unleashed US demand for goods propelled HFC into the suburbs, and by 1960 it had 1,000 branch offices and was advertising on television.

In the conglomerate-crazed 1960s, HFC, viewing itself broadly as a retailer of money, began to diversify into other kinds of retailing: hardware stores (Coast-to-Coast, 1961), variety chains (Ben Franklin and TG&Y, 1965), vacuum jugs (King-Seeley Thermos, 1968), and car rentals (National, 1969). HFC also bought a savings and loan company, 4 banks, and Alexander Hamilton Life (1977). This diversification strategy benefited the company in the 1970s, when rising inflation rates made Household's traditional short-term, fixed-rate loans less profitable.

The company adopted Household International as its corporate name in 1981. In 1984 chairman Donald Clark thwarted an $8 billion takeover by dissident shareholders by adopting a "poison pill" that, after a takeover, would have let stockholders buy stock in the resulting company for half price. In the mid-1980s Clark refocused the company on financial services, particularly consumer banking, and began divesting its noncore operations, jettisoning retailing, transportation, and manufacturing, including the 1989 spinoff of 3 companies, Eljer, Scotsman, and Schwitzer. Between 1985 and 1988 it bought several finance companies and banks, including BGC Finance in Australia.

In 1993 Household joined a consortium led by Goldman, Sachs that bought ITT's unsecured consumer loan portfolio, which HFC services.

In addition to the divestiture of several businesses, the 1994–95 restructuring included the streamlining of Household's back-office operations, which consolidated its processing operations along business lines. At the same time the company moved most Canadian processing operations to the US and servicing for all HFC-originated loans was moved to a single site in Illinois, while billing, payment, and check processing operations were moved to 4 regional processing centers.

William Aldinger, formerly of Wells Fargo, became president and CEO in 1994, taking over executive duties from Chairman Clark.

NYSE symbol: HI
Fiscal year ends: December 31

WHO

Chairman: Donald C. Clark, age 63, $1,877,119 pay
President and CEO: William F. Aldinger, age 47,
$685,770 pay
**Group Executive, US BankCard and Household Retail
Services:** Joseph W. Saunders, age 49, $778,805 pay
Group Executive, US Consumer Finance and Canada:
Robert F. Elliott, age 54, $644,371 pay
**Group Executive, Household Bank, f.s.b. and HFC
Bank (UK):** Lawrence N. Bangs, age 58
Chairman, Alexander Hamilton Life Insurance: Richard
H. Headlee, age 64
SVP and CFO: David A. Schoenholz, age 43
VP and General Counsel: Kenneth H. Robin, age 48
VP and Chief Information Officer: David B. Barany,
age 51
VP Corporate Communications: Michael H. Morgan,
age 40
VP Human Resources: Colin P. Kelly, age 52
Auditors: Arthur Andersen & Co, SC

WHERE

HQ: 2700 Sanders Rd., Prospect Heights, IL 60070
Phone: 847-564-5000
Fax: 847-205-7452

Household International operates 759 offices in Canada,
the UK, and the US.

	1994 Sales		1994 Operating Income	
	$ mil.	% of total	$ mil.	% of total
US	3,969	86	512	94
Canada	239	5	(17)	—
UK	322	7	31	6
Australia	73	2	2	0
Total	**4,603**	**100**	**528**	**100**

WHAT

	1994 Assets	
	$ mil.	% of total
Cash & equivalents	541	2
Government securities	431	1
Mortgage-backed securities	2,892	8
Corporate bonds	4,502	13
Other securities	819	2
Credit receivables	20,778	61
Mortgage & policy loans	235	1
Other	4,140	12
Total	**34,338**	**100**

	1994 Sales		1994 Operating Income	
	$ mil.	% of total	$ mil.	% of total
Finance & banking	4,012	87	448	85
Individual life insurance	591	13	80	15
Total	**4,603**	**100**	**528**	**100**

Selected Subsidiaries
Alexander Hamilton Life Insurance Co. of America
Household Bank, f.s.b. (full-service consumer banking)
Household Bank, NA (MasterCard and VISA accounts)
Household Commercial Financial Services, Inc.
Household Finance Corp. (consumer credit, home
equity loans)
Household Retail Services, Inc. (revolving credit
administration for retailers)

KEY COMPETITORS

ADVANTA	Countrywide	General Electric
American Express	Credit	Great Western
AT&T Corp.	Dean Witter,	MBNA
BankAmerica	Discover	Prudential
Beneficial	Equifax	Transamerica
Chase Manhattan	First Chicago	Wells Fargo
Citicorp	First USA	
CoreStates Financial	Ford	

HOW MUCH

	Annual Growth	1985	1986	1987	1988	1989	1990	1991	1992	1993	1994
Sales ($ mil.)	3.5%	3,383	2,741	3,441	2,637	3,490	4,320	4,594	4,181	4,455	4,603
Net income ($ mil.)	9.1%	168	248	222	310	240	235	150	191	299	368
Income as % of sales	—	5.0%	9.0%	6.5%	11.8%	6.9%	5.4%	3.3%	4.6%	6.7%	8.0%
Earnings per share ($)	10.6%	1.41	2.57	2.66	3.21	3.07	2.88	1.55	1.93	2.85	3.50
Stock price – high ($)	—	21.69	26.25	31.25	30.50	32.75	26.63	31.50	30.25	40.44	39.75
Stock price – low ($)	—	14.19	19.56	16.25	19.75	23.19	9.69	13.75	20.75	26.94	28.50
Stock price – close ($)	6.5%	21.13	23.88	19.94	28.44	25.94	16.44	25.63	29.63	32.63	37.13
P/E – high	—	15	10	12	10	11	9	20	16	14	11
P/E – low	—	10	8	6	6	8	3	9	11	10	8
Dividends per share ($)	3.6%	0.89	0.91	0.95	1.02	1.07	1.08	1.11	1.14	1.17	1.22
Book value per share ($)	4.1%	15.85	14.28	14.47	17.03	16.91	19.02	19.17	19.41	21.92	22.78
Employees	(6.5%)	28,300	21,419	22,029	10,000	14,500	14,500	14,500	13,397	16,900	15,500

1994 Year-end:
Debt ratio: 91.3%
Return on equity: 17.2%
Cash (mil.): $541
Long-term debt (mil.): $10,274
No. of shares (mil.): 97
Dividends
  Yield: 3.3%
  Payout: 34.9%
Market value (mil.): $3,587
Assets (mil.) $34,338

**Stock Price History
High/Low 1985–94**

HYATT CORPORATION

OVERVIEW

Chicago-based Hyatt Corporation is one of the largest hotel operators in the US. Led by CEO Jay Pritzker, the company is a subsidiary of H Group Holding, which is owned by the Pritzker family, one of the US's wealthiest families (with a net worth estimated at $4.4 billion by *Forbes*). Through Hyatt Hotels Corp. the company manages 104 hotels in North America and the Caribbean. Hyatt International runs more than 60 hotels overseas.

Long known for superlative service, Hyatt introduced many amenities (free shampoo, restricted-access floors) that have been copied by other hotels. However, by the early 1990s many of the company's contractees began to complain that Hyatt was concentrating more on adding luxuries than on generating profits. The company began a major restructuring focused on cutting costs. Some of the company's amenities were trimmed. For example, at the Chicago Hyatt Regency if guests want their beds turned down at night, they now have to ask. The change has saved the hotel more than $200,000 a year. The company has also reduced middle management and centralized much of its purchasing. Overall it has saved $100 million annually.

The company is now focusing on expansion. It has begun selectively franchising the Hyatt name, is entering the time-share business, and has some 30 hotel projects in development.

WHEN

In 1881 Nicholas Pritzker left Kiev for Chicago, where he began his progeny's ascent to the ranks of America's wealthiest families.

Nicholas's son A. N. left the family law practice in the 1930s and began investing in a variety of businesses. He turned a 1942 investment (Cory Corporation) worth $25,000 into $23 million by 1967.

After WWII, A. N.'s son Jay followed in his father's wheeling-and-dealing footsteps. In 1953, with the help of his father's banking connections, Jay purchased Colson Company and recruited his brother Bob, an industrial engineer, to restructure a company that made tricycles and navy rockets. By 1990 Jay and Bob had added 60 industrial companies, with annual sales exceeding $3 billion, to the entity they called the Marmon Group.

In 1957 Jay bought a hotel called Hyatt House, located near the Los Angeles airport, from Hyatt von Dehn. Jay had added 5 locations by 1961 and brought his gregarious youngest brother, Donald, to California to manage the hotel company.

In 1967 the Pritzkers took the company public, but the move that opened new vistas for the hotel chain was the purchase of an 800-room hotel in Atlanta that both Hilton and Marriott had turned down. John Portman's design, incorporating a 21-story atrium, a large fountain, and a revolving rooftop restaurant, became a Hyatt trademark.

The Pritzkers formed Hyatt International in 1969 to operate hotels overseas, and the company grew rapidly during the 1970s in the US and abroad. Donald Pritzker died in 1972, and his successor ran up some questionable expenses. This prompted the family to move the corporate offices to Chicago in 1977 and to take the company private in 1979. In 1980 Hyatt built its first Park Hyatt, a European-style super-luxury hotel, near the Water Tower in Chicago. The company opened its next Park Hyatt, in Washington, DC, in 1986.

Much of Hyatt's growth in the 1970s came from contracts to manage, under the Hyatt banner, hotels built by other investors. In the 1980s Hyatt's cut on those contracts shrank, and it launched its own hotel and resort developments under Nick Pritzker, a cousin to Jay and Bob. In 1988, with US and Japanese partners, it built the $360 million Hyatt Regency Waikoloa on Hawaii's Big Island. At the time the resort was, according to *FORTUNE*, the most expensive hotel ever built.

Through Hyatt subsidiaries the Pritzkers bought bedraggled Braniff Airlines in 1983 as it emerged from bankruptcy. After a failed 1987 attempt to merge the airline with Pan Am, the Pritzkers sold Braniff in 1988.

In 1989 Hyatt launched Classic Residence by Hyatt, a group of upscale retirement communities. In 1993 Hyatt sold the majority of its 85% interest in Ticketmaster to Paul Allen, cofounder of Microsoft. That same year Donald Trump sued Hyatt, alleging that the hotelier was trying to squeeze him out of his 50% stake in New York City's Grand Hyatt. In 1994 Hyatt sued Trump, claiming that "The Donald" was trying to lessen his financial woes by blocking renovations on the Grand Hyatt and that he had turned over his share of the hotel to 2 of his creditors.

In 1995 Hyatt signed deals to manage Makkah Hyatt Regency in Saudi Arabia and the Hyatt Regency Baku in Azerbaijan.

Private company
Fiscal year ends: January 31

WHO

Chairman and CEO: Jay A. Pritzker, age 72
President: Thomas V. Pritzker, age 44
SVP and CFO: Ken Posner
SVP Planning and Human Resources: Larry Deans
SVP Sales and Marketing: Jim Evans
Chairman, Hyatt Hotels Corp.: Darryl Hartley-Leonard
President, Hyatt Hotels Corp.: Doug Geoga, age 39
President, Classic Residence: Penny S. Pritzker
President, Marmon Group: Robert Pritzker, age 68
EVP, Hyatt Hotels Corp.: Albert J. Kelly
General Counsel: Michael Evanoff
Auditors: KPMG Peat Marwick LLP

WHERE

HQ: 200 W. Madison, Chicago, IL 60606
Phone: 312-750-1234
Fax: 312-750-8550
Reservations: 800-233-1234

Through its domestic division, Hyatt Corporation operates hotels across the US. Hyatt's international division is responsible for the company's network of foreign-based hotels, found worldwide.

Selected Hotels
Bali Hyatt
Grand Hyatt Hong Kong
Grand Hyatt New York
Grand Hyatt San Francisco
Hyatt Regency Atlanta
Hyatt Regency Austin
Hyatt Regency Baku
Hyatt Regency Belgrade
Hyatt Regency Buenos Aires
Hyatt Regency Casablanca
Hyatt Regency Chicago
Hyatt Regency Dubai
Hyatt Regency Istanbul
Hyatt Regency Jerusalem
Haytt Regency Paris
Hyatt Regency Riyadh
Makkah Hyatt Regency
Park Hyatt Tokyo
UN Plaza-Park Hyatt Hotel

WHAT

Subsidiaries
Hyatt Hotels Corp.
  Classic Residence by Hyatt (upscale retirement communities)
  Grand Hyatt
  Hyatt
  Hyatt Hotels International
  Hyatt Regency
  Park Hyatt
Spectacor Management Group (50%, arena management)

Related Pritzker Businesses
American Medical International (hospitals)
Conwood Co. (tobacco products)
Dalfort Corp. (aircraft maintenance)
Hawthorn Suites (lodging)
Itel Corp. (minority interest, railroad cars)
Marmon Group (over 60 industrial companies)
Penguin Realty Associates LP
Royal Caribbean Cruises Ltd. (50%, cruise line)
Tampa Bay Hockey Group (applicant for National Hockey League franchise)
Ticketmaster Corp. (15%, ticket sales)

KEY COMPETITORS

Accor	HFS
American Express	Hilton
Bally	ITT Corp.
Bass	Loews
Canadian Pacific	Marriott International
Carlson	Nestlé
Carnival Corp.	Ogden
Delaware North	Promus
Dial	Rank
Dole	Ritz-Carlton
Doubletree	Trump Organization
Forte	Walt Disney
Four Seasons	Westin Hotel
Helmsley	Wyndham Hotels

HOW MUCH

	Annual Growth	1986	1987	1988	1989	1990	1991	1992	1993	1994	1995
Estimated sales ($ mil.)	—	2,000	2,300	2,330	2,400	3,101	2,915	1,350[1]	1,460[1]	950[1]	1,240[1]
Employees	5.1%	30,000	30,000	40,000	40,000	55,195	49,820	51,275	52,275	52,275	47,000

Estimated Sales
($ mil.)
1986–95

HYATT
HOTELS & RESORTS

3,500
3,000
2,500
2,000
1,500
1,000
500
0

[1] Does not include revenue for franchised or managed hotels

IGA, INC.

OVERVIEW

IGA (which stands for both International Grocers Alliance and Independent Grocers Alliance) is the world's largest voluntary supermarket network. The group includes about 3,600 supermarkets in 49 US states and 13 foreign countries. It is owned by its 20 wholesale distributors, including such giants as Fleming Companies and SUPERVALU. IGA members receive such services as insurance, equipment, and advertising and also have access to IGA Brand private-label foods.

Led by Baptist minister Thomas Haggai, IGA also developed a marketing program, with the slogan "Hometown Proud," centering on community service in members' market areas.

Although IGA has lost members in the US in recent years, either because of store closings or because stores failed to meet IGA's $35,000-per-week minimum sales requirement, IGA has expanded rapidly overseas in the last few years. In 1995 it became the first US grocer to enter China and Singapore.

WHEN

IGA was founded in Chicago in 1926 by a group led by accountant Frank Grimes. During the 1920s chain stores began to dominate the grocery store industry. Grimes, who did accounting for many grocery wholesalers, saw an opportunity to develop a network of independent grocers that could compete with the burgeoning chains. Grimes and 5 associates — Gene Flack, Louis Groebe, W. K. Hunter, H. V. Swenson, and William Thompson — created IGA.

Their idea was to "level the playing field" for independent grocers and chain stores by taking advantage of the lowered costs from large-volume buying and mass marketing. IGA originally acted as a purchasing agent for its wholesalers, but that duty was eventually passed to the wholesalers. The group's first member was Poughkeepsie, New York–based grocery distributor W. T. Reynolds Company and the 69 grocery stores that it serviced.

IGA focused on adding distributors and retailers, and it soon added wholesaler Fleming-Wilson (now the Fleming Companies) and Winston & Newell (now SUPERVALU). The group was able to weather the Depression by developing its brand image. In 1930 it hired Babe Ruth as a spokesman. Other spokesmen during the period included Jackie Cooper, Jack Dempsey, and Popeye (the Sailor Man). IGA also sponsored a radio program called the *IGA Home Town Hour*.

During the 1940s the company expanded and also developed new store formats for its members. In 1945 it introduced the Foodliner format, a large-store design with a minimum of 4,000 square feet. Foodliner stores were designed to exceed $7,500 in sales a week. In 1946 IGA introduced the Precision Store. The stores were 30 feet by 100 feet, and were designed so that customers had to walk past all of the other merchandise in the store to get to the frequently visited dairy and bread sections.

Frank Grimes retired as president in 1951. He was succeeded by his son, Don. Under Don Grimes the company continued to expand. He was succeeded in 1968 by Richard Jones, head of IGA member J. M. Jones Co.

In 1976 Thomas Haggai was named chairman of the company. A Baptist minister, radio commentator, and former CIA employee, Haggai was not the target of any headhunter search. He came to the attention of Frank Grimes in 1960 when he praised Christian Scientists in one of his radio broadcasts. Grimes, a Christian Scientist, asked Haggai to speak at an IGA convention and eventually asked him to join the IGA board. Haggai, who became CEO in 1986, tightened the restrictions for IGA members, weeding out many of the smaller, low-volume mom-and-pop stores that had made up much of the group's network.

Haggai also began a push for international expansion. In 1988 IGA signed a deal with Japanese food company C. Itoh to open a distribution outlet in Tokyo. That same year the company moved into Australia when Sydney's Davids Distribution joined its distribution network. In 1990 IGA entered the Papua New Guinea market, and in 1991 it expanded further in Australia, when Perth's Foodland Associated joined IGA.

In 1994 the group licensed grocery stores in Anguilla, Antigua, St. Thomas, and Trinidad. That same year it signed a deal with Hong Kong–based distributor Pearl River Distribution to move IGA's operations into China. Also in 1994 the group launched its first line of private-label products for the ethnic food market, introducing several Mexican food products, including tortilla chips, salsa, refried beans, and frozen burritos.

In 1995 IGA signed a partnership with Singapore's largest grocery store chain, NTUC Fairprice Co-operative Ltd., giving it 47 stores in the Singapore market.

Cooperative
Fiscal year ends: December 31

WHO

Chairman and CEO: Thomas S. Haggai
EVP and COO: Larry Willis
EVP, IGA International: Roger Romrell
VP Finance and Information Systems (HR): James Anderson
VP Insurance: Mary Castro
Director Events: Barbara Wiest
Director IGA Brand: Patrick Sylvester
Director Insurance: Dorothy Rasmussen
Director Communications: Kevin Burkum
Controller: John Baloun

WHERE

HQ: 8725 W. Higgins Rd., Chicago, IL 60631-2773
Phone: 312-693-4520
Fax: 312-693-4533

IGA has operations in 49 states (Hawaii excluded), Anguilla, Antigua, Australia, Canada, China, Indonesia, Japan, Malaysia, Papua New Guinea, Singapore, South Korea, Thailand, Trinidad, and the US Virgin Islands.

	Sales % of total
US	64
Canada	25
Other countries	11
Total	**100**

WHAT

Distributor/Owners
Bozzuto's, Inc.
C.I. Foods Systems Co., Ltd.
The Copps Corporation
Davids Ltd.
Fairway Foods of Michigan, Inc.
Fleming Companies, Inc.
Foodland Associated Ltd.
Great North Foods
Ira Higdon Grocery Co.
Merchants Distributors, Inc.
Nash Finch Co.
Pearl River Distribution Ltd.
Rand's Incorporated
Richford, Inc.
Sunkyong Distribution Ltd.
Super Food Services, Inc.
SUPERVALU INC.
T. J. Morris Co.
Tripifoods, Inc.
W. Lee Flowers & Co., Inc.

Selected Programs and Services
Advertising
Employee benefits
Equipment
Hometown Proud
Hometown Trees
IGA Brand
IGA Grocergram (in-house magazine)
Meetings/events
Public relations
Red Oval Family
Uniforms

KEY COMPETITORS

Albertson's	George Weston	Randall's
American Stores	Giant Food	Red Apple
Associated Grocers	Golub	Royal Ahold
Associated Wholesale	Grand Union	Safeway
Grocers	Great A&P	Stop & Shop
Big V Supermarkets	H. E. Butt	Supermarkets
Bruno's	Hy-Vee Stores	General
Daiei	Ito-Yokado	Waban
Delchamps	Kroger	Wal-Mart
DeMoulas	Megafood Stores	Wegmans
Super Markets	Pathmark	Whole Foods
Food Lion	Price/Costco	Winn-Dixie
Food Town	Publix	Yucaipa

HOW MUCH

	Annual Growth	1985	1986	1987	1988	1989[1]	1990[1]	1991[1]	1992	1993	1994
Sales ($ mil.)	10.0%	—	—	—	—	10,400	11,100	11,500	15,900	16,500	17,000
Employees	—	—	—	—	—	—	—	—	—	—	130,000

Sales ($ mil.)
1989–94

18,000
16,000
14,000
12,000
10,000
8,000
6,000
4,000
2,000
0

[1] Excluding Canada

ILLINOIS TOOL WORKS INC.

OVERVIEW

The name is misleading. Illinois Tool Works (ITW) covers more than Illinois and makes more than a single tool. ITW makes an extensive range of equipment for the automotive, construction, food and beverage, and general industrial markets worldwide.

ITW operates in 2 business segments (Engineered Components and Industrial Systems and Consumables), making plastic and metal fastening components and assemblies, fastening tools, gears and switches, adhesives and polymers, packing systems and consumer packaging products, paint finishing and static control systems and products, quality assurance products, and arc welding equipment.

ITW has developed its various business units as small, decentralized structures in order to be responsive to its customers.

The company, which operates 261 units in 33 countries, has seen its sales buoyed by the worldwide resurgence of the automotive and construction markets. These 2 markets accounted for 63% of 1994 revenues in the Engineered Components segment.

The Smith family (descendants of the company founder) owns 37% of ITW.

WHEN

In the early years of the 20th century, Byron Smith, founder of Chicago's Northern Trust Company, recognized that rapid industrialization was outgrowing the capacity of small shops to supply machine tools. Smith encouraged 2 of his 4 sons to launch Illinois Tool Works in 1912.

One Smith brother, Harold C., became president of ITW in 1915 and expanded its product line into automotive parts. WWI boosted company business and profits.

ITW developed the Shakeproof fastener, the first twisted-tooth lock washer, in 1923. When Harold C. died in 1936, the torch passed to his son Harold B., who decentralized the company and exhorted salesmen to learn customers' businesses so well that they could develop solutions even before the customer recognized the problems. As WWII spurred demand for the company's products, Smith plowed profits back into research.

In the 1950s the company began exploring plastics and combination metal-and-plastic fasteners as well as electrical controls and instruments, becoming a leader in miniaturization. Its major breakthrough came in the early 1960s with the development of flexible plastic collars to hold 6-packs of beverage cans. This item, under a new division called Hi-Cone, was ITW's most profitable offering.

Smith gave up his board chairmanship in 1970 and turned the CEO slot over to Silas Cathcart. Smith's son, another Harold B., was president and COO until 1981 (he remains on the board of directors and is chairman of the board's executive committee). By the early 1980s ITW had become bureaucratic and susceptible to foreign competition. It was forced to lower prices to hold on to customers. Wary after the 1982 recession, ITW hired John Nichols as CEO.

After Nichols and his staff analyzed Japanese production methods and studied profiles in business publications, ITW adopted 3 manufacturing concepts — in-lining, the 80/20 rule, and focused factories. In-lining boosts productivity by concentrating the steps of production; the 80/20 rule, recognizing that 20% of customers account for 80% of orders, takes advantage of economies of scale in large orders; and focused factories are decentralized facilities that empower and challenge workers.

Nichols broadened the company's product line and doubled ITW's size by buying 27 companies, the largest being Signode Industries for $524 million (1986). Nichols broke Signode into smaller units, speeding development of 20 new products.

ITW acquired Ransburg Corporation (electrostatic finishing systems, 1989) and the DeVilbiss division of Eagle Industries (1990), merging the 2 to form its Finishing Systems and Products division.

In 1993 ITW acquired ownership of the Miller Group, a maker of arc welding equipment and related systems, through a stock swap. That same year the firm also made a number of small acquisitions, which included Pro/Mark (high-quality, thermally applied graphics) and the Edgeboard product line (pallet packaging items) from Sonoco.

An increased growth in car building in Europe in 1994 (11%) caused revenues of the company's engineered components segment to grow dramatically. That year 76% of ITW's international revenues derived from its European operations.

Following its tradition of promoting from within, ITW in 1995 named president James Farrell as CEO, replacing John Nichols. Nichols will retire from the position of chairman in 1996.

WHO

Chairman of the Executive Committee: Harold B.
Smith, age 61
Chairman: John D. Nichols, age 64, $1,402,067 pay
VC: H. Richard Crowther, age 62, $569,398 pay
President and CEO: W. James Farrell, age 52,
$542,050 pay (prior to promotion)
EVP: Frank S. Ptak, age 51, $387,165 pay
EVP: Gunter A. Berlin, age 62
EVP: F. Ronald Seager, age 54
EVP: Russell M. Flaum, age 44
SVP and Controller: Michael W. Gregg, age 59
SVP, General Counsel, and Secretary: Stewart S.
Hudnut, age 55
SVP Human Resources: John Karpan, age 54
VP Patents and Technology: Thomas W. Buckman,
age 57
VP Research and Advanced Development: Donald L.
VanErden, age 59
Auditors: Arthur Andersen & Co, SC

WHERE

HQ: 3600 W. Lake Ave., Glenview, IL 60025-5811
Phone: 847-724-7500
Fax: 847-657-4261

The company operates 172 plants and offices in the US.
Major international offices and plants are located in
Australia, Belgium, Canada, France, Germany, Ireland,
Italy, Japan, Malaysia, Spain, Switzerland, and the UK.

	1994 Sales		1994 Operating Income	
	$ mil.	% of total	$ mil.	% of total
US	2,229	64	361	72
International	1,232	36	138	28
Total	**3,461**	**100**	**499**	**100**

WHAT

	1994 Sales		1994 Operating Income	
	$ mil.	% of total	$ mil.	% of total
Engineered Components	1,828	53	275	55
Industrial Systems & Consumables	1,633	47	224	45
Total	**3,461**	**100**	**499**	**100**

Engineered Components
Adhesives, polymers, and
application systems
Arc welding equipment
Automobile exterior door
handle assemblies
Collated nails and staples
Fastener systems
Insert molding products
Metal screws

Industrial Systems and Consumables
Electrostatic and
conventional, liquid
and powder finishing
spray guns
Hot stamp imprinters
Metallic foils
Paint curing systems
Paper packaging systems
Plastic multipack ring
carriers and application
systems
Resealable plastic bags
Strapping machinery

KEY COMPETITORS

Armstrong World
BASF
Ciba-Geigy
Cooper
Industries
DuPont
Elco Industries
Emerson
Giddings & Lewis
W. R. Grace
Hoechst
Ingersoll-Rand

Manville
3M
Morton
PPG
Premark
SPS Technologies
Stanley Works
Textron
TriMas
Tyco International
Union Carbide

HOW MUCH

	Annual Growth	1985	1986	1987	1988	1989	1990	1991	1992	1993	1994
Sales ($ mil.)	21.6%	596	961	1,698	1,930	2,173	2,544	2,640	2,812	3,159	3,461
Net income ($ mil.)	27.2%	32	80	106	140	164	182	181	192	207	278
Income as % of sales	—	5.3%	8.3%	6.3%	7.3%	7.5%	7.2%	6.8%	6.8%	6.5%	8.0%
Earnings per share ($)	25.4%	0.32	0.78	1.03	1.33	1.53	1.68	1.63	1.72	1.83	2.45
Stock price – high ($)	—	9.06	13.38	24.75	21.88	23.75	28.69	34.69	35.31	40.50	45.50
Stock price – low ($)	—	6.81	7.75	12.63	15.13	16.50	19.63	22.81	28.50	32.50	37.00
Stock price – close ($)	19.6%	8.75	12.97	16.50	17.38	22.44	24.13	31.88	32.63	39.00	43.75
P/E – high	—	28	17	24	17	16	17	21	21	22	19
P/E – low	—	21	10	12	11	11	12	14	17	18	15
Dividends per share ($)	15.0%	0.17	0.18	0.20	0.22	0.27	0.33	0.40	0.45	0.49	0.60
Book value per share ($)	14.5%	4.00	4.65	5.87	7.05	8.12	9.95	10.88	11.94	11.12	13.53
Employees	11.5%	7,300	13,700	13,600	14,200	15,700	18,400	18,700	17,800	19,000	19,500

1994 Year-end:
Debt ratio: 18.1%
Return on equity: 36.0%
Cash (mil.): $77
Current ratio: 2.01
Long-term debt (mil.): $273
No. of shares (mil.): 114.0
Dividends
Yield: 1.4%
Payout: 24.5%
Market value (mil.): $4,986

**Stock Price History
High/Low 1985–94**

IMC GLOBAL INC.

OVERVIEW

Rock on, IMC. Northbrook, Illinois–based IMC Global is one the world's largest phosphate rock and potash mining companies, with mining operations in the US and Canada. IMC upgrades phosphate rocks into phosphate chemicals (including uranium) and potash (the common salts of potassium, used worldwide in fertilizers). It is a joint venture partner (with Freeport-McMoRan Resource Partners, L.P.) in IMC-Agrico Company, the US's #1 producer and distributor of phosphate crop nutrients and IMC's top source of revenues.

The company also makes high-value crop nutrients under the Rainbow brand that are marketed primarily in the Southeast. In addition, IMC has a 25% interest in joint ventures mining for natural gas, oil, and sulfur in the Gulf of Mexico. It operates an extensive North American rail transportation system,

including the maintenance of 2,400 railroad cars, to enable efficient customer service. IMC operates a railcar repair facility in Georgia. International sales are conducted through one Canadian and 3 US export associations.

IMC-Agrico's annual concentrated phosphate production capacity is 4 million tons of phosphoric acid, which accounts for 32% of US capacity and 11% of world capacity. IMC's potash products are sold worldwide, with 33% of 1995 sales generated by foreign markets, including Australia, China, Japan, Korea, Malaysia, New Zealand, and South America.

With an eye to expanding global sales, IMC set up a World Food Production Conference in Beijing in 1995 to support its China market strategy. It is also exploring marketing opportunities for crop nutrients in India with the assistance of Indian company E.I.D. Parry.

WHEN

At the end of the 19th century, farmers in North America and Europe began to switch from traditional fertilizers to commercial chemical fertilizers (incorporating the nutrient elements of nitrogen, phosphorus, and potassium). In 1897, engineering graduate Thomas Meadows and his brother-in-law Oscar Dortch formed T.C. Meadows & Co. in Tennessee to exploit the local phosphorus-rich phosphate rock. At that time major sources for potassium (potash) and nitrogen (nitrates) were located only in such distant locations as Germany and Chile. The company, renamed United States Agricultural Corporation in 1899, began mining in Florida, which was soon to develop into the major center of the US phosphate industry.

Waldemar Schmidtmann, whose father controlled a major German potash mine, joined Meadows and Dortch in 1909 to form International Agricultural Corporation (IAC), which acquired the elder Schmidtmann's German potash holdings. Despite the import ban during WWI, IAC's German potash supplies gave it a jump over other US companies still searching for a US potash source. IAC pioneered a method of separating phosphate rocks from surrounding debris in 1929, doubling the life of rock reserves. By 1939 it had emerged as the world's largest phosphate rock producer. US potash was commercially developed by the Union Potash Company in the late 1930s, and IAC bought the firm in 1939.

In 1941 IAC changed its name to International Mineral & Chemical (IMC) and shifted

its headquarters from Atlanta to Chicago. After WWII the use of Western farming techniques (such as commercial fertilizer use) by heavily populated markets in Asia helped IMC sustain 20 years of growth. With a 1963 joint venture with Northern Natural Gas of Omaha to build an ammonia plant, IMC made a belated entry into the nitrates market. (IMC exited the ammonia business in 1992.)

The dominance of Communist-bloc fertilizer firms in markets outside the US in the 1970s and 1980s, combined with the downward slide of fertilizer prices and growing public concern about the health risks of nonorganic fertilizers, caused IMC to suffer financially. In 1986 new chairman George Kennedy diversified IMC with the purchases of Mallinckrodt (pharmaceuticals) and Pitman-Moore (animal health products).

Kennedy formed a holding company and made subsidiaries Mallinckrodt, IMC Fertilizer, and Pitman-Moore separate businesses. He then took IMC Fertilizer public in 1988 and established its headquarters in Northbrook, Illinois. The company continued to struggle in the early 1990s as plant explosions, lawsuits, and depressed prices hurt its financial performance. In 1993 it pooled its phosphate assets with those of Freeport-McMoRan Resource Partners, L.P., creating IMC-Agrico. Wendell Bueche took over as chairman and CEO that year. In 1994 the company changed its name to IMC Global.

In 1995 IMC opened an office in Hong Kong to strengthen its ties with China.

WHO

Chairman and CEO: Wendell F. Bueche, age 64,
$990,040 pay
President and COO: James D. Speir, age 55,
$540,435 pay
EVP and CFO: Robert C. Brauneker, age 57,
$430,040 pay
SVP: C. Steven Hoffman, age 46, $371,840 pay
SVP, Secretary, and General Counsel: Marschall I.
Smith, age 50, $336,680 pay
SVP Business Development: Robert M. Felsenthal,
age 43
SVP Human Resources: Allen C. Miller, age 49
VP North American Sales: Brian S. Turner, age 43
VP and Treasurer: Peter Hong, age 37
Auditors: Ernst & Young LLP

WHERE

HQ: 2100 Sanders Rd., Northbrook, IL 60062-6146
Phone: 847-272-9200
Fax: 847-205-4805

The company mines and processes potash in the US and
Canada.

| | 1995 Sales | |
	$ mil.	% of total
US	1,061	52
Far East	644	31
Canada	184	9
Latin America	122	6
Europe	27	1
Other regions	12	1
Adjustments	(126)	—
Total	**1,924**	**100**

WHAT

| | 1995 Sales | |
	$ mil.	% of total
Concentrated phosphates	1,248	65
Potash	249	13
Phosphate rock	231	12
High-value crop nutrients	115	6
Uranium	11	1
Other	70	3
Total	**1,924**	**100**

Major Products
High-value crop nutrients
Natural gas
Oil
Phosphate rock and concentrated phosphates
Potash
Sulfur
Uranium

Selected Joint Ventures
IMC-Agrico Co. (phosphate crop nutrient production,
marketing and distribution; 56.5% IMC, 43.5%
Freeport-McMoRan Resource Partners, L.P.)
Main Pass 299 sulfur mine (25%)

KEY COMPETITORS

Arcadian
Enterprise Miniere Et Chimique
First Mississippi
Kali und Salz Beteiligings
Mines de Potasse D'Alsace
Mycogen
Norsk Hydro
Nu-West Industries
Rich Coast
Tenneco
Terra Industries
Tessenderlo Chemie

HOW MUCH

	Annual Growth	1986	1987	1988	1989	1990	1991	1992	1993	1994	1995[1]
Sales ($ mil.)	9.3%	866	876	1,086	1,222	1,106	1,131	1,059	897	1,442	1,924
Net income ($ mil.)	—	(35)	27	97	137	83	96	91	(120)	(4)	121
Income as % of sales	—	—	3.1%	9.0%	11.2%	7.5%	8.5%	8.6%	—	—	6.6%
Earnings per share ($)	1.5%	—	—	1.94	2.64	1.57	1.93	2.06	(2.72)	(0.07)	2.04
Stock price – high ($)	—	—	—	22.56	24.88	19.31	30.00	34.00	23.63	24.63	27.31
Stock price – low ($)	—	—	—	11.44	15.63	15.19	16.50	18.63	12.19	15.38	20.63
Stock price – close ($)	3.0%	—	—	22.06	16.88	17.44	28.38	21.31	22.69	21.88	27.06
P/E – high	—	—	—	12	9	12	16	17	—	—	13
P/E – low	—	—	—	6	6	10	9	9	—	—	10
Dividends per share ($)	(14.3%)	—	—	0.44	0.39	0.54	0.54	0.54	0.41	0.00	0.15
Book value per share ($)	2.1%	—	—	11.19	14.54	15.56	16.12	13.96	9.76	11.12	12.92
Employees	2.5%	—	5,600	5,500	6,000	6,000	6,000	5,400	5,200	6,500	6,800

1995 Year-end:
Debt ratio: 40.7%
Return on equity: 17.1%
Cash (mil.): $196
Current ratio: 2.00
Long-term debt (mil.): $516
No. of shares (mil.): 59
Dividends
  Yield: 0.6%
  Payout: 7.4%
Market value (mil.): $1,598

Stock Price History[1]
High/Low 1988–95

[1] 1995 stock prices are through fiscal year-end (June 30).

INLAND STEEL INDUSTRIES, INC.

OVERVIEW

Inland Steel Industries is a holding company with 3 operating units that make and sell steel (Inland Steel Co.), distribute industrial materials nationally (Inland Materials Distribution Group, Inc.), and trade steel and other industrial materials internationally (Inland International, Inc.).

The US's 5th largest integrated steel manufacturer, Inland Steel Co. produced 5.5% (5.5 million tons) of all US steel in 1994. It is a leading supplier to the automotive, appliance, and office furniture industries. Inland Materials Distribution Group, the nation's largest metals distributor, operates 56 US steel service centers (Joseph T. Ryerson & Son) and metals distribution and processing centers (J.M. Tull Metals Company). As part of a strategy to widen its markets internationally, the parent company created Inland International in 1994

to sell, trade, and distribute steel products and other industrial materials worldwide.

In 1994 an upswing in the US helped Inland earn its first profit in 5 years. The company also has closed unprofitable operations, sold off noncore businesses, and pursued new markets abroad. Now Inland is aggressively seeking growth opportunities in emerging markets around the world. It created a joint venture (Ryerson de México) in 1994 with Altos Hornos de México, Mexico's biggest steel company, and another (Ryerson de China) in 1995 with China's #3 steelmaker, Baoshan Iron and Steel, to set up distribution centers. Inland also has expressed an interest in India. In early 1995 Inland formed a joint venture in Hong Kong with South African Macsteel and Canada's Federal Industries to handle exports of steel and other industrial products.

WHEN

In 1893, 8 partners purchased 40 freight cars of used steel-making machinery from bankrupt Chicago Steel and established Inland Steel in the Chicago Heights area. By 1894 Inland was selling agricultural implements (plows, etc.).

In 1901 the Lake Michigan Land Company offered 50 acres of land at Indiana Harbor to any company that would spend $1 million to develop the land by building an open-hearth steel mill. Inland raised the money and built Indiana Harbor Works and in 1906 bought the Laura Ore iron mine in Minnesota.

Inland grew steadily and then in 1916 began a rapid expansion to meet the WWI demand for steel. By 1920 Inland was producing 2% of American steel. After converting back to peacetime production, Inland began producing rails (1922).

During the Great Depression, Inland turned to the lighter steel (tinplate, sheets) used in consumer goods. In 1931 the company, under chairman L. E. Block, built facilities to make strip, sheet, and plate steel. Inland bought Joseph T. Ryerson & Son (steel warehousing) in 1935 and Wilson & Bennett Manufacturing (later renamed Inland Steel Containers) in 1939. The company introduced Ledloy (a steel/lead alloy machining metal) in 1938.

Inland again turned to wartime production in the 1940s. In 1947 the company expanded the capacity of its rolling mills and introduced its line of galvanized steel sheets (marketed under the TI-CO trade name) in 1951. In 1957 Inland built its skyscraper headquarters (one

of the first constructed using external columns and stainless steel) in Chicago.

Inland became a billion-dollar company in 1966. The 1970s brought a steel boom but when the boom ended in the 1980s, Inland suffered big losses.

In 1986 Inland reorganized as a holding company to separate its steel manufacturing operations from its more profitable steel distribution division. The company also acquired J.M. Tull Metals from Bethlehem Steel. During the late 1980s Inland increasingly turned its attention to the production of custom work (such as painted steel for appliances).

Inland entered into joint ventures with Nippon Steel in 1987 and 1989 to build and operate a cold rolling mill (I/N Tek, 60% owned) and a coating facility (I/N Kote, 50%). The I/N Tek plant began operation in 1990 and I/N Kote in late 1991. Inland's 1991 closure of a structural steel mill removed the company from structural steel manufacturing.

In May 1993 Inland and the United Steelworkers agreed on a 6-year contract with a no-layoff clause. The company also closed a 69-oven facility for producing coke (a material used as fuel for steelmaking) to comply with federal clean air requirements.

In 1994 Inland created a 3rd operating unit, Inland International, and new divisions, among them Inland International Trading and Ryerson de México, to help sell and distribute its products to a wide range of industrial customers worldwide.

NYSE symbol: IAD
Fiscal year ends: December 31

WHO

Chairman, President, and CEO: Robert J. Darnall,
age 56, $965,389 pay
EVP; President and CEO, Inland Steel Co.: Maurice S.
Nelson Jr., age 57, $772,848 pay
**SVP and CFO; President and COO, Inland
International Inc.:** Earl L. Mason, age 47,
$513,881 pay
**SVP; President and COO, Inland Materials Distribution
Group, Inc.:** Neil S. Novich, age 40
**VP Corporate Development, General Counsel, and
Secretary:** David B. Anderson, age 52, $456,333 pay
VP Finance: Jay E. Dittus, age 62
VP Information Technology: H. William Howard, age 60
VP Human Resources: Judd R. Cool, age 59
Auditors: Price Waterhouse LLP

WHERE

HQ: 30 W. Monroe St., Chicago, IL 60603
Phone: 312-346-0300
Fax: 312-899-3197

The company produces all of its raw steel at Indiana
Harbor Works in East Chicago, Indiana. It operates 54
steel service centers nationwide.

WHAT

	1994 Sales		1994 Operating Income	
	$ mil.	% of total	$ mil.	% of total
Steel mfg.	2,487	53	149	60
Materials distribution	2,198	47	98	40
Adjustments	(188)	—	2	—
Total	**4,497**	**100**	**249**	**100**

	1994 Shipments
	% of total
Automotive	32
Steel service centers	29
Steel converters/processors	12
Appliance	9
Industrial, electrical & farm machinery	8
Construction & contractors' products	2
Other	8
Total	**100**

Major Subsidiaries and Affiliates

Inland International, Inc. (international marketing,
trading, and distribution)
I.M.F. Steel International Ltd. (50%, industrial
metals and services)
Inland Industries de México SA de CV
Inland International Trading, Inc. (international
purchasing and exporting services)
Ryerson de México (50%, service centers, Mexico)

Inland Materials Distribution Group, Inc.
J.M. Tull Metals Co., Inc. (metals distribution)
Joseph T. Ryerson & Son, Inc. (steel service centers)
Ryerson Coil Processing Co.

Inland Steel Co. (steel production)
I/N Kote (50%, steel finishing)
I/N Tek (60%, steel finishing)
Inland Steel Bar Co. (high-quality steel bars)
Inland Steel Flat Products Co. (sheet and steel plate)

KEY COMPETITORS

AK Steel	Cargill	National Steel
Alcan	Earle Jorgensen	Nucor
Alcoa	Holdings	Oregon Steel
Allegheny Ludlum	Friedrich Krupp	Mills
A.M. Castle	Hyundai	Phelps Dodge
Anglo American	IRI	Reynolds Metals
Armco	LTV	Thyssen
ASARCO	Mitsubishi	USX–U.S. Steel
Bethlehem Steel	Mitsui	Weirton Steel
Broken Hill		

HOW MUCH

	Annual Growth	1985	1986	1987	1988	1989	1990	1991	1992	1993	1994
Sales ($ mil.)	4.6%	2,999	3,173	3,453	4,068	4,147	3,870	3,405	3,494	3,888	4,497
Net income ($ mil.)	—	(147)	35	112	249	120	(21)	(275)	(159)	(38)	107
Income as % of sales	—	—	1.1%	3.2%	6.1%	2.9%	—	—	—	—	2.4%
Earnings per share ($)	—	(6.14)	0.95	3.09	6.99	3.15	(1.41)	(9.88)	(5.83)	(1.96)	1.70
Stock price – high ($)	—	26.00	28.38	35.25	42.63	48.50	36.38	26.13	27.00	35.00	42.00
Stock price – low ($)	—	19.50	14.50	17.00	27.50	31.38	20.88	17.38	16.25	20.00	29.38
Stock price – close ($)	5.0%	22.63	18.88	30.38	41.50	33.75	24.75	21.63	22.63	33.13	35.13
P/E – high	—	—	30	11	6	15	—	—	—	—	25
P/E – low	—	—	15	6	4	10	—	—	—	—	17
Dividends per share ($)	(100.0%)	0.38	0.00	0.00	0.75	1.40	1.40	0.15	0.00	0.00	0.00
Book value per share ($)	(11.8%)	34.20	32.85	36.15	42.50	43.00	41.27	31.10	6.01	7.79	11.06
Employees	(4.9%)	24,413	22,668	20,740	20,639	20,715	20,154	18,600	17,180	16,200	15,500

1994 Year-end:
Debt ratio: 58.9%
Return on equity: 23.9%
Cash (mil.): $107
Current ratio: 1.91
Long-term debt (mil.): $706
No. of shares (mil.): 45
Dividends
  Yield: —
  Payout: —
Market value (mil.): $1,565

**Stock Price History
High/Low 1985–94**

JOHNSON PUBLISHING COMPANY

OVERVIEW

Chicago-based Johnson Publishing is the leading US publisher of black-oriented magazines and America's 2nd largest black-owned business (after TLC Beatrice). Owned and controlled by John Johnson and his family, the company launched the first magazine for blacks in the 1940s and later branched into other magazines, broadcasting, insurance, and black-oriented beauty products and fashions. Today the company publishes *Ebony*, the cornerstone of the Johnson empire, with more than 11 million readers; *Jet*, which reaches nearly 9 million readers; and *EM* (Ebony Male), a magazine for men. The company also owns a radio station (WLOU-AM in Louisville) and produces hair care products (Supreme Beauty) and cosmetics (Fashion Fair and Eboné). Since 1978 the company has sponsored the "American Black Achievement Awards," a nationally syndicated TV special.

The company's book division features works by black authors. Johnson Publishing also produces Ebony Fashion Fair, which is billed as the world's biggest traveling fashion show. The company recently sold its 2 Chicago radio stations and expected to introduce its first foreign edition of *Ebony* in South Africa in late 1995.

Founder Johnson, now 77, still heads the company, but Johnson's daughter and heir apparent, Linda Rice, handles the day-to-day operations.

WHEN

John Johnson launched his publishing business in 1942 while still in college in Chicago. The idea for a magazine oriented to blacks came to him while he was working part-time for Supreme Life Insurance Co. of America, where one of his jobs was to clip news articles about the black community from magazines and newspapers. With $500 his mother raised by mortgaging family furniture, Johnson mailed a $2 charter subscription offer to potential subscribers. He got 3,000 replies and with that $6,000 printed the first issue of *Negro Digest*, patterned after *Reader's Digest*. Within a year circulation was 50,000.

In 1945 Johnson started *Ebony* magazine, which was immediately popular and is still Johnson's premier publication. *Ebony* (like *Life*, but focusing on black culture and achievements) and *Jet* (a celebrity-oriented magazine started in 1951) were the only publications for US blacks for 20 years.

In the early days Johnson was unable to obtain advertising, so he formed his own mail-order business called Beauty Star and advertised its products (dresses, wigs, hair care products, and vitamins) through his magazines. He won his first major account, Zenith Radio, in 1947; Johnson landed Chrysler in 1954 after he sent a salesman to Detroit every week for 10 years.

By the 1960s Johnson had become one of the most prominent black men in America. In 1963 he posed with John F. Kennedy to publicize a special issue of *Ebony* celebrating the Emancipation Proclamation. *Negro Digest*, renamed *Black World*, became known for its provocative articles, but its circulation dwindled from 100,000 to 15,000. Johnson stopped publishing the magazine in 1975. In the meantime US magazine publishers named Johnson Publisher of the Year in 1972.

Unable to find the proper makeup for his *Ebony* models, Johnson founded his own cosmetics business, Fashion Fair Cosmetics, in 1973. Fashion Fair competed successfully against Revlon (which introduced cosmetic lines for blacks) and another black cosmetics company, Johnson Products (unrelated) of Chicago. By 1982 sales for the Fashion Fair division alone were more than $30 million.

In 1973 Johnson also launched *Ebony Jr!* (since discontinued), a black preteens magazine, designed to provide "positive black images." Johnson bought radio stations WJPC (Chicago's first black-owned station; sold in 1995) and WLOU (Louisville) in 1974 and WLNR (Lansing, Illinois) in the mid-1980s (merged into WJPC in 1992). In 1984 Johnson Publishing passed Motown Industries to become the largest black-owned business in America. In 1987 *Black Enterprise* magazine selected John Johnson as Entrepreneur of the Decade.

Johnson and the company sold their controlling interest in Illinois's last minority-owned insurance company (and Johnson's first employer), Supreme Life Insurance, to Unitrin in 1991. That same year the company and Spiegel announced a joint venture to develop black women's fashions. The 2 companies launched a mail-order catalog, called *E Style*, in 1993 and a credit card to go with it in 1994. Johnson Publishing teamed up with South African company Publico and Real Africa Investments in 1995 with plans to launch its South African edition of *Ebony*.

Private company
Fiscal year ends: December 31

WHO

Chairman and CEO: John H. Johnson, age 77
President and COO: Linda Johnson Rice, age 36
Secretary and Treasurer: Eunice W. Johnson, age 73
Controller: Gregory Robertson
Editor, *Ebony*: Lerone Bennett Jr.
Personnel Director: La Doris Foster

WHERE

HQ: Johnson Publishing Company, Inc.,
    1820 S. Michigan Ave., Chicago, IL 60605
Phone: 312-322-9200
Fax: 312-322-0918

WHAT

Business Lines

Beauty Aids
Eboné Cosmetics
Fashion Fair Cosmetics
Supreme Beauty Products Co.
    Duke (hair care for men)
    Raveen (hair care for women)

Books
Johnson Publishing Co. Book Division

Fashion
E Style (women's apparel, accessories, and home
    fashions catalog; joint venture with Spiegel)
Ebony Fashion Fair (traveling fashion show)

Magazines
Ebony
EM (Ebony Male)
Jet

Radio Station
WLOU (AM), Louisville

Television Production
"American Black Achievement Awards"

KEY COMPETITORS

Advance Publications
Amway
Avon
BET
Body Shop
Colgate-Palmolive
Cox Enterprises
Essence Communications
Estée Lauder
Forbes
Gannett
Gillette
Hearst
Knight-Ridder
Lagadère Group
L'Oréal
MacAndrews & Forbes
New York Times
Pavion
Procter & Gamble
Reader's Digest
Rodale Press
Soft Sheen Products
Strickland and Co.
Time Warner
Tribune
Unilever
Walt Disney
Washington Post
Zuckerman Media Properties

HOW MUCH

	Annual Growth	1985	1986	1987	1988	1989	1990	1991	1992	1993	1994
Sales ($ mil.)	7.9%	155	174	202	217	241	252	261	274	294	307
Employees	4.4%	1,802	1,828	1,903	2,364	2,370	2,382	2,710	2,785	2,600	2,662

Sales ($ mil.)
1985–94

KEMPER NATIONAL INSURANCE COS.

OVERVIEW

Kemper National Insurance Companies unites most of the property/casualty businesses formerly held by Kemper Corp. Over a 6-year period beginning in 1989, Kemper Corp. sold these businesses to majority-owner Lumbermens Mutual and spun off its money-losing brokerage businesses. In 1994 both GE and Conseco tried to acquire Kemper Corp. (GE withdrew its offer and Conseco shareholders nixed the deal as dilutive.) Kemper Corp.'s remains (asset management and life insurance) were acquired by Zurich Insurance.

Disentangling Kemper National and Kemper Corp. was a long operation that finally culminated in 1995, when Kemper Corp.'s chairman, David Mathis, assumed the chairmanship of Kemper National, a mutual.

Kemper National's lead entity (and Kemper Corp.'s predecessor), Lumbermens Mutual, is again the parent of several property/casualty companies. Other fields include workers' compensation (Kemper is the 4th largest such insurer), health care, and reinsurance.

Recently, Kemper National has lagged behind that of the industry, partly because of internal inefficiencies. Kemper has been addressing these problems by instituting internal cost controls and by building fee income through expansion of claim, loss control, and managed-care services.

WHEN

James Kemper started Lumbermens Mutual in 1912 to provide workers' compensation to Illinois lumberyard owners. The 26-year-old insurance agent perceived a niche after yard owners complained they were being overcharged because insurers classed lumberyards with the much more dangerous business of logging. In 1913 Kemper expanded coverage to fire insurance for lumberyards by founding National Underwriters.

Lumbermens began growing, opening offices in Philadelphia, Boston, and Syracuse. By 1921 the company was based in Chicago.

The company was one of the first auto insurers in the US, and in 1926 Kemper formed a company specifically for personal and commercial auto insurance, American Motorists Insurance Co. (AMICO). In the early 1930s the company added boiler and machinery, surety bond, and inland marine insurance. As subsidiaries blossomed, they all began to be known as the Kemper companies.

The Kemper family was active in philanthropy, founding a traffic safety institute at Northwestern University in the 1930s and endowing a scholarship fund.

In 1957 Lumbermens began offering ocean marine coverage and began advertising on national television, sponsoring sports events. The Kemper group of companies added Federal Kemper Life Assurance in 1961 and American Protection Insurance in 1962. In 1964 the company introduced Highly Protected Risk commercial insurance coverage.

In response to concerns about the organizational difficulties of a mutual company owning so many subsidiaries, in 1967 Lumbermens formed Kemperco, Inc., a public holding company (later Kemper Corp.), with Lumbermens owning a controlling interest. In 1981, at age 94, James Kemper died.

In the 1980s Kemper began its drive to become a financial services powerhouse, buying brokerages Prescott, Ball & Turben (1982), Loewi (1982), and Boettcher (1985).

In 1989 Kemper Corp. began selling property/casualty operations back to Lumbermens (for stock, decreasing Lumbermens's interest in Kemper Corp.) because the cyclic losses inherent in that type of insurance were a drag on quarter-by-quarter earnings growth. It also embarked on a reorganization that gave Kemper Corp. and Kemper National Insurance Cos. (a new entity) separate management and separate boards of directors. In 1992 the chairmanships of the companies were separated.

Kemper National was formed just as the property/casualty industry was about to be hit by the longest and costliest string of natural disasters in the 20th century. Hurricanes in Florida, floods on the Mississippi and Missouri Rivers, and earthquakes in California pummeled the industry, hitting Kemper National hard. But returns on its investments carried the company through.

In 1993 Kemper Corp. — by then a financial services company — sold National Loss Control Service (risk management) and Kemper Reinsurance to Lumbermens in exchange for most of Lumbermens's remaining stock in Kemper, reducing its interest in Kemper Corp. from 38% to about 4%.

The next year Kemper National was devastated by rising interest rates (in addition to being forced to raise its reserves for unresolved Superfund liabilities) that caused income to plummet. In 1995, however, interest rates fell again and nature stayed quiet.

Mutual company
Fiscal year ends: December 31

WHO

Chairman: David B. Mathis, age 57
President and COO: Alfred K. Kenyon, age 60
EVP and CFO: Walter L. White
EVP: James S. Kemper III
EVP: Elizabeth M. Lindner
EVP: Peter T. Standbridge
VP Compensation and Benefits: Sally Bullen
VP Personal Lines: Joseph J. Kondratowicz
VP Personal Lines: Louis V. LaPaglia
VP Administration: Frederic C. McCullough
VP Special Risks Underwriting: Mark D. O'Brien
VP Human Resources: Robert L. Davis
General Counsel: John K. Conway
Treasurer: Robert B. Stacy
Auditors: KPMG Peat Marwick LLP

WHERE

HQ: Kemper National Insurance Companies,
One Kemper Dr., Long Grove, IL 60049
Phone: 847-320-2000
Fax: 847-320-2494

Kemper National operates in all 50 states and the District of Columbia and has offices in Australia, Belgium, Bermuda, Canada, France, Germany, Japan, Singapore, and the UK.

WHAT

	1994 Assets	
	$ mil.	% of total
Cash & equivalents	63	1
US government securities	1,466	17
State, county & municipal bonds	824	9
Other bonds	2,141	24
Preferred stocks	173	2
Common stocks	1,419	16
Real estate	126	1
Mortgage loans & other investments	572	6
Premiums in transmission	1,782	20
Other	390	4
Total	**8,956**	**100**

	1994 Sales	
	$ mil.	% of total
Lumbermens Mutual	1,633	45
American Manufacturers	734	20
Other	1,234	35
Total	**3,601**	**100**

	1994 Sales	
	$ mil.	% of total
Premiums	3,010	84
Investments	423	12
Fees	168	4
Total	**3,601**	**100**

Subsidiaries and Affiliates
American Manufacturers Mutual Insurance Co.
American Motorists Insurance Co.
American Protection Insurance Co.
Kemper International
Kemper Lloyd's Insurance Co.
Kemper National Services (managed care, workers' compensation coverage)
Kemper Reinsurance
Kemper Risk Management Services (reducing workplace injuries, claims management)
Lumbermens Mutual Casualty Co.
National Loss Control Service Corp. (risk management, corporate claims, industrial hygiene)

KEY COMPETITORS

Acordia
AIG
Allmerica Insurance
Allstate
American Re
Chubb
CNA Financial
FHP International
General Re
Hartford Steam Boiler Inspection
Liberty Mutual
Lincoln National
Mutual of Omaha
St. Paul Cos.
Transamerica
Travelers
USAA
USF&G

HOW MUCH

	Annual Growth	1985	1986	1987	1988	1989	1990	1991	1992	1993	1994
Assets ($ mil.)	9.8%	3,850	4,690	5,280	5,680	6,640	7,330	8,190	8,460	9,137	8,956
Net income ($ mil.)	(2.4%)	31	189	210	145	157	(71)	41	86	119	25
Income as % of assets	—	0.8%	4.0%	4.0%	2.6%	2.4%	—	0.5%	1.0%	1.3%	0.3%
Employees	(7.8%)	—	—	—	—	—	—	—	—	9,000	8,295

1994 Year-end:
Equity as % of assets: 20.0%
Return on equity: 1.4%
Return on assets: 0.3%
Sales ($ mil.): $3,601

Assets ($ mil.)
1985–94

LEO BURNETT COMPANY, INC.

OVERVIEW

As the creator of Charlie Tuna, the Jolly Green Giant, the Keebler Elves, the Pillsbury Doughboy, and Tony the Tiger, the Leo Burnett Company was once known as the Critter Shop. The advertising agency, based in Chicago, has always prided itself on its homespun ideas that connect consumers to their clients' products with a folksy familiarity, as opposed to the glitz and glamour produced by many Madison Avenue shops.

The old-fashioned firm has usually stayed above the frenzy generated by the cutthroat tactics of agencies prowling for new accounts. Burnett has a small client list — only about 30 domestic clients — but it's a blue-chip list with

loyalty. Green Giant, Kellogg, and Pillsbury have been with the agency for more than 40 years, and, like other Burnett clients, they are big spenders of advertising dollars.

Global growth was all the rage among larger agencies in the early 1990s, but Burnett avoided rushing into new markets. Instead, the agency followed its multinational clients (notably Philip Morris and Procter & Gamble) as they expanded across borders. In 1995 the company announced plans for major expansion in central and eastern Europe and in the Middle East.

Burnett is a private company whose stock is held by its employees.

WHEN

In 1935 Leo Burnett left Erwin Wasey & Company, then one of America's top advertising agencies, to form his own ad firm. He opened his office in Chicago with 8 staffers, 3 clients (the Minnesota Valley Canning Company, Hoover, and Realsilk Hosiery), and a bowl of red apples on the receptionist's desk as a gesture of hospitality. Early on, a journalist summed up the prevailing attitude about the agency's chances of success during the Depression by saying, "It won't be long 'til Leo Burnett is *selling* apples on the street corner instead of giving them away." But Burnett soon rewarded Minnesota Valley's loyalty by creating the Jolly Green Giant campaign, and the apples have remained a symbol of his success.

However, the agency's national success was not immediate. Not until 1949, when the firm landed the Pillsbury Family Flour account (then worth $7 million), did Burnett hit the big time. Soon after, accounts from Kellogg and the New York–based Tea Council were acquired, instantly garnering respect from the advertising mecca of Madison Avenue.

Burnett shunned the flashy sophistication used by many New York firms and instead, using Midwestern warmth and personality, tried to convey the "inherent drama" of a product. This strategy proved itself repeatedly in ads such as United Airlines's "Fly the Friendly Skies," but it was most successful with Philip Morris, which hired the agency in the 1950s to bolster sales of one of its minor brands, Marlboro. Burnett created the Marlboro man and transformed the filter cigarette targeted mainly at women into a rugged, full-flavored smoke. Annual sales rocketed from 500 million cigarettes to 22.5 billion in

just 3 years. Marlboro went on to become the world's best-selling cigarette.

By 1962 the agency had additional offices in Detroit, Hollywood, New York, and Toronto. That year it expanded overseas, buying an interest in British firm Legget Nicholson and Partners. In 1967 Burnett merged with D. P. Brother & Co. of Detroit, which handled the Oldsmobile account for General Motors. In 1971 Leo Burnett died.

Throughout the 1970s the agency grew, not by adding many new clients but by helping improve the sales of its existing clients, many of which were large, consumer-oriented companies that constantly introduced new products, such as Keebler and Procter & Gamble. By 1980 Burnett passed $1 billion in billings.

During the 1980s the agency adopted a slightly more aggressive approach, wresting the McDonald's account from Needham. But the firm's client list remained relatively short. By 1990 the domestic arm of Burnett had only 31 clients, while many similar-sized agencies had over 100 clients.

In 1991 Burnett won accounts for Miller Lite, Sony, and Nintendo despite a recession that dramatically reduced revenues at other firms. However, by 1993 the agency began to experience its own troubles as several clients chose to use services such as promotions and direct mail, switching to agencies with strengths in these areas. Burnett also suffered the loss of several key personnel while in the midst of changes to offer a broader range of services.

Although Burnett lost the Sony account in 1994, it rebounded in 1995, adding Coca-Cola's Fruitopia account and United Distillers's Johnnie Walker account.

Private company
Fiscal year end: December 31

WHO

Chairman and Chief Creative Director: Richard B. Fizdale
President and CEO: William T. Lynch
Group President and Deputy Chief Creative Officer: Michael B. Conrad
Group President and CFO: Roger A. Haupt
Group President, The Americas: James M. Jenness
Group President, Asia/Pacific: James G. Oates
Group President, Europe/Middle East/Africa: Kerry M. Rubie
Corporate VC and Director Corporate Planning: Albert C. M. Winninghoff
Corporate VC; Director Creative Services, Leo Burnett U.S.A.: Robert D. Nolan
Chief Creative Officer, Leo Burnett U.S.A.: Robert H. Welke
EVP Human Resources and Law, Worldwide: Michael Breslin

WHERE

HQ: 35 W. Wacker Dr., Chicago, IL 60601
Phone: 312-220-5959
Fax: 312-220-6533

Worldwide Offices

Argentina	France	Netherlands	South Africa
Australia	Germany	New Zealand	South Korea
Belgium	Greece	Norway	Spain
Brazil	Guatemala	Pakistan	Sweden
Bulgaria	Hong Kong	Panama	Switzerland
Canada	Hungary	Peru	Taiwan
Chile	India	Philippines	Thailand
China	Indonesia	Poland	Turkey
Colombia	Italy	Portugal	UK
Costa Rica	Japan	Puerto Rico	Ukraine
Czech	Kazakhstan	Romania	United Arab
Republic	Kuwait	Russia	Emirates
Denmark	Latvia	Saudi Arabia	Uruguay
Dominican	Lebanon	Singapore	US
Republic	Malaysia	Slovakia	Venezuela
Egypt	Mexico	Slovenia	Vietnam

	1994 Billings	
	$ mil.	% of total
International	2,366	52
US	2,226	48
Total	**4,592**	**100**

WHAT

Selected Services
Advertising
Brand consulting
Direct mail
Interactive media services
Market research
Media buying
Promotional services
Public relations

US Clients (Year Assigned)
Allstate Insurance Cos. (1957)
Ameritech (1994)
The Amurol Confections Co. (1988)
Arthur Andersen (1994)
The Beef Industry Council (1991)
Coca-Cola (1995)
Commonwealth Edison Co. (1954)
Dean Witter, Discover & Co. (1988)
First Brands Corp. (1961)
Fruit of the Loom (1992)
Green Giant (1935)
Hallmark Cards (1988)
J. M. Smucker Co. (1994)
Keebler Co. (1968)
Kellogg Co. (1949)
Kraft Foods (1984)
Maytag (1955)
McDonald's (1982)
Nintendo (1991)
Oldsmobile division of General Motors (1934)
Philip Morris (1954)
The Pillsbury Co. (1944)
Procter & Gamble (1952)
Reebok (1993)
Rockport (1994)
Samsonite (1983)
Sealy (1990)
True Value Hardware Stores (1994)
United Airlines (1965)
United Distillers North America (1968)
Walt Disney (1994)

KEY COMPETITORS

Bozell	Interpublic Group
Cordiant	N W Ayer
Creative Artists	Omnicom Group
D'Arcy Masius	True North
Dentsu	WPP Group
Grey Advertising	Young & Rubicam

HOW MUCH

	Annual Growth	1985	1986	1987	1988	1989	1990	1991	1992	1993	1994
Sales ($ mil.)	10.8%	269	293	338	430	487	538	577	560	549	675
Employees	4.0%	—	—	4,795	—	5,700	6,200	6,314	—	6,581	6,308

Sales ($ mil.)
1985–94

700	
600	
500	
400	
300	
200	
100	
0	

THE MARMON GROUP

Like a great linebacker, the Marmon Group may be big, but it is all muscle. The Chicago-based company is one of the 25 largest private firms in the US. Its holdings include 60 autonomous manufacturing and service companies.

Several of the group's companies lead their respective industries, including Getz Bros., the US's largest export marketer and distributor of noncommodity goods; Long-Airdox, one of the world's largest suppliers of underground mining equipment; Marmon/Keystone, a leading distributor of steel, aluminum, and nickel alloy tubing; and Trans Union Corp., the country's leading consumer credit reporting agency. The Marmon roster is filled out with an industrialist's all-star team of cable, caster, screw, valve,

and wheel manufacturers and distributors. The group operates more than 400 facilities in over 30 countries.

Coaching the Marmon team are brothers Jay and Robert Pritzker. Jay (also founder and chairman of the Hyatt Hotels Corp.) is the Marmon Group's chairman; Robert is president and CEO. The brothers (who also own stakes in Royal Caribbean Cruises and chewing tobacco maker Conwood) are worth more than $4.4 billion, according to *Forbes*.

Recent acquisitions spotlight 2 trends in the Marmon Group's growth: the firm is expanding internationally, and it is boosting its presence in industries such as mining equipment and casters where it is already established.

Although the history of the Marmon Group officially begins in 1953, the company's roots are in the Chicago law firm Pritzker and Pritzker, started by Nicholas Pritzker in 1902. Through the firm the family gained connections with the First National Bank of Chicago, which Nicholas's son, A. N., used to get a line of credit to begin acquiring real estate. By 1940 the firm had stopped accepting outside clients in order to concentrate on the family's growing investment portfolio.

In 1953 A. N.'s oldest son, Jay, wanted to buy Colson Company, a small, money-losing manufacturer, and he used his father's connections with the First National Bank to get the loan. Jay's brother, Robert, a graduate of the Illinois Institute of Technology with a degree in industrial engineering, took charge of Colson and turned the company around. Soon Jay began acquiring more companies for his brother to manage.

In 1963 the brothers paid $2.7 million for about 45% of the Marmon-Herrington Co. (whose predecessor, Marmon Motor Car, built the car that in 1911 won the first Indianapolis 500). The family now had a name for their industrial holdings — the Marmon Group.

The Marmon Group became a public company in 1966 when it merged with boot- and spring-maker Fenestra. However, Jay began to take greater control of the group through a series of stock purchases, and in 1971 the Marmon Group was private once again.

In 1973 the group began to acquire stock in Cerro Corp., which had operations in mining, manufacturing, trucking, and real estate, and by 1976 the group had bought all of that company. The brothers sold Cerro's trucking sub-

sidiary, ICX, in 1977 and bought organ maker Hammond Corp., along with Wells Lamont, Hammond's glove-making subsidiary.

In 1981 the Marmon Group acquired conglomerate Trans Union Corp. for $688 million. Trans Union brought the group businesses with a variety of operations, including railcar and equipment leasing, credit information services, international trading, and water and wastewater treatment systems.

The Pritzkers made a foray into the airline business in 1984, buying Braniff Airlines. After unsuccessfully bidding for Pan Am in 1987, they sold Braniff in 1988. Disappointments in other Pritzker businesses didn't slow the Marmon Group, which added to its transportation equipment business in 1984 when it acquired Altamil Corp., a maker of products for the trucking and aerospace industries. In 1990 the Marmon Group bought the Winamac Spring Division from Masco Industries.

In honor of its 40th anniversary, the company sponsored a car, the Marmon Wasp II, at the 1993 Indianapolis 500. That same year the Pritzkers sold Ticketmaster to Microsoft cofounder Paul Allen, retaining a minority interest. The next year Mexican banking authorities stymied an attempt by Trans Union to establish a credit reporting system with the Association of Mexican Bankers.

In 1995 the Pritzkers continued to wheel and deal, selling Arzco Medical Systems and buying (through group subsidiaries) mine equipment and service providers National Mine Service (Pennsylvania) and the Anderson Group (Scotland). The Marmon Group also bought the Anbuma Group, a Belgian distributor of steel tubing.

Private company
Fiscal year ends: December 31

WHO

Chairman: Jay A. Pritzker, age 73
President and CEO: Robert A. Pritzker, age 69
EVP, Treasurer, and CFO: Robert C. Gluth
SVP: Gerald T. Shannon
VP, General Counsel, and Secretary: Robert W. Webb
Personnel Director: George Frese
Auditors: Ernst & Young LLP

WHERE

HQ: 225 W. Washington St., Chicago, IL 60606
Phone: 312-372-9500
Fax: 312-845-5305

The Marmon Group operates worldwide.

	1994 Sales % of total
US	74
Other countries	26
Total	**100**

WHAT

	1994 Sales % of total
Manufacturing	50
Services	50
Total	**100**

Selected Member Companies
Alaron Inc. (consumer electronics)
Am-Safe, Inc. (aircraft passenger seat belts)
The Anbuma Group (steel tubing distribution)
Anderson Copper and Brass Co. (brass connectors and valves)
Anderson Group Ltd. (underground coal mining machinery and mineral handling equipment, precision gearing components, conveyor belt components)
Atlas Bolt & Screw Co. (aluminum, steel, and stainless steel fasteners)
Cerro Copper Products (copper refining and extrusion, copper plumbing tube manufacture)
Cerro Metal Products Co. (brass products)
Colson Caster Corp. (casters, wheels, and rubber bumpers)

L.A. Darling Co. (store fixtures)
Detroit Steel Products (springs for trucks and trailers)
Eagle-Gypsum Products (gypsum mining and gypsum wallboard manufacture)
Ecodyne Ltd. (water and wastewater treatment equipment)
EcoWater Systems, Inc. (residential water treatment and purification systems)
Fontaine Industries, Inc. (specialty truck and truck conversion products)
Getz Bros. & Co., Inc. (international marketing and distribution)
The Graver Co. (water and wastewater equipment and systems)
Huron Steel Co., Inc. (steel service center)
Jamesway Incubator Co. Ltd. (poultry incubators)
Kangol Ltd. (headwear)
Long-Airdox Co. (mining equipment and systems)
Medical Device Technologies, Inc. (biopsy devices)
Meyer Material Co. (ready-mix concrete)
MicroAire Surgical Instruments, Inc. (surgical devices)
National Mine Service, Inc. (mining products and safety equipment)
Pan American Screw (screw manufacturing and sales)
Perfection Hy-Test Co. (new and rebuilt automobile clutches)
Procor Ltd. (railcar leasing in Canada)
Robertson Whitehouse Inc. (standard and specialty fasteners)
Solidstate Controls, Inc. (uninterruptible power supplies)
Spectrum Labs, Inc. (water, soil, and hazardous waste testing)
Sterling Crane (mobile crane rentals)
TIE/Communications, Inc. (telecommunications and information distribution hardware and software)
Trackmobile, Inc. (in-plant and switching yard railcar moving equipment)
Trans Union Corp. (consumer credit reporting service)
Union Tank Car Co. (rail tank car manufacture and leasing)
Wells Lamont Corp. (recreational and work gloves)

KEY COMPETITORS

American Consumer
Anixter International
Cawsl
Eaton
Equifax
Illinois Tool Works

Ingersoll-Rand
ITT Industries
Masco
PACCAR
Peerless Mfg.
Peerless Tube
Playtex

Quanex
SPS Technologies
Thiokol
Terex
TRW
US Filter
Wolverine Tube

HOW MUCH

	Annual Growth	1985	1986	1987	1988	1989	1990	1991	1992	1993	1994
Sales ($ mil.)	7.5%	2,767	2,878	3,239	3,507	3,841	3,846	3,867	4,008	4,319	5,301
Net income ($ mil.)	10.5%	114	116	144	204	206	125	126	145	207	280
Income as % of sales	—	4.1%	4.0%	4.5%	5.8%	5.4%	3.3%	3.3%	3.6%	4.8%	5.3%
Employees	0.4%	27,095	26,910	25,545	25,005	25,074	26,705	27,050	27,000	27,700	28,000

MARMON

Net Income ($ mil.) 1985–94

MCDONALD'S CORPORATION

OVERVIEW

If old McDonald had this farm, he'd be singing M-O-N-E-Y. Based in Oak Brook, Illinois, McDonald's is the largest global food service retailer and the US's most profitable retailer over the past decade. The company's brand name is the world's 2nd most recognized (after Coca-Cola).

McDonald's operates more than 15,000 restaurants (2nd only to PepsiCo) and has a 21% share of the US fast-food restaurant business. It has responded to the competitive US fast-food marketplace by redesigning its menus to stress value and choice. An annual advertising budget of over $1.4 billion keeps product awareness high, while movie tie-ins (including one with *Batman Forever* in 1995) and video offerings add merchandising to the mix.

With profits in the US climbing slowly, McDonald's continues to look abroad for growth. It plans to open between 1,200 and 1,500 new restaurants in 1995, most outside the US, where less competition, lighter market saturation, and high name recognition have already brought success. Its overseas restaurants (about 1/3 of its total) account for half its profits. To heat up US operations, the company shuffled its management in late 1995. EVP Patrick Flynn was given the title of Senior Operating Officer and the task of "driving the strategic agenda for the US business."

The company and its affiliates operate only about 30% of all McDonald's restaurants. Franchisees control the rest under agreements that generally last 20 years.

WHEN

The first McDonald's opened in 1948 in San Bernardino, California. In 1954 owners Dick and Mac McDonald signed a franchise agreement with 52-year-old Ray Kroc (a malt machine salesman). A year later Kroc opened his first restaurant in Des Plaines, Illinois. By 1957 Kroc was operating 14 McDonald's restaurants in Illinois, Indiana, and California. The company sold its 100 millionth hamburger in 1958 and opened its 100th restaurant in 1959. Kroc bought out the McDonald brothers for $2.7 million in 1961.

In 1962 McDonald's adopted the golden arches as its company trademark. The company served its billionth hamburger live on the "Art Linkletter Show" in 1963. Ronald McDonald made his debut that year, as did the company's first new menu item — the Filet-O-Fish sandwich. In 1965 McDonald's went public, and Kroc ran the first McDonald's TV ads. In 1967 the company opened its first stores outside the US (in Canada).

In 1968 McDonald's added the Big Mac to its menu and opened its 1,000th restaurant. The company's advertising began featuring the slogan "You deserve a break today — so get up and get away to McDonald's" in 1970.

During the 1970s McDonald's grew at the rate of about 500 restaurants per year. New menu items included the Quarter Pounder (1972), the Egg McMuffin (pioneering breakfast fast food, 1973), and Happy Meals (1979). The first Ronald McDonald House (residence for families of hospitalized children) opened in 1974. That year Fred Turner, longtime operations chief and Kroc protégé, was named CEO. (Turner became chairman in 1977, with Kroc

staying on as senior chairman until his death in 1984.) In 1975, the year the drive-thru appeared, McDonald's formed the National Operators Advisory Board (NOAB) in response to operators unhappy with the franchising system. (NOAB gave some power back to them.) By 1978 McDonald's had over 5,000 restaurants, with sales exceeding $3 billion.

After introducing Chicken McNuggets in 1983, McDonald's became the first fast-food chain to provide customers with a list of its products' ingredients (1986). In 1987 it started serving salads, and in 1989 McDonald's served its 75 billionth hamburger.

At the end of the 1980s, growing competition in the domestic market slowed the company's US sales growth to about 5% per year. McDonald's responded by adding "value menus" and the unsuccessful McLean Deluxe, a low-fat hamburger (1991). Franchisees were also granted leeway to experiment with decor and new menu items.

In 1993 McDonald's opened its first restaurants inside Wal-Mart stores, an experimental joint venture between the 2 US business giants. By 1994 more than 30 Wal-Marts shared space with McDonald's.

Also in 1994 a jury awarded Stella Liebeck about $2.7 million after she sued McDonald's for severe burns she received when she spilled hot coffee on herself. The award was later reduced to less than $600,000 following a settlement.

In 1996 McDonald's will open its first restaurants in India. Menus will include chicken and fish sandwiches and vegetable nuggets but no beef.

NYSE symbol: MCD
Fiscal year ends: December 31

WHO

Senior Chairman: Fred L. Turner, age 62
Chairman and CEO: Michael R. Quinlan, age 51, $1,948,875 pay
VC and CFO: Jack M. Greenberg, age 53, $1,142,353 pay
President and CEO, USA: Edward H. Rensi, age 51, $1,196,837 pay
President and CEO, International: James R. Cantalupo, age 52, $1,183,219 pay
SEVP and Chief Marketing Officer: Paul D. Schrage, age 60, $755,872 pay
EVP and Chief Operations Officer: Thomas W. Glasgow Jr., age 48
EVP and Senior Operating Officer: Patrick J. Flynn, age 53
SVP, General Counsel, and Secretary: Shelby Yastrow
SVP (Personnel): Stanley R. Stein
Auditors: Ernst & Young LLP

WHERE

HQ: McDonald's Plaza, Oak Brook, IL 60521
Phone: 708-575-3000
Fax: 708-575-3392 (Stockholder Relations)

McDonald's has restaurants in 79 countries.

	1994 No. of Restaurants
US	9,744
Japan	1,133
Canada	717
Germany	570
UK	526
Australia	454
France	350
Brazil	149
The Netherlands	110
Other countries	1,452
Total	**15,205**

	1994 Sales		1994 Operating Income	
	$ mil.	% of total	$ mil.	% of total
US	4,155	50	1,130	50
Europe/Africa/ Middle East	2,605	31	672	30
Asia/Pacific	731	9	243	11
Canada	546	7	117	5
Latin America	284	3	79	4
Total	**8,321**	**100**	**2,241**	**100**

WHAT

	1994 Restaurants	
	No.	% of total
Operated by franchisees	10,458	69
Operated by the company	3,083	20
Operated by affiliates	1,664	11
Total	**15,205**	**100**

	1994 Sales	
	$ mil.	% of total
Company restaurants	5,793	70
Fees from franchised restaurants	2,528	30
Total	**8,321**	**100**

Major Products

Big Mac	French fries
Chicken McNuggets	Milkshakes
Egg McMuffin	Quarter Pounder
Filet-O-Fish	Salads

KEY COMPETITORS

Blimpie	Foodmaker	ShowBiz Pizza
Boston Chicken	Grand	Shoney's
Checkers	Metropolitan	Sonic Corp.
Drive-In	Imasco	Subway
CKE Restaurants	Little Caesars	Triarc
Dairy Queen	PepsiCo	Wendy's
Domino's Pizza	Rally's	Whataburger
Flagstar	Restaurant Co.	

HOW MUCH

	Annual Growth	1985	1986	1987	1988	1989	1990	1991	1992	1993	1994
Sales ($ mil.)	9.4%	3,695	4,144	4,894	5,566	6,142	6,640	6,695	7,133	7,408	8,321
Net income ($ mil.)	12.2%	433	480	549	646	727	802	860	959	1,083	1,224
Income as % of sales	—	11.7%	11.6%	11.2%	11.6%	11.8%	12.1%	12.8%	13.4%	14.6%	14.7%
Earnings per share ($)	13.0%	0.56	0.63	0.73	0.86	0.98	1.10	1.18	1.30	1.46	1.68
Stock price – high ($)	—	9.09	12.80	15.28	12.75	17.44	19.25	19.94	25.19	29.56	31.38
Stock price – low ($)	—	5.69	8.13	7.84	10.19	11.50	12.50	13.06	19.13	22.75	25.56
Stock price – close ($)	14.0%	9.00	10.16	11.00	12.03	17.25	14.56	19.00	24.38	28.50	29.25
P/E – high	—	16	20	21	15	18	18	17	19	20	19
P/E – low	—	10	13	11	12	12	11	11	15	16	15
Dividends per share ($)	9.7%	0.10	0.11	0.12	0.14	0.16	0.17	0.18	0.20	0.21	0.23
Book value per share ($)	13.6%	2.84	3.22	3.86	4.54	4.63	5.55	6.33	7.30	7.91	8.95
Employees	2.4%	148,000	159,000	159,000	169,000	176,000	174,000	168,000	166,000	169,000	183,000

1994 Year-end:
Debt ratio: 41.2%
Return on equity: 20.7%
Cash (mil.): $180
Current ratio: 0.30
Long-term debt (mil.): $2,935
No. of shares (mil.): 694
Dividends
   Yield: 0.8%
   Payout: 13.7%
Market value (mil.): $20,291

Stock Price History High/Low 1985–94

MONTGOMERY WARD HOLDING CORP.

OVERVIEW

One of the largest department store operators in the US, Chicago-based Montgomery Ward operates 402 Montgomery Ward department stores and Lechmere superstores in 43 states. The company also runs Montgomery Ward Direct (a catalog company) and 13 outlet stores that sell overstocked items.

Led by CEO and firebrand Bernard Brennan — who owns about 40% of Ward's stock and whose brother, Edward, chairs crosstown rival Sears — Montgomery Ward saw profits rise 14% in 1994 after 2 years in the doldrums. Brennan reformulated the company's strategy in the late 1980s, when insiders took the company private in a $3.8 billion LBO, one of the

largest in US history. Brennan introduced brand-name merchandise to the stores and established specialty departments, including Electric Avenue (appliances and electronics) and Home Ideas (home furnishings). These departments are distinct and often have separate entrances.

The company is entering the home-shopping business. In 1994 it introduced "The Electric Avenue & More," a home-shopping TV program. That same year the company bought a 4.7% stake in Value Vision International. Montgomery Ward has an option to buy up to 49% of the home-shopping cable company.

WHEN

Aaron Montgomery Ward started the Chicago company that bears his name in 1872. It was the world's first general merchandise mail-order concern. Before, farmers had bought goods from general stores or peddlers. Ward provided them with an inexpensive way to shop. In 1873 brother-in-law George Thorne became Ward's partner. In 1875 the company pioneered the "Satisfaction Guaranteed or Your Money Back" policy.

In 1893 Thorne bought a controlling interest in the company. By 1900 Ward's sales had fallen behind flamboyant Chicago rival Sears (founded in 1893). In 1904 Ward introduced what is believed to be the first company magazine edited by employees without a company-dictated policy. Profits surpassed $1 million for the first time in 1909, and the following year George Thorne retired, leaving 5 sons in control of the company. In 1913 Ward died; Charles Thorne became president. He moved to chairman 3 years later, and his brother Robert became president. In 1919 Ward went public; Robert Wood took over.

From 1920 to 1924 Ward's sales grew by 48%, versus Sears's 16% decrease. Wood wanted Ward to develop retail stores, but the company wanted to remain in the mail-order business, so in 1924 Wood left and went to work for Sears. In 1926 Ward opened its first retail store in Plymouth, Indiana.

In 1931 Sewell Avery became CEO; he ended 4 years of losses with a profitable 1934. Avery refused to turn over the company to federal control during a WWII labor dispute, and President Franklin Roosevelt had National Guardsmen carry Avery out of his office. Avery, who had correctly predicted the Great Depression, was convinced a recession would

follow WWII and canceled expansion plans, so Ward missed the postwar boom.

After Avery's departure (1955), Ward started an expansion program that included new stores in Alaska and the company's first major distribution center (1958). In 1968 the company merged with Container Corporation of America. In 1974 Mobil Oil acquired 54% control of Ward, acquiring 100% by 1976. Mobil made huge loans to the company in hopes of making Ward profitable.

In 1985 Mobil put Ward up for sale and brought in Bernard Brennan — who had worked for Sears before 1976, joined Ward in 1982, and quit after disputes with then-CEO Stephen Pistner in 1983 — to lead the company. Brennan and other senior managers led a $3.8 billion LBO in 1988. Brennan sold Ward's credit card business to General Electric Capital for $716 million in cash and assumption of $1.7 billion in debt. In 1990 president Bernard Andrews left Ward and joined consumer electronics retailer Circuit City.

In 1994 Ward agreed to buy Lechmere, an appliance and consumer electronics retailer founded in 1913, with 24 stores in the Northeast and $800 million in annual sales.

Between 1993 and 1994, 3 people held the post of president, and Brennan's fiery temper is said to be the cause of the turnover. Brennan finally talked Bernard Andrews into returning to Ward as president.

However, in 1995 Andrews resigned from the company. Some insiders say Brennan's intrusive management style forced Andrews to leave again, but because former executives are offered lucrative severance packages to keep quiet, little is known about the revolving door in Montgomery Ward's executive offices.

Private company
Fiscal year ends: Saturday nearest December 31

WHO

Chairman and CEO: Bernard F. Brennan, age 56, $1,515,600 pay
VC Operations and Catalog: Richard M. Bergel, age 59, $762,500 pay
Chairman and CEO, Signature Financial Marketing: G. Joseph Reddington, age 53, $660,000 pay
EVP, Secretary, and General Counsel: Spencer H. Heine, age 52, $468,447 pay
EVP, CFO, and Assistant Secretary: John L. Workman, age 43
EVP Merchandise and Store Operations: Edwin G. Pohlmann, age 47
EVP Marketing, Sales Promotion, and Business Development: Gene C. McCaffery, age 49
EVP Apparel: Robert F. Connolly, age 51
EVP Human Resources, Montgomery Ward: Robert A. Kasenter, age 48
Auditors: Arthur Andersen & Co, SC

WHERE

HQ: One Montgomery Ward Plaza, Chicago, IL 60671-0042
Phone: 312-467-2000
Fax: 312-467-3975

	No. of Stores
California	57
Texas	45
Illinois	36
Florida	22
New York	18
Virginia	17
Maryland	16
Michigan	16
Pennsylvania	14
Colorado	13
Massachusetts	13
Arizona	11
Other states	124
Total	**402**

WHAT

	1994 Sales	
	$ mil.	% of total
Retail merchandising	6,573	93
Direct marketing	465	7
Total	**7,038**	**100**

Retail Specialties
The Apparel Store (includes the Kids Store)
Auto Express (tires, batteries, parts, and service)
Electric Avenue (electronics and major appliances)
Gold 'N Gems (jewelry)
Home Ideas (home furnishings)
Rooms & More (home furnishings)

Subsidiaries
Lechmere, Inc. (retailer with stores in the Northeast)
Montgomery Ward Direct L.P. (50% partnership with Fingerhut Cos., Inc., specialty catalog)
Signature Group
(Montgomery Ward Auto Club, life/health insurance, and direct-mail marketing)

KEY COMPETITORS

50-Off Stores	Lands' End
AAA	Levitz
Ames	L.L. Bean
AutoZone	May
Best Buy	Melville
Best Products	Men's Wearhouse
Bradlees	Pennzoil
Caldor	Pep Boys
Circuit City	Price/Costco
Damark Intl.	Schottenstein
Dayton Hudson	Sears
Dillard	Service Merchandise
Federated	Spiegel
The Gap	Sun Television & Appliance
Good Guys	TJX
Hanover Direct	Venture Stores
J. Crew	Wal-Mart
J. C. Penney	Woolworth
Kmart	

HOW MUCH

	Annual Growth	1985	1986	1987	1988	1989	1990	1991	1992	1993	1994
Sales ($ mil.)	3.0%	5,388	4,870	5,024	5,567	5,461	5,584	5,654	5,781	6,002	7,038
Net income ($ mil.)	—	(298)	110	130	146	151	153	135	100	101	115
Income as % of sales	—	—	2.3%	2.6%	2.6%	2.8%	2.7%	2.4%	1.7%	1.7%	1.6%
Earnings per share ($)	(0.4%)	—	—	—	2.74	2.71	2.79	2.40	2.01	2.29	2.68
Dividends per share ($)	—	—	—	—	—	—	—	—	0.25	0.50	0.50
Book value per share ($)[1]	19.2%	—	—	—	—	5.74	8.61	10.39	12.11	13.61	13.82
Employees	(2.1%)	71,200	56,300	52,300	65,000	67,000	66,300	62,400	62,300	51,350	58,600

1994 Year-end:
Debt ratio: 39.7%
Return on equity: 18.9%
Cash (mil.): $350
Current ratio: —
Long-term debt (mil.): $309
No. of shares (mil.): 44
Dividend payout
  Class A: 18.7%
  Class B: 21.7%
Total assets (mil.): $4,540

Net Income ($ mil.) 1985–94

[1] Approximate for both class A and class B

MORTON INTERNATIONAL, INC.

OVERVIEW

Morton International's successful diversification has rubbed salt into the wounds of its competitors. The salt maker, whose "Umbrella Girl" logo is one of the most famous brand icons in the US, also manufactures specialty chemicals for a variety of applications. Products include adhesives for food packaging, liquid plastic coatings for autos, electronic materials used in printed circuit boards, and dyes used in inks.

The company's Automotive Safety Products division is the US's leading air bag maker. US legislation requiring air bags on both the passenger's and the driver's sides by 1999 have helped boost division sales lately. The division produced over 11 million air bags in 1994 and won major contracts to provide air bags for cars sold in Europe and Japan. In addition to

these contracts, favorable conditions in the US have Morton executives anticipating further solid sales gains.

The company's salt unit is a consistent cash generator. Morton's table salt remains the #1 seller in the US. The company also sells table salt under the Windsor label in Canada and sells salt for water conditioning, highway/ice control, and industrial and chemical uses. Recurring storms in the Ohio Valley and the eastern US in 1994 created a strong demand for the firm's highway/ice control salt.

The company's largest business segment, Specialty Chemicals, has benefited from an improving US economy, opportunities in Europe and Southeast Asia, and lower costs from streamlined operations; it posted a 14% increase in sales in 1995.

WHEN

Alonzo Richmond started Richmond & Company, agents for Onondaga Salt, in Chicago in 1848. During the first year Richmond received 36,656 barrels of salt for packing from Onondaga Lake near Syracuse.

In 1867 the company became Haskins, Martin & Wheeler, and the salt supply came by boat from lumber towns in northern Michigan. In 1886 Joy Morton became the controlling owner of Haskins, Martin & Wheeler (renamed Joy Morton & Company). The company remained a sales agency until 1890, when it built its first salt evaporation plant in Wyandotte, Michigan. In 1910 the company was renamed Morton Salt Company. In 1914, after 3 years of advertisements featuring the Morton Salt girl holding an umbrella, the company added its now-well-known slogan, "When it rains it pours."

Morton expanded nationwide with 8 production centers in the 1940s. It also bought a Louisiana salt plant (1947) for salt cake (paper making) and muriatic acid (steel production). In 1951 the company purchased Edwal Laboratories, an Illinois manufacturer of photographic chemicals, and introduced Morton Pellets, salt for recharging home water softeners. In 1954 Morton purchased the Canadian Salt Company Ltd.

In the 1960s Morton diversified by purchasing Adcote Chemicals (1964, commercial adhesives), Simoniz (1965, waxes), and Williams Hounslow (1967, food and cosmetic dyes). In 1969 Morton merged with Norwich Pharmacal, maker of drugs (Pepto-Bismol, Chloraseptic) and household cleaners (Fantastik,

Spray'N Wash), to form Morton-Norwich Products, Inc. During the 1970s the company organized into 4 divisions: salts, pharmaceuticals, household products, and specialty chemicals. In 1982 the company sold its Norwich-Eaton Pharmaceuticals division to Procter & Gamble for $371 million. Later that year Morton-Norwich bought Thiokol, Inc., a rocket and chemical manufacturer, to form Morton Thiokol, Inc.

The company successfully applied Thiokol's propulsion knowledge to develop automobile air bags. However, then-CEO Charles Locke was concerned that aerospace represented about 45% of sales but only 28% of profits in 1987. By 1989 salt and specialty chemicals outperformed aerospace by an even wider margin, and the company spun off the aerospace division into a new company, Thiokol Corporation. Morton International retained the salt, chemical, and air bag businesses.

In 1990 Morton bought Whitaker Corporation (coatings, adhesives). Morton formed a joint venture with Germany's Robert Bosch to produce air bags for the European market, and it sold its food and cosmetic colors business in 1991. In 1992 Morton Bendix, a joint venture with the Bendix Safety Restraints Group of AlliedSignal, opened an air bag module assembly plant in Tennessee.

To support the rapid growth in the European air bag market, the company acquired air bag production facilities in Germany and Amsterdam in 1994.

In 1995 Morton won a contract to supply passenger-side air bags for GM's C/K trucks.

NYSE symbol: MII
Fiscal year ends: June 30

WHO

Chairman and CEO: S. Jay Stewart, age 57,
$1,353,333 pay
President and COO: William E. Johnston Jr., age 55,
$637,250 pay (prior to promotion)
VP; President, Adhesives and Specialty Polymers:
Thomas S. Russell, age 50, $457,083 pay
VP Legal Affairs and General Counsel: James R. Stanley,
age 63, $435,600 pay
VP; President, Coatings: Stephen A. Gerow, age 52,
$421,955 pay
VP; President, Salt: Walter W. Becky II, age 52
VP; President, Electronic Materials: Daniel D. Feinberg
VP; President, Specialty Chemical Products: James J.
Fuerholzer, age 59
VP; President, Automotive Safety Products: Fred J.
Musone, age 51
VP Finance and CFO: Thomas F. McDevitt, age 55
VP Human Resources: Christopher K. Julsrud, age 48
Auditors: Ernst & Young LLP

WHERE

HQ: 100 N. Riverside Plaza, Chicago, IL 60606-1596
Phone: 312-807-2000
Fax: 312-807-2241

Morton operates facilities in the US, the Bahamas,
Belgium, Canada, France, Germany, Italy, Japan, Mexico,
the Netherlands, and the UK.

	1995 Sales		1995 Operating Income	
	$ mil.	% of total	$ mil.	% of total
US	2,646	79	467	82
Europe	465	14	62	11
Canada/Bahamas	185	6	35	6
Other regions	30	1	3	1
Adjustments	29	—	—	—
Total	**3,355**	**100**	**567**	**100**

WHAT

	1995 Sales		1995 Operating Income	
	$ mil.	% of total	$ mil.	% of total
Specialty chemicals	1,565	47	224	39
Automotive safety products	1,226	36	227	40
Salt	535	16	117	21
Interest & other	29	1	—	—
Total	**3,355**	**100**	**568**	**100**

Specialty Chemicals
Automotive coatings
Industrial adhesives
Industrial coatings
Liquid and dry film
photoresists
Liquid colorants
Organic specialties
Packaging adhesives
Performance chemicals
Plastic additives
Polymers and sealants
Powder coatings
Process chemicals and
ancillary products for
printed circuit boards
Specialty dyes
Thermoplastic
polyurethanes

Traffic markings
Water-based polymers

Automotive Safety Products
Driver-side and passenger-
side air bag inflators and
modules

Salt
Agricultural salt
Food/chemical processing
salt
Highway/ice control salt
(SAFE-T-SALT)
Morton and Windsor table
salts
Private-label table salt
Water conditioning salt

KEY COMPETITORS

American Home
Products
ARCO
Ashland Inc.
Atlantic Richfield
BASF
Bayer
Breed Technologies
Cargill
Ciba-Geigy

Dow Chemical
DuPont
FMC
Hercules
Hitachi
Hoechst
Imperial Chemical
3M
Mobil

PPG
Rhône-Poulenc
Safety
Components
Sherwin-
Williams
TRW
Union Carbide
W. R. Grace

HOW MUCH

	Annual Growth	1986	1987	1988	1989	1990	1991	1992	1993	1994	1995[1]
Sales ($ mil.)	14.1%	1,023	1,104	1,262	1,422	1,657	1,929	2,078	2,331	2,878	3,355
Net income ($ mil.)	14.1%	90	105	116	97	135	138	145	127	227	294
Income as % of sales	—	8.8%	9.5%	9.2%	6.8%	8.1%	7.2%	7.0%	5.4%	7.9%	8.8%
Earnings per share ($)	13.4%	0.63	0.74	0.81	0.68	0.93	0.95	0.98	0.86	1.51	1.96
Stock price – high ($)	—	—	—	—	13.96	15.83	19.42	21.63	33.54	37.25	32.00
Stock price – low ($)	—	—	—	—	10.50	11.17	12.88	16.92	19.25	25.50	26.25
Stock price – close ($)	16.1%	—	—	—	11.96	15.21	19.38	20.29	31.17	28.50	29.25
P/E – high	—	—	—	—	21	17	20	22	39	25	16
P/E – low	—	—	—	—	16	12	14	17	22	17	13
Dividends per share ($)	—	—	—	—	0.00	0.29	0.31	0.32	0.32	0.37	0.44
Book value per share ($)	10.2%	—	—	—	6.27	7.00	7.61	8.40	8.20	9.48	11.22
Employees	5.9%	7,700	7,700	7,800	8,400	9,700	10,200	10,700	11,900	13,100	13,800

1995 Year-end:
Debt ratio: 13.6%
Return on equity: 19.2%
Cash (mil.): $88
Current ratio: 2.11
Long-term debt (mil.): $219
No. of shares (mil.): 148.3
Dividends
Yield: 1.5%
Payout: 22.4%
Market value (mil.): $4,338

Stock Price History[1]
High/Low 1989–95

40
35
30
25
20
15
10
5
0

[1] 1995 stock prices are through fiscal year-end (June 30).

MOTOROLA, INC.

OVERVIEW

Wireless communications pioneer Motorola is running rings around the competition. The Schaumburg, Illinois–based company is leading a consortium that will ring the planet with low-orbit satellites to provide instant global telecommunications services by 1998. Motorola owns 30% of the project, called Iridium, which also involves BCE, Ericsson, Lockheed, Raytheon, and Sprint.

Motorola manufactures a wide range of products, including semiconductors, computers and microcomputer boards, cellular telephones (#1 producer worldwide), pagers (85% of the global market), and data communications equipment. The company also makes electronic systems and controls for aerospace, automotive, communications, lighting, military, navigation, and transportation industry customers.

In 1988 Motorola won the first Malcolm Baldrige Quality Award. The company invests heavily in both quality management (employees receive 40 hours of training each year through "Motorola University") and technology development (the company was granted 940 patents granted in 1994).

With contracts in countries such as China, Colombia, India, and Malaysia, Motorola is taking wireless phone service to areas where traditional wired service is underdeveloped and revenue potential is enormous. The company is also supplying pagers and paging infrastructure to India's first commercial paging service, which started in early 1995.

WHEN

Two individuals share primary responsibility for shaping Motorola. The first, Paul Galvin, founded Galvin Manufacturing in Chicago in 1928. The following year he began producing car radio receivers and trying to develop a mobile radio for the police. The 2nd key figure, Daniel Noble, was a professor working on mobile design when he met Galvin, who persuaded him to join the company in 1940. That same year Motorola developed the first handheld 2-way radio for the US Army.

In 1947 Galvin renamed the company Motorola, after its car radios. That same year Noble established an Arizona research laboratory to pursue defense contracts for radio communications. Radios and TVs required vacuum tubes, which Motorola had to purchase. Noble persuaded Galvin to invest R&D dollars in solid-state devices, and in the late 1950s Motorola turned to semiconductors. The company began manufacturing integrated circuits and microprocessors, which allowed it to market outside its auto industry mainstay. Galvin died in 1959, and his son Robert became CEO. Noble continued as chairman of the science committee. In 1965 Motorola debuted the 8-track tape player for automobiles.

In the 1970s Motorola changed focus. The company launched its 6800 microprocessor and sold its TV business to Matsushita (Japan) in 1974, then began investing in the data communications market for hardware (such as modems) through the acquisitions of Codex (1977) and Universal Data Systems (1978). In 1987 Motorola made its last car radio.

Robert Galvin's chosen successor, George Fisher, took over in 1990. That same year

Motorola organized the $3.4 billion Iridium project, an ambitious scheme to create a global satellite system capable of handling digital service to hand-held telephones, faxes, and pagers without using land-based stations; commercial service is expected in 1998. In 1991 Motorola formed a partnership with IBM and Apple to develop the PowerPC chip. That same year Motorola started making electronic ballasts for lighting systems.

In 1993 the company acquired Lexicus (handwriting-recognition software for pen-based computers) and purchased a 40% interest in Monterrey, Mexico–based CedeTel, a regional cellular phone service.

Galvin's son Christopher was widely expected to be Fisher's successor until Fisher jumped to Eastman Kodak in 1993 after only 3 years at Motorola's helm. Gary Tooker became CEO, and Christopher took over the #2 spot. In 1993 William Weisz was made chairman, a position now separate from management.

In 1994 Motorola joined with Apple and IBM to develop the PowerPC microprocessor. The company sold its US 800MHz mobile radio business to Nextel for a minority stake in Nextel valued at $1.7 billion.

In 1995 Motorola began shipping its handheld Envoy wireless communicator, used to exchange electronic messages and receive stock updates. That year Motorola completed a DRAM plant in Japan (a joint venture with Toshiba). It also signed 4 technology agreements for Chinese projects, including joint ventures with Leshan Radio and Panda Electronics Group, and it announced plans to build a $720 million computer chip plant in Tianjin.

WHO

Chairman: William J. Weisz, age 67
VC: John F. Mitchell, age 66, $1,320,000 pay
VC and CEO: Gary L. Tooker, age 55, $1,980,000 pay
President and COO: Christopher B. Galvin, age 44, $1,488,667 pay
EVP; President and General Manager, General Systems Sector: Edward F. Staiano, age 58, $1,263,000 pay
EVP and CFO: Carl F. Koenemann, age 56
EVP; Manager, Semiconductor Products Sector: Thomas D. George, age 54
EVP; President and General Manager, Land Mobile Products Sector: Merle Gilmore, age 46
EVP; President and General Manager, Messaging, Information, and Media Sector: Robert L. Growney, age 52
EVP; President and General Manager, Government and Space Technology Group: David G. Wolfe, age 59
EVP and Director, Automotive, Energy, and Controls Group: Frederick T. Tucker, age 54
EVP; Director Human Resources: James Donnelly, age 55
Auditors: KPMG Peat Marwick LLP

WHERE

HQ: 1303 E. Algonquin Rd., Schaumburg, IL 60196
Phone: 847-576-5000
Fax: 847-576-8003

Motorola has manufacturing facilities in the US and 18 foreign countries.

	1994 Sales		1994 Operating Income	
	$ mil.	% of total	$ mil.	% of total
US	16,297	56	1,932	60
Other countries	12,758	44	1,292	40
Adjustments	(6,810)	—	(353)	—
Total	**22,245**	**100**	**2,871**	**100**

WHAT

	1994 Sales		1994 Operating Income	
	$ mil.	% of total	$ mil.	% of total
General systems	8,613	35	1,214	41
Semiconductors	6,936	28	996	34
Communications	5,776	24	589	20
Govt. & systems technology	829	3	(55)	—
Other products	2,434	10	156	5
Adjustments	(2,343)	—	(29)	—
Total	**22,245**	**100**	**2,871**	**100**

Selected Products
Cellular infrastructure equipment systems
Computers and microcomputers
Electronic ballasts for fluorescent lighting
High-speed leased-line and dial modems
Microprocessors, microcontrollers, gate arrays, and motherboards
Radio-telephone products (cellular and cordless telephones)
Two-way radios (mobile and portable), radio paging products and services, and wireless data systems
X.25 networking equipment

KEY COMPETITORS

AMD	Hitachi	Robert Bosch
Analog Devices	Hyundai	Samsung
Apple	IBM	Siemens
AT&T	Intel	Silicon Graphics
Chips and Technologies	LG Group	Texas Instruments
Cirrus Logic	Matsushita	Thomson SA
Cyrix	Mitsubishi	Toshiba
DEC	National Semiconductor	Trimble Navigation
Eaton	NEC	U.S. Robotics
Ericsson	Nokia	Westinghouse
Fujitsu	Oki	Zoom
Harris	Philips	Telephonics
Hewlett-Packard	Pioneer	

HOW MUCH

	Annual Growth	1985	1986	1987	1988	1989	1990	1991	1992	1993	1994
Sales ($ mil.)	16.9%	5,443	5,888	6,707	8,250	9,620	10,885	11,341	13,303	16,963	22,245
Net income ($ mil.)	40.7%	72	194	308	445	498	499	454	576	1,022	1,560
Income as % of sales	—	1.3%	3.3%	4.6%	5.4%	5.2%	4.6%	4.0%	4.3%	6.0%	7.0%
Earnings per share ($)	36.6%	0.16	0.39	0.60	0.86	0.96	0.95	0.86	1.08	1.78	2.65
Stock price – high ($)	—	10.19	12.50	18.50	13.66	15.63	22.09	17.81	26.59	53.75	61.13
Stock price – low ($)	—	7.28	8.41	8.75	8.97	9.88	12.28	11.44	16.06	24.38	42.13
Stock price – close ($)	22.0%	9.72	8.91	12.44	10.50	14.59	13.09	16.31	26.13	46.13	58.00
P/E – high	—	64	33	31	16	16	23	21	25	30	23
P/E – low	—	46	22	15	10	10	13	13	15	14	16
Dividends per share ($)	7.6%	0.16	0.16	0.16	0.16	0.19	0.19	0.19	0.19	0.22	0.31
Book value per share ($)	13.9%	4.79	5.37	5.83	6.51	7.29	8.08	8.76	9.54	11.50	15.47
Employees	4.3%	90,200	94,400	97,700	102,000	104,000	105,000	103,000	107,000	120,000	132,000

1994 Year-end:
Debt ratio: 18.3%
Return on equity: 20.1%
Cash (mil.): $1,059
Current ratio: 1.51
Long-term debt (mil.): $1,127
No. of shares (mil.): 588
Dividends
 Yield: 0.5%
 Payout: 11.7%
Market value (mil.): $34,104

**Stock Price History
High/Low 1985–94**

NAVISTAR INTERNATIONAL

OVERVIEW

Chicago-based Navistar is the US's #1 maker of heavy- and medium-sized trucks (27% of the 1994 market) and the leading supplier of school bus chassis. The company also builds diesel engines for its vehicles and sells engines to original equipment makers. In addition, Navistar provides financing and insurance to both dealers and customers.

After years of losses, Navistar is starting to rally. In 1994 the company made its first profit since 1989. Navistar has been adding new shifts, overtime, and more employees at some of its manufacturing plants to match an upsurge in demand. The company also rolled out some improved products in 1994, such as new engines and larger sleeping compartments — amenities trucking companies want in order to attract drivers. Also that year Navistar produced its first fully electronic diesel engine. The company is continuing to upgrade its engines, which it started doing in 1993.

However, Navistar is still hobbled by the expense of retiree health care costs, although it cut its health and operational costs $280 million over the last 2 years. The company has set cost reduction goals that include simplifying its products, using fewer parts, and reducing development times.

WHEN

Cyrus McCormick, the Virginia-born inventor who perfected the reaper in 1831, moved west and set up his first factory in Chicago in 1846. To compete with other manufacturers, McCormick offered such innovations as the installment plan, a written guarantee, and factory-trained repairmen. In 1886 a strike at the Chicago works in favor of the 8-hour workday led to the infamous Haymarket Square riot. In 1902, with the backing of J. P. Morgan, McCormick merged with Deering and several smaller firms to form International Harvester (IH). The new enterprise controlled 85% of US harvester production.

IH set up its first overseas factory in 1905 in Sweden. In 1906 Harvester entered the tractor industry and in 1907 began production of the Auto Buggy, forerunner of the truck. By 1910 the firm was annually producing 1,300 trucks and 1,400 tractors and had reached over $100 million in sales.

In 1913 Cyrus Jr. (Cyrus Sr. had died in 1884) borrowed $5 million from John D. Rockefeller and gained control of the company. The new general manager, Alexander Legge (also president from 1922 to 1929), introduced the Farmall, the first all-purpose tractor, in 1924. In 1928 IH began production of a heavy truck with a 4-cylinder engine, and by 1937 it was the top US producer of medium and heavy trucks.

In the post-WWII industry boom, IH's neglect of product development and capital improvement, combined with the effects of overdiversification, caused market share to decline for most of its products. The company sold more trucks than agricultural equipment for the first time in 1955. IH lost its lead in agricultural equipment to John Deere in 1958. During the 1960s IH lost its medium industry sales leadership to Ford, and the company's construction equipment business, although buoyed by the 1952 acquisition of the Payloader, consistently lost market share.

A 6-month strike by the UAW in 1980, coupled with a recession, sent IH to the edge of bankruptcy. Between 1980 and 1982 the company lost $2.3 billion. Restructuring, IH sold the construction equipment division to Dresser Industries in 1982. In 1985 Tenneco bought the agricultural equipment business and the International Harvester name. By 1986 the number of employees had dropped 85%, and plants had decreased from 48 worldwide to 6 in North America.

The company was renamed Navistar in 1986. By 1987 it had redesigned 85% of its truck line. In 1989 Navistar introduced a 9-speed heavy truck transmission (developed jointly with Dana), the first all-new design in more than 25 years. In 1991 Navistar raised its stake in Mexican truck maker Dina Camiones to 17% and inked OEM deals for its engines with Perkins Group (UK) and Perkins's North American distributor, Detroit Diesel. The next year Navistar announced it would recall up to 185,000 school buses after one failed a federal safety test.

A boom in demand for heavy trucks in 1992 and 1993 resulted in Navistar's retail deliveries rising nearly 33%. Also in 1993 the company started a program to increase fuel efficiency and torque in its engines. That same year Navistar introduced 3 new 6-cylinder engines for its line of medium trucks. In 1994 Navistar was the first truck maker to offer a one-million-mile warranty for its heavy trucks.

In early 1995 chairman and CEO James Cotting stepped down, relinquishing his posts to John Horne, Navistar's president and COO.

WHO

Chairman, President, and CEO: John R. Horne, age 56, $543,000 pay (prior to promotion)
EVP and CFO: Robert C. Lannert, age 54, $393,833 pay
Group VP; General Manager Financial Services: John J. Bongiorno, $313,420 pay
Group VP Truck Businesses: David J. Johanneson
Group VP Sales and Distribution: James T. O'Dare Jr.
Group VP; General Manager Engine and Foundry: Daniel C. Ustian
Group VP International Operations: Dennis W. Webb
SVP and General Counsel: Robert A. Boardman, age 47, $310,510 pay
SVP Employee Relations and Administration: John M. Sheahin
VP Truck Engineering: Kirk A. Gutmann
VP and Treasurer: Thomas M. Hough
VP and Controller: Robert I. Morrison
Auditors: Deloitte & Touche LLP

WHERE

HQ: Navistar International Corporation,
455 N. Cityfront Plaza Dr., Chicago, IL 60611
Phone: 312-836-2000
Fax: 312-836-2192

Navistar has 7 manufacturing and assembly plants in the US and one in Canada. The company sells its products through approximately 951 dealers in North America and exports trucks and parts to more than 77 countries around the world.

	1994 Sales	
	$ mil.	% of total
US	4,670	91
Canada	483	9
Adjustments	184	—
Total	**5,337**	**100**

WHAT

	1994 Sales	
	$ mil.	% of total
Manufacturing	5,153	96
Financial services	152	3
Other	32	1
Total	**5,337**	**100**

	1994 Sales
	% of total
Heavy trucks	42
Medium trucks	32
Replacement parts	14
Engines	12
Total	**100**

Navistar International Transportation Corp.
Diesel engines
Replacement parts
School bus chassis
Trucks

Navistar Financial Corporation
Customer financing
Dealer financing
Insurance

KEY COMPETITORS

Blue Bird	Mitsubishi
Caterpillar	Nissan
Cummins Engine	Oshkosh Truck
Daimler-Benz	PACCAR
Fiat	Peugeot
Ford	Renault
General Motors	Saab-Scania
Harley-Davidson	Tata
Hino	Volvo
Isuzu	

HOW MUCH

	Annual Growth	1985	1986	1987	1988	1989	1990	1991	1992	1993	1994
Sales ($ mil.)	4.7%	3,508	3,357	3,530	4,080	4,023	3,643	3,259	3,875	4,694	5,337
Net income ($ mil.)	—	(463)	(2)	146	244	87	(11)	(165)	(212)	(273)	82
Income as % of sales	—	—	—	4.1%	6.0%	2.2%	—	—	—	—	1.5%
Earnings per share ($)	—	(36.70)	(1.80)	5.00	8.40	2.30	(1.60)	(7.70)	(9.50)	(8.63)	0.72
Stock price – high ($)	—	112.50	116.25	87.50	73.75	70.00	46.25	42.50	41.25	33.75	26.63
Stock price – low ($)	—	65.00	41.25	30.00	31.25	32.50	20.00	21.25	17.50	19.25	12.25
Stock price – close ($)	(17.5%)	85.00	47.50	42.50	53.75	38.75	22.50	26.25	22.50	23.63	15.13
P/E – high	—	—	—	18	9	30	—	—	—	—	37
P/E – low	—	—	—	6	4	14	—	—	—	—	17
Dividends per share ($)	—	0.00	0.00	0.00	0.00	0.00	0.00	0.00	0.00	0.00	0.00
Book value per share ($)	—	(138.07)	(27.76)	14.98	24.10	26.43	22.80	13.27	3.66	7.09	7.71
Employees	(1.3%)	16,836	14,997	14,918	15,719	14,118	14,071	13,472	13,945	13,612	14,910

1994 Year-end:
Debt ratio: 59.9%
Return on equity: 14.9%
Cash (mil.): $557
Current ratio: 1.59
Long-term debt (mil.): $696
No. of shares (mil.): 74
Dividends
  Yield: —
  Payout: —
Market value (mil.): $1,125

**Stock Price History
High/Low 1985–94**

NIPSCO INDUSTRIES, INC.

OVERVIEW

NIPSCO has divided its sales forces and is battling with itself in a rehearsal for the expected war of retail competition. The Hammond, Indiana–based holding company owns several utility and nonutility subsidiaries, including Northern Indiana Public Service Company. Northern Indiana's electric division generates, distributes, and sells electricity to more than 400,000 customers in northern Indiana; its gas division, along with NIPSCO subsidiaries Kokomo Gas and Fuel Co. and Northern Indiana Fuel and Light Co., distributes and sells natural gas to nearly 700,000 customers in the same area. NIPSCO's nonutility subsidiaries engage in activities such as cogeneration and gas brokering in the Midwest and overseas.

In 1994 NIPSCO CEO Gary Neale declared, "Anyone who doesn't think that retail wheeling [competition] is coming hasn't lived on

this planet in the last year." Neale reinforced these words with actions: Northern Indiana's electric and gas utility was divided into competing units — each with its own sales force. NIPSCO diversified its corporate culture (and ended its monopoly-driven inertia) by replacing about 25–30% of its utility employees with marketing specialists and people from the banking, medical, and pipeline industries. The rest of its workforce was retrained.

Neale wants to grow earnings 10% annually by lowering costs, moving into new markets, acquiring other utilities, and developing new products and services (such as home security, gas appliance repair, and electric sales during peak demand periods). He plans to add 250,000 new customers within 5 years, in part through the anticipated growth of Hammond as a bedroom community for nearby Chicago.

WHEN

The earliest of NIPSCO Industries' ancestors was the South Bend (Indiana) Gas Light Co., which was founded in 1868 by the Studebaker brothers (of later auto fame) to supply manufactured gas.

In 1886 natural gas was discovered near Kokomo, Indiana, which led to a boom in northern Indiana's use of the fuel. By the turn of the century steel plants and other industries set up along the shore of Lake Michigan in northwestern Indiana (known as the Calumet region) and neighboring Illinois, fueling the area's growth and demand for power.

Another of NIPSCO's forebears was the Hammond Illuminating Co., formed in 1901. Hammond soon changed its name to South Shore Gas and Electric Co. and acquired a neighboring utility. In 1909 the Northern Indiana Gas and Electric Co. was founded by merging South Shore with other utilities in the Calumet region. In 1910 Northern Indiana acquired South Bend (which had changed its name to South Bend and Mishawaka Gas Co.).

The 3rd and last of NIPSCO's predecessors was the Calumet Electric Co., formed in 1912. Over the years the company built transmission lines to serve outlying towns and acquired several utilities. By the early 1920s Calumet Electric was acquired by utility magnate Samuel Insull as part of his huge Midland Utilities holding company. In 1923 Insull added Northern Indiana Gas and Electric. In 1926 those 2 utilities were merged to form Northern Indiana Public Service Company. NIPSCO acquired its present service territory

in 1930 when it swapped some areas with another Midland subsidiary. Despite the Depression, NIPSCO rapidly expanded its generating capacity.

By 1947 the Public Utility Holding Company Act of 1935 (which inaugurated the present era of regulated regional monopolies) had forced Midland to divest NIPSCO. In the 1950s and 1960s the firm built 2 power plants and signed a contract with a Houston gas company that tripled NIPSCO's natural gas supply.

Demand for electricity continued to rise, and in 1970 NIPSCO applied for a permit to build a nuclear unit at its Bailly plant (Porter County), estimated to cost $180 million. In 1976 NIPSCO brought the coal-fired Schahfer power plant (Jasper County) online. By 1981 the nuke's projected cost had risen to $2.1 billion, prompting its abandonment. In 1987 the firm reorganized and formed a holding company, NIPSCO Industries.

The National Energy Policy Act of 1992 fundamentally changed the electric industry by allowing wholesale competition. That same year, NIPSCO acquired Kokomo Gas and Fuel and Northern Indiana Fuel and Light. In 1993 NIPSCO brought a pulverized tire–fueled power plant into service in England.

Gary Neale became head of NIPSCO in 1993 and instituted a new strategy intended to prepare the company for greater competition. In 1995 the company announced plans to build 3 cogeneration facilities, which will produce nearly 300 megawatts for 3 major steel plants in northwestern Indiana.

NYSE symbol: NI
Fiscal year ends: December 31

WHO

Chairman, President, and CEO: Gary L. Neale, age 54, $690,000 pay
EVP, CFO, and Treasurer: Stephen P. Adik, age 51, $287,000 pay
EVP and COO, Electric: Patrick J. Mulchay, age 52, $245,000 pay
EVP and COO, Gas: Jeffrey W. Yundt, age 49, $245,000 pay
VP Human Resources: Owen C. Johnson Jr., age 48
Auditors: Arthur Andersen & Co, SC

WHERE

HQ: 5265 Hohman Ave., Hammond, IN 46320-1775
Phone: 219-853-5200
Fax: 219-647-5589

NIPSCO subsidiary Crossroads Pipeline Co. owns a 202-mile natural gas pipeline running from northwestern Indiana to Cygnet, Ohio. NIPSCO Development Co., owns a 325,000-square-foot office building in Merrillville, Indiana. Northern Indiana Public Service Co. owns and operates 4 coal-fired and 2 hydroelectric power plants in Indiana.

WHAT

	1994 Electric Generating Capacity	
	MW	% of total
Coal-fired steam	3,059	90
Gas turbine	203	6
Gas-fired steam	120	4
Hydroelectric	10	—
Total	**3,392**	**100**

	1994 Electricity Marketed	
	kWh (mil.)	% of total
Industrial	9,542	61
Commercial	2,737	18
Residential	2,552	16
Wholesale	564	4
Street lighting	55	—
Other	86	1
Total	**15,536**	**100**

	1994 Sales	
	$ mil.	% of total
Electric utility operations		
Industrial	450	27
Residential	260	16
Commercial	238	14
Wholesale	22	1
Other	24	1
Subtotal	**994**	**59**
Gas operations		
Residential	449	27
Commercial	153	9
Industrial	76	5
Gas transported	34	2
Other	(30)	—
Subtotal	**682**	**41**
Total	**1,676**	**100**

Selected Nonutility Subsidiaries
NIPSCO Capital Markets, Inc. (funding agent for subsidiaries' business ventures)
NIPSCO Development Company, Inc. (develops cogeneration, environmental, and real estate projects)
NIPSCO Energy Services, Inc. (coordinates energy-related diversification; owns subsidiaries Crossroads, Fuel, NETCO, and NI-TEX)

KEY COMPETITORS

American Electric
Central Illinois Public Service
CINergy
Indiana Energy
Indiana Municipal Power
IPALCO Enterprises
Unicom
Wabash Valley Power

HOW MUCH

	Annual Growth	1985	1986	1987	1988	1989	1990	1991	1992	1993	1994
Sales ($ mil.)	(1.4%)	1,909	1,626	1,452	1,524	1,560	1,521	1,535	1,582	1,678	1,676
Net income ($ mil.)	4.8%	107	(14)	65	123	137	125	133	137	156	164
Income as % of sales	—	5.6%	—	4.5%	8.1%	8.8%	8.2%	8.7%	8.6%	9.3%	9.8%
Earnings per share ($)	9.5%	1.10	(0.57)	0.53	1.41	1.72	1.81	1.94	2.00	2.31	2.48
Stock price – high ($)	—	12.88	13.50	18.50	14.13	19.63	19.25	27.00	26.63	34.88	33.00
Stock price – low ($)	—	8.38	9.38	8.00	8.63	13.13	15.75	18.50	22.50	26.13	26.13
Stock price – close ($)	13.0%	9.88	11.75	8.50	13.88	19.38	18.88	25.75	26.50	32.88	29.75
P/E – high	—	12	—	35	10	11	11	14	13	15	13
P/E – low	—	8	—	15	6	8	9	10	11	11	11
Dividends per share ($)	(0.9%)	1.56	0.00	0.15	0.45	0.84	1.04	1.16	1.24	1.32	1.44
Book value per share ($)	2.6%	13.73	13.16	13.13	14.03	13.92	14.64	15.17	15.73	16.63	17.34
Employees	(2.9%)	5,774	5,695	5,172	4,946	4,825	4,547	4,600	4,648	4,602	4,441

1994 Year-end:
Debt ratio: 54.0%
Return on equity: 14.9%
Cash (mil.): $40
Current ratio: 0.51
Long-term debt (mil.): $1,180
No. of shares (mil.): 64
Dividends
  Yield: 4.8%
  Payout: 58.1%
Market value (mil.): $1,901

**Stock Price History
High/Low 1985–94**

NORTHERN TRUST CORPORATION

OVERVIEW

Northern Trust Corp. is one of Chicago's most venerable financial institutions and one of the few that have not yet been acquired by an out-of-town bank.

The company's flagship operation is Northern Trust Co., which provides banking and trust services (administration of trusts and estates, stock transfer and registration, and investment management) to businesses, financial institutions, and well-off individuals in the Chicago area. Its Arizona, California, Florida, and Texas banks provide the same services in those regions. It is one of the leading master trustees for company pension and profit-sharing plans.

Through its other subsidiaries, Northern Trust provides international banking and trust, brokerage, leasing and lease financing, and pension and retirement services. One of

its subsidiaries manages real estate foreclosures from loans gone bad.

In 1994 Northern Trust restructured its internal operations into two broad categories. Corporate and Institutional Services integrates all facets of business-to-business operations in order to offer seamless service to (and generate more income from) clients by addressing the full range of their needs rather than having each department focus on its own narrow function. Personal Financial Services does the same for individual clients.

Northern Trust intends to grow through expansion within the states where it currently does business (many of which, such as Florida and Arizona, are meccas for well-off retirees).

The founding Smith family is represented on the board by Harold Smith, who controls almost 7% of the company.

WHEN

In 1885 Byron Smith took time off from his banking career to take care of some family matters. Friends turned to him for advice on trust and estate matters, and it occurred to Smith that there was a market for such services within a banking framework.

Bank regulation was unfamiliar and suspect in the 1880s, so Smith used Northern Trust to test the validity of new Illinois banking and trust administration rules by arranging for the state to reject his charter application. The regulations were upheld. Northern Trust opened in 1889 in one of Chicago's newfangled skyscrapers, the Rookery, designed by Louis Sullivan. With capital of $1 million — 40% from Smith and the rest from the likes of Marshall Field (retailing), Martin Ryerson (steel), and Philip Armour (meat) — the bank attracted $138,000 in deposits on its first day.

Northern Trust was an aggressive advertiser, using direct mail and newspapers, and was one of the first banks to hire an ad agency. In 1893 the bank received another boost when it was asked to operate a branch bank at the Columbian Exposition. By 1896 the bank was firmly established; Smith began taking a salary and the company issued its first dividend. Ten years later the bank built itself a home, a granite edifice that conveys strength and solidity.

The bank began buying commercial paper in 1912, joined the Federal Reserve System in 1917, and became a custodian for expropriated German assets during WWI. Byron Smith died in 1914 and was succeeded by his son, Solomon, who had begun working at the bank

in 1899. Solomon's tenure lasted until 1963, when he retired at age 86.

The bank rejected the get-rich-quick ethos of the 1920s and was in such good shape during the Depression that at the conclusion of Franklin Roosevelt's 8-day bank holiday in 1933 it experienced a reverse run, with people clamoring to make deposits. During the Depression, the bank administered the scholarship fund that helped Ronald Reagan attend Eureka College. By 1941 almost half of Northern Trust's commercial deposits originated outside the Chicago area. The bank kept growing during the war and, soon after, pioneered automated statements.

Solomon was succeeded in 1963 by his son, Edward. (He retired in 1979.) Edward oversaw the company's expansion overseas (Northern Trust International was formed in 1968) and out of state (Florida in 1971, Arizona in 1974). The company's business was also helped by the 1974 passage by Congress of ERISA, which required company retirement plans to be overseen by an outside custodian. In 1981 Illinois began allowing intrastate branch banking, and Northern Trust expanded within the Chicago area.

During the 1980s the bank expanded into California (1988) and Texas (1989). In 1987 Northern Trust had a loss, in part due to defaults on loans to developing countries. It navigated the recession of the late 1980s and early 1990s and continued to expand. In 1995 it received permission to provide trust services throughout Canada.

Nasdaq symbol: NTRS
Fiscal year ends: December 31

WHO

Chairman and CEO: William A. Osborn, age 47,
$635,000 pay (prior to promotion)
President and COO: Barry G. Hastings, age 47,
$600,000 pay (prior to promotion)
SEVP and CFO: Perry R. Pero, age 55, $485,500 pay
EVP, General Counsel, and Secretary: Peter L. Rossiter,
age 46, $393,750 pay
**EVP Institutional Financial Services, Corporate and
Institutional Services Unit:** J. David Brock, age 50
EVP Worldwide Operations: James J. Mitchell, age 52
SVP and Chief Investment Officer: James M. Snyder,
age 48
SVP Human Resources: William Setterstrom
Auditors: Arthur Andersen & Co, SC

WHERE

HQ: 50 S. LaSalle St., Chicago IL 60675
Phone: 312-630-6000
Fax: 312-630-1512

Northern Trust operates in Arizona, California, Florida,
Georgia, Illinois, New York, Texas, and Washington in
the US as well as Canada, the Cayman Islands, France,
Hong Kong, and the UK.

	1994 Pretax Income	
	$ mil.	% of total
Europe	19	39
Latin America	12	25
North America	9	19
Asia/Pacific	8	17
Total	**48**	**100**

WHAT

	1994 Assets	
	$ mil.	% of total
Cash & equivalents	3,844	21
US Treasurys	938	5
Mortgage-backed securities	3,252	17
State & municipal bonds	474	3
Other securities	389	2
Net loans & leases	8,446	45
Other	1,219	7
Other	**18,562**	**100**

	1994 Sales	
	$ mil.	% of total
Income from loans & leases	500	34
Income from securities	235	16
Interest on bank deposits	98	7
Other interest	16	1
Trust fees	453	30
Commissions & trading	18	1
Other	159	11
Total	**1,479**	**100**

Selected Subsidiaries
Berry, Hartell, Evers & Osborne, Inc. (investment
management company)
Hazelhurst & Associates, Inc. (retirement benefit
services)
MFC Co., Inc. (holder of defaulted properties)
NorLease, Inc. (leasing and lease financing)
Northern Futures Corp.
Northern Trust Banks (banking and trust services)
Northern Trust Co., Canada (banking & trust services)
Northern Trust International Banking Corp.
(international operations)

KEY COMPETITORS

BankAmerica
Bank of Montreal
Bankers Trust
Chase Manhattan
Citicorp
First Chicago
Republic New York
Transamerica

HOW MUCH °

	Annual Growth	1985	1986	1987	1988	1989	1990	1991	1992	1993	1994
Assets ($ mil.)	10.6%	7,500	9,090	9,326	9,904	10,938	11,789	13,193	14,960	16,903	18,562
Net income ($ mil.)	20.5%	34	52	(65)	109	113	115	127	150	168	182
Income as % of assets	—	0.5%	0.6%	—	1.1%	1.0%	1.0%	1.0%	1.0%	1.0%	1.0%
Earnings per share ($)	18.4%	0.69	1.08	(1.59)	2.13	2.01	2.05	2.27	2.64	2.95	3.16
Stock price – high ($)	—	9.46	15.67	17.01	15.84	23.64	22.51	34.68	43.19	50.50	43.25
Stock price – low ($)	—	6.59	9.42	10.09	12.34	14.76	13.01	18.01	32.68	37.00	32.25
Stock price – close ($)	15.7%	9.42	13.05	12.01	14.84	20.59	19.68	33.27	42.00	39.63	35.00
P/E – high	—	14	15	—	7	12	11	15	16	17	14
P/E – low	—	10	9	—	6	7	6	8	12	13	10
Dividends per share ($)	12.3%	0.31	0.31	0.31	0.33	0.41	0.51	0.56	0.64	0.74	0.88
Book value per share ($)	10.6%	8.29	9.10	7.19	9.05	10.55	11.57	14.11	15.91	18.42	20.53
Employees	4.2%	4,551	4,645	5,291	5,387	5,600	5,784	5,798	6,249	6,259	6,608

1994 Year-end:
Equity as % of assets: 6.9%
Return on equity: 17.4%
Return on assets: 1.0%
Long-term debt (mil.): $792
No. of shares (mil.): 54
Dividends
  Yield: 2.5%
  Payout: 27.8%
Market value (mil.): $1,893
Sales (mil.): $1,479

Stock Price History
High/Low 1985–94

NORTHWESTERN UNIVERSITY

OVERVIEW

Northwestern University is recognized as one of the leading institutions of higher learning in the US. The university's more than 17,000 full-time and part-time students do their course work on 2 campuses located next to Lake Michigan.

The larger of the 2 campuses is located in Evanston, Illinois, and includes Northwestern's college of arts and sciences; the schools of education, engineering, speech, and journalism; and graduate schools. The university's Chicago campus includes Northwestern's schools of law, medicine, and dentistry, as well as other graduate programs and several hospitals of the McGaw Medical Center.

Northwestern is best known for its journalism and drama programs (famous graduates include Charlton Heston, Warren Beatty, Cloris Leachman, and columnist Bob Greene) as well as its programs in engineering, business, music, and health services administration. A private institution, the university gets most of its revenue from tuition and student fees and government grants.

WHEN

In 1850 Northwestern University's founders met in a law office over a hardware store in downtown Chicago. All devout Methodists, the group included 3 lawyers, 2 businessmen, a physician, and 3 clergymen. Their goal was to create an institution of higher learning to serve the original Northwest Territory. (Created by an act of Congress in 1787, it included what became Ohio, Indiana, Illinois, Michigan, Wisconsin, and part of Minnesota.) The university was chartered in 1851, and in 1853 it acquired 379 acres of property north of Chicago on Lake Michigan. The board of trustees decided to name the area Evanston, after one of the school's founders, John Evans.

Northwestern began classes in the fall of 1855 in a 3-story frame building. The first class had 2 professors and an enrollment of 10 students (only 4 of whom were present the first day — some things never change).

By 1869 Northwestern had more than 100 students. That year the board of trustees decided to admit women to the university for the first time. In 1870 Northwestern signed an affiliation agreement with the Chicago Medical College (founded in 1859), and it continued to expand its curriculum. In 1873 it signed an agreement with the original University of Chicago (no relation to the current institution) to create the Union College of Law. When the University of Chicago closed in 1886 because of financial difficulties, Northwestern took control of the law school. That same year it added the Illinois College of Pharmacy as a university department, and it also began creating its dental school.

In 1891, led by new president Henry Wade Rogers, Northwestern reorganized, consolidating its affiliated professional schools (dentistry, law, medicine, and pharmacy) into the university. By that year Northwestern had a total enrollment of more than 2,000.

By 1900 Northwestern had grown to become the 3rd largest university in the US, after Harvard and Michigan, with an enrollment of 2,700. The university continued to grow rapidly, and by 1920 it had nearly 7,000 students. That year the university acquired land on the corner of Chicago Avenue and Lakeshore Drive to create a single campus for its Chicago schools. In 1926 the primary buildings on the campus were completed and the schools moved into their new facilities. In that decade the university created the Medill School of Journalism, named for Joseph Medill, founder of the *Chicago Tribune*, and it established the School of Education as a separate unit of the university.

Northwestern suffered a temporary drop in enrollment during the early 1930s because of the Depression, but it began to rebound later in the decade. During WWII much of the university's focus was on military training, with civilian classes cut back considerably. The end of WWII brought a jump in enrollment as veterans took advantage of the college scholarships offered by the G.I. Bill.

During the 1950s, 1960s, and 1970s the university undertook a major construction program, including filling in part of Lake Michigan to expand the campus during the early 1960s.

In 1985, in an effort to attract more high-tech industries, Northwestern and the city of Evanston began developing a research center in downtown Evanston on land next to the university. Northwestern's graduate school of business was named #1 in the US by *Business Week* in 1988, 1990, and 1992.

In 1994 Henry Bienen, a dean at Princeton, was named president of Northwestern. In 1995 the Northwestern Wildcat football team, long the doormat of the Big 10, won the conference championship and went to the Rose Bowl.

Private university
Fiscal year ends: August 31

WHERE

HQ: 1801 Hinman Ave., PO Box 3060, Evanston, IL
60204-3060
Phone: 847-491-7271
Fax: 847-491-2376

Campuses

Chicago
Dental School
Graduate School
Managers' Program of the J. L. Kellogg School of
Management
Medical School
School of Law
University College (continuing education)

Evanston
College of Arts and Sciences
Graduate School
J. L. Kellogg Graduate School of Management
Medill School of Journalism
Robert R. McCormick School of Engineering and
Applied Science
School of Education and Social Policy
School of Music
School of Speech

WHAT

1994 Revenues

	$ mil.	% of total
Tuition & fees	272	40
Grants & contracts	142	21
Sales & service	127	19
Investment income	49	7
Private gifts	28	4
Other	58	9
Total	**676**	**100**

1994 Expenditures

	$ mil.	% of total
Instruction	242	33
Research	122	17
Scholarships & fellowships	79	11
Maintenance of plant	46	6
Auxiliaries	41	6
Student services & academic support	40	5
Debt service	26	4
Administration & other	129	18
Total	**725**	**100**

1994 Degrees Conferred

	No.
Bachelor's	1,882
Master's	2,115
Doctorate	320
First professional	438
Certificate/diploma	67
Total	**4,822**

1995 Freshman Enrollment

	% of total
Midwest	52
Middle Atlantic states	14
West	13
South	8
New England	5
Southwest	4
Foreign	4
Total	**100**

HOW MUCH

	Annual Growth	1985	1986	1987	1988	1989	1990	1991	1992	1993	1994
Revenues ($ mil.)	7.1%	—	391	404	436	502	515	550	587	628	676
Endowment ($ mil.)	12.4%	—	—	—	517	573	572	581	647	717	1,045
Full-time enrollment	1.4%	12,283	12,515	12,655	12,788	12,980	13,158	13,267	13,618	13,711	13,946
Faculty[1]	4.0%	1,597	1,601	1,599	1,726	2,071	2,124	2,135	2,203	2,313	2,280
Employees	0.0%	—	—	—	—	—	—	—	—	5,650	5,650

Revenues ($ mil.)
1986–94

[1] Excluding part of medical school faculty for 1985–88

OUTBOARD MARINE CORPORATION

OVERVIEW

Waukegan-based Outboard Marine Corporation (OMC) is the company that invented the out-board motor and, in the process, recreational boating. It is the world's largest manufacturer of outboard motors and the US's 2nd largest boat builder, after Brunswick. OMC's major brands include well-known Chris-Craft and Grumman boats as well as Evinrude and Johnson outboard motors. In addition to aluminum boats, its products include fiberglass runabouts, cruisers, and fishing boats, under such names as Four Winns, Sunbird, Stratos, and Hydra-Sports. OMC's products are sold through a worldwide network of dealers. In 1994, 75% of sales were from the US.

OMC has had more than its share of turbulence. Intense competition and depressed markets have forced the company to reorganize, lay off about 5,000 employees, and close some plants. The company lost more than $325 million over 4 years, and the COO resigned when OMC's board said it wanted an outsider to replace 16-year veteran James Chapman as chairman and CEO; former Whirlpool executive Harry Bowman was hired in early 1995.

OMC is developing a new generation of outboard engines, slated for production in 1996, that meet stringent federal clean air requirements but also boost performance, use less fuel, and are more easily serviced.

WHEN

In 1903 Ole Evinrude helped design Harley-Davidson's first carburetor. His outboard-motor design provided the basis for Evinrude Motor Company, which he formed in Milwaukee in 1907. Evinrude sold the company to Chris Meyer (1914) and in 1921 formed ELTO Outboard Motor Company, producing a motor 33% lighter than the Evinrude.

In 1926 gasoline-engine pioneer Briggs & Stratton bought Evinrude Motor but sold it in 1929 to Briggs's cofounder Stephen Briggs, who formed a syndicate with Ole Evinrude called the Outboard Motors Corporation. OMC introduced electric-starting outboards in 1930 and fully enclosed engines (for safety and noise reduction) in 1934. In 1935 OMC bought Johnson Motors (Sea Horse outboards).

After WWII OMC discontinued the ELTO line and in 1952 bought power-mower maker RPM Manufacturing of Lamar, Missouri. OMC renamed the mowers Lawn-Boy, and by 1957 Lawn-Boy mowers led the nation in power-mower sales.

Foreign sales, an important revenue source from early on, tripled between 1949 and 1956, the year the company adopted its present name. Between 1956 and 1958 OMC bought Industrial Engineering, Canada's largest chain-saw manufacturer (renamed Pioneer Chain Saw, sold to Electrolux in 1977); acquired Cushman Motor Works, makers of lightweight vehicles such as golf carts; and introduced the first mass-produced, die-cast, aluminum V-engine (a V-4).

In the 1960s OMC entered new product fields, most importantly stern-drive marine engines. In 1967 the company introduced an all-electronic outboard ignition, now the industry standard. Additionally, OMC acquired

Trade Winds (marine products) and Ryan Equipment (turf-care equipment).

OMC expanded its marine business in the 1980s. In 1985 the company introduced the first V-8 outboard engine. Between 1986 and 1989 OMC spent approximately $230 million acquiring 10 boat manufacturers (including Chris-Craft and Donzi). In 1989 OMC sold both Cushman (to Ransomes America for $150 million) and Lawn-Boy (to Toro for $85 million). The boating industry boomed from 1982 to June 1989, carrying OMC to record profits in 1988.

In 1990 OMC continued to buy boat makers, acquiring Grumman's aluminum boat operations, Topaz Marine, and 4 other boat-building businesses located in Canada, Australia, and France.

OMC launched the Roughneck line of aluminum boats in 1991 and began distributing replacement parts for competitors' engines through the OMC dealer network in 1992. The company entered a 10-year agreement in 1993 with Genmar Industries to "pre-rig" or factory-install controls for OMC's Evinrude and Johnson outboard engines. That same year OMC lost a large outboard supply agreement with Tracker Marine, a major boat manufacturer.

In 1994 the company sold its Adventurent boat rental subsidiary to Nino Martini, that company's president. Also that year OMC closed 3 manufacturing plants.

In 1995 OMC formed a joint venture with Volvo to consolidate 2 separate stern drives as one brand, the Volvo Penta Cobra SX. OMC's 1995 earnings edged up to $51 million, on increased sales of $1.23 billion.

NYSE symbol: OM
Fiscal year ends: September 30

WHO

Chairman, President, and CEO: Harry W. Bowman, age 51
VP; President, OMC International Group: Ronald J. Jensen, age 45, $306,313 pay
VP; President, OMC Fishing Boat Group, Inc.: L. Earl Bentz, age 42, $305,522 pay
VP; President, OMC Aluminum Boat Group, Inc.: William J. Ek, age 58, $259,684 pay
VP and Controller: James R. Maurice, age 53
VP and General Counsel: D. Jeffrey Baddeley, age 56, $267,273 pay
VP Manufacturing and Engineering: John D. Flaig, age 47
VP Sales and Marketing: David R. Lumley, age 40
Secretary and Senior Counsel: Howard Malovany, age 44
Treasurer: Christopher R. Sachs, age 42
VP Human Resources: Richard H. Medland, age 52
Auditors: Arthur Andersen & Co, SC

WHERE

HQ: 100 Sea Horse Dr., Waukegan, IL 60085
Phone: 847-689-6200
Fax: 847-689-5555

Outboard Marine operates 16 US plants and 10 plants in Australia, Brazil, Canada, China, France, Hong Kong, Mexico, and Sweden.

	1994 Sales		1994 Operating Income	
	$ mil.	% of total	$ mil.	% of total
US	805	75	56	—
Europe	87	8	(6)	—
Other regions	186	17	23	—
Adjustments	—	—	(27)	—
Total	**1,078**	**100**	**46**	**—**

WHAT

	1994 Sales	
	$ mil.	% of total
Engine products	574	53
Boats & packages	504	47
Total	**1,078**	**100**

Aluminum Boat Group
Grumman boats and canoes
Lowe
Princecraft
Roughneck
Sea Nymph
Suncruiser pontoon boats

Fishing Boat Group
Hydra-Sports
Javelin
Quest
Stratos

International Group
Chris-Craft boats
Evinrude outboards
Four Winn boats
Haines Hunter boats
Johnson outboards
OMC SysteMatched parts and accessories
Princecraft/Springbok boats

Ryds boats
Sea Nymph boats
Seabird boats
Seaswirl boats
Stacer boats
Sunbird boats

Marine Power Products Group
Evinrude outboards
Johnson outboards
OMC Cobra stern drives
OMC King Cobra stern drives
OMC SysteMatched parts and accessories
OMC TurboJet drive systems

Recreational Boat Group
Chris-Craft
Four Winns
Seaswirl
Sunbird

KEY COMPETITORS

Bombardier
Brunswick
Fountain Powerboat
Genmar
Honda
MacAndrews & Forbes
Meridian Sports
Polaris
Suzuki
Yamaha

HOW MUCH

	Annual Growth	1985	1986	1987	1988	1989	1990	1991	1992	1993	1994
Sales ($ mil.)	2.3%	880	972	1,289	1,605	1,464	1,146	984	1,065	1,035	1,078
Net income ($ mil.)	5.7%	29	11	47	72	70	(77)	(86)	2	(165)	49
Income as % of sales	—	3.3%	1.1%	3.6%	4.5%	4.8%	—	—	0.2%	—	4.5%
Earnings per share ($)	2.7%	1.74	0.66	2.56	3.74	3.64	(3.98)	(4.42)	0.10	(8.42)	2.22
Stock price – high ($)	—	31.50	38.50	38.00	35.50	46.00	28.25	19.38	26.63	25.25	25.88
Stock price – low ($)	—	19.63	23.88	16.25	21.88	25.00	9.00	11.50	15.13	15.25	17.38
Stock price – close ($)	(3.9%)	28.00	27.00	21.88	31.00	26.00	13.50	17.63	21.75	22.38	19.63
P/E – high	—	18	58	15	10	13	—	—	—	—	12
P/E – low	—	11	36	6	6	7	—	—	151	—	8
Dividends per share ($)	(2.0%)	0.48	0.64	0.64	0.70	0.80	0.80	0.50	0.40	0.40	0.40
Book value per share ($)	(8.3%)	22.77	23.14	26.67	30.47	33.08	28.93	23.88	23.31	8.13	10.45
Employees	(0.4%)	8,800	9,117	11,500	12,903	13,418	10,830	8,449	8,410	8,074	8,500

1994 Year-end:
Debt ratio: 46.1%
Return on equity: 26.2%
Cash (mil.): $80
Current ratio: 1.84
Long-term debt (mil.): $178
No. of shares (mil.): 20
Dividends
  Yield: 2.0%
  Payout: 18.0%
Market value (mil.): $393

Stock Price History High/Low 1985–94

PREMARK INTERNATIONAL, INC.

OVERVIEW

The party may be over at Premark. The company, based in Deerfield, Illinois, announced in late 1995 that it would spin off its Tupperware division, which accounts for about 56% of operating income, (and still markets its plastic containers through "Tupperware parties," 12 million of which were held last year at homes, offices, and social clubs worldwide). Premark cited differences in operating characteristics and management needs between its other businesses and Tupperware as the reason for the separation.

Premark's other divisions include its Food Equipment Group, which sells commercial food preparation appliances, such as mixers and meat saws, under the brand names

Vulcan, Foster, and Adamatic; and the Consumer and Decorative Products division, which sells laminates, floor tile, hardwood flooring, small appliances, and physical fitness equipment.

Premark, which stands for "premier trademarks," considers its brands to be its principal asset. Besides Tupperware, the company's Hobart (commercial food equipment) and West Bend (small appliances) remain 2 of the best-known brand names in their categories. Premark hopes to make more of its brands available internationally.

Premark's chairman, Warren Batts, will also be Tupperware's chairman and CEO. James Ringler will become CEO of Premark.

WHEN

Premark's story begins with Justin Dart, a native of Illinois who, after graduating from Northwestern in the 1920s, married (and then divorced) the daughter of Walgreen Company's founder, Charles Walgreen. When Walgreen died in 1939, Dart became general manager of the company but left in 1941 to join United Drugs, a Boston-based drug company started in 1903. Dart took control of United Drugs in 1943, moving its headquarters from Boston to Los Angeles in 1945.

Boasting Rexall as a major brand, the company adopted the name Rexall Drug in 1947. Dart led Rexall through a series of acquisitions, including Tupper Corporation, former DuPont chemist Earl Tupper's plastic container company (Tupperware, 1958); Ralph Wilson Plastics, a decorative laminated plastics manufacturer (Wilsonart, 1966); and West Bend, a cookware maker (1968). The company adopted the name Dart Industries in 1969.

Dart sold its Rexall division, the last vestige of the original drug company, in 1977 and bought P. R. Mallory and Company, maker of Duracell batteries, in 1978.

In 1980 the company merged with Kraft, the Chicago food conglomerate, to form Dart & Kraft. Founded in 1903 by cheese wholesaler James Kraft, Kraft merged with rival cheesemaker Phenix Cheese in 1928 to form Kraft-Phenix. In 1930 the company was acquired by National Dairy Products Corporation, which adopted the name Kraftco (1969) and then Kraft, Inc. (1976) to take advantage of the name value of its best-known products. After the Dart-Kraft merger, John Richman, CEO of Kraft since 1979, became chairman

and CEO of Dart & Kraft. Dart acted as an advisor to the company until his death in 1984.

Warren Batts, former CEO of Mead, became president and COO of Dart & Kraft in 1981. That year the company bought Hobart Corporation, maker of commercial kitchen equipment, including KitchenAid appliances (sold in 1986). Other purchases included Precor (fitness equipment, 1984) and Vulcan-Hart (gas stoves, 1986).

In 1986 the company decided to spin off its nonfood divisions. Tupperware, Hobart, Vulcan-Hart, Ralph Wilson Plastics, and West Bend became Premark International, a new company headed by Batts. Kraft kept all of its pre-1980 assets and Duracell batteries. Premark has since acquired several businesses, including Tibbals (oak flooring, 1988) and Florida Tile (decorative tiles, 1990).

Premark sought to expand its marketing options by starting Tupperware Express, which delivered (and eventually would have sold) merchandise directly to customers. In 1992, however, Premark announced that shipping costs for Tupperware Express were prohibitive and began trying out other delivery systems. Domestic Tupperware sales, which had been sluggish, began to turn around in 1993 as the company expanded its sales force by 27% and improved its use of promotions. Sales continued to improve in 1994. That year Tupperware introduced about 100 new products worldwide and started TupperKids, an extension of its toy business that includes lunch boxes, educational games, and a series of tapes and books.

In 1995 Tupperware's sales rose in Asia, Europe, and Latin America.

NYSE symbol: PMI
Fiscal year ends: Last Saturday in December

WHO

Chairman and CEO: Warren L. Batts, age 62, $2,365,833 pay
President and COO: James M. Ringler, $1,429,500 pay
EVP; President, Tupperware Worldwide: E. V. Goings, age 49, $1,676,763 pay
SVP and CFO: Lawrence B. Skatoff, age 55, $827,500 pay
SVP, General Counsel, and Secretary: John M. Costigan, age 52
SVP Human Resources: James C. Coleman, age 55
Group VP and President, Food Equipment Group: Joseph W. Deering, age 54, $818,565 pay
Corporate VP and President, The West Bend Company: Thomas W. Kieckhafer, age 56
VP Planning: Isabelle C. Goossen, age 43
VP and Treasurer: Lisa Kearns Richardson, age 42
Auditors: Price Waterhouse LLP

WHERE

HQ: 1717 Deerfield Rd., Deerfield, IL 60015
Phone: 847-405-6000
Fax: 847-405-6013

Premark manufactures products in 15 countries and markets them in over 100.

	1994 Sales		1994 Operating Income	
	$ mil.	% of total	$ mil.	% of total
US	1,898	55	151	42
Europe	939	27	139	39
Asia/Pacific	378	11	48	14
Latin America & Canada	236	7	18	5
Total	**3,451**	**100**	**356**	**100**

WHAT

	1994 Sales		1994 Operating Income	
	$ mil.	% of total	$ mil.	% of total
Tupperware	1,333	39	199	56
Food equipment	1,135	33	81	23
Other	983	28	76	21
Total	**3,451**	**100**	**356**	**100**

Operations and Selected Brand Names

Tupperware
TupperCare
TupperKids
Tuppertoys
Tupperware
Tupperwave

Food Equipment
Adamatic
Foster
Hobart
Still
Tasselli
Vulcan
Wolf

Consumer and Decorative Products
Florida Tile (decorative tile)
Gibraltar (surfacing products)
Hartco (flooring installation)
Precor (fitness equipment)
West Bend (appliances)
Wilsonart (laminates)

Principal Subsidiaries
Dart Industries Inc. (Tupperware)
Florida Tile Industries, Inc.
Precor, Inc.
Premark FEG Corp.
Ralph Wilson Plastics Co.
The West Bend Co.

KEY COMPETITORS

Amway	Hasbro	Owens-Illinois
Armstrong World	Home	Rubbermaid
Avon	Interiors &	Scotsman
Black & Decker	Gifts	Soloflex
CML Group	Mattel	Sunbeam-Oster
Color Tile	Middleby	Toastmaster
Corning	3M	Tyco Toys
Dal-Tile	Mobil	U. S. Industries
AB Electrolux	Nautilus	Whitman
Gillette	Acquisition	

HOW MUCH

	Annual Growth	1985	1986	1987	1988	1989	1990	1991	1992	1993	1994
Sales ($ mil.)	7.7%	1,763	1,959	2,197	2,397	2,592	2,721	2,816	2,946	3,097	3,451
Net income ($ mil.)	13.9%	70	(98)	72	121	78	52	102	5	173	226
Income as % of sales	—	4.0%	—	3.3%	5.1%	3.0%	1.9%	3.6%	0.2%	5.6%	6.5%
Earnings per share ($)	17.1%	0.82	(1.44)	1.04	1.75	1.12	0.82	1.63	0.07	2.58	3.39
Stock price – high ($)	—	—	10.75	15.88	18.13	21.00	15.50	20.31	25.63	41.88	48.00
Stock price – low ($)	—	—	8.75	9.25	11.06	14.69	6.38	8.13	14.88	19.13	33.50
Stock price – close ($)	20.9%	—	9.81	11.19	15.75	15.38	8.69	20.31	20.31	40.13	44.75
P/E – high	—	—	—	15	10	19	19	13	—	16	14
P/E – low	—	—	—	9	6	13	8	5	—	7	10
Dividends per share ($)	—	—	0.00	0.13	0.23	0.36	0.42	0.42	0.46	0.53	0.74
Book value per share ($)	7.7%	—	8.42	9.84	11.14	11.76	12.33	13.44	11.17	12.72	15.22
Employees	1.1%	—	22,000	22,800	24,000	24,700	25,400	24,000	24,000	24,000	24,000

1994 Year-end:
Debt ratio: 17.5%
Return on equity: 25.3%
Cash (mil.): $121
Current ratio: 1.38
Long-term debt (mil.): $122
No. of shares (mil.): 64
Dividends
  Yield: 1.7%
  Payout: 21.8%
Market value (mil.): $2,859

Stock Price History High/Low 1986–94

THE QUAKER OATS COMPANY

OVERVIEW

Does Passion Supreme go well with oatmeal? Can the staid Quaker Man and the flamboyant Snapple Lady find true happiness together? And how does Gatorade spokesman Michael Jordan fit into it? These were the questions on everyone's lips when Quaker Oats (the grain products and good-for-you-drinks company) paid a whopping $1.7 billion for the new-age noncarbonated drinks pioneer Snapple.

The Snapple purchase in 1994 stretched Quaker's resources because, in addition to the purchase price itself, the entrepreneurial Snapple needed an overhaul in its distribution and marketing operations. Problems in these areas, as well as increased competition in its field, had contributed to a falling market share. Quaker expects that its strength in supermarket distribution (gained through Gatorade's dominance of the sports drink area) will mean increased sales in the long run. However, Snapple's greatest distribution was in single-serving bottles for cooler-case sales, with which Quaker has little experience. Gatorade and Snapple make up 40% of sales; Quaker is the US's #3 beverage company, behind Coca-Cola and PepsiCo.

To help pay for the purchase, Quaker decided in 1995 to exit several businesses, including its European and US pet foods (sold to Dalgety of the UK and to Heinz); Van Camp's beans and Wolf Brand chili (sold to ConAgra); and its Mexican chocolate business (sold to Nestlé). The remaining focus is on grain-based foods and noncarbonated drinks.

In October 1995 Philip Marineau resigned as president of Quaker, although both he and the company denied that he was taking the fall for the troubled Snapple business.

WHEN

The familiar, friendly Quaker Man of the Quaker Oats Company was first used as a trademark in 1877 by Henry Crowell at his Quaker Mill in Ravenna, Ohio. Crowell was one of 7 prominent millers who formed the American Cereal Company of Chicago in 1891. Called by some the "oatmeal trust," the company changed its name to the Quaker Oats Company in 1901 and adopted Crowell's Quaker Man as its logo.

The company was an immediate success. Crowell's creative marketing practices and powerful sales staff covered the nation with the image of the Quaker Man — on billboards, in magazines, in newspapers, on cards on subways and streetcars, and in coupon promotions and miniature samples left on doorsteps — extolling the virtues of oatmeal to a newly health-conscious public. Crowell was an early advertising innovator.

Robert Stuart, another founder, consolidated mill operations to 2 locations: a large mill in Akron, Ohio, and his own mill in Cedar Rapids, Iowa, which he modernized and expanded. The company prospered and by 1911 was diversifying its product line with such purchases as animal feed and grocery items. Sales reached $123 million in 1918. In 1925 Quaker bought Aunt Jemima pancake flour, one of its most successful brands.

The company remained under Stuart family management until 1953. Cap'n Crunch cereal was introduced in 1963. Robert Stuart, son of a previous president, became CEO in 1966 and embarked on a program of diversification.

Acquisitions included Fisher-Price toys (1969, sold 1991), restaurants, and candies.

William Smithburg became CEO in 1979 and continued to diversify (clothiers, opticians). The company bought Stokely-Van Camp in 1983 for $238 million and kept its top brands of canned beans and Gatorade sports beverage. In 1986 the company paid $801 million for Anderson, Clayton & Company, a Houston food products company with such brands as Seven Seas salad dressings, Chiffon margarine, and Igloo ice chests (all later sold), as well as Gaines dog food. Smithburg began to refocus the company on foods.

Following a down year in 1990, Quaker reinforced its back-to-basics food strategy by increasing its advertising budget, reformulating its dog foods, and launching new products. Continuing to emphasize its core food categories, in 1993 Quaker sold Sutherland Foods, a British maker of sandwich filling products, and purchased the Chico-San rice cake brand from the Heinz Company. In 1994 the company announced a plan to consolidate manufacturing and cut employment. The costs of these actions were dwarfed by those associated with the Snapple purchase later that year. The company also formed a joint venture with a Taiwanese firm to sell All-In-One cereal and Mighty pudding in China.

The restructuring continued in 1995 when Quaker combined its cereal, snack, and convenience food divisions into one organization and eliminated duplicate administration, marketing, and supply functions.

NYSE symbol: OAT
Fiscal year ends: June 30

	1995 Sales		1995 Operating Income	
	$ mil.	% of total	$ mil.	% of total
US and Canada	4,624	73	974	63
Europe	1,106	17	483	31
Latin America and Pacific	635	10	93	6
Total	**6,365**	**100**	**1,550**	**100**

WHO

Chairman and CEO: William D. Smithburg, age 57, $855,014 pay
EVP Worldwide Beverages: James F. Doyle, age 43, $550,360 pay
EVP International Quaker Food Products: Barbara A. Allen, age 42
EVP US and Canadian Quaker Food Products: Douglas W. Mills, age 49
SVP Finance and CFO: Robert S. Thomason, age 50, $401,220 pay
SVP Law and Corporate Affairs: Luther C. McKinney, age 64, $368,682 pay
SVP Human Resources: Douglas J. Ralston, age 50
VP Corporate Planning: Jeffrey A. Atkins, age 46
VP and Treasurer: Janet K. Cooper, age 42
VP and Corporate Controller: Thomas L. Gettings, age 38
VP General Corporate Counsel and Corporate Secretary: R. Thomas Howell Jr., age 53
VP Corporate Tax: W. Stephen Perry, age 53
VP and Chief Customer Officer: John A. Boynton, age 41
VP Investor Relations and Corporate Communications: Margaret M. Eichman
VP Government and Community Relations: Penelope C. Cate
Auditors: Arthur Andersen & Co, SC

WHERE

HQ: Quaker Tower, PO Box 049001, 321 N. Clark St., Chicago, IL 60604-9001
Phone: 312-222-7111
Fax: 312-222-8304

Quaker operates in Argentina, the Benelux countries, Brazil, Colombia, France, Germany, Italy, Mexico, the UK, the US, and Venezuela, and its products are sold through marketing agreements throughout the world.

WHAT

Selected Brand Names

Cereals
Cap'n Crunch
Life
Quaker 100% Natural
Quaker Kids' Choice
Quaker MultiGrain
Quaker Oat Squares
Quaker Oatmeal
Quaker Oats
Quaker Toasted Oatmeal

Other Food Products
Ardmore Farms (citrus juice)
Arnie's Bagelicious Bagels
Aunt Jemima
Burry (cookies and crackers)

Celeste (pizza)
Chico-San (rice cakes)
Continental Coffee
Gatorade
Golden Grain (pasta)
Maryland Club (food service coffee)
Near East (grain-based dishes)
Nile Spice
Noodle Roni
Petrofsky's bagels
Proof & Bake (frozen foods)
Quaker Caramel Corn Cakes
Quaker Chewy Granola Bars
Quaker Rice Cakes
Rice-A-Roni
Snapple

KEY COMPETITORS

Borden
Cadbury Schweppes
Celestial Seasonings
Coca-Cola
ConAgra
Dole
General Mills
Grand Metropolitan
Grist Mill
Ferolito, Vultaggio
Heinz
Hershey
Inflo Holdings
Kellogg
Mars
Nestlé
PepsiCo
Philip Morris
Procter & Gamble
Ralcorp
RJR Nabisco

HOW MUCH

	Annual Growth	1986	1987	1988	1989	1990	1991	1992	1993	1994	1995[1]
Sales ($ mil.)	6.3%	3,671	4,421	5,330	5,724	5,031	5,491	5,576	5,731	5,955	6,365
Net income ($ mil.)	18.2%	180	244	256	203	169	206	248	287	232	806
Income as % of sales	—	4.9%	5.5%	4.8%	3.5%	3.4%	3.7%	4.4%	5.0%	4.0%	12.7%
Earnings per share ($)	20.4%	1.13	1.55	1.60	1.28	1.08	1.33	1.63	1.97	1.68	6.00
Stock price – high ($)	—	22.44	28.81	30.75	34.44	29.75	37.88	37.19	30.19	42.50	37.50
Stock price – low ($)	—	13.69	15.88	19.25	24.81	20.50	23.88	25.13	30.19	29.69	30.38
Stock price – close ($)	5.6%	20.00	20.81	26.56	28.88	26.44	37.44	32.50	35.50	30.75	32.63
P/E – high	—	20	19	19	27	28	29	23	20	25	6
P/E – low	—	12	10	12	19	19	18	16	15	18	5
Dividends per share ($)	14.2%	0.34	0.39	0.48	0.58	0.68	0.76	0.84	0.94	11.04	1.12
Book value per share ($)	5.2%	4.95	6.47	7.88	7.22	6.73	5.90	5.52	3.97	3.34	7.80
Employees	(5.9%)	29,500	30,800	31,300	31,700	28,200	20,900	21,100	20,200	20,000	17,000

1995 Year-end:
Debt ratio: 58.4%
Return on equity: 108.0%
Cash (mil.): $102
Current ratio: 0.73
Long-term debt (mil.): $1,103
No. of shares (mil.): 134
Dividends
  Yield: 3.4%
  Payout: 18.7%
Market value (mil.): $4,371

Stock Price History[1]
High/Low 1986–95

[1] 1995 stock prices are through fiscal year-end (June 30).

ROTARY INTERNATIONAL

OVERVIEW

Headquartered in Evanston, Illinois, Rotary International has more than 1.2 million members in over 27,000 clubs in 151 countries. It is the oldest, most international service organization in the world, and it has served as a model for many other service clubs.

The organization's motto, "Service Above Self," exemplifies Rotary's dedication to its "four avenues" of club, vocational, community, and international service. The organization promotes high ethical standards in business and international understanding, goodwill, and peace.

Rotary operates through local clubs, in which membership is by invitation only. These clubs are organized into 515 districts worldwide. Rotary is governed by a 18-member elected board of directors. Although the executive officers are paid, the president performs his largely promotional duties at his own expense.

Each local club chooses its own service activities, but Rotary International encourages clubs to concentrate on hunger, the environment, illiteracy, drug abuse, childhood immunization, and service for youths and the elderly. Through the Rotary Foundation, Rotary provides scholarships and humanitarian grants. Its Ambassadorial Scholarship program is the world's largest privately sponsored scholarship program. Its PolioPlus program has raised more than $240 million to support an immunization program to eradicate polio. In 1995 the Rotary won the Audrey Hepburn Child Advocacy Award for the work performed by the program.

WHEN

On February 23, 1905, 4 small businessmen — a lawyer, a tailor, an engineer, and a coal dealer — met at Madame Galli's restaurant in Chicago. The lawyer, 37-year-old Paul Percy Harris, who was new to Chicago and pined for the close ties of his native Racine, Wisconsin, proposed that they form an organization dedicated to fellowship and the mutual business advantage of its members (no 2 of whom were to be from the same profession or business). The club soon assumed another objective, service, which now dominates its activities.

At first known as "the Conspirators," the club later took the name Rotary from the practice of rotating the meeting venue among members' places of business.

Harris refused to hold any office in the Rotary Club of Chicago until 1907, when he became president. By 1910 there were 16 clubs (including the first non-US one in Winnipeg) and 1,500 Rotarians. To reflect its wider geographical base, the club was renamed the National Association of Rotary Clubs. A London club opened in 1911, and 2 other UK clubs followed. In 1912 the organization became the International Association of Rotary Clubs, adopting its present name in 1922. The Rotary Foundation was established in 1917 to further international understanding.

During WWI and WWII Rotary aided war victims and helped establish UNESCO in 1945. Rotary lost a number of clubs in Eastern Europe during and after WWII.

By the 1950s Rotary was a fixture of American life. It excluded women because their presence at meetings was deemed a threat to the tranquility of its male members' marriages. Rotary was frowned on by the Catholic Church, which deemed it a secret society like the Freemasons. Thus it was a club of Protestant, family-oriented businessmen who, in the US, were mostly Republicans. Membership continued to grow, to roughly 682,000 by 1970 and 876,000 by 1980. In 1986 Rotary established the Village Corps to promote self-help community service projects.

In the 1980s a California club admitted a woman; Rotary disciplined the club, which sued for the right to admit women under a California civil rights law — and lost. Upon appeal, the US Supreme Court ruled in 1987 that Rotary is a business organization and must admit women. While many protested that this violated members' rights of free association, others believed it would revitalize the clubs. In 1989 Rotary extended its welcome to women worldwide.

Also in 1989 Rotary's board of directors fired the general secretary and eliminated 5 managerial positions to curb overspending and to reduce what had become a bureaucracy. More management changes came in 1993 when Spencer Robinson quit the general secretary post and was replaced by Herbert Pigman and when Mary Wolfenberger became the Rotary's first woman CFO.

In 1995 the Rotary Club of Ulan Bator, the first club in Mongolia, was admitted for membership. That same year the Rotary returned to Cambodia, after interrupting its operations there in 1977 because of unstable political conditions.

Service organization
Fiscal year ends: June 30

WHO

General Secretary: Geoffrey Large
President: Herb Brown
President-Elect: Luis Giay
VP: Richard Slager
CFO: Mary Wolfenberger
Treasurer: Reijiro Hattori
Director Human Resources: Calvin Henderson
Auditors: Deloitte & Touche LLP

WHERE

HQ: One Rotary Center, 1560 Sherman Ave., Evanston, IL 60201
Phone: 847-866-3000
Fax: 847-328-8554

Rotary International has 27,300 clubs in 151 countries.

WHAT

	1995 Revenues	
	$ mil.	% of total
Dues	37	62
Magazine, publications & supplies	8	14
International convention	5	8
One Rotary Center tenants	4	6
Investments	3	5
Other	3	5
Total	**60**	**100**

	1995 Foundation Program Expenditures	
	$ mil.	% of total
PolioPlus (eradication program)	20	39
Scholarships	19	36
Humanitarian	8	15
Group study	5	10
Total	**52**	**100**

Prominent Members

US Presidents
Dwight Eisenhower
Warren Harding
Herbert Hoover
John Kennedy
Richard Nixon
Franklin Roosevelt
Harry Truman
Woodrow Wilson

Politicians
Winston Churchill
J. William Fulbright
Mark Hatfield
Wayne Morse
Adlai Stevenson
Earl Warren

Literary Figures
Thomas Mann
Norman Vincent Peale
James Whitcomb Riley

Business Leaders
Frank Borman
Raymond Firestone
Connie Mack
Charles Walgreen

Royalty
Prince Bernhard (The Netherlands)
King Carl XVI Gustav (Sweden)
King Hassan II (Morocco)
Prince Philip (England)
Prince Rainier (Monaco)

Others
Neil Armstrong
Admiral Richard Byrd
Gordon Cooper
Albert Schweitzer
Alan Shepard

HOW MUCH

	Annual Growth	1986	1987	1988	1989	1990	1991	1992	1993	1994	1995
Revenues ($ mil.)	6.9%	33	30	29	31	40	46	51	52	59	60
Rotary Foundation assets ($ mil.)	14.5%	125	162	248	302	336	356	369	394	396	423
Foundation program expenditures ($ mil.)	(5.4%)	—	—	—	—	—	65	71	66	54	52
Membership (thou.)	1.7%	1,013	1,039	1,057	1,077	1,125	1,143	1,157	1,174	1,201	1,176
Employees	(5.4%)	—	—	—	487	532	—	554	617	450	350

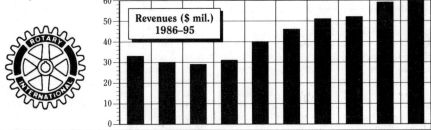

Revenues ($ mil.)
1986–95

R. R. DONNELLEY & SONS COMPANY

OVERVIEW

Chicago-based R. R. Donnelley & Sons is the largest supplier of commercial print and related services in the US. Although its prepress, presswork, and binding operations now account for over 90% of revenues, Donnelley stays in the forefront of printing technology by creating integrated manufacturing platforms. Donnelley's view is that electronics and print coexist, and that each spurs the other's growth — computer documentation involves more than just printed manuals; Donnelley also reproduces the accompanying software.

The company operates 3 sectors. Commercial Print (61% of sales) covers magazine, catalog, newspaper insert, and directory printing, as well as their digital versions. Networked Services (32% of sales) controls the company's book publishing, computer documentation, CD-ROM and diskette replication, and financial printing. This sector's software services unit is the world's #1 provider of software distribution services.

The 3rd sector is Information Resources (7% of sales). Its Metromail unit provides, enhances, and manages consumer mailing lists and offers cross-reference and on-line services, while its information services unit offers digital and on-demand printing, sophisticated graphics design and management, and CD-ROM production, among other services.

Donnelley is the #1 supplier of Microsoft's printed matter and handles disk duplication and order fulfillment for other software companies.

WHEN

In 1864 Richard Robert Donnelley, an emigre Canadian printer, joined Chicago publishers Edward Goodman and Leroy Church. Their partnership became the Lakeside Publishing and Printing Co. in 1870. The company produced a variety of periodicals and some of the first inexpensive paperback books. The new Lakeside Building was destroyed in the 1871 Chicago Fire, but by 1873 it had reopened.

By 1877 Lakeside no longer existed, but its paperback subsidiary survived as Donnelley, Loyd & Co. Donnelley bought out his partners in 1879 and separated the printing component (reorganized as R. R. Donnelley & Sons in 1882) from publishing (Chicago Directory Co.). Chicago Directory became the Reuben H. Donnelley Corp. (1916), named for a Donnelley son. In 1961 Dun & Bradstreet bought Reuben H. Donnelley Corp.

Before 1900 Donnelley had printed telephone books and the Montgomery Ward catalog. In 1910 it began printing the *Encyclopædia Britannica*. In 1927 it won the contract to print *Time*. The firm's innovation in high-speed printing was a major factor in Henry Luce's 1936 decision to begin *Life*.

For most of Donnelley's history, family members have served as chairman and president. An in-law, Charles Haffner (chairman, 1952–1964), took the company public in 1956. The first outsider to become chairman was Charles Lake (1975). Family members are still active in the company.

In the last 2 decades, Donnelley acquired printing companies in the UK (Ben Johnson, 1978; Index Press and Thompson Photo Litho, 1985), Japan (Dowa Insatsu, 1988), and Ireland (Irish Printers, 1989). During the 1980s Donnelley developed the Selectronic process, which can tailor editions of magazines and catalogs to small target audiences. In 1987 it bought Metromail, the largest US mailing list business, which in 1991 generated a national telephone directory with 77 million names and addresses on 9 CD-ROMs. In 1990 it acquired high-quality printer Meredith/Burda and Business Mail Data Services, a UK equivalent of Metromail.

A 1991 partnership with French publisher Hachette brought Donnelley into the continental European market. A Singapore plant, opened in 1991, made it possible to offer a full range of computer hardware and software documentation services. A new plant in Mexico allowed Donnelley to enter the lucrative children's book business, and its Japanese unit produced a video catalog of US direct-mail products for Japanese customers.

The company closed its Southside Chicago plant — its oldest — in 1993 when one customer, Sears, canceled its catalog.

In 1994 Donnelley invested in Nimbus CD International (CD-ROM manufacturing) to expand its software fulfillment abilities. The company also bought 51% of Chilean printer Editorial Lord Cochrane. In late 1994 Donnelley won a 10-year, $2.5 billion contract to print telephone directories for SBC Communications, Southwestern Bell's parent.

In 1995, to further expand its capacity, Donnelley merged its software operations with Corporate Software to form the $1.3 billion company Stream International, a mail-order software retailer.

NYSE symbol: DNY
Fiscal year ends: December 31

WHO

Chairman and CEO: John R. Walter, age 48,
$1,294,316 pay
VC: James R. Donnelley, age 59
EVP; Sector President, Information Resources: Rory J.
Cowan, age 42, $564,772 pay
EVP and CFO: Cheryl A. Francis
EVP; Sector President, Commercial Print: Jonathan P.
Ward, age 40, $433,891 pay
EVP; Sector President, Networked Services: W. Ed
Tyler, age 42, $385,503 pay
SVP and General Counsel: T. J. Quarles, age 45
SVP Strategy, Human Resources, and Communication:
Steven J. Baumgartner, age 43
President, Telecommunications Unit: E. Patrick Duffy,
age 53
Auditors: Arthur Andersen & Co, SC

WHERE

HQ: 77 W. Wacker Dr., Chicago, IL 60601
Phone: 312-326-8000
Fax: 312-326-8543

WHAT

	1994 Sales
	% of total
Catalogs, inserts & specialty products	31
Magazines	18
Global software services	14
Books	13
Directories	12
Financial printing	5
Other	7
Total	**100**

Commercial Print Sector
Magazine publishing services (consumer and trade
magazine printing, prepress services, editorial and
advertorial versioning, and pool shipping distribution)
Merchandise media (catalog and retail printing, prepress
services, specialty printing, direct marketing services,
customized versioning, and distribution)
Telecommunications (telephone directory printing,
digital directories, and digital ad-production systems)

Information Resources Sector
Information services (marketing communication,
database management and digital printing services,
creative design, interactive services, and graphics
management services)
Metromail (information for direct marketing; mailing
list and database development, management, and
enhancement; cross-reference products; and on-line
services)

Networked Services Sector
Book publishing services (book printing and binding,
distribution and fulfillment, and direct marketing)
Financial services (corporate and municipal financial
printing, mutual fund marketing and distribution
support, personalized on-demand printing, and equity
and debt issue typesetting and printing)
Global software services (computer documentation
localization, printing and binding; CD-ROM and
diskette replication, packaging, licensing, fulfillment,
and distribution; and mail-order software)

KEY COMPETITORS

ADVO	Dun & Bradstreet	Sullivan Graphics
American Business	Graphic	Taylor Corp.
Information	Industries	Treasure Chest
Banta	Merrill Corp.	Advertising
Bertelsmann	Moore	U S WEST
Bowne	NYNEX	Valassis Comm.
Cadmus	Quad/Graphics	Webcraft
Communications	Quebecor	Technologies
Courier	Ringier	World Color Press

HOW MUCH

	Annual Growth	1985	1986	1987	1988	1989	1990	1991	1992	1993	1994
Sales ($ mil.)	10.2%	2,038	2,234	2,483	2,878	3,122	3,498	3,915	4,193	4,388	4,889
Net income ($ mil.)	6.9%	148	158	178	205	222	226	205	235	121	269
Income as % of sales	—	7.3%	7.1%	7.2%	7.1%	7.1%	6.5%	5.2%	5.6%	2.8%	5.5%
Earnings per share ($)	6.8%	0.97	1.01	1.15	1.32	1.43	1.45	1.32	1.51	0.79	1.75
Stock price – high ($)	—	16.13	20.00	22.63	19.38	25.63	26.25	25.63	33.75	32.75	32.50
Stock price – low ($)	—	11.50	14.63	12.75	14.88	17.13	17.13	19.38	23.75	26.13	26.88
Stock price – close ($)	7.1%	15.88	15.38	16.31	17.31	25.63	19.88	25.00	32.75	31.13	29.50
P/E – high	—	17	20	20	15	18	18	19	22	41	19
P/E – low	—	12	15	11	11	12	12	15	16	33	15
Dividends per share ($)	8.4%	0.29	0.32	0.35	0.39	0.44	0.48	0.50	0.51	0.54	0.60
Book value per share ($)	8.9%	5.87	6.34	7.45	8.34	9.28	10.30	11.14	11.93	11.96	12.63
Employees	8.3%	19,100	20,600	22,000	24,500	26,100	27,500	29,100	30,400	32,100	39,000

1994 Year-end:
Debt ratio: 38.6%
Return on equity: 27.2%
Cash (mil.): $21
Current ratio: 1.69
Long-term debt (mil.): $1,212
No. of shares (mil.): 153
Dividends
  Yield: 2.2%
  Payout: 36.6%
Market value (mil.): $4,516

**Stock Price History
High/Low 1985–94**

SAFETY-KLEEN CORP.

OVERVIEW

It's a messy world, and Safety-Kleen hopes to clean up. The company is the world's leading provider of cleaning services for parts and tools. Safety-Kleen markets its services primarily to small businesses such as auto repair shops, dry cleaners, and printers, providing collection, disposal, and recycling of lubricants, solvents, and industrial fluids.

In 1994 and 1995 the company expanded its photochemical waste services with the purchase of Boston Recovery, a photochemical processing and silver recovery service, and Drew Resource, a photoprocessing equipment and service provider based in California. Also in 1995 Safety-Kleen acquired the parts cleaner business of Sparkle Corp.

Safety-Kleen earnings looked dull in the early 1990s, but a companywide restructuring has improved profitability. Profits were also helped by new products, including the Green Machine, a cyclonic parts cleaner introduced in 1994. In 1995 the company added an aqueous parts cleaner for brakes in response to an upcoming OSHA regulation.

Safety-Kleen, North America's largest used-oil re-refiner, operates 12 solvent recycling centers, 2 used-oil re-refineries, and 3 fuel-blending facilities (fluids are refined for reuse or blended for making asphalt or as furnace fuel). In 1994 the company processed over 230 million gallons of used industrial fluids and had over 585,000 parts cleaners in place.

WHEN

Safety-Kleen's business originated in the 1950s with Milwaukee inventor Ben Palmer's "red sink on a drum" parts cleaning system. Palmer's sink was mounted on a barrel of solvent. A small electric motor allowed the user to spray solvent over mechanical parts. The solvent went back into the drum, while dirt was captured by a filter. Safety-Kleen was established in 1963 to provide this system to Milwaukee garages. Once a drum of solvent was used, Safety-Kleen would replace the contaminated liquid with a barrel of fresh solvent. Instead of dumping the used solvent, as was common, the company recycled it for reuse.

In 1968 Donald Brinckman bought the company for Chicago Rawhide Manufacturing. It was spun off as a separate company in 1974.

During the 1970s Safety-Kleen fanned out across the country, offering its services on a free trial basis. Business boomed, with several years of record earnings. The company gained a reputation on Wall Street for its extraordinary earnings gains. Safety-Kleen claims to be the only publicly held company ever to garner profit gains of more than 20% for 18 years in a row (1971–88).

In 1980 the company expanded into the paint refinishing market with the purchase of American Impacts, a producer of buffing pads. Safety-Kleen branched into the dry-cleaning fluid recovery market in 1984 and in 1987 bought Breslube Enterprises, North America's largest refiner of used lubricating oil. The company spent around $300 million on new refineries in the late 1980s. Changes in government regulations in the early 1980s that required companies with as little as 220 pounds of liquid waste a month to dispose of it

suitably were a tremendous stimulus to Safety-Kleen's business. The company also began offering parts washing services for the industrial market and developed a grease-collecting filter for use in kitchens. It sold its restaurant services business in 1988.

Safety-Kleen continued to expand during the 1980s with a string of fluid-recovery acquisitions, including Custom Organics (1985), McKesson Envirosystems (1987), and Solvents Recovery Service of New Jersey (1989). In 1989 Donald Brinckman, CEO since 1968, was named CEO of the Decade by *Financial World*.

The company also formed joint ventures in European markets, buying out its German operation in 1990 and its other European partners in 1991. Also in 1991 the company paid $1.3 million in fines to the State of California for alleged violations of hazardous waste laws. In 1992 Safety-Kleen got a business boost when the EPA created new (and rigid) rules for disposing of motor oil.

In 1993 the company named John "Jack" Johnson, formerly with Arco Chemical Company, as president and COO. The company took a restructuring charge in late 1993 to cover the replacement of its existing machines, the closing of a recycling plant, and worker layoffs.

In 1994 Safety-Kleen introduced a new parts cleaner, the Green Machine, which filters and recycles the solvent, requiring fewer service calls and costing customers less.

Johnson became CEO in 1995. Also that year the company expanded its sorbent (absorbent and adsorbent) services and introduced a collection service for used disposable towels contaminated with industrial fluids.

NYSE symbol: SK
Fiscal year ends: Saturday nearest December 31

Chairman: Donald W. Brinckman, age 64, $578,000 pay
President and CEO: John G. "Jack" Johnson Jr., age 54, $440,561 pay
SVP Processing, Engineering, and Oil Recovery: Joseph Chalhoub, age 49, $250,014 pay
SVP Sales and Service: David A. Dattilo, age 54, $247,350 pay
SVP Finance and Secretary: Robert W. Willmschen Jr., age 47, $242,106 pay
SVP Marketing Services and Customer Care: Michael H. Carney, age 47
SVP Environment, Health, and Safety: Scott E. Fore, age 40
SVP Strategic/Environmental Planning: F. Henry Habicht II, age 41
SVP Operations and Information: William P. Kasko, age 52
SVP and General Counsel: Hyman K. Bielsky, age 40
SVP Human Resources: Robert J. Burian, age 57
Auditors: Arthur Andersen & Co, SC

WHERE

HQ: 1000 N. Randall Rd., Elgin, IL 60123
Phone: 847-697-8460
Fax: 847-468-8560

Safety-Kleen offers its services through a network of 236 branch facilities in North America and Europe. The company licenses operations in Israel, Japan, and Korea.

	1994 Sales		1994 Net Income	
	$ mil.	% of total	$ mil.	% of total
US	649	82	47	95
Europe	85	11	2	3
Canada	57	7	1	2
Total	**791**	**100**	**50**	**100**

WHAT

	1994 Sales	
	$ mil.	% of total
North America		
Automotive/retail repair services	238	30
Industrial services	222	28
Oil recovery services	118	15
Other service areas	128	16
European services	85	11
Total	**791**	**100**

Business Units

Envirosystems Service (large-scale waste recovery and processing)

Oil Recovery Services (serves automotive garages/dealers by collecting and recycling used lubricating oil)

Small Quantity Generator Resource Recovery Services
Automotive/retail repair services (provides machines and solvents that clean and degrease small parts and equipment)
Dry cleaner services (collects and recycles dry-cleaning waste)
Imaging services (collects and recycles photochemicals and recovers silver)
Industrial services (markets parts-cleaning services and fluid-recovery services to industrial customers)
Paint refinishing services (provides machines and solvents that clean paint spray guns for auto paint shops and car dealers)

KEY COMPETITORS

Allied Waste
American Waste
Bechtel
Browning-Ferris
Conrail
Harding Associates
International Recovery
Morrison Knudsen
Ogden
Parsons
Republic Environmental
WMX Technologies

HOW MUCH

	Annual Growth	1985	1986	1987	1988	1989	1990	1991	1992	1993	1994
Sales ($ mil.)	15.2%	221	255	334	417	478	589	695	795	796	791
Net income ($ mil.)	8.5%	24	28	35	42	46	55	52	45	(101)	50
Income as % of sales	—	10.6%	11.1%	10.5%	10.1%	9.6%	9.4%	7.4%	5.7%	—	6.3%
Earnings per share ($)	6.6%	0.49	0.57	0.71	0.85	0.91	1.05	0.90	0.78	(1.76)	0.87
Stock price – high ($)	—	12.13	17.24	26.35	23.51	25.85	29.85	37.88	32.25	24.75	18.50
Stock price – low ($)	—	9.34	11.46	14.80	14.51	15.84	18.26	22.00	22.63	13.13	12.75
Stock price – close ($)	2.8%	11.46	14.84	21.68	16.17	20.34	26.18	25.75	23.75	16.25	14.75
P/E – high	—	25	30	37	28	28	28	42	41	—	21
P/E – low	—	19	20	21	17	17	17	24	29	—	15
Dividends per share ($)	13.0%	0.12	0.14	0.16	0.26	0.24	0.27	0.32	0.34	0.36	0.36
Book value per share ($)	12.6%	2.36	2.83	3.66	4.36	5.13	7.58	8.14	8.53	6.29	6.86
Employees	9.6%	2,898	3,300	3,900	4,300	5,000	5,800	6,500	6,800	6,600	6,600

1994 Year-end:
Debt ratio: 42.6%
Return on equity: 13.2%
Cash (mil.): $21
Current ratio: 1.15
Long-term debt (mil.): $284
No. of shares (mil.): 57.8
Dividends
  Yield: 2.4%
  Payout: 41.4%
Market value (mil.): $852

**Stock Price History
High/Low 1985–94**

SARA LEE CORPORATION

OVERVIEW

If you've had one too many slices of Sara Lee's cheesecake, don't despair. Just head on over to your supermarket meat case and pick up some fat-free Ball Park hot dogs, and then on to sundries for some Hanes Her Way Smooth Illusions pantyhose (they'll hide those extra few pounds) and a pair of Hanes Briefs for your significant other. If you have time, you can stop at the department store for a Playtex 18-Hour Bra, some Isotoner gloves, and a new Coach bag. When you're done shopping, Chicago-based Sara Lee Corp. will be a little richer.

Although Sara Lee is best known for its frozen baked goods and other foods, its busi-nesses include personal and household goods, food services (through its PYA/Monarch opera-tions), and direct sales of toiletries, jewelry, and other personal items.

Most of the company's operations have grown in recent years, but sheer hosiery has gotten snagged by the recent worldwide trend toward a more casual lifestyle. The change has been so devastating that the company restruc-tured the personal products division to con-solidate operations and shift production to trouser socks and tights.

The son of Sara Lee CEO John Bryan, John Bryan III, was named president and CEO of the company's Bryan Foods segment in 1995.

WHEN

Sara Lee Corporation began in 1939 when businessman Nathan Cummings bought the C. D. Kenny Company, a Baltimore wholesaler of coffee, tea, and sugar. Cummings soon pur-chased several grocery firms and later changed the company's name to Consolidated Grocers (1945). In 1946 the company's stock was listed on the New York Stock Exchange. The com-pany was renamed Consolidated Foods Corpo-ration (CFC) in 1954.

In 1956 CFC purchased the Kitchens of Sara Lee, a Chicago bakery founded by Charles Lubin in 1951. Lubin had introduced Sara Lee cheesecake (named after his daughter) in 1949, and it became his most popular product. He remained with Consolidated Foods, suc-cessfully building the frozen desserts market under the Sara Lee brand name.

Focusing primarily on food and grocery concerns, Cummings broadened his invest-ments by buying and selling an array of food companies, grocery stores, and producers of personal care and consumer products. Pur-chases included Piggly Wiggly Midwest super-markets (1956) and Eagle Food Centers (1961). The company's Eagle Complex, which included Piggly Wiggly and Eagle stores, drug-stores, and photo supply stores, was sold in 1968. The company also bought Shasta Water Company in 1960 (sold in 1985), Chicken De-light food franchises (bought in 1965, sold in 1979), and Electrolux Corporation (bought in 1968, sold in 1987). Cummings served as president until 1970.

The company continued to buy and sell a long list of businesses in the US and Europe. Its operations have included foods, beverages, grocery stores, apparel, appliances, food ser-vices, and chemicals. In 1962 Consolidated Foods made its first European acquisition and began to build its international markets. Some of its major purchases included Douwe Egberts (coffee, tea, and tobacco; Holland; 1978), Nicholas Kiwi (shoe care and pharma-ceuticals, Australia, 1984), Akzo Con-sumenten Produkten (food, household, and personal care products; Holland; 1987), Dim (hosiery and underwear, France, 1989), and Pretty Polly (hosiery, UK, 1991).

Some major US company purchases were Hanes Corporation (1979), Jimmy Dean Meat Company (1984), and Champion Products (athletic knitwear, 1989).

Consolidated Foods changed its name to Sara Lee Corporation in 1985, using one of its most respected brand names to enhance the public's awareness of the company.

In the 1990s Sara Lee bought Playtex Ap-parel, kosher meat producer Bessin, the Euro-pean bath and body care lines of SmithKline Beecham, the consumer food group of BP Nu-trition, and the Filodoro Group, an Italian hosiery maker. The company also signed bas-ketball superstar Michael Jordan to promote Hanes knit products and Ball Park franks.

After years of acquisitions, Sara Lee found itself (like some of its most devoted custom-ers) just a bit overweight. In 1993 the com-pany embarked on a plan to trim operations and cut more than 8,000 employees.

The next year it entered into a joint venture with Mexican meat processor Kir Alimentos, a major producer of ham and luncheon meats.

As part of its restructuring, the company has upgraded some of its technical systems. In 1995 it agreed to replace several information systems in its bakery division with a single manufacturing management system by Oracle.

NYSE symbol: SLE
Fiscal year ends: Saturday nearest June 30

WHO

Chairman and CEO: John H. Bryan, age 58, $2,039,521 pay
VC, CFO, and Administrative Officer: Michael E. Murphy, age 58, $1,187,642 pay
EVP: C. Steven McMillan, age 49, $1,071,599 pay
EVP: Donald J. Franceschini, age 59, $1,027,924 pay
SVP: Frank L. Meysman, age 43, $811,685 pay
SVP and CFO: Judith A. Sprieser, age 42
SVP, Secretary, and General Counsel: Janet L. Kelly, age 37
SVP Corporate Development: Mark J. McCarville, age 48
SVP Human Resources: Gary C. Grom, age 48
VP Investor Relations and Corporate Affairs: Janet E. Bergman, age 36
VP Public Responsibility: Elynor A. Williams, age 48
Auditors: Arthur Andersen & Co, SC

WHERE

HQ: 3 First National Plaza, Chicago, IL 60602-4260
Phone: 312-726-2600
Fax: 312-726-3712

Sara Lee operates 310 food and consumer product plants in 27 states and 35 other nations.

	1995 Sales		1995 Operating Income	
	$ mil.	% of total	$ mil.	% of total
US	10,659	60	880	55
Europe	5,484	31	564	36
Asia/Pacific & Latin America	1,160	7	101	6
Other regions	439	2	51	3
Adjustments	(23)	—	(377)	—
Total	**17,719**	**100**	**1,219**	**100**

WHAT

	1995 Sales		1995 Operating Income	
	$ mil.	% of total	$ mil.	% of total
Personal products	7,151	40	658	41
Meats & bakery	6,110	34	383	24
Coffee & grocery	2,777	16	374	24
Home/personal care	1,691	10	181	11
Adjustments	(10)	—	(377)	—
Total	**17,719**	**100**	**1,219**	**100**

Selected Brand Names

Clothing/ Hosiery	Merrild	Biotex
Bali	Pickwick	Bloo Ultra 5
Champion	**Foods**	Bloom
Dim	Ball Park	Brylcreem
Donna Karan	Bryan	Catch
Hanes	Duyvis	Endust
L'eggs	Hillshire Farm	Sanex
Liz Claiborne	Jimmy Dean	Vapona
Playtex	Mr. Turkey	Zwitsal
Princesa	Sara Lee	**Leather Goods**
	Sinai 48	Coach
Coffee/Tea		
Douwe Egberts	**Home/Personal Care**	**Shoe Care**
Marcilla	Ambi-Pur	Kiwi
	Behold	Tana

KEY COMPETITORS

American Home Products	General Mills	Philip Morris
Amway	Gillette	Procter & Gamble
Bristol-Myers Squibb	Hormel	Quaker Oats
Campbell Soup	IBP	RJR Nabisco
Coca-Cola	Johnson & Johnson	S.C. Johnson
Colgate-Palmolive	Kellogg	Thorn Apple
CPC	LVMH	TLC Beatrice
Danskin	Maidenform	Vendôme
Fruit of the Loom	Nestlé	Warnaco Group
	PepsiCo	Warner-Lambert

HOW MUCH

	Annual Growth	1986	1987	1988	1989	1990	1991	1992	1993	1994	1995[1]
Sales ($ mil.)	9.3%	7,938	9,155	10,424	11,718	11,606	12,382	13,243	14,580	15,536	17,719
Net income ($ mil.)	14.9%	223	267	325	396	441	499	732	678	210	776
Income as % of sales	—	2.8%	2.9%	3.1%	3.4%	3.8%	4.0%	5.5%	4.7%	1.4%	4.4%
Earnings per share ($)	13.3%	0.51	0.59	0.71	0.88	0.94	1.05	1.50	1.37	0.43	1.57
Stock price – high ($)	—	9.20	12.28	12.88	16.88	16.69	29.06	32.44	31.13	26.00	29.00
Stock price – low ($)	—	5.89	6.63	8.22	10.72	12.06	14.81	23.31	21.00	19.35	24.25
Stock price – close ($)	14.4%	8.47	8.81	10.50	16.75	15.88	28.94	30.00	25.00	25.25	28.25
P/E – high	—	18	21	18	19	18	28	22	23	60	18
P/E – low	—	12	11	12	12	13	14	16	15	45	15
Dividends per share ($)	15.0%	0.19	0.23	0.28	0.33	0.39	0.45	0.61	0.56	0.63	0.67
Book value per share ($)	13.1%	2.70	3.20	3.56	4.21	4.97	5.48	7.05	7.31	6.92	8.20
Employees	6.2%	87,000	92,400	85,700	101,800	107,800	113,400	128,000	138,000	145,900	149,100

1995 Year-end:
Debt ratio: 39.7%
Return on equity: 21.4%
Cash (mil.): $202
Current ratio: 1.02
Long-term debt (mil.): $1,817
No. of shares (mil.): 480.7
Dividends
  Yield: 2.4%
  Payout: 42.7%
Market value (mil.): $13,579

Stock Price History[1]
High/Low 1986–95

[1] 1995 stock prices are through fiscal year-end (July 1).

SEARS, ROEBUCK AND CO.

OVERVIEW

Sears single-handedly lessened the nation's landfill "crisis" when it discontinued its "Great American Wish Book" catalog in 1993. Since then the company has been shedding its other weighty operations, including Dean Witter, Discover, as part of a plan to focus on its core Merchandise Group, which operates a network of mall-based department stores and free-standing stores in the US, Canada, and Mexico.

In 1995 Sears spun off Allstate (it owned 80%), the nation's largest publicly held property and casualty insurance company, with over 20 million customers and over $20 billion in sales. Allstate has suffered heavy losses because of the recent floods and earthquakes in California. Sears does plan on keeping its 50% stake in Prodigy, an on-line computer net-work, and its automotive division, which includes Western Auto, an operator of 633 stores (including 118 Tire America and 125 NTW stores). Sears also operates hardware stores and Homelife furniture stores. Despite losing all this weight, Sears is still the largest company based in the Chicago area.

The company's commitment to its retail operations is paying off. Same-store sales climbed 8.3% in 1994, due in part to improved apparel sales.

In 1995 Sears agreed to have Jiffy Lube (a Pennzoil unit) open oil change centers inside Sears Auto Centers. Also, CEO Edward Brennan announced his retirement. Arthur Martinez, chairman and CEO of the Sears Merchandise Group, will replace Brennan.

WHEN

In 1886 Richard W. Sears, a railway agent in Minnesota, bought a shipment of watches being returned to the maker. He started the R. W. Sears Watch Company 6 months later, moved to Chicago (home of mail order pioneer Montgomery Ward), and in 1887 hired watch-maker Alvah C. Roebuck. Sears sold the watch business in 1889 and 2 years later formed another mail order business that became Sears, Roebuck, and Company in 1893. The company issued its first general catalog in 1896, offering low prices and money-back guarantees to the farmers who were Sears's principal customers.

Roebuck left the company in 1895, and Sears found 2 new partners: Aaron Nussbaum (who left in 1901) and Julius Rosenwald. In 1906 Sears went public to raise money for expansion. Differences soon arose between Sears and Rosenwald; Sears departed in 1908 and Rosenwald became president.

Anticipating the changes that the automobile would bring to rural life, Sears opened its first retail store in 1924 so that farmers could drive to town to buy merchandise; in 1925 Sears brought out a line of tires under the name Allstate. Auto insurance (named after the tire) followed in 1931.

The company bought Homart Development (shopping centers, 1959) and several savings and loans. The Sears Tower — the world's tallest building — opened in 1973. After struggling through the high interest rates and low growth of the late 1970s, Sears decided to diversify into financial services and in 1981 acquired Coldwell Banker (real estate sales) and Dean Witter Reynolds (stock broker-age). Under the Dean Witter umbrella, Sears launched the Discover Card in 1985. But the financial operations never created any synergy for Sears and detracted from retailing.

In reaction to falling market share in the 1980s, Sears lurched from retail strategy to retail strategy, going up and down market, diversifying into auto supplies and repairs, and neglecting its department stores.

In 1992 Sears Auto Centers in California came under fire when it was alleged that salespeople sold unneeded auto parts and services in order to build their commissions. Sears tried to change the commission system, but some salespeople remained on commission, and the system was quietly revamped.

In 1992 Sears entered into a joint venture with IBM, its partner in the on-line service Prodigy, to form Advantis, a voice-and-data network services company. In 1993 Sears agreed to sell its Eye Care Centers of America stores, sold the last part of Coldwell Banker that it owned, and disposed of Dean Witter, Discover in a combination IPO and spinoff.

In 1994 the company transferred ownership of the Sears Tower, in Chicago, to a trust. The deal, which will enable a 3rd party to become owner of the building in 2003, relieved Sears of about $850 million in debt. That same year the company added 3.4 million square feet of apparel space to its stores. Sears also introduced national brands to go along with its own private-label clothing.

In 1995 the company announced its intention to divest Homart, its real estate subsidiary with about $2 billion in assets.

WHO

Chairman, President, and CEO: Edward A. Brennan, age 61, $1,483,805 pay
VC and Acting CFO: James M. Denny, age 62, $973,455 pay
Chairman and CEO, Sears Merchandise Group: Arthur C. Martinez, age 55, $2,050,746 pay
EVP Administration (HR): Anthony J. Rucci
SVP, General Counsel, and Secretary: David Shute, age 64
VP and Treasurer: Alice M. Peterson, age 42
VP Public Affairs: Gerald E. Buldak, age 50
Auditors: Deloitte & Touche LLP

WHERE

HQ: Sears Tower, Chicago, IL 60684
Phone: 312-875-2500
Fax: 312-875-8351

Sears operates 1,940 Homelife, Sears, Western Auto, and other retail stores in the US; 1,548 Sears and catalog stores in Canada; and 47 stores in Mexico.

	1994 Sales		1994 Operating Income	
	$ mil.	% of total	$ mil.	% of total
Merchandising				
US	29,376	54	1,484	84
Other countries	3,649	7	60	3
Allstate	21,464	39	227	13
Other	110	—	(59)	—
Adjustments	(40)	—	—	—
Total	**54,559**	**100**	**1,712**	**100**

WHAT

	1994 Sales		1994 Pretax Income	
	$ mil.	% of total	$ mil.	% of total
Merchandising	33,025	61	1,544	78
Property & liability insurance	18,607	34	108	5
Life insurance	2,856	5	334	17
Corporate	110	—	(59)	—
Adjustments	(39)	—	(215)	—
Total	**54,559**	**100**	**1,712**	**100**

Selected Stores

Sears catalog stores
Sears department stores
Sears Hardware stores
Sears Homelife furniture stores
Western Auto Supply Co.
 NTW
 Tire America

KEY COMPETITORS

Ace Hardware	Goodyear	Montgomery
Ames	Home Depot	Ward
AutoZone	J. Crew	Office Depot
Best Buy	J. C. Penney	Pep Boys
Best Products	Kmart	Service
Black & Decker	Lands' End	Merchandise
Bradlees	Levitz	Servistar
Brown Group	L.L. Bean	Sherwin-Williams
Caldor	Lowe's	Spiegel
Carson Pirie Scott	May	Stanley Works
Circuit City	Maytag	Toys "R" Us
Cotter & Company	McCrory	Venture Stores
Dayton Hudson	Men's Wearhouse	Waban
Dillard	Mercantile	Wal-Mart
Edison Brothers	Stores	Whitman
Federated	Monro Muffler	Woolworth
The Gap	Brake	

HOW MUCH

	Annual Growth	1985	1986	1987	1988	1989	1990	1991	1992	1993	1994
Sales ($ mil.)	3.3%	40,715	44,282	48,440	50,251	53,794	55,972	57,242	52,345	50,838	54,559
Net income ($ mil.)	1.2%	1,303	1,351	1,649	1,032	1,446	892	1,279	(2,059)	2,374	1,454
Income as % of sales	—	3.2%	3.1%	3.4%	2.1%	2.7%	1.6%	2.2%	—	4.7%	2.7%
Earnings per share ($)	0.4%	3.53	3.62	4.30	2.71	4.30	2.63	3.71	(5.65)	6.13	3.66
Stock price – high ($)	—	41.13	50.38	59.50	46.25	48.13	41.88	43.50	48.00	60.13	55.13
Stock price – low ($)	—	30.88	35.88	26.00	32.25	36.50	22.00	24.38	37.00	39.88	42.13
Stock price – close ($)	1.9%	39.00	39.75	33.50	40.88	38.13	25.38	37.88	45.50	52.88	46.00
P/E – high	—	12	14	14	17	11	16	12	—	10	15
P/E – low	—	9	10	6	12	9	8	7	—	7	12
Dividends per share ($)	(1.1%)	1.76	1.76	1.94	2.00	2.00	2.00	2.00	2.00	1.60	1.60
Book value per share ($)	(1.8%)	31.70	33.98	35.76	37.75	39.77	34.10	40.29	27.89	29.58	26.91
Employees	(2.8%)	466,000	485,400	501,100	520,000	500,000	460,000	450,000	403,000	359,000	360,570

1994 Year-end:
Debt ratio: 61.2%
Return on equity: 12.9%
Cash (mil.): $1,421
Current ratio: —
Long-term debt (mil.): $10,854
No. of shares (mil.): 352
Dividends
 Yield: 2.2%
 Payout: 43.7%
Market value (mil.): $16,178

Stock Price History
High/Low 1985–94

SERVICEMASTER LIMITED PARTNERSHIP

OVERVIEW

ServiceMaster uses divine inspiration to help it do the dirty work. The company, whose first principle is "to honor God in all we do," is a leading provider of professional cleaning services (ServiceMaster and Res/Com), termite and pest control (Terminix), maid services (Merry Maids), lawn care (TruGreen-ChemLawn), and home appliance repair warranties (American Home Shield). These consumer services are offered through a worldwide network of company-owned and franchised branches. The company is based in Downers Grove, Illinois.

ServiceMaster also provides health care, educational, and industrial facilities with supportive management services, such as plant operations and maintenance, housekeeping and custodial, laundry and linen, and grounds and landscaping services. It operates child care centers and provides food services for schools, too.

Part of ServiceMaster's success stems from its training, which uses videotapes and manuals that break down such tasks as mopping a floor into 5-minute steps. By standardizing manual chores and using state-of-the-art equipment (battery-powered vacuum cleaners and lighter mops, for example), the company ensures high productivity and quality.

The other key to the company's success is its ability to motivate its workers. Although ServiceMaster doesn't impose Christianity on its workers, its managers use the faith's values to treat all of its workers with dignity, from executives to janitors. According to chairman William Pollard, "When you have people identifying with the mission of the organization, when they see something beyond the paycheck, then they are motivated to do a better job." And cleanliness, after all, is next to godliness.

WHEN

Marion Wade founded a carpet-cleaning and mothproofing business in 1929. After a 1944 accident with cleaning chemicals nearly cost him his sight, he looked to God for direction. Wade subsequently met Kenneth Hansen, a graduate of the religious Wheaton College, and the 2 incorporated a cleaning company in 1947. They were joined in 1954 by Kenneth Wessner, another Wheaton graduate, and in 1958 they named the company ServiceMaster, to reflect their business expertise and their credo of "Service to the Master."

The company successfully franchised its cleaning business in places as far away as the UK, but its real business inspiration came from a nun who suggested that ServiceMaster offer its services to hospitals. The company's first hospital contract came in 1962. That same year ServiceMaster went public.

The 1970s were a time of profound advancement: ServiceMaster averaged more than 25% annual growth in earnings for the decade. Although the company sold thousands of consumer cleaning franchises, most of its revenues were coming from the health care services division. ServiceMaster's scrupulous cleaning methods converted many hospitals to outsourcing these services. Chairman Wade died in 1973.

As the 1980s unfolded, revenue growth slowed due to stern cost-control measures in health care institutions. In order to maintain its upward path and meet a company goal of $2 billion in revenues by 1990 (it fell one year short), ServiceMaster needed to diversify.

The company began supplying its cleaning services to schools and other institutions and then moved into food services. In order to fund acquisitions in new lines of business, ServiceMaster altered its previous policy of abstaining from the use of long-term debt. The company was also converted in 1986 to a publicly traded limited partnership, eliminating its federal tax burden. This move freed up cash that, along with borrowings, was used that year to acquire Terminix (then the 2nd largest pest control company in the US), and American Food Management (which supplied food service management to colleges).

In 1988 the company purchased Merry Maids, a franchisor of professional maid services. ServiceMaster continued its march into the home services industry with the acquisition of American Home Shield, a provider of home warranty contracts, in 1989. The following year it acquired control of TruGreen, and in 1992 the company added ChemLawn to its professional lawn care operations. The company also branched into child care services.

In 1992 shareholders approved a plan to convert the company from a limited partnership back into a corporation; this is expected to occur at the end of 1997.

With the financial rewards of domestic expansion, ServiceMaster took its crusade for cleanliness to Europe by acquiring pest control companies in the UK and the Netherlands in 1994. In 1995 it formed a joint venture with Tarmac, a leading provider of total facilities management in the UK.

NYSE symbol: SVM
Fiscal year ends: December 31

WHO

Chairman: C. William Pollard, age 56
VC: Charles W. Stair, age 54
President and CEO: Carlos H. Cantu, age 61,
$962,500 pay
**President and COO, International and New Business
Development:** Robert D. Erickson, age 51,
$539,000 pay
President and CEO, Diversified Health Services: Jerry
D. Mooney, age 41, $470,000 pay
President and COO, Consumer Services: Robert F.
Keith, age 38, $425,000 pay
President and COO, Management Services: Brian D.
Oxley, age 44
SVP and General Counsel: Vernon T. Squires, age 60,
$418,000 pay
SVP and CFO: Ernest J. Mrozek, age 41
VP People Management: Debra Kass
Auditors: Arthur Andersen & Co, SC

WHERE

HQ: One ServiceMaster Way, Downers Grove, IL 60515
Phone: 708-271-1300
Fax: 708-271-2710

ServiceMaster provides its services through a network
of 4,800 service centers and to 2,200 facilities in the
US and 28 foreign countries.

WHAT

	1994 Sales	
	$ mil.	% of total
Management services	1,823	61
Consumer services	1,041	35
Other	121	4
Total	**2,985**	**100**

Selected Businesses

Consumer Services
American Home Shield Corp.
Merry Maids
ServiceMaster Consumer Services Co.
ServiceMaster Residential/Commercial Services
The Terminix International Co.
TruGreen-ChemLawn

Diversified Health Services
ServiceMaster Diversified Health Services Co.
ServiceMaster Home Health Care Services, Inc.

International and New Business Development
ServiceMaster Child Care Services, Inc.
ServiceMaster International and New Business
Development

Management Services
CMI Group
ServiceMaster Business & Industry Group
ServiceMaster Education Management Services
ServiceMaster Energy Management Services
ServiceMaster Healthcare Management Services
ServiceMaster Management Services Co.
ServiceMaster Manufacturing Services

Joint Ventures
Daka Restaurants L.P.
ServiceMaster of Canada Limited
Tarmac ServiceMaster Limited

KEY COMPETITORS

ABM Industries
All Green
ARAMARK
Barefoot
Chemed
Children's Discovery
  Centers of America
Consolidated Food Service

Delaware North
Ecolab
Flagstar
KinderCare
La Petite Academy
Morrison Restaurants
Rollins

HOW MUCH

	Annual Growth	1985	1986	1987	1988	1989	1990	1991	1992	1993	1994
Sales ($ mil.)	12.9%	1,002	1,123	1,425	1,531	1,609	1,826	2,110	2,489	2,759	2,985
Net income ($ mil.)	17.5%	33	33	60	65	68	83	86	130	146	140
Income as % of sales	—	3.3%	2.9%	4.2%	4.2%	4.2%	4.6%	4.1%	5.2%	5.3%	4.7%
Earnings per share ($)	16.7%	0.45	0.45	0.85	0.90	0.93	1.17	1.19	1.71	1.90	1.81
Stock price – high ($)	—	11.34	11.90	14.24	12.62	10.79	10.57	17.35	19.93	31.00	28.38
Stock price – low ($)	—	7.79	8.79	9.12	9.73	9.29	8.79	9.79	14.67	17.68	21.50
Stock price – close ($)	10.4%	10.01	9.45	10.57	10.07	9.57	10.51	16.57	18.51	27.38	24.38
P/E – high	—	25	26	17	14	12	9	15	12	16	16
P/E – low	—	17	20	11	11	10	8	8	9	9	12
Dividends per share ($)	11.7%	0.34	0.38	0.67	0.75	0.78	0.82	0.85	0.79	0.89	0.92
Book value per share ($)	15.8%	1.08	0.46	0.60	0.73	0.58	1.35	1.68	2.82	3.78	4.04
Employees	16.9%	8,410	12,291	14,861	17,000	15,300	17,500	21,300	28,000	32,400	34,300

1994 Year-end:
Debt ratio: 56.2%
Return on equity: 46.9%
Cash (mil.): $14
Current ratio: 1.09
Long-term debt (mil.): $387
No. of shares (mil.): 76
Dividends
  Yield: 3.8%
  Payout: 50.8%
Market value (mil.): $1,853

Stock Price History
High/Low 1985–94

SPECIALTY FOODS CORPORATION

OVERVIEW

Specialty Foods Corporation is a $2 billion holding company that came into being when hungry investors led by Texas billionaire Robert Bass helped themselves to 8 major American food companies previously owned by Beledia N.V., of the Netherlands. Included in the company's 3 broad product categories — bakery, specialty foods, and cheese and meat — are bagels, breads, cheeses, cookies, meats, pickles, and snack foods produced for distribution to wholesalers, retail grocers, and club stores in the US and Canada.

The Deerfield, Illinois–based company's Metz Bakery Group distributes breads and sweets under the Taystee, Holsum, and D'Italiano brands in the Midwest; sourdough French bread under the Parisian, Colombo, and Toscana brands in California; cookies under the Mother's, Mrs. Wheatly's, and Bakery

Wagon labels in the western US; and a full range of bakery products under the Gai's, Country Hearth, and Langendorf labels in the Pacific Northwest.

Specialty Foods's cheese and meat operation includes Stella Foods, one of the nation's largest cheese makers (with 14 plants nationwide producing Italian and other specialty cheeses under the Frigo, Lorraine, and Stella labels), and H&M Food Systems, a maker of precooked meats for the food service market.

The company's specialty foods category consists of pickle and spice manufacturer and marketer B&G/DSD; the original bagel chip maker, Burns & Ricker; and the 29 Andre Boudin Sourdough Bakeries and Cafes.

Certain they have not bitten off more than they can chew, company executives plan growth through additional acquisitions.

WHEN

Specialty Foods Corporation was founded in June 1993, when an investor group comprising Haas Wheat & Partners; Keystone, Inc. (formerly the Robert M. Bass Group); Acadia Partners, L.P.; UBS Capital Corporation; and Donaldson, Lufkin & Jenrette joined together to buy the North American food businesses of Beledia N.V., of the Netherlands, a subsidiary of Artal Group, of Belgium. The acquisition included 8 companies (all acquired by Beledia in the previous 7 years and assembled for Specialty by the New York–based Invus Group).

The companies, with combined annual revenues of about $2 billion, included B&G/DSD, a Roseland, New Jersey–based manufacturer of pickles, peppers, and spices, founded in 1889, with distribution to retail grocers in New York City and direct store delivery of dry goods to stores from Massachusetts to Pennsylvania; Burns & Ricker, a Paterson, New Jersey–based snack food maker now run by B&G/DSD; Gordon's Wholesale of Des Moines, Iowa, a distributor of candy, tobacco, and foodstuffs (sold in 1994); H&M Food Systems, a Fort Worth, Texas–based manufacturer of precooked pizza toppings and meats for Mexican food, founded in 1983; and Metz Baking Company of Sioux City, Iowa, a wholesale baker serving the Midwest. Also included were Mother's Cake and Cookie Co., an Oakland, California–based cookie maker founded in 1914 by Mique Wheatley after he bought a cookie recipe from an elderly couple and began daily delivery of the fresh-baked treats to local grocers; the Pacific Coast Baking Co., the

owner of the San Francisco French Bread Company, one of the nation's leading wholesale producers of sourdough French bread and operator of the Andre Boudin Sourdough Bakeries and Cafes chain and of Gai's Seattle French Baking Company, a baker serving the Pacific Northwest; and Stella Foods, the largest specialty Italian cheese producer in the US, based in Green Bay, Wisconsin.

Thomas Herskovits, the former president of Kraft General Foods Frozen Products and Dairy Groups, was named Specialty Foods's president and CEO in November 1993. The company established its corporate headquarters in the Chicago area.

Since its inception, Specialty Foods has shuffled its baking business a couple of times. The bakeries were initially regrouped as the Western Bakery Group in October 1993. In 1994 Specialty Foods acquired the Bagel Place, adding the California-based bagel and "energy bar" producer to its operations. In January 1995 the company made a move to streamline its extensive bakery operations, announcing the creation of a single, integrated national baking company to be run by Metz and called the Metz Bakery Group. Only Mother's Cake & Cookie Co. (which launched an international expansion campaign with distribution to Canada, Japan, Mexico, Russia, and Saudi Arabia in 1994) and the Andre Boudin retail chain were to remain separate.

Herskovits has said acquisitions will drive future growth. The company hopes to become a $4 billion firm in the next 5 years.

Private company
Fiscal year ends: December 31

WHO

Chairman: Robert B. Haas, age 47
President and CEO: Thomas Herskovits, age 48,
$900,000 pay
COO: Paul J. Liska, age 39, $395,000 pay
VP, Secretary, and General Counsel: John E. Kelly,
age 42, $470,000 pay
VP Marketing and Strategy: Robert E. Baker, age 48,
$240,000 pay
VP Human Resources: John R. Reisenberg, age 50
CEO and COO, Metz Bakery Group: Henry J. Metz,
age 44, $395,000 pay
President and CEO, Stella Foods, Inc.: Lawrence S.
Benjamin, age 39
President and CEO, H&M Food Systems Co., Inc.:
Richard G. Scalise, age 40
CEO, B&G/DSD, Inc.: Leonard S. Polaner, age 63
Auditors: KPMG Peat Marwick LLP

WHERE

HQ: 520 Lake Cook Rd., Ste. 520, Deerfield, IL
60015-4927
Phone: 847-267-3000
Fax: 847-267-0015

WHAT

	1994 Sales	
	$ mil.	% of total
Bakery	861	43
Cheese & meat	941	48
Other specialty food	177	9
Total	**1,979**	**100**

Companies and Brands
Andre Boudin Sourdough Bakeries and Cafes, Inc.
B&G/DSD, Inc. (pickles, peppers, spices, and dry goods)
Burns & Ricker, Inc. (baked premium snack products)
  Biscotti
  Mini-Bagel Crisps
  Pita Crisps
  Tuscany Toast
H&M Food Systems Co., Inc. (precooked meats)
Metz Bakery Group
  Colombo
  Country Hearth
  D'Italiano
  Egekvist
  Gai's
  Holsum
  Langendorf
  Master
  Old Home
  Parisian
  Taystee
  Toscana
Mother's Cake and Cookie Co.
  Bakery Wagon
  Mother's
  Mrs. Wheatly's
Stella Foods, Inc. (specialty cheeses)
  Frigo
  Lorraine
  Stella

KEY COMPETITORS

Campbell Soup
Campbell Taggart
ConAgra
CooperSmith
CPC Intl.
Dean Foods
Flowers Indus.
General Mills
GF Industries
Inflo Holdings

Interstate Bakeries
Land O'Lakes
Mars
PepsiCo
Philip Morris
Piemonte Foods
Powerfood Inc.
Quaker Oats
RJR Nabisco
Universal Foods

HOW MUCH

	Annual Growth	1985	1986	1987	1988	1989	1990	1991	1992	1993	1994
Sales ($ mil.)	16.1%	—	—	—	—	939	1,170	1,383	1,637	1,998	1,979
Net income ($ mil.)	—	—	—	—	—	(7)	(7)	3	11	(14)	(21)
Income as % of sales	—	—	—	—	—	—	—	0.2%	0.6%	—	—
Employees	(0.4%)	—	—	—	—	—	—	—	14,000	13,100	13,900

Net Income
($ mil.)
1989–94

SPIEGEL, INC.

Spiegel is one of the largest specialty retailers in the US. Although largely known for its flagship catalog, the company also sells clothes through its Newport News catalog (moderately priced women's apparel) and its Eddie Bauer subsidiary, which operates 356 stores in the US, Canada, and Japan, as well as its own catalogs (Eddie Bauer, Eddie Bauer Home, AKA Eddie Bauer, and The Complete Resource [combining the 3 concepts]). In sum, Spiegel's catalog circulation neared 340 million in 1994. The company operates 13 Spiegel outlet stores as well.

Spiegel saw its earnings drop by nearly 1/2 in 1994. The disappointing results were due to unseasonably warm weather, and thus weak demand for winter apparel, and start-up costs for its new common catalog distribution center. Spiegel plans to fill orders from all its separate catalogs through this center, bringing the company closer to its long-term goal: to be a low-cost operator.

Spiegel no longer depends on demographics for marketing and merchandising decisions but rather on its sophisticated database of customer buying habits. Besides being used to predict customers' future purchases, the database helps Spiegel decide where to place new stores, targeting areas with high concentrations of its catalog customers.

Spiegel is expanding internationally. In 1994 Eddie Bauer began distributing catalogs in Germany and opened 3 stores in Tokyo.

A few weeks after his release from a Confederate prison, Joseph Spiegel established a home furnishings store in Chicago in 1865. New railroads and an influx of immigrants contributed to the city's bustle and to the burgeoning sales of Spiegel's enterprise. In 1871 Spiegel's store was razed in the Great Chicago Fire, but because he had stored much of his wares in his backyard, he was soon back in business. Spiegel's business grew quickly and in 1905, at his son Arthur's suggestion, and probably to compete with the other 2 local mail order giants, Montgomery Ward and Sears, he began offering mail order sales to customers in rural areas.

Arthur soon took over, and in 1912 the company began selling women's clothing. Spiegel's focus shifted to its catalog business, and during the Depression it sold its retail operations. The company pioneered many catalog innovations: it was the first to use photographs in catalogs, to publish a Christmas catalog, and to offer credit, a novel service that was the main driver behind Spiegel's mail order business.

Credit restrictions during WWII brought the company back to retailing. While the stores increased sales, they were not as profitable as the catalogs, and in 1953 Spiegel once again returned to solely mail order sales.

Spiegel was bought by Beneficial Corporation in 1965. By the mid-1970s the company was facing tough competition from 4 other catalogers: Sears, J. C. Penney, Montgomery Ward, and Aldens, each virtually identical. To set itself apart, Spiegel targeted more upscale consumers, shifting from "mass to class." By 1985 it was selling apparel by Liz Claiborne, Calvin Klein, and Ralph Lauren.

In 1982 Spiegel was acquired by European catalog company Otto Versand. Sales tripled in 4 years. Although the company went public in 1987, Otto Versand chairman Michael Otto controlled the voting stock.

Spiegel bought Eddie Bauer in 1988. Eddie Bauer had founded his business in 1928 after a bout with hypothermia, when the wool clothing he had worn on a fishing trip proved inadequate. Upon his return he invented the Skyline, a goose down–insulated jacket, which was so popular that the air force contracted Bauer to provide down-insulated flight suits during WWII. Mail order operations began in 1946, and the company grew into a network of retail stores.

In 1990 Spiegel acquired First Consumer National Bank, the basis of its credit card operations. In 1993 it bought New Hampton (now Newport News), which publishes catalogs aimed at lower-middle-market shoppers.

Spiegel joined with Time Warner in 1993 to create a new shopping channel, Catalog 1, offering goods to a more affluent clientele than most such services. It began test marketing in 4 areas in early 1994. However, after disappointing sales results, the company discontinued television production of Catalog 1 in 1995 and reduced its programming from 24 hours a day to just 2 hours on Saturday.

Also in 1995 Eddie Bauer launched a new line of stores called AKA Eddie Bauer, specializing in upscale dress for men and women. This new concept feature's its own specialty catalogs.

Nasdaq symbol: SPGLA
Fiscal year ends: December 31

Chairman: Michael Otto, age 51
VC, President, and CEO: John J. Shea, age 56,
  $836,250 pay
President, Eddie Bauer: Richard T. Fersch,
  $550,000 pay
EVP Merchandise: David C. Moon, age 52, $310,900 pay
SVP Operations and Information Services: Kenneth A.
  Bochenski, age 52, $314,500 pay
SVP Human Resources: Harold S. Dahlstrand,
  age 50
VP Manufacturing: Alois J. Lohn, age 60, $370,500 pay
VP Finance and CFO: James W. Sievers, age 52
VP Corporate Planning: Stanley D. Leibowitz, age 43
VP Advertising: Davia L. Kimmey, age 41
VP, Secretary, and General Counsel: Michael R. Moran,
  age 48
Treasurer: John R. Steele, age 42
Auditors: KPMG Peat Marwick LLP

WHERE

HQ: 3500 Lacey Rd., Downers Grove, IL 60515-5432
Phone: 708-986-8800
Fax: 708-769-3101

In addition to catalog sales, Spiegel operates 356
Eddie Bauer stores in Canada, Japan, and the US and
13 Spiegel outlet stores.

WHAT

	1994 Sales	
	$ mil.	% of total
Catalog	1,742	58
Retail	965	32
Finance & other	309	10
Total	**3,016**	**100**

	1994 Sales	
		% of total
Apparel		68
Household furnishings & other general merchandise		32
Total		**100**

	1994 Stores
	No.
Eddie Bauer — retail	318
Eddie Bauer — outlet	38
Spiegel outlet	13
Total	**369**

Selected Subsidiaries
Cara Corp. (information management)
Eddie Bauer, Inc.
First Consumers National Bank (credit cards)
Newport News, Inc. (moderately priced women's
  apparel)
Spiegel Credit Corporation
Spiegel Properties Inc.

KEY COMPETITORS

50-Off Stores	Home Shopping	Montgomery
L. L. Bean	Network	Ward
Blair	J. Crew	Neiman Marcus
Brown Group	J. C. Penney	Nordstrom
Comcast	Kmart	Polo/Ralph
Dayton Hudson	Lands' End	Lauren
Dillard	Lechters	REI
Edison Brothers	The Limited	Ross Stores
Federated	L.L. Bean	Sears
Fingerhut	Luxottica	Stein Mart
The Gap	May	Talbots
Hanover Direct	Melville	Wal-Mart
	Mercantile Stores	Woolworth

HOW MUCH

	Annual Growth	1985	1986	1987	1988	1989	1990	1991	1992	1993	1994
Sales ($ mil.)	15.3%	836	985	927	1,402	1,696	1,993	1,976	2,219	2,596	3,016
Net income ($ mil.)	7.5%	13	36	41	57	73	62	17	39	48	25
Income as % of sales	—	1.6%	3.7%	4.4%	4.1%	4.3%	3.1%	0.9%	1.8%	1.9%	0.8%
Earnings per share ($)	3.4%	0.17	0.46	0.51	0.59	0.71	0.59	0.17	0.38	0.47	0.23
Stock price – high ($)	—	—	—	7.63	5.63	11.56	13.50	10.50	9.00	23.38	26.75
Stock price – low ($)	—	—	—	3.50	3.88	4.44	4.88	5.38	5.00	7.75	8.75
Stock price – close ($)	13.4%	—	—	4.19	4.56	10.13	6.75	6.63	8.50	22.50	10.13
P/E – high	—	—	—	15	10	16	23	62	24	50	116
P/E – low	—	—	—	7	7	6	8	32	13	16	38
Dividends per share ($)	—	—	—	0.00	0.12	0.18	0.18	0.18	0.18	0.20	0.20
Book value per share ($)	10.4%	—	—	2.67	3.44	3.97	4.38	4.31	4.55	5.32	5.35
Employees	15.2%	5,500	—	6,000	9,000	10,500	12,300	12,000	13,500	16,700	19,700

1994 Year-end:
Debt ratio: 70.4%
Return on equity: 4.4%
Cash (mil.): $33
Current ratio: 3.04
Long-term debt (mil.): $1,300
No. of shares (mil.): 108
Dividends
  Yield: 2.0%
  Payout: 87.0%
Market value (mil.): $1,096

Stock Price History High/Low 1987–94

STONE CONTAINER CORPORATION

OVERVIEW

After overexpansion and slumping paper prices almost broke Stone Container in the early 1990s, Stone is on a roll again. The 1994 surge in paper prices is lifting the once-sinking Stone toward profitability.

The company is the world's largest producer of paperboard and paper packaging; it is the #1 producer of containerboard and corrugated containers as well as bags and sacks (such as those used in supermarkets and 20-pound bags of Purina dog food). In addition, Stone Container is major producer of newsprint, uncoated groundwood paper, and market pulp and makes lumber, plywood, and veneer at 16 North American mills. The company operates in Latin America, Europe, Australia, and the Far East as well. Foreign sales accounted for 27% of total 1994 revenue.

Stone Container's financial problems stem from its 1989 purchase of Consolidated-

Bathhurst (renamed Stone-Consolidated) for $2.2 billion. Shortly after the acquisition, prices for newsprint produced by Stone-Consolidated softened, and the company began negotiating with lenders. In recent years the company has taken measures to lighten its debt load, including selling off assets, issuing new debt, and selling stock.

The Stone family, which holds several key executive positions, owns about 15% of the company's common stock. Led by Roger Stone's unsinkable optimism, the company reckons to make $1 billion in net profit on $10 billion sales in 1998.

The company is leaving no stone unturned in its twin strategies of decreasing debt and increasing sales. In 1994 the company restructured $2.5 billion of its debt, and CEO Stone is looking to the expanding demand for boxes in Europe and Asia to keep sales growing.

WHEN

Go to America, Joseph Stone's mother told him in 1888. There's nothing for you in Russia, she said.

Stone moved to the US, first to Philadelphia, then to Chicago. In 1926, with $2,300 he scraped together from savings and from sons Norman and Marvin, he launched J.H. Stone & Sons as a jobber for shipping supplies such as wrapping paper and tissue. A 3rd son, Jerome, joined the business in 1928, the same year the little company (first year sales: $68,000) began jobbing corrugated boxes. During the Depression the Stone firm suffered a shortage of corrugated boxes, and when a supplier offered to sell the Stones used box-making equipment, they paid $7,200 for it. In 1938 the Stones built a 150,000-square-foot plant to manufacture corrugated boxes. They paid the $382,000, 20-year note off in 3 years, because, as Marvin Stone would recall later, "we . . . did not view business debt as virtue."

Stone bought a Philadelphia corrugated box company (1943), incorporated as Stone Container Corp. (1945), and went public (1947). In the early 1960s the company launched its South Carolina Industries affiliate to manufacture kraft linerboard.

Roger Stone, Marvin's son, became president in 1975. In 1979 Stone Container's board of directors turned down a $125 million purchase offer from Boise Cascade. Under Roger the company shifted from target to marksman, picking off distressed companies during industry slumps. Using junk bond financing, Stone Container paid $509 million for Continental Group's forest products unit (1983), $426 million for the brown paper business of Champion (1986), and $760 million for Southwest Forest Industries (1987).

In 1989 Stone Container bought Consolidated-Bathhurst of Canada, a leading maker of newsprint, in an all-cash $2.2 billion deal, seeing in Consolidated-Bathhurst's European subsidiaries a beachhead for gaining entry into the European market. But when prices slumped and interest expense skyrocketed, Stone Container suffered. In 1993 Stone sold to the public 25% of its stake in the Canadian subsidiary, raising $462 million.

In 1990 the company pushed into the recycling market, entering a joint venture with WMX (Paper Recycling International) and beefing up its recycling capacity at plants in Germany, Connecticut, and Montana. In 1993, as part of its effort to shore up its balance sheet, the company sold its interest in Titan, a Mexican corrugated container firm, and 2 short-line railroads for $125 million. In 1994 the company raised $962 million by selling 16.5 million shares of common stock and another $710 million by issuing debt.

The company sold 2 Detroit area container plants in 1994 to Laimbeer Packaging and closed 3 solid wood products operations in the Pacific Northwest.

NYSE symbol: STO
Fiscal year ends: December 31

WHO

Chairman, President, and CEO: Roger W. Stone, age 60, $730,000 pay
President and CEO, Stone-Consolidated: James Doughan, age 61, $678,412 pay
EVP Corporate Administration: Morty Rosenkranz, age 67, $420,000 pay
EVP, CFO, and Chief Planning Officer: Arnold F. Brookstone, age 65, $322,000 pay
SVP and General Manager, North American Containerboard, Paper and Pulp: James B. Heider, age 51, $285,000 pay
SVP and General Manager, Industrial and Retail Packaging Division: Thomas W. Cadden Sr., age 61
SVP and General Manager, Forest Products Division: Gerald M. Freeman, age 58
VP, Secretary, and Counsel: Leslie T. Lederer, age 47
VP Human Resources and Benefits Administration: Gayle M. Sparapani
Auditors: Price Waterhouse LLP

WHERE

HQ: 150 N. Michigan Ave., Chicago, IL 60601-7568
Phone: 312-346-6600
Fax: 312-580-4919

Stone Container has more than 125 plants in the US, 27 in Canada, 16 in Germany, 2 in Australia, 2 in Belgium, 2 in Costa Rica, 2 in the UK, 6 in France, and one each in Mexico, the Netherlands, and Venezuela.

	1994 Sales		1994 Operating Income	
	$ mil.	% of total	$ mil.	% of total
US	4,188	73	344	91
Canada	942	16	20	5
Europe	619	11	15	4
Total	**5,749**	**100**	**379**	**100**

WHAT

	1994 Sales		1994 Operating Income	
	$ mil.	% of total	$ mil.	% of total
Paperboard & paper packaging	4,199	73	354	94
White paper & pulp	1,550	27	25	6
Total	**5,749**	**100**	**379**	**100**

Paperboard and Paper Packaging
Bags and sacks
Boxboard
Containerboard
Corrugated containers
Folding cartons
Kraft paper

White Paper and Pulp
Market pulp
Newsprint
Uncoated paper

Wood Products
Lumber
Plywood
Veneer

KEY COMPETITORS

Arjo Wiggins
Appleton
Boise Cascade
Bowater
Burhmann-Tetterode
Champion International
Consolidated Papers
Fletcher Challenge
Fort Howard
Georgia-Pacific
International Paper

James River
Jefferson Smurfit
Kimberly-Clark
Longview Fibre
Manville
Mead
Potlatch
Scott
Stora
Temple-Inland
Union Camp
Westvaco
Weyerhaeuser
Willamette Industries

HOW MUCH

	Annual Growth	1985	1986	1987	1988	1989	1990	1991	1992	1993	1994
Sales ($ mil.)	18.7%	1,229	2,032	3,233	3,743	5,330	5,756	5,384	5,521	5,060	5,749
Net income ($ mil.)	—	4	35	161	342	286	95	(49)	(170)	(319)	(190)
Income as % of sales	—	0.3%	1.7%	5.0%	9.1%	5.4%	1.7%	—	—	—	—
Earnings per share ($)	—	0.09	0.73	2.65	5.58	4.67	1.56	(0.78)	(2.59)	(4.59)	(2.30)
Stock price – high ($)	—	13.17	20.00	38.83	39.50	36.38	25.25	26.00	32.63	19.50	21.13
Stock price – low ($)	—	8.00	11.38	15.33	20.67	22.13	8.13	9.00	12.50	6.38	9.63
Stock price – close ($)	3.8%	12.38	18.95	24.02	31.37	23.41	11.27	25.37	16.75	9.63	17.38
P/E – high	—	—	27	15	7	8	16	—	—	—	—
P/E – low	—	—	16	6	4	5	5	—	—	—	—
Dividends per share ($)	(100.0%)	0.19	0.19	0.25	0.35	0.70	0.71	0.71	0.35	0.00	0.00
Book value per share ($)	(2.0%)	7.08	9.92	12.40	17.73	22.50	24.34	22.12	13.91	6.91	5.90
Employees	13.4%	9,400	15,500	18,800	20,700	32,600	32,300	31,800	31,200	29,000	29,100

1994 Year-end:
Debt ratio: 89.9%
Return on equity: —
Cash (mil.): $109
Current ratio: 1.76
Long-term debt (mil.): $4,432
No. of shares (mil.): 90
Dividends
  Yield: —
  Payout: —
Market value (mil.): $1,571

Stock Price History High/Low 1985–94

TOPCO ASSOCIATES, INC.

OVERVIEW

Skokie, Illinois–based Topco is one of the top companies in the business of supplying supermarkets with processed, preserved, and perishable foods as well as pharmaceuticals, paper products, and cosmetics. A member-owned cooperative, it has 46 member organizations across the US, including supermarket chains Giant Eagle (based in Pennsylvania), Meijer (Michigan), Penn Traffic (New York), Randall's Food Markets (Texas), Schnuck Markets (Missouri), and Smith's Food & Drug Centers (Utah).

Topco is the leading provider of private-label products to supermarkets, a growth area in that business. Topco's private labels include Food Club (breakfast cereals and processed foods), Jungle Land (children's health and personal care items), Mega (processed foods), PAWS Professional (pet food), and Valu Time (processed foods). The company is also pioneering the branding of perishables (such as baked goods, fresh meat, produce, and seafood), an area of marketing that is only in its infancy. In 1995 it launched a pilot program to provide its clients with better analysis of meat products sales data.

Topco has a size advantage that allows it to pass on lower product, equipment, and service costs to its members through large-volume purchases on their behalf. The company is also upgrading its information technology to increase efficiency.

WHEN

Food Cooperatives was founded in Wisconsin in 1944. A few years later it decided to merge with Top Frost Foods, with which it had some members in common. After negotiations led by Food Cooperatives executive John Hayes, the merger was completed with the creation of Topco in 1950. (According to legend, the company's new name, "Topco" was either a combination of the names of the 2 founding cooperatives or an abbreviation for "top companies.") The member companies involved in the merger included Alpha Beta, Big Bear, Brockton Public Market, Fred Meyer, Furr's, Hinky Dinky, Penn Fruit Company, and Star Markets. Hayes was appointed general manager, and Sam Cooke of Penn Fruit was made president.

The company initially sold basic commodities to private-label retailers, adding fresh produce in 1958. In 1960 Topco expanded its product line further, moving into general merchandise, health and beauty care items, and store equipment. In 1961, when Topco moved its headquarters to Skokie, revenues topped the $100 million mark.

During the 1960s other leading supermarkets, including Giant Eagle, King Soopers, McCarty-Holman, and Tom Thumb, joined the cooperative. Also that decade the company came under attack from the Justice Department when it was accused of antitrust activity in granting its members exclusive distribution rights for Topco-branded products. The case went all the way to the Supreme Court, which in 1972 found against the company. In light of the ruling, Topco agreed to sell products under the private labels of its members.

In the late 1970s the company introduced Valu Time, the first nationally marketed line of branded generic products. This concept was then adopted by many US supermarkets. By 1979 Topco surpassed $1 billion in annual revenues.

By the end of the 1980s, Topco's membership had expanded to include Carr-Gottstein, Fry's, Randall's, Red Food Stores, Riser Foods, Riverside Markets, Pueblo, Schnuck Markets, and Smith's Food & Drug Centers. In 1988 Topco introduced World Classics, a premium quality line of high-volume, high-margin products that are packaged and promoted as national brands.

During the early 1990s the company ran through a number of CEOs. In 1990 Robert Seelert replaced 10-year CEO Marcel Lussier. In 1992 John Beggs took over, and in 1993 Steven Rubow was handed the reins. The early 1990s also saw rapid growth, with 20 new members bringing the company's total to 46 by 1995. During this period annual sales jumped from $2.4 billion to $3.7 billion.

Topco also expanded internationally, with the membership of Oshawa Group (Canada), the associate membership of Seiyu (Japan), and a sales campaign in Mexico.

In 1993 the company rolled out a new line of upscale cosmetics and hair and skin care products. This product line, called TC Color Shop, offers 84 different cosmetic items to supermarket shoppers.

In 1995 Topco succeeded in having the upscale Kings Super Markets drop its private-label allegiance with distributor White Rose and sign on with Topco.

Cooperative
Fiscal year ends: March 31

Chairman: David Dillon
President and CEO: W. Steven Rubow
SVP and CFO: Steven K. Lauer
SVP Planning and Development: Frank G. Mayes
SVP Branded Goods: Dan Mazur
SVP Perishables: Russell Wolfe
VP Produce and Floral Operations: Ron Bajda
VP Grocery Procurement: Jon Fruh
VP Member Development: Ken Guy
VP HBC/GM/Pharmacy: Jim Wisner
VP Support Services: Jack Zrency
VP Logistics: Jay Zwart
VP Human Resources and Administration: Ronald Ficks
Auditors: KPMG Peat Marwick LLP

WHERE

HQ: 7711 Gross Point Rd., Skokie, IL 60077-2697
Phone: 847-676-3030
Fax: 847-676-4949

Topco distributes processed, preserved, and perishable foods as well as paper products, cosmetics, and pharmaceuticals to its 46 supermarket members in Canada, Japan, and the US.

WHAT

Selected Products
Breakfast cereals (Food Club)
Canned vegetables (Mega)
Children's health and personal care items (Jungle Land)
Cleaning supplies (Top Crest)
Flowers
Frozen food
Fruit juice (Valu Time)
Perishables
Pet food (PAWS Professional)
Pharmaceuticals
Seafood

Member Companies
Ahold USA
    BI-LO, Inc./Red Food
    Finast
    First National Supermarkets, Inc.
    Giant Food Stores, Inc.
    Tops Markets, Inc.

Big Y Foods, Inc.
C&S Wholesale Grocers, Inc.
Carr-Gottstein Foods Company, Inc.
Delchamps, Inc.
Dillon Companies, Inc.
    City Market, Inc.
    Dillon Stores
    Dillon Stores – Springfield Division
    Fry's Food Stores of Arizona, Inc.
    King Soopers, Inc.
Dominick's Finer Foods, Inc.
Eagle Food Centers, Inc.
F.A.B., Inc.
The Fred W. Albrecht Grocery Co.
Furr's Supermarkets, Inc.
Giant Eagle, Inc.
Gooding's Supermarkets, Inc.
Haggen, Inc.
Kings Super Markets, Inc.
K-VA-T Food Stores
McCarty-Holman Company, Inc.
Meijer, Inc.
Nugget Distributors, Inc.
The Oshawa Group, Ltd.
    Oshawa Foods
Penn Traffic Co.
    Big Bear Stores Co.
    Grand Union Co.
    P&C/Quality Markets/Insalaco
    Riverside Markets
Pueblo International
    Xtra Super Food Centers
Quality Food Centers, Inc.
Randall's Food Markets, Inc.
    Tom Thumb Food & Pharmacy
Riser Foods, Inc.
Schnuck Markets, Inc.
Schultz Sav-O Stores, Inc.
Seiyu America, Inc.
Shaw's Supermarkets, Inc.
Smith's Food & Drug Centers, Inc.
Star Market Companies, Inc.
Ukrop's Super Markets, Inc.
Victory Holdings, Inc.
    Great American Victory Markets, Inc.
    New Almacs, Inc.

KEY COMPETITORS

Fleming	GSC	Spartan Stores
Foodland	Enterprises	SUPERVALU
Distributors	Nash Finch	Wal-Mart
Grocers Supply	Shurfine	White Rose

HOW MUCH

	Annual Growth	1986	1987	1988	1989	1990	1991	1992	1993	1994	1995
Sales ($ mil.)	8.6%	1,800	1,900	2,100	2,200	2,400	2,600	2,900	3,000	3,500	3,700
Employees	8.3%	—	—	—	—	375	400	400	375	400	375

Sales ($ mil.) 1986–95

Topco.

TRIBUNE COMPANY

OVERVIEW

Chicago's Tribune Company is a multimedia information and entertainment giant. It gathers, packages, and delivers information to 60% of US households via newspapers, radio, TV, and, lately, cyberspace. Tribune is the US's 13th largest media company, with 3 major daily newspapers (*Chicago Tribune*, Ft. Lauderdale's *Sun-Sentinel*, and the *Orlando Sentinel*); 8 TV stations (in Los Angeles, New York, Philadelphia, Chicago, and other cities); and 6 radio stations (in New York, Chicago, and other cities). Publishing accounted for 60% of sales and 68% of operating profits in 1994. The company also owns various book publishing companies (including Compton's and Contemporary Books), produces and syndicates TV, radio, and on-line programming, and owns a major league baseball team (Chicago Cubs). Tribune has radio and TV broad-

cast rights for 7 of the 28 major league baseball teams. It also owns other daily and weekly newspapers and has a stake in cable TV.

Tribune continues to extend its reach for new markets and information sources. In 1994 the company bought Farm Journal Inc., publisher of the country's leading farm magazine and 4 other agribusiness magazines; acquired a minority stake in Qwest Broadcasting, which buys TV and radio stations; bought The Wright Group, a publisher of educational materials; took a minority stake in Checkfree, an on-line bill-paying and collection service; and bought Boston's leading TV newscast and movie station, WLVI. To focus on information and entertainment, Tribune in 1995 agreed to sell QUNO Corp., its publicly traded newsprint affiliate located in Canada, to Donohue Inc. for $806.7 million.

WHEN

Tribune Company had its beginnings as the *Chicago Tribune*, which produced 400 newspapers on its first day in 1847. Joseph Medill, a promoter who, some say, gave the Republican party its name, became part owner and editor in 1855. He spent the next 44 years building the *Tribune* into a conservative newspaper.

Medill reportedly warned that Chicago was a fire hazard just a month before the Great Fire of 1871. He rallied his employees to publish the paper despite being burned out of their building. Medill died in 1899 and was succeeded by son-in-law Robert Patterson and grandson Medill McCormick. In 1914 his other 2 grandsons, Robert McCormick and Joseph Patterson, took over the newspaper.

McCormick, great-nephew of the inventor of the harvest machine, built the *Tribune* into the self-proclaimed "World's Greatest Newspaper," whose acronym, WGN, became part of the company's subsequent radio and TV station call letters. Patterson left for New York in 1919 to found the *News*, later the *Daily News*.

In 1924 the company branched into radio by starting WGN, which became the first radio station to broadcast the World Series, Indianapolis 500, and Kentucky Derby. WGN moved into TV broadcasting in 1948, the same year the paper prematurely published its "Dewey Defeats Truman" headline.

McCormick took over the *Daily News* when Patterson died in 1946 and ran both papers from Chicago. He remained at that post until his death in 1955.

Tribune expanded its radio and TV broadcasting outside of Chicago. It founded WPIX-TV in New York (1948) and bought TV stations in Denver (1965), New Orleans (1983), Atlanta (1984), Los Angeles (1985), Philadelphia (1992), and Boston (1994). The company also bought newspapers in Florida (Ft. Lauderdale, 1963; Orlando, 1965), California (Los Angeles, 1973, sold 1985; Escondido, 1977; Palo Alto, 1978, closed 1993), and Virginia (Newport News, 1986).

Tribune diversified with news and entertainment programming, beginning Independent Network News in 1980 (shut down, 1990) and the Tribune Broadcasting Co. in 1981. That same year it bought the Chicago Cubs baseball team from chewing gum maker Wm. Wrigley. Tribune went public in 1983.

A protracted strike at the *Daily News* prompted Tribune to sell the newspaper in 1991. Also that year Tribune began a series of investments in on-line technology companies, buying a stake in America Online, with which it launched the local Chicago Online.

In 1993 Tribune bought Compton's Multimedia Publishing Group and print-based Contemporary Books. In 1994 it acquired The Wright Group for its New Media & Education group and joined with Time Warner to form a prime-time network.

John Madigan was named CEO in 1995. That year Tribune agreed to sell its Compton's subsidiary to SoftKey, an educational software maker, for $106.5 million in SoftKey stock and the assumption of $17 million in debt.

NYSE symbol: TRB
Fiscal year ends: Last Sunday in December

WHO

Chairman: Charles T. Brumback, age 66, $1,261,806 pay
President and CEO: John W. Madigan, age 57,
$839,616 pay (prior to promotion)
EVP Media Operations: James C. Dowdle, age 61,
$770,000 pay
EVP Tribune Broadcasting Co.: Dennis J. FitzSimons,
age 44, $600,431 pay
EVP Tribune Publishing Co.: Joseph D. Cantrell, age 50
EVP and General Manager, New Media/Education:
Robert D. Bosau, age 48
SVP Development: David D. Hiller, age 41, $454,923 pay
SVP and CFO: Donald C. Grenesko, age 46
SVP Information Systems: John S. Kazik, age 52
SVP Administration (HR): John T. Sloan, age 43
VP and General Counsel: James E. Cushing Jr.
Auditors: Price Waterhouse LLP

WHERE

HQ: 435 N. Michigan Ave., Chicago, IL 60611
Phone: 312-222-9100
Fax: 312-222-0449

Tribune media properties are located in 11 states.

WHAT

	1994 Sales		1994 Operating Income	
	$ mil.	% of total	$ mil.	% of total
Publishing	1,293	60	288	68
Broadcasting & Entertainment	764	35	132	31
New Media/Education	98	5	3	1
Other	—	—	(26)	—
Total	**2,155**	**100**	**397**	**100**

Selected Publishing Operations
Alternate Postal Delivery (private mail delivery)
America Online (6%) and Chicago Online
Chicago Tribune (682,000 daily circulation)
Knight-Ridder/Tribune Information Services (50%)
The Orlando Sentinel (269,000 daily circulation)
The Orlando Sentinel Online (electronic publishing)
Peapod (minority stake; grocery shopping by computer)
Picture Network International (52%; electronic photo
archive marketing system)
Real Estate Information Connection (50%)
StarSight Telecast (TV guide and VCR recording)
Sun-Sentinel (Ft. Lauderdale; 266,000 daily circulation)
Tribune Interactive Network Services
Tribune Media Services

Selected Broadcasting and Entertainment Operations
Chicago National League
Ball Club, Inc. (baseball)
CLTV News (cable TV news)
Farm Journal Inc.
(agribusiness magazine)
KCTC (AM), Sacramento
KEZW (AM), Denver
KOSI (FM), Denver
KTLA-TV, Los Angeles
KWGN-TV, Denver
KYMX (FM), Sacramento

Tribune Entertainment
Co. (TV programming)
TV Food Network (31%)
WGN (AM), Chicago
WGN-TV, Chicago
WGNO-TV, New Orleans
WGNX-TV, Atlanta
WLVI-TV, Boston
WPHL-TV, Philadelphia
WPIX-TV, New York
WQCD (FM), New York

New Media/Education
Compton's Multimedia Publishing Group (CD-ROMs)
Contemporary Books, Inc. (trade book publisher)
The Wright Group (educational materials)

KEY COMPETITORS

Advance
Publications
Associated Press
Capital Cities/ABC
CBS
Chris-Craft
Cox
Dow Jones

Encyclopædia
Britannica
Gannett
General Electric
Hearst
Lagardère
Microsoft
New York Times

News Corp.
Reuters
Sony
Time Warner
Times Mirror
UPI
Viacom
Washington Post

HOW MUCH

	Annual Growth	1985	1986	1987	1988	1989	1990	1991	1992	1993	1994
Sales ($ mil.)	1.2%	1,938	2,030	2,160	2,335	2,455	2,353	2,035	2,109	1,953	2,155
Net income ($ mil.)	7.7%	124	293	142	210	242	(64)	142	137	189	242
Income as % of sales	—	6.4%	14.4%	6.6%	9.0%	9.9%	—	7.0%	6.5%	9.7%	11.2%
Earnings per share ($)	8.0%	1.53	3.63	1.80	2.78	3.00	(1.22)	1.83	1.70	2.36	3.07
Stock price – high ($)	—	28.94	39.00	49.75	43.00	63.13	48.25	48.38	50.75	61.25	64.50
Stock price – low ($)	—	16.00	24.75	28.63	33.75	36.38	31.25	33.13	38.75	48.00	48.88
Stock price – close ($)	7.8%	27.88	28.50	41.00	38.88	47.38	35.25	41.00	48.00	60.13	54.75
P/E – high	—	19	11	28	16	21	—	26	30	26	21
P/E – low	—	11	7	16	12	12	—	18	23	20	16
Dividends per share ($)	10.6%	0.42	0.50	0.60	1.00	0.88	0.96	0.96	0.96	0.96	1.04
Book value per share ($)	6.7%	11.19	13.91	14.35	15.88	10.63	6.49	7.84	8.72	16.36	19.98
Employees	(6.2%)	18,700	17,300	16,800	16,800	17,100	16,100	12,900	12,400	9,900	10,500

1994 Year-end:
Debt ratio: 24.8%
Return on equity: 19.9%
Cash (mil.): $22
Current ratio: 1.03
Long-term debt (mil.): $411
No. of shares (mil.): 67
Dividends
  Yield: 1.9%
  Payout: 33.9%
Market value (mil.): $3,652

**Stock Price History
High/Low 1985–94**

UAL CORPORATION

OVERVIEW

Shuttle, not subtle. United Airlines (the operational arm of UAL Corporation) and the #2 US airline (after American) has challenged #8 Southwest Airlines at its own game by introducing a no-frills shuttle service in the western US. United began in October 1994 with 184 daily flights; its service jumped to 304 by the end of the year and is putting the squeeze on Southwest's profits.

United Airlines serves 152 airports in 30 countries and operates a fleet of 543 aircraft. Its major hub airports are at Chicago; Denver; San Francisco; Washington, DC; London; and Tokyo.

On July 12, 1994, United Airlines's stockholders approved a plan ceding 55% of the company to its employees in exchange for $4.8 billion in wage concessions and changes in work rules. The radical restructuring worked. Since the buyout the firm has reduced its costs and improved its efficiency; on-time performances have reached a record level.

The buyout came after 3 years of losses totaling more than $800 million, caused in part by fare wars with competitors and the growth of a generation of small, short-haul airlines.

In 1994 United formed a joint service agreement with Lufthansa German Airlines, giving United passengers connections on Lufthansa flights (and vice versa) to 40 destinations worldwide.

In an expansive mode since the 1994 buyout, United inaugurated service to its 12th Latin American destination — Lima, Peru — in 1995. United also plans to initiate nonstop service to a number of Canadian cities.

WHEN

In 1929 aircraft designer Bill Boeing (Boeing Airplane and Transport) and engine designer Fred Rentschler (Pratt & Whitney) merged their companies to form United Aircraft and Transport. Renamed United Air Lines in 1931, the New York–based company offered one of America's first coast-to-coast airline services. In 1934 United's manufacturing and transportation divisions split, and former banker Bill Patterson became president of the latter (United Airlines), moving it to Chicago.

Under Patterson (1934–63), United was slow to use new technology, offering jet service in 1959, later than American, its leading rival. Still, in 1961 United became the US's #1 airline after buying Capital Airlines, which added Washington, DC, and points along the Great Lakes and in Florida to its network.

The company bought the Westin Hotel Company in 1970 and named Westin president Eddie Carlson as United's CEO in 1971. Another hotelier, Richard Ferris, became CEO in 1979. Hoping to build United into a travel conglomerate, Ferris spent $2.3 billion buying Hertz Corporation (1985), Pan Am's Australian and Asian routes (1986), and Transworld's Hilton International (1987). In 1987, after spending an additional $7.3 million to change United's name to Allegis Corporation, Ferris resigned when Coniston Partners, the company's largest shareholder, threatened to oust the board and liquidate the company. Assuming its old name under Stephen Wolf (former Flying Tigers chief), United sold its hotels and car rental business as well as 50% of its computer reservation partnership (Covia).

A 1989 takeover bid by Los Angeles billionaire Marvin Davis led to a management and union buyout plan, which failed in 1989. Another union buyout attempt failed the next year. United then reached an accord with Coniston, which sold most of its stake in UAL in exchange for 2 seats on the board.

In 1990 United received DOT permission to fly from Chicago to Tokyo. In 1991 and 1992 United bought Pan Am's London and Paris routes, most of Pan Am's Latin American routes, and its Los Angeles–Mexico City route. UAL bought Air Wis (owner of Air Wisconsin, one of its feeders) in 1992.

Throughout 1993 United sought to negotiate a buyout with its unions. Early in the year it canceled plans to hire 1,900 new employees, instead laying off 2,800 and cutting US management salaries and directors' fees.

Finally, the 1993 sale of United's kitchen operations to Dial's Dobbs Houses (eliminating 5,800 union jobs) and the announcement of plans to start up a subsidiary short-haul airline brought the pilots and machinists (but not the flight attendants) back to the table.

Despite improved job performance after the buyout, the company is not out of the woods yet. United expects to incur $124 million in costs caused by overruns and delays at the new Denver International Airport. Even so, United has ambitious expansion plans; while its rivals are shrinking services, United plans to increase its capacity by 3% in 1995.

NYSE symbol: UAL
Fiscal year ends: December 31

Chairman and CEO, UAL and United Airlines: Gerald
Greenwald, age 59, $3,975,821 pay
President, UAL and United Airlines: John A.
Edwardson, age 45, $2,372,094 pay
**EVP Corporate Affairs and General Counsel, UAL and
United Airlines:** Stuart I. Oran, age 44, $1,687,865 pay
EVP; EVP Operations, United Airlines: Joseph R.
O'Gorman Jr., age 51, $556,945 pay
EVP; EVP Marketing and Planning, United Airlines:
James M. Guyette, age 50, $555,296 pay
SVP Finance and CFO; SVP Finance, United Airlines:
Douglas A. Hacker, age 39
SVP International, United Airlines: James E. Goodwin
SVP, United Airlines; President, Shuttle by United:
Alan B. Magary
SVP People, United Airlines: Paul G. George, age 43
Auditors: Arthur Andersen & Co, SC

WHERE

HQ: 1200 Algonquin Rd., Elk Grove Township,
IL 60007; PO Box 66919, Chicago, IL 60666
Phone: 847-952-4000
Fax: 847-952-7578
Reservations: 800-241-6522

United serves 152 airports in 30 countries.

Hub Locations

Chicago, IL	San Francisco, CA
Denver, CO	Tokyo, Japan
London, UK	Washington, DC

	1994 Sales	
	$ mil.	% of total
US	9,030	65
Other countries	4,920	35
Total	**13,950**	**100**

WHAT

	1994 Sales	
	$ mil.	% of total
Passengers	12,295	88
Cargo	685	5
Contract services & other	970	7
Total	**13,950**	**100**

Major Subsidiaries and Affiliates
Air Wis Services, Inc.
Apollo Travel Services Partnership (77%)
Four Star Insurance Company, Ltd.
Galileo International Partnership (38%)
Mileage Plus, Inc.
UAL Leasing Corporation
U-C Corp.
United Airlines, Inc.

	Aircraft	
	Owned	Leased
A320	—	21
Boeing 727	50	25
Boeing 737	82	145
Boeing 747	23	28
Boeing 757	33	55
Boeing 767	22	20
DC-10	18	21
Total	**228**	**315**

KEY COMPETITORS

Air Canada	Hawaiin	Northwest Airlines
Air France	Airlines	Qantas
Alaska Air	IRI	SAS
All Nippon Airways	JAL	Singapore Airlines
America West	Kiwi	Southwest Airlines
AMR	KLM	Swire Pacific
British Airways	Korean Air	TWA
Continental	Mesa Air	USAir
Airlines	Midwest	Valuejet
Delta	Express	Virgin Group

HOW MUCH

	Annual Growth	1985	1986	1987	1988	1989	1990	1991	1992	1993	1994
Sales ($ mil.)	9.1%	6,383	9,196	8,292	8,982	9,794	11,037	11,663	12,890	14,511	13,950
Net income ($ mil.)	—	(49)	12	(4)	600	324	94	(332)	(417)	(50)	77
Income as % of sales	—	—	0.2%	—	6.7%	3.3%	0.9%	—	—	—	0.6%
Earnings per share ($)	—	(3.43)	0.25	(0.08)	20.20	14.96	4.33	(14.13)	(17.34)	(3.40)	0.76
Stock price – high ($)	—	59.50	64.38	105.88	110.00	294.00	171.00	161.50	159.00	155.50	150.00
Stock price – low ($)	—	39.75	46.25	52.25	68.50	105.25	84.25	109.00	103.00	110.75	83.13
Stock price – close ($)	6.5%	49.75	52.25	71.50	109.50	171.25	110.13	145.75	126.13	146.00	87.38
P/E – high	—	—	—	—	6	20	40	—	—	—	—
P/E – low	—	—	—	—	3	7	20	—	—	—	—
Dividends per share ($)	(100.0%)	1.00	1.00	0.75	0.00	0.00	0.00	0.00	0.00	0.00	0.00
Book value per share ($)	—	44.50	45.69	51.50	56.76	71.64	76.34	67.21	29.11	24.55	(99.94)
Employees	5.8%	47,000	59,000	64,000	66,000	69,000	74,000	79,000	84,000	83,400	77,900

1994 Year-end:
Debt ratio: 100.0%
Return on equity: —
Cash (mil.): $1,532
Current ratio: 0.65
Long-term debt (mil.): $2,887
No. of shares (mil.): 12
Dividends
  Yield: —
  Payout: —
Market value (mil.): $1,087

Stock Price History
High/Low 1985–94

UNICOM CORPORATION

OVERVIEW

Unicom is the holding company for Commonwealth Edison (ComEd), the 4th largest publicly owned electric utility in the US. ComEd's service area covers the northern portion of Illinois (including Chicago) — representing about 70% of the state's population. Nuclear power plants are the company's main source of power, generating about 71% of its electricity in 1994.

Unicom was formed in 1994 as a holding company for all of ComEd's operations in order to provide more flexibility as the company prepares to deal with increased competition created by deregulation. The company formed Unicom Enterprises to handle its unregulated businesses, including Unicom Thermal, which provides cooling services to large buildings in downtown Chicago. Unicom Enterprises also plans to offer power plant design and construction services and energy consulting services. Its R&D department is developing large-scale energy storage technology.

Unicom's profits rebounded in 1994 after settlements of Illinois Supreme Court rate orders led to an annual rate reduction of more than $300 million and customer refunds totaling more than $1.3 billion. In 1994 the company filed for a $469 million increase, and in 1995 the Illinois Commerce Commission granted a $303 million increase. However, with deregulation on the horizon, ComEd's rates, which are 30% higher than neighboring utilities, could put the company at a competitive disadvantage.

WHEN

A group of Chicago businessmen formed Western Edison Light in 1882. It was reorganized as Chicago Edison by its 39 shareholders in 1887, and under the leadership of Samuel Insull, it bought its main competitor, Chicago Arc Light & Power, in 1893. In 1898 the company created a holding company, Commonwealth Electric, to buy other power companies in the Chicago area. Commonwealth and Chicago Edison merged in 1907 to form Commonwealth Edison.

In 1912 ComEd finished its Northwest Station — then the largest steam generator ever built — and followed it with the even more powerful Crawford Station in 1924. ComEd also continued to buy other utilities and by 1933 consisted of 77 separate companies.

ComEd bought the Public Service Company of Northern Illinois (1937) and Chicago District Electric Generating Corporation (1939), which, combined with Western United Gas & Electric and Illinois Northern Utility (both bought in 1950), created one unit providing power in northern Illinois (outside Chicago). ComEd consolidated its position in Chicago through other purchases, including Produce Terminal Corporation (1956) and Central Illinois Electric and Gas (1966).

In 1960 ComEd opened the world's first full-scale, privately owned nuclear facility (Dresden Station) and by 1974 had built 7 nuclear plants. That year the company bought the Cotter Corporation, a Colorado uranium mining company, to provide low-cost fuel for its nuclear plants. In 1976 ComEd bought mining rights to 8,200 coal-rich acres in Wyoming, and in 1979 the company formed Edison Development Canada to explore for uranium deposits in Newfoundland.

Although touted as one of the US's best-run nuclear utilities during the mid-1980s, ComEd drew criticism in later years from environmental and consumer groups for its heavy investment in nuclear construction, which has resulted in some of the highest utility bills in the US. In 1984 and 1985, 2 nuclear plants went on-line, but when construction costs skyrocketed in 1986, the Illinois Commerce Commission (ICC) threatened to revoke licenses for 2 other nuclear plants (Byron 2 and Braidwood 1 & 2) still under construction. These went into service in 1987 and 1988, costing a total of $7.1 billion.

ComEd applied to the ICC for rate increases to pay for the new plants, but the ICC deemed the plants not 100% "used and useful." In 1991 ComEd received a rate increase, to be phased in over 3 years; however, later that year the Illinois Supreme Court remanded the increase and suspended the 2nd and 3rd phases.

In 1993 ComEd reached 2 settlements involving 6 rate- and fuel-related cases, including the Byron and Braidwood rate matters. The company agreed to cut its annual electric rates by $339 million and to refund $1.37 billion to customers — the largest refund in utility history.

In 1995 the Nuclear Regulatory Commission (NRC) announced it would levy a $100,000 fine against ComEd. The NRC said workers at the company's Braidwood nuclear power plant left a monitoring system used to detect hydrogen gas leaks disconnected for 3 months.

WHO

Chairman and CEO: James J. O'Connor, age 58, $1,258,642 pay
President: Samuel K. Skinner, age 56, $1,146,086 pay
SVP: Thomas J. Maiman, age 56, $423,378 pay
SVP: Michael J. Wallace, age 47, $393,492 pay
SVP: Cordell Reed, age 57, $356,937 pay
SVP: Robert J. Manning, age 52
SVP: Donald A. Petkus, age 53
VP and CFO: John C. Bukovski, age 52
VP and General Counsel: Pamela B. Strobel, age 42
VP Customer Service: K. Edward Bartels
Treasurer: Dennis F. O'Brien, age 49
Secretary: David A. Scholz, age 53
Comptroller: Roger F. Kovak, age 46
VP Human Resources: J. Stanley Graves
Auditors: Arthur Andersen & Co, SC

WHERE

HQ: One First National Plaza, 37th Fl., 10 S. Dearborn St., PO Box 767, Chicago, IL 60690-0767
Phone: 312-394-4321
Fax: 312-394-3110

Generating Facilities

Fossil Fuels	Nuclear
Collins (near Morris, IL)	Braidwood (near Braidwood, IL)
Crawford (Chicago)	
Fisk (Chicago)	Byron (near Byron, IL)
Joliet 6, 7 & 8 (near Joliet, IL)	Dresden (near Morris, IL)
Kincaid (near Taylorville, IL)	
Powerton (near Pekin, IL)	LaSalle County (near Seneca, IL)
State Line (Hammond, IN)	
Waukegan (Waukegan, IL)	Quad-Cities (75%, near Cordova, IL)
Will County (near Lockport, IL)	Zion (Zion, IL)

WHAT

	1994 Sales	
	$ mil.	% of total
Residential	2,274	36
Small commercial & industrial	1,917	31
Large commercial & industrial	1,381	22
Public authorities	453	7
Sales for resale	187	3
Electric railroads	26	—
Provisions for refunds	(16)	—
Other	56	1
Total	**6,278**	**100**

	1994 Fuel Sources
	% of total
Nuclear	71
Coal	25
Natural gas	3
Oil	1
Total	**100**

Subsidiaries
Commonwealth Edison Co.
Commonwealth Edison Co. of Indiana, Inc.
Cotter Corp.
Edison Development Co.
Unicom Enterprises Inc.
Unicom Thermal Technologies Inc.

KEY COMPETITORS

Becthel	Nipsco
Duke Power	Peoples Energy
Fluor	Peter Kiewiet Sons'
General Electric	Southern Co.
Nicor	Westinghouse

HOW MUCH

	Annual Growth	1985	1986	1987	1988	1989	1990	1991	1992	1993	1994
Sales ($ mil.)	2.6%	4,964	5,479	5,674	5,613	5,751	5,262	6,276	6,026	5,260	6,278
Net income ($ mil.)	(10.4%)	956	1,050	1,086	738	694	128	95	514	103	355
Income as % of sales	—	19.3%	19.2%	19.1%	13.1%	12.1%	2.4%	1.5%	8.5%	2.0%	5.7%
Earnings per share ($)	(10.4%)	4.45	4.69	4.73	3.01	2.83	0.22	0.08	2.08	0.17	1.66
Stock price – high ($)	—	32.88	35.75	38.00	33.38	40.75	37.88	42.63	40.13	31.63	28.75
Stock price – low ($)	—	27.00	28.63	25.25	22.75	32.13	27.25	33.63	21.75	22.88	20.63
Stock price – close ($)	(2.2%)	29.38	33.88	27.50	33.00	37.63	34.75	39.88	23.25	28.13	24.00
P/E – high	—	7	8	8	11	14	—	—	19	—	17
P/E – low	—	6	6	5	8	11	—	—	11	—	12
Dividends per share ($)	(6.7%)	3.00	3.00	3.00	3.00	3.00	3.00	3.00	2.65	1.60	1.60
Book value per share ($)	(1.8%)	29.96	31.60	33.27	32.85	32.68	29.97	26.98	26.76	25.40	25.42
Employees	(0.1%)	18,634	18,429	17,898	17,867	17,649	18,087	19,551	19,870	19,265	18,460

1994 Year-end:
Debt ratio: 59.6%
Return on equity: 6.5%
Cash (mil.): $126
Current ratio: 0.91
Long term debt (mil.): $7,453
No. of shares (mil.): 214
Dividends
  Yield: 6.7%
  Payout: 96.4%
Market value (mil.): $5,144

Stock Price History High/Low 1985–94

Note: Figures for 1985–93 are for Commonwealth Edison.

THE UNIVERSITY OF CHICAGO

OVERVIEW

Despite its reputation for a rigorous core curriculum based on the classics, the University of Chicago is encouraging its students to lighten up. The private, nonsectarian institution has let Barnes & Noble take over a campus bookstore, and a Starbucks coffeehouse has appeared — all in an effort to warm up social life on the cold shores of Lake Michigan.

With the university's students having an average Scholastic Assessment Test score of 1,350 (against a national average of 910), it's no wonder they have a single-minded focus on academics; more than 90% plan to go on to graduate studies. The university is devoted to medical, scientific, and academic research.

Many distinguished scholars have been associated with the university, including 65 Nobel laureates (such as Milton Friedman, James Watson, and Saul Bellow). In 1995 Robert Lucas became the 5th University of Chicago Nobel Prize winner in economics in 6 years.

Among the university's strongest disciplines are sociology (in which it was a pioneer), archaeology, economics, and the sciences. It also operates one of the largest and most active university presses in the country.

Despite the university's early reputation as a hotbed of radicalism, the Chicago school of thought is now characterized by a free-market, conservative philosophy — i.e, lots of study.

WHEN

The first University of Chicago was a small Baptist school (1858–86). The name was appropriated later, when a $600,000 gift from John D. Rockefeller, $400,000 in contributions from members of the American Baptist Education Society, and land donated by department store owner Marshall Field made possible the creation of the University of Chicago in 1891.

William Rainey Harper, a noted Bible scholar, was the university's first president. On October 1, 1892, the university opened with a faculty of 103, including 8 former college presidents, and 594 students. As it grew the university took over property that had been used in the Columbian Exposition of 1892–93, eventually surrounding the fair's former main thoroughfare, the Midway.

While intellectual in outlook, the university organized its first football team, under famed coach Amos Alonzo Stagg, the day it opened. Its first games were against high school and YMCA teams, and at times the coach had to play in order to field enough men. The team won one game its first season. Improving in later seasons and earning the nickname "Monsters of the Midway," the team became a member of the Big 10. It later relapsed to its losing ways and withdrew from intercollegiate play in 1939.

So enthusiastic was the response to the new university that, 4 years after its founding, its enrollment of 1,815 exceeded Harvard's. By 1907 enrollment was 5,038, of whom 4.3% were women. Rockefeller continued to contribute to the university (calling his $36 million of contributions the best investment he ever made), enabling the university to expand in size and intellectual influence under Harper and his successor, Harry Pratt Judson.

The university's greatest intellectual flowering came with Robert Maynard Hutchins's presidency (1929-51), during which he revolutionized the university and American higher education by insisting on the study of original sources (the Great Books) and competency testing through comprehensive exams. He organized the college and graduate divisions into their present structure, reaffirming the role of the university as a place for intellectual exploration rather than vocational training. It was during his tenure, in 1942, that the nuclear age began, when Enrico Fermi created the first self-sustaining nuclear chain reaction in the abandoned football stadium.

From the 1950s through the 1970s, the university consolidated its position as one of the world's great centers of learning and successfully stemmed the tide of urban decay encroaching on its South Side Chicago campus. During this time it purchased and restored Frank Lloyd Wright's famed Robie House (now used by the alumni association), built the Joseph Regenstein Library (1970), and reinstated intercollegiate football (1969).

From 1978 to 1992 the university was led by Hanna Holborn Gray, the first woman president of a major university. In 1992 Gray retired and was succeeded by Hugo Sonnenschein. The beginning of his tenure coincided with a period of financial difficulty for the university, which has operated at a deficit since 1992. The university has cut costs because of a reduced rate of income growth. However, a 5-year fund-raising goal of $500 million (set in 1991) was met in 1995. University trustees raised the ante to $650 million to fund endowed faculty positions, student scholarships, and a new athletic complex.

Private university
Fiscal year ends: June 30
Motto: *Crescat scientia vita excolatur*;
Let knowledge grow from more to more,
and so be human life enriched.

WHO

President: Hugo F. Sonnenschein
Provost: Geoffrey R. Stone
VP and CFO: Lawrence J. Furnstahl
VP Administration and General Counsel: Arthur M. Sussman
VP Development and Alumni Relations: Randy L. Holgate
VP Investments: Gary B. Helms
VP (HR): JoAnn Shaw
Auditors: KPMG Peat Marwick LLP

WHERE

HQ: 5801 S. Ellis Ave., Chicago, IL 60637
Phone: 312-702-1234
Fax: 312-702-8324

The university's main campus is in Hyde Park on Chicago's South Side; it also maintains a downtown Chicago campus and owns Yerkes Observatory in Williams Bay, Wisconsin.

WHAT

	1995 Revenues	
	$ mil.	% of total
Hospital sales & services	521	40
Tuition & fees	205	15
Government grants	139	11
Auxiliary activities	127	9
Professional fees	120	9
Private gifts, grants & contracts	62	5
Endowment income	61	5
Other	78	6
Total	**1,313**	**100**

Selected Degrees 1994–95

	No. of recipients
Bachelor of Arts	733
Bachelor of Science	48
Master of Arts	
Divinity	39
Fine Arts	7
Humanities	131
Public Policy Studies	51
Social Sciences	231
Social Service Administration	122
Teaching	11
Master of Science	
Biological Sciences	20
Physical Sciences	104
Master of Business Administration	1,067
Master of Divinity	14
Master of Laws	38
Doctor of Law	176
Doctor of Medicine	99
Doctor of Ministry	2
Doctor of Philosophy	
Biological Sciences	45
Business	15
Divinity	19
Humanities	61
Physical Sciences	83
Social Sciences	139

A total of 3,260 degrees were awarded in 1994–95.

Selected Affiliated Institutions

Argonne National Lab.
Bergmann Gallery
Court Theatre
Enrico Fermi Institute
James Franck Institute
Laboratory School
Midway Studios
National Opinion Research Center
Office of Continuing Education
Oriental Institute
Smart Museum
The University of Chicago Medical Center
The University of Chicago Press
Yerkes Observatory

HOW MUCH

	Annual Growth	1986	1987	1988	1989	1990	1991	1992	1993	1994	1995
Revenues ($ mil.)	3.0%	—	—	1,066	1,134	1,370	1,054	1,113	1,150	1,216	1,313
Enrollment	2.1%	9,783	10,217	10,431	10,625	10,950	11,063	9,432	10,231	11,472	11,825
Annual tuition ($)	8.4%	9,600	11,352	12,120	12,030	14,895	—	—	—	18,930	19,875
Endowment ($ mil.)[1]	6.2%	801	914	898	974	1,093	1,081	1,151	1,224	1,224	1,378
Faculty	0.9%	1,156	1,166	1,178	1,200	1,193	1,200	1,490	1,843	1,232	1,257
Employees	(3.7%)	—	—	—	—	—	—	—	11,800	—	10,954

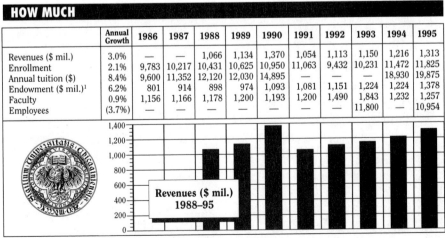

Revenues ($ mil.)
1988–95

[1] Market value

USG CORPORATION

OVERVIEW

Sheetrock is the bedrock of USG's business. USG is a holding company for a number of leading makers, marketers, and distributors of building materials. Its main subsidiary, United States Gypsum, is the world's leading manufacturer of gypsum wallboard, supplying about 33% of the US demand for wallboard. USG's L&W Supply Corp. is the US's leading distributor of wallboard (9% market share) and related building materials, operating 139 distribution centers in 34 states. The firm's USG Interiors subsidiary is the leading US manufacturer of acoustic ceiling grids and the #2 producer of acoustic ceiling panels.

Internationally, USG owns a Mexican gypsum products maker (Yeso Panamericano) and holds a 76% stake in CGC, the largest producer of gypsum wallboard in eastern Canada. The company coordinates its international marketing and manufacturing of building materials through USG International. This arm of USG makes acoustical ceiling tile, gypsum products, access floors, joint treatment, and ceiling grid suspension systems in 7 plants and 8 distribution facilities in 12 countries for markets in Europe, the Middle East, Latin America, and the Pacific.

Strong housing demand in 1994 had the wallboard industry posting price increases and running at 95% capacity. United States Gypsum shipped a record 7.7 billion square feet of wallboard in that same year.

WHEN

In 1901, 35 companies joined to form the largest gypsum-producing and -processing company in the industry, headquartered in Chicago. Sewell Avery became CEO in 1905 and led the company until 1951.

U.S. Gypsum started producing lime in 1915 and paint in 1924. By 1931 the company had diversified into insulating board production and the metal lath field and added 2 lime companies and 2 gypsum concerns.

In 1931 Avery became chairman of Montgomery Ward, managing both companies simultaneously. U.S. Gypsum continued making profits and paying dividends throughout the Great Depression. The company entered the asphalt roofing and mineral wool business in 1933, began making hardboard from highly compressed wood fibers in 1934, and entered the asbestos-cement siding field in 1937.

Beginning in the late 1960s, U.S. Gypsum diversified into the building materials and remodeling businesses, acquiring A.P. Green Refractories (1967; brick, tile, and accessories), Wallace Manufacturing (1970, prefinished wood panels), Chicago Mastic (1971; mastics, cements, and adhesives), Kinkead Industries (1972, steel doors and frames), and various smaller businesses. In 1971 U.S. Gypsum formed L&W Supply.

Following the 1984 purchase of the Masonite Corp. for $380 million, the company adopted its present name (1985). USG acquired Donn (remodeling materials) in 1986 and DAP (caulk and sealants) in 1987 for a total of $260 million.

In 1987 USG led a $776 million buyback of 20% of its stock to ward off a takeover attempt. In 1988 Desert Partners of Midland, Texas, tried another takeover, foiled 9 months later when shareholders approved a management plan to keep control of USG. The plan included taking on $2.5 billion of new debt, a $37-per-share payout, and a payment-in-kind debenture of $5 per share.

After completing virtually all asset sales envisioned in the plan by the end of 1989, USG became about 25% smaller. Proceeds from the sale of Masonite (to International Paper), Kinkead, and Marlite netted a total of $560 million and were used to repay debt.

In February 1991 USG defaulted on about $40 million of scheduled payments to bondholders and banks. USG sold its profitable DAP unit to the UK's Wassall for $90 million. (USG had bought DAP in 1987 for $123 million.) In 1991 USG deferred paying banks $27 million in interest due.

In 1993 the company filed one of the largest prepackaged Chapter 11 bankruptcy cases on record. With creditors having agreed to the reorganization plan in advance of the filing, the company was able to win court approval within 37 days. As a result of the restructuring, USG cut its debt by $1.4 billion and its annual interest payments by $200 million. In early 1994 USG sold 7.9 million new shares, raising $224 million to further reduce its debt.

Industrywide, demand for gypsum wallboard in the repair/remodel market was up 7% in 1994 and is anticipated to grow in 1995. The company is planning to expand its ceiling tile capacity by adding a line at its Greenville, Mississippi, ceiling tile plant. USG is also investing $32.5 million to increase wallboard capacity at 9 plants, adding a total of 600 million square feet of new capacity.

NYSE symbol: USG
Fiscal year ends: December 31

WHO

Chairman: Eugene B. Connolly, age 63, $1,435,366 pay
President, CEO, and COO: William C. Foote, age 44, $802,016 pay
Group VP North American Gypsum; President and CEO, United States Gypsum: Donald E. Roller, age 57, $604,160 pay
Group VP Worldwide Ceilings and International; President and CEO, USG Interiors: J. Bradford James, age 48
SVP Worldwide Manufacturing and Technology: P. Jack O'Bryan, age 59, $595,827 pay
SVP and Chief Administrative Officer: Harold E. Pendexter Jr., age 60, $583,820 pay
SVP and CFO: Richard H. Fleming, age 47
SVP and General Counsel: Arthur G. Leisten, age 53
VP R&D: Brian W. Burrows, age 55
VP Human Resources – Operations; VP Human Resources, Worldwide Ceilings: S. Gary Snodgrass, age 43
Auditors: Arthur Andersen & Co, SC

WHERE

HQ: 125 S. Franklin St., Chicago, IL 60606-4678
Phone: 312-606-4000
Fax: 312-606-4093

USG operates more than 50 plants in 12 nations.

	1994 Sales		1994 Operating Income	
	$ mil.	% of total	$ mil.	% of total
US	2,008	83	94	90
Canada	164	7	2	2
Other countries	228	10	8	8
Adjustments	(110)	—	—	—
Total	**2,290**	**100**	**104**	**100**

WHAT

	1994 Sales		1994 Operating Income	
	$ mil.	% of total	$ mil.	% of total
Gypsum products	1,325	51	176	—
Building products distribution	659	26	10	—
Ceiling products	594	23	(38)	—
Adjustments	(288)	—	(44)	—
Total	**2,290**	**100**	**104**	**—**

Principal Subsidiaries

CGC Inc. (76%, gypsum and building products, Canada)
L&W Supply Corp. (gypsum board and building materials distribution)
United States Gypsum Co. (gypsum products for construction and industrial markets)
USG Interiors, Inc. (ceiling, wall, and floor systems)
USG International (access floors, acoustical tile, gypsum products, and suspended ceilings)
Yeso Panamericano, SA (gypsum wallboard, joint compound, acoustical ceiling tile, and construction metals; Mexico)

KEY COMPETITORS

American Biltrite
Armstrong World
Cameron Ashley
Caraustar
Centex Construction Products
Dal-Tile
Domtar
Fletcher Challenge
General Electric
Georgia-Pacific
Hanson
Imperial Chemical
Jim Walter
Manville
Maxim Group
3M
Moore-Handley
National Gypsum
Patrick Industries
PPG
Premark
Republic Gypsum
Saint-Gobain
Sherwin-Williams
Wickes Lumber
Wolohan Lumber

HOW MUCH

	Annual Growth	1985	1986	1987	1988	1989	1990	1991	1992	1993	1994
Sales ($ mil.)	2.9%	1,769	2,122	2,254	2,070	2,007	1,915	1,712	1,777	1,916	2,290
Net income ($ mil.)	—	208	230	173	67	20	(54)	(141)	(191)	511	(92)
Income as % of sales	—	11.8%	10.8%	7.6%	3.2%	1.0%	—	—	—	27.8%	—
Earnings per share ($)	—	—	—	—	—	—	—	—	—	11.45	(2.14)
Stock price – high ($)	—	—	—	—	—	—	—	—	—	30.50	36.00
Stock price – low ($)	—	—	—	—	—	—	—	—	—	9.63	17.25
Stock price – close ($)	(33.3%)	—	—	—	—	—	—	—	—	29.25	19.50
P/E – high	—	—	—	—	—	—	—	—	—	—	—
P/E – low	—	—	—	—	—	—	—	—	—	—	—
Dividends per share ($)	—	—	—	—	—	—	—	—	—	0.00	0.00
Book value per share ($)	—	—	—	—	—	—	—	—	—	(3.61)	(0.18)
Employees	(0.9%)	13,400	15,300	15,900	15,300	13,400	12,700	11,800	11,850	13,400	12,300

1994 Year-end:
Debt ratio: 100.0%
Return on equity: —
Cash (mil.): $197
Current ratio: 1.42
Long-term debt (mil.) $1,077
No. of shares (mil.): 45
Dividends
  Yield: —
  Payout: —
Market value (mil.): $879

**Stock Price History
High/Low 1993–94**

WALGREEN CO.

OVERVIEW

Apparently Walgreen has prescribed itself a growth hormone. The suburban Chicago–based company is the largest drugstore chain in the US (at least until the Rite Aid–Revco merger goes through), filling more prescriptions than any other retailer. But it is looking to get even bigger.

Led by CEO Daniel Jorndt, Walgreen plans to open 200 stores a year through the end of the decade and to be operating 3,000 stores by the year 2000. The company has momentum on its side — 20 straight years of record sales and earnings — with sales up 11% to $9.2 billion in 1994. That year Walgreen was named to *FORTUNE* magazine's list of "Most Admired Corporations in America" for the first time.

To compete more effectively, the company has spent more than $1 billion over the last 5 years on remodeling its stores, adding new technology, and improving its distribution systems. It recently introduced Intercom Plus, which allows customers to request refills 24 hours a day via a touch-tone telephone. The orders are automatically entered into the store's computer system. Walgreen hopes the new system will boost orders per day by as much as 60%.

Walgreen has used changes in the retail pharmacy industry to its advantage over the last few years. As more and more customers use managed care or drug benefit plans, the company has worked to sign up these providers to increase its customer base and sales of its nonprescription items, such as cosmetics, cigarettes, and liquor. As a dominant player in the retail prescription business, Walgreen is now renegotiating contracts with many managed care providers in order to boost profits.

WHEN

In 1901 Chicago pharmacist Charles Walgreen borrowed $2,000 from his father for a down payment on his first drugstore. In 1909 Walgreen sold a half interest in his first store and bought a 2nd, where he installed a large soda fountain and began serving lunches. In 1916, 9 stores consolidated under the corporate name Walgreen Co. By 1920 there were 20 stores in Chicago, with sales of $1.55 million. The firm was first listed on the NYSE in 1927. In 1929 the chain's 397 stores in 87 cities had sales of $47 million.

During the Great Depression the company did comparatively well. Although average sales per store dropped between 1931 and 1935, per-store earnings went up, thanks to a chainwide emphasis on efficiency. By 1940 Walgreen had 489 stores, but the chain shrank during WWII when unprofitable stores were closed.

The 1950s saw a major change in the way retailers did business. Walgreen was an early leader in self-service merchandising. The company opened its first self-serve store in 1952 and had 22 by the end of 1953, leading the industry. Between 1950 and 1960, as small, older stores were replaced with larger, more efficient, self-service units, the total number of stores in the chain increased only about 10%, but sales grew by more than 90%.

By 1960 Walgreen had 451 stores, half of which were self-service. In 1962 the company bought 3 Globe discount department stores in Houston. By 1966 there were 13 Globes in the Southwest doing over $120 million in annual sales, but these survived only 11 years. During the 1960s soda fountains in the stores proved unprofitable and were phased out.

The 1970s and 1980s saw rapid growth and modernization in the chain. In 1973 company management organized a planning committee to boost Walgreen's sagging return on investment. After a customer survey characterized the stores as "junky, disorganized, and hard-to-shop," Walgreen modernized them and emphasized health aid and pharmacy business. In 1986 the company purchased Medi Mart.

Responding to the public's demand for convenient shopping and its own desire for greater efficiency, Walgreen began linking its stores through a satellite network in 1989.

The company began Pharmacy Mail services to serve the growing mail-order drug business in 1991. In 1992 it completed the installation of point-of-sale inventory tracking equipment in all of its stores.

In 1993 the company organized a subsidiary, Healthcare Plus, and established a $15 million distribution center to focus on large, national accounts with state-of-the-art mail service capabilities.

Walgreen and an alliance of independent drugstores helped set up Pharmacy Direct Network in 1994 to compete in the rapidly growing field of managing prescription drug programs for group health plans. It also opened its 2,000th store, in Cleveland.

In 1995 Walgreen opened a new distribution center in Woodland, California. In fiscal 1995 the company earned $321 million on sales of $10.4 billion.

NYSE symbol: WAG
Fiscal year ends: August 31

Chairman and CEO: Charles R. Walgreen III, age 58,
$1,130,489 pay
President and COO: L. Daniel Jorndt, age 53,
$816,756 pay
EVP Store Operations: Glenn S. Kraiss, age 61,
$465,970 pay
EVP Marketing: Vernon A. Brunner, age 54,
$465,970 pay
SVP and CFO: Roger Polark, age 46
SVP Distribution: John R. Brown, age 58
SVP Facilities Development: William A. Shiel, age 43
SVP Human Resources: John A. Rubino, age 53
VP and Treasurer: W. Lynn Earnest, age 51
VP, General Counsel, and Secretary: Julian A. Oettinger,
age 55
Auditors: Arthur Andersen & Co, SC

WHERE

HQ: 200 Wilmot Rd., Deerfield, IL 60015
Phone: 847-940-2500
Fax: 847-940-2804

	1994 Stores	
	No.	% of total
Florida	326	17
Illinois	313	16
Texas	189	10
California	117	6
Arizona	110	6
Wisconsin	108	5
Indiana	94	5
Tennessee	69	3
Massachusetts	67	3
Other states & Puerto Rico	575	29
Total	**1,968**	**100**

1994 Sales by Geographical Area

	% of total
South & Southeast	28
Midwest (except Chicago)	21
Southwest	18
Chicago & suburbs	14
West	10
East	9
Total	**100**

WHAT

	Estimated 1994 Sales by Product Class
	% of total
Prescription drugs	41
General merchandise	24
Nonprescription drugs	13
Liquor & beverages	9
Cosmetics & toiletries	9
Tobacco products	4
Total	**100**

Subsidiary
Walgreens Healthcare Plus (mail-order pharmacy)

KEY COMPETITORS

Albertson's	Merck
American Stores	Pathmark
Bruno's	Phar-Mor
Drug Emporium	Price/Costco
Eckerd	Publix
Eli Lilly	Pueblo Xtra
Fiesta Mart	Randall's
Fred Meyer	Revco
H. E. Butt	Rite Aid
Imasco	Safeway
J. C. Penney	Thrifty PayLess
Kmart	Vons
Kroger	Wal-Mart
Longs	Whole Foods Market
Meijer	Winn-Dixie
Melville	Yucaipa

HOW MUCH

	Annual Growth	1985	1986	1987	1988	1989	1990	1991	1992	1993	1994
Sales ($ mil.)	12.6%	3,162	3,661	4,282	4,884	5,380	6,048	6,733	7,475	8,295	9,235
Net income ($ mil.)	13.0%	94	103	104	129	154	175	195	221	245	282
Income as % of sales	—	3.0%	2.8%	2.4%	2.6%	2.9%	2.9%	2.9%	3.0%	3.0%	3.1%
Earnings per share ($)	12.8%	0.77	0.84	0.84	1.05	1.25	1.42	1.58	1.78	1.98	2.28
Stock price – high ($)	—	15.13	19.75	22.44	18.69	25.13	26.63	38.63	44.50	44.63	45.38
Stock price – low ($)	—	10.75	12.13	12.38	13.56	15.00	19.94	24.69	30.38	35.38	33.75
Stock price – close ($)	13.4%	14.06	16.19	15.38	15.13	23.38	25.69	38.00	43.63	40.88	43.63
P/E – high	—	20	24	27	18	20	19	24	25	23	20
P/E – low	—	14	14	15	13	12	14	16	17	18	15
Dividends per share ($)	13.6%	0.21	0.24	0.27	0.29	0.33	0.39	0.45	0.51	0.60	0.66
Book value per share ($)	14.0%	3.92	4.50	5.06	5.79	6.69	7.70	8.79	10.02	11.20	12.79
Employees	5.8%	37,200	42,100	45,300	43,800	46,500	48,500	51,000	53,500	57,700	61,900

1994 Year-end:
Debt ratio: 0.0%
Return on equity: 19.1%
Cash (mil.): $108
Current ratio: 1.59
Long-term debt (mil.): $0
No. of shares (mil.): 123
Dividends
  Yield: 1.5%
  Payout: 28.9%
Market value (mil.): $5,370

Stock Price History
High/Low 1985–94

WHITMAN CORPORATION

OVERVIEW

Combining Pepsi bottling with muffler sales and walk-in refrigerator making sounds like a difficult challenge, but Chicago-based Whitman Corporation has made a success of it. Its Pepsi-Cola General Bottlers is the largest independent Pepsi bottler in the US; its Midas International is the largest franchised network for servicing mufflers in the world; and its Hussmann Corp. produces merchandising and refrigeration systems for the commercial food industry.

The bottling division operates in 12 states in the Midwest and Southeast. It has grown by acquisition and by the increase of Pepsi's share of the US soft drink market. Some 34% of the division's sales come from noncola product distribution. In 1994 it expanded its operations to Poland. Midas is also expanding in Europe and plans to double its European chain to 600 units by the year 2000.

Southeastern Asset Management, an investment firm, owns 9.5% of Whitman.

WHEN

Whitman Corporation is a very different business from its grandparent company, the Illinois Central Railroad. Started in 1851 with a 3.6 million–acre land grant, Illinois Central became one of the nation's 10 largest rail systems. In 1901, its 50th year, it boasted 4,200 rail miles, a $32 million income, and freight and passenger service in 13 states. Its famous passenger trains included the Green Diamond (Chicago to St. Louis) and the Diamond Special and City of New Orleans (Chicago to New Orleans). Passenger service, no longer profitable, was sold to Amtrak in 1971. In 1972 the company (renamed Illinois Central Industries in 1962) acquired the Gulf, Mobile and Ohio Railroad (Chicago to Mobile, Alabama), and the railroad was renamed Illinois Central Gulf (ICG).

The company maintained its focus on railroads until William Johnson, former president of Railway Express Agency, became president in 1966. Johnson served as president for 21 years, transforming it into a multinational conglomerate that was renamed IC Industries in 1975. IC bought numerous companies, including Pepsi-Cola General Bottlers (1970); Midas International auto muffler shops (1972); and the venerable St. Louis company, Pet Inc. (1978). Pet had begun in 1885 as an evaporated milk company and had made substantial diverse purchases of its own, including Hussmann Refrigeration, a leading producer of refrigeration systems for grocery stores; Downyflake Foods; Stuckey roadside candy stores; and chocolate company Stuart F. Whitman and Son.

By the late 1970s the ICG railroad provided only 1% of the company's pretax profits. IC was determined to sell it, but it wasn't until 1989 that IC spun off ICG to its stockholders. In the interim IC sold many of its real estate holdings, and ICG's trackage shrank by 2/3.

A private concern, Prospect Group, bought the railroad within a month of the spinoff.

The company changed its name in 1988 to Whitman Corporation (after Pet's well-known chocolate brand) to reflect its concentration on consumer goods and services. In the 1980s Whitman sold 65 companies, including its Pneumo Abex aerospace operations (for $1.2 billion, 1988). In the same time period, Whitman has bought 98 companies, including Orval Kent (refrigerated salad products, 1988) and Van de Kamp's Frozen Seafoods (1989). In 1989 Whitman announced plans to sell Hussmann but, lacking an acceptable offer, decided in 1990 to keep the unit.

In an attempt to restructure, the company spun off its Pet food unit to shareholders, losing such brands as Old El Paso (Mexican foods), Progresso (Italian foods), and Whitman Chocolates (sold to Russell Stover Candies in 1993). The company also pared jobs to reduce debt. Whitman purchased 39 European muffler shops and 3 Pepsi franchises in the early 1990s.

In 1993 Pepsi General began work on a $7.5 million line at its Munster, Indiana, plant for production of Lipton Original Tea. Hussmann introduced Protocol, a refrigeration system that doesn't use CFCs, and continued to upgrade its largest plant (in Bridgeton, Missouri). In 1993 and 1994 Whitman took steps to reduce its heavy debt, refinancing $360 million that is expected to cut annual interest costs by $12 million.

In 1994 Hussmann completed development of medium-temperature refrigerated cases, as part of its new product line called Impact. That same year Hussmann set up a joint venture with Luoyang Refrigeration Machinery Factory, China's #1 maker of commercial refrigerators. Hussmann plans to begin production there in 1995.

NYSE symbol: WH
Fiscal year ends: December 31

WHO

Chairman and CEO: Bruce S. Chelberg, age 60,
$1,160,417 pay
EVP (CFO): Thomas L. Bindley, age 51,
$657,500 pay
SVP and Controller: Frank T. Westover
SVP Human Resources: Lawrence J. Pilon, age 46
VP; President and CEO, Pepsi-Cola General Bottlers:
Gerald A. McGuire, age 63, $560,250 pay
VP; President and CEO, Midas Intl Corp.: John R.
Moore, age 59, $531,000 pay
VP; President and CEO, Hussmann Corp.: J. Larry
Vowell, age 54, $405,166 pay
VP Secretary and General Counsel: William B. Moore
VP and Treasurer: Kathleen R. Gannon
VP Taxes: Louis J. Corna
Auditors: KPMG Peat Marwick LLP

WHERE

HQ: 3501 Algonquin Rd., Rolling Meadows, IL 60008
Phone: 847-818-5000
Fax: 847-818-5045 (Corporate Affairs)

Whitman's Pepsi operations are located in 12
midwestern and southeastern states and in Poland.
Midas has 2,575 shops in the US and 13 other countries.
Hussmann has operations in Canada, Mexico, the UK,
and the US and joint ventures in Asia and Europe.

	1994 Sales		1994 Operating Income	
	$ mil.	% of total	$ mil.	% of total
US	2,236	83	312	91
Other countries	472	17	31	9
Adjustments	(49)	—	(16)	—
Total	**2,659**	**100**	**327**	**100**

WHAT

	1994 Sales		1994 Operating Income	
	$ mil.	% of total	$ mil.	% of total
Pepsi General	1,256	47	185	54
Hussmann	860	32	83	24
Midas	543	21	75	22
Other	—	—	(16)	—
Total	**2,659**	**100**	**327**	**100**

**Pepsi-Cola General
Bottlers, Inc.**
All-Sport
A&W Root Beer
Caffeine Free Pepsi
Canada Dry
Dad's Root Beer
Diet Pepsi
Dr Pepper
Hawaiian Punch
Lipton's Tea
Mountain Dew
Ocean Spray
Pepsi
Seven-Up

Slice
Wild Cherry Pepsi

Hussmann Corporation
Bottle coolers
Commercial/industrial
refrigeration systems
HVAC equipment
Refrigerated display cases
Storage coolers
Walk-in coolers

**Midas International
Corporation**
Auto service shops

KEY COMPETITORS

American Standard
Bridgestone
Cadbury Schweppes
Celestial Seasonings
Coca-Cola
Coca-Cola Bottling
of Chicago
Coca-Cola Enterprises
Cott
AB Electrolux
Fedders
Ferolito, Vultaggio
GKN
Goodyear

Lennox International
Meineke
Middleby
Monro Muffler
Montgomery Ward
National Beverage
Nestlé
Premark
Quaker Oats
Scotsman Industries
Sears
Triarc
United Technologies
York International

HOW MUCH

	Annual Growth	1985	1986	1987	1988	1989	1990	1991	1992	1993	1994
Sales ($ mil.)	(5.5%)	4,405	4,222	4,027	3,583	3,986	2,305	2,393	2,388	2,530	2,659
Net income ($ mil.)	(4.9%)	163	(126)	252	210	191	19	98	60	106	103
Income as % of sales	—	3.7%	—	6.3%	5.9%	4.8%	0.8%	4.1%	2.5%	4.2%	3.9%
Earnings per share ($)	3.5%	0.71	(0.54)	1.03	0.91	0.70	(0.08)	0.92	0.56	0.99	0.97
Stock price – high ($)	—	9.40	14.06	19.10	17.25	17.71	13.77	14.13	16.38	17.00	18.00
Stock price – low ($)	—	6.22	8.25	10.36	13.72	12.73	7.87	8.22	12.25	12.75	14.75
Stock price – close ($)	7.7%	8.88	10.65	15.22	16.55	13.31	8.33	13.38	14.75	16.25	17.25
P/E – high	—	13	—	19	19	25	—	15	29	17	19
P/E – low	—	9	—	10	15	18	—	9	22	13	15
Dividends per share ($)	0.0%	0.32	0.35	0.39	0.43	0.46	0.48	0.37	0.25	0.28	0.32
Book value per share ($)	(3.8%)	7.40	6.30	6.79	3.91	1.78	1.61	4.32	4.47	4.83	5.24
Employees	(10.9%)	43,050	38,162	15,174	15,099	15,165	15,219	14,703	14,374	14,868	15,271

1994 Year-end:
Debt ratio: 59.5%
Return on equity: 19.3%
Cash (mil.): $71
Current ratio: 1.46
Long-term debt (mil.): $723
No. of shares (mil.): 106
Dividends
Yield: 1.9%
Payout: 33.0%
Market value (mil.): $1,820

**Stock Price History
High/Low 1985–94**

WICKES LUMBER COMPANY

OVERVIEW

Wickes Lumber is going pro. While the Home Depots and Builders Squares of the building materials world have found their niche by selling to do-it-yourselfers working on their homes, Wickes is concentrating its sales on professional contractors. The Vernon Hills, Illinois–based company makes more than 3/4 of its sales to building and remodeling professionals, and the rest are to what it calls "serious do-it-yourselfers" who are working on major projects.

Wickes operates more than 130 building supply centers located primarily in the midwestern and northeastern US. Its stores sell wood products, such as lumber, plywood, and siding; other building materials, including roofing, doors, and insulation; and such supplies as paint, tools, and floor coverings.

Led by CEO Steven Wilson, whose investment firm, Riverside Group, owns 39.3% of the company, Wickes is looking to expand in its Midwest and Northeast strongholds and increase its presence in the South by acquiring existing building supply companies in those areas. The company is also working to boost its service to builders of multifamily structures, restaurants, motels, and other light commercial properties.

WHEN

Wickes Lumber's roots go back to a Flint, Michigan, foundry and machine shop started by Henry Dunn Wickes in 1854. Two years later he was joined by his brother Edward and by H. W. Wood. They established the Genesee Iron Works to provide equipment and repairs for the rapidly growing Michigan lumber industry. In 1864 the Wickes brothers bought out Wood and changed the company's name to Wickes Bros. Iron Works. Business took off after they developed a steam-powered mill saw that revolutionized the lumber business.

As the Michigan lumber industry began to decline, Wickes Bros. diversified, selling reconditioned equipment from shuttered sawmills and expanding into other types of machinery, including steam boilers, which powered the company's growth in the early part of the 20th century. Wickes Bros. slumped during the Depression, but military orders during WWII helped it rebound.

In 1952 Joseph McMullin, who ran lumber-buying operations for a group of grain elevators that Wickes Bros. had bought in 1950, convinced the company's board of directors to give him about $15,000 to open an outlet to sell retail building supplies. McMullin took unused space in a grain terminal in Bay City, Michigan. Dubbed the Bay City Cash Way Company, the store revolutionized the building supplies business. The store offered a one-stop shop with a large inventory at prices much lower than those at the small, independent lumberyards that were its main competitors.

The Bay City store was an immediate success. In 1953 the company opened a 2nd store in Kalamazoo, Michigan. Riding the post-WWII building boom, Cash Way grew rapidly. By 1962, when Cash Way was renamed Wickes Lumber, it had 41 stores in the midwestern and eastern US.

Wickes Lumber continued to grow during the 1960s. In 1964 it expanded into the Southeast with the acquisitions of the 19-store Varina Wholesale Builders Supply chain and the 18-store Ross Builders Supplies chain. By 1970 the company had 213 building supply outlets in 32 states.

In 1971 Wickes Companies was formed as a holding company for the various Wickes operations. While the retail lumber business was expanding, Wickes Companies was moving into a range of businesses, including retail furniture, consumer credit, modular housing, and commercial construction.

In 1978 Wickes Lumber acquired home improvement retailer Builders Emporium, and by 1981 the company had 280 building centers. However, the expensive acquisition of supermarket and drugstore company Gamble-Skogmo, coupled with a recession, put Wickes Companies in jeopardy. In 1982 the parent filed for bankruptcy. It sold off many of its operations and emerged from bankruptcy in 1985. Several acquisitions following the reorganization left the company deeply in debt, and in 1988 Wickes Companies sold Wickes Lumber to management for about $306 million in an LBO. The deal included 233 building supply stores and 10 component factories.

To pay down the debt left over from the LBO, Wickes began to sell off some of its stores. In 1991 Steven Wilson's Riverside Group acquired a major stake in the company. Wilson became CEO, and he continued a strategy of closing or selling unprofitable stores. Wickes went public in 1993.

In 1995 the company acquired Lappo Lumber, which had 2 stores in Michigan.

Nasdaq symbol: WIKS
Fiscal year ends: Last Saturday in December

Chairman and CEO: J. Steven Wilson, age 51,
$850,000 pay
VC, General Counsel, and Secretary: Kenneth M.
Kirschner, age 52
President and COO: Douglas J. Woods, age 50,
$444,900 pay
SVP, CFO, and Treasurer: George A. Bajalia, age 37,
$228,600 pay
VP Merchandising: Robert W. Rowatt, age 49,
$175,198 pay
VP Business Development: George C. Finkenstaedt,
age 43, $168,250 pay
VP Marketing and Sales: Robert F. Sherlock, age 39
VP Information Systems: Gene L. Curtin, age 47
VP Human Resources: E. Trevor Dignall, age 47
Auditors: Coopers & Lybrand L.L.P.

WHERE

HQ: 706 Deerpath Dr., Vernon Hills, IL 60061
Phone: 847-367-3400
Fax: 847-367-3750

	1994 Stores
	No.
Michigan	27
Wisconsin	15
Indiana	13
New York	12
Ohio	11
Pennsylvania	9
Illinois	5
Alabama	4
Kentucky	4
Maine	4
Other states	26
Total	**130**

WHAT

	1994 Sales
	% of total
Residential contractors	51
Retail consumers	22
Repair & remodeling professionals	17
Commercial contractors	10
Total	**100**

	1994 Sales
	% of total
Wood products	52
Hardlines	14
Other building materials	34
Total	**100**

Wood Products
Lumber
Plywood
Roof and floor trusses
Sheathing
Siding
Specialty lumber
Treated lumber

Hardlines
Cabinets
Electrical supplies
Floor coverings
Hardware

Lighting products
Paint
Plumbing supplies
Tools

Other Building Materials
Doors
Drywall
Insulation
Moldings
Roofing
Vinyl siding
Windows

KEY COMPETITORS

84 Lumber
Ace Hardware
Cotter & Co.
D.I.Y. Home Warehouse
Foxworth-Galbraith Lumber
Hechinger
Home Depot
Kmart

Lowe's
McCoy
Menard
Payless Cashways
Sears
Servistar
Sherwin-Williams
Wal-Mart

HOW MUCH

	Annual Growth	1985	1986	1987	1988	1989	1990	1991	1992	1993	1994
Sales ($ mil.)	(0.3%)	—	—	—	—	1,002	847	746	745	847	987
Net income ($ mil.)	—	—	—	—	—	(11)	(15)	(22)	6	8	28
Income as % of sales	—	—	—	—	—	—	—	—	0.8%	1.0%	2.8%
Earnings per share ($)	116.4%	—	—	—	—	—	—	—	0.98	1.34	4.59
Stock price – high ($)	—	—	—	—	—	—	—	—	—	18.25	24.75
Stock price – low ($)	—	—	—	—	—	—	—	—	—	12.25	10.00
Stock price – close ($)	(42.7%)	—	—	—	—	—	—	—	—	17.88	10.25
P/E – high	—	—	—	—	—	—	—	—	—	14	5
P/E – low	—	—	—	—	—	—	—	—	—	9	2
Dividends per share ($)	—	—	—	—	—	—	—	—	—	0.00	0.00
Book value per share ($)	1,550.2%	—	—	—	—	—	—	—	—	0.30	4.94
Employees	10.5%	—	—	—	—	—	—	—	—	4,092	4,523

1994 Year-end:
Debt ratio: 87.5%
Return on equity: 175.5%
Cash (mil.): $2
Current ratio: 3.15
Long-term debt (mil.): $211
No. of shares (mil.): 6
Dividends
  Yield: —
  Payout: —
Market value (mil.): $63

Stock Price History
High/Low 1993–94

WM. WRIGLEY JR. COMPANY

OVERVIEW

Chicago-based Wm. Wrigley Jr. is the world's #1 chewing gum maker and a giant in the US, commanding a 49% share of the domestic gum market. Wrigley derives 90% of its revenues from gum. Its products include such popular brands as Juicy Fruit, Doublemint, Freedent, and top seller Extra sugar-free gum. Overseas, these and other brands are manufactured in 9 factories and sold in more than 120 countries. International sales accounted for 44% of 1994 revenues.

Wrigley has maintained low prices to foil competitors and increase its customer base. The company also has benefited from automation and declining costs of such materials as

gum base and corn syrup. It is building new plants in Poland and India and expanding its Alsace manufacturing plant in France to meet the demand in Eastern Europe and Russia, which accounts for almost half of its sales growth. Sales of sugar-free gum, overseas and at home, outpaced shipments of regular gum for the first time in 1994. Wrigley's success, however, has attracted imitators. Japanese confectionary Sun Kotobuki plans to make a knockoff of Wrigley's Doublemint gum in Vietnam.

Wrigley still has no long-term debt. CEO William Wrigley, grandson of the founder, owns roughly 1/4 of the company.

WHEN

William Wrigley Jr. started his career at 13 when, following his expulsion from school, his father put him to work at the family's soap factory in Philadelphia. After a year Wrigley was promoted to the sales staff, where he was very successful selling door-to-door.

In 1891 he opened, in Chicago, an office of his father's soap company. Wrigley learned to promote his products with free premiums, such as cookbooks. When he began offering customers chewing gum made of spruce gum and paraffin by Zeno Manufacturing (1892), he received numerous requests to buy the gum. At the time chicle (a naturally sweet gum base from Central America) was being imported for the rubber industry. Wrigley successfully gambled on the idea that chicle would work as a main ingredient in chewing gum.

By 1893 Wrigley had introduced Spearmint and Juicy Fruit and was selling only gum. He offered dealers sales incentives such as counter scales, cash registers, and display cases for volume purchases. In 1898 he merged with Zeno to form Wm. Wrigley, Jr. & Co. By 1910 Spearmint gum was the leading US brand, and Wrigley began to expand into Canada (1910), Australia (1915), and Great Britain (1927).

The Wrigley family bought real estate, including Catalina Island (1919) and the Arizona Biltmore Hotel (1931); built the Wrigley Building (1924); and purchased the Chicago Cubs (1924, sold 1981). Wrigley was keen on advertising. He plastered simple messages on huge billboards and used twins to promote Doublemint gum in the 1930s. By the time of his death in 1932, when son Philip took over, the company was the largest single-product advertiser.

For over 75 years Wrigley made 3 gums: Spearmint, Juicy Fruit, and Doublemint (introduced in 1914). Unable to obtain the proper ingredients during WWII, Wrigley produced inferior gum under a different label but kept the Wrigley brand alive with a picture of his former gum and the ad slogan "Remember this Wrapper." It worked: After the war Wrigley's popularity increased. The company did not raise its original 5¢ price until 1971, when management grudgingly went to 7¢.

By 1974 Wrigley faced competition from sugar-free gums. Despite declining market share, management refused to bring out a sugar-free gum at that time, instead introducing Freedent for denture wearers. Later the company introduced Big Red (1975); Orbit, a sugar-free gum (1977); and Hubba Bubba (1978; through Amurol, bought in 1958). Philip died in 1977, and a 3rd-generation Wrigley (William) took over.

In 1984 Wrigley introduced a new sugar-free gum, Extra. In 1991 the company launched Michael Jordan Hang Time shredded bubble gum, a sugar-free version of Freedent, and a bubble gum version of Extra.

The company has made rapid inroads overseas, particularly in Eastern Europe, establishing operations in Hungary, Slovenia, and the Czech Republic. In 1993 the company opened a new chewing gum factory in China.

In 1994 Wrigley began an ambitious construction program to build new factories in the US and abroad and sold its Singapore affiliate for a $38 million profit. Wrigley also launched its first new sugar-based chewing gum in nearly 20 years, Winterfresh, which has been very successful without undermining sales of other company brands.

NYSE symbol: WWY
Fiscal year ends: December 31

WHO

President and CEO: William Wrigley, age 61, $475,000 pay
EVP: R. Darrell Ewers, age 61, $376,500 pay
Group VP International: Douglas S. Barrie, age 61, $324,833 pay
Group VP Marketing: Ronald O. Cox, age 56, $276,500 pay
SVP and CFO: John F. Bard, age 53, $261,000 pay
SVP Manufacturing: Martin J. Geraghty, age 58
VP Treasurer: Dushan Petrovich, age 41
VP Personnel: David E. Boxell, age 53
Auditors: Ernst & Young LLP

WHERE

HQ: 410 N. Michigan Ave., Chicago, IL 60611
Phone: 312-644-2121
Fax: 312-644-0097 (Marketing)

The company has operations in 27 countries.

	1994 Sales		1994 Operating Income	
	$ mil.	% of total	$ mil.	% of total
North America	938	55	177	50
Europe	573	33	107	30
Other regions	200	12	70	20
Adjustments	(50)	—	1	—
Total	**1,661**	**100**	**356**	**100**

WHAT

US Brands (Gum)	Non-US Brands (Gum)
Big Red	Arrowmint
Doublemint	Big Boy
Extra	Big G
Freedent	Cool Crunch
Juicy Fruit	Dulce 16
Spearmint	Freedent
Winterfresh	Hubba Bubba
	Juicy Fruit

Amurol Products   Orbit
Co. Brands   P.K.
Big League Chew
Bubble Tape   **Real Estate**
Hubba Bubba   Wrigley Building, Chicago

US Subsidiaries and Divisions
Amurol Confections Co. (children's bubble gum and candy)
Four-Ten Corporation
L.A. Dreyfus Co. (chewing gum base)
Northwestern Flavors, Inc. (flavorings)
Wrico Packaging (wrapping supplies)

KEY COMPETITORS

Cadbury Schweppes
Hauser Chemical
Hercules
Hershey
IFF
Mars
Marvel
Nabisco Holdings
Roche
Tootsie Roll
Warner-Lambert

HOW MUCH

	Annual Growth	1985	1986	1987	1988	1989	1990	1991	1992	1993	1994
Sales ($ mil.)	11.6%	620	699	781	891	993	1,111	1,149	1,287	1,429	1,661
Net income ($ mil.)	20.4%	44	54	70	87	106	117	129	149	175	231
Income as % of sales	—	7.0%	7.7%	9.0%	9.8%	10.7%	10.6%	11.2%	11.5%	12.2%	13.9%
Earnings per share ($)	21.6%	0.34	0.43	0.56	0.73	0.90	1.00	1.09	1.27	1.50	1.98
Stock price – high ($)	—	5.27	8.66	11.82	13.65	17.90	19.73	26.97	39.88	46.13	53.88
Stock price – low ($)	—	3.19	4.58	6.49	10.66	11.82	14.57	16.36	22.10	29.50	38.13
Stock price – close ($)	28.5%	5.16	7.62	11.51	12.03	17.86	17.07	26.89	32.63	44.13	49.38
P/E – high	—	16	20	21	19	20	20	25	31	31	27
P/E – low	—	9	11	12	15	13	15	15	17	20	19
Dividends per share ($)	20.3%	0.17	0.21	0.28	0.36	0.45	0.49	0.55	0.62	0.75	0.90
Book value per share ($)	12.6%	2.04	2.31	2.39	2.59	2.91	3.41	3.94	4.27	4.94	5.92
Employees	2.5%	5,600	5,500	5,500	5,500	5,750	5,850	6,250	6,400	6,700	7,000

1994 Year-end:
Debt ratio: 0.0%
Return on equity: 36.5%
Cash (mil.): $128
Current ratio: 2.97
Long-term debt (mil.): $0
No. of shares (mil.): 116
Dividends
  Yield: 1.8%
  Payout: 45.5%
Market value (mil.): $5,738

Stock Price History
High/Low 1985–94

WMX TECHNOLOGIES, INC.

OVERVIEW

Too many irons in the incinerator has management reeling at WMX, the world's largest waste collection and disposal company. To rescue its fragmented worldwide operations, WMX is taking a long look at its components, acquiring new businesses that complement the company's core segments (spending nearly $173 million for 46 businesses in 1994), and shedding weak units (about 10 in 1994).

To boost its share of the growing recycling market, WMX bought Resource Recycling Technologies, an East Coast operator of recycling facilities, in 1995. The addition could also help WMX win municipal refuse contracts.

In a move to tighten its operations, the company purchased the outstanding shares of spinoff Chemical Waste Management in 1994.

It also repurchased the publicly held shares of Rust International in 1995. WMX still has 2 public subsidiaries: Wheelabrator Technologies and Waste Management International.

Also in 1995 WMX agreed to sell Rust's hazardous waste and nuclear remediation business to OHM Corp., an Ohio-based pollution services company. The transaction gives Rust about 37% of OHM's stock. WMX's hazardous waste segment has been especially troublesome, with capacity outstripping volume. The company took a $91 million charge in the first quarter of 1995 to write down its investments in hazardous waste–handling equipment.

In 1995 WMX's North American operations served 11.3 million residential and 1 million commercial and industrial customers.

WHEN

In 1956 Dean L. Buntrock joined Ace Scavenger Service (Illinois), which had 12 collection trucks and $750,000 per year in revenues. Under Buntrock's leadership the company expanded into Wisconsin.

In the early 1970s a growing number of waste service companies were forming. In 1971 Waste Management, Inc., emerged when Buntrock joined forces with H. Wayne Huizenga, who had bought 2 waste routes in Broward County, Florida, in 1962. Both companies had grown rapidly during the 1960s, as concern with air quality prompted bans on residential and industrial on-site waste burning. Waste Management, with customers in Florida, Illinois, Indiana, Minnesota, Ohio, and Wisconsin, reported earnings of $1.2 million its first year. In the 1970s it made acquisitions in Michigan, New York, Ohio, Pennsylvania, and Canada.

In 1975 the company bid on and won a contract in Riyadh, Saudi Arabia (service started in 1978), and formed its international subsidiary. Other foreign contracts followed, and the company now operates in 20 foreign countries, including Argentina, Australia, Germany, Italy, the Netherlands, New Zealand, and Venezuela. Waste Management also divided into specialty areas, forming Chemical Waste Management (1975) and offering site cleanup services (ENRAC, 1980) and low-level nuclear waste disposal (Chem-Nuclear Systems, 1982). Expansion in this period included a great coup — the acquisition of 60% of competitor SCA of Boston (1984).

Huizenga retired from his trash-hauling business in 1983 and soon purchased Block-

buster Video, the #1 video rental chain in the country (now a unit of Viacom, Inc.).

During the 1980s the company established joint ventures for the sale of recyclable materials with DuPont, Stone Container Corporation, and American National Can. Its partnership with the Henley Group created Wheelabrator Technologies (22% owned in 1988, now 57% owned). In 1989 Waste Management contracted to dispose of approximately 90% of the waste from the *Exxon Valdez* oil spill. In 1991 Waste Management International and Wessex Waste Management, a UK-based water company, formed a joint venture, creating UK Waste Management Ltd.

For many years the company has been targeted, and in some cases fined, for violation of antitrust laws and pollution ordinances. The company has also challenged ordinances, including an Alabama tax charging $72 per ton on waste brought into a company-owned site from out-of-state. In 1992 the court found in Chemical Waste Management's favor.

In 1993 Waste Management became WMX Technologies and opened the most modern hazardous-waste treatment plant in the world: a $150 million plant in Hong Kong. That same year the company spun off Rust International.

Wheelabrator's Air Pollution Control unit was awarded a $40 million contract in 1994 to build a trio of 750-foot chimneys for the Salt River Project in Page, Arizona.

In a move aimed at breaking into New York City's lucrative refuse market, in 1995 WMX agreed to purchase a majority interest in a 14-acre solid-waste transfer station located in the Bronx.

NYSE symbol: WMX
Fiscal year ends: December 31

WHO

Chairman and CEO: Dean L. Buntrock, age 63,
$2,520,000 pay
President and COO: Phillip B. Rooney, age 50,
$2,029,280 pay
SVP, Treasurer, and CFO: James E. Koenig, age 47,
$750,000 pay
SVP Corporate and Public Affairs: D. P. Payne, age 52
VP, General Counsel, and Secretary: Herbert A. Getz,
age 39, $502,500 pay
VP, Controller, and Principal Accounting Officer:
Thomas C. Hau, age 59
VP and Chief Environmental Officer: Donald A.
Wallgren, age 53
**VP Technology Development and Management;
President and CEO, Rust, International, Inc.:** Rodney
C. Gilbert, age 55
VP Communications: William J. Plunkett
VP Human Resources: Edward Kalebich
Auditors: Arthur Andersen & Co, SC

WHERE

HQ: 3003 Butterfield Rd., Oak Brook, IL 60521
Phone: 708-572-8800
Fax: 708-572-3094

The company has over 12 million residential clients and
municipal and commercial accounts in the US and 21
foreign countries.

	1994 Sales		1994 Operating Income	
	$ mil.	% of total	$ mil.	% of total
US	7,947	79	1,496	85
Europe	1,504	15	198	11
Other regions	646	6	74	4
Total	**10,097**	**100**	**1,768**	**100**

WHAT

	1994 Sales		1994 Operating Income	
	$ mil.	% of total	$ mil.	% of total
Solid waste	5,118	49	1,066	60
Intl. waste mgmt.	1,711	16	236	13
Engineering/ construction	1,683	16	97	6
Water treatment/ air quality	1,324	13	290	16
Hazardous waste	649	6	89	5
Adjustments	(388)	—	(10)	—
Total	**10,097**	**100**	**1,768**	**100**

Selected Services
Air quality (pollution control technologies)
Chemical waste (transport, treatment, and disposal)
Hazardous and low-level radioactive waste (collection,
transportation, treatment, and resource recovery)
Solid waste (collection, transport, disposal, recycling,
and energy recovery)
Trash-to-energy (power facilities)
Water and wastewater (treatment facilities)

Selected Subsidiaries
Chemical Waste Management (CWM; 100%, hazardous
waste management services)
Rust International (100% [CWM owns 56%,
Wheelabrator owns 40%]; engineering, construction,
and environmental and infrastructure consulting
services; remediation and related on-site services)
Waste Management International (56%; collection,
processing, transfer, and disposal services)
Wheelabrator Technologies (57%; air, energy, and water
treatment services)

KEY COMPETITORS

Allwaste	CSX	Ogden
Bechtel	EnviroSource	Safety-Kleen
Browning-Ferris	Halliburton	TRW
Canadian	Mid-American	USA Waste
Pacific	Waste	Services

HOW MUCH

	Annual Growth	1985	1986	1987	1988	1989	1990	1991	1992	1993	1994
Sales ($ mil.)	22.5%	1,625	2,018	2,758	3,566	4,459	6,034	7,551	8,661	9,136	10,097
Net income ($ mil.)	18.4%	172	371	327	464	562	709	606	921	453	784
Income as % of sales	—	10.6%	18.4%	11.9%	13.0%	12.6%	11.8%	8.0%	10.6%	5.0%	7.8%
Earnings per share ($)	15.9%	0.43	0.88	0.73	1.03	1.22	1.49	1.23	1.86	0.93	1.62
Stock price – high ($)	—	9.50	14.94	24.25	21.38	15.75	20.38	28.63	32.63	40.25	30.75
Stock price – low ($)	—	5.44	8.63	13.50	13.50	15.75	20.38	28.63	32.00	23.00	22.63
Stock price – close ($)	12.7%	8.88	13.91	18.81	20.69	35.00	35.00	42.13	40.00	26.38	26.13
P/E – high	—	22	17	33	21	29	31	36	25	43	19
P/E – low	—	13	10	19	15	17	19	27	17	25	14
Dividends per share ($)	20.7%	0.11	0.13	0.17	0.17	0.21	0.27	0.34	0.40	0.48	0.58	0.60
Book value per share ($)	14.4%	2.79	3.67	4.19	4.82	5.88	7.52	8.37	8.81	8.60	9.38
Employees	15.8%	19,800	24,485	30,650	36,750	42,640	62,050	63,040	67,200	72,600	74,400

1994 Year-end:
Debt ratio: 60.4%
Return on equity: 18.0%
Cash (mil.): $142
Current ratio: 0.97
Long-term debt (mil.): $6,044
No. of shares (mil.): 484
Dividends
  Yield: 2.3%
  Payout: 37.0%
Market value (mil.): $12,645

Stock Price History
High/Low 1985–94

W.W. GRAINGER, INC.

OVERVIEW

Skokie, Illinois–based W.W. Grainger is a major US distributor of maintenance, repair, and operating supplies and equipment to commercial, contractor, industrial, and institutional clients, including hospitals and restaurants. Among the products it distributes are electric motors, fixtures for manufacturing facilities, heating and refrigeration equipment, power tools, and plumbing supplies. The company is 10.2% owned by chairman David Grainger, the son of the founder.

Grainger has positioned itself as a single-source option for its customers. To this end, the company is forming alliances with distributors in product categories where Grainger's own product line is limited, such as ball bearings, power transmission products, electrical supplies, fasteners, industrial plastics, pipes, valves, and fittings.

The company traditionally served small-scale industrial contractors, but it has expanded to serve large companies with multiple locations. Grainger sells its products through a nationwide network of 337 branches (retail outlets). Each branch tailors its inventory to the preferences of local customers and actual product demand. Grainger's *General Catalog* (published continually since 1927) offers over 61,000 separate items.

In 1994 the company opened zone distribution centers in Atlanta and Dallas. These centers provide regional warehouse support to branch locations in their respective regions, enabling speedy delivery of items to customers.

WHEN

In 1919 William W. Grainger graduated from the University of Illinois with an electrical engineering degree. Working as a motor designer and salesman, he saw the market opportunity to develop a wholesale electric motor sales and distribution company. He set up an office in Chicago in 1927 and incorporated the business a year later. With his sister Margaret and 2 employees, Grainger shipped out motors to mail-order customers. Sales were generated primarily through postcard mailers and an 8-page catalog called the *MotorBook*.

In the late 1920s and 1930s, city utilities and factories shifted from direct current to alternating current power systems. Uniform DC-powered assembly lines gave way to individual workstations, each powered by a separate AC motor. This burgeoning market opened the way for distributors like Grainger to tap into segments that high-volume manufacturers found difficult to reach. In the early 1930s Grainger opened offices in Atlanta, Dallas, Philadelphia, and San Francisco. By 1936 Grainger had opened 15 sales branches.

The company entered a boom period after WWII. By 1949 it had established 39 branches in 30 states. Sales grew from $8 million in 1948 to $18 million in 1952. In 1953 the company opened 5 regional warehouses, in Chicago, New York (and later Cranford, New Jersey), Oakland, Fort Worth, and Memphis (and later Atlanta), to bring its supplies closer to its branches. The company continued to expand geographically in the 1950s and 1960s. It went public in 1967.

William Grainger led the company until his retirement in 1968, when he was succeeded as CEO by his son David. The company expanded into electric motor manufacturing with the purchase of the Doerr Companies in 1969. In 1979 Grainger opened its 150th branch and moved its head office to Skokie, Illinois.

The company's distribution became decentralized with the opening of its 1.4 million-square-foot automated regional distribution center in Kansas City in 1983. Grainger passed $1 billion in sales in 1984. The company sold its Doerr Electric subsidiary to Emerson Electric in 1986 for $24.3 million.

After its first-ever market research study in 1986, Grainger computerized its branch operations and opened 36 branches in 1987 and 55 in 1988.

In 1989 the company made its first acquisition in 17 years with the purchase of Vonnegut Industrial Products for $9 million. In 1990 it acquired Bossert Industrial Supply and Allied Safety.

In 1991 Grainger purchased Ball Industries, a California distributor of sanitary and janitorial supplies.

The company completed the acquisition of Lab Safety Supply for $161 million in 1992. Grainger began integrating its sanitary supply business with its core activities in 1993 and in 1994 announced plans to similarly integrate its Allied Safety (safety products and related equipment) and Bossert (production consumable products) units.

In 1995 Grainger named its president, Richard Keyser, as CEO, replacing David Grainger, who remained as chairman. This marked the first time in the company's history that a Grainger was not in the CEO position.

NYSE symbol: GWW
Fiscal year ends: December 31

WHO

Chairman: David W. Grainger, age 67, $964,000 pay
VC (CFO): Jere D. Fluno, age 53, $1,148,880 pay
President and CEO: Richard L. Keyser, age 52, $1,148,880 pay
SVP Marketing and Sales: Donald E. Bielinski, age 45, $540,608 pay
SVP, General Counsel, and Secretary: James M. Baisley, age 62, $441,817 pay
SVP Product Development: John W. Slayton Jr., age 49
VP Distribution Operations: Richard H. Hantke, age 56
VP; General Manager, Integrated Supply: Michael R. Knight, age 46
VP; General Manager, Direct Sales: John J. Rozwat, age 56
VP; General Manager, Direct Marketing: John A. Schweig, age 37
VP Product Line Development: Fred E. Loepp
VP Information Services: James T. Ryan, age 36
VP Financial Services: Paul J. Wallace, age 48
VP Financial Reporting and Investor Relations: Robert D. Pappano
VP; President, Lab Safety Supply: Peggy H. Stich
VP Real Estate: Richard D. Quast
VP Human Resources: Gary J. Goberville
Auditors: Grant Thornton LLP

WHERE

HQ: 5500 W. Howard St., Skokie, IL 60077-2699
Phone: 847-982-9000
Fax: 847-982-3489

The company has general offices in Chicago and Niles, Illinois, and regional distribution centers in Greenville County, South Carolina; Kansas City, Missouri; and Niles, Illinois. It also has 3 zone distribution centers and 337 branch locations nationwide.

WHAT

	1994 Branch Locations	
	No.	% of total
Company-owned	256	76
Leased	81	24
Total	**337**	**100**

Selected Products

Air compressors	Lighting fixtures and components
Air tools and spray painting equipment	Liquid pumps
Air-conditioning and refrigeration equipment	Material handling and storage equipment
Blowers	Motor controls
Computer supplies	Office equipment
Electric motors	Plant and office maintenance equipment
Fans	Power and hand tools
Gas engine–driven power plants	Power generating plants
Gear motors	Power transmission components
Heating equipment and controls	Safety products
Hydraulic equipment	Shop tools
Janitorial supplies	

Brand Names
Dayton (electric motors and ventilatic ipment)
Demco (power transmission belts)
Dem-Kote (spray paints)
Speedaire (air compressors)
Teel (liquid pumps)

Selected Subsidiaries
Lab Safety Supply, Inc.
Parts Company of America

KEY COMPETITORS

American Standard	Fastenal	lunkin
Baldor Electric	Figgie	iley Works
Bearings	Home Depot	Distributors
Black & Decker	Kaman	en
Emerson Electric	Kmart	

HOW MUCH

	Annual Growth	1985	1986	1987	1988	1989	1990	1991	1992	1993	1994
Sales ($ mil.)	12.0%	1,092	1,160	1,321	1,536	1,728	1,935	2,077	2,364	2,628	3,023
Net income ($ mil.)	6.6%	72	86	91	109	120	127	128	137	149	128
Income as % of sales	—	6.6%	7.4%	6.9%	7.1%	6.9%	6.6%	6.1%	5.8%	5.7%	4.2%
Earnings per share ($)	8.1%	1.24	1.49	1.57	1.96	2.20	2.31	2.37	2.58	2.88	2.50
Stock price – high ($)	—	20.06	23.25	35.88	33.75	33.13	39.19	55.50	61.00	66.75	69.13
Stock price – low ($)	—	13.72	18.63	21.56	24.63	26.25	27.19	30.25	39.00	51.63	51.50
Stock price – close ($)	13.0%	19.19	21.75	29.38	26.94	32.25	33.19	54.25	60.00	57.50	57.75
P/E – high	—	16	16	23	17	15	17	23	24	23	28
P/E – low	—	11	13	14	13	12	12	13	15	18	21
Dividends per share ($)	9.7%	0.34	0.36	0.39	0.43	0.50	0.57	0.61	0.65	0.71	0.78
Book value per share ($)	9.5%	8,96	10.07	10.49	11.69	13.43	15.07	16.26	17.78	18.58	20.35
Employees	9.1%	5,195	5,578	6,258	7,209	7,646	8,649	8,778	9,643	10,219	11,343

1994 Year-end:
Debt ratio: 3.6%
Return on equity: 13.0%
Cash (mil.): $15
Current ratio: 2.10
Long-term debt (mil.): $1
No. of shares (mil.): 51
Dividends
  Yield: 1.4%
  Payout: 31.2%
Market value (mil.): $2,931

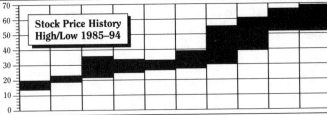

Stock Price History
High/Low 1985–94

ZENITH ELECTRONICS CORPORATION

OVERVIEW

Zenith is one company that's never going to overlook the Big Picture — especially not with the large-screen television market expected to explode over the next few years. The Glenview, Illinois, company sold a record number of TVs in 1994, outstripping the industry's overall unit sales growth of 10% and recording a near-doubling of sales of large-screen models. However, Zenith's 6-year money-losing streak continued, like a never-ending rerun.

The channel changed in July 1995 with the announcement that Zenith — the last US manufacturer of color televisions and picture tubes — was selling a majority stake to South Korea's LG Electronics for $350 million.

In addition to standard TVs, VCRs, and cable boxes, Zenith is pushing projection TVs, high-definition televisions (HDTV, to be introduced

to the US in 1997), and newly developed sets that operate in the 3 major broadcast systems used throughout North and South America. The company is tuning in to opportunities offered by cable and telephone companies, too. In 1996 it plans to offer TVs incorporating services available through the AT&T Home Information Center, and Zenith's *ScreenPlay* software now allows cable operators to create custom video displays for their customers.

Opportunities outside the US beckon also. NAFTA has created higher demand for picture tubes, and in 1995 the company struck a deal for a Canadian cable operator to use its HomeWorks Universal high-speed modem for an IBM work-at-home program in Ontario.

In 1995 Zenith president Albin Moschner replaced Jerry Pearlman as CEO.

WHEN

In 1915 Karl Hassel and R. H. G. Mathews, 2 ham radio operators, formed Chicago Radio Laboratory. In 1918 they began manufacturing radio equipment. In 1921 they were joined by Eugene McDonald Jr., a wealthy investor, who formed Zenith Radio Corporation (named after the call letters 9ZN of Hassel's amateur radio station) in 1923 to act as the sales agent for Chicago Radio Laboratory. Zenith was an early innovator in radio, developing the first portable radio (1924), the first home receiver to run on alternating current (1926), and the first push-button radio (1927). The Great Depression caused sales to drop 80%, but the company survived. It started a radio station and a TV station and began making hearing aids prior to WWII. During the war the company produced radar and communications equipment.

In 1948 Zenith bought the Rauland Corporation, which manufactured picture tubes, and produced its first black-and-white television sets. In 1956 Zenith's Robert Adler invented the first practical television remote control device. By 1959 the company was the black-and-white sales leader. In 1961 Zenith introduced its first line of color televisions. In the same year the FCC adopted Zenith's system for broadcasting FM radio in stereo.

During the 1970s and 1980s, Zenith faced the challenge of low-priced Japanese imports. Though it led the market in color television sales from 1972 to 1978, prices were held down by the Japanese "dumping" of television sets in the US market (selling sets in America for less than their cost). Under the pressure of

falling prices, the company moved some manufacturing operations to Mexico and Taiwan. Zenith chairman John Nevin lobbied Congress and filed suits against the Japanese TV manufacturers, eventually winning the battle but losing market share.

In 1979, moving away from radio and TV, Zenith acquired the Heath Company, makers of microcomputers and do-it-yourself electronics kits. Zenith's Data Systems subsidiary grew from sales of $10 million in 1980 to over $1 billion in 1989 on the strength of government and university contracts for its IBM-compatible personal computers; during that time, in 1984, the company changed its name to Zenith Electronics Corporation. In 1989 Zenith sold all computer operations, including the industry-leading laptop computer business, to Groupe Bull of France, using the proceeds to retire much of its debt. That year Zenith entered a joint venture with AT&T to develop an HDTV broadcast system.

In 1992 the company began consolidating its Mexican manufacturing operations, reorganizing its distribution, and cutting employment by about 1/5. Zenith sold its high-resolution monochrome monitor business in 1993 and its switch-mode power supply business in 1994. Its HDTV system was chosen in 1994 as the industry standard by a coalition of 3 groups that developed the systems. The company has benefited from the passage of NAFTA, which has lowered the duty on parts going to and from its Mexican manufacturing facilities.

Zenith plans to offer its first digital video disc (DVD) players in mid-1996.

NYSE symbol: ZE
Fiscal year ends: December 31

Chairman: Jerry K. Pearlman, age 55, $458,333 pay
CEO and President: Albin F. Moschner, age 42,
$276,667 pay (prior to promotion)
**EVP Sales and Marketing; President, Zenith Sales
Company:** Gerald M. McCarthy, age 53, $212,000 pay
SVP Finance and CFO: Kell B. Benson, age 47,
$157,833 pay
SVP Operations: Philip S. Thompson, age 45
SVP and General Counsel: Richard F. Vitkus, age 55
VP Human Resources: Michael J. Kaplan, age 55,
$137,167 pay
VP and Controller: Richard C. Lueck, age 51
**VP Research and Development and Network Systems
Engineering:** John W. Bowler
VP Consumer Products Sales: Larry G. Cockrell
Auditors: Arthur Andersen & Co., SC

WHERE

HQ: 1000 Milwaukee Ave., Glenview, IL 60025-2493
Phone: 847-391-7000
Fax: 847-391-8334 (Public Relations)

Zenith operates from 20 locations in the US: 6 produc-
tion, research, and administration facilities in the
Chicago area, 5 warehouses in Texas, one warehouse in
Arizona, and 8 domestic distribution centers throughout
the country. The company also has 15 locations in
Mexico, 3 in Canada, and one purchasing office in
Taiwan.

	1994 Sales		1994 Pretax Income	
	$ mil.	% of total	$ mil.	% of total
US	1,365	93	(8.4)	—
Other countries	104	7	(6.1)	—
Total	**1,469**	**100**	**(14.5)**	**—**

WHAT

Selected Products
Analog set-top boxes
Digital set-top boxes
High-definition television systems
HomeWorks high-speed cable modems
Large-screen televisions
Multistandard televisions
Picture tubes
Projection televisions
Remote controls
ScreenPlay software
StarSight interactive on-screen program guide
Television cabinets
Television/videocassette recorder combinations
Videocassette recorders

KEY COMPETITORS

ADC Telecommunications	NEC
Antec	Philips
Bose	Pioneer
Compaq	Recoton
Curtis Mathes	Samsung
DEC	Sanyo
Gemstar	Scientific-Atlanta
General Electric	Sharp
General Instrument	Siemens
Harman International	Sony
Hitachi	Sun Microsystems
IBM	Thomson S.A.
International Jensen	Toshiba
Matsushita	Universal Electronics
Mitsubishi	Yamaha
Motorola	

HOW MUCH

	Annual Growth	1985	1986	1987	1988	1989	1990	1991	1992	1993	1994
Sales ($ mil.)	(1.1%)	1,624	1,892	2,363	2,686	1,549	1,410	1,322	1,244	1,228	1,469
Net income ($ mil.)	7.0%	(8)	(10)	(19)	5	(68)	(63)	(52)	(106)	(97)	(14)
Income as % of sales	—	—	—	—	0.2%	—	—	—	—	—	—
Earnings per share ($)	0.3%	(0.33)	(0.43)	(0.78)	(0.20)	(2.56)	(2.36)	(1.79)	(3.59)	(3.01)	(0.34)
Stock price – high ($)	—	25.00	29.88	33.63	30.00	21.50	13.63	9.38	11.13	10.50	14.13
Stock price – low ($)	—	16.25	17.88	10.00	13.50	11.50	4.00	5.13	5.00	5.75	7.00
Stock price – close ($)	(6.1%)	20.50	21.88	14.75	19.00	12.75	6.63	7.38	5.88	7.00	11.63
P/E – high	—	—	—	—	150	—	—	—	—	—	—
P/E – low	—	—	—	—	68	—	—	—	—	—	—
Dividends per share ($)	—	0.00	0.00	0.00	0.00	0.00	0.00	0.00	0.00	0.00	0.00
Book value per share ($)	(13.7%)	18.90	18.49	18.45	18.84	14.90	12.33	10.60	6.94	4.25	5.00
Employees	(4.2%)	33,000	37,000	35,000	36,000	32,000	27,000	27,700	25,000	22,100	22,500

1994 Year-end:
Debt ratio: 44.4%
Return on equity: —
Cash (mil.): $9
Current ratio: 1.94
Long-term debt (mil.): $182
No. of shares (mil.): 46
Dividends
    Yield: —
    Payout: —
Market value (mil.): $531

**Stock Price History
High/Low 1985–94**

Selected Chicago Companies

ADVANCE ROSS CORPORATION

OVERVIEW

In 1996 Advance Ross was purchased by CUC International. Advance Ross owns European Tax-free Shopping (ETS), the world's leading consumer value-added tax (VAT) refund service. ETS relieves travelers of the burden of filing refund forms for items purchased at any of 90,000 affiliated merchants and allows them to receive their refunds at airport booths as they leave the country. Advance Ross also owns PPC Industries, a designer and maker of industrial pollution control devices.

The company's predecessor was started in 1914 as H.M. Byllesby & Co., a utility engineering company. By 1940 it had become an investment banking firm with which J. Patrick Lannan was associated. In 1958 Lannan merged 2 of the company's holdings, Advance Aluminum Castings and Ross Electronics, to form Advance Ross, which became a holding company for interests that included mineral-rich land and makers of airline crew seats, home electronics, and TV components. In the 1960s the company started making pollution control equipment; the other operations have since ceased. Lannan died in 1983, leaving his heirs and associates battling for control of the $100 million in assets he left to a Florida art foundation. CEO Harve Ferrill is the former son-in-law of the founder.

Advance Ross repositioned itself with the 1992 purchase of ETS, a small Swedish VAT refund company (in 1995 Sweden joined the EU, so its people are no longer eligible for the refunds). Aggressive marketing has lifted the number of affiliated merchants to 90,000 and expanded ETS worldwide. ETS is highly dependent on seasonal tourism and the vagaries of currency exchange rates.

In 1994 Washington State regulators sued Advance Ross to recover part of the $6 million cost of cleaning up of coal tar spilled by a PPC predecessor company between 1910 and 1924.

WHO

Chairman and CEO: Harve A. Ferrill, age 62, $662,500 pay
President and COO: Paul G. Yovovich, age 41, $475,003 pay
EVP Finance and Treasurer: Randy M. Joseph, age 36, $110,000 pay
Secretary and Assistant Treasurer: Constance Schirmer
Auditors: Deloitte & Touche LLP

WHERE

HQ: 233 S. Wacker Dr., Ste. 9700, Chicago, IL 60606-6502
Phone: 312-382-1100   **Fax:** 312-382-1109

	1994 ETS Sales
	% of total
Japan	18
Russia	10
United States	10
Germany	5
Hong Kong	3
Egypt	2
Poland	2
Switzerland	2
Thailand	2
Other countries	46
Total	**100**

WHAT

	1994 Sales	
	$ mil.	% total
ETS services	56.9	87
Pollution control equipment	9.6	13
Total	**66.5**	**100**

Selected Affiliated Stores

Armani	KaDeWe
Chanel	Karstadt
Gucci	Loewe
Harrods	Marks & Spencer

KEY COMPETITORS

Governmental customs services
Local VAT refund operators

HOW MUCH

Subsidiary FY ends: December 31	Annual Growth	1989	1990	1991	1992	1993	1994
Sales ($ mil.)	89.8%	2.7	5.5	17.6	11.0	50.3	66.5
Net income ($ mil.)	75.4%	0.5	2.7	7.3	0.7	5.1	8.3
Income as % of sales	—	18.5%	49.1%	41.5%	6.4%	10.1%	12.6%
Earnings per share ($)	71.5%	0.13	0.69	1.97	0.18	1.19	1.93
Stock price – high ($)	—	7.50	5.88	6.00	8.19	18.63	30.25
Stock price – low ($)	—	4.50	4.13	4.25	4.38	6.50	14.75
Stock price – close ($)	31.6%	5.06	5.19	4.69	7.88	18.63	20.00
P/E – high	—	58	9	3	46	16	16
P/E – low	—	35	6	2	24	6	8
Dividends per share ($)	—	0.00	0.00	0.00	0.00	0.00	0.00
Book value per share ($)	21.7%	3.58	4.28	6.24	5.48	6.55	9.73
Employees	78.6%	18	23	31	196	253	327

1994 Year-end:
Debt ratio: 24.9%
Return on equity: 29.7%
Cash (mil.): $13.5
Current ratio: 1.91
Long-term debt (mil.): $6.7
No. of shares (mil.): 3.4
Dividends
  Yield: —
  Payout: —
Market value (mil.): $69.0

ALTERNATIVE RESOURCES

ALTERNATIVE RESOURCES

OVERVIEW

Alternative Resources Corporation (ARC) is taking advantage of the trends toward downsizing and the outsourcing of information services tasks in large corporations. Offering cost-effective alternatives to in-house computer operations, ARC provides technical resources in 5 areas: mainframe operations, desktop to workstation computing, voice and data communications, help desk, and client/server. The company has a roster of more than 25,000 technical professionals for both short-term and long-term contracts with 600 of North America's largest companies. ARC serves its clients through a network of 40 branch offices and 4 client support sites in the US and Canada. EDS, ARC's #1 customer, accounted for 12% of revenues in 1994.

The company was founded in 1988 by Larry Kane, a 27-year veteran of the information technology industry, and investor Wind Point Partners. By the end of 1991 the company had 15 centers across the US, reflecting the success of ARC's flexible package of outsourcing options. The company's Smartsourcing option, which gives clients outside technical personnel while allowing them to maintain strategic control and management of a project, proved popular. ARC added 4 more offices in 1992, 5 in 1993, and 9 more in 1994, including its first Canadian site (in Toronto). ARC went public in 1994; Wind Point owns 25%, Kane 16%.

ARC is pursuing an aggressive expansion strategy, targeting new clients in its core market (*FORTUNE* 1000 firms with complex information service operations) and adding account managers to its branch offices. It is also targeting middle market firms (with sales between $50 million and $100 million). ARC plans to double the number of its branch offices by the year 2000.

In early 1995 ARC opened offices in Boca Raton, Florida; Colorado Springs, Colorado; Kansas City, Missouri; and Milwaukee.

WHO

Chairman, President, and CEO: Larry I. Kane, age 54, $240,000 pay
VP Operations: Lisa A. DesCoteaux, age 36, $162,000 pay
VP Finance, CFO, Secretary, and Treasurer: Michael E. Harris, age 34, $150,000 pay
VP Human Resources: Silvia U. Masini, age 40, $100,000 pay
Auditors: KPMG Peat Marwick LLP

WHERE

HQ: Alternative Resources Corporation, 75 Tri-State International, Ste. 100, Lincolnshire, IL 60069
Phone: 847-317-1000   **Fax:** 847-317-1008

WHAT

	1994 Sales	
	$ mil.	% of total
Tactical staffing	64.6	68
Strategic staffing	28.8	31
Professional services	1.1	1
Total	**94.5**	**100**

Selected Services
Data center consulting services (information services operations consulting)
Smartsourcing (client-managed outsourcing personnel)
Stategic resources (projects requiring technical personnel for at least one year)
Tactical resources (short- to long-term assignments of technical personnel)

KEY COMPETITORS

Brandon Systems
Cambridge Horizons
Computer Horizons
Computer Sciences
Corporate Staffing Resources
DEC
Hewlett-Packard
IBM
Keane
Kelly Services
Manpower
Olsten
On Assignment
Robert Half
Technalysis
Uniforce Temporary

HOW MUCH

Nasdaq symbol: ALRC FY ends: December 31	Annual Growth	1989	1990	1991	1992	1993	1994
Sales ($ mil.)	100.4%	2.9	7.6	13.9	27.9	53.1	94.5
Net income ($ mil.)	—	(0.4)	(0.8)	0.0	1.6	3.2	6.2
Income as % of sales	—	—	—	—	5.7%	6.1%	6.6%
Earnings per share ($)	93.1%	—	—	—	0.11	0.24	0.41
Stock price – high ($)		—	—	—	—	—	15.88
Stock price – low ($)		—	—	—	—	—	8.13
Stock price – close ($)		—	—	—	—	—	15.75
P/E – high		—	—	—	—	—	39
P/E – low		—	—	—	—	—	20
Dividends per share ($)		—	—	—	—	—	0.00
Book value per share ($)		—	—	—	—	—	1.35
Employees	60.1%	—	—	—	—	208	333

1994 Year-end:
Debt ratio: 0.0%
Return on equity: 36.2%
Cash (mil.): $9.2
Current ratio: 4.23
Long-term debt (mil.): $0.0
No. of shares (mil.): 14.8
Dividends
  Yield: —
  Payout: —
Market value (mil.): $232.8

AMERICAN BAR ASSOCIATION

OVERVIEW

What do you call 200 lawyers at the bottom of the ocean? Some would say it's a good start, but the roughly 350,000 members of the American Bar Association (ABA) may beg to differ. The ABA is the largest voluntary professional association in the world. Membership is open to members of state and territory bars in good standing. Other legal professionals, such as legal assistants and educators, can become associates. The ABA has more than 80 commissions, committees, and task forces, which deal with specific legal issues and make policy recommendations. The association gets most of its revenues from dues but also earns more than $7 million from the publication of nearly 100 periodicals.

In 1878 Simeon Baldwin, then a faculty member at Yale Law School, proposed a meeting to organize an association of American lawyers. In August of that year, 100 lawyers from 21 states met in Saratoga, New York, and drafted the constitution for the American Bar Association. Its objectives were "to advance the science of jurisprudence, promote the administration of justice and uniformity of legislation throughout the union, uphold the honor of the profession of the law, and encourage cordial intercourse among members." The ABA started with 289 members.

As the ABA grew it became more influential. Since the early 1950s, US presidents and the Senate have consulted its Federal Judiciary Committee on the qualifications of potential judicial appointments. The ABA's power in that process was criticized in the mid-1980s as unduly political.

In 1992, when a policy was adopted to oppose laws restricting abortion rights, more than 3,000 lawyers canceled their membership. One year later, the Massachusetts School of Law sued the ABA, claiming that its law school–accrediting practices were an attempt to control salaries, employment conditions, and tuitions. In 1995 the ABA agreed to change its accreditation process after the Justice Department said the association had requirements that raised costs without improving the quality of legal education. Also in 1995, Roberta Cooper Ramo was elected as the ABA's first female president.

WHO

President: Roberta Cooper Ramo
Executive Director: Robert A. Stein
General Counsel: Darryl Depriest
Associate Executive Director, Policy and Governance Group: Marina B. Jacks
Associate Executive Director, Governmental Affairs and Public Services Group: Robert D. Evans
Associate Executive Director, Financial Resources Group: John E. Hanle Jr.
Associate Executive Director, Administration: Elain Weiss
Editor and Publisher, *ABA Journal*: Gary Hengstler
Director Human Resources: Nina B. Eidell
Auditors: Ernst & Young LLP

WHERE

HQ: 750 N. Lake Shore Dr., Chicago, IL 60611
Phone: 312-988-6179 **Fax:** 312-988-5100

WHAT

	1994 Revenues	
	$ mil.	% of total
Dues	58.8	52
Grants & contributions	15.2	13
Meeting fees	13.3	12
Publications	7.4	6
Advertising	5.6	5
Other	13.8	12
Total	**114.1**	**100**

Selected Committees, Commissions, and Other Entities
Amicus Curiae Briefs
Ethics and Professional Responsibility
Federal Judiciary
Group and Prepaid Legal Services
Impaired Attorneys
Law Library of Congress
Lawyer Competence
Lawyer Referral and Information Service
Lawyers' Professional Liability
Legal Aid and Indigent Defendants
Legal Assistance for Military Personnel
Legal Problems of the Elderly
Medical Professional Liability
Opportunities for Minorities in the Profession
Professional Discipline
Women in the Profession

KEY COMPETITORS

Nolo Press
Reed Elsevier
Thomson Corp.

Viacom
West Publishing
Wolters Kluwer

HOW MUCH

Trade association FY ends: August 31	Annual Growth	1989	1990	1991	1992	1993	1994
Revenues ($ mil.)	5.9%	85.7	90.1	105.4	111.0	110.3	114.1
Membership	0.1%	346,007	350,990	357,993	362,104	357,032	348,568
Employees	—	—	—	—	—	—	700

AMERICAN CLASSIC VOYAGES CO.

OVERVIEW

American Classic operates 2 cruise lines. The Delta Queen Steamboat Co. is the #1 provider of overnight passenger cruises in the continental US. It operates 3 paddle wheel–driven boats that cruise the Mississippi, Ohio, and other rivers. American Hawaii Cruises operates 2 cruise ships that sail around the Hawaiian Islands. The company also owns the Maison Dupuy Hotel in New Orleans. An investment group controlled by famed Chicago investor Sam Zell and board member Ann Lurie owns 45.9% of the company.

American Classic traces its roots back to 1890, when steamboat captain Gordon Greene acquired the *H. K. Bedford* to haul freight and passengers on US rivers. The Greene Line began to focus more on passengers as newer forms of transportation took over the freight business. In 1946 the company bought the steamboat *Delta Queen* (built in 1927 to travel between Sacramento and San Francisco), which it moved to the Mississippi River. In 1976 the company (which had changed its name to the Delta Queen Steamboat Co.) launched a 2nd luxury steamboat, the *Mississippi Queen*. Delta Queen went public in 1992.

The company focused on offering nostalgic river cruises that included everything from barbershop quartets and ice cream socials to concerts by the Glenn Miller Orchestra. It expanded into the Hawaiian Islands in 1993 when it acquired bankrupt American Global Line, which operated inter-island cruises.

In 1994 the company changed its name to American Classic Voyages. That same year it traded lawsuits with Newport News Shipyard over Newport News's renovation of American Classic's cruise ship the *S. S. Independence*, which was cited by the Coast Guard for 157 deficiencies following the renovation.

In 1995 the company launched its 3rd riverboat, the *American Queen*.

WHO

Chairman: Samuel Zell, age 53
President and CEO: Philip C. Calian, age 32
EVP Operations American Hawaii; President and COO, American Hawaii Cruises: R. Anthony McKinnon, age 55, $280,000 pay
EVP Operations Delta Queen; President and COO, The Delta Queen Steamboat Co.: Jeffrey D. Krida, age 49, $200,031 pay
EVP, CFO, and Treasurer: Steven M. Isaacson, age 40, $185,000 pay
VP and General Counsel: Jordan B. Allen, age 32
VP Human Resources, The Delta Queen Steamboat Co.: Craig T. Keller
Auditors: KPMG Peat Marwick LLP

WHERE

HQ: 2 N. Riverside Plaza, Chicago, IL 60606
Phone: 312-258-1890   **Fax:** 312-466-6001

WHAT

Cruise Lines

American Hawaii Cruises
Constitution (682 feet, 788 passengers)
Independence (682 feet, 802 passengers)

The Delta Queen Steamboat Co. (Arkansas, Atchafalaya, Cumberland, Mississippi, Ohio, and Tennessee Rivers)
American Queen (418 feet, 436 passengers)
Delta Queen (285 feet, 174 passengers)
Mississippi Queen (382 feet, 414 passengers)

Hotel

Maison Dupuy Hotel (New Orleans, 198 rooms)

KEY COMPETITORS

Accor
Carlson
Carnival Corp.
Europa Cruises
Hilton
Hyatt
ITT Corp.
Marriott International
Royal Caribbean Cruises

HOW MUCH

Nasdaq symbol: AMCV FY ends: December 31	Annual Growth	1989	1990	1991	1992	1993[1]	1994
Sales ($ mil.)	39.8%	—	51.2	61.7	66.7	109.0	195.2
Net income ($ mil.)	—	—	2.0	2.3	9.2	3.8	(1.0)
Income as % of sales	—	—	3.9%	3.8%	13.8%	3.4%	—
Earnings per share ($)	—	—	0.31	0.60	0.81	0.32	(0.07)
Stock price – high ($)	—	—	—	—	16.25	22.58	19.50
Stock price – low ($)	—	—	—	—	9.75	11.38	12.00
Stock price – close ($)	0.9%	—	—	—	13.25	17.38	13.50
P/E – high	—	—	—	—	20	71	—
P/E – low	—	—	—	—	12	36	—
Dividends per share ($)	100.0%	—	—	—	0.04	0.12	0.16
Book value per share ($)	24.6%	—	—	—	3.84	6.18	5.97
Employees	90.9%	—	—	—	617	1,849	2,248

1994 Year-end:
Debt ratio: 44.2%
Return on equity: —
Cash (mil.): $12.2
Current ratio: 0.32
Long-term debt (mil.): $65.0
No. of shares (mil.): 13.8
Dividends
 Yield: 1.2%
 Payout: —
Market value (mil.): $185.8

[1] 9-month fiscal year

ANDREW CORPORATION

OVERVIEW

Getting away from it all is becoming increasingly difficult, thanks to Andrew Corporation, a global manufacturer and supplier of telecommunications system equipment and service. Andrew's major wireless communications markets include cellular phone, land mobile radio, and long distance companies; other corporations; and domestic and foreign governments. The company's products include equipment for TV broadcasting, for military radar and communications systems, and for corporate data networks. Andrew has manufacturing, distribution, sales, and engineering offices in 16 countries. New markets include South America and Russia.

Andrew has shown a profit every year since its founding as a partnership in 1937. It was incorporated in 1947. The market slowdown of the mid-1980s and consequent drop in sales and profits resulted in management's restructuring the company in order to take advantage of potential cellular and computer network markets. To bolster the company's networking business, Andrew acquired KMV Systems in 1989 and Emerald Technology in 1990.

Andrew continues to take advantage of the rapidly growing personal communications market. In 1993 Andrew received a record-setting order ($42.8 million) with the signing of a deal to help build Argentina's cellular phone network. Operations in Russia include joint ventures to help build that country's telecommunications infrastructure, including recently completed digital fiber-optic networks in Moscow and St. Petersburg.

Andrew set record highs for orders in fiscal 1995, with net income increasing 53% to $67.8 million and sales hitting $626.5 million, a 12% increase. Cellular, land mobile, and broadcast markets led an upsurge but were offset by lower revenues from the network and defense businesses.

WHO

Chairman, President, and CEO: Floyd L. English, age 60, $1,527,955 pay
Group VP Network Group and Corporate Marketing: John B. Scott, age 53, $481,134 pay
Group VP Communications Products: Thomas E. Charlton, age 58, $474,594 pay
VP Finance and Administration and CFO: Charles R. Nicholas, age 48, $586,908 pay
VP Corporate Research and Development: Eric L. Brooker, age 67
Auditors: Ernst & Young LLP

WHERE

HQ: 10500 W. 153rd St., Orland Park, IL 60462
Phone: 708-349-3300   **Fax:** 708-349-5943

	1994 Sales	
	$ mil.	% of total
US	415.5	74
Europe	94.6	17
Australasia	29.3	6
Canada	19.1	3
Total	**558.5**	**100**

WHAT

	1994 Sales	
	$ mil.	% of total
Commercial	457.8	83
Network	52.2	9
Government	43.6	8
Adjustments	4.9	—
Total	**558.5**	**100**

Selected Products
Commercial (microwave antenna systems, coaxial cable systems and bulk cables, antennas)
Network (local-area network gateways, terminal emulators, file transfer software, adapter cards)
Government (electronic scanning and communication receivers, specialized microwave antenna systems)

KEY COMPETITORS

Alcatel Alsthom	IBM	Nippon Steel
Ericsson	Mitsubishi	Vertex Communications

HOW MUCH

Nasdaq symbol: ANDW FY ends: September 30	Annual Growth	1989	1990	1991	1992	1993	1994
Sales ($ mil.)	13.1%	301.9	366.0	416.2	442.0	430.8	558.5
Net income ($ mil.)	22.3%	16.2	18.2	22.2	25.0	27.9	44.4
Income as % of sales	—	5.4%	5.0%	5.3%	5.7%	6.5%	7.9%
Earnings per share ($)	25.8%	0.54	0.60	0.76	0.87	1.09	1.70
Stock price – high ($)	—	5.83	5.78	8.17	10.83	19.33	53.75
Stock price – low ($)	—	4.00	3.44	4.44	4.94	8.67	24.00
Stock price – close ($)	57.2%	5.44	4.86	7.56	10.83	17.11	52.25
P/E – high	—	11	10	11	12	18	32
P/E – low	—	7	6	6	6	8	14
Dividends per share ($)	—	0.00	0.00	0.00	0.00	0.00	0.00
Book value per share ($)	12.0%	6.06	6.68	7.59	7.85	8.72	10.68
Employees	0.4%	2,870	3,200	3,370	3,040	2,294	2,924

1994 Year-end:
Debt ratio: 15.5%
Return on equity: 18.0%
Cash (mil.): $40.3
Current ratio: 2.84
Long-term debt (mil.): $45.5
No. of shares (mil.): 25.5
Dividends
  Yield: —
  Payout: —
Market value (mil.): $1,334.7
R&D as % of sales: 4.6%

CAPSURE HOLDINGS CORP.

OVERVIEW

Capsure Holdings is an insurance holding company whose subsidiaries focus on specialty insurance. United Capitol (bought in 1990) writes policies for clients like asbestos abatement companies, whose high risks command high premiums. In the 1990s this niche was unexpectedly competitive, which kept premium rates low. Western Surety (bought in 1992) handles low-risk policies, mainly small-fidelity and noncontract surety bonds, and errors and omissions insurance. Capsure's 3rd major subsidiary, Universal Surety (bought in 1994), writes small-contract and other surety bonds, primarily in Texas. Capsure operates in all 50 states through 120,000 agents.

The company is the successor of Nucorp, Inc., a small oil and gas company that declared bankruptcy in 1982. After Nucorp emerged from bankruptcy in 1986 with about $300 million in tax-loss carryforwards, Chicago financier Sam Zell added Nucorp to his portfolio. Zell, a renowned bottom-feeder, redirected Nucorp's development from fuels to insurance, buying United Capitol and Western Surety, one of the largest writers of miscellaneous bonds in the US. In 1993 the company sold its oil and gas interests and changed its name to Capsure (combining *Capital* and *Surety*). Zell's entities, Equity Holdings and Equity Group Investments, control about 26% of Capsure.

Capsure's strategy is to grow by acquisitions, but increasing competition for acquisitions in the quickly-consolidating insurance industry has made bargains hard to come by, slowing external growth; in addition, there has been little growth in existing businesses. Natural disasters (including earthquakes and floods) in the 1990s dragged down United Capitol's (and therefore Capsure's) earnings in 1994 despite the application of the remaining Nucorp tax losses to increase income.

WHO

Chairman and CEO: Samuel Zell, age 53, $150,000 pay
President; Chairman, President, and CEO, United Capitol: Bruce A. Esselborn, age 52, $500,000 pay
President and CEO, Western Surety Company: Joe P. Kirby, age 41, $500,000 pay
EVP, General Counsel, and Secretary, Western Surety Company: Dan L. Kirby, age 48, $500,000 pay
SVP and CFO: Mary Jane Robertson, $230,000 pay
VP and General Counsel: Kelly L. Stonebraker, age 40
Director of Human Resources: Laura Rode
Auditors: Coopers & Lybrand L.L.P.

WHERE

HQ: 2 North Riverside Plaza, Chicago, IL 60606
Phone: 312-879-1900   **Fax:** 312-454-9946

WHAT

	1994 Assets	
	$ mil.	% of total
Cash & equivalents	4.1	1
Mortgage-backed derivatives	42.7	8
Collateralized mortage obligations	113.9	21
Asset-backed securities	59.7	11
Other investments	85.5	15
Goodwill	84.1	15
Other	163.4	29
Total	**553.4**	**100**

	1994 Sales	
	$ mil.	% of total
Net premiums	92.5	82
Investment & other income	20.2	18
Total	**112.7**	**100**

Primary Subsidiaries
United Capitol Insurance Co.
Universal Surety of America
Western Surety Co.

KEY COMPETITORS

Capital Guaranty
Chubb
CIGNA
Executive Risk
Mountbatten
Old Republic
Penn-America
USF&G

HOW MUCH

NYSE symbol: CSH FY ends: December 31	Annual Growth	1989	1990	1991	1992	1993	1994
Assets ($ mil.)	72.1%	36.7	194.3	197.2	417.6	530.1	553.4
Net income ($ mil.)	83.1%	0.7	5.3	7.2	10.7	16.3	14.4
Income as % of assets	—	2.0%	2.7%	3.7%	2.6%	3.1%	2.6%
Earnings per share ($)	46.7%	0.14	0.62	0.79	0.88	1.08	0.95
Stock price – high ($)	—	9.88	9.38	9.00	14.38	19.38	16.13
Stock price – low ($)	—	5.50	4.63	4.25	6.88	12.25	12.13
Stock price – close ($)	13.2%	7.88	5.13	7.13	13.63	13.50	14.63
P/E – high	—	71	15	11	16	18	17
P/E – low	—	39	8	5	8	11	13
Dividends per share ($)	0.00	0.00	0.00	0.00	0.00	0.00	0.00
Book value per share ($)	23.7%	5.04	6.25	7.63	8.89	13.80	14.61
Employees	151.2%	6	49	52	543	574	600

1994 Year-end:
Equity as % of assets: 40.6%
Return on equity: 6.7%
Return on assets: 2.8%
Long-term debt (mil.): $71.0
No. of shares (mil.): 15.4
Dividends
    Yield: —
    Payout: —
Market value (mil.): $225.1
Sales (mil.): $112.7

CDW COMPUTER CENTERS, INC.

OVERVIEW

Things are on the upswing at CDW Computer Centers, a national direct marketer of microcomputer products at discount prices. CDW (short for computer discount warehouse) has increased the number and frequency of its catalog mailings, expanded its ad space in national computer magazines (*PC World*, *PC Magazine*, and *Mac World*), added new multimedia products to its line of more than 20,000 items related to DOS/Windows and Macintosh-based microcomputers, and expanded its staff of account executives to handle the growth. CDW operates 2 retail showrooms in the Chicago area in addition to its direct-mail business. Founder Michael Krasny owns 68% of the company stock.

Krasny started CDW in 1983 at age 29. Weary of selling used cars at his father's Chicago lot, Krasny quit but soon ran out of money and was forced to sell his personal computer. A classified ad in the *Chicago Tribune* generated phenomenal response, and Krasny's computer sold almost instantly. When calls kept coming in, Krasny bought more computers and sold them to people responding to the original ad, and his mail-order business was under way. The company's first catalog was launched in 1987, and its first retail showroom opened in Chicago in 1989. CDW went public in 1993 and completed a secondary offering in 1994.

The company's move to its new Buffalo Grove, Illinois, headquarters in 1994 more than doubled its warehouse, office, and showroom space, but additional space is already being sought in anticipation of growth.

CDW planned to diversify with more emphasis on multimedia and videoconferencing products while hiring additional account executives to service the increased volume. The company believes Microsoft's Windows 95 will be a boon to sales of more powerful CPUs and accessories.

WHO

Chairman, CEO, Secretary, and Treasurer: Michael P. Krasny, age 41, $471,311 pay
President: Gregory C. Zeman, age 36, $1,079,164 pay
CFO: Harry J. Harczak Jr., age 38
VP Operations: Daniel B. Kass, age 38, $519,941 pay
VP Human Resources: Mary C. Gerlits, age 36, $151,165 pay
VP Finance, Controller, and Chief Accounting Officer: Daniel F. Callen, age 37, $150,060 pay
VP Purchasing: Paul A. Kozak, age 30
Auditors: Coopers & Lybrand L.L.P.

WHERE

HQ: 1020 E. Lake Cook Rd., Buffalo Grove, IL 60089
Phone: 847-465-6000   **Fax:** 847-465-6800

WHAT

	1994 Sales % of total
Notebook & laptop computers	23
Printers	17
Software	11
Data storage devices	8
Desktop computers	8
Network products	8
Video	8
Add-on boards/memory	7
Communications	6
Other accessories	4
Total	**100**

KEY COMPETITORS

Circuit City
Compaq
CompUSA
Damark
DEC
Dell
Egghead
ELEK-TEK
Gateway 2000
Global Direct Mail
IBM
InaCom
Inmac
Intelligent Electronics
Micro Center
Micro Warehouse
MicroAge
PC Connection
Tandy
Tiger Direct
Vanstar

HOW MUCH

Nasdaq symbol: CDWC FY ends: December 31	Annual Growth	1989	1990	1991	1992	1993	1994	1994 Year-end:
Sales ($ mil.)	49.3%	—	83.1	101.5	138.6	270.9	413.3	Debt ratio: 0.0%
Net income ($ mil.)	78.2%	—	1.2	3.7	1.3	12.6	12.1	Return on equity: 31.2%
Income as % of sales	—	—	1.4%	3.7%	0.9%	4.7%	2.9%	Cash (mil.): $22.6
Earnings per share ($)	1.1%	—	—	—	—	0.90	0.91	Current ratio: 3.22
Stock price – high ($)	—	—	—	—	—	14.25	34.75	Long-term debt (mil.): $0.0
Stock price – low ($)	—	—	—	—	—	6.75	13.38	No. of shares (mil.): 13.8
Stock price – close ($)	143.8%	—	—	—	—	14.00	34.13	Dividends
P/E – high	—	—	—	—	—	16	38	Yield: —
P/E – low	—	—	—	—	—	8	15	Payout: —
Dividends per share ($)	—	—	—	—	—	0.00	0.00	Market value (mil.): $470.9
Book value per share ($)	135.5%	—	—	—	—	1.72	4.05	
Employees	48.6%	—	80	100	135	247	390	

CELEX GROUP, INC.

OVERVIEW

"Success is a journey, not a destination" is a favorite slogan at Celex Group, and it should know. The company is a leading maker of personal motivation and self-improvement products such as posters, desktop art, personalized gifts and awards, apparel, greeting cards, and coffee mugs adorned with a variety of mottos ("Energy and persistence will conquer all things," and "It takes both rain and sunshine to make a rainbow"). It also sells audiotapes by such motivational speakers as Zig Ziglar and Anthony Robbins. Celex sells its products through more than 90 company-owned and franchised Successories stores, through a Successories catalog, and through licensed domestic and international distributors. Founder and CEO Mac Anderson owns 17.9% of the company.

Anderson founded the company in 1985 to sell wall plaques and other gifts to corporations for their top-performing employees. He began to add other products to his line, and in 1988 he introduced his first catalog. The company went public in 1990 (and began trading on NASDAQ in 1993). It opened its first retail store, in Naperville, Illinois, in 1991.

Celex grew rapidly as the company expanded both its product lines and its target markets. The retail stores expanded the company's reach beyond corporate customers to include general consumers looking for a motivational boost.

In 1995 the company found out that the successful journey can have some serious bumps in the road. Celex posted a $7.7 million loss after insufficient management controls led to inventory problems, including difficulties with order fulfillment during the Christmas season and inventory discrepancies that forced the company to restate earnings. Celex shuffled its management and introduced new inventory control systems.

WHO

Chairman and CEO: Arnold M. "Mac" Anderson, age 49, $175,000 pay
President, COO, and CFO: James M. Beltrame, age 51
SVP and Creative Director: Michael H. McKee, age 41, $100,000 pay
SVP Business Development: Peter C. Walts, age 34
SVP Direct Marketing: Neil J. Sexton, age 36
Director Personnel: Linda Sondgeroth
Auditors: Price Waterhouse LLP

WHERE

HQ: 919 Springer Dr., Lombard, IL 60148
Phone: 708-953-8440   **Fax:** 708-953-2110

	1995 US Stores
	No.
California	9
Illinois	9
Florida	8
Indiana	6
New York	5
Georgia	4
Michigan	4
Texas	4
Other states	43
Total	**92**

WHAT

	1995 Sales
	% of total
Retail sales	48
Direct marketing	47
Wholesale, international & other	5
Total	**100**

KEY COMPETITORS

American Greetings
Baldwin Cooke
Cole National
Cyrk
Gibson Greetings
Hallmark
HA-LO
Nightingale-Conant
Tandycrafts

HOW MUCH

Nasdaq symbol: CLXG FY ends: April 30	Annual Growth	1990	1991	1992	1993	1994	1995
Sales ($ mil.)	52.5%	5.3	5.6	5.7	13.3	29.8	44.1
Net income ($ mil.)	—	(1.0)	0.6	0.1	1.0	2.2	(7.7)
Income as % of sales	—	—	10.9%	1.8%	7.7%	7.4%	—
Earnings per share ($)	—	(0.39)	0.23	0.04	0.30	0.50	(1.60)
Stock price – high ($)[1]	—	—	—	—	3.67	18.00	22.00
Stock price – low ($)[1]	—	—	—	—	0.67	10.83	12.00
Stock price – close ($)[1]	82.2%	—	—	—	5.50	24.17	18.25
P/E – high	—	—	—	—	12	36	—
P/E – low	—	—	—	—	2	22	—
Dividends per share ($)	—	—	—	—	0.00	0.00	0.00
Book value per share ($)	27.3%	—	—	—	1.40	3.47	2.27
Employees	69.8%	—	—	—	179	388	516

[1] Stock prices are for the prior calendar year.

1995 Year-end:
Debt ratio: 44.7%
Return on equity: —
Cash (mil.): $1.2
Current ratio: 2.02
Long-term debt (mil.): $8.3
No. of shares (mil.): 5.1
Dividends
  Yield: —
  Payout: —
Market value (mil.): $93.4

CHICAGO BEARS FOOTBALL CLUB, INC.

OVERVIEW

"You're the pride and joy of Illinois, Chicago Bears, bear down." So goes the last line of the fight song for one of the most storied teams in NFL history. One of the league's oldest surviving franchises, the Bears have won 8 NFL championships, and its rosters have included such legends as Red Grange, Dick Butkus, Gale Sayers, and Walter Payton. The team gets most of its revenue from the NFL's TV contract, which is shared by the league's 30 teams. The club is headed by chairman Ed McCaskey, grandson of founder George "Papa Bear" Halas. The Bears are owned primarily by the McCaskey family.

In 1920 A. E. Staley, owner of Staley Starchworks, asked Halas to run his team, the Decatur Staleys, in the newly formed American Professional Football Association (which changed its name to the NFL in 1922). In 1921 Staley gave the team to Halas. The team moved to Chicago and began playing at Wrigley Field. In 1922 it changed its name to the Chicago Bears. The Bears won their first NFL championship in 1932, and the "Monsters of the Midway" (a name borrowed from the then forlorn University of Chicago football team) remained dominant through the early 1960s. The team moved to Soldier Field in 1971 and began a resurgence in the early 1980s after hiring former Bear player Mike Ditka to coach the team in 1982. Led by Ditka, the team won the Super Bowl in 1986. After a 5-11 record in 1992, Ditka was fired in early 1993. He was replaced by Dave Wannstedt.

Like many sports teams these days, the Bears are seeking ways to boost revenues in other areas. McCaskey has for years been trying to get a new stadium with money-generating luxury skyboxes. Proposals have included remodeling Soldier Field and constructing a new domed stadium. In 1995 a group of investors proposed building a 75,000-seat, open-air stadium in Gary, Indiana, and hoped to lure the Bears across the state line to play in it.

WHO

Chairman: Edward W. McCaskey, age 76
President and CEO: Michael B. McCaskey, age 52
VP Operations and CFO: Ted Phillips, age 38
VP: Tim McCaskey
Director Administration (HR): Tim LeFevour, age 39
Director Marketing and Broadcasting: Ken Valdiserri, age 37
Director Public Relations: Bryan Harlan, age 33
Controller: Scott Worthem, age 29
Head Coach: David R. Wannstedt, age 43
Director Player Personnel: Rod Graves, age 36

WHERE

HQ: Halas Hall, 250 N. Washington Rd., Lake Forest, IL 60045
Phone: 847-295-6600   **Fax:** 847-295-5238

The Bears compete in the Central Division of the National Football Conference. They play their home games at Soldier Field in Chicago.

WHAT

	1995 Sales	
	$ mil.	% of total
Media revenues	41.3	63
Gate receipts	15.3	24
Stadium revenues	6.0	9
Other	2.5	4
Total	**65.1**	**100**

1994 Offense
Passing touchdowns (19)
Rushing touchdowns (10)
Return touchdowns (1)
Field goals (21)
Yards gained
  Passing (3,091)
  Rushing (1,588)

1994 Defense
Interceptions (12)
Quarterback sacks (28)
Yards allowed
  Passing (3,087)
  Rushing (1,922)

KEY COMPETITORS

Detroit Lions
Green Bay Packers
Minnesota Vikings
Tampa Bay Buccaneers

HOW MUCH

Private company FY ends: Last day of Feb.	Annual Growth	1990	1991	1992	1993	1994	1995
Sales ($ mil.)	6.6%	—	50.4	56.6	55.8	65.4	65.1
Player costs ($ mil.)	15.8%	—	20.4	22.4	28.8	35.3	36.7
Total attendance	(1.0%)	489,976	481,018	491,778	478,507	465,832	468,015
Games won	—	6	11	11	5	7	9
Games lost	—	10	5	5	11	9	7
Division finish	—	4	2	2	3	3	2
Winning percentage	—	.375	.688	.688	.313	.438	.563
Employees	—	—	—	—	—	—	150

Note: Fiscal-year numbers are for the prior calendar-year schedule.

CRAIN COMMUNICATIONS INC

OVERVIEW

The Crains have been whooping it up in the publishing business for 8 decades. Owned and managed by family members, Crain Communications specializes in the publication of business, consumer, and trade journals in both the US and Europe. Chicago-based Crain publishes about 2 dozen magazines and journals, including its flagship magazine, *Advertising Age*, and business journals (*Crain's Chicago Business, Crain's Cleveland Business, Crain's Detroit Business*, and *Crain's New York Business*). It also publishes industry-specific magazines such as *American Laundry Digest, Automotive News, Modern Healthcare*, and *Urethanes Technology* (Europe). Crain also owns a Florida radio station (WWUS) and a news service, and it rents out its subscriber database.

The firm was founded by Gustavus Dedman (G. D.) Crain in 1916 in Louisville, Kentucky, with a staff of 3. It produced 2 publications — *Class* (later renamed *Business Marketing*) and *Hospital Management* (sold in the 1950s) — and relocated to Chicago later that year.

In 1930 the company launched *Advertising Age* and adopted the name Advertising Publications Inc. Over time the company broadened its publications beyond advertising, and in 1969 it changed its name to Crain Communications, Inc.

G. D. Crain continued to lead the company until his death in 1973. That year, veteran employee Sidney Bernstein, who had served as president since 1964, gave up the presidency to Rance Crain, G. D.'s elder son. Crain's widow, Gertrude, became chairman, and Keith Crain (Rance's brother) was subsequently appointed VC.

In 1986 Crain purchased *Media World*, the #1 UK media magazine at that time. By the early 1990s the company was publishing 3 magazines in Europe. The company bought *RCR Radio Communications Report* (wireless communications) in 1992. The next year, in a move beyond its standard publishing format, it began sending daily fax updates to subscribers on electronic media and auto industry news.

Never afraid to stick its neck out, Crain launched a new magazine in 1995, *Waste News*, covering the waste disposal business.

WHO

Chairman: Gertrude R. Crain
VC: Keith E. Crain
President: Rance E. Crain
EVP Operations: William A. Morrow
SVP International: Joseph C. Cappo
Treasurer: Mary Kay Crain
Secretary: Merillee P. Crain
Director Personnel: Frances Scott

WHERE

HQ: 740 N. Rush St., Chicago, IL 60611-2590
Phone: 312-649-5200   **Fax:** 312-280-3179

WHAT

Crain Communications Inc
Advertising Age
Automotive News
AutoWeek
Business Insurance
Business Marketing
Crain's Chicago Business
Crain's Cleveland Business
Crain's Detroit Business
Crain's New York Business
Detroit Monthly
Electronic Media
Euromarketing
European Rubber Journal
Modern Healthcare
Pensions & Investments
Plastics News
Rubber & Plastics News
TIRE BUSINESS
Urethanes Technology (Europe)
Waste News

Crain Associated Enterprises, Inc.
American Clean Car
American Coin-Op
American Drycleaner
American Laundry Digest
RCR Radio Communications Report

Other Activities
Crain News Service
Crain Subscription Services
Crain's List Rental Service
WWUS-FM

KEY COMPETITORS

Advance Publications
Advanstar
Cowles Media
Dow Jones
K-III
Lagardère
McGraw-Hill
Pittway
Reed Elsevier
VNU

HOW MUCH

Private company FY ends: December 31	Annual Growth	1989	1990	1991	1992	1993	1994
Sales ($ mil.)	3.3%	145.0	150.0	145.0	151.6	157.0	170.7
Employees	(1.8%)	1,026	998	945	970	953	939

DEVRY INC.

OVERVIEW

Education is all business at DeVry Inc., one of North America's largest operators of accredited proprietary business/technical colleges. It runs 14 DeVry Institutes (technical associate and BS degrees), 17 Keller Graduate School of Management centers (MBAs and other management degrees) in the US and Canada, and Corporate Educational Services (CES, on-site training for businesses and government). Cofounders Dennis Keller and Ronald Taylor own 14.8% and 6.2% of the company, respectively.

DeVry Institutes was founded in 1931 by Herman DeVry as a mail-order electronics-repair school. It was later acquired by Bell & Howell, a pioneer in movie cameras and projection equipment. Keller, a Princeton graduate and University of Chicago MBA, met Taylor, with degrees from Harvard and Stanford, when they worked for Bell & Howell. In 1973 they quit to create a private business school, focusing on working adults. In 1987 Keller and Taylor bought DeVry and combined it with their graduate business school under the DeVry name; it went public in 1991.

DeVry has fought the prejudice of the educational establishment against proprietary schools by thinking of its students as customers. It offers them the services they need (flexible payment and scheduling plans; practical, accredited programs developed in cooperation with industry and taught by business professionals; and placement assistance — 91% of graduates are placed in their fields) at prices up to 60% less than at traditional institutions. The company intends to profit from the increasingly technical nature of work and the baby boomlet of the 1980s and 1990s, which will increase the number of people seeking post–high school education. In 1994 and 1995 DeVry opened a new center in Long Beach, California, and 2 in Ontario, Canada.

WHO

Chairman and CEO: Dennis J. Keller, age 54, $732,175 pay
President and COO: Ronald L. Taylor, $732,175 pay
SVP: Norman C. Metz, age 47, $231,000 pay
SVP: O. John Skubiak, age 45, $175,000 pay
SVP: David C. MacFarlane, age 51, $150,960 pay
VP, CFO, and Controller: Norman M. Levine, age 52
VP, General Counsel, and Secretary: Marilynn J. Cason
Director Human Resources: Carl A. Weinstein
Auditors: Price Waterhouse LLP

WHERE

HQ: One Tower Ln., Oakbrook Terrace, IL 60181-4624
Phone: 708-571-7700   **Fax:** 708-571-0317

DeVry operates in Arizona, California, Georgia, Illinois, Missouri, New Jersey, Ohio, Texas, and Wisconsin and in Alberta and Ontario, Canada.

	1995 Sales		1995 Pretax Income	
	$ mil.	% of total	$ mil.	% of total
US	205.4	90	23.3	91
Canada	23.2	10	2.4	9
Total	**228.6**	**100**	**25.7**	**100**

WHAT

	1995 Sales	
	$ mil.	% of total
Tuition	207.5	91
Other educational	19.9	9
Interest	1.2	0
Total	**228.6**	**100**

Degree-granting Schools
DeVry Institutes of Technology
Keller Graduate School of Management, Inc.

KEY COMPETITORS

Apollo Group	Computer	FlightSafety
Berlitz	Learning	ITT Educational
Canterbury	Centers	Services
Corporate	Educational	National Education
Services	Alternatives	

HOW MUCH

NYSE symbol: DV FY ends: June 30	Annual Growth	1990	1991	1992	1993	1994	1995[1]	1995 Year-end: Debt ratio: 46.5%
Sales ($ mil.)	7.8%	156.7	163.1	179.2	191.9	211.4	228.6	Return on equity: 48.9%
Net income ($ mil.)	—	(9.2)	(3.6)	5.9	9.4	12.2	14.9	Cash (mil.): $46.4
Income as % of sales	—	—	—	3.3%	4.9%	5.8%	6.5%	Current ratio: 1.19
Earnings per share ($)	—	(4.01)	(1.50)	0.36	0.57	0.73	0.89	Long-term debt (mil.): $33.0
Stock price – high ($)	—	—	8.13	10.88	14.94	16.75	21.50	No. of shares (mil.): 16.6
Stock price – low ($)	—	—	4.38	6.63	9.75	11.75	15.25	Dividends
Stock price – close ($)	30.6%	—	6.88	10.06	14.00	15.50	20.00	Yield: —
P/E – high	—	—	—	30	26	23	24	Payout: —
P/E – low	—	—	—	18	17	16	17	Market value (mil.): $332.3
Dividends per share ($)	—	—	0.00	0.00	0.00	0.00	0.00	
Book value per share ($)	—	—	(1.58)	0.08	0.66	1.38	2.29	
Employees	8.5%	—	2,720	2,900	3,130	3,275	3,770	

[1] 1995 stock prices are through fiscal year-end (June 30).

ELEK-TEK, INC.

OVERVIEW

Home Sweet Home is more than a song for ELEK-TEK — it's also a retail strategy. The Skokie-based company, which sells computer hardware and software through retail stores, mail order, and a direct-sales force, is working to build its business in the home computer market. But while about half of its sales come from 7 retail stores, ELEK-TEK has struggled to keep up in this highly competitive market.

In 1979, when PCs were in their infancy, Hal Goldman (then in his mid-20s) went into the mail-order computer business with his father, Morton. ELEK-TEK soon became a well-known and well-regarded reseller, and it opened a single retail outlet. In 1982 the company opened its first "superstore" (a mere 18,000 square feet) in Lincolnwood, Illinois. The concept was a success, but growth was slow; it did not open another store until 1987. Nevertheless, the chain dominated the Chicago market against such national competition as Radio Shack and ComputerLand. The company opened another store in 1991 and one in 1992. ELEK-TEK went public in 1993 and used the proceeds to pay down debt, open a store in Indianapolis, and remodel its stores to further differentiate it from the national warehouse-type stores that by 1993 had penetrated the Chicago market.

In 1994 ELEK-TEK opened a store in Kansas and one in Colorado. That same year the company suffered a blow when Hal Goldman killed himself and Morton (who owns about 30% of the firm) retired. SVP Cameron Estes, the heir to much of Hal Goldman's 40% interest in the company, became CEO.

Estes plans to continue ELEK-TEK's 3-channel distribution, but to boost sales at its superstores (which had a 1.3% drop in same-store sales in 1994), he announced plans in 1995 to launch children's departments in 5 stores, increase advertising, improve customer service, and give stores a more "open" feel.

WHO

President, CEO, and Treasurer: Cameron B. Estes Jr., age 51, $208,146 pay
VP Merchandising and Secretary: Steven M. Goodman, age 35, $161,994 pay
VP and CFO: John M. Lader, age 43, $146,495 pay
VP Human Resources: Rory K. Zaks, age 38
Auditors: Coopers & Lybrand L.L.P.

WHERE

HQ: 7350 N. Linder Ave., Skokie, IL 60077
Phone: 847-677-7660   **Fax:** 847-677-1081

	1994 Stores
	No.
Illinois	4
Colorado	1
Indiana	1
Kansas	1
Total	**7**

WHAT

	1994 Sales	
	$ mil.	% of total
Retail	157.5	52
Mail order	86.1	28
Direct sales	62.0	20
Total	**305.6**	**100**

KEY COMPETITORS

Anam Group	Dataflex	MicroAge
Applied Computer	Egghead	NeoStar
Technology	Entex	Office Depot
Best Buy	Gateway 2000	OfficeMax
CDW Computer	Global	PC and Mac
Centers	Directmail	Connection
Circuit City	Inmac	Random Access
CompUSA	Intelligent	Software
Creative	Electronics	Spectrum
Computers	IPC Technology	Staples
CyberSource	Liuski	Tandy Corp.
Damark	International	Tiger Direct
Data Storage	Micro Warehouse	Vanstar
Marketing		

HOW MUCH

Nasdaq symbol: ELEK FY ends: December 31	Annual Growth	1989	1990	1991	1992	1993	1994
Sales ($ mil.)	25.3%	99.1	138.4	148.7	176.8	222.2	305.6
Net income ($ mil.)	16.4%	1.6	2.7	1.7	2.1	4.5	3.5
Income as % of sales	—	1.6%	1.9%	1.2%	1.5%	2.0%	1.1%
Earnings per share ($)	3.8%	—	—	—	0.51	0.78	0.55
Stock price – high ($)	—	—	—	—	—	17.75	19.00
Stock price – low ($)	—	—	—	—	—	9.25	7.00
Stock price – close ($)	(51.8%)	—	—	—	—	17.63	8.50
P/E – high	—	—	—	—	—	23	35
P/E – low	—	—	—	—	—	12	13
Dividends per share ($)	—	—	—	—	—	0.00	0.00
Book value per share ($)	18.5%	—	—	—	—	2.96	3.51
Employees	11.9%	—	—	—	—	788	882

1994 Year-end:
Debt ratio: 58.1%
Return on equity: 17.0%
Cash (mil.): $8.2
Current ratio: 1.85
Long-term debt (mil.): $29.6
No. of shares (mil.): 6.3
Dividends
  Yield: —
  Payout: —
Market value (mil.): $53.6

ENCYCLOPÆDIA BRITANNICA, INC.

Encyclopædia Britannica sells the oldest continuously published encyclopedia in the world. But if the medium is the message, then the message from the last few years of declining sales is that the publisher is being outmaneuvered by its competitors in the emerging medium of electronic publishing. The company sells its encyclopedias and other products (such as *Merriam-Webster* dictionaries) to consumers, libraries, and research centers. In 1994 it expanded into electronic publishing, offering CD-ROMs and online versions of its products. The firm is owned by the William Benton Foundation, a nonprofit corporation connected to the University of Chicago. In 1995 an investment group led by Jacob E. Safra agreed to purchase the company for an undisclosed amount.

Encyclopædia Britannica was founded in Scotland in 1768 by engraver Andrew Bell and printer Colin Macfarquhar. The first edition, edited by William Smellie of the University of Edinburgh, included articles by Benjamin Franklin and John Locke. Ownership moved across the Atlantic in 1901 when American businessmen Horace Hooper and Walter Jackson purchased the company. Sears operated the company for over 20 years until 1943, when ownership transferred to master salesman William Benton (of Benton & Bowles advertising agency fame). Under Benton the company built up a nationwide sales force with a hard-sell reputation. It moved into multimedia with the 1989 release of *Compton's MultiMedia Encyclopedia*. But subsequent declining sales led the firm to sell Compton's NewMedia division to Chicago's Tribune for $57 million in 1993. The Tribune sold it to software publisher Softkey in 1995.

The reference book publisher belatedly reentered electronic publishing in 1994. But while Encyclopædia Britannica's CD-ROM version sells for $995, Microsoft's *Encarta* sells for $100. Competitors are undercutting its print versions too. K-III sells its set of *Funk & Wagnalls* encyclopedias for under $150; the *Encyclopædia Britannica* costs around $2,000.

In 1995 the company launched a version of *Britannica* on the Internet and tied up a deal to provide online content on Time Warner's Pathfinder Internet web site.

President and CEO: Joseph J. Esposito, age 44
EVP International: Thomas A. Gies
EVP, Secretary, and General Counsel: William J. Bowe
CFO: James E. Goulka
VP and Controller: Nancy Wilke
VP Human Resources: Karl Steinberg
Treasurer: Thomas B. Digan

HQ: 310 S. Michigan Ave., Chicago, IL 60604
Phone: 312-347-7000   **Fax:** 312-347-7135

	1995 North American Sales
	% of total
Print encyclopedias & other	84
CD-ROM encyclopedias	16
Total	**100**

Selected Products
Audiovisual learning aids
Dictionaries (*Merriam-Webster*)
Encyclopedias
   CD-ROM versions
   Online versions
   Print versions
Films
Reading instruction
Reference books

Subsidiaries
Encyclopædia Britannica International, Ltd.
Encyclopædia Britannica North America (EBNA)
   Advanced Technology Group
   Britannica Home Library Service, Inc.
   Britannica Publishing Division
   Encyclopædia Britannica Educational Corporation
   Merriam-Webster, Inc.

Advance Publications
Berkshire Hathaway
Franklin Electronic Publishers
Houghton Mifflin
K-III
Lagardere
Microsoft
Oxford University Press
Softkey
Thomson Corp.
Time Warner
Viacom

Private company FY ends: September 30	Annual Growth	1990	1991	1992	1993	1994	1995
Estimated sales ($ mil.)	(9.0%)	650.0	627.0	586.0	540.0	453.0	405.0
Employees	13.0%	1,247	1,260	2,000	2,350	2,350	2,300

17 68

ENVIRODYNE INDUSTRIES, INC.

OVERVIEW

Envirodyne's success in wrapping up the global food industry, and its money troubles, have helped make it an acquisition candidate. The Oak Brook, Illinois–based holding company owns 3 subsidiaries: Clear Shield National, a leading manufacturer of disposable plastic cutlery; Sandusky Plastics, a maker of molded plastic dairy containers; and Viskase, a leading worldwide producer of cellulosic (nonedible) meat casings and plastic food wrap. Chairman Donald Kelly owns about 10% of Envirodyne's stock, and Avram Glazer (an Envirodyne director and president of Zapata Corp.) holds 31%.

In 1970 Ronald Linde founded Envirodyne as a Los Angeles environmental engineering firm. In 1977, after building sales to $24 million, Linde acquired the much larger Chicago-based Wisconsin Steel. Linde closed the bankrupted steel firm 2 years later, and Envirodyne's stock price plunged to 12 cents. The firm rebounded, however, with the purchase of Clear Shield National in 1983. Linde added Viskase in 1986 and Sandusky in 1988.

Kelly, who had guided an LBO of Beatrice Companies and sold off its pieces in 1986 (netting investors $3 billion), formed an investment firm in 1988 and soon took aim at Envirodyne. He led a $900 million LBO of the company and took it private in 1989.

A worldwide recession brought financial troubles that spun the company into bankruptcy in early 1993. By the end of the year, however, Envirodyne emerged from Chapter 11 as a public company. Its strategy became quite simple: focus on building the market share of its core businesses. The firm planned to offer niche products for specific customer needs and improve plant efficiency.

In 1995 Glazer contemplated acquiring Envirodyne as part of an effort to shift Zapata Corp. (founded by George Bush) from the natural gas industry into the food industry.

WHO

Chairman, President, and CEO: Donald P. Kelly, age 73, $450,000 pay
EVP and COO: F. Edward Gustafson, age 53, $390,000 pay
EVP and CFO: John S. Corcoran, age 52, $390,000 pay
VP, Secretary, and General Counsel: Stephen M. Schuster, age 38, $214,636 pay
VP Human Resources: Gordon R. Miller
Auditors: Coopers & Lybrand L.L.P.

WHERE

HQ: 701 Harger Rd, Ste. 190, Oak Brook, IL 60521
Phone: 708-571-8800   **Fax:** 708-571-0959

Envirodyne has 21 factories in Brazil, Canada, France, Mexico, Puerto Rico, the UK, and the US. Clear Shield National's headquarters is in Wheeling, Illinois. Sandusky's main office is in Sandusky, Ohio. Viskase's world headquarters is in Chicago, and its European headquarters is in Paris.

	1994 Sales	
	$ mil.	% of total
North/South American operations	423.0	70
European operations	184.4	30
Other & eliminations	(8.4)	—
Total	**599.0**	**100**

WHAT

Subsidiaries
Clear Shield National (drinking straws, plastic cutlery)
Sandusky (thermoformed and injection-molded plastic containers, trays, and inserts for yogurt, cottage cheese, and take-home foods)
Viskase (cellulogic casings for bologna and hot dogs and specialty film products including PERFLEX heat-shrinkable bags)

KEY COMPETITORS

Ball	Liqui-Box
Bemis	Sealed Air
Continental Can	Silgan Holdings
Dart Container	Sonoco Products
James River	

HOW MUCH

Nasdaq symbol: EDYN FY ends: Last Sat. in Dec.	Annual Growth	1989	1990	1991	1992	1993	1994	1994 Year-end: Debt ratio: 79.2%
Sales ($ mil.)	2.7%	523.1	544.1	544.0	575.7	587.4	599.0	Return on equity: — Cash (mil.): $7.3
Net income ($ mil.)	—	(19.2)	(15.2)	(31.8)	(37.0)	(98.6)	(3.6)	Current ratio: 1.69
Income as % of sales	—	—	—	—	—	—	—	Long-term debt (mil.): $489.4
Earnings per share ($)	—	—	—	—	—	—	0.27	No. of shares (mil.): 13.5
Stock price – high ($)	—	—	—	—	—	—	11.25	Dividends
Stock price – low ($)	—	—	—	—	—	—	3.50	Yield: —
Stock price – close ($)	—	—	—	—	—	—	4.13	Payout: —
P/E – high	—	—	—	—	—	—	42	Market value (mil.): $55.7
P/E – low	—	—	—	—	—	—	13	
Dividends per share ($)	—	—	—	—	—	—	0.00	
Book value per share ($)	—	—	—	—	—	—	10.01	
Employees	1.3%	4,600	4,600	4,600	4,500	4,900	4,900	

EQUITY GROUP INVESTMENTS, INC.

OVERVIEW

Equity Group is the top-tier entity in Chicago financier Sam Zell's network of business holdings. The partnership stands at the top of a complex web of service relationships (such as accounting, tax services, and administration) that generate revenues for Equity Holdings, its officers, and its directors. Zell's holdings make him the US's largest office-property owner.

Sam Zell and his college buddy and partner, Robert Lurie, began managing student housing in the 1960s. Soon they graduated to investing in residential properties, forming Equity Financial and Management Co. Their empire of distressed properties grew in the 1970s, as Zell made the deals and Lurie made the deals work.

In the 1980s they began making corporate acquisitions with Great American Management and Investment, a foundering real estate management company. As their interest in the company grew, they transformed it into an investment company. Later targets included Itel (now Anixter International) and Nucorp (an oil and gas company, now Capsure Holdings, an insurance company). In each case the true attraction was tax loss carryforwards that could be applied against future earnings.

Lurie died in 1990; his estate continues to share in most Zell enterprises. Also in 1990 Zell formed Zell/Chilmark Fund L.P. with David Schulte. Capitalized at $1 billion, the Zell/Chilmark fund soon owned or controlled companies like Broadway Stores (formerly Carter Hawley Hale), Schwinn, Sealy, and Revco (sold to Rite Aid in 1995). Some (such as Broadway Stores, which was sold in 1995 to Federated) showed little improvement under Zell/Chilmark, prompting speculation that Zell had stretched himself too thin. To combat this perception, Zell has built up the management of some of these companies.

In the 1990s Zell formed 4 real estate funds with Merrill Lynch. He also tried in 1995 to gain control of the company that owns Rockefeller Center's mortgage but lost out to a group led by Goldman Sachs. This is just one example of the growing competition for distressed assets that threatens the strategy behind the growth of the Zell empire.

WHO

Chairman; Chairman, Anixter International, Inc., Capsure Holdings Corp., and Great American Management and Investment, Inc: Samuel Zell, age 54
President and CEO, Equity Group Investments: Sheli Z. Rosenberg, age 53
President and CEO, Anixter International, Inc.; President and CEO, Great American Management and Investment, Inc.: Rod F. Dammeyer, age 54

WHERE

HQ: 2 N. Riverside Plaza, Chicago, IL 60606
Phone: 312-454-1800　　**Fax:** 312-454-1063

WHAT

Selected Affiliates
Anixter International, Inc. (25.8%)
Arlington Leasing Co.
Capsure Holdings Corp. (19.8%, insurance)
CFI Industries, Inc. (67%, plastic packaging)
The Delta Queen Steamboat Co. (45.9%, riverboat cruises)
Equity Holdings L.P.
　Equity Financial and Management Co. (real estate management)
　Equity Institutional Investors Inc. (partnership management)
　Equity Office Holdings L.L.C.
　Equity Properties and Development L.P. (shopping centers)
Equity Residential Properties Trust (13.3%, apartments)
Great American Management and Investment, Inc. (72.3%)
Manufactured Home Communities, Inc. (10.6%, mobile home communities REIT)
Riverside Partners (real estate partnership)
Zell/Chilmark Fund L.P. (investment vulture fund)
　Jacor Communications Inc. (65%, radio stations)
　Midway Airlines Corp.
　Quality Food Centers Inc. (27.6%, supermarkets)
　Scott Sports Group (Schwinn bicycles)
　Sealy Corp. (mattresses)
Zell/Merrill Lynch Real Estate Funds (4 funds)

KEY COMPETITORS

Alexander Hagen	Edper Group	Melvin Simon
Amli Residential	Goldman Sachs	Patricof & Co.
Apollo Advisers	Investcorp	Stein & Co.
Bain Capital	JMB Realty	Thomas Lee
Carlyle Group	Jupiter Industries	Trump
Clayton, Dubilier	KKR	White River Corp.

HOW MUCH

Private company	Annual Growth	1989	1990	1991	1992	1993	1994
Estimated net worth of Sam Zell ($ mil.)[1]	30.1%	—	—	400.0	425.0	750.0	880.0

[1] Estimated by *Forbes*

FIRST ALERT, INC.

OVERVIEW

Death comes from silent stalkers stealing through the house at night. First Alert is the guardian against these killers — smoke, carbon monoxide (CO), and radon. The company, with an 80% market share, is the leading maker of residential smoke and gas alarms. It also makes rechargeable flashlights, fire extinguishers, and escape ladders.

Harold Burke, Howard Roberts, and Wayne Kimberlin founded BRK Electronics in 1958. Ten years later, they produced the first Underwriters Laboratories–approved battery-operated commercial smoke alarm. The next year the founders sold the company to Pittway. In 1974 Pittway let Sears market BRK's residential smoke detectors under its own name. BRK introduced the First Alert brand in 1976. It was soon the market leader. In 1992 Pittway sold BRK to management in an LBO financed by the Thomas H. Lee Co., which now controls 53% of the company. In 1994 the company went public as First Alert.

The firm has benefited from the increasing desire for home safety in the wake of high-profile disasters. The MGM Grand fire and other blazes in the 1970s and 1980s helped spur building code requirements for smoke detectors, and the 1994 death of tennis star Vitas Gerulaitis did the same for CO detectors.

In 1994 Chicago became the first (and so far the only) major city to require CO detectors. But First Alert's early detectors were too sensitive and produced a flurry of false alarms (and a flurry of emergency calls to the city). This problem has been fixed in newer detectors.

Although 92% of US households have a smoke detector, First Alert hopes to boost the percentage of multiple alarms and to increase sales overseas, where penetration is low.

In 1995 First Alert introduced a new tamper-resistant alarm powered by lithium batteries, which can last for up to 10 years.

WHO

Chairman and CEO: Malcolm Candlish, age 59, $471,667 pay
President and COO: James S. Amtmann, age 47
SVP, CFO, Treasurer, and Secretary: Gary L. Lederer, age 44, $226,583 pay
VP Sales: William K. Brouse, age 46, $142,683 pay
VP Marketing: Richard F. Timmons, age 44, $136,183 pay
VP Operations: Fred W. Higgenbottom, age 46, $128,003 pay
Manager Human Resources: Lisa Reynolds
Auditors: Price Waterhouse LLP

WHERE

HQ: 780 McClure Rd., Aurora, IL 60504-2495
Phone: 708-851-7330   **Fax:** 708-851-7538

	1994 Sales		1994 Operating Income	
	$ mil.	% of total	$ mil.	% of total
US	244.4	85	35.2	98
Europe	21.8	8	(0.8)	—
Other regions	20.0	7	0.5	2
Adjustments	(37.8)	—	—	—
Total	**248.4**	**100**	**34.9**	**100**

WHAT

Products
Carbon monoxide detectors
Electronic and mechanical timers
Fire escape ladders
Fire extinguishers
Fire-resistant safes
Infrared motion detectors
Radon detectors
Rechargeable flashlights and lanterns
Smoke detectors

KEY COMPETITORS

Aim Safety
American Sensors
Gentex
Nighthawk Systems
Pittway

HOW MUCH

Nasdaq symbol: ALRT FY ends: December 31	Annual Growth	1989	1990	1991	1992	1993	1994
Sales ($ mil.)	18.3%	107.3	107.7	123.7	131.1	157.6	248.4
Net income ($ mil.)	76.5%	1.0	2.7	7.3	1.2	8.0	17.6
Income as % of sales	—	1.0%	2.5%	5.9%	0.9	5.1%	7.1%
Earnings per share ($)	206.2%	—	—	—	0.08	0.25	0.75
Stock price – high ($)	—	—	—	—	—	—	22.50
Stock price – low ($)	—	—	—	—	—	—	8.75
Stock price – close ($)	—	—	—	—	—	—	14.63
P/E – high	—	—	—	—	—	—	30
P/E – low	—	—	—	—	—	—	12
Dividends per share ($)	—	—	—	—	—	—	0.00
Book value per share ($)	—	—	—	—	—	—	4.66
Employees	2.7%	—	—	—	—	2,040	2,095

1994 Year-end:
Debt ratio: 14.2%
Return on equity: 21.7%
Cash (mil.): $1.1
Current ratio: 1.91
Long-term debt (mil.): $15.8
No. of shares (mil.): 20.5
Dividends
　Yield: —
　Payout: —
Market value (mil.): $299.2
R&D as % of sales: 0.7%
Advertising as % of sales: 12.9%

FOLLETT CORPORATION

OVERVIEW

Follett Corporation is the oldest and largest operator of college bookstores in the US, with more than 400 stores serving colleges and universities in 46 states. The company is privately owned and managed by the Follett family, which has been involved with the company for 4 generations. Follett's stores don't rely solely on students' cravings for knowledge. About 1/3 of its on-campus business derives from food, snacks, and other nontextbook items. Follett is expanding into custom academic publishing, establishing many copy centers on campuses. The company is also a leading wholesaler of books to elementary and high school libraries.

Follett began in 1873 as a small bookstore opened by the Reverend Charles Barnes in his home in Wheaton, Illinois. C. W. Follett acted as both salesman and stock clerk. In 1917 Follett bought into the company when Barnes's son, William, moved to New York (he started what became one of Follett's biggest competitors, Barnes & Noble). Follett took control of the company in 1923 and later brought his own sons into the business. During WWII the company began publishing children's books, which were in demand because of a shortage of metal toys.

C. W. died in 1952, and his son, Dwight, took over. In 1957 the firm organized into divisions, and Follett Corporation was created as the parent company. During the 1960s Follett developed the first multiracial textbook series, depicting ethnically diverse characters. Dwight built Follett to $50 million in annual sales by 1977, when he retired. He was succeeded by his son, Robert, who led the company through tremendous growth in the 1980s. In 1990 Follett acquired Brennan College Service, adding 57 stores to its chain. Robert's son-in-law Richard Traut, named chairman in 1994, was the first person without the Follett name to hold that position.

Follett prides itself on its ability to process orders quickly. The company ships more than 95% of all book orders in less than a month.

In 1994 Follett introduced Sneak Preview Plus, a CD-ROM product designed to enhance the acquisition process in libraries. That year Follett also launched a custom academic publishing line.

WHAT

Chairman: Richard M. Traut
President and CEO: P. Richard Litzsinger
EVP: Laverne Hosek
VP Finance and CFO: Kenneth J. Hull
VP Operations: Richard Waichler
Treasurer: Robert O'Brian
Director Human Resources: Louis Monosealco
Auditors: Arthur Andersen & Co, SC

WHERE

HQ: 2233 West St., River Grove, IL 60171-1895
Phone: 708-583-2000   **Fax:** 708-452-9347

Divisions

Follett Campus Resources
2211 West St., River Grove, IL 60171-1800

Follett College Stores
400 W. Grand Ave., Elmhurst, IL 60126

Follett Collegiate Graphics
2233 West St., River Grove, IL 60171-1895

Follett Educational Services
5563 S. Archer Ave., Chicago, IL 60638

Follett Library Resources
4506 Northwest Hwy., Crystal Lake, IL 60014

Follett Software Company
809 N. Front St., McHenry, IL 60050

WHAT

Selected Products and Services
Custom academic course packs
Data management systems for libraries
On-campus reprographics
Software development for libraries
Textbook distribution
Wholesale books
Workbook (elementary and high school use) distribution

KEY COMPETITORS

Baker & Taylor
Barnes & Noble
Borders
Crown Books
Data Research
Ingram
Kinko's
McGraw-Hill

HOW MUCH

Private company FY ends: March 31	Annual Growth	1990	1991	1992	1993	1994	1995
Sales ($ mil.)	15.7%	343.3	432.2	548.7	611.9	646.4	712.8
Employees	11.4%	4,200	5,758	6,198	6,500	6,800	7,200

GENERAL BINDING CORPORATION

OVERVIEW

General Binding is a leading manufacturer/marketer of business machines that bind and laminate sheets of paper. It also makes paper shredders. These products are manufactured in 18 plants in the US and abroad and sold through a network of sales staff, dealers, distributors, and wholesale stationers. The Northbrook, Illinois–based firm sells to the business, commercial, education, and government markets. It sells 35% of its products internationally.

The company was founded in 1947, when William Lane and 2 partners bought a Chicago bindery. General Binding expanded in 1962 by acquiring Virginia Laminating, and it bought U.S. RingBinder in 1977. The company explored computers in 1981, teaming with NorthStar Computers as an OEM; poor performance drained profits, and the company pulled out in 1984, a year after William Lane III was elected chairman. In 1985 it had greater OEM success under an agreement to make and use VeloBind's rigid plastic binding strips.

The 1-Step, a binding machine introduced in 1988, was the company's first product sold through office supply stores. When the company bought Loose Leaf Metals Co. from Varlen Corp. in 1989 and purchased VeloBind in late 1991, it absorbed significant competitors. With VeloBind in the fold (after federal antitrust negotiations), General Binding has worked on new products and markets.

The company wrapped itself around another competitor in 1993, purchasing the Bates Manufacturing Company — a 100-year-old maker of staplers, card files, and 3-hole punches — for $5 million. In 1994 General Binding acquired binding machine and paperpunch maker Sickinger for $4.9 million.

In 1995 the company launched a foil imprinter that allows clients to create personalized covers that incorporate one of General Binding's 6 foil colors.

WHO

Chairman: William N. Lane III, age 51, $200,000 pay
VC: Rudolph Grua, age 66, $386,667 pay
President and CEO: Govi C. Reddy, age 50, $208,750 pay
SVP North American Operations: Elliott L. Smith, age 60, $211,000 pay
SVP International Operations: Steven R. Baumhardt, age 46, $203,000 pay
SVP Corporate Development: Walter M. Hebb, age 55
VP North American Sales: John G. Lindroth, age 57
VP, Secretary, and General Counsel: Steven Rubin
VP and CFO: Edward J. McNulty, age 55
Director Human Resources: Gary Smith
Auditors: Arthur Andersen & Co, SC

WHERE

HQ: One GBC Plaza, Northbrook, IL 60062-4195
Phone: 847-272-3700   **Fax:** 847-272-1389

	1994 Sales	
	$ mil.	% of total
US	274.3	65
Other countries	146.1	35
Total	**420.4**	**100**

WHAT

	1994 Sales
	% of total
Binding products	51
Laminating products	31
Ring metals	8
Service	6
Shredding products	4
Total	**100**

Brand Names	Selected Products
Bates	Binding systems
GBC	Electric punches
Shredmaster	Laminating films
Sickinger	Ring metals
U.S. RingBinder	Shredding machines
VeloBind	Staplers

KEY COMPETITORS

Gradco Systems	KOA Holdings	Standard Register
Jacobs Management	Mead	Xerox

HOW MUCH

Nasdaq symbol: GBND FY ends: December 31	Annual Growth	1989	1990	1991	1992	1993	1994
Sales ($ mil.)	8.2%	283.7	303.7	311.2	368.6	376.1	420.4
Net income ($ mil.)	(4.8%)	20.1	13.7	12.6	16.7	15.0	15.7
Income as % of sales	—	7.1%	4.5%	4.0%	4.5%	4.0%	3.7%
Earnings per share ($)	(4.5%)	1.26	0.86	0.80	1.06	0.95	1.00
Stock price – high ($)	—	30.25	28.25	20.50	21.50	19.25	22.00
Stock price – low ($)	—	17.67	13.00	10.75	14.50	11.50	14.38
Stock price – close ($)	(5.8%)	26.25	16.00	18.75	19.25	15.75	19.50
P/E – high	—	24	33	26	20	20	22
P/E – low	—	14	15	13	14	12	14
Dividends per share ($)	8.7%	0.27	0.29	0.33	0.37	0.40	0.41
Book value per share ($)	6.4%	6.56	7.16	7.53	8.08	8.47	8.96
Employees	(0.6%)	3,332	3,207	3,537	3,363	3,199	3,226

1994 Year-end:
Debt ratio: 32.0%
Return on equity: 11.4%
Cash (mil.): $5.6
Current ratio: 2.02
Long-term debt (mil.): $42.0
No. of shares (mil.): 15.7
Dividends
  Yield: 2.1%
  Payout: 40.5%
Market value (mil.): $307.1

HA-LO INDUSTRIES, INC.

OVERVIEW

"Most of the world will take anything if it's free," observes HA-LO founder Lou Weisbach, so he gives it to them. Weisbach is the Santa Claus of corporate giveaways — the pens, hats, key rings, paperweights, and coffee mugs emblazoned with a company's name, logo, or message that are given as gifts to customers. Based in the suburban Chicago area, HA-LO is one of the nation's top 20 promotional and specialty advertisers and was the first public company in this fastest-growing segment of the advertising industry. HA-LO has 525 independent sales representatives and offices in most major US cities. Customers include *FORTUNE* 500 clients (such as Time Warner, Quaker Oats, and Apple Computer) and sports teams (including the Chicago Cubs, Chicago Bulls, and California Angels). Weisbach owns 47% of HA-LO's stock.

Weisbach founded the company in 1972 when he was 23, only 3 years after finishing college, by borrowing $3,500 from his mother. He first sold calendars to beauty shops and butchers. Weisbach named the company for himself and his brother, Hal. It grew slowly for 20 years; in 1992 it went public, raising $7.9 million. Within 2 years HA-LO had bought several smaller, related companies and tripled its sales to $69 million. In 1995 HA-LO bought Leshore Calgift, one of the US's leading specialty advertisers, which added 200 salespeople nationwide and a sales office in Los Angeles.

HA-LO wants to be a national-level company in what is a highly fragmented industry, made up mostly of small vendors. HA-LO has moved into corporate fulfillment programs, which warehouse and distribute, as needed, a wide variety of items featuring a company's logo; the company pays for the products as well as an annual fee for the service. It is also tackling larger markets, such as New York and Dallas, to boost annual sales.

WHO

Chairman, President, and CEO: Lou Weisbach, age 46, $500,000 pay
EVP: David C. Robbins, age 42, $555,000 pay
VP Finance, Treasurer, and CFO: Richard A. Magid, age 36, $128,636 pay
VP Administration and Secretary: Barbara G. Berman, age 50, $108,866 pay
Director Administration and Human Resources: Sabina Filipovic
Auditors: Arthur Andersen & Co, SC

WHERE

HQ: 5980 Touhy Ave., Niles, IL 60714
Phone: 847-647-2300   **Fax:** 847-647-5999

WHAT

Selected Customers

Abbott Labs	Kraft
Andersen Consulting	Metropolitan Life
Apple Computer	Montgomery Ward
California Angels	Motorola
Chicago Bulls	Quaker Oats
Chicago Cubs	Reynolds Metals
Detroit Tigers	*Sports Illustrated*
FMC Corp.	Time Warner
Helene Curtis	Turner Broadcasting
Kemper Financial	U.S. Cellular

Selected Promotional Products

Calendars	Desk accessories	Luggage tags
Clocks	Hats	Pens
Coffee mugs	Jackets	Pocket knives
Crystalware	Key chains	T-shirts

Services

Corporate fulfillment	Events by HA-LO (event
Corporate logo design	organizing and promoting)
Custom products	Graphics and typesetting

KEY COMPETITORS

Baldwin Cooke	Fast Advertising	Pharmaceutical
Benham Advertising	Jayline	Marketing
Celex Group	Maritz	Premiere
CSA Promotions	Mickelberry	Merchandising
Cyrk		TRY-AD

HOW MUCH

Nasdaq symbol: HALO FY ends: December 31	Annual Growth	1989	1990	1991	1992	1993	1994
Sales ($ mil.)	39.2%	13.1	17.5	22.4	23.5	35.7	68.6
Net income ($ mil.)	—	(0.1)	(0.1)	0.8	0.5	0.2	1.3
Income as % of sales	—	—	—	3.7%	2.0%	0.6%	1.9%
Earnings per share ($)	—	(0.02)	(0.02)	0.30	0.16	0.05	0.30
Stock price – high ($)	—	—	—	—	7.50	7.00	7.75
Stock price – low ($)	—	—	—	—	5.50	3.63	5.50
Stock price – close ($)	(0.9%)	—	—	—	6.63	5.50	6.50
P/E – high	—	—	—	—	47	140	26
P/E – low	—	—	—	—	34	73	18
Dividends per share ($)	—	—	—	—	0.00	0.00	0.00
Book value per share ($)	13.3%	—	—	—	1.59	1.71	2.03
Employees	47.4%	—	—	—	75	137	202

1994 Year-end:
Debt ratio: 60.2%
Return on equity: 15.9%
Cash (mil.): $0.0
Current ratio: 2.01
Long-term debt (mil.): $12.0
No. of shares (mil.): 4.4
Dividends
  Yield: —
  Payout: —
Market value (mil.): $28.4

HARPO ENTERTAINMENT GROUP

OVERVIEW

Harpo Entertainment is the umbrella company that produces and syndicates TV shows, films, and other media offerings for founder, owner, chairman, and CEO Oprah Winfrey (Harpo is Oprah spelled backwards). An entertainment dynamo, Winfrey is the first black female and the 3rd woman in US history (after Mary Pickford and Lucille Ball) to own her own production studio. Winfrey is the nation's #1 TV talk show host. *The Oprah Winfrey Show*, the highest-rated talk show in TV history, is seen by 15 million viewers on 210 US TV stations and in over 117 foreign countries. Winfrey is also an acclaimed actress whose performance in *The Color Purple* won her an Oscar nomination.

Winfrey began her broadcasting career in 1973 at age 19 as a news anchor at Nashville's WTVF-TV. She became an evening news co-anchor in Baltimore, where she was recruited to co-host WJZ-TV's local talk show, *People Are Talking*. In the early 1980s Winfrey moved to Chicago to host ABC affiliate WLS-TV's *AM Chicago*, which quickly became the city's top morning talk show. Renamed *The Oprah Winfrey Show*, the program was expanded to an hour. What made *Oprah* distinctive from other talk shows was its focus on ordinary people.

Harpo was founded in 1986, the same year Winfrey's agent Jeffrey Jacobs (now Harpo's president) obtained syndication rights to *Oprah* and started distributing it through King World Productions. Winfrey's exposure in *The Color Purple* boosted her ratings when *Oprah* debuted nationally that year in 138 cities. Winfrey obtained ownership rights to the program in 1988. In 1990 Harpo Films was created, and Winfrey bought a Chicago studio to produce *Oprah*.

Winfrey is contemplating other media ventures (such as fitness videos, prime-time TV interviews, online services, and acting) to expand on her popular brand name. Winfrey's ratings have slipped amid competition from a spate of new talk shows and the O.J. Simpson trial and after she abandoned seamier topics. In 1995 she agreed to continue hosting her daytime show for at least another 2 years but also signed with Capital Cities/ABC to produce or star in 6 made-for-TV movies over 3 years.

WHO

Chairman and CEO: Oprah Winfrey, age 41
President: Jeffrey Jacobs
Director of Media and Corporate Relations: Deborah Johns
President, Harpo Productions: Tim Bennett
CFO: Doug Pattison
VP Development and Production: Kate Forte
Director of Development, Harpo Films: Valerie Scoon

WHERE

HQ: 110 N. Carpenter St., Chicago, IL 60607
Phone: 312-633-1000   **Fax:** 312-633-1111

Harpo has offices in Chicago and Los Angeles.

WHAT

Harpo Films (film and TV production company, based in Los Angeles)
Oprah Online (online talk show on America Online, underwritten with Capital Cities/ABC)
Oprah Winfrey Presents (made-for-TV films)
The Oprah Winfrey Show (daily TV talk show)

KEY COMPETITORS

All American Communications
Dick Clark Productions
DreamWorks SKG
Hearst
International Family Entertainment
Kushner-Lock
Lagardère
LIN Television
MacAndrews & Forbes
News Corp.
Sony
Spelling Entertainment
Time Warner
Tribune
Turner Boardcasting
Viacom
Walt Disney

HOW MUCH

Private company FY ends: December 31	Annual Growth	1989	1990	1991	1992	1993	1994
Sales ($ mil.)	6.9%	—	—	—	105.0	110.1	120.0
Employees	4.4%	—	—	—	—	135	141

IDEX CORPORATION

OVERVIEW

The fluid handling of a series of acquisitions has enabled IDEX to emerge as a leader in several niches in the fluid handling and industrial products markets. Its fluid handling division (which accounts for 69% of sales) makes industrial pumps, compressors, controls, and fire-fighting pumps. The industrial products division makes items such as steel banding and metal fabricating equipment. IDEX's 11 business units include Band-It, Corken, Hale Products, and Lubriquip. The company is 29.9%-owned by KKR Associates.

IDEX is the successor of Houdaille (pronounced "WHO-dye") Industries, which took its name from Maurice Houdaille, the French inventor of recoilless artillery used in WWI. After the war a US firm bought the name and the rights to Houdaille's patented rotary shock absorber. By the 1930s Houdaille was the #1 US maker of shock absorbers. During WWII it was involved in the building of the atomic bomb. With the trend toward in-house manufacture by the auto giants in the 1950s, the company diversified into industrial and construction products, pumps, and machine tools. Facing difficult economic conditions and the threat of an unfriendly takeover, Phil Reilly (Houdaille's CEO-nominee) and investors Kohlberg, Kravis and Roberts led the company private in 1979 in the first LBO of any company worth more than $100 million.

In 1987 IDEX (an acronym for Innovation, Diversity, and EXcellence) was formed to buy back 7 units it had sold to the British TI Group earlier that year. In 1989 IDEX went public. Following the IPO, the company pursued an aggressive acquisition strategy. Purchases included Corken (1991), Devjo's Pump Group (now Viking Pump, 1992), Signfix (1993), and Hale Products (1994).

In 1995 the company acquired Micropump, a leading manufacturer of small, magnetically driven pumps, for $32 million.

WHO

Chairman, President, and CEO: Donald N. Boyce, age 56, $825,000 pay
SVP Operations and COO: Frank J. Hansen, age 53, $325,000 pay
SVP Finance, CFO, and Secretary: Wayne P. Sayatovic, age 49, $320,400 pay
VP; Group Executive and President, Hale Products: Wade H. Roberts, age 48, $278,600 pay
VP; Group Executive: Mark W. Baker, age 47
VP Human Resources: Jerry N. Derck
Auditors: Deloitte & Touche LLP

WHERE

HQ: 630 Dundee Rd., Northbrook, IL 60062
Phone: 847-498-7070   **Fax:** 847-498-3940

WHAT

	1994 Sales	
	$ mil.	% of total
Fluid handling	275.5	69
Industrial products	124.0	31
Total	**399.5**	**100**

Business Units
Band-It (stainless steel bands, buckles, preformed clamps, and installation tools)
Corken (compressors, vane and turbine pumps, and valves)
Hale Products (truck-mounted and portable fire pumps)
Lubriquip (lubrication systems, forcefeed lubricators, and metering devices)
Pulsafeeder (pumps)
Signfix (sign-mounting systems)
Vibratech (dampers and energy absorption devices)
Viking Pump (positive replacement rotary gear, pumps, and electronic controls)
Warren Rupp (air pumps)

KEY COMPETITORS

Autoclave Engineers	General Signal	Newflo
BW/IP	Goulds Pumps	NYCOR
Cooper Industries	Handy & Harman	Osmonics
Dresser	Haskel	Robbins &
Falcon Building	Hayward	Myers
Gardner Denver	Industries	Roper
Machinery	Illinois Tool Works	Industries

HOW MUCH

NYSE symbol: IEX FY ends: December 31	Annual Growth	1989	1990	1991	1992	1993	1994
Sales ($ mil.)	12.6%	221.1	228.4	228.2	277.1	308.6	399.5
Net income ($ mil.)	13.2%	18.1	17.8	17.1	15.2	25.3	33.6
Income as % of sales	—	8.2%	7.8%	7.5%	5.5%	8.2%	8.4%
Earnings per share ($)	9.6%	1.09	1.10	1.01	0.80	1.31	1.72
Stock price – high ($)	—	11.25	11.63	13.38	15.88	24.00	29.25
Stock price – low ($)	—	9.25	6.88	6.38	11.13	14.63	22.63
Stock price – close ($)	20.1%	11.25	7.13	11.13	15.88	23.88	28.13
P/E – high	—	10	11	13	20	18	17
P/E – low	—	8	6	6	14	11	13
Dividends per share ($)	—	0.00	0.00	0.00	0.00	0.00	0.00
Book value per share ($)	—	(1.44)	(0.26)	1.98	3.11	4.39	6.10
Employees	8.4%	2,000	2,000	2,000	2,400	2,500	3,000

1994 Year-end:
Debt ratio: 59.1%
Return on equity: 33.6%
Cash (mil.): $6.3
Current ratio: 2.18
Long-term debt (mil.): $168.2
No. of shares (mil.): 19.1
Dividends
  Yield: —
  Payout: —
Market value (mil.): $536.6

INFORMATION RESOURCES, INC.

OVERVIEW

Chicago-based Information Resources, Inc. (IRI), is the world's 2nd largest marketing research firm (after Dun & Bradstreet's Northbrook-based A. C. Nielsen). The company uses product bar codes to translate purchases at supermarket chains, drugstores, mass merchandisers, convenience stores, and warehouse clubs into an extensive database, which clients use to follow sales of their brands (as well as their competitors') and track consumer purchasing trends. IRI also markets analytical software that helps clients with planning, testing, and evaluating sales.

IRI was founded in 1977 by current VC Gerald Eskin and John Malec (who left in 1990 when IRI spun off its computerized shopping carts as VideOcart; that company went bankrupt in 1993). Dun & Bradstreet, parent of archrival Nielsen, offered to buy IRI in 1987. The FTC nixed the merger for antitrust reasons, and IRI, which had spent heavily to expand, was left with a depressed stock price and much debt. The company made a profit again in 1990 when it merged with Arbitron. Since then, IRI and Nielsen have vied for the industry's top spot. Hostilities have included swiping personnel and major clients, such as Bristol-Meyers Squibb (from IRI to Nielsen) and Campbell Soup (from Nielsen to IRI).

In 1994 the company moved into Japan, Mexico, and Venezuela but lost $8.9 million because of other expansion costs, product delays, and shareholder litigation. That year IRI began seeking a hefty equity investor. In 1995 IRI expanded into the Middle East and Canada and sold its online analytical processing business to Oracle for $100 million, which will be used to support more overseas growth. The company also replaced chairman Gian Fulgoni with Thomas Wilson, a company director and former McKinsey & Co. senior partner, to shore up shareholder confidence; Fulgoni remains as president and CEO.

WHO

Chairman: Thomas W. Wilson Jr., age 63
VC: Gerald J. Eskin, age 60
President and CEO: Gian M. Fulgoni, age 47, $330,750 pay
EVP and CFO: Gary M. Hill
EVP Human Resources: Gary Newman
Secretary and General Counsel: Edward S. Berger, age 54
President International Information Services Group: Randall S. Smith, age 43, $275,465 pay
President and CEO, IRI North America Group: George R. Garrick, age 42
Auditors: Grant Thornton LLP

WHERE

HQ: 150 N. Clinton St., Chicago, IL 60661
Phone: 312-726-1221   **Fax:** 312-726-0360

	1994 Sales		1994 Operating Profit	
	$ mil.	% of total	$ mil.	% of total
US	318.1	84	23.5	—
Other countries	58.5	16	(18.2)	—
Total	**376.6**	**100**	**5.3**	**—**

WHAT

	1994 Sales	
	$ mil.	% of total
Information services	257.4	68
Software products	119.2	32
Total	**376.6**	**100**

Selected Products and Services
BehaviorScan (test marketing system)
InfoScan (scanner-based data service)
InfoScan Census (chainwide purchase measurements)
IRI Software (business analysis and management software)
QScan (chainwide purchase information)
Towne-Oller (tracking of health and beauty products)

KEY COMPETITORS

Advanced Promotion
Catalina Marketing
Comshare
Dun & Bradstreet
Heritage Media
Hyperion Software
Maritz

HOW MUCH

Nasdaq symbol: IRIC FY ends: December 31	Annual Growth	1989	1990	1991	1992	1993	1994
Sales ($ mil.)	22.5%	136.4	166.7	207.7	276.4	334.5	376.6
Net income ($ mil.)	—	(13.6)	4.2	14.2	19.2	22.2	(8.9)
Income as % of sales	—	—	2.5%	6.8%	6.9%	6.6%	—
Earnings per share ($)	—	(0.80)	0.15	0.63	0.78	0.82	(0.34)
Stock price – high ($)	—	14.88	16.63	29.25	36.25	44.75	39.75
Stock price – low ($)	—	9.00	7.75	9.13	18.50	27.00	11.25
Stock price – close ($)	1.3%	12.88	10.00	27.50	31.50	38.50	13.75
P/E – high	—	—	111	46	47	55	—
P/E – low	—	—	52	15	24	33	—
Dividends per share ($)	—	0.00	0.00	0.00	0.00	0.00	0.00
Book value per share ($)	23.9%	2.94	3.46	5.42	7.82	9.00	8.58
Employees	20.5%	2,500	3,000	3,679	4,707	5,800	6,360

1994 Year-end:
Debt ratio: 12.8%
Return on equity: —
Cash (mil.): $11.8
Current ratio: 1.95
Long-term debt (mil.): $31.5
No. of shares (mil.): 26.5
Dividends
  Yield: —
  Payout: —
Market value (mil.): $364.3
R&D as % of sales: 6.2%

JOHN D. MACARTHUR FOUNDATION

OVERVIEW

The John D. and Catherine T. MacArthur Foundation, one of the largest private philanthropic organizations in the US, awards grants to groups and individuals worldwide for efforts to improve the human condition.

The foundation distributes grants through 8 diverse programs, ranging from the General Program, which supports diversity in the media, to the Health Program, which funds research on midlife development. Money is also awarded through foundationwide initiatives, which address problems that fall within the scope of 2 or more of the 8 programs.

The MacArthur Fellows Program has drawn the most attention for bestowing what the press calls "genius awards." Fellows receive $30,000–$75,000 annually for 5 years to pursue creative projects. The amount of money is determined by the person's age. Fellowships have been given to people ranging from a clown to a binder of rare books.

Not long after trustees began making awards, the foundation became known as one of the most bizarre in the US. In recent years, however, it has received credit for supporting interesting projects.

The foundation was established by an eccentric billionaire who enjoyed making money more than spending it. John D. MacArthur, one of the richest men in America, made a fortune after he bought Bankers Life & Casualty Company of Chicago and sold mail-order insurance at the end of the Depression. He later became the largest landowner in Florida.

To avoid taxes, MacArthur used most of his $2.5 billion estate to establish a foundation named after himself and his 2nd wife. After MacArthur's death in 1978, the foundation's board of trustees found no guidelines other than his brief statement: "I figured out how to make the money, you boys figure out how to spend it."

The foundation's trustees continue to modify programs. In 1994 the focus of the General Program was extended to protect the rights of refugees, and the Education Program was revised to support research on professional development of teachers and principals.

WHO

Chairman: Elizabeth J. McCormack
President: Adele Simmons
SVP: Victor Rabinowitch
VP and CFO: Lawrence L. Landry
VP Public Affairs; Director, General Program: Woodward A. Wickham
VP Community Affairs; Director, Community Initiatives Program: Rebecca R. Riley
VP Human Resources and Administration: William E. Lowry
General Counsel: Joshua J. Mintz

WHERE

HQ: The John D. and Catherine T. MacArthur Foundation, 140 S. Dearborn St., Ste. 1100, Chicago, IL 60603
Phone: 312-726-8000   **Fax:** 312-920-6258

WHAT

	1994 Summary of Grants	
	$ mil.	% of total
General	23.8	17
Community Initiatives	22.6	16
Health	21.9	16
Peace & International Cooperation	20.5	14
World Environment & Resources	16.2	11
Population	12.5	9
Education	11.7	9
MacArthur Fellows	6.5	4
Foundation-wide Initiatives	5.3	4
Total	**141.0**	**100**

Programs
General (diversity in the media and rights of refugees)
Community Initiatives (community development and cultural activities in Chicago and Palm Beach County, Florida)
Health (research on mental health, human development, and biology of parasitic diseases)
Peace and International Cooperation (training, research, and public education)
World Environment and Resources (conservation, public education, policy studies, and projects related to environmental issues in the tropics)
Population (reproductive rights and women's reproductive health)
Education (professional development of educators, education standards, and student assessment)
MacArthur Fellows (fellowships for creativity)

HOW MUCH

Private institution FY ends: December 31	Annual Growth	1989	1990	1991	1992	1993	1994
Assets ($ bil.)	(1.9%)	3.2	3.1	3.3	2.9	3.1	2.9
Revenues ($ mil.)	(6.4%)	—	—	236.2	223.6	280.0	194.0
Net income before grants ($ mil.)	(11.8%)	—	—	177.6	158.2	210.9	121.9
Grants ($ mil.)	(1.5%)	151.7	148.1	141.3	154.4	151.2	141.0
Employees	12.6%	127	147	183	197	213	230

THE JOHN D. AND CATHERINE T.
MACARTHUR FOUNDATION

LETTUCE ENTERTAIN YOU ENTERPRISES

OVERVIEW

Lettuce Entertain You Enterprises tosses in a lot of fun at its 40 restaurants (under different names) in Arizona, Illinois, Minnesota, and Washington. (Licensees operate 2 more in Japan.) Most are in the Chicago area and all reflect the creative genius of company co-founder Richard Melman, among the nation's most successful restaurateurs.

Melman began adding pizazz to restaurants in 1971 when he and real estate developer Jerry Orzoff opened the popular R.J. Grunts in Chicago. For an encore, they unveiled restaurants with such whimsical names as Fritz That's It! (1973), Jonathan Livingston Seafood (1975), and Lawrence of Oregano (1976).

Melman lost his friend and mentor when Orzoff died of a heart attack in 1981. In recent years Melman has operated his company with the help of 25 partners. They oversee restaurants that embrace a variety of themes and cuisines, ranging from the 4-star French bistro Ambria to Bub City — a cross between a Southern crab shack and a Texas barbecue joint.

Melman continues to introduce innovative dining concepts such as one called foodlife, which features 11 kiosks in Chicago's upscale Water Tower Place mall, offering fresh, healthy food from a wide range of ethnic cuisines. In addition, foodlife offers a retail and carryout market.

Although Melman prefers one-of-a-kind restaurants, most of those opened in the mid-1990s have been duplicates of existing eateries. Also, for the first time, most of the new ones have been outside of Chicago.

A few Lettuce Entertain You ventures were unsuccessful. In the 1980s Melman failed to revive the troubled Playboy Clubs, Jim McMahon's bar and restaurant, and the Wrigley Building restaurant. Several restaurants that were opened in the 1970s, including Jonathan Livingston Seafood, didn't survive new dining trends in the 1990s.

Melman says he plans to open restaurants in more cities and to clone more of the concepts. Although the company doesn't strive for big profits or rapid expansion, he says the company likely will grow faster when he and yet-to-be-named partners form joint ventures for new eateries.

WHO

President and CEO: Richard Melman, age 53
CFO: Jay Steiber
EVP: Manford Joast
EVP: Robert Wattel
VP Human Resources: Susan Southgate-Fox

WHERE

HQ: Lettuce Entertain You Enterprises, Inc., 5419 N. Sheridan Rd., Chicago, IL 60640
Phone: 312-878-7340
Fax: 312-878-7667

Lettuce Entertain You has 40 restaurants in Arizona, Illinois, Minnesota, and Washington. Licensees operate 2 restaurants in Japan.

	1994 Company-Owned Restaurants	
	No.	% of total
Illinois	35	88
Arizona	2	5
Minnesota	2	5
Washington	1	2
Total	**40**	**100**

WHAT

Selected Restaurants
Ambria (fine French cuisine)
Brasserie Jo (Alsatian French fare)
Bub City (Southern-style seafood and Texas barbecue)
Cafe Ba-Ba-Reeba! (tapas bar and regional and traditional Spanish dishes)
Corner Bakery (traditional old-world bread shop)
foodlife (variety of fresh, healthy food)
Hat Dance (classic Mexican cuisine)
The Original A-1 (Texas mesquite grilling and traditional Mexican fare)
Papagus Greek Taverna (traditional Greek cuisine)
The Pump Room (American cuisine)
Shaw's Crab House and Blue Crab Lounge (fresh seafood)

KEY COMPETITORS

Applebee's
Bob Evans
Boston Chicken
Brinker
Buffets
Carlson
Cracker Barrel
DAKA International
Darden Restaurants
Family Restaurants
Lone Star Steakhouse
Metromedia
Morrison Restaurants
Outback Steakhouse
Restaurant Co.

HOW MUCH

Private company FY ends: December 31	Annual Growth	1989	1990	1991	1992	1993	1994
Sales ($ mil.)	6.8%	90	—	—	—	112	125
Employees	7.6%	2,500	2,500	2,500	3,000	3,000	3,600

MERCURY FINANCE COMPANY

OVERVIEW

Mercury Finance will help you finance a Mercury — or a Chevy, Honda, or Mercedes. The company is the US's largest independent provider of used-car loans, with a network of 260 offices serving more than 5,000 car dealers. It also makes cash loans and works with retailers to underwrite the sales of appliances and other household goods. Through its subsidiaries Gulfco Life and Mercury Life, the company provides credit, health, and life insurance to borrowers.

Mercury was formed in 1984 by John Brincat, a former marine, to make small, short-term loans to US military personnel. Brincat persuaded First Illinois Corp. of Evanston, Illinois, to form Mercury as a subsidiary. The company's first office was near the main gate of Pensacola (Florida) Naval Air Station. In 1989 Mercury was spun off and listed on the NYSE, its stock was distributed to First Illinois shareholders, and First Illinois was dissolved. At the same time, First Illinois Life Insurance became Mercury Life Insurance. Chicago investor, octogenarian, and noted art collector Daniel Terra is Mercury's chairman and owns 16% of its stock.

In 1993 Mercury bought Gulfco Investment Inc., the Louisiana-based parent of Gulfco Finance (consumer loans) and Gulfco Life Insurance. Gulfco's operations are concentrated in Louisiana, Mississippi, and Texas.

Mercury added 31 new offices in 1994. That same year it acquired Midland Finance Co. of Chicago, which specializes in sales financing contracts and consumer loans. The company also favorably renegotiated its own credit backing at 18 US and foreign banks.

With the lease-car industry pumping "preowned" cars into the marketplace, Mercury will continue to focus on car loans, which accounted for 85% of 1994 receivables. It plans to add 30 or more new offices in 1995, primarily in the northeast and northwest US.

WHO

Chairman: Daniel J. Terra, age 83
President and CEO: John N. Brincat, age 58, $1,738,670 pay
SVP, Controller, and Secretary: James A. Doyle, age 47, $268,617 pay
VP Operations: Richard P. Bosson, age 52, $175,839 pay
VP Operations: John J. Pratt, age 55, $175,596 pay
VP, Treasurer, and CFO: Charley A. Pond, age 49, $170,324 pay
VP Administration: Jeffrey R. Brincat, age 32
VP Operations: John N. Brincat Jr., age 33
VP Marketing: Edward G. Stautzenbach, age 56
Director Human Resources: Robert Lutgen
Auditors: KPMG Peat Marwick LLP

WHERE

HQ: 40 Skokie Blvd., Ste. 200, Northbrook, IL 60062
Phone: 847-564-3720   Fax: 847-564-3758

WHAT

	1994 Receivables % of total
Sales finance	89
Consumer loans	11
Total	**100**

Selected Products

Consumer financing	Insurance (credit life,
Automobile loans	accident, health, and
Direct cash loans	property to borrowers)
Sales finance contracts	Gulfco Life
	Mercury Life

KEY COMPETITORS

Aegis Consumer Funding	Jayhawk Acceptance
Americredit	Monaco Finance
Beneficial	Money Store
CenCor	National Auto Credit
Citicorp	Olympic Financial
Cole Taylor	Regional Acceptance
Credit Acceptance	Search Capital
Dealer Alliance Credit	TFC Enterprises
First Merchants	Union Acceptance
Household International	Unitrin
	World Acceptance

HOW MUCH

NYSE symbol: MFN FY ends: December 31	Annual Growth	1989	1990	1991	1992	1993	1994
Sales ($ mil.)	28.1%	73.3	94.8	115.5	141.9	194.4	252.5
Net income ($ mil.)	37.8%	17.4	23.2	32.8	45.7	64.9	86.5
Income as % of sales	—	23.7%	24.5%	28.4%	32.2%	33.3%	34.3%
Earnings per share ($)	35.8%	0.16	0.21	0.29	0.39	0.56	0.74
Stock price – high ($)	—	3.17	3.80	9.61	12.66	20.38	19.13
Stock price – low ($)	—	1.78	2.25	2.84	7.78	11.25	11.13
Stock price – close ($)	35.8%	2.81	3.14	9.47	11.16	19.13	13.00
P/E – high	—	20	18	33	32	36	26
P/E – low	—	11	11	10	20	20	15
Dividends per share ($)	—	0.00	0.07	0.09	0.14	0.20	0.29
Book value per share ($)	31.8%	0.50	0.65	0.93	1.26	1.67	1.99
Employees	25.1%	490	550	650	780	1,200	1,500

1994 Year-end:
Debt ratio: 76.7%
Return on equity: 41.1%
Cash (mil.): $20.0
Long-term debt (mil.): $750.8
No. of shares (mil.): 114.2
Dividends
    Yield: 2.2%
    Payout: 39.2%
Market value (mil.): $1,485.1
Total assets: $1,036.4

METRA

OVERVIEW

While seeking to raise a head of steam with higher fares, Metra is rolling ahead with plans to open the first new Chicago commuter rail line since 1928. Metra (short for Metropolitan Rail), the commuter rail division of the Regional Transportation Authority, provides rail service to, from, and around Chicago via 12 lines that radiate from the central business district. Its new line northwest to Antioch, Illinois, will begin service in 1996.

By the 1970s, after a century of service, the railroads that helped build Chicago into a Midwest transportation hub were losing money. Passenger traffic had declined as automobile use climbed. However, alternate forms of transportation received a boost when the 1973 OPEC oil embargo squeezed gasoline supplies. That same year the Regional Transportation Authority (RTA) was created to coordinate Chicago-area mass transit.

Three years later the RTA began forming service contracts with commuter railroads, but the RTA's role shifted in 1981 when a railroad company withdrew from its service agreement. No other firms could be induced to take over, so the RTA created the Northeast Illinois Railroad Corp. (NIRC) to operate the commuter line.

In 1983 the Illinois General Assembly authorized 3 decentralized service boards under RTA's umbrella: NIRC was reorganized as the Metropolitan Rail Division (Metra) to manage commuter rail operations. Jeffrey Ladd became Metra's chairman. In 1987 Metra acquired Illinois Central Gulf's main electrical railway line and its southern branches (now Metra Electric), greatly expanding its intercity and suburban service.

In 1989 a bond issue was passed, providing $450 million to Metra for capital improvements. Metra's on-time performance steadily improved, peaking at 97% in 1993 — the highest of any US commuter railroad.

However, in 1995 the worst accident in the agency's history occurred when a school bus was struck by a commuter train, killing 7 students. The wreck fueled debate regarding the need for more grade separations.

WHO

Chairman: Jeffrey R. Ladd
VC: Gerald A. Porter
Executive Director: Philip A. Pagano
Director: Joseph A. Tecson
Director: Donald A. Udstuen
Director: Robert A. Wislow
Treasurer: Lowell E. Anderson
Secretary: W. Warren Nugent
Director Human Resources: Barbara Akins
Auditors: Deloitte & Touche LLP

WHERE

HQ: 547 W. Jackson, Chicago, IL 60661
Phone: 312-322-6900   **Fax:** 312-322-6765

Metra provides service to 215 stations in Chicago, its suburbs, and regional towns in Cook, Du Page, Kane, Lake, McHenry, and Will counties in Illinois. Metra also provides service to 13 stations in South Bend, Indiana, and Kenosha, Wisconsin. The authority owns or leases 1,189 track miles and has 505 route miles.

WHAT

1995 Rolling Stock
Metra owns 130 locomotives, 171 cab cars, 223 electric cars, and 524 trailer cabs

	1994 Passenger Trips	
Line	No. (mil.)	% of total
Union Pacific	25.2	34
Burlington Northern	13.2	18
Electric District	11.5	15
Milwaukee District	11.3	15
Rock Island	8.2	11
South Shore	3.5	5
SouthWest Service	1.5	2
Heritage Corridor	0.3	0
Total	**74.7**	**100**

	1994 Operating Expenses
	% of total
Transportation	31
Equipment	21
Way & structure	18
Fuels	6
Claims	4
Union Station	2
Other	18
Total	**100**

HOW MUCH

Transportation authority FY ends: December 31	Annual Growth	1989	1990	1991	1992	1993	1994
Total revenue[1] ($ mil.)	2.4%	172.0	178.1	180.7	183.7	184.1	193.4
Passenger rev. ($ mil.)	1.4%	151.1	154.7	154.1	156.4	156.3	161.6
Op. expenses ($ mil.)	3.1%	278.5	294.7	295.5	309.3	312.9	327.0
Employees	—	—	—	—	—	—	2,400

[1] Does not include government funding

Metra

MOLEX INCORPORATED

OVERVIEW

Molex is a leading global manufacturer of electronic, electrical, and fiber-optic connectors and switches. Its components are used in a variety of products, including automobiles, computers, household appliances, medical equipment, and office electronics. The Lisle, Illinois–based company makes 50,000 different products, which it sells primarily to OEMs.

In 1938 Frederick Krehbiel mixed coal tar and asbestos to create a thick, black substance he called Molex. The stuff was soon being used in many products, including plastic flower pots, toys, the US Army's land mines (a coating of Molex masked the mines from the enemy's metal detectors), and as sheathing for electrical components. Frederick's son, John Sr., joined the company in the late 1940s and changed its focus to connectors (the product called Molex would soon become obsolete).

The company entered the international connectors market in 1968 and incorporated in 1972. During the 1970s Molex expanded globally, and by the 1980s it was the world's 10th largest manufacturer of electronic connectors. In the late 1980s the company went on a spending binge, acquiring stakes in a variety of small companies and investing millions in new products and plants. The Krehbiel family, including John Sr.'s sons Fred (chairman) and John Jr. (president), owns about 30% of Molex.

During the early 1990s Molex jumped on the emerging technologies bandwagon with new products for cable television, computer networking, and telecommunications.

In 1995 Molex continued to expand its presence in the computer networking market with the acquisition of Mod-Tap W. Corp., a maker of cabling systems used in LANs. Advances in automotive electronics are also playing a role in the growth of Molex, which in 1995 won a $150 million, 3-year contract from General Motors.

WHO

Chairman and CEO: Frederick A. Krehbiel, age 54, $965,019 pay
President: John H. Krehbiel Jr., age 58, $834,740 pay
VP; President, Molex Far East – North Operations; President, Molex Japan: Goro Tokuyama, age 61, $1,013,774 pay
VP; President, Molex European Operations: Werner W. Fichtner, age 52, $817,333 pay
VP International Operations: J. Joseph King, age 51, $659,909 pay
VP, CFO, and Treasurer: John C. Psaltis, age 55
Corporate VP Human Resources: Kathi M. Regas, age 39
Auditors: Deloitte & Touche LLP

WHERE

HQ: 2222 Wellington Ct., Lisle, IL 60532
Phone: 708-969-4550   **Fax:** 708-969-1352

Molex operates 44 manufacturing facilities in 21 countries. The company's overseas headquarters are located in Munich, Singapore, and Tokyo.

WHAT

	1995 Sales % of total
Computers/business equipment/ telecommunications	48
Home entertainment/home appliances	32
Automotive	12
Other	8
Total	**100**

Selected Customers

Apple	General Motors	Motorola
AT&T	Hewlett-Packard	Philips
Canon	IBM	Sony
Compaq	JVC	Xerox
Ford	Matsushita	

KEY COMPETITORS

Altron	Methode	Robinson
AMP	Electronics	Nugent
Augat	3M	SCI Systems
ITT Corp.	Parlex	Thomas & Betts

HOW MUCH

Nasdaq symbol: MOLX FY ends: June 30	Annual Growth	1990	1991	1992	1993	1994	1995[1]
Sales ($ mil.)	15.0%	594.4	708.0	776.2	859.3	964.1	1,197.7
Net income ($ mil.)	15.8%	59.6	64.6	67.5	74.7	94.9	124.0
Income as % of sales	—	10.0%	9.1%	8.7%	8.7%	9.8%	10.4%
Earnings per share ($)	15.2%	0.61	0.67	0.69	0.76	0.96	1.24
Stock price – high ($)	—	24.58	18.56	20.22	24.48	28.80	31.41
Stock price – low ($)	—	8.45	11.27	15.11	16.48	19.36	24.80
Stock price – close ($)	21.1%	11.91	18.30	17.05	22.72	27.59	31.00
P/E – high	—	40	28	29	32	30	25
P/E – low	—	14	17	22	22	20	20
Dividends per share ($)	24.6%	0.01	0.01	0.01	0.02	0.03	0.03
Book value per share ($)	17.3%	4.94	5.65	6.72	7.62	8.87	10.97
Employees	7.2%	6,700	6,900	7,400	7,671	8,167	9,500

1995 Year-end:
Debt ratio: 0.7%
Return on equity: 12.5%
Cash (mil.): $313.1
Current ratio: 2.78
Long-term debt (mil.): $8.1
No. of shares (mil.): 101.0
Dividends
  Yield: 0.1%
  Payout: 2.4%
Market value (mil.): $3,130.4
R&D as % of sales: 6.5%

[1] 1995 stock prices are through fiscal year-end (June 30).

MORNINGSTAR, INC.

OVERVIEW

Mutual funds have gone supernova and Morningstar is hot. The biweekly *Morningstar Mutual Funds* is the top mutual fund report. The company also publishes information on closed-end funds, variable annuities/life, and equities. Morningstar built its popularity by providing one-page, statistic- and analysis-rich profiles of its subjects. Information is available in print, on CD-ROM, and online.

Morningstar (the name was inspired by the last line in Thoreau's *Walden*: "The sun is but a morning star.") was founded in 1984 by Joseph Mansueto. After earning an MBA at the University of Chicago in 1980 and working as an analyst at money management firm Harris Associates, Mansueto used his savings to launch the quarterly *Mutual Fund Sourcebook*. The early 1980s boom in mutual funds spurred interest in Morningstar's product; 2 years later the company added the biweekly mutual fund report. The company gained recognition in 1985 when *Business Week* used it as a resource for an issue on mutual funds. Mansueto owns the company.

Morningstar's product line has grown to 10 print and 6 CD-ROM titles. In 1991 the company added a biweekly analysis of Japanese stocks (discontinued in 1994, Morningstar's only failure to date). In 1992 the company introduced a CD-ROM database covering more than 2,200 mutual funds along with a program that allows users to compare, evaluate, and track them. The following year Canadian funds were added to Morningstar reports, and in 1994 the company launched a publication on American Depository Receipts (ADRs).

Morningstar has also been creating an investors' database of US companies. In 1994 it moved closer to achieving this goal with the acquisition of MarketBase, which compiles data on the stocks of 6,000 US firms.

By the end of 1994, *Morningstar Mutual Funds* had 35,000 subscribers at $395 a year. The monthly newsletter *5-Star Investor* had 78,000 subscribers. In an ongoing feud, rival Value Line has accused Morningstar of copying its format, while Morningstar has accused Value Line of plagiarizing its analyses.

In 1995 Dow Jones entered negotiations to acquire a 20% stake in Morningstar.

WHO

CEO: Joseph Mansueto
President: Donald Phillips
CFO: Patrick Geddes
COO: Liz Michaels
Controller: Joseph Sutton
Publisher, Managed Products: John Rekenthaler
Publisher, Equity Products: Cathy Gillis
Managing Editor, ADRs: Rika Yoshida
Editor, ADRs: Haywood Kelly
Editor, Closed-End Funds: Gregg Wolper
Editor, Annuities and Life: Jennifer Strickland
Auditors: Deloitte & Touche LLP

WHERE

HQ: 225 W. Wacker Dr., Chicago, IL 60606-1224
Phone: 312-696-6000   **Fax:** 312-696-6001

WHAT

Selected Products

Mutual Funds
5-Star Investor (monthly newsletter covering 500 funds)
Morningstar Mutual Fund 500 (annual book covering 500 funds)
Morningstar Mutual Funds (biweekly report covering 1,500 funds)
Morningstar No-Load Funds (monthly report covering 650 funds)
Morningstar OnDemand (as-needed fax or mail report covering 1,500 funds)
Mutual Funds OnDisc (monthly, quarterly, or annual CD-ROM covering 5,700 funds)
Mutual Fund Performance Report (monthly, quarterly, or annual book covering 5,700 funds and 1,500 money market funds)

Other
The Dow Jones Guide to the World Stock Market (book; published in association with Dow Jones & Co.)
Morningstar ADRs (biweekly report covering 700 stocks)
Morningstar Closed-End Funds (biweekly report covering 350 funds)
Morningstar Variable Annuities/Life (biweekly report covering 790 subaccounts and 80 policies)
U.S. Equities OnFloppy (weekly, monthly, quarterly, or annual disk covering 6,000 stocks)
Variable Annuity/Life Performance Report (monthly, quarterly, or annual report covering 2,500 subaccounts)

KEY COMPETITORS

Bloomberg
CDA/Weisenberger
Dun & Bradstreet
Lipper Analytical
McGraw-Hill
Micropal
Pearson
Value Line

HOW MUCH

Private company FY ends: December 31	Annual Growth	1990	1991	1992	1993	1994	1995
Sales ($ mil.)	68.9%	2.4	4.5	11.2	21.2	32.0	33.0[1]
Employees	58.5%	35	70	190	280	380	350

[1] Estimated

PC QUOTE, INC.

OVERVIEW

Like a determined David among many Goliaths, little PC Quote has come out swinging in the competition to supply financial market data to commercial and individual customers. The secret behind the company's ability to capture such big-league partners as Charles Schwab and Microsoft (which in 1995 contracted with the company to provide data for its Microsoft Network online service) is its transmission system, HyperFeed. This system allows PC Quote to supply its data instantaneously via satellite rather than over phone lines. Unlike that of many competitors, PC Quote's data is manipulable by clients' systems instead of being confined to a rigid format. Two strategic allies, Bridge Information Systems (which provides international financial data) and National Computer Systems (which provides on-site customer assistance) own 21.8% and 14.3% of PC Quote, respectively.

On-Line Response, PC Quote's predecessor, built the world's first real-time option analysis system in 1975. In 1980 the company was incorporated with current chairman Louis Morgan as president. It became PC Quote in 1983 and went public in 1984. Although the company garnered a clientele of banks and financial institutions, it remained unprofitable, despite a cash infusion from investor and ally Bridge, because of high product development costs. The company introduced HyperFeed in 1989. In the 1990s PC Quote has concentrated on global expansion and on transforming itself to a mature growth organization from an entrepreneurial company.

In 1995, in addition to the partnership with Microsoft, PC Quote forged alliances with Time Warner (for Time Warner's new interactive cable system) and with News Corp./MCI Online Ventures, a new joint venture focusing on interactive information services for the Internet.

WHO

Chairman, CEO, and Treasurer: Louis J. Morgan, age 58, $225,463 pay
CFO: Richard F. Chappetto, age 45, $147,658 pay
SVP: James M. Yates
VP Development and Design: Michael J. Kreutzjans, $123,140 pay
VP Sales: Jerry M. Traver
Corporate Secretary (HR): Darlene Czaja
Auditors: Coopers & Lybrand L.L.P.

WHERE

HQ: 300 S. Wacker Dr., Ste. 300, Chicago, IL 60606
Phone: 312-913-2800 **Fax:** 312-913-2900

PC Quote has offices in Chicago, Los Angeles, New York, and San Diego in the US and in Caracas, Guatemala City, London, Manila, Singapore, Taipei, and Toronto.

WHAT

	1994 Sales	
	$ mil.	% of total
Services to nonaffiliates	9.5	74
Services to Bridge Information Systems	3.4	26
Total	**12.9**	**100**

Selected Products
HyperFeed (digital data transmission product)
InvestorVison/QuoteBlaster (stock data software)
PC QUOTE (real-time stock and commodity trading data software)
PC Quote for Windows (Windows-compatible version)
PriceWare (asset pricing service)
QuoteLan (for networks)
QuoteWare (data interfaces with user systems)

News Services Available Through PC Quote
COMTEX OmniNews
Dow Jones News Services
Futures World News

KEY COMPETITORS

ADP	Global Market Information
Bloomberg	Reuters
Data Broadcasting	Security APL
Dow Jones	Telekurs

HOW MUCH

AMEX symbol: PQT FY ends: December 31	Annual Growth	1989	1990	1991	1992	1993	1994
Sales ($ mil.)	7.2%	9.1	10.0	10.2	11.0	12.2	12.9
Net income ($ mil.)	—	(0.4)	(1.4)	(0.5)	0.1	0.2	0.3
Income as % of sales	—	—	—	—	0.9%	1.6%	2.5%
Earnings per share ($)	—	(0.06)	(0.21)	(0.08)	0.01	0.03	0.04
Stock price – high ($)	—	4.63	2.38	1.06	1.75	3.75	3.13
Stock price – low ($)	—	1.88	0.81	0.63	0.63	0.75	1.00
Stock price – close ($)	(6.8%)	2.13	0.81	0.63	0.69	2.13	1.50
P/E – high	—	—	—	—	175	125	78
P/E – low	—	—	—	—	63	25	25
Dividends per share ($)	—	0.00	0.00	0.00	0.00	0.00	0.00
Book value per share ($)	(5.0%)	0.89	0.67	0.60	0.61	0.64	0.69
Employees	(1.0%)	80	85	68	68	79	76

1994 Year-end:
Debt ratio: 27.3%
Return on equity: 6.5%
Cash (mil.): $1.4
Current ratio: 0.78
Long-term debt (mil.): $0.9
No. of shares (mil.): 7.0
Dividends
 Yield: —
 Payout: —
Market value (mil.): $10.5
R&D as % of sales: 5.2%

PITTWAY CORPORATION

OVERVIEW

Pittway has grown alarmingly in recent years. Fueled by a growing sense of personal insecurity, the Chicago-based company's fire and burglar alarm businesses have prospered over the past 5 years. Pittway's Ademco subsidiary is the world's #1 burglar and fire alarm system maker, with over 23% of the US market. Pittway's other business line, trade magazine publishing (23% of 1994 revenues), has had flat sales over the past 5 years. Its Penton Publishing subsidiary publishes 43 national business and trade publications, such as *Air Transport World* and *Industry Week*. Pittway also has holdings in real estate.

The company is developing systems that integrate various alarms and controls (e.g., video cameras and burglar and fire alarms) into single operating systems. It is expanding its wireless alarm systems business (only 15% of the market in 1994). Pittway is also growing internationally. It opened sales offices in Brazil, France, and Mexico in 1994.

Pittway has its roots in the Standard Gas and Electric Company, formed in the 1920s. The Pittsburgh Railways Company, Standard Gas's streetcar operation, was spun off in 1950. Neison Harris, a veteran of the beauty product supply business, gained a controlling interest in Pittsburgh Railway in the early 1960s and diversified the company. In 1963 he bought Ademco, a leading alarm maker, and in 1967 he changed the company's name to Pittway. Pittway acquired Patterson Publishing in 1968 and Penton Publishing in 1976. After diversifying into packaging and consumer electronics, Pittway spun off these lines in the early 1990s to focus on its 2 core businesses. Harris's son King is CEO. Members of the Harris family hold 52.8% of company stock.

In 1995 the company announced plans to begin operating a joint venture manufacturing plant with China's leading maker and distributor of smoke detectors.

WHO

Chairman: Neison Harris, age 79
VC; Chairman and CEO, Ademco Security Group: Leo A. Guthart, age 57, $655,000 pay
President and CEO: King Harris, age 51, $700,000 pay
VP; President and COO, Penton Publishing: Daniel J. Ramella, age 42, $400,000 pay
VP; President, Pittway Systems Technology Group: Fred Conforti, age 53, $360,000 pay
VP; Chairman and CEO, Penton Publishing: Sal F. Marino, age 74, $315,000 pay
Financial VP and Treasurer: Paul R. Gauvreau, age 55
Auditors: Price Waterhouse LLP

WHERE

HQ: 200 S. Wacker Dr., Ste. 700, Chicago, IL 60606-5802
Phone: 312-831-1070   **Fax:** 312-831-0808

WHAT

	1994 Sales		1994 Operating Income	
	$ mil.	% of total	$ mil.	% of total
Alarm & other security products	600.6	77	45.2	80
Publishing	176.7	23	11.0	20
Adjustments	0.7	—	(6.3)	—
Total	**778.0**	**100**	**49.9**	**100**

Ademco Security Group	**Pittway Real Estate**
Ademco Hong Kong Ltd.	**Pittway Systems**
ADI (Ademco Distribution Inc.)	**Technology Group**
Fire Burglary Instruments	Nesco
Penton Publishing, Inc.	Notifier/Fire-Lite Alarms
Curtin & Pease/Peneco, Inc.	System Sensor Division
Penton Learning Systems, Inc.	Xetron Division

KEY COMPETITORS

ADT	Knogo North America
Advanstar Communications	McGraw-Hill
Alert Centre	Miller Freeman
Code-Alarm	Publications
Crain Communications	Napco Security Systems
Detection Systems	Protection One
First Alert	Reed Elsevier
K-III	Winner International

HOW MUCH

AMEX symbol: PRYA FY ends: December 31	Annual Growth	1989	1990	1991	1992	1993	1994
Sales ($ mil.)	(1.7%)	847.6	944.1	981.6	568.3	650.1	778.0
Net income ($ mil.)	6.5%	32.7	24.1	25.5	47.4	31.2	44.8
Income as % of sales	—	3.9%	2.6%	2.6%	8.3%	4.8%	5.8%
Earnings per share ($)	6.2%	2.38	1.74	1.85	3.42	2.24	3.22
Stock price – high ($)	—	—	21.63	17.50	20.00	34.00	40.75
Stock price – low ($)	—	—	11.50	11.25	15.75	18.50	31.50
Stock price – close ($)	35.7%	—	11.50	16.56	19.00	34.00	39.00
P/E – high	—	—	12	10	6	15	13
P/E – low	—	—	7	6	5	8	10
Dividends per share ($)	—	—	7.71	0.45	0.75	0.35	0.40
Book value per share ($)	(4.4%)	—	28.13	28.90	30.09	20.95	23.53
Employees	(9.1%)	8,700	8,500	8,300	4,500	4,800	5,400

1994 Year-end:
Debt ratio: 14.7%
Return on equity: 14.4%
Cash (mil.): $44.7
Current ratio: 1.98
Long-term debt (mil.): $5.1
No. of shares (mil.): 13.9
Dividends
  Yield: 1.0%
  Payout: 12.4%
Market value (mil.): $543.7

PLATINUM TECHNOLOGY, INC.

PLATINUM technology, inc., is fattening its share of the open systems computing market by gobbling up software companies — 11 in 1995 alone. PLATINUM (long dependent on mainframe database software) is using its acquisitions to build a new systems management framework called P.O.E.M.S. (PLATINUM Open Enterprise Management System). P.O.E.M.S. lets a company integrate its multiple software platforms (including MVS, UNIX, and Windows) into a custom environment. Among PLATINUM's recent acquisitions are Answer Systems (help-desk software), Locus (open systems software consulting), and Trinzic (client/server application development tools).

Andrew "Flip" Filipowski started PLATINUM (with several partners) in 1987 after being forced out of DBMS Inc., a software firm he had founded in 1979 (DBMS was acquired by Computer Associates in 1990). PLATINUM's aim was to improve DB2, IBM's relational database manager that supplanted older hierarchical systems. (DB2's complexity spawned a number of performance-enhancing products by independent software developers.) Struggling at first, Filipowski gained market share by deeply discounting his product. PLATINUM went public in 1991. That year the company completed an agreement with IBM whereby PLATINUM paid 10% of its revenues from certain software in return for access to IBM's database research program. By 1994 the company had also forged strategic systems support alliances with Oracle, Sybase, and Gupta Corp.

By mid-1995 PLATINUM offered more than 100 software products for data manipulation and systems management. The company continues to add options to P.O.E.M.S., which may soon encompass the OS/2, AS400, and VMS platforms. Also in 1995 PLATINUM said it would participate in Oracle's Warehouse Technology Initiative, bringing advanced relational database technology to P.O.E.M.S. users.

Chairman, President, and CEO: Andrew J. Filipowski, age 43, $1,418,245 pay
EVP Product Development and COO: Paul L. Humenansky, age 37, $816,679 pay
EVP, CFO, Treasurer, and Secretary: Michael P. Cullinane, age 44, $730,024 pay
EVP Sales: Thomas A. Slowey, age 33, $640,637 pay
EVP International Operations: Paul A. Tatro, age 37, $499,750 pay
Director Human Resources: Jennifer Werneke
Auditors: KPMG Peat Marwick LLP

HQ: 1815 S. Meyers Rd., Oakbrook Terrace, IL 60181
Phone: 708-620-5000   **Fax:** 708-691-0710

	1994 Sales	
	$ mil.	% of total
Software	60.6	63
Maintenance	29.6	31
Educational services	5.5	6
Total	**95.7**	**100**

Selected Acquisitions
Altai (automated operations software, 1995)
Aston Brooke (database management tools, 1994)
BrownStone Solutions (relational database repositories, 1995)
Datura (client/server software, 1993)
Dimeric Development (Oracle database software, 1994)
RelTech Group (relational database repositories, 1995)
Software Interfaces (database access software, 1995)
SQL Software (database management tools, 1995)
ViaTech Development (UNIX software, 1995)

American Software
BMC Software
Borland
Candle Corp.
Computer Associates
Computer Data Systems
Compuware
IBM
Informix
LEGENT
OpenVision
Oracle
Progress Software
Sequent
Software AG
Sybase

Nasdaq symbol: PLAT FY ends: December 31	Annual Growth	1989	1990	1991	1992	1993	1994
Sales ($ mil.)	74.0%	6.0	15.2	28.8	49.0	62.2	95.7
Net income ($ mil.)	—	0.2	2.2	5.1	9.3	3.0	(3.2)
Income as % of sales	—	3.3%	14.5%	17.7%	19.0%	4.8%	—
Earnings per share ($)	—	0.02	0.14	0.25	0.43	0.14	(0.16)
Stock price – high ($)	—	—	—	23.50	25.25	25.00	23.75
Stock price – low ($)	—	—	—	9.00	11.25	7.25	10.00
Stock price – close ($)	2.1%	—	—	21.25	20.25	10.75	22.63
P/E – high	—	—	—	94	59	179	—
P/E – low	—	—	—	36	26	52	—
Dividends per share ($)	—	—	—	0.00	0.00	0.00	0.00
Book value per share ($)	28.3%	—	—	2.57	3.13	3.46	5.43
Employees	78.5%	41	71	163	245	382	743

1994 Year-end:
Debt ratio: 0.0%
Return on equity: —
Cash (mil.): $79.4
Current ratio: 2.72
Long-term debt (mil.): $0.0
No. of shares (mil.): 24.2
Dividends
  Yield: —
  Payout: —
Market value (mil.): $546.6
R&D as % of sales: 14.5%

PLAYBOY ENTERPRISES, INC.

OVERVIEW

Built on its well-known magazine (which is known for its well-built centerfolds), Playboy Enterprises is a global publishing, entertainment, and licensing company with related operations in international and domestic cable TV networks, movies, TV programming, videos, CD-ROMS, direct marketing, and name-brand retail products (apparel, spirits, and condoms, among others). Though it is the world's leading men's magazine, with 3 million readers, *Playboy* is still shunned by some advertisers. US circulation is half its 1972 peak, and lately profits have been hurt by higher paper and postage costs. Hugh Hefner owns 70% of company voting stock.

Playboy was started in 1953 by Hefner, a former copywriter at *Esquire*, who mortgaged some belongings, borrowed $6,000 from friends, and threw in $600 of his own. The first issue, which was put together on Hefner's kitchen table, sold 51,000 copies, earning enough to publish a 2nd issue. Hefner epitomized the *Playboy* lifestyle, living among "playmates" in a 48-room mansion (now a dormitory for the Art Institute of Chicago). The Playboy Club, which opened in 1960, was the most successful nightclub chain in history for more than 20 years (the last club closed in 1986). In 1971 the company went public.

In 1982, when Hefner's daughter Christie was named Playboy president, the company began to diversify and greatly expand overseas. That year Playboy launched a national pay cable TV service and home video business. The company agreed to form its first overseas TV network in 1995 with Flextech. Also that year it returned to the casino business when a consortium that includes Playboy was awarded a gaming license on the Greek isle of Rhodes. The company is looking for investors to help Playboy's international expansion.

WHO

Founder, Chairman Emeritus, and Editor in Chief: Hugh M. Hefner, age 69, $498,493 pay
Chairman, President, and CEO: Christie Hefner, age 42, $714,332 pay
EVP Finance and Operations and CFO: David I. Chemerow, age 44, $452,778 pay
EVP and General Counsel: Howard Shapiro, age 48
EVP Publishing Group and Publisher *Playboy*: Richard Kinsler
VP Human Resources: Denise M. Bindelglass
Auditors: Coopers & Lybrand L.L.P.

WHERE

HQ: 680 N. Lake Shore Dr., Chicago, IL 60611
Phone: 312-751-8000   **Fax:** 312-751-2818

WHAT

	1995 Sales		1995 Pretax Income	
	$ mil.	% of total	$ mil.	% of total
Publishing	127.3	51	10.7	—
Catalog	61.4	25	5.2	—
Entertainment	51.7	21	1.0	—
Product marketing	6.8	3	3.4	—
Adjustments	—	—	(17.9)	—
Total	**247.2**	**100**	**2.4**	**—**

Selected Products
900 number (*Playboy*-related audiotext services)
AdulTVision (pay-per-view TV channel)
Books (anthologies and compilations from *Playboy*)
Critics' Choice Video (movie and video catalog)
Playboy (US editions plus 16 foreign editions)
Playboy catalog (clothes, gifts, and collectibles)
The Playboy Electronic Datebook (PC-based daily planner)
Playboy Home Video
Playboy Late Night (weekly TV series)
Playboy Television (cable TV network)

KEY COMPETITORS

Advance Publications	Hearst	Viacom
General Media	Time Warner	Walt Disney
Graff Pay-Per-View	Turner Broadcasting	

HOW MUCH

NYSE symbol: PLA FY ends: June 30	Annual Growth	1990	1991	1992	1993	1994	1995[1]
Sales ($ mil.)	8.1%	167.7	174.0	193.7	214.9	219.0	247.2
Net income ($ mil.)	(36.8%)	6.2	4.5	3.5	0.4	(17.0)	0.6
Income as % of sales	—	3.7%	2.6%	1.8%	0.2%	—	0.3%
Earnings per share ($)	—	0.33	0.24	0.19	0.02	(0.86)	(0.03)
Stock price – high ($)	—	7.63	8.50	9.50	11.00	11.00	10.63
Stock price – low ($)	—	3.13	3.88	5.88	6.63	6.00	7.38
Stock price – close ($)	14.5%	4.00	6.88	7.38	11.00	9.50	7.88
P/E – high	—	23	35	50	550	—	—
P/E – low	—	9	16	31	331	—	—
Dividends per share ($)	—	0.00	0.00	0.00	0.00	0.00	0.00
Book value per share ($)	4.1%	1.93	2.14	2.33	2.78	2.32	2.36
Employees	1.1%	561	586	616	628	583	593

1995 Year-end:
Debt ratio: 11.3%
Return on equity: 1.3%
Cash (mil.): $1.5
Current ratio: 1.17
Long-term debt (mil.): $0.7
No. of shares (mil.): 20.0
Dividends
  Yield: —
  Payout: —
Market value (mil.): $157.4

[1] 1995 stock prices are through fiscal year-end (June 30).

QUILL CORPORATION

OVERVIEW

Lincolnshire–based Quill Corporation is the nation's largest independent mail-order distributor of office products. The company supplies computer and school products as well. Quill markets its goods to more than 750,000 businesses through semiannual catalogs (listing more than 9,500 products) and sales flyers.

The company was started in 1956 by Jack Miller, who sold office supplies from a phone in his father's poultry shop on Chicago's North Side. A year later he was joined by his brother Harvey. In 1974 their brother Arnold sold his California CPA practice to join Quill, which by then operated out of a 37,000-square-foot facility in Northbrook. In 1985 the company finished a $9 million expansion of its current headquarters, giving it a total of 401,000 square feet.

With the advent in the late 1980s of office supply superstores such as Office Depot, Quill was forced to improve its operations. The company lowered its prices and simplified its pricing strategy (giving the customers the lowest price advertised in any of its catalogs). Quill reduced its costs with better targeting of its catalogs and flyers and improved shipping with state-of-the-art distribution centers (Quill has 4 centers across the US and one in Canada). Despite competitive pressures the company continued its strong growth.

In 1991 Quill entered the retail markets with the purchase of Aaron's Office Furniture Warehouse, a 5-store chain in Chicago. (The name was changed to Quill's Office Furniture, and a 6th store was opened in 1994.) In 1992 the company won a major victory in a Supreme Court case, *Quill Corporation v. North Dakota Department of Revenue*. The court held that without congressional authorization, state governments could not force out-of-state mail-order companies to collect taxes from in-state customers unless the company operated a store or employed salespeople in that state.

In 1995 Quill branched out into the school supplies mail-order business. Marketed to elementary and secondary schools, colleges, and vocational schools, Quill catalogs include audio/visual equipment, computer and printer supplies, and furniture, as well as chalk, crayons, scissors, and rulers.

WHO

President: Jack Miller
VP Human Resources: Philip Petrilli
CFO and Treasurer: Arnold Miller
Secretary: Harvey L. Miller
Director Advertising: Lowell Meyers

WHERE

HQ: 100 Schelter Rd., Lincolnshire, IL 60069-3621
Phone: 847-634-6650   **Fax:** 847-634-5816

Distribution Centers
Canton, Georgia
Lebanon, Pennsylvania
Lincolnshire, Illinois
Ontario, California
Mississauga, Ontario

WHAT

Furniture
Microcomputer supplies
Office supplies
School supplies

KEY COMPETITORS

Best Buy
Boise Cascade Office Products
Circuit City
CompUSA
Corporate Express
Damark
Dayton Hudson
ELEK-TEK
Fay's
Global Directmail
Inmac
Intelligent Electronics
Kmart
Micro Warehouse
Office Depot
OfficeMax
P.C. Richard
Price/Costco
Sears
Staples
Tandy Corp.
Viking Office Products
Wal-Mart

HOW MUCH

Private company FY ends: December 31	Annual Growth	1989	1990	1991	1992	1993	1994
Sales ($ mil.)	9.1%	270.0	289.0	310.1	341.0	384.0	418.0
Employees	2.9%	1,084	1,120	1,123	1,156	1,163	1,248

QUIXOTE CORPORATION

OVERVIEW

Quixote (Kee-ho-tay) is composed of 3 major subsidiaries: Disc Manufacturing, Inc. (DMI), which holds 15% of the CD-ROM market and is the largest independent maker of audio compact discs; Energy Absorption Systems, a leading maker of highway crash cushions and safety products; and Legal Technologies, Quixote's weak link, a supplier of legal and court-reporting software and hardware.

CEO Philip Rollhaus gave up aspirations of becoming a novelist and founded Quixote in 1969 to market a plastic energy-absorbing bumper for autos. When the automakers failed to show interest, the bumper technology was reapplied to cushioning objects that vehicles might hit. In 1975 Quixote ventured into optical disc technology and produced the first US-made audio CD. It acquired Stenograph, a pioneer and leading maker of court-reporting machines, 4 years later. Legal Technologies was formed in 1993 to serve as an umbrella for several companies that specialize in particular areas of the legal market, including jury research and trial consulting, shorthand machines, and legal software.

DMI warns that as the selling prices of music CDs and CD-ROMs continue to decline, future profit margins will diminish. To combat that, DMI is increasing volume. In 1995 DMI secured manufacturing contracts with Rand McNally Media and Eastman Kodak and continued its 3-year, $65 million expansion program, which will double capacity to 200 million discs a year by 1997. The Bertelsmann Music Group, which includes the RCA label, accounted for 38% of DMI's revenue in 1995.

In April 1995 Energy Absorption acquired a 40% interest in Quantic Industries, a manufacturer of electronic and pyrotechnic devices for the aerospace and defense industries as well as automobile airbag systems.

WHO

Chairman, President, and CEO: Philip E. Rollhaus Jr., age 61, $560,000 pay
EVP Finance; President, Disc Manufacturing, Inc.: Myron R. Shain, age 55, $305,000 pay
EVP and Secretary; President, Legal Technologies, Inc.: James H. DeVries, age 63, $300,000 pay
President, Energy Absorption Systems, Inc.: George D. Ebersole, age 59, $335,000 pay
President, Stenograph Corporation: Michael J. La Forte Jr., age 49, $257,250 pay
Office Manager (HR): Dorothy French
Auditors: Coopers & Lybrand L.L.P.

WHERE

HQ: One E. Wacker Dr., Chicago, IL 60601
Phone: 312-467-6755   **Fax:** 312-467-1356

WHAT

	1995 Sales		1995 Operating Income	
	$ mil.	% of total	$ mil.	% of total
Compact discs	87.3	47	8.7	42
Legal technologies	51.6	28	(7.6)	—
Hwy. safety devices & plastic prods.	46.5	25	11.8	58
Adjustments	—	—	(3.7)	—
Total	**185.4**	**100**	**9.2**	**100**

Compact Discs
CD-ROMs
Optical discs

Stenograph Machines and Related Products
Discovery software
Premier Power software
Stentura 6000
Stentura 8000

Highway Safety Devices and Plastic Products
Highway crash cushions
Mobile traffic barriers
Truck-mounted attenuators

KEY COMPETITORS

Bertelsmann
Matsushita
Philips
Sony
Stimsonite
Thorn EMI
Time Warner

HOW MUCH

Nasdaq symbol: QUIX FY ends: June 30	Annual Growth	1990	1991	1992	1993	1994	1995[1]
Sales ($ mil.)	23.0%	65.8	111.8	129.4	145.1	176.9	185.4
Net income ($ mil.)	3.7%	5.0	1.9	8.3	9.4	11.6	6.0
Income as % of sales	—	7.7%	1.7%	6.4%	6.4%	6.6%	3.2%
Earnings per share ($)	1.4%	0.68	0.26	1.07	1.17	1.37	0.73
Stock price – high ($)	—	6.50	13.25	15.75	18.00	22.75	12.75
Stock price – low ($)	—	4.13	3.38	9.50	11.75	10.75	9.25
Stock price – close ($)	22.0%	4.63	13.00	13.75	17.75	11.00	12.50
P/E – high	—	10	51	15	15	17	17
P/E – low	—	6	13	9	10	8	13
Dividends per share ($)	—	0.00	0.00	0.00	0.20	0.22	0.00
Book value per share ($)	14.3%	3.84	3.40	4.51	5.53	6.94	7.49
Employees	8.8%	1,048	988	986	1,156	1,586	1,599

[1] 1995 stock prices are through fiscal year-end (June 30).

1995 Year-end:
Debt ratio: 53.9%
Return on equity: 10.5%
Cash (mil.): $2.2
Current ratio: 1.26
Long-term debt (mil.): $68.0
No. of shares (mil.): 7.9
Dividends
  Yield: —
  Payout: —
Market value (mil.): $98.3
R&D as % of sales: 1.9%

RAND MCNALLY & COMPANY

OVERVIEW

Rand McNally guides more than lost highway travelers. The Skokie, Illinois, company is the world's largest commercial mapmaker — only the Bible outsells its road atlases. However, cartography accounts for less than half of the firm's sales. The privately held company is the 3rd largest printer of children's books and it also provides logistical services, book services, publishing, docusystems, and media services. Its DocuSystems business is the world's leading supplier of baggage tags and tickets for airline and surface transportation.

William Rand cofounded a small print shop with the *Chicago Tribune* in 1856 and 2 years later hired Andrew McNally as an assistant. In 1868 Rand bought the newspaper's share and formed a new company with McNally as his partner. The 2 began making timetables and railway tickets and published their first book, a Chicago business directory, in 1870. One year later the Chicago fire nearly destroyed their print shop, but the firm recovered quickly, issuing its first *Railway Guide* that same year. The company's first map appeared in an edition of the guide a few years later; Rand McNally printed the poems of Robert Browning between the trains' schedules. The company was incorporated in 1880, and McNally bought Rand's share of the business in 1894 upon Rand's retirement. The firm has been held by the McNally family ever since. In the last 50 years, Rand McNally has been profitable every year except 1991 and 1992, when restructuring and accounting changes resulted in modest losses and when the breakup of the Soviet Union led to slow map sales.

In 1994 Rand McNally introduced TripMaker, a vacation-planning software program on CD-ROM. By late 1995 the multimedia program was trampling a 3-year-old Microsoft product. In 1995 Rand McNally won a 10-year contract to create maps and indexes for the *Reader's Digest Illustrated Atlas of the World*. That same year the firm began a joint venture with Italian publisher De Agostini to provide geographic information for print and electronic media worldwide. The 1996 edition of TripMaker covered all of North America and included an improved map interface, views of 30 cities, and a restaurant and hotel guide.

WHO

Chairman and CEO: Andrew McNally IV
President and COO: John S. Bakalar
President, Publishing and New Media Division: Henry J. Feinberg, age 43
President, Book Services: William C. Korner
President, Media Services: James T. Thaden
President, DocuSystems: Thomas J. Breen
VP and CFO: James J. Habschmidt
VP Corporate Relations and Secretary: Edward C. McNally
Chief Cartographer: Michael W. Dobson
VP Human Resources and General Counsel: Kurt D. Steele
Director Corporate Communications: Tony Garel
Auditors: Arthur Andersen & Co, SC

WHERE

HQ: 8255 N. Central Park Ave., Skokie, IL 60076-2970
Phone: 847-329-8100   **Fax:** 847-673-0539

WHAT

Book Services	Publishing
Book manufacturing	Atlases
Information product	Catalogs
support	Children's books
	Globes
DocuSystems	Maps
Airline and surface	Reference books
transportation tickets	
Baggage tags	**Software**
Debit cards	Quick Reference Atlas
Specialty labels	StreetAtlas
Transit passes	TripMaker
	US geography screensaver
Media Services	World Atlas
Custom packaging	
Logistical services	

KEY COMPETITORS

American Automobile Association
American Map Corp.
Automap Inc.
Brøderbund
DeLorme Mapping
Gousha
Hammond
MapInfo
Michelin
Microsoft
Mobil
Strategic Mapping
Stream International
Time Warner

HOW MUCH

Private company FY ends: December 31	Annual Growth	1989	1990	1991	1992	1993	1994
Estimated sales ($ mil.)	12.2%	247.0	262.0	306.9	341.9	395.0	439.0
Estimated employees	1.0%	4,000	4,200	4,200	4,200	4,200	4,200

 RAND McNALLY

SCOTSMAN INDUSTRIES, INC.

OVERVIEW

This Scotsman likes the cold. Scotsman Industries is the world's largest ice machine maker and is a leading US manufacturer of food preparation workstations and refrigerators. The company also makes drink dispensing equipment (it holds leading market positions in the UK), exhaust hoods, and other niche products for food service outlets. Scotsman (which earned 1/4 of its 1994 sales in Europe) primarily sells to commercial customers in the food service, hospitality, beverage, and health care industries in 60 countries. The company's commercial ice machine business accounted for 57% of 1994 sales. Officers and directors hold about 18% of Scotsman.

The company was spun off from Household International (the parent of Household Finance, which had diversified into manufacturing in the late 1960s) in 1989, borrowing $57.5 million from its former parent in the process. Led by Richard Osborne, EVP of Household's manufacturing subsidiary before the spin-off, Scotsman restructured, consolidated plants, disposed of noncore assets, and beefed up its marketing operations. In 1992 Scotsman acquired US ice-maker manufacturer Crystal Tips and also obtained exclusive rights to sell large-capacity flake ice machines made by Howe. In 1993 the company acquired Simag, an Italian ice machine maker, for approximately $5.5 million.

Scotsman expanded its market share in 1994 with the acquisition of Delfield Co. (refrigerated food service equipment) and Whitlenge Drink Equipment (drink dispensing equipment, UK) for $69.3 million. The company plans to acquire other firms in the US and Europe as the manufacturing base in the food service industry consolidates, and it is also looking to other markets for expansion.

In 1995 Scotsman acquired a 40% interest in an ice machine joint venture in China, with Xinle, part of the Chinese Aerospace Agency.

WHO

Chairman, President, and CEO: Richard C. Osborne, age 51, $520,000 pay
EVP; Managing Director, Frimont, SpA, and Castel MAC, SpA: Emanuele Lanzani, age 60, $222,194 pay
VP Finance and Secretary: Donald D. Holmes, age 57, $220,768 pay
VP; President and CEO, The Delfield Co.: Kevin E. McCrone, age 46, $205,972 pay
VP Human Resources: Richard M. Holden, age 44
General Manager, Castel MAC, SpA: Paolo Faenza, age 55, $168,836 pay
Auditors: Arthur Andersen & Co, SC

WHERE

HQ: 775 Corporate Woods Pkwy., Vernon Hills, IL 60061
Phone: 847-215-4500   **Fax:** 847-913-9844

	1994 Sales	
	$ mil.	% of total
US	201.7	76
Europe	64.9	24
Total	**266.6**	**100**

WHAT

	1994 Sales
	% of total
Commercial ice machines	57
Food preparation & storage equipment	28
Drink dispensing equipment	12
Other	3
Total	**100**

Selected Subsidiaries
Booth (Crystal Tips ice machines)
Castel MAC SpA (ice machines, Italy)
Delfield Co. (refrigerated food service equipment)
Frimont SpA (ice machines, Italy)
Whitlenge Drink Equipment (drink dispensing equipment, UK)

KEY COMPETITORS

AB Electrolux	Maytag	Remcor
IMI	NYCOR	Whitman
Manitowoc	Premark	

HOW MUCH

NYSE symbol: SCT FY ends: Sun. nearest Dec. 31	Annual Growth	1989	1990	1991	1992	1993	1994
Sales ($ mil.)	8.9%	174.4	179.9	164.1	168.7	164.0	266.6
Net income ($ mil.)	11.3%	7.5	7.4	(1.7)	6.4	7.4	11.9
Income as % of sales	—	4.3%	4.1%	—	3.8%	4.5%	4.8%
Earnings per share ($)	9.4%	0.86	1.05	(0.24)	0.90	1.06	1.35
Stock price – high ($)	—	15.00	10.50	9.63	10.63	14.50	18.25
Stock price – low ($)	—	8.88	4.63	6.00	7.13	9.13	13.00
Stock price – close ($)	10.8%	10.25	6.88	8.13	9.38	14.13	17.13
P/E – high	—	17	10	—	12	14	14
P/E – low	—	10	4	—	8	9	10
Dividends per share ($)	14.9%	0.05	0.10	0.10	0.10	0.10	0.10
Book value per share ($)	24.8%	3.45	4.75	4.39	4.31	4.85	10.45
Employees	13.7%	1,150	1,100	1,075	1,027	915	2,182

1994 Year-end:
Debt ratio: 50.5%
Return on equity: 19.8%
Cash (mil.): $9.8
Current ratio: 1.88
Long-term debt (mil.): $85.2
No. of shares (mil.): 8.3
Dividends
　Yield: 0.6%
　Payout: 7.4%
Market value (mil.): $141.6
R&D as % of sales: 1.9%

SPORTMART, INC.

OVERVIEW

From hiking to cycling, from soccer to skating, Sportmart has the goods. The Wheeling-based company is one of the leading sporting goods superstore retailers in the US, and it is the market leader in each of its developed markets, including Chicago, Los Angeles, and San Francisco/Sacramento. A pioneer of the sporting goods superstore concept, Sportmart stocks about 65,000 different products in stores that average about 42,000 square feet. Stores are broken up into "concept shops" such as the Cheering Section (licensed apparel), the Fairway (golf equipment), and the Campsite (outdoor equipment and apparel). Sportmart also operates 4 No Contest athletic footwear and apparel stores in St. Louis and Bloomington, Minnesota. Cofounder and CEO Larry Hochberg and his family control 48% of the company's stock (60% of voting shares).

A former executive with toy retailer Children's Bargain Town, Hochberg sold his stake in that company to a predecessor of Toys "R" Us in 1969. In 1970 he and Sanford Cantor, who had also worked at Children's Bargain Town, founded Sportmart. They opened their first store in Niles in 1971. Sportmart opened 4 more stores in the Chicago area during the 1970s. In 1982 it moved into Southern California, opening 2 stores in the Los Angeles area. Sportmart expanded into San Diego in 1988 and San Francisco in 1992. By 1992 it had 26 superstores. That year the company went public.

Since its IPO, Sportmart has expanded rapidly to compete with other sporting goods superstore chains, including market leader Sports Authority. In 1992 and 1993 the company moved into Minneapolis, Portland, and Seattle, and it expanded into Columbus, Ohio.

Sportmart continues to grow rapidly. In 1995 it moved into Toronto.

WHO

Chairman and CEO: Larry J. Hochberg, age 57, $360,776 pay
VC and Secretary: Sanford Cantor, age 61, $220,848 pay
President: Andrew S. Hochberg, age 33, $206,370 pay (prior to promotion)
EVP Marts: John A. Lowenstein, age 33
SVP and CFO: Thomas T. Hendrickson, age 40
SVP Merchandising: Mark Scott
VP and General Counsel: Gregory E. Fix, age 36
VP Human Resources: Joseph A. DeFalco Jr., age 41
Auditors: Coopers & Lybrand L.L.P.

WHERE

HQ: 1400 S. Wolf Rd., Ste. 200, Wheeling, IL 60090
Phone: 847-520-0100   **Fax:** 847-520-1570

	1995 Superstores
	No.
Chicago	17
Los Angeles	14
San Francisco/Sacramento	10
Minneapolis	4
Seattle	3
Toronto	3
Other cities	6
Total	**57**

WHAT

	1995 Sales
	% of total
Fitness equipment, in-line skates, outdoor equipment & other sports equipment	53
Sportswear & athletic apparel	26
Athletic footwear	21
Total	**100**

KEY COMPETITORS

Athlete's Foot	Leonard Green &	Sports &
Finish Line	Partners	Recreation
G. I. Joe's	L. L. Bean	Sports Authority
J. C. Penney	Oshman's	Wal-Mart
Kmart	Sporting Goods	Woolworth

HOW MUCH

Nasdaq symbol: SPMT FY ends: Sun. nearest Jan. 31	Annual Growth	1990	1991	1992	1993	1994	1995	1995 Year-end: Debt ratio: 34.0%
Sales ($ mil.)	19.6%	173.3	187.2	216.0	250.5	338.4	424.2	Return on equity: 8.7%
Net income ($ mil.)	28.5%	2.6	3.0	5.8	5.9	7.9	8.9	Cash (mil.): $3.2
Income as % of sales	—	1.5%	1.6%	2.7%	2.3%	2.3%	2.1%	Current ratio: 2.05
Earnings per share ($)	5.9%	—	—	0.69	0.66	0.77	0.82	Long-term debt (mil.): $31.1
Stock price – high ($)[1]		—	—	—	—	—	17.50	No. of shares (mil.): 12.8
Stock price – low ($)[1]		—	—	—	—	—	10.25	Dividends
Stock price – close ($)[1]		—	—	—	—	—	11.13	Yield: —
P/E – high		—	—	—	—	—	21	Payout: —
P/E – low		—	—	—	—	—	13	Market value (mil.): $141.9
Dividends per share ($)		—	—	—	—	—	0.00	
Book value per share ($)		—	—	—	—	—	8.40	
Employees	24.4%	—	—	2,343	2,998	3,804	4,512	

[1] Stock prices are for the prior calendar year.

SPYGLASS, INC.

OVERVIEW

If you want to cruise the information super-highway, you need a vehicle, a software program called a browser. Spyglass's Mosaic (formerly called Enhanced Mosaic) is one of the most widely used browsers on the giant network of linked multimedia databases called the World Wide Web. Naperville, Illinois–based Spyglass licenses its Mosaic software to more than 36 companies, which embed the program into their own products. CompuServe uses Spyglass Mosaic to give its subscribers access to the Web; Alis Technologies uses the program in its new multilingual browser.

Spyglass was started in 1990 by University of Illinois master of science graduate Tim Krauskopf and others to commercialize technology from the university's National Center for Supercomputing Applications (NCSA). In 1991 Krauskopf recruited Doug Colbeth from Stellar/Stardent to raise venture capital for the fledgling company. Spyglass's expertise with graphical software and its relationship with NCSA prompted the university in 1994 to choose the company as a partner for commercializing Mosaic, which had been developed with public funds and was being distributed for free. Later that year Spyglass licensed a commercial version of the program (Spyglass Enhanced Mosaic) for use in products by such industry giants as IBM (OS/2 Warp operating system), AT&T (NetWare Connect Services), DEC (Pathworks), Ventana Communications (Internet Membership Kit and Mosaic Quick Tour software), CompuServe (Spry's Internet-in-a-Box and Air Mosaic), and NEC.

In 1995 Spyglass released the upgraded version 2.1 of Spyglass Mosaic, which provides secure checking and credit card transactions over the Internet (using the open standard Secure Transaction Technology developed by Microsoft and Visa International). That same year an agreement with Microsoft put Spyglass Mosaic features into the Windows 95 operating system. The company also sold its visual data analysis software (including Plot, Slicer, and Transform) and announced that it would expand its marketing efforts in Europe and Asia.

Spyglass went public in mid-1995 at $17 a share. It ended fiscal 1995 with revenues of $10.35 million, nearly triple 1994 revenues.

WHO

President and CEO: Douglas P. Colbeth, age 39, $130,500 pay
EVP Marketing: Marcus C. Miller, age 40
EVP Business Development: Michael F. Tyrrell, age 36
VP Research and Development and Chief Technical Officer: Tim Krauskopf, age 31, $83,000 pay
VP Sales: Thomas Banahan
Treasurer, Controller, and Secretary: Thomas S. Lewicki, age 40, $55,000 pay
Product Manager: Dan Johnson
Director Business Development: Andrew Parker
Director Public Relations: Randy Pitzer
Office Manager: Kathy Jacob
Auditors: Price Waterhouse LLP

WHERE

HQ: Naperville Corporate Ctr., 1230 E. Diehl Rd., Ste. 304, Naperville, IL 60563
Phone: 708-505-1010   **Fax:** 708-505-4944

Spyglass has sales offices in California and Massachusetts and an R&D facility in Illinois.

WHAT

	1995 Sales	
	$ mil.	% of total
World Wide Web technology	8.9	85
Data visualization products	1.5	15
Total	**10.4**	**100**

Products
Spyglass Mosaic (graphical interface software for the World Wide Web)
Spyglass Server (World Wide Web database management and access control software)

Selected Licensing Partners

Alis Technologies	Microsoft	PSI
Corel	NEC	Quarterdeck
DEC	Oracle	Ventana Media
Firefox	O'Reilly & Associates	

KEY COMPETITORS

America Online	NETCOM	Silicon Graphics
Apple	NetManage	Sun
CERN	Netscape	Microsystems
Cornell University	Network	University
Frontier	Computing	of Kansas
Technologies	OpenMarket	Verity
Intercon	Oracle	
Systems	Prodigy	

HOW MUCH

Nasdaq symbol: SPYG FY ends: September 30	Annual Growth	1990	1991	1992	1993	1994	1995
Sales ($ mil.)	146.4%	0.1	0.6	0.9	1.4	3.6	10.4
Net income ($ mil.)	—	(0.3)	(0.8)	(0.6)	(0.6)	1.1	2.2
Income as % of sales	—	—	—	—	—	29.6%	21.1%
Employees	128.3%	—	—	—	14	48	73

SPYGLASS

SYSTEM SOFTWARE ASSOCIATES, INC.

OVERVIEW

System Software Associates (SSA) is a leading provider of cost-effective business information systems. The company's integrated product line, the Business Planning and Control System, provides business process re-engineering and integration of operations, such as configurable manufacturing processes, global financial solutions, and supply chain management. Other offerings include interoperable tool set products (known as AS/SET) and electronic data interchange products. SSA sells through a network of 150 affiliate software firms in 70 countries and a worldwide office system.

Roger Covey started SSA in 1981. The company grew by offering products for IBM's AS computers and by developing strong relationships with affiliates (software and professional services firms that market SSA products after being trained by SSA). The company went public in 1987, using the proceeds to acquire 3 of its affiliates. In 1991 Covey turned the reins over to Larry Ford, a former IBM executive.

SSA's strategy is to provide open systems software that is platform independent. Its object-based software architecture runs on several servers, including IBM AS/400, UNIX–based RS/6000, and HP 9000.

In 1994 SSA entered into an alliance with Hewlett-Packard (a leader in commercial UNIX systems) to provide solutions to business problems worldwide. That same year, after a 3-year absence during which he studied Chinese art, SSA founder and 32.5% owner Covey got back in the CEO saddle again. Covey pushed Ford into the VC position.

In 1995 SSA teamed up with Netherlands-based Harbinger Corp. (commerce software) to develop AS/400 products. Also that year the company acquired Softwright, the leading provider of business object technology and systems in Europe. In 1995 revenue rose to $394.4 million and profits more than doubled to $34.1 million.

WHO

Chairman and CEO: Roger E. Covey, age 40
VC: Larry J. Ford, age 53, $385,000 pay
President and COO: Terence H. Osborne, age 56, $444,833 pay (prior to promotion)
VP North America: Terry E. Notari, age 56, $290,000 pay (prior to promotion)
VP and CFO: Joseph J. Skadra, age 53
Director Human Resources: Mark Ugol
Auditors: Price Waterhouse LLP

WHERE

HQ: 500 W. Madison St., 32nd Fl., Chicago, IL 60661
Phone: 312-641-2900   **Fax:** 312-474-7500

	1994 Sales		1994 Operating Income	
	$ mil.	% of total	$ mil.	% of total
US	165.6	45	22.4	90
Europe & Mideast	119.4	32	1.9	8
Other regions	82.6	23	0.5	2
Adjustments	(33.2)	—	—	—
Total	**334.4**	**100**	**24.8**	**100**

WHAT

	1994 Sales	
	$ mil.	% of total
License fees	239.5	72
Client services & other	94.9	28
Total	**334.4**	**100**

Business Planning and Control System (BPCS)
  Product Applications
Distribution and logistics
Financial
Manufacturing
Retrieval

Interoperable Tool Set Products
AS/SET software development tools
Electronic Data Interchange (EDI) Products

KEY COMPETITORS

American Software	Computer Associates	Oracle
Arthur Andersen	Dun & Bradstreet	PeopleSoft
BMC Software	Fourth Shift	Sterling
BT	General Electric	Software

HOW MUCH

Nasdaq symbol: SSAX FY ends: October 31	Annual Growth	1989	1990	1991	1992	1993	1994
Sales ($ mil.)	28.6%	95.0	124.2	149.1	228.8	263.4	334.4
Net income ($ mil.)	6.8%	11.1	16.4	16.7	26.6	23.4	15.4
Income as % of sales	—	11.7%	13.2%	11.2%	11.6%	8.9%	4.6%
Earnings per share ($)	6.3%	0.42	0.61	0.63	0.99	0.86	0.57
Stock price – high ($)	—	9.26	12.78	16.56	25.33	25.50	18.00
Stock price – low ($)	—	5.14	5.67	5.56	11.83	10.00	10.63
Stock price – close ($)	12.0%	8.81	12.00	15.50	23.50	15.25	15.50
P/E – high	—	22	21	26	26	30	32
P/E – low	—	12	9	9	12	12	19
Dividends per share ($)	—	0.00	0.00	0.12	0.12	0.12	0.12
Book value per share ($)	23.8%	1.46	2.13	2.60	3.03	3.76	4.25
Employees	33.6%	420	560	760	1,260	1,560	1,790

1994 Year-end:
Debt ratio: 22.2%
Return on equity: 14.3%
Cash (mil.): $60.2
Current ratio: 1.64
Long-term debt (mil.): $32.7
No. of shares (mil.): 27.0
Dividends
  Yield: 0.8%
  Payout: 21.1%
Market value (mil.): $425.2
R&D as % of sales: 10.5%

TECHNOLOGY SOLUTIONS COMPANY

OVERVIEW

Technology Solutions Co. (TSC) is a management consulting firm that designs computer information systems, primarily for large corporations. It has 5 areas of practice: applications and training (systems installation and instruction), call center (development of telecommunications systems for marketing and customer service businesses), financial services (development of transaction processing systems), managed health care (cost control, workflow, and treatment evaluation systems), and products (systems consulting).

When Arthur Young (now Ernst & Young) rejected Albert Beedie's proposal to restructure its systems integration division in 1988, Beedie quit and formed TSC (taking along 10 of Arthur Young's top executives and spawning lawsuits). The company went public in 1991. In 1992, hoping to speed the transition from an entrepreneurial to a corporate culture, Beedie hired Melvyn Bergstein as co-CEO. But the company soon began splitting into Beedie and Bergstein camps, impairing effectiveness and causing defections. After the firm's top client, Northrop (23% of all sales), left, the board asked both men to leave. Beedie left, but Bergstein had to be removed forcibly and took 28 staff members with him (he later filed a wrongful termination suit, winning on several counts).

New management under William Waltrip (formerly of Unifax) stopped the flood of staff departures by offering big bonuses. It did away with the "rainmaker" approach to client recruitment, which depended on the personal contacts of top executives, and enlisted the aid of all employees in selling services. Back on track, the company began expanding in the US and started a subsidiary in Mexico to help service its 1995 strategic alliance with German systems maker SAP.

WHO

Chairman: William H. Waltrip, age 57, $490,000 pay
President and CEO: John T. Kohler, age 48, $850,000 pay
EVP: James S. Carluccio, age 41, $790,000 pay
EVP; President, TSC de México SA de CV: Jack N. Hayden, age 48, $538,000 pay
EVP and Call Center Practice Area Leader: Kelly D. Conway, age 38, $484,000 pay
VP and CFO: Martin T. Johnson, age 44
VP, General Counsel, and Secretary: Paul R. Peterson, age 52
Director Human Resources: Debbie Steele
Auditors: Price Waterhouse LLP

WHERE

HQ: 205 N. Michigan Ave., Ste. 1500, Chicago, IL 60601
Phone: 312-861-9600   **Fax:** 312-861-9601

Technology Solutions has offices in Atlanta, Chicago, Dallas, Los Angeles, New York, and Philadelphia in the US and in Mexico City.

WHAT

Areas of Practice
Applications and training
Call center (telecommunications services)
Financial services (front office and administration; transaction processing, clearance, and settlement; reporting; real-time trading)
Managed health care (workload and technology evaluation, specialist and hospital cost control)
Products (systems & business consulting)

KEY COMPETITORS

American Management	DEC
Arthur Andersen	Dun & Bradstreet
Booz, Allen	EDS
Cambridge Technology	Ernst & Young
Partners	IBM
Cap Gemini	KPMG
Computer Sciences	Perot Systems
Computer Task Group	Price Waterhouse
Coopers & Lybrand	SHL Systemhouse
Deloitte & Touche	Unisys

HOW MUCH

Nasdaq symbol: TSCC FY ends: May 31	Annual Growth	1990	1991	1992	1993	1994	1995[1]
Sales ($ mil.)	8.5%	43.9	52.4	71.0	62.5	53.2	65.8
Net income ($ mil.)	0.8%	3.2	8.5	12.1	5.7	0.0	3.4
Income as % of sales	—	7.4%	16.2%	17.0%	9.1%	0.1%	5.1%
Earnings per share ($)	2.5%	0.31	0.81	1.01	0.46	0.00	0.35
Stock price – high ($)	—	—	25.75	30.75	15.00	9.25	10.25
Stock price – low ($)	—	—	17.25	6.75	7.00	4.75	7.25
Stock price – close ($)	(22.3%)	—	25.75	14.00	9.00	7.75	9.38
P/E – high	—	—	32	30	33	—	29
P/E – low	—	—	21	7	15	—	21
Dividends per share ($)	—	—	0.00	0.00	0.00	0.00	0.00
Book value per share ($)	34.3%	—	1.79	1.79	6.01	5.55	5.83
Employees	6.8%	—	325	473	317	274	423

[1] 1995 stock prices are through fiscal year-end (May 31).

1995 Year-end:
Debt ratio: 3.3%
Return on equity: 6.4%
Cash (mil.): $17.3
Current ratio: 2.80
Long-term debt (mil.): $0.0
No. of shares (mil.): 8.9
Dividends
  Yield: —
  Payout: —
Market value (mil.): $83.2

TELEPHONE AND DATA SYSTEMS, INC.

OVERVIEW

The phones are ringing off the wall at Telephone and Data Systems (TDS), one of the largest non-Bell telephone companies in the US. TDS's 81.3%-owned United States Cellular Corporation subsidiary services 478,000 wireless phones. The fast-growing subsidiary is now the largest contributor to TDS's total revenues, with 45% of sales. The TDS Telecommunications subsidiary operates 96 local telephone companies with more than 420,000 access lines in 29 states. American Paging, an 82.5%-owned subsidiary, services 652,800 pager customers from 36 sales and service operating centers. TDS also operates several service subsidiaries that provide engineering, data processing, custom printing, telephone answering, and other products and services. Founder and chairman Roy Carlson and his family own about 52% of TDS stock.

Carlson ran another phone company for 20 years before selling it to Contel in 1966 for $30 million. He then formed TDS, starting operations in 1969 with 10 telephone companies servicing fewer than 20,000 access lines in Wisconsin. His son Ted joined him in 1974. American Paging was established in 1981 to capitalize on an FCC decision allowing telephone companies to provide radio paging services outside their service areas. US Cellular was founded in 1983.

TDS has acquired 26 telephone companies since 1987, primarily in rural areas and small cities, where the company generates one of the highest revenues-per-subscriber ratios in the market. TDS's cellular phone markets increased from 33 in 1988 to 207 in 1994. It added more than 260 new cell sites and 142,000 new customers to its network in 1994.

In 1995 TDS acquired 4 nonwireline cellular systems serving Iowa, North Carolina, and Virginia in an exchange of assets with Centennial Cellular. It made a bid for Camden Telephone, a firm with cellular assets in Indiana.

WHO

Chairman: Leroy T. "Roy" Carlson, age 78, $335,000 pay
President and CEO: Leroy T. "Ted" Carlson Jr., age 48, $445,000 pay
President, TDS Telecommunications Corporation: James Barr III, age 55, $297,100 pay
President, United States Cellular Corporation: H. Donald Nelson, age 61, $295,200 pay
EVP Finance and CFO: Murray L. Swanson, age 53, $283,750 pay
President, American Paging, Inc.: John R. Schaaf, age 49, $212,550 pay
VP Human Resources: C. Theodore Herbert, age 59
Auditors: Arthur Andersen & Co, SC

WHERE

HQ: 30 N. LaSalle St., Ste. 4000, Chicago, IL 60602-2587
Phone: 312-630-1900   **Fax:** 312-630-1908

WHAT

	1994 Sales	
	$ mil.	% of total
Cellular telephone	332.4	45
Telephone	306.3	42
Radio paging	92.1	13
Total	**730.8**	**100**

Cellular Telephone
United States Cellular
  Corporation (81.3%)

Telephone
TDS Telecommunications
  Corporation

Radio Paging
American Paging, Inc.
  (82.5%)

Service Companies
Integrated
  Communications
  Services, Inc.
  (telemessaging systems)
Suttle Press, Inc.
  (commercial printing)
TDS Computing Services,
  Inc. (information
  systems)

KEY COMPETITORS

AirTouch	Century	Page America
Ameritech	Telephone	Paging Network
Arch	GTE	SBC
Communications	Metrocall	Communications
AT&T Corp.	Nextel	Sprint
Bell Atlantic	NYNEX	U S WEST
BellSouth		

HOW MUCH

AMEX symbol: TDS FY ends: December 31	Annual Growth	1989	1990	1991	1992	1993	1994	1994 Year-end: Debt ratio: 31.3%
Sales ($ mil.)	25.0%	239.7	294.6	354.0	456.1	590.7	730.8	Return on equity: 4.5%
Net income ($ mil.)	40.0%	11.1	27.2	21.1	38.5	33.9	60.5	Cash (mil.): $24.7
Income as % of sales	—	4.6%	9.2%	6.0%	8.4%	5.7%	8.3%	Current ratio: 0.54
Earnings per share ($)	25.0%	0.35	0.86	0.59	0.91	0.67	1.07	Long-term debt (mil.): $536.5
Stock price – high ($)	—	46.50	48.00	40.38	41.25	57.00	51.50	No. of shares (mil.): 54.9
Stock price – low ($)	—	26.88	21.75	28.50	30.13	33.25	35.50	Dividends
Stock price – close ($)	(0.1%)	46.38	34.25	35.50	40.63	52.13	46.13	Yield: 0.8%
P/E – high	—	133	56	68	45	85	48	Payout: 33.6%
P/E – low	—	77	25	48	33	50	33	Market value (mil.): $2,531.0
Dividends per share ($)	6.7%	0.26	0.28	0.30	0.32	0.34	0.36	
Book value per share ($)	14.5%	12.00	14.17	18.46	21.27	24.15	26.85	
Employees	15.7%	2,562	2,954	3,297	3,803	4,343	5,322	

TELLABS, INC.

OVERVIEW

Tellabs makes voice and data transmission products, traditionally for telephone companies. But new markets are calling, including cable TV systems that want to offer phone service via cable lines and phone companies that want to transmit video over phone lines.

Tellabs (shortened from Telecommunications Laboratories) was founded in 1975 by CEO Michael Birck, VP Charles Cooney, and several others. Birck, a former Bell Labs employee, developed an echo suppressor on the company's homemade workbench. Increased use of satellites for phone transmission created a market for the product. Tellabs went public in 1980. Birck owns 11.4% of Tellabs's stock.

The creation of the RBOCs and several new long-distance services in the mid-1980s created a surge of new competitors; Tellabs's sales rose but profits fell. The company restructured for efficiency, boosted R&D spending, and refocused on high-end products. In 1987 a $10 million contract from Sprint for digital echo cancellers helped revive Tellabs, which began marketing to overseas telecommunications services and making strategic acquisitions, including Delta Communications (Ireland, 1987).

In 1991 Tellabs introduced its TITAN digital cross-connect products for routing and switching voice and data transmissions at very high speeds. In 1993 it acquired Martis Oy, a Finnish telecommunications manufacturer whose DXX multiplexer (which allows 2 or more signals to travel over a single circuit) for data and phone networks is now one of Tellabs's top products.

Tellabs continued its global expansion in 1994 with contracts from phone providers in Namibia and Singapore. It also introduced an asynchronous transfer mode (ATM) switch and CABLESPAN, a voice-over-cable product. In 1995 Tellabs penned an OEM agreement whereby Swedish telecommunications equipment maker Ericsson will market DXX cross-connect equipment to Vodafone Australia.

WHO

Chairman: Frederick A. Krehbiel, age 53
President and CEO: Michael J. Birck, age 57, $536,304 pay
CFO; President, Tellabs International: Peter A. Guglielmi, age 53, $335,385 pay
EVP; President, Tellabs Operations: Brian J. Jackman, age 54, $335,385 pay
VP Sales and Service, Tellabs Operations: Charles C. Cooney, age 54, $233,462 pay
VP, General Counsel, and Secretary: Carol Coghlan Gavin, age 39
Director Compensation, Benefits, and Human Resources: Dave Southard
Auditors: Grant Thornton LLP

WHERE

HQ: 4951 Indiana Ave., Lisle, IL 60532
Phone: 708-969-8800　　**Fax:** 708-852-7346

WHAT

	1994 Sales % of total
Digital systems products	46
Managed digital networks	27
Network access products	26
Other	1
Total	**100**

Selected Products
Digital cross-connect systems (cross-connect systems and network management platforms)
Managed digital networks (multiplexers, packet switches, and network management systems)
Network access systems (products for digital signal processing, special services, and local access)

KEY COMPETITORS

ADC Telecom.	Coherent	Newbridge
ADTRAN	Communications	Networks
Alcatel Alsthom	DSC	Nokia
Ascend	Communications	Oki
Communications	Fujitsu	PairGain
Ascom Timeplex	General DataComm	Philips
AT&T Corp.	Motorola	Siemens
Aydin	NEC	Teltrend

HOW MUCH

Nasdaq symbol: TLAB FY ends: Fri. nearest Dec. 31	Annual Growth	1989	1990	1991	1992	1993	1994
Sales ($ mil.)	22.2%	181.3	211.0	212.8	258.6	320.5	494.2
Net income ($ mil.)	59.1%	7.1	8.1	6.6	16.9	30.5	72.4
Income as % of sales	—	3.9%	3.8%	3.1%	6.5%	9.5%	14.6%
Earnings per share ($)	51.6%	0.10	0.11	0.09	0.20	0.35	0.80
Stock price – high ($)	—	2.42	2.52	3.67	4.40	13.59	28.00
Stock price – low ($)	—	1.38	1.40	2.04	2.63	3.17	10.94
Stock price – close ($)	78.0%	1.56	2.50	3.61	4.13	11.81	27.88
P/E – high	—	24	23	41	22	39	35
P/E – low	—	14	13	23	13	9	14
Dividends per share ($)	—	0.00	0.00	0.00	0.00	0.00	0.00
Book value per share ($)	16.1%	1.59	1.70	1.80	2.01	2.41	3.35
Employees	5.0%	2,029	2,127	2,094	2,000	2,370	2,585

1994 Year-end:
Debt ratio: 1.0%
Return on equity: 29.0%
Cash (mil.): $51.5
Current ratio: 2.68
Long-term debt (mil.): $2.9
No. of shares (mil.): 87.3
Dividends
　Yield: —
　Payout: —
Market value (mil.): $2,433.6
R&D as % of sales: 13.1%

TELULAR CORPORATION

OVERVIEW

When a terrorist bomb knocked out phone lines at the World Trade Center in 1993, Telular helped get emergency calls through. The Buffalo Grove, Illinois–based company's "black box" allows traditional phone, fax, and video equipment to transmit over wireless networks. Telular products are also used at remote locations and in emerging countries where telephone infrastructure is limited. Now the company wants to sell its products to homeowners in the US, where most cellular calls are made during the day, making system access much cheaper during off-hours.

Telular was founded in 1986 by chairman Bill De Nicolo to capitalize on a device created by Mississippi inventor Bill West. Its products were originally used for emergency communications and wireless alarms, but in 1992 former Skytel executive James Phillips became Telular's president and led its development of telecommunications products. Richard Gerstner, a former IBM VP (and older brother of IBM CEO Louis Gerstner), became Telular's president and CEO in 1993. The company went public in 1994. Motorola owns 20.5% of the stock; De Nicolo owns 19.8%.

Telular has been struggling after spending heavily to sell its products in emerging nations and to protect its core technology. After years of costly litigation, in 1994 and 1995 Telular won a series of victories upholding its principal patent. It has had less luck in less-developed countries, which are opting for fully wireless telephone systems. To stem losses, Telular has cut management and formed strategic relationships with such major cellular providers as Alcatel and several RBOCs. In 1994 Alcatel accounted for 11% of the company's revenues.

In mid-1995 Telular indicated it was looking for a merger or acquisition partner. The company ended fiscal 1995 with a loss of $19.7 million on revenues of $33 million.

WHO

Chairman: William L. De Nicolo, age 48, $12,923 pay
President and CEO: Richard T. Gerstner, age 55, $223,433 pay
SVP: Stephen P. Wolfe, age 38, $193,650 pay
SVP Quality and Information Services: Frank R. Brletich, age 48, $157,500 pay
VP Corporate Development: Patrick L. Murtha, age 44, $123,000 pay
SVP and CFO: Daniel O. Wagster, age 38
SVP Marketing and Sales: Michael J. Quinlan, age 53
VP Development and Technology: George Claudio Jr., age 34
Director Human Resources: Marci Feldman
Auditors: Ernst & Young LLP

WHERE

HQ: 920 Deerfield Parkway, Buffalo Grove, IL 60089
Phone: 847-465-4500   **Fax:** 847-465-4501

Telular has regional sales offices in Florida, Singapore, and the UK. It operates manufacturing facilities in Georgia, Illinois, and Puerto Rico.

WHAT

Selected Products

CelDock products (allow certain cellular phones to interconnect with traditional wired, customer-owned, on-site equipment)
CelSwitch products (monitor existing telephone lines and switch the attached standard phone equipment to the cellular network in the event of line failure)
PhoneCell products (enable traditional wired, customer-owned, on-site equipment to operate over cellular systems)
TelGuard products (allow signals to be transmitted over a cellular network when the wiring in a traditional system has been cut or otherwise fails)

KEY COMPETITORS

Adage	Coded	Nera AS
Alpha	Communication	P-Com
Industries	DSC	Spectrum
Cincinnati	Emcee Broadcast	Information
Microwave	ITI Technical	Stanford Telecom

HOW MUCH

Nasdaq symbol: WRLS FY ends: September 30	Annual Growth	1989	1990	1991	1992[1]	1993	1994	1994 Year-end: Debt ratio: 0.0%
Sales ($ mil.)	43.6%	—	4.2	3.1	3.1	6.6	17.7	Return on equity: —
Net income ($ mil.)	—	—	0.6	0.6	(1.4)	(3.7)	(27.9)	Cash (mil.): $36.2
Income as % of sales	—	—	14.3%	20.3%	—	—	—	Current ratio: 10.36
Earnings per share ($)	—	—	—	—	—	(0.18)	(1.25)	Long-term debt (mil.): $0.0
Stock price – high ($)	—	—	—	—	—	—	24.50	No. of shares (mil.): 22.6
Stock price – low ($)	—	—	—	—	—	—	6.00	Dividends
Stock price – close ($)	—	—	—	—	—	—	6.25	Yield: —
P/E – high	—	—	—	—	—	—	—	Payout: —
P/E – low	—	—	—	—	—	—	—	Market value (mil.): $141.3
Dividends per share ($)	—	—	—	—	—	—	0.00	R&D as % of sales: 9.4%
Book value per share ($)	—	—	—	—	—	—	2.49	
Employees	—	—	—	—	—	—	273	

[1] 9-month fiscal year

TNT FREIGHTWAYS CORPORATION

OVERVIEW

Since its launching as an independent company in 1992, TNT has exploded, now posting sales in excess of $1 billion. The Rosemont, Illinois–based company, through its 6 regional trucking subsidiaries, provides less-than-truckload (LTL) services to manufacturers, retailers, and other clients across the country (including Alaska). Holland Motor Express, TNT's largest subsidiary, serves the central US with terminals in 17 states and accounts for 44% of total revenues. Together, its 6 companies make TNT #1 in US regional trucking.

The company is focusing on strengthening its national dominance of the regional trucking market (the fastest-growing part of the trucking industry). In 1994 it established new terminals in the Southeast and Alaska. That year it also set up a partnership with X-Press Freight Forwarders to serve Puerto Rico.

TNT Freightways was originally the American subsidiary of Australian-based trucking giant TNT Limited, founded by Ken Thomas in 1946. That company first entered the US market with the purchase of California trucking firm Walkup's Merchant Express in 1969. TNT Limited's early incursions in the union-dominated US trucking industry were troubled by strikes, arson, and mysterious bombings. But from 1980 on, trucking deregulation and market conditions that favored competition allowed the company to expand rapidly. It acquired Holland Motor Express in 1984 and Big State Freight Lines (now Bestway), Dugan Truck Lines, and Reddaway Truck Line in 1989. In 1990 it purchased United Truck Lines. Plunging profits outside the US in the early 1990s led TNT Limited to spin off TNT Freightways in 1992, with Campbell Carruth (CEO since 1985) in charge.

In 1995 TNT Freightways teamed with Direct Container Line to provide direct international LTL service. It also won a 5-year contract to provide trucking services for W.R. Grace.

WHO

Chairman: Morley Koffman, age 65
President and CEO: J. Campbell Carruth, age 64, $775,000 pay
SVP; President, TNT Holland: Michael J. Gorno, age 60, $520,753 pay
SVP Finance and CFO: Christopher L. Ellis, age 50, $347,000 pay
SVP: Peter D. Boulais, age 50
Controller and Principal Accounting Officer: Robert S. Owen
Executive Secretary (HR): Rosemary Marziarka
Auditors: KPMG Peat Marwick LLP

WHERE

HQ: 9700 Higgins Rd., Ste. 570, Rosemont, IL 60018
Phone: 847-696-0200   **Fax:** 847-696-2080

WHAT

Trucking Subsidiaries	1994 Sales	
	$ mil.	% of total
Holland	448.0	44
Red Star	179.0	18
Reddaway	113.9	11
Bestway	110.9	11
Dugan	67.4	7
United	45.7	4
Others	51.6	5
Total	**1,016.5**	**100**

Services
General commodities delivery
Overnight delivery
Second-day freight delivery

KEY COMPETITORS

Airborne Freight
American Freightways
American President
Arkansas Best
BNSF
Canadian Pacific
C.H. Robinson
Conrail
Consolidated Freightways
DHL
FedEx
Harper Group
Hub Group
J.B. Hunt
Roadway
Schneider National
Southern Pacific Rail
UPS
Yellow Corp.

HOW MUCH

Nasdaq symbol: TNTF FY ends: Sat. nearest Dec. 31	Annual Growth	1989	1990	1991	1992	1993	1994
Sales ($ mil.)	20.3%	402.9	524.6	646.1	800.0	898.9	1,016.5
Net income ($ mil.)	13.7%	16.9	14.4	16.0	21.1	27.3	32.1
Income as % of sales	—	4.2%	2.8%	2.5%	2.6%	3.0%	3.2%
Earnings per share ($)	16.8%	0.67	0.57	0.63	0.79	1.20	1.45
Stock price – high ($)	—	—	—	—	14.33	27.50	29.75
Stock price – low ($)	—	—	—	—	9.33	12.00	19.25
Stock price – close ($)	35.3%	—	—	—	14.00	27.00	25.63
P/E – high	—	—	—	—	18	23	21
P/E – low	—	—	—	—	12	10	13
Dividends per share ($)	15.0%	—	—	—	0.28	0.37	0.37
Book value per share ($)	(10.3%)	—	—	—	12.69	9.01	10.20
Employees	14.3%	6,246	8,704	9,236	10,221	11,089	12,184

1994 Year-end:
Debt ratio: 33.7%
Return on equity: 16.5%
Cash (mil.): $2.1
Current ratio: 1.22
Long-term debt (mil.): $105.7
No. of shares (mil.): 20.4
Dividends
  Yield: 1.4%
  Payout: 25.5%
Market value (mil.): $522.9

TOOTSIE ROLL INDUSTRIES, INC.

OVERVIEW

The chewy, chocolate-flavored Tootsie Roll turns 100 in 1996. Some 37 million of the sugar- and corn syrup–based, bite-sized bullets roll out of Tootsie Roll Industries' plants each day, along with some 16 million lollipops (Charms, Charms Blow Pops, Tootsie Pops) and a host of other confectionary delights, such as Cella's chocolate-covered cherries, Junior Mints, Mason Dots, and Sugar Daddies. The closely held candy maker (66% of Tootsie Roll Industries is owned by the husband-and-wife, CEO-and-president team of Melvin and Ellen Gordon and their family) has made a mint off its trademark candy-cum-American icon, posting an increase in earnings each year since 1979. Acquisitions of established candy brands have bolstered gains. Tootsie Roll's products are distributed in the US, Mexico, and Canada, and the company opened an office in Hong Kong in 1993.

Founded in 1896 when Austrian immigrant Leo Hirshfield created the Tootsie Roll (a treat he named for the daughter he fondly called "Tootsie"), the company in 1897 merged with New York candy maker Stern & Staalberg and was renamed the Sweets Company of America in 1922, the same year it went public. Tootsie Rolls were included in GI rations in WWII, and by the 1950s, under the direction of Ellen Gordon's father, William Rubin, Tootsie Roll had become a household name. The company changed its name to Tootsie Roll Industries in 1966. In 1972 it bought the Mason division of Candy Corp. of America, maker of Mason Crows and Dots. Tootsie Roll acquired Cella Confectioners in 1985; its largest competitor, Charms Co., for $65 million in 1988; and Warner-Lambert's caramel and chocolate brands (Junior Mints, Sugar Babies) for an estimated $82 million in 1993.

In 1995 Tootsie Roll released 2 new products, the What a Melon Blow Pop and the Caramel Apple Pop.

WHO

Chairman and CEO: Melvin J. Gordon, age 75, $1,085,000 pay
President and COO: Ellen R. Gordon, age 63, $1,015,000 pay
VP Manufacturing: John W. Newlin Jr., age 58, $498,000 pay
VP Marketing and Sales: Thomas E. Corr, age 46, $451,000 pay
VP Finance: G. Howard Ember Jr., age 42, $298,000 pay
Director Personnel: Maurice Buddemeier
Auditors: Price Waterhouse LLP

WHERE

HQ: 7401 S. Cicero Ave., Chicago, IL 60629
Phone: 312-838-3400   **Fax:** 312-838-3564

	1994 Sales	
	$ mil.	% of total
US	268.5	90
Mexico & Canada	28.4	10
Total	**296.9**	**100**

WHAT

Products

Blow Pop	Pom Poms
Cella's	Sugar Babies
(chocolate-covered cherries)	Sugar Daddy
Charleston Chew	Tootsie Frooties
Charms	Tootsie Pop
Junior Mints	Tootsie Roll
Mason Crows	Tootsie Roll Flavor Roll
Mason Dots	Zip-A-Dee-Doo-Da-Pops

KEY COMPETITORS

Archibald Candy	Mars
Berkshire Hathaway	Nestlé
Borden	Philip Morris
Cadbury Schweppes	RJR Nabisco
Campbell Soup	Topps
Farley Foods	Unilever
Ferrara Pan Candy	Warner-Lambert
General Mills	World's Finest Chocolate
Hershey	Wrigley
Kellogg	

HOW MUCH

NYSE symbol: TR FY ends: December 31	Annual Growth	1989	1990	1991	1992	1993	1994	1994 Year-end:
Sales ($ mil.)	10.6%	179.3	194.3	207.9	245.4	259.6	296.9	Debt ratio: 10.3% Return on equity: 16.8%
Net income ($ mil.)	13.4%	20.2	22.6	26.5	32.0	35.4	37.9	Cash (mil.): $16.5
Income as % of sales	—	11.3%	11.6%	12.3%	13.1%	13.7%	12.8%	Current ratio: 4.53
Earnings per share ($)	14.2%	0.90	1.01	1.21	1.52	1.68	1.75	Long-term debt (mil.): $27.5
Stock price – high ($)	—	16.13	21.56	33.31	38.67	39.30	36.41	No. of shares (mil.): 21.7
Stock price – low ($)	—	10.16	13.38	15.84	27.34	30.41	26.22	Dividends
Stock price – close ($)	14.3%	15.28	17.58	32.59	35.47	33.47	29.86	Yield: 0.6%
P/E – high	—	18	21	28	25	23	21	Payout: 10.9%
P/E – low	—	11	13	13	18	18	15	Market value (mil.): $647.8
Dividends per share ($)	13.7%	0.10	0.10	0.11	0.13	0.17	0.19	
Book value per share ($)	17.2%	5.02	6.17	7.25	8.88	10.08	11.08	
Employees	4.0%	1,400	1,450	1,500	1,500	1,700	1,700	

TRUE NORTH COMMUNICATIONS INC.

OVERVIEW

True North, based in Chicago, is the parent company for advertising agencies Foote, Cone & Belding; Borders, Perrin and Norrander (a regional agency operating mainly in the Pacific Northwest); and Mojo (one of Australia's largest agencies). True North also owns 49% of Publicis-FCB, a joint venture for its European operations.

FCB's predecessor, Lord & Thomas, was founded in 1873 by Daniel Lord. In 1881, after several ephemeral partnerships, Ambrose Thomas joined the company. Albert Lasker took over the company in 1906. In 1943 it passed to 3 managers, Emerson Foote, Fairfax Cone, and Don Belding, and became one of the top agencies worldwide. The firm was an early proponent of using radio for advertising, and as early as 1945 it recognized the potential of television for advertising.

In 1988 FCB put its European operations into a joint venture with Publicis, a French ad agency (Publicis owns 20% of True North). By the early 1990s FCB, though still large, seemed to have lost its identity. In 1991 Bruce Mason took over and began remaking the firm. In 1994 the name True North was chosen for the new parent company because, according to Mason, it connotes an "immutable reference point when you're trying to find yourself."

True North teamed with R/GA Media Group, a multimedia production company, in 1994 to create TN Technologies. This division uses a digital network that allows the creation of communications campaigns from multiple locations worldwide. Other operations include TN Services (which will consolidate administration) and TN Media (a media buyer that will serve companies unrelated to FCB).

In 1995 True North won accounts with Viacom's Blockbuster Music (with estimated billings of $35 million) and Seagram's Tropicana juices (worth $25 million).

WHO

Chairman and CEO: Bruce Mason, age 55, $1,230,000 pay
VC: Craig R. Wiggins, age 49, $820,000 pay
President and COO, FCB North America: Jack Balousek, age 49, $920,000 pay
President, FCB International: Harry Reid
EVP and CFO: Terry M. Ashwill, age 50, $770,000 pay
Director Global Marketing Planning: Laurel Cutler, age 68, $665,000 pay
VP and General Counsel: Mary A. Carragher
VP and Director Human Resources: Paul Sollitto
Auditors: Arthur Andersen & Co, SC

WHERE

HQ: 101 E. Erie St., Chicago, IL 60611-2897
Phone: 312-751-7000 **Fax:** 312-751-3501

	1994 Sales		1994 Pretax Income	
	$ mil.	% of total	$ mil.	% of total
US	306.7	76	57.9	99
Other countries	97.0	24	0.6	1
Adjustments	—	—	(22.5)	—
Total	**403.7**	**100**	**36.0**	**100**

WHAT

Services	Selected Clients
Advertising	AT&T
Direct marketing	Clorox
Media buying	Columbia Sportswear
Public relations	Levi Strauss
Research and market studies	Nabisco
Sales promotion	Qantas Airways

KEY COMPETITORS

Bozell	Interpublic Group
Cordiant	Leo Burnett
Creative Artists	N W Ayer
D'Arcy Masius	Omnicom Group
Dentsu	WPP Group
Grey Advertising	Young & Rubicam

HOW MUCH

NYSE symbol: TNO FY ends: December 31	Annual Growth	1989	1990	1991	1992	1993	1994
Sales ($ mil.)	4.4%	326.1	338.1	342.0	353.3	372.7	403.7
Net income ($ mil.)	9.0%	19.6	21.6	(19.1)	18.0	25.7	30.3
Income as % of sales	—	6.0%	6.4%	—	5.1%	6.9%	7.5%
Earnings per share ($)	6.7%	0.97	1.05	0.90	0.83	1.15	1.34
Stock price – high ($)	—	16.00	15.06	13.75	15.75	24.00	24.00
Stock price – low ($)	—	11.25	8.88	9.31	11.50	14.75	19.94
Stock price – close ($)	8.0%	14.63	10.13	12.75	15.69	24.00	21.50
P/E – high	—	16	14	15	19	21	18
P/E – low	—	12	8	10	14	13	15
Dividends per share ($)	0.0%	0.60	0.60	0.60	0.60	0.60	0.60
Book value per share ($)	1.2%	8.34	8.76	7.26	7.95	8.58	8.85
Employees[1]	4.2%	7,002	8,484	7,922	7,842	8,059	8,583

1994 Year-end:
Debt ratio: 8.0%
Return on equity: 14.8%
Cash (mil.): $77.1
Current ratio: 0.96
Long-term debt (mil.): $5.5
No. of shares (mil.): 22.8
Dividends
  Yield: 2.8%
  Payout: 44.8%
Market value (mil.): $504.8

[1] Includes Publicis-FCB joint venture

UNDERWRITERS LABORATORIES INC.

OVERVIEW

If you aren't shocked by the thousands of new electrical products introduced each year, you can thank Underwriters Laboratories (UL). Based in Northbrook, UL is the world's largest independent testing lab. Each year more than 77,000 products are subjected to burning, stretching, pummeling, and other abuse to determine compliance with product safety standards. The UL standards are voluntary for manufacturers, but products carrying the UL label have a significant advantage in the marketplace over untested products. Accordingly, manufacturers are willing to pay UL, a not-for-profit corporation, to conduct the tests and make surprise inspections to ensure continued compliance.

In 1893 William Merrill, an expert electrical investigator, was asked by the Chicago Board of Fire Underwriters to inspect a dazzling display called the Palace of Electricity at that year's World's Fair. In 1894 Merrill, realizing the need in the new electrical industry for standardization and supervision, founded the Underwriters' Electrical Bureau, which furnished fire risk data to insurers. Incorporated in 1901 as Underwriters Laboratories, it expanded its performance testing into other areas, such as auto parts, fire extinguishers, telephone wiring, and even airline pilot certification (which the government later took over). Merrill died in 1923. UL now has 5 departments: electrical; fire protection; burglary protection and signaling; casualty and chemical hazards; and heating, air conditioning, and refrigeration.

Since the end of WWII, UL has attempted to establish international standards to facilitate global trade. This would bring UL significantly more testing service business from foreign companies exporting goods into the US and from US companies selling goods abroad.

In 1993 UL introduced the UL mark for Canada (the C-UL), indicating compliance with Canadian standards. It was the first UL designation outside of the US. Later that year UL signed an agreement with the Mexican certification organization, ANCE, allowing UL to help manufacturers obtain the certification mark for Mexico, the NOM mark. In 1994 UL signed testing agreements with India and China.

WHO

President and CEO: Tom Castino, $305,000 pay
SVP Certification Operations: Don Mader
SVP Administrative Operations and Corporate Secretary: Ken Melnick
SVP Field Operations: Bob Levine
VP Local Engineering and Field Services: Al Bernardi
VP Engineering: Jim Beyreis
VP Follow-Up Services: Joe Bhatia
VP External Affairs: Bob Harris
VP and Treasurer: Larry Newman
VP and General Counsel: Debra Rade
Director Human Resources: Howard Simon
Auditors: Grant Thornton LLP

WHERE

HQ: 333 Pfingsen Rd., Northbrook, IL 60062-2096
Phone: 847-272-8800   **Fax:** 847-272-8129

UL operates 5 full-service laboratories and nearly 200 inspection centers, serving manufacturers in 74 countries.

Laboratory Locations
Camas, Washington
Melville, New York
Northbrook, Illinois
Research Triangle Park, North Carolina
Santa Clara, California

WHAT

Subsidiaries
UL de México, SA de CV
UL International Ltd. (Hong Kong)
UL International Services Ltd. (Korea, Singapore, and Taiwan)
UL Japan Co., Ltd.

UL Designations
UL certified (product meets standards set by another authority)
UL listed (product meets UL standards and can be used by itself)
UL recognized (component product meets UL standards)

KEY COMPETITORS

Canadian Standards Association
Factory Mutual Research Corp.
Inchcape

HOW MUCH

Not-for-profit corporation FY ends: December 31	Annual Growth	1989	1990	1991	1992	1993	1994
Sales ($ mil.)	8.3%	185.0	203.0	224.0	244.0	261.0	275.0
Net surplus ($ mil.)	—	—	—	—	—	—	17.2
Employees	(0.5%)	4,000	3,900	4,000	4,200	4,100	3,900

UNITED STATES CELLULAR

OVERVIEW

US Cellular wants to change the country's crazy-quilt pattern of cellular telephone franchises. The Chicago-based company provides cellular phone service to more than 615,000 subscribers in small cities and rural and suburban areas. US Cellular has been consolidating its 149 markets into "clusters" through acquisitions and exchanges with other franchisees. To pay for its acquisitions, the company is selling noncore franchises. US Cellular believes that geographic consolidation will help it boost its name recognition while cutting costs.

LeRoy Carlson, a Chicago-based investor, formed Telephone and Data Systems (TDS) in 1968 from the 50 rural phone companies he owned. As the cellular telephone industry picked up steam, TDS sought to acquire franchises, spending $250,000 to develop its first application. In 1983 TDS established United States Cellular as a subsidiary. Carlson challenged larger franchise applicants in order to gain networks in Tulsa and Knoxville; both systems began operating in 1985. US Cellular went public in 1988. Through TDS, Carlson owns 81% of the company's stock and controls 96% of its voting rights. He is a company director, and his son, LeRoy Jr., is chairman.

Like much of its industry, US Cellular is waiting for a shakeout of rival digital telecommunications technologies (time division multiple access [TDMA] versus the newer code division multiple access [CDMA]). The company currently uses TDMA but plans to incorporate CDMA.

In the meantime, US Cellular is continuing to consolidate its holdings. In 1995 it acquired markets in Virginia and Iowa and made exchanges that added 8 markets in Florida, Iowa, Texas, and Virginia. Also in 1995 Wal-Mart agreed to let US Cellular sell phones at kiosks in 80 Wal-Mart stores.

WHO

Chairman: LeRoy T. Carlson Jr., age 48, $171,756 pay
President and CEO: H. Donald Nelson, age 61, $295,226 pay
VP Engineering: Richard W. Goehring, age 45, $211,269 pay
VP Finance and CFO: Kenneth R. Meyers, age 41, $165,067 pay
VP Operations, Central Region: Joyce V. Gab Kneeland, age 37, $165,067 pay
VP Market and Business Development: Edward W. Towers, age 47
VP Information Services: James D. West, age 42
VP Human Resources: Douglas S. Arnold, age 40
Auditors: Arthur Andersen & Co, SC

WHERE

HQ: United States Cellular Corporation, 8410 W. Bryn Mawr, Ste. 700, Chicago, IL 60631
Phone: 312-399-8900   **Fax:** 312-399-8936

The company provides cellular telephone service through 790 cell sites in 37 states.

Selected Major Markets

Baton Rouge, LA	Manchester-Nashua, NH
Davenport, IA	Meade, KY
Des Moines, IA	Northampton, NC
Evansville, IN	Peoria, IL
Knoxville, TN	Tulsa, OK

WHAT

	1994 Sales	
	$ mil.	**% of total**
Services	318.6	96
Equipment	13.8	4
Total	**332.4**	**100**

KEY COMPETITORS

AirTouch	CommNet Cellular	SBC
ALLTEL	GTE	Communications
AT&T Corp.	InterCel	Sprint
Bell Atlantic	MCI	U S WEST
BellSouth	Nationwide	Vanguard
Centennial	Cellular	Cellular
Cellular	Palmer Wireless	WorldCom

HOW MUCH

AMEX symbol: USM FY ends: December 31	Annual Growth	1989	1990	1991	1992	1993	1994
Sales ($ mil.)	52.5%	40.3	63.0	99.5	164.1	247.3	332.4
Net income ($ mil.)	—	(18.3)	(14.7)	(24.4)	6.2	(25.4)	16.4
Income as % of sales	—	—	—	—	3.8%	—	4.9%
Earnings per share ($)	—	(0.65)	(0.51)	(0.63)	0.11	(0.45)	0.21
Stock price – high ($)	—	41.38	33.63	24.63	24.25	39.25	35.25
Stock price – low ($)	—	20.25	12.75	14.88	17.50	20.75	22.38
Stock price – close ($)	1.0%	31.13	19.00	21.00	21.88	35.00	32.75
P/E – high	—	—	—	—	—	—	168
P/E – low	—	—	—	—	—	—	107
Dividends per share ($)	—	0.00	0.00	0.00	0.00	0.00	0.00
Book value per share ($)	35.5%	2.87	3.88	6.67	7.63	12.55	13.09
Employees	—	—	—	—	—	—	2,250

1994 Year-end:
Debt ratio: 22.0%
Return on equity: 5.8%
Cash (mil.): $5.8
Current ratio: 0.66
Long-term debt (mil.): $290.6
No. of shares (mil.): 83.6
Dividends
  Yield: —
  Payout: —
Market value (mil.): $2,737.1

U.S. ROBOTICS, INC.

When computers talk, U.S. Robotics wants to be there. This Skokie, Illinois–based company is the world's 2nd largest supplier of data communication products, such as modems, LAN access products, and WAN hubs. (First place goes to Taiwan-based GVC Technologies.) With its 1995 acquisition of Megahertz, U.S. Robotics is now the leading producer of credit card–sized modems for mobile computing.

In 1975 CEO Casey Cowell, a University of Chicago graduate with a degree in economics, teamed up with fellow Chicago graduates Paul Collard (who later left the firm) and Steve Muka (who died in 1985) to go into the budding computer field. U.S. Robotics (its name was inspired by a company in Isaac Asimov's book *I, Robot*) first produced an acoustic coupler that connected computers over phone lines via the handsets. In 1976 an FCC ruling allowed non-AT&T products to be plugged into phone lines, freeing the company to move into modems. U.S. Robotics grew quickly, first as a distributor and from 1988 on as a manufacturer of its own products, climbing to the #2 position in high-end modems (after Motorola). U.S. Robotics went public in 1991. Cowell owns about 5.3% of the company's stock.

U.S. Robotics has been riding the wave of people and businesses rushing onto the Internet via online services by providing faster, lower-priced modems for PCs. In 1994 modem sales accounted for over half of the company's total revenue. Also in 1994 it introduced the NETServer/2 network connector and FAXserver, a fax tool for networks.

In 1995 the company introduced products that are compatible with ISDN, a technology being adopted by companies to facilitate high-speed Internet access. U.S. Robotics ended fiscal 1995 with $889.3 million in sales. Employment rose to 4,000; profits were also up — to $89.2 million.

WHO

Chairman, President, and CEO: Casey G. Cowell, age 42, $1,455,965 pay
EVP International Operations: John McCartney, age 42, $1,091,974 pay
EVP Sales and Marketing: Jonathan N. Zakin, age 45, $1,091,974 pay
SVP Operations and CFO: Ross W. Manire, age 42, $479,299 pay
VP Advanced Development: Dale M. Walsh, age 58, $347,456 pay
VP, General Counsel, and Secretary: George A. Vinyard, age 45
VP Human Resources: Elizabeth S. Ryan
Auditors: Grant Thornton LLP

WHERE

HQ: 8100 N. McCormick Blvd., Skokie, IL 60076
Phone: 847-982-5010   **Fax:** 847-982-5235

	1994 Sales	
	$ mil.	% of total
US	281.2	74
Other countries	97.5	26
Total	**378.7**	**100**

WHAT

Selected Products
Courier and Sportster desktop and PCMCIA modems
Enterprise Network Hubs and shared-access products for LANs
MobileLAN remote-access servers
PCMCIA Ethernet adapters and Ethernet modems
Total Control hubs for WANs

KEY COMPETITORS

3Com	Cirrus Logic	Matsushita
Apex Data	DATA RACE	Motorola
Apple	Global Village	Multi-Tech
Asanté	GVC Technologies	Proteon
Ascend	Hayes	Shiva
Communications	Microcomputer	Tandem
AT&T Systems	HyperMedia	Zoom
Bay Networks	IBM	Telephonics
Boca Research	Intel	

HOW MUCH

Nasdaq symbol: USRX FY ends: Sun. nearest Sept. 30	Annual Growth	1989	1990	1991	1992	1993	1994
Sales ($ mil.)	58.8%	37.5	56.4	78.8	112.4	189.2	378.7
Net income ($ mil.)	68.7%	1.9	4.7	7.3	10.9	17.0	26.4
Income as % of sales	—	5.2%	8.4%	9.3%	9.7%	9.0%	7.0%
Earnings per share ($)	64.5%	0.17	0.44	0.78	1.00	1.40	2.05
Stock price – high ($)	—	—	—	16.75	24.25	35.25	46.00
Stock price – low ($)	—	—	—	12.25	13.38	17.00	24.00
Stock price – close ($)	39.3%	—	—	16.00	20.50	34.63	43.25
P/E – high	—	—	—	21	24	25	22
P/E – low	—	—	—	16	13	12	12
Dividends per share ($)	—	—	—	0.00	0.00	0.00	0.00
Book value per share ($)	61.1%	—	—	2.86	6.25	9.35	11.96
Employees	47.2%	210	316	402	479	755	1,451

1994 Year-end:
Debt ratio: 29.9%
Return on equity: 21.4%
Cash (mil.): $37.5
Current ratio: 4.15
Long-term debt (mil.): $60.3
No. of shares (mil.): 11.8
Dividends
  Yield: —
  Payout: —
Market value (mil.): $511.4
R&D as % of sales: 6.2%
Advertising as % of sales: 3.9%

VITALINK PHARMACY SERVICES, INC.

OVERVIEW

Naperville, Illinois–based Vitalink provides institutional pharmacy services to prisons and to institutional health facilities including nursing homes, assisted-living complexes, and centers for the developmentally disabled. The company's pharmacies meet various institutions' specific needs for all aspects of dispensing and monitoring medications in a complex, highly regulated environment for institutional residents. Vitalink provides, on a daily basis, medication for about 42,000 patients and fills about 9,000 prescriptions. Its subsidiary, Vitalink Infusion Services, provides infusion of nutrition and drugs in an institutional setting or at home to individuals eligible under Medicare.

The company was originally incorporated in 1967. In 1981, as part of Americana Healthcare Corporation, it was acquired by a subsidiary of Manor Care, one of the largest publicly owned long-term care providers in the US. In 1992 Manor Care spun off its pharmacy services and changed the newly public company's name to Vitalink.

Manor Care still owns about 82% of Vitalink and is its primary customer, accounting for 49% of its revenue. However, this dependence on Manor Care is dropping.

Vitalink plans to further penetrate existing markets, target non–Manor Care facilities, and buy institutional pharmacies in both new and current markets. The company's efforts are likely to be boosted by the growing elderly population and the trend toward cutting costs through early discharge of hospital patients into alternative settings.

In 1995 Vitalink acquired the institutional pharmacy business of San Antonio–based Parker's Pharmacy for $2.4 million. It also acquired Home Intravenous Care, of Loveland, Colorado, for $2.4 million.

WHO

Chairman and CEO: Donald C. Tomasso, age 50
VC: Stewart Bainum Jr., age 49
President and COO: Donna DeNardo, age 43, $253,285 pay
SVP Operations: Vincent C. DiTrapano, age 49, $192,061 pay
VP Finance and CFO: Scott T. Macomber, age 40, $166,320 pay
Secretary: James H. Rempe, age 65
Treasurer: James A. MacCutcheon, age 43
VP Human Resources and Administration: Stephen A. Thompson
Auditors: Arthur Andersen Co, SC

WHERE

HQ: 1250 E. Diehl Road, Ste. 208, Naperville, IL 60563
Phone: 708-505-1320   **Fax:** 708-505-1319

Vitalink operates 18 institutional pharmacies and 2 infusion pharmacies in 13 states.

WHAT

	1995 Revenues
	% of total
Prescription management	74
Infusion therapy	16
Medical supplies & other	7
Consultation	3
Total	**100**

	1995 Payer Mix
	% of total
Private	64
Medicaid	29
Medicare	7
Total	**100**

KEY COMPETITORS

American Home Patient	Grancare
Apria	Horizon/CMS Healthcare
Caremark	Omnicare
Coram	U.S. HomeCare
Geriatric Medical	

HOW MUCH

Nasdaq symbol: VTLK FY ends: May 31	Annual Growth	1990	1991	1992	1993	1994	1995[1]
Sales ($ mil.)	43.6%	18.4	27.3	40.2	65.7	98.6	112.3
Net income ($ mil.)	34.4%	2.7	3.8	5.5	7.3	9.2	11.7
Income as % of sales	—	14.5%	13.8%	13.7%	11.2%	9.3%	10.4%
Earnings per share ($)	29.6%	0.23	0.33	0.46	0.53	0.66	0.84
Stock price – high ($)	—	—	—	18.00	13.25	15.50	17.00
Stock price – low ($)	—	—	—	10.25	7.50	8.50	11.75
Stock price – close ($)	9.9%	—	—	12.63	9.88	14.25	16.75
P/E – high	—	—	—	39	25	23	20
P/E – low	—	—	—	22	14	13	14
Dividends per share ($)	—	—	—	0.00	0.00	0.00	0.00
Book value per share ($)	17.9%	—	—	3.16	3.68	4.34	5.18
Employees	30.2%	—	270	300	530	700	775

1995 Year-end:
Debt ratio: 0.0%
Return on equity: 17.6%
Cash (mil.): $0.2
Current ratio: 3.32
Long-term debt (mil.): $0.0
No. of shares (mil.): 14.0
Dividends
  Yield: —
  Payout: —
Market value (mil.): $234.1

[1] 1995 stock prices are through fiscal year-end (May 31).

WISCONSIN CENTRAL TRANSPORTATION

OVERVIEW

With train operations in Canada and New Zealand and its head office adjacent to O'Hare airport, Wisconsin Central Transportation Corp. (WCTC) is bigger than its name implies. WCTC is the largest regional railroad in the US, operating 215 locomotives and 10,715 railcars on 2,817 miles of track, primarily in Wisconsin and contiguous states. A holding company, WCTC has 7 subsidiaries, including Fox Valley & Western (FV&W), WCL Railcars, and Algoma Central Railway (ACRI). WCTC , which carries only freight, also holds a 29% share in New Zealand Rail, a 2,500-mile-long railroad providing service throughout New Zealand. Principal cities served by WCTC are Chicago; Duluth, Minnesota/Superior, Wisconsin; Green Bay; Milwaukee; Minneapolis/St. Paul; and Sault Ste. Marie, Ontario.

Backed financially by former Wisconsin governor Richard Ogilvie, railroad industry veterans Edward Burkhardt and Thomas Power formed WCTC in 1987 to buy Soo Line's Lake States Transportation unit. WCTC bought an additional Soo line in Wisconsin in 1991. The firm went public that year. CEO Burkhardt holds 7.1% of the company.

WCTC accelerated its expansion strategy following its IPO. It purchased a Wisconsin line from Chicago and North Western in 1992 and in 1993 paid Itel $62.2 million for 3 Midwestern railroads (renamed Fox Valley & Western). WCTC expanded its reach halfway around the world that year, buying 29% of the monopoly New Zealand Rail.

In 1995 WCTC increased its Canadian business by acquiring the 332 route miles of rail lines, plus locomotives and railcars, of Algoma Central Corp. for approximately $8.2 million, giving WCTC service between Sault Ste. Marie and Hearst, Ontario. WCTC is looking at further international growth. In 1995 it met with the UK transport secretary to discuss a possible bid for all 3 of British Rail's freight firms.

WHO

President and CEO: Edward A. Burkhardt, age 56, $1,217,193 pay
EVP and CFO: Thomas F. Power Jr., age 54, $479,618 pay
VP Engineering, WCL, FV&W, and ACRI: Glenn J. Kerbs, age 54, $174,181 pay
VP Marketing, WCL, FV&W, and ACRI: William R. Schauer, age 50, $170,395 pay
VP Finance: Walter C. Kelly, age 51, $168,674 pay
Assistant VP Human Resources: David French
Auditors: KPMG Peat Marwick LLP

WHERE

HQ: Wisconsin Central Transportation Corporation, 6250 N. River Rd., Ste. 9000, Rosemont, IL 60018
Phone: 847-318-4600   **Fax:** 847-318-4618

WHAT

Freight Transported	1994 Sales % of total
Paper	14
Chemicals & petroleum products	13
Wood pulp	13
Clay products & granules	10
Food & grain	8
Other	42
Total	**100**

Selected Subsidiaries and Affiliates
Algoma Central Railway Inc.
Fox Valley & Western Ltd.
New Zealand Rail Ltd. (29%)
Sault Ste. Marie Bridge Co.
WC Canada Holdings, Inc.
WCL Railcars, Inc.
Wisconsin Central International, Inc.
Wisconsin Central Ltd. (WCI)

KEY COMPETITORS

Burlington Northern
Canadian Pacific
Consolidated Freightways
CSX
Heartland Express
Hub Group
Illinois Central
J. B. Hunt
RailTex
TNT Freightways
Union Pacific
Yellow Corp.

HOW MUCH

Nasdaq symbol: WCLX FY ends: December 31	Annual Growth	1989	1990	1991	1992	1993	1994	1994 Year-end:
Sales ($ mil.)	15.8%	101.3	113.3	113.7	124.4	151.7	211.1	Debt ratio: 35.0%
Net income ($ mil.)	45.9%	5.8	7.5	8.6	10.9	18.8	38.3	Return on equity: 22.5%
Income as % of sales	—	5.7%	6.6%	7.6%	8.8%	12.4%	18.1%	Cash (mil.): $5.2
Earnings per share ($)	26.3%	0.72	0.95	0.79	0.84	1.14	2.31	Current ratio: 0.74
Stock price – high ($)	—	—	—	10.75	18.63	30.00	48.25	Long-term debt (mil.): $102.5
Stock price – low ($)	—	—	—	8.50	10.00	17.88	29.00	No. of shares (mil.): 16.6
Stock price – close ($)	60.3%	—	—	10.00	18.00	29.88	41.25	Dividends
P/E – high ($)	—	—	—	14	22	26	21	Yield: —
P/E – low ($)	—	—	—	11	12	16	13	Payout: —
Dividends per share ($)	—	—	—	0.00	0.00	0.00	0.00	Market value (mil.): $686.7
Book value per share ($)	25.8%	—	—	5.74	8.11	9.04	11.44	
Employees	14.0%	866	1,030	931	1,033	1,373	1,667	

WMS INDUSTRIES INC.

OVERVIEW

The pinball wizards at WMS Industries set off the tilt buzzer in 1995 when the company's $127 million bid to acquire Bally Gaming was thwarted by rival Alliance Gaming's superior offer. WMS is the world's #1 pinball machine maker. It also makes coin-operated arcade games, lottery terminals, and slot machines. It owns and operates the Condado Plaza and El San Juan Hotel/Casinos, and it has a stake in El Conquistador Resort.

WMS traces its roots to the Automatic Amusement Company, founded by Harry Williams in the 1930s. Williams took a franchise in 1929 for a coin-operated game called Jai Alai, and he soon produced his first game, called Advance. He followed with several industry innovations, including the "tilt" mechanism and, in 1933, electricity. In 1964 his company, Williams Electronics, was acquired by jukebox maker Seeburg Corp. Seeburg was bought by Xcor, led by Chicago wheeler-dealer Louis Nicastro, in the 1970s. Williams became a public company in 1974. After Seeburg went bankrupt in 1980, it spun off Williams, and Nicastro became CEO. (Son Neil is now president and co-CEO.) Former Viacom CEO Sumner Redstone holds 24.6% of the company.

Williams changed its name to WMS in 1987, and in 1988 it acquired the amusement game lines of rival Bally/Midway, enhancing its position as a world leader in arcade gaming. In 1990 WMS moved its headquarters from New York to Chicago. It also moved into hotel and casino management that year.

In 1994 WMS created a joint venture (Williams/Nintendo) to market games for all Nintendo platforms and moved into the home video game market when it acquired Tradewest Inc. In 1995 WMS's Mortal Kombat III sold 250,000 units in its first weekend on the market, for $15 million, making it one of the US's top-selling video games of 1995.

WHO

Chairman and Co-CEO: Louis J. Nicastro, age 67, $982,500 pay
VC: Norman J. Menell, age 63
President, Co-CEO, and COO: Neil D. Nicastro, age 38, $1,021,600 pay
VP Finance, CFO, Treasurer, and Chief Accounting Officer: Harold H. Bach Jr., age 63, $317,800 pay
VP, Secretary, and General Counsel: Barbara M. Norman, age 57, $177,200 pay
VP and General Manager Coin-Op Amusement Games Operations: Kenneth J. Fedesna, age 45
Director Human Resources: Michael Sirchio
Auditors: Ernst & Young LLP

WHERE

HQ: 3401 N. California Ave., Chicago, IL 60618
Phone: 312-961-1111   **Fax:** 312-961-1090

WHAT

	1995 Sales	
	$ mil.	% of total
Amusement games	314.5	82
Condado Plaza	57.5	15
Williams Hospitality	13.4	3
Total	**385.4**	**100**

Selected Gaming Subsidiaries
Condado Plaza Hotel & Casino
Midway Manufacturing Co. (coin-operated video games)
Williams Electronic Games, Inc. (pinball games)
WMS Gaming Inc. (slot machines and video lottery terminals)

Selected Gaming Products

Casino gaming machines	Video arcade games
Home video games	Video lottery terminal
Pinball games	games

KEY COMPETITORS

7th Level	Hilton	SEGA
Acclaim	HFS	Sodak Gaming
Entertainment	Hyatt	Stuart Enterprises
Alliance Gaming	id Software	Thorn EMI
Anchor Gaming	International Game	Time Warner
Brøderbund	Technology	Video Lottery
Electronic Arts	Jackpot Enterprises	Technologies

HOW MUCH

NYSE symbol: WMS FY ends: June 30	Annual Growth	1990	1991	1992	1993	1994	1995[1]
Sales ($ mil.)	21.2%	147.1	161.2	227.0	331.1	358.2	385.4
Net income ($ mil.)	—	(10.3)	10.9	25.2	30.7	28.5	19.2
Income as % of sales	—	—	6.7%	11.1%	9.3%	8.0%	5.0%
Earnings per share ($)	—	(0.62)	0.64	1.21	1.31	1.19	0.80
Stock price – high ($)	—	5.56	14.50	25.00	34.00	29.88	24.25
Stock price – low ($)	—	1.75	1.63	13.38	17.13	15.88	16.25
Stock price – close ($)	61.0%	1.81	13.94	23.63	28.75	18.63	19.63
P/E – high	—	—	23	21	26	25	30
P/E – low	—	—	3	11	13	13	20
Dividends per share ($)	—	0.00	0.00	0.00	0.00	0.00	0.00
Book value per share ($)	66.4%	0.68	1.32	5.59	6.48	7.53	8.65
Employees	7.6%	1,041	1,118	1,556	1,848	2,080	3,381

1995 Year-end:
Debt ratio: 30.2%
Return on equity: 9.8%
Cash (mil.): $93.8
Current ratio: 0.66
Long-term debt (mil.): $84.4
No. of shares (mil.): 24.1
Dividends
  Yield: —
  Payout: —
Market value (mil.): $473.1

[1] 1995 stock prices are through fiscal year-end (June 30).

ZEBRA TECHNOLOGIES CORPORATION

OVERVIEW

Zebra Technologies has no intention of changing its stripes. Exploiting the worldwide trend toward standardization of bar code labels, Zebra, which designs, manufactures, and distributes printers for computerized bar codes, is leading the herd of automatic identification system makers with a 30% market share. In addition to its computerized bar code label and ticket printing systems, Zebra sells ink ribbons and label/ticketing paper stock to support these systems. Overseas sales account for 40% of total revenues.

The company was founded in 1969 as Data Specialties, Inc. (DSI), with $1,000 from current CEO Edward Kaplan and current EVP Gerhard Cless, to make machines that punched holes in paper and read paper tape. In 1982 the company introduced its first bar code printer, which used a dot matrix system. In 1986 DSI introduced the first thermal transfer bar code printer and, to emphasize the company's new focus, changed its name to Zebra Technologies to convey the image of stripes found on bar codes. The company went public in August 1991 and made a 2nd offering in March 1993. Kaplan and Cless control a majority of the voting stock.

In 1987 Zebra started a 5-year transition to shift most of its manufacturing base from Japan back to the US, which at the time amused many American business analysts. In 1991 the company opened a UK office, and in 1993 it acquired a plant in Preston, UK, to better serve the growing European market.

Despite the recent resignation of 6 senior employees (4 of whom joined rival companies), Kaplan is confident of the company's continued growth. Kaplan gave up the day-to-day management of Zebra in 1995 in order to focus on acquisitions. The company is pushing a marketing strategy to increase its share of the low end of the bar code machine market, where it lags behind #1 Datamax.

WHO

Chairman and CEO: Edward L. Kaplan, age 52, $315,268 pay
President: Jeffrey K. Clements, age 48
EVP and Secretary: Gerhard Cless, age 55, $233,968 pay
SVP Marketing: Jack A. LeVan, age 40
CFO and Treasurer: Charles R. Whitchurch, age 48, $148,064 pay
VP Corporate Development: John H. Kindsvater Jr., age 53, $132,059 pay
VP Sales: Thomas C. Beusch, age 42
VP Technology Development: Clive P. Hohberger, age 52
Director Human Resources: Ellen Barnes
Auditors: KPMG Peat Marwick LLP

WHERE

HQ: 333 Corporate Woods Pkwy., Vernon Hills, IL 60061
Phone: 847-634-6700   **Fax:** 847-634-1830

	1994 Sales	
	$ mil.	% of total
US	64.5	60
Other countries	42.6	40
Total	**107.1**	**100**

WHAT

	1994 Sales	
	$ mil.	% of total
Printers	68.5	64
Supplies	28.9	27
Other	9.7	9
Total	**107.1**	**100**

Products
Label printing systems (18 thermal transfer bar code label printers, ranging in price from $1,395 to $10,245)
Media supplies (ink ribbons and label/ticketing stock)

KEY COMPETITORS

Datamax	Litton Industries	TEC
DH Technology	Pitney Bowes	Toshiba
Eltron	Sato	Western Atlas

HOW MUCH

Nasdaq symbol: ZBRA FY ends: December 31	Annual Growth	1989	1990	1991	1992	1993	1994
Sales ($ mil.)	29.0%	30.0	38.0	45.6	58.7	87.5	107.1
Net income ($ mil.)	30.7%	5.5	6.6	8.5	11.8	18.3	21.1
Income as % of sales	—	18.5%	17.5%	18.6%	20.1%	20.9%	19.7%
Earnings per share ($)	30.1%	—	0.61	0.75	0.99	1.52	1.75
Stock price – high ($)	—	—	—	19.00	24.75	60.75	57.25
Stock price – low ($)	—	—	—	14.50	14.50	20.25	23.50
Stock price – close ($)	32.6%	—	—	16.75	24.00	56.63	39.06
P/E – high	—	—	—	25	25	40	33
P/E – low	—	—	—	19	15	13	13
Dividends per share ($)	—	—	—	0.00	0.00	0.00	0.00
Book value per share ($)	38.5%	—	—	2.56	3.52	5.05	6.82
Employees	35.8%	—	—	200	294	380	501

1994 Year-end:
Debt ratio: 0.4%
Return on equity: 29.5%
Cash (mil.): $54.2
Current ratio: 7.13
Long-term debt (mil.): $0.2
No. of shares (mil.): 12.0
Dividends
  Yield: —
  Payout: —
Market value (mil.): $470
R&D as % of sales: 5.4%

Key Chicago Companies

A. EPSTEIN & SONS INTERNATIONAL, INC.

600 W. Fulton St.
Chicago, IL 60661
Phone: 312-454-9100
Fax: 312-559-1217

CEO: Mickey Kupperman
CFO: Alfred Altschul
HR: Michele DeClecq
Employees: 600

1994 Sales: $55 million
1-Yr. Sales Change: -3.5%
Ownership: Privately Held

Engineering & architectural services

A. FINKIL & SONS COMPANY

2011 N. Southport Ave.
Chicago, IL 60614
Phone: 312-975-2500
Fax: 312-975-2602

CEO: Charles W. Finkil
CFO: Joe Curci
HR: —
Employees: 400

1994 Sales: $67.3 million
1-Yr. Sales Change: 10.5%
Ownership: Privately Held

Steel - ingots & open die forgings

AAR CORP.

1111 Nicholas Blvd.
Elk Grove Village, IL 60007
Phone: 847-439-3939
Fax: 847-439-3955

CEO: Ira A. Eichner
CFO: Timothy Romenesko
HR: Robert Naughton
Employees: 1,940

1995 Sales: $451.4 million
1-Yr. Sales Change: 10.7%
Exchange: NYSE
Symbol: AIR

Aerospace - buys, sells & trades aircraft components in the aftermarket; remanufactures aircraft parts

A B DICK COMPANY

5700 W. Touhy Ave.
Niles, IL 60714
Phone: 312-763-1900
Fax: 312-647-8369

CEO: Ronald Peterson
CFO: Richard Cleys
HR: Susan Leri
Employees: 3,000

1994 Sales: $479.7 million
1-Yr. Sales Change: 6.6%
Ownership: Subsidiary

Office equipment, copiers & printers; subsidiary of The General Electric Company PLC

ABBOTT LABORATORIES

100 Abbott Park Rd.
Abbott Park, IL 60064-3500
Phone: 708-937-6100
Fax: 708-937-1511

CEO: Duane L. Burnham
CFO: Gary P. Coughlan
HR: Ellen M. Walvoord
Employees: 49,464

1994 Sales: $9,156 million
1-Yr. Sales Change: 8.9%
Exchange: NYSE
Symbol: ABT

Drugs, hospital equipment, pesticides, consumer health care products (Murine, Selsun Blue) & nutritional supplements (Similac)

 See pages 34–35 for a full profile of this company.

ABC RAIL PRODUCTS CORPORATION

200 S. Michigan Ave., 13th Fl.
Chicago, IL 60604-2402
Phone: 312-322-0360
Fax: 312-322-0377

CEO: Donald W. Grinter
CFO: D. Chisholm MacDonald
HR: Joseph A. Parsons
Employees: 1,402

1995 Sales: $243.2 million
1-Yr. Sales Change: 29.9%
Exchange: Nasdaq
Symbol: ABCR

Transportation equipment - freight rail equipment

ACE HARDWARE CORPORATION

2200 Kensington Ct.
Oak Brook, IL 60521
Phone: 708-990-6600
Fax: 708-573-4894

CEO: Dave Hodnik
CFO: Rita D. Kahle
HR: Fred J. Neer
Employees: 3,664

1994 Sales: $2,326.1 million
1-Yr. Sales Change: 15.3%
Ownership: Cooperative

Building products - member-owned hardware wholesale cooperative

 See pages 36–37 for a full profile of this company.

ACME METALS INCORPORATED

13500 S. Perry Ave.
Riverdale, IL 60627-1182
Phone: 708-849-2500
Fax: 708-841-6010

CEO: Brian W. H. Marsden
CFO: Jerry F. Williams
HR: Gerald J. Shope
Employees: 2,750

1994 Sales: $522.9 million
1-Yr. Sales Change: 14.3%
Exchange: Nasdaq
Symbol: ACME

Metal processing & fabrication

ADLER PLANETARIUM

1300 S. Lake Shore Dr.
Chicago, IL 60605
Phone: 312-922-7827
Fax: 312-322-2257

CEO: Paul H. Knappenberger Jr.
CFO: Edward J. Williams
HR: Maguerite E. Dawson
Employees: 130

1994 Sales: $6.1 million
1-Yr. Sales Change: —

Planetarium & museum

ADMIRAL MAINTENANCE SERVICE L.P.

4343 W. Touhy Ave.
Lincolnwood, IL 60646
Phone: 847-675-6000
Fax: 847-675-6033

CEO: Richard K. Fiedler
CFO: Richard K. Fiedler
HR: —
Employees: 2,100

1994 Sales: $39.4 million
1-Yr. Sales Change: 5.1%
Ownership: Privately Held

Building - contract janitorial, window washing & metal maintenance services

ADVANCE MECHANICAL SYSTEMS, INC.

2001 Estes Ave.
Elk Grove Village, IL 60007
Phone: 847-593-2510
Fax: 847-593-2536

CEO: John J. Nowicki
CFO: Robert Blumenthal
HR: —
Employees: 225

1994 Sales: $46.5 million
1-Yr. Sales Change: -4.3%
Ownership: Privately Held

Building - mechanical contractor

ADVANCE ROSS CORPORATION

233 S. Wacker Dr., Ste. 9700
Chicago, IL 60606-6502
Phone: 312-382-1100
Fax: 312-382-1109

CEO: Harve A. Ferrill
CFO: Randy M. Joseph
HR: Randy M. Joseph
Employees: 327

1994 Sales: $66.5 million
1-Yr. Sales Change: 32.2%
Ownership: Subsidiary

Financial services - value-added tax refund service for corporate clients; electrostatic precipitator systems (acquired by CUC International)

 **See page 190 for a full profile of this company.**

ADVANTIS

231 N. Martingale Rd.
Schaumburg, IL 60173
Phone: 847-240-3000
Fax: 847-340-3868

CEO: Syd N. Heaton
CFO: Patrick M. Kerin
HR: Jim P. Doyle
Employees: 3,000

1994 Sales: $1,135 million
1-Yr. Sales Change: 3.2%
Ownership: Joint Venture

Telecommunications services - data communications & networking services; joint venture between IBM & Sears, Roebuck

ADVOCATE HEALTH CARE

2025 Windsor Dr.
Oak Brook, IL 60521-1586
Phone: 708-572-9393
Fax: 708-990-5025

CEO: Richard R. Risk
CFO: Lawrence Majka
HR: Ben Grigaliunas
Employees: 20,400

1994 Sales: $697.6 million
1-Yr. Sales Change: 6.4%
Ownership: Privately Held

Hospitals - not-for-profit system serving the Chicagoland area (Christ Hospital & Medical Center, Lutheran General Hospital, Ravenswood Hospital Medical Center, Good Samaritan Hospital)

AGI, INC.

1950 N. Ruby St.
Melrose Park, IL 60160
Phone: 708-344-9100
Fax: 708-344-9113

CEO: Richard Block
CFO: Dave Underwood
HR: Marie Renteria
Employees: 400

1994 Sales: $74.5 million
1-Yr. Sales Change: 3.3%
Ownership: Privately Held

Containers - full-service packaging for the entertainment, cosmetics & toiletries, multimedia & food industries

AIRWAYS TRANSPORTATION GROUP OF COMPANIES

4025 N. Mannheim Rd.
Schiller Park, IL 60176
Phone: 847-678-2300
Fax: 847-678-2600

CEO: Michael Zaransky
CFO: Michael Zaransky
HR: Rosalind Zaransky
Employees: 360

1994 Sales: $36.8 million
1-Yr. Sales Change: 6.7%
Ownership: Privately Held

Diversified operations - auto leasing & sales; airport parking; limousine sevices

A. J. GERRARD & COMPANY

400 E. Touhy Ave.
Des Plaines, IL 60018
Phone: 847-299-8000
Fax: 847-803-5250

CEO: Tony Tako
CFO: Pete Rocush
HR: Rick Davidson
Employees: 600

1994 Sales: $145 million
1-Yr. Sales Change: 7.4%
Ownership: Privately Held

Tools, machinery & packaging material

AL BASKIN COMPANY

500 Joliet Rd.
Willowbrook, IL 60522
Phone: 708-789-0130
Fax: 708-789-6806

CEO: Scott Baskin
CFO: Rick Anglin
HR: Lynn Denton
Employees: 1,000

1994 Est. Sales: $81.6 mil.
1-Yr. Sales Change: 6.0%
Ownership: Privately Held

Retail - clothing stores in Illinois, Minnesota, Missouri, Georgia & Texas (Mark Shale)

ALBERTO-CULVER COMPANY

2525 Armitage Ave.
Melrose Park, IL 60160-1163
Phone: 708-450-3000
Fax: 708-450-3354

CEO: Howard B. Bernick
CFO: William Cernugel
HR: Douglas E. Meneely
Employees: 9,300

1995 Sales: $1,358.2 million
1-Yr. Sales Change: 11.7%
Exchange: NYSE
Symbol: ACV

Cosmetics & toiletries - shampoos (Alberto VO5, Bold Hold, Consort, Alberto Balsam); cash-and-carry beauty supply stores (#1 worldwide: Sally Beauty Supply)

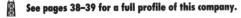 **See pages 38–39 for a full profile of this company.**

ALEXIAN BROTHERS HEALTH SYSTEM

600 Alexian Way
Elk Grove Village, IL 60007
Phone: 847-437-5500
Fax: 847-981-5766

CEO: Philip Kennedy
CFO: Gary Eiler
HR: Roger Johnson
Employees: 2,300

1994 Sales: $302.8 million
1-Yr. Sales Change: 5.6%

Hospitals - not-for-profit system with 3 hospitals

ALLIANT FOODSERVICE INC.

One Parkway Dr. North	CEO: James A. Miller	1994 Sales: $4,100 million
Deerfield, IL 60015	CFO: Jack A. Peterson	1-Yr. Sales Change: 7.9%
Phone: 847-405-8500	HR: George Arseneau	Ownership: Privately Held
Fax: 847-405-8980	Employees: 9,000	

Food - exclusive distributor of Kraft products

 See pages 40–41 for a full profile of this company.

ALLIED PRODUCTS CORPORATION

10 S. Riverside Plaza	CEO: Richard A. Drexler	1994 Sales: $215.5 million
Chicago, IL 60606	CFO: Kenneth B. Light	1-Yr. Sales Change: -1.1%
Phone: 312-454-1020	HR: —	Exchange: NYSE
Fax: 312-454-1511	Employees: 1,600	Symbol: ADP

Diversified operations - farm equipment, tool & die equipment & insulation

ALLSCRIPS PHARMACEUTICALS, INC.

1033 Butterfield Rd.	CEO: Michael E. Carr	1994 Sales: $59 million
Vernon Hills, IL 60061	CFO: Greg Cull	1-Yr. Sales Change: —
Phone: 847-680-3515	HR: Sheryl Kemble	Ownership: Privately Held
Fax: 847-680-7935	Employees: 148	

Business services - pharmacy benefit management

THE ALLSTATE CORPORATION

Allstate Plaza	CEO: Jerry D. Choate	1994 Sales: $21,464.3 mil.
Northbrook, IL 60062	CFO: Thomas J. Wilson	1-Yr. Sales Change: 2.5%
Phone: 847-402-5000	HR: Joan M. Crockett	Exchange: NYSE
Fax: 847-402-0045	Employees: 46,300	Symbol: ALL

Insurance - home & auto (#2 in US)

 See pages 42–43 for a full profile of this company.

ALTERNATIVE RESOURCES CORPORATION

75 Tri-State Intl., Ste. 100	CEO: Larry I. Kane	1994 Sales: $94.5 million
Lincolnshire, IL 60069	CFO: Bradley K. Lamers	1-Yr. Sales Change: 78.0%
Phone: 847-317-1000	HR: Silvia U. Masini	Exchange: Nasdaq
Fax: 847-317-1008	Employees: 333	Symbol: ALRC

Personnel - employment services to information processing centers

 See page 191 for a full profile of this company.

A.M. CASTLE & CO.

3400 N. Wolf Rd.
Franklin Park, IL 60131
Phone: 847-455-7111
Fax: 847-455-0587

CEO: Richard G. Mork
CFO: Edward F. Culliton
HR: Thomas D. Prendergast
Employees: 1,200

1994 Sales: $536.6 million
1-Yr. Sales Change: 13.2%
Exchange: AMEX
Symbol: CAS

Metal products - distribution of round, hexagon, square & flat bars, tubing, shapes & coil

AM INTERNATIONAL, INC.

1800 W. Central Rd.
Mount Prospect, IL 60056
Phone: 847-292-0600
Fax: 847-818-3438

CEO: Jerome D. Brady
CFO: Thomas D. Rooney
HR: Brian Valentine
Employees: 3,400

1995 Sales: $509.5 million
1-Yr. Sales Change: 20.8%
Exchange: AMEX
Symbol: AM

Office equipment & supplies - equipment, supplies & services to the graphics industry

AMCOL INTERNATIONAL CORPORATION

1500 W. Shure Dr., Ste. 500
Arlington Heights, IL 60004-7803
Phone: 847-394-8730
Fax: 847-870-6436

CEO: John Hughes
CFO: Paul G. Shelton
HR: Steve Alexander
Employees: 1,328

1994 Sales: $265.4 million
1-Yr. Sales Change: 21.1%
Exchange: Nasdaq
Symbol: ACOL

Metal ores

AMERICAN BAR ASSOCIATION

750 N. Lake Shore Dr.
Chicago, IL 60611
Phone: 312-988-6179
Fax: 312-988-5100

CEO: Robert A. Stein
CFO: John E. Hanley Jr.
HR: Nina B. Eidell
Employees: 750

1994 Sales: $112.9 million
1-Yr. Sales Change: —
Ownership: Privately Held

National professional legal association with approximately 370,000 members (#1 voluntary professional association worldwide); magazine & book publishing (ABA Press)

 **See page 192 for a full profile of this company.**

AMERICAN CLASSIC VOYAGES CO.

Two N. Riverside Plaza
Chicago, IL 60606
Phone: 312-258-1890
Fax: 312-466-6151

CEO: Philip C. Calian
CFO: Philip C. Calian
HR: Amy Klein-Alter
Employees: 2,248

1994 Sales: $195.2 million
1-Yr. Sales Change: 79.1%
Exchange: Nasdaq
Symbol: AMCV

Leisure & recreational services - paddlewheel steamboat cruises (Delta Queen) & ocean cruises (American Hawaii)

 **See page 193 for a full profile of this company.**

AMERICAN HEALTHCARE PROVIDERS, INC.

4801 Southwick Dr.
Matteson, IL 60443
Phone: 708-503-5000
Fax: 708-508-5001

CEO: Asif A. Sayeed
CFO: Ramesh Joshi
HR: —
Employees: 170

1994 Sales: $51.2 million
1-Yr. Sales Change: 14.5%
Ownership: Privately Held

Managed health care services

AMERICAN LABELMARK COMPANY

5724 N. Pulaski Rd.
Chicago, IL 60646
Phone: 312-478-0900
Fax: 312-478-6054

CEO: Dwight Curtis
CFO: Alan Schoen
HR: Peggy Boyd
Employees: 300

1994 Sales: $40 million
1-Yr. Sales Change: 3.1%
Ownership: Privately Held

Printing - commercial labels; marking products distribution

AMERICAN MEDICAL ASSOCIATION

515 N. State St.
Chicago, IL 60610
Phone: 312-464-5000
Fax: 312-464-4184

CEO: Lonnie R. Bristow
CFO: Bill Zimmerman
HR: —
Employees: 1,100

1994 Sales: $186.6 million
1-Yr. Sales Change: —
Ownership: Privately Held

National voluntary service association of physicians with nearly 300,000 members; publisher of scientific & medical information (#1 worldwide: Journal of the American Medical Association, Archives of Surgery, American Medical News)

AMERIHOST PROPERTIES, INC.

2400 E. Devon Ave., Ste. 280
Des Plaines, IL 60018-4617
Phone: 847-298-4500
Fax: 847-298-4505

CEO: Michael P. Holtz
CFO: Russell J. Cerqua
HR: Bill Roclaw
Employees: 1,900

1994 Sales: $43.3 million
1-Yr. Sales Change: 26.2%
Exchange: Nasdaq
Symbol: HOST

Hotels & motels (AmeriHost Inns)

AMERIN CORPORATION

200 E. Randolph Dr.
Chicago, IL 60601
Phone: 312-540-0078
Fax: 312-540-0564

CEO: Gerald L. Friedman
CFO: George G. Freudenstein
HR: Tammy Sjurson
Employees: 70

1994 Sales: $10.5 million
1-Yr. Sales Change: 98.1%
Exchange: Nasdaq
Symbol: AMRN

Financial - mortgage insurance

AMERITECH CORPORATION

30 S. Wacker Dr.
Chicago, IL 60606
Phone: 312-750-5000
Fax: 312-207-1601

Utility - telephone

CEO: Richard C. Notebaert
CFO: Oren G. Shaffer
HR: Walter M. Oliver
Employees: 63,594

1994 Sales: $12,570 million
1-Yr. Sales Change: 7.3%
Exchange: NYSE
Symbol: AIT

🏢 **See pages 44–45 for a full profile of this company.**

AMITY PACKING COMPANY

210 N. Green St.
Chicago, IL 60607
Phone: 312-942-0270
Fax: 312-942-0413

Food - fresh & frozen meat

CEO: Terry Samuel
CFO: Brian Tyler
HR: Rick Voelker
Employees: 200

1994 Sales: $101 million
1-Yr. Sales Change: 5.2%
Ownership: Privately Held

AMLI RESIDENTIAL PROPERTIES TRUST

125 S. Wacker Dr., Ste. 3100
Chicago, IL 60606
Phone: 312-984-5037
Fax: 312-443-0909

Real estate investment trust - apartment communities

CEO: Allan J. Sweet
CFO: Stephen C. Ross
HR: —
Employees: 400

1994 Sales: $66.2 million
1-Yr. Sales Change: 15.1%
Exchange: NYSE
Symbol: AML

AMOCO CORPORATION

200 E. Randolph Dr.
Chicago, IL 60601
Phone: 312-856-6111
Fax: 312-856-2460

Oil & gas - US integrated

CEO: H. Laurance Fuller
CFO: John L. Carl
HR: R. Wayne Anderson
Employees: 43,205

1994 Sales: $30,162 million
1-Yr. Sales Change: 6.1%
Exchange: NYSE
Symbol: AN

🏢 **See pages 46–47 for a full profile of this company.**

AMSTED INDUSTRIES INCORPORATED

205 N. Michigan Ave., 44th Fl.
Chicago, IL 60601
Phone: 312-645-1700
Fax: 312-819-8425

Machinery - railroad & industrial equipment, building products

CEO: Gordon R. Lohman
CFO: Gerald K. Walter
HR: Gary B. Montgomery
Employees: 9,000

1994 Sales: $1,030 million
1-Yr. Sales Change: 18.6%
Ownership: Privately Held

ANCILLA SYSTEMS

1000 S. Lake Park Ave.
Hobart, IN 46342
Phone: 219-947-8500
Fax: 219-947-4149

Health care - home

CEO: Monica Rawn
CFO: Monica Rawn
HR: Cheryl Auge
Employees: 4,500

1994 Sales: $385.5 million
1-Yr. Sales Change: -6.3%
Ownership: Privately Held

ANDREW CORPORATION

10500 W. 153rd St.
Orland Park, IL 60462
Phone: 708-349-3300
Fax: 708-349-5943

Telecommunications equipment - antennas & radar systems

CEO: Floyd L. English
CFO: Charles R. Nicholas
HR: —
Employees: 26,118

1995 Sales: $626.5 million
1-Yr. Sales Change: 11.9%
Exchange: Nasdaq
Symbol: ANDW

 See page 194 for a full profile of this company.

ANIXTER INTERNATIONAL, INC.

2 N. Riverside Plaza
Chicago, IL 60606
Phone: 312-902-1515
Fax: 312-902-1573

Diversified operations - marine construction; rail car leasing (formerly Itel)

CEO: Rod F. Dammeyer
CFO: Dennis J. Letham
HR: Alan Drizd
Employees: 4,200

1994 Sales: $1,732.6 million
1-Yr. Sales Change: -1.3%
Exchange: NYSE
Symbol: AXE

ANTEC CORPORATION

2850 W. Golf Rd.
Rolling Meadows, IL 60008
Phone: 847-439-4444
Fax: 847-439-8527

Telecommunications equipment - equipment & wiring for cable TV applications

CEO: John Egan
CFO: Lawrence A. Margolis
HR: Jim Bauer
Employees: 695

1994 Sales: $553.5 million
1-Yr. Sales Change: 29.4%
Exchange: Nasdaq
Symbol: ANTC

AON CORPORATION

123 N. Wacker Dr.
Chicago, IL 60606
Phone: 312-701-3000
Fax: 312-701-3100

Insurance - accident & health

CEO: Patrick G. Ryan
CFO: Harvey N. Medvin
HR: Stephen C. Taylor
Employees: 18,000

1994 Sales: $4,156.9 million
1-Yr. Sales Change: 8.1%
Exchange: NYSE
Symbol: AOC

 See pages 48–49 for a full profile of this company.

APTARGROUP, INC.

475 W. Terra Cotta Ave.
Crystal Lake, IL 60014
Phone: 815-477-0424
Fax: 815-477-0481

CEO: Ervin J. LeCoque
CFO: Stephen J. Hagge
HR: Lawrence Lowrimore
Employees: 3,300

1994 Sales: $474.3 million
1-Yr. Sales Change: 15.3%
Exchange: NYSE
Symbol: ATR

Pumps & seals - aerosol valves, pumps & dispensers

ARCHIBALD CANDY CORPORATION

1137 W. Jackson Blvd.
Chicago, IL 60607
Phone: 312-243-2700
Fax: 312-243-5504

CEO: Thomas Quinn
CFO: Joseph S. Secker
HR: Maryann Munson
Employees: 3,354

1994 Sales: $115.7 million
1-Yr. Sales Change: 2.8%
Ownership: Privately Held

Food - boxed candies (Fannie May & Fanny Farmer)

ARROW CHEVROLET, INC.

14640 S. Cicero Ave.
Midlothian, IL 60445
Phone: 708-389-0600
Fax: 708-389-7354

CEO: Cary E. Frank
CFO: Gary Dunn
HR: Angie Renes
Employees: 190

1994 Sales: $106.2 million
1-Yr. Sales Change: 18.8%
Ownership: Privately Held

Retail - new & used cars

THE ART INSTITUTE OF CHICAGO

111 S. Michigan Ave.
Chicago, IL 60603
Phone: 312-443-3600
Fax: 312-443-0849

CEO: James N. Wood
CFO: Barry L. Swenson
HR: Marion L. Alt
Employees: 1,900

1995 Sales: $105.3 million
1-Yr. Sales Change: 8.9%
Ownership: Privately Held

Art museum & school

ARTHUR ANDERSEN & CO, SC

69 W. Washington St.
Chicago, IL 60602-3094
Phone: 312-580-0069
Fax: 312-507-2548

CEO: Lawrence A. Weinbach
CFO: John D. Lewis
HR: Peter Pesce
Employees: 82,121

1995 Sales: $8,100 million
1-Yr. Sales Change: 20.2%
Ownership: Privately Held

Business services - accounting & technical consulting

 See pages 50–51 for a full profile of this company.

ARTHUR J. GALLAGHER & CO.

2 Pierce Place
Itasca, IL 60143-3141
Phone: 708-773-3800
Fax: 708-285-4000

Insurance - brokerage

CEO: J. Patrick Gallagher Jr.
CFO: Michael J. Cloherty
HR: Bette Brinkerhoff
Employees: 3,300

1994 Sales: $356.4 million
1-Yr. Sales Change: 12.2%
Exchange: NYSE
Symbol: AJG

ARTISTIC IMPRESSIONS INC.

240 Cortland Ave.
Lombard, IL 60148
Phone: 708-916-0050
Fax: 708-916-1478

Retail - paintings & lithography through home parties

CEO: Bart Breighner
CFO: Julie Lamoureaux
HR: Joy Jensen
Employees: 90

1995 Sales: $20 million
1-Yr. Sales Change: 11.1%
Ownership: Privately Held

ARTRA GROUP INCORPORATED

500 Central Ave.
Northfield, IL 60093
Phone: 847-441-6650
Fax: 847-441-6959

Diversified operations - costume jewelry; flexible packaging products to the fast-food, bakery, microwave popcorn, supermarket & theater industries

CEO: John J. Harvey
CFO: James D. Doering
HR: Robert Gruber
Employees: 1,600

1994 Sales: $152.1 million
1-Yr. Sales Change: -4.7%
Exchange: NYSE
Symbol: ATA

ASAP SOFTWARE EXPRESS, INC.

850 Asbury Dr.
Buffalo Grove, IL 60089
Phone: 847-465-3710
Fax: 847-465-3277

Computers - PC software distribution

CEO: Scott Wald
CFO: David Polster
HR: Michelle Avastasi
Employees: 150

1994 Est. Sales: $200 mil.
1-Yr. Sales Change: —
Ownership: Privately Held

ATLAS LIFT TRUCK RENTALS & SALES, INC.

5050 N. River Rd.
Schiller Park, IL 60176
Phone: 847-678-3450
Fax: 847-678-9557

Leasing - forklifts, construction equipment & material handling products & systems

CEO: Howard Bernstein
CFO: Larry Hirsch
HR: Chris Kozlowski
Employees: 172

1994 Sales: $54 million
1-Yr. Sales Change: 20.0%
Ownership: Privately Held

AURORA EBY-BROWN CO.

280 W. Schuman Blvd., Ste. 280
Naperville, IL 60566
Phone: 708-778-2800
Fax: 708-778-2835

CEO: Thomas Wake
CFO: Jeff Adams
HR: Steve Bundy
Employees: 1,327

1994 Sales: $1,450 million
1-Yr. Sales Change: 39.4%
Ownership: Privately Held

Wholesale distribution - tobacco & tobacco products including cigarettes, cigars & snuff

AVONDALE FINANCIAL CORP.

20 N. Clark St.
Chicago, IL 60602
Phone: 312-782-6200
Fax: 312-782-0724

CEO: Robert S. Engleman Jr.
CFO: Robert S. Engleman Jr.
HR: —
Employees: 113

1995 Sales: $34 million
1-Yr. Sales Change: 0.3%
Exchange: Nasdaq
Symbol: AVND

Banks - Midwest (Avondale Federal Savings Bank)

AXIA, INC.

2001 Spring Rd.
Oak Brook, IL 60521
Phone: 708-571-3350
Fax: 708-571-3360

CEO: Dennis W. Sheehan
CFO: Lyle J. Frye
HR: LaRue Carlson
Employees: 889

1994 Sales: $81.3 million
1-Yr. Sales Change: -7.4%
Ownership: Privately Held

Diversified operations - coated wire racks used in dishwashers; drywall tools; packaging machinery;
material handling & storage equipment

BAGCRAFT CORPORATION OF AMERICA

3900 W. 43rd St.
Chicago, IL 60632
Phone: 312-254-8000
Fax: 312-254-8204

CEO: Mark Santacrose
CFO: Mike Ardnino
HR: Charles Gaul
Employees: 1,088

1994 Sales: $125 million
1-Yr. Sales Change: 4.1%
Ownership: Privately Held

Containers - flexible packaging; water-soluble ink

BAIRD & WARNER, INC.

200 W. Madison St.
Chicago, IL 60606
Phone: 312-368-1855
Fax: 312-368-1490

CEO: Stephen W. Baird
CFO: Jeff Edgar
HR: Norbert Michalak
Employees: 1,445

1994 Sales: $86.3 million
1-Yr. Sales Change: -3.6%
Ownership: Privately Held

Real estate operations - residential & commercial brokerage

BAKER & MCKENZIE

130 E. Randolph Dr.	CEO: John C. Klotsche	1995 Sales: $594 million
Chicago, IL 60601	CFO: Robert S. Spencer	1-Yr. Sales Change: 8.8%
Phone: 312-861-8800	HR: Mary Weis	Ownership: Privately Held
Fax: 312-861-8823	Employees: 5,248	

Law firm

 See pages 52–53 for a full profile of this company.

BALLY ENTERTAINMENT CORPORATION

8700 W. Bryn Mawr Ave.	CEO: Arthur M. Goldberg	1994 Sales: $942.3 million
Chicago, IL 60631	CFO: Lee S. Hillman	1-Yr. Sales Change: -28.6%
Phone: 312-399-1300	HR: Harold Morgan	Exchange: NYSE
Fax: 312-693-2982	Employees: 11,200	Symbol: BLY

Gambling resorts & casinos in Atlantic City (Bally's Park Place, The Grand), Las Vegas (Bally's Las Vegas), New Orleans & Tunica, Mississippi

 See pages 54–55 for a full profile of this company.

BANKERS LIFE HOLDING CORPORATION

222 Merchandise Mart Plaza	CEO: Barth T. Murphy	1994 Sales: $1,437.9 million
Chicago, IL 60654-2076	CFO: Fred E. Crosley	1-Yr. Sales Change: -1.3%
Phone: 312-396-6000	HR: Kathi Slomka	Exchange: NYSE
Fax: 312-396-5970	Employees: 1,950	Symbol: BLH

Insurance - accident & health

BANYAN INVESTMENT FUNDS

150 S. Wacker Dr.	CEO: Philip H. Brady Jr.	1994 Sales: $12.8 million
Chicago, IL 60606	CFO: William M. Karnes	1-Yr. Sales Change: —
Phone: 312-553-9800	HR: —	
Fax: 312-553-0450	Employees: —	

Series of publicly traded real estate investment trusts

BAXTER INTERNATIONAL INC.

One Baxter Pkwy.	CEO: Vernon R. Loucks Jr.	1994 Sales: $9,324 million
Deerfield, IL 60015	CFO: Harry Jansen Kraemer Jr.	1-Yr. Sales Change: 5.0%
Phone: 847-948-2000	HR: Herbert E. Walker	Exchange: NYSE
Fax: 847-948-2887	Employees: 53,500	Symbol: BAX

Medical products & health services

 See pages 56–57 for a full profile of this company.

BECO GROUP

200 S. Prospect Rd.
Park Ridge, IL 60068
Phone: 847-825-8000
Fax: 847-692-0620

CEO: Leonard A. Wislow
CFO: Leonard A. Wislow
HR: Angela Kabbes
Employees: 50

1994 Sales: $66 million
1-Yr. Sales Change: 3.6%
Ownership: Privately Held

Personnel - temporary employment services

BEER ACROSS AMERICA

55 Albrecht Dr.
Lake Bluff, IL 60044
Phone: 847-604-8008
Fax: 847-639-0029

CEO: Bob Baubien
CFO: Steve Sprindis
HR: Pete Gault
Employees: 110

1994 Est. Sales: $16 mil.
1-Yr. Sales Change: —
Ownership: Privately Held

Beverages - beer-, wine- & coffee-of-the-month mail-order clubs (Beer Across America, International Wine Cellars, CoffeeQuest)

BELL & HOWELL HOLDINGS COMPANY

5215 Old Orchard Rd.
Skokie, IL 60077-1076
Phone: 847-470-7100
Fax: 847-470-9825

CEO: William J. White
CFO: Nils A. Johansson
HR: Maria T. Rubly
Employees: 5,791

1994 Sales: $720.3 million
1-Yr. Sales Change: 6.6%
Exchange: NYSE
Symbol: BHW

Diversified operations - publishing; information systems; mail handling equipment; online service (UMI)

 See pages 58–59 for a full profile of this company.

BELL BANCORP, INC.

79 W. Monroe St.
Chicago, IL 60603
Phone: 312-346-1000
Fax: 312-346-0102

CEO: Robert G. Rowen
CFO: John C. Savio
HR: Kathryn Banky
Employees: 364

1995 Sales: $118 million
1-Yr. Sales Change: -3.6%
Exchange: Nasdaq
Symbol: BELL

Banks - Midwest

BEN FRANKLIN RETAIL STORES, INC.

500 E. North Ave.
Carol Stream, IL 60188-2168
Phone: 708-462-6100
Fax: 708-462-6243

CEO: Bob Kendig
CFO: David A. Brainard
HR: Michele Benoit
Employees: 1,974

1995 Sales: $354.8 million
1-Yr. Sales Change: 5.0%
Exchange: Nasdaq
Symbol: BFRS

Retail - discount & variety

BERLIN INDUSTRIES, INC.

175 Mercedes Dr.
Carol Stream, IL 60188
Phone: 708-682-0600
Fax: 708-682-5928

CEO: Ed Majerczak
CFO: Steve Schmitt
HR: Mike Chieslewicz
Employees: 400

1994 Sales: $80 million
1-Yr. Sales Change: 26.2%
Ownership: Privately Held

Printing - full-service commercial

BERLIN PACKAGING CORPORATION

111 N. Canal St.
Chicago, IL 60606
Phone: 312-876-9292
Fax: 312-876-9290

CEO: Andrew T. Berlin
CFO: Gordon Anderson
HR: Sandy Mandell
Employees: 180

1994 Sales: $105 million
1-Yr. Sales Change: 5.0%
Ownership: Privately Held

Containers - glass, plastic & metal

BIGSBY & KRUTHERS, INC./KNOT SHOPS

57 W. Grand
Chicago, IL 60610
Phone: 312-440-1700
Fax: 312-644-0404

CEO: Gene Silverberg
CFO: Dulcie Truitt
HR: —
Employees: 194

1994 Sales: $50 million
1-Yr. Sales Change: 22.0%
Ownership: Privately Held

Retail - apparel for big & tall men (Bigsby & Kruthers) & neckware (Knot Shops)

BINKS MANUFACTURING COMPANY

9201 W. Belmont Ave.
Franklin Park, IL 60131-2887
Phone: 847-671-3000
Fax: 847-671-6489

CEO: Burke B. Roche
CFO: Jeffrey W. Lemajeur
HR: James E. Lindquist
Employees: 1,682

1994 Sales: $243.6 million
1-Yr. Sales Change: 15.8%
Exchange: AMEX
Symbol: BIN

Spray finishing & coating application equipment, including spray guns & nozzles

BIO-LOGIC SYSTEMS CORPORATION

One Bio-Logic Plaza
Mundelein, IL 60060
Phone: 847-949-5200
Fax: 847-949-8615

CEO: Gabriel Raviv
CFO: Charles Z. Weingarten
HR: Faith Curtis
Employees: 82

1995 Sales: $12.1 million
1-Yr. Sales Change: 13.1%
Exchange: Nasdaq
Symbol: BLSC

Medical instruments - integrated family of electrodiagnostic testing systems

BLISS & LAUGHLIN INDUSTRIES INC.

281 E. 155th St.
Harvey, IL 60426
Phone: 708-333-1220
Fax: 708-333-1228

Steel - production

CEO: Gregory H. Parker
CFO: George W. Fleck
HR: Richard M. Bogdon
Employees: 437

1995 Sales: $169.4 million
1-Yr. Sales Change: 11.2%
Exchange: Nasdaq
Symbol: BLIS

BLUE CROSS AND BLUE SHIELD ASSOCIATION

676 N. St. Clair St.
Chicago, IL 60611
Phone: 312-440-6000
Fax: 312-440-6609

Insurance - prepaid health care plans

CEO: Patrick A. Hays
CFO: David Murdoch
HR: Kris Kurschner
Employees: 146,352

1994 Sales: $71,414 million
1-Yr. Sales Change: 0.4%
Ownership: Privately Held

See pages 60–61 for a full profile of this company.

BOB O'CONNOR FORD

2601 W. 95th St.
Evergreen Park, IL 60642
Phone: 708-423-3500
Fax: 708-423-3553

Retail - new & used cars

CEO: Robert E. O'Connor
CFO: Robert E. O'Connor
HR: Pat O'Connor
Employees: 185

1994 Sales: $75 million
1-Yr. Sales Change: 45.6%
Ownership: Privately Held

BODINE ELECTRIC COMPANY

2500 W. Bradley Place
Chicago, IL 60618
Phone: 312-478-3515
Fax: 312-478-3146

Machinery - fractional horsepower AC & DC motors & controls

CEO: John R. Bodine
CFO: David Dahl
HR: Denise Taylor
Employees: 525

1994 Sales: $53 million
1-Yr. Sales Change: 10.4%
Ownership: Privately Held

BOISE CASCADE OFFICE PRODUCTS CORPORATION

800 W. Bryn Mawr Ave.
Itasca, IL 60143
Phone: 708-773-5000
Fax: 708-773-3607

Retail - direct mail sales of office supplies & furniture

CEO: Peter G. Danis
CFO: Carol B. Moerdyk
HR: John Love
Employees: 3,120

1994 Sales: $908.5 million
1-Yr. Sales Change: 33.1%
Exchange: NYSE
Symbol: BOP

BORG-WARNER AUTOMOTIVE, INC.

200 S. Michigan Ave.
Chicago, IL 60604
Phone: 312-322-8500
Fax: 312-322-8849

CEO: John F. Fiedler
CFO: Robin J. Adams
HR: Geraldine Kinsella
Employees: 7,330

1994 Sales: $1,223.4 million
1-Yr. Sales Change: 24.2%
Exchange: NYSE
Symbol: BWA

Automotive & trucking - components & systems

 See pages 62–63 for a full profile of this company.

BORG-WARNER SECURITY CORPORATION

200 S. Michigan Ave.
Chicago, IL 60604
Phone: 312-322-8500
Fax: 312-322-8849

CEO: Donald C. Trauscht
CFO: Timothy Wood
HR: John D. O'Brien
Employees: 91,698

1994 Sales: $1,792.9 million
1-Yr. Sales Change: 1.6%
Exchange: NYSE
Symbol: BOR

Protection - guard, alarm, armored transportation & courier services

 See pages 64–65 for a full profile of this company.

BRADNER CENTRAL COMPANY

333 S. Desplaines St.
Chicago, IL 60661-5596
Phone: 312-454-1852
Fax: 312-454-0783

CEO: Terence J. Shea
CFO: Bernard J. Tarte Jr.
HR: Susan A. Trush
Employees: 187

1995 Est. Sales: $400 mil.
1-Yr. Sales Change: 33.6%
Ownership: Privately Held

Paper-distribution

BRESLER'S INDUSTRIES, INC.

999 E. Touhy Ave.
Des Plaines, IL 60018
Phone: 847-298-1100
Fax: 847-298-0697

CEO: David Lasky
CFO: Dennis Rissman
HR: Pat Haas
Employees: 58

1994 Sales: $45.8 million
1-Yr. Sales Change: 0.7%
Ownership: Privately Held

Business services - franchisor of quick-service ice cream & yogurt shops

BROOK FURNITURE RENTAL, INC.

2301 E. Oakton St.
Arlington Heights, IL 60005
Phone: 847-593-0343
Fax: 847-593-0883

CEO: Robert W. Crawford Jr.
CFO: John Luttrell
HR: —
Employees: 400

1994 Sales: $45.2 million
1-Yr. Sales Change: 0.0%
Ownership: Privately Held

Leasing - residential, office & convention furniture

BROOKFIELD FARMS, INC.

219 N. Green St.
Chicago, IL 60607
Phone: 312-829-4900
Fax: 312-829-4788

Food - meat processing

CEO: Frank Swan
CFO: Erwin Raybin
HR: Tom Fitzgibbons
Employees: 125

1994 Sales: $48 million
1-Yr. Sales Change: 4.3%
Ownership: Privately Held

BRUNSWICK CORPORATION

One N. Field Ct.
Lake Forest, IL 60045-4811
Phone: 847-735-4700
Fax: 847-735-4765

Leisure & recreational products - boats, sporting goods & bowling center

CEO: Peter N. Larson
CFO: Peter B. Hamilton
HR: Kenneth B. Zeigler
Employees: 20,800

1994 Sales: $2,700.1 million
1-Yr. Sales Change: 22.4%
Exchange: NYSE
Symbol: BC

 See pages 66–67 for a full profile of this company.

BRUSS COMPANY

3548 N. Kostner Ave.
Chicago, IL 60641
Phone: 312-282-2900
Fax: 312-282-6966

Food - meat processing & distribution

CEO: Dan Timm
CFO: Dan Timm
HR: Phil Rizzo
Employees: 265

1994 Sales: $90 million
1-Yr. Sales Change: 13.9%
Ownership: Privately Held

BT OFFICE PRODUCTS INTERNATIONAL, INC.

2150 E. Lake Cook Rd.
Buffalo Grove, IL 60089
Phone: 847-808-3000
Fax: 847-808-3011

Office products (Masterbrand, BT Masterbrand, Classic) & office furniture distribution

CEO: Rudolf A. J. Huyzer
CFO: John J. McKiernan
HR: Rhonda Barnes
Employees: 4,000

1994 Sales: $789.5 million
1-Yr. Sales Change: 34.5%
Exchange: NYSE
Symbol: BTF

BUDGET RENT A CAR CORPORATION

4225 Naperville Rd.
Lisle, IL 60532
Phone: 708-955-1900
Fax: 708-955-7799

Leasing - car & truck rental

CEO: William N. Plamondon
CFO: Kevin M. McShea
HR: Gene Williams
Employees: 8,700

1994 Sales: $1,081 million
1-Yr. Sales Change: 6.2%
Ownership: Privately Held

 See pages 68–69 for a full profile of this company.

BURNHAM BROADCASTING COMPANY

980 N. Michigan Ave.
Chicago, IL 60611
Phone: 312-787-9800
Fax: 312-787-3964

Broadcasting - TV stations

CEO: Peter B. Desnoes
CFO: Tyler Sheffield
HR: —
Employees: 500

1994 Sales: $76.5 million
1-Yr. Sales Change: 8.5%
Ownership: Privately Held

BUTERA FINER FOODS, INC.

One Clock Tower Plaza
Elgin, IL 60120
Phone: 847-741-1010
Fax: 847-741-9674

Retail - supermarkets

CEO: Paul Butera
CFO: Joseph Butera
HR: Gwen Houston
Employees: 1,000

1994 Est. Sales: $133 mil.
1-Yr. Sales Change: -5.0%
Ownership: Privately Held

CALUMET BANCORP, INC.

1350 E. Sibley Blvd.
Dolton, IL 60419
Phone: 708-841-9010
Fax: 708-841-9312

Banks - Midwest

CEO: Thaddeus Walczak
CFO: John L. Garlanger
HR: Deborah V. Cattoni
Employees: 142

1994 Sales: $39.2 million
1-Yr. Sales Change: -3.4%
Exchange: Nasdaq
Symbol: CBCI

CAMBRIDGE HOMES, INC.

800 S. Milwaukee Ave.
Libertyville, IL 60048
Phone: 847-362-9100
Fax: 847-362-9102

Building - single-family homes & townhouses

CEO: Richard J. Brown
CFO: Russ Schlatter
HR: —
Employees: 320

1995 Est. Sales: $220 mil.
1-Yr. Sales Change: —
Ownership: Privately Held

CAPITOL CONSTRUCTION GROUP, INC.

1400 S. Wols Rd.
Wheeling, IL 60090
Phone: 847-215-2500
Fax: 847-215-5331

Building - general contractor & construction management

CEO: Larry Belcaster
CFO: David Radomski
HR: Valerie Sobieski
Employees: 120

1994 Sales: $90 million
1-Yr. Sales Change: 50.0%
Ownership: Privately Held

CAPSURE HOLDINGS CORP.

2 N. Riverside Plaza
Chicago, IL 60606
Phone: 312-879-1900
Fax: 312-454-0614

CEO: Samuel Zell
CFO: Mary Jane Robertson
HR: Laura Rode
Employees: 600

1994 Sales: $112.7 million
1-Yr. Sales Change: 3.9%
Exchange: NYSE
Symbol: CSH

Insurance - property & casualty; oil & gas production

 See page 195 for a full profile of this company.

CAREMARK INTERNATIONAL INC.

2215 Sanders Rd., Ste. 400
Northbrook, IL 60062
Phone: 847-559-4700
Fax: 847-559-4792

CEO: C. A. Lance Piccolo
CFO: Thomas W. Hodson
HR: Kent J. DeLucenay
Employees: 9,150

1994 Sales: $2,426 million
1-Yr. Sales Change: 36.0%
Exchange: NYSE
Symbol: CK

Health care - outpatient & home

 See pages 70–71 for a full profile of this company.

CARQUEVILLE/TCR GRAPHICS, INC.

2200 Estes Ave.
Elk Grove Village, IL 60007
Phone: 847-439-8700
Fax: 847-228-3953

CEO: Patrick Carney
CFO: John Nowicki
HR: —
Employees: 217

1994 Sales: $31.3 million
1-Yr. Sales Change: 4.3%
Ownership: Privately Held

Printing - commercial, specializing in labels, brochures & annual reports

CB BANCORP, INC.

126 E 4th St.
Michigan City, IN 46360
Phone: 219-873-2800
Fax: 219-873-2851

CEO: Joseph F. Heffernan
CFO: George L. Koehm
HR: Carlyne Graves
Employees: 61

1995 Sales: $10.2 million
1-Yr. Sales Change: -17.1%
Exchange: Nasdaq (SC)
Symbol: CBCO

Banks - Midwest

CBI INDUSTRIES, INC.

800 Jorie Blvd.
Oak Brook, IL 60521-2268
Phone: 708-572-7000
Fax: 708-572-7405

CEO: John E. Jones
CFO: George L. Schueppert
HR: Stephen M. Duffy
Employees: 14,440

1994 Sales: $1,890.9 million
1-Yr. Sales Change: 13.1%
Exchange: NYSE
Symbol: CBI

Diversified operations - heavy construction (Chicago Bridge & Iron); industrial gases (Liquid Carbonic)

 See pages 72–73 for a full profile of this company.

CC INDUSTRIES, INC.

222 N. LaSalle St.
Chicago, IL 60601
Phone: 312-855-4000
Fax: 312-236-7074

CEO: William H. Crown
CFO: Paul Dwyer
HR: Patricia Slizewski
Employees: 5,449

1994 Sales: $502 million
1-Yr. Sales Change: 8.4%
Ownership: Privately Held

Diversified operations - manufacturing; real estate development

CCC INFORMATION SERVICES, INC.

444 Merchandise Mart
Chicago, IL 60654
Phone: 312-222-4636
Fax: 312-527-2298

CEO: David M. Phillips
CFO: Gary J. Bjarnson
HR: Kathy Sfikas
Employees: 846

1994 Sales: $88.4 million
1-Yr. Sales Change: 41.0%
Ownership: Privately Held

Computers - automotive claims software & proprietary information

CCH INCORPORATED

2700 Lake Cook Rd.
Riverwoods, IL 60015-3888
Phone: 847-267-7000
Fax: 847-267-2873

CEO: Oakleigh B. Thorne
CFO: John I. Abernethy
HR: Judith Kohn
Employees: 5,290

1994 Sales: $578.8 million
1-Yr. Sales Change: 0.2%
Exchange: Nasdaq
Symbol: CCHIA

Publishing - legal information; corporate services; computer software

 See pages 74–75 for a full profile of this company.

CDW COMPUTER CENTERS, INC.

1020 E. Lake Cook Rd.
Buffalo Grove, IL 60089
Phone: 847-465-6000
Fax: 847-465-6800

CEO: Michael P. Krasny
CFO: Harry J. Harczak Jr.
HR: Mary C. Gerlits
Employees: 390

1994 Sales: $413.3 million
1-Yr. Sales Change: 52.6%
Exchange: Nasdaq
Symbol: CDWC

Computers - direct marketer of computers, peripherals & software

 See page 196 for a full profile of this company.

CELEX GROUP INC.

919 Springer Dr.
Lombard, IL 60148
Phone: 708-953-1222
Fax: 708-953-2110

CEO: Arnold M. "Mac" Anderson
CFO: James M. Beltrame
HR: Linda Sondgeroth
Employees: 516

1995 Sales: $44.1 million
1-Yr. Sales Change: 48.0%
Exchange: Nasdaq
Symbol: CLXG

Retail - motivational & gift products (Successories)

 See page 197 for a full profile of this company.

CELOZZI-ETTLESON CHEVROLET, INC.

155 E. Roosevelt Rd.
Elmhurst, IL 60126
Phone: 708-279-5200
Fax: 708-832-2310

Retail - new & used cars

CEO: Nick A. Cellozzi
CFO: Robert Cartlend
HR: —
Employees: 221

1994 Est. Sales: $141.6 mil.
1-Yr. Sales Change: 6.9%
Ownership: Privately Held

CENTERPOINT PROPERTIES CORPORATION

401 N. Michigan Ave., 30th Fl.
Chicago, IL 60611
Phone: 312-346-5600
Fax: 312-456-7696

Real estate investment trust - industrial real estate

CEO: John S. Gates Jr.
CFO: Paul S. Fisher
HR: —
Employees: 95

1994 Sales: $33.8 million
1-Yr. Sales Change: 275.6%
Exchange: AMEX
Symbol: CNT

CENTRAL GROCERS COOPERATIVE, INC.

3701 N. Centrella St.
Franklin Park, IL 60131
Phone: 847-678-0660
Fax: 847-678-1606

Food - wholesale to grocers

CEO: John Cortesi
CFO: Jane Hidalgo
HR: Annalee Robish
Employees: 260

1994 Sales: $412 million
1-Yr. Sales Change: 10.2%
Ownership: Cooperative

CERTIFIED GROCERS MIDWEST, INC.

One Certified Dr.
Hodgkins, IL 60525
Phone: 708-579-2100
Fax: 708-354-8570

Food - cooperative distributing food & nonfood products to grocery stores

CEO: Elwood F. Winn
CFO: Ed Bradley
HR: Marcy Meister
Employees: 700

1994 Sales: $700.8 million
1-Yr. Sales Change: 9.8%
Ownership: Cooperative

CF INDUSTRIES, INC.

One Salem Lake Dr.
Long Grove, IL 60047
Phone: 847-438-9500
Fax: 847-438-0211

Chemicals - fertilizers

CEO: Robert C. Liuzzi
CFO: Stephen R. Wilson
HR: William G. Eppel
Employees: 1,471

1994 Sales: $1,182.9 million
1-Yr. Sales Change: 30.6%
Ownership: Privately Held

CFC INTERNATIONAL, INC.

500 State St.	CEO: Roger F. Hruby	1994 Sales: $27.8 million
Chicago Heights, IL 60411	CFO: Dennis W. Lakomy	1-Yr. Sales Change: 9.9%
Phone: 708-891-3456	HR: Susan Contri	Exchange: Nasdaq
Fax: 708-758-5989	Employees: 182	Symbol: CFCI

Paper & paper products - multilayered holographic coatings for protective & informative purposes

CFI INDUSTRIES, INC.

935 W. Union Ave.	CEO: Robert W. George	1995 Sales: $31.3 million
Wheaton, IL 60187	CFO: Robert W. Zimmer	1-Yr. Sales Change: 9.1%
Phone: 708-668-2838	HR: Gary Kent	Exchange: Nasdaq
Fax: 708-668-2804	Employees: 250	Symbol: CFIB

Paper & paper products

CHAMPION PARTS, INC.

2525 22nd St.	CEO: Thomas W. Blashill	1994 Sales: $95.3 million
Oak Brook, IL 60521	CFO: Mark Smetana	1-Yr. Sales Change: -4.7%
Phone: 708-573-6600	HR: Mark Smetana	Exchange: Nasdaq
Fax: 708-573-0348	Employees: 1,470	Symbol: CREB

Automotive & trucking - replacement parts

CHARLES INDUSTRIES LTD.

5600 Apollo Dr.	CEO: Joseph T. Charles	1994 Sales: $90 million
Rolling Meadows, IL 60008	CFO: Robert Novak	1-Yr. Sales Change: 13.2%
Phone: 847-806-6300	HR: —	Ownership: Privately Held
Fax: 847-806-6231	Employees: 975	

Telecommunications equipment - power & electrical components

CHAS. LEVY COMPANIES

1200 N. North Branch	CEO: Carol G. Kloster	1995 Sales: $320 million
Chicago, IL 60622	CFO: Carol G. Kloster	1-Yr. Sales Change: 5.7%
Phone: 312-440-4400	HR: Jim Crawford	Ownership: Privately Held
Fax: 312-440-4434	Employees: 2,000	

Wholesale distribution - books & magazines

CHEMCENTRAL CORPORATION

7050 W. 71st St.	CEO: H. Daniel T. Wenstrup	1994 Sales: $745 million
Bedford Park, IL 60499	CFO: Arlen L. Haines	1-Yr. Sales Change: 10.4%
Phone: 708-594-7000	HR: Dave Friede	Ownership: Privately Held
Fax: 708-594-6328	Employees: 834	

Wholesale distribution - industrial chemicals

CHERNIN'S SHOES, INC.

1001 S. Clinton St.	CEO: Steven Larrick	1994 Sales: $80 million
Chicago, IL 60607	CFO: James Lubinski	1-Yr. Sales Change: 0.0%
Phone: 312-922-5900	HR: Dan Naslund	Ownership: Privately Held
Fax: 312-922-3673	Employees: 325	

Retail - shoes

THE CHERRY CORPORATION

3600 Sunset Ave.	CEO: Peter B. Cherry	1995 Sales: $339.2 million
Waukegan, IL 60087-3298	CFO: Dan A. King	1-Yr. Sales Change: 23.2%
Phone: 847-662-9200	HR: Nancy Guarascio	Exchange: Nasdaq
Fax: 847-360-3508	Employees: 3,986	Symbol: CHERB

Electrical components - automotive switching devices; keyboards, switches & semiconductors for the computer industry

CHICAGO AIRPORT SYSTEM

Terminal 2, O'Hare Airport	CEO: David R. Mosena	1994 Sales: $419.8 million
Chicago, IL 60666	CFO: Dwain Hawthorne	1-Yr. Sales Change: 6.1%
Phone: 312-686-8060	HR: Mike Cummings	
Fax: 312-686-6234	Employees: 2,614	

Transportation - airport management (O'Hare, Midway, Meigs)

CHICAGO BEARS FOOTBALL CLUB INC.

250 N. Washington Rd.	CEO: Michael McCaskey	1995 Sales: $65.1 million
Lake Forest, IL 60045	CFO: Ted Phillips	1-Yr. Sales Change: -0.5%
Phone: 847-295-6600	HR: Tim LeFevour	Ownership: Privately Held
Fax: 847-295-5238	Employees: 150	

Leisure & recreational services - professional football team

 See page 198 for a full profile of this company.

CHICAGO BLACK HAWKS HOCKEY TEAM INC.

1901 W. Madison St.	CEO: William Wirtz	1994 Sales: $42.6 million
Chicago, IL 60612	CFO: Robert Rinkus	1-Yr. Sales Change: 1.2%
Phone: 312-455-7000	HR: —	Ownership: Subsidiary
Fax: 312-455-7041	Employees: 24	

Leisure & recreational services - professional hockey team; subsidiary of Wirtz Corporation

CHICAGO BULLS

1901 W. Madison St.	CEO: Jerry Reinsdorf	1994 Sales: $57.5 million
Chicago, IL 60612	CFO: Irwin Mandel	1-Yr. Sales Change: 14.3%
Phone: 312-455-4000	HR: Steve Schanwald	Ownership: Privately Held
Fax: 312-455-4196	Employees: 75	

Leisure & recreational services - professional basketball team

CHICAGO CORPORATION

208 S. La Salle St.	CEO: John A. Wing	1994 Sales: $185 million
Chicago, IL 60604	CFO: Wilbert A. Thiel	1-Yr. Sales Change: 7.4%
Phone: 312-855-7600	HR: Diane Denk	Ownership: Privately Held
Fax: 312-984-6781	Employees: 908	

Financial - securites & commodities brokerage; investment banking

CHICAGO DOCK AND CANAL TRUST

455 E. Illinois, Ste. 565	CEO: Charles R. Gardner	1995 Sales: $22.4 million
Chicago, IL 60611	CFO: David R. Tinkham	1-Yr. Sales Change: 8.2%
Phone: 312-467-1870	HR: —	Exchange: Nasdaq
Fax: 312-467-9647	Employees: 8	Symbol: DOCKS

Real estate investment trust - commercial real estate

CHICAGO FAUCET COMPANY

2100 S. Clearwater Dr.	CEO: Alan Lougee	1994 Est. Sales: $31.5 mil.
Des Plaines, IL 60018	CFO: Dan Felde	1-Yr. Sales Change: 5.0%
Phone: 847-803-5000	HR: Dennis Matha	Ownership: Privately Held
Fax: 847-298-6485	Employees: 365	

Building products - plumbing equipment

CHICAGO HEIGHTS STEEL COMPANY

211 E. Main St.
Chicago Heights , IL 60411
Phone: 708-756-5660
Fax: 708-756-5628

Steel - production

CEO: Frank L. Corral
CFO: Richard Gollner
HR: Michael Wrona
Employees: 345

1994 Sales: $65 million
1-Yr. Sales Change: 16.1%
Ownership: Privately Held

CHICAGO NATIONAL LEAGUE BALL CLUB INC.

1060 W. Addison St.
Chicago, IL 60613
Phone: 312-404-2827
Fax: 312-404-4111

CEO: Andrew MacPhail
CFO: Margaret Durkin
HR: Janice Maltby
Employees: 1,000

1994 Sales: $53.8 million
1-Yr. Sales Change: -35.0%
Ownership: Subsidiary

Leisure & recreational services - professional baseball team (Chicago Cubs); subsidiary of Tribune
Company

CHICAGO NATURAL GAS, INC.

345 N. Canal St.
Chicago, IL 60606
Phone: 312-527-4100
Fax: 312-321-0013

CEO: David Rubenstein
CFO: David Rubenstein
HR: David Rubenstein
Employees: 10

1994 Sales: $50 million
1-Yr. Sales Change: 4.2%
Ownership: Privately Held

Natural gas sales & distribution; energy cogeneration; energy consulting

CHICAGO RIVET & MACHINE COMPANY

901 Frontenac Rd., PO Box 3061
Naperville, IL 60566
Phone: 708-357-8500
Fax: 708-983-9314

Metal products - fasteners

CEO: John A. Morrissey
CFO: John C. Osterman
HR: —
Employees: 261

1994 Sales: $23 million
1-Yr. Sales Change: 12.7%
Exchange: AMEX
Symbol: CVR

CHICAGO WHITE SOX

333 W. 35th St.
Chicago, IL 60616
Phone: 312-924-1000
Fax: 312-451-5116

CEO: Jerry Reinsdorf
CFO: Howard Pizer
HR: Moira Foy
Employees: 75

1994 Sales: $45.5 million
1-Yr. Sales Change: -42.3%
Ownership: Privately Held

Leisure & recreational services - professional baseball team

CHT CORPORATION

816 W. Armitage Ave.	CEO: Charles H. Trotter	1995 Sales: $3.8 million
Chicago, IL 60614	CFO: Russell C. Drew	1-Yr. Sales Change: 26.7%
Phone: 312-248-6228	HR: Patricia Mowen	Ownership: Privately Held
Fax: 312-248-6088	Employees: 50	

Retail - fine dining restaurant (Charlie Trotter's)

CIRCUIT SYSTEMS, INC.

2350 E. Lunt Ave.	CEO: D. S. Patel	1995 Sales: $59.6 million
Elk Grove Village, IL 60007	CFO: Dilip S. Vyas	1-Yr. Sales Change: -1.3%
Phone: 847-439-1999	HR: William Blair	Exchange: Nasdaq
Fax: 847-437-5910	Employees: 540	Symbol: CSYI

Electrical components - single-sided, double-sided & multilayer printed circuit boards

C. J. VITNER COMPANY

4202 W. 45th St.	CEO: William A. Vitner	1994 Sales: $48.2 million
Chicago, IL 60632	CFO: Patrick Hugdin	1-Yr. Sales Change: 1.5%
Phone: 312-523-7900	HR: Joan Zelinski	Ownership: Privately Held
Fax: 312-523-9143	Employees: 380	

Snack foods manufacturing & distribution

CLARK FOODSERVICE INC.

950 Arthur Ave.	CEO: Don J. Hindman	1994 Sales: $350 million
Elk Grove Village, IL 60007	CFO: Gerry DeMatteo	1-Yr. Sales Change: 1.4%
Phone: 847-956-1730	HR: —	Ownership: Privately Held
Fax: 847-956-0199	Employees: 800	

Food - wholesale to grocers

CLASSICS INTERNATIONAL ENTERTAINMENT, INC.

919 N. Michigan Ave., Ste. 3400	CEO: Richard S. Berger	1994 Sales: $5.4 million
Chicago, IL 60611	CFO: James M. Dore	1-Yr. Sales Change: 25.6%
Phone: 312-482-9006	HR: Lawrence A. Strauss	Exchange: Nasdaq (SC)
Fax: 312-664-5269	Employees: 93	Symbol: CIEI

Retail - comic-book stores (Dream Factory, Moondog's); comic-book publishing (First Classics)

CNA FINANCIAL CORPORATION

CNA Plaza	CEO: Laurence A. Tisch	1994 Sales: $10,999.5 mil.
Chicago, IL 60685	CFO: Peter E. Jokiel	1-Yr. Sales Change: -0.1%
Phone: 312-822-5000	HR: Floyd E. Brady	Exchange: NYSE
Fax: 312-822-6419	Employees: 15,600	Symbol: CNA

Insurance - property & casualty

See pages 76–77 for a full profile of this company.

COBRA ELECTRONICS, INC.

6500 W. Cortland St.	CEO: Jerry Kalov	1994 Sales: $82.1 million
Chicago, IL 60635	CFO: Gerald M. Laures	1-Yr. Sales Change: -16.9%
Phone: 312-889-8870	HR: Celeste Boucher	Exchange: Nasdaq
Fax: 312-889-1678	Employees: 150	Symbol: COBR

Consumer electronic products - answering machines, cordless phones & audio equipment

COCA-COLA BOTTLING CO. OF CHICAGO

7400 N. Oak Park Ave.	CEO: Marvin J. Herb	1994 Sales: $705 million
Niles, IL 60714	CFO: Jerry Moza	1-Yr. Sales Change: -11.1%
Phone: 312-775-0900	HR: Robert T. Palo	Ownership: Privately Held
Fax: 312-647-7104	Employees: 4,200	

Beverages - soft drink bottling

COLE TAYLOR FINANCIAL GROUP, INC.

350 E. Dundee Rd., Ste. 300	CEO: Jeffrey W. Taylor	1994 Sales: $143.8 million
Wheeling, IL 60090-3199	CFO: J. Christopher Alstrin	1-Yr. Sales Change: 20.3%
Phone: 847-459-1111	HR: Jean C. Schmidt	Exchange: Nasdaq
Fax: 847-459-5860	Employees: 760	Symbol: CTFG

Banks - Midwest (Cole Taylor Bank, Cole Taylor Finance Co.)

COLUMBIA PIPE & SUPPLY COMPANY

1120 W. Pershing Rd.	CEO: William D. Arenberg	1994 Sales: $70 million
Chicago, IL 60609	CFO: Steve Harrison	1-Yr. Sales Change: 16.7%
Phone: 312-927-6600	HR: Steve Harrison	Ownership: Privately Held
Fax: 312-927-6091	Employees: 215	

Building products - plumbing & heating equipment distribution

COMARK, INC.

444 Scott Dr.
Bloomingdale, IL 60108
Phone: 708-924-6670
Fax: 708-924-6790

CEO: Chuck Rolande
CFO: Phil Courtland
HR: Chris Schuver
Employees: 472

1994 Sales: $411 million
1-Yr. Sales Change: 38.4%
Ownership: Privately Held

Computers - software, computer & peripherals dealer & distributor

COMDISCO, INC.

6111 N. River Rd.
Rosemont, IL 60018
Phone: 847-698-3000
Fax: 847-518-5440

CEO: Jack Slevin
CFO: John J. Vosicky
HR: Lucie A. Buford
Employees: 2,000

1995 Sales: $2,240 million
1-Yr. Sales Change: 6.8%
Exchange: NYSE
Symbol: CDO

Leasing - computers

 See pages 78–79 for a full profile of this company.

CONTINENTAL MATERIALS CORPORATION

225 W. Wacker Dr., 18th Fl.
Chicago, IL 60606
Phone: 312-541-7200
Fax: 312-541-7201

CEO: James G. Gidwitz
CFO: Joseph J. Sum
HR: —
Employees: 713

1994 Sales: $75.3 million
1-Yr. Sales Change: 20.5%
Exchange: AMEX
Symbol: CUO

Building products - a/c & heating

CONTINENTAL MOTORS GROUP

5901 S. La Grange Rd.
Countyside, IL 60525
Phone: 708-352-9200
Fax: 708-352-2022

CEO: John F. Weinberger
CFO: John F. Weinberger
HR: Lois Cates
Employees: 300

1994 Sales: $133 million
1-Yr. Sales Change: 12.7%
Ownership: Privately Held

Retail - new & used cars

CONTINENTAL WEB PRESS, INC.

1430 Industrial Dr.
Itasca, IL 60143
Phone: 708-773-1903
Fax: 708-773-1909

CEO: Kenneth W. Field
CFO: John DeBerge
HR: Michele Krahn
Employees: 425

1994 Sales: $78 million
1-Yr. Sales Change: 4.0%
Ownership: Privately Held

Printing - commercial web offset printing

CORCOM, INC.

844 E. Rockland Rd.
Libertyville, IL 60048-1298
Phone: 847-680-7400
Fax: 847-680-8169

CEO: Werner E. Neuman
CFO: Thomas J. Buns
HR: Sherril Bishop
Employees: 588

1994 Sales: $26.7 million
1-Yr. Sales Change: 3.1%
Exchange: Nasdaq
Symbol: CORC

Electrical components - frequency interference filters & power entry devices

COTTER & COMPANY

8600 Bryn Mawr Ave.
Chicago, IL 60631
Phone: 312-695-5000
Fax: 312-695-6524

CEO: Daniel A. Cotter
CFO: Kerry J. Kirby
HR: Pat Kelley
Employees: 4,200

1994 Sales: $2,574.5 million
1-Yr. Sales Change: 6.3%
Ownership: Cooperative

Building products - member-owned hardware wholesale cooperative (True Value)

 See pages 80–81 for a full profile of this company.

COVENANT MINISTRIES OF BENEVOLENCE

5145 N. California Ave.
Chicago, IL 60625
Phone: 312-878-8200
Fax: 312-878-2617

CEO: Rolland S. Carlson
CFO: Philip R. Melchert
HR: —
Employees: 3,500

1995 Sales: $238.4 million
1-Yr. Sales Change: 6.1%
Ownership: Privately Held

Hospitals - not-for-profit system with 2 hospitals (Emanuel Medical Center in Turlock, CA; Swedish Covenant Hospital in Chicago) & 13 retirement centers in the Chicago area, California, Connecticut, Florida, Minnesota & Washington

C. P. HALL COMPANY

311 S. Wacker Dr.
Chicago, IL 60606
Phone: 312-554-7400
Fax: 312-554-7499

CEO: George A. Vincent
CFO: James Klusendorf
HR: James Roach
Employees: 250

1994 Sales: $100 million
1-Yr. Sales Change: 16.3%
Ownership: Privately Held

Chemicals - specialty additives & industrial chemicals

CRAIN COMMUNICATIONS, INC.

740 N. Rush St.
Chicago, IL 60611
Phone: 312-649-5200
Fax: 312-280-3179

CEO: Gertrude R. Crain
CFO: Mary K. Crain
HR: Frances Scott
Employees: 939

1994 Sales: $170.7 million
1-Yr. Sales Change: 8.7%
Ownership: Privately Held

Publishing - business, trade & consumer periodicals

 See page 199 for a full profile of this company.

CUMMINS-AMERICAN CORPORATION

891 Freehangill	CEO: William Jones	1994 Est. Sales: $88.4 mil.
Prospect, IL 60056	CFO: Mark Gray	1-Yr. Sales Change: 6.3%
Phone: 708-299-9550	HR: Joe Panaralle	Ownership: Privately Held
Fax: 708-299-4940	Employees: 626	

Banks - Midwest (Glenview State Bank); coin counters, shredders & bill scanners (Cummins-Allison Corporation)

DADE INTERNATIONAL, INC.

1717 Deerfield Rd.	CEO: Scott Garrett	1994 Sales: $624 million
Deerfield , IL 60015	CFO: Kinzie Weimer	1-Yr. Sales Change: —
Phone: 708-267-5300	HR: Kim Griffin	Ownership: Privately Held
Fax: 708-267-6014	Employees: 4,000	

Medical products - health care diagnostic systems, including blood-test machines

DAUBERT INDUSTRIES, INC.

One Westbrook Corporate Ctr.	CEO: M. Lawrence Garman	1994 Sales: $110.1 million
Westchester, IL 60154	CFO: Sidney A. Scott	1-Yr. Sales Change: 10.8%
Phone: 708-409-5000	HR: William Gaeth	Ownership: Privately Held
Fax: 708-409-5155	Employees: 472	

Chemicals - film, protective & release coatings; packaging materials & sealants

DEAN FOODS COMPANY

3600 N. River Rd.	CEO: Howard M. Dean	1995 Sales: $2,630.2 million
Franklin Park, IL 60131	CFO: Dale I. Hecox	1-Yr. Sales Change: 8.2%
Phone: 312-625-6200	HR: Jerry Berger	Exchange: NYSE
Fax: 708-928-8621	Employees: 11,800	Symbol: DF

Food - dairy & specialty food products

 See pages 82–83 for a full profile of this company.

DEKALB GENETICS CORPORATION

3100 Sycamore Rd.	CEO: Bruce P. Bickner	1995 Sales: $319.4 million
DeKalb, IL 60115-9917	CFO: Thomas R. Rauman	1-Yr. Sales Change: -0.6%
Phone: 815-758-3461	HR: Theresa Brown	Exchange: Nasdaq
Fax: 815-758-3711	Employees: 1,800	Symbol: SEEDB

Agricultural operations - development & marketing of seed including corn, soybeans, sorghum, alfalfa & sunflowers; hybrid swine breeding stock

DELPHI INFORMATION SYSTEMS, INC.

3501 Algonquin Rd.	CEO: David J. Torrence	1995 Sales: $53 million
Rolling Meadows, IL 60008	CFO: Daniel F. Dunne	1-Yr. Sales Change: -1.1%
Phone: 847-506-3100	HR: Alan E. Drizd	Exchange: Nasdaq (SC)
Fax: 847-590-8280	Employees: 461	Symbol: DLPH

Computers - management information software for independent property & casualty insurance agencies & brokerages

DEPAUL UNIVERSITY

One E. Jackson Blvd.	CEO: John Minogue	1994 Sales: $168.1 million
Chicago, IL 60604	CFO: Ken McHugh	1-Yr. Sales Change: 11.0%
Phone: 312-362-8000	HR: Carole Schor	
Fax: 312-362-5116	Employees: 2,950	

Jesuit-run Catholic university offering 109 undergraduate & 34 graduate degree programs

DESKS, INC.

2323 W. Pershing Rd.	CEO: Robert A. Stacey	1994 Sales: $39.2 million
Chicago, IL 60609	CFO: Greg Erazmus	1-Yr. Sales Change: 14.6%
Phone: 312-523-3375	HR: Greg Erazmus	Ownership: Privately Held
Fax: 312-650-9633	Employees: 76	

Retail - office furniture

DESOTO, INC.

16750 S. Vincennes Rd.	CEO: John R. Phillips	1994 Sales: $87.2 million
South Holland, IL 60473	CFO: Anne E. Eisele	1-Yr. Sales Change: -13.8%
Phone: 708-331-8800	HR: Cheryl Davis	Exchange: NYSE
Fax: 708-210-0345	Employees: 417	Symbol: DSO

Soap & cleaning preparations - private label & contract household cleaning products

DEVRY INC.

One Tower Ln.	CEO: Dennis J. Keller	1995 Sales: $228.6 million
Oakbrook Terrace, IL 60181-4624	CFO: Norman M. Levine	1-Yr. Sales Change: 8.1%
Phone: 708-571-7700	HR: Carl A. Weinstein	Exchange: Nasdaq
Fax: 708-571-0317	Employees: 3,770	Symbol: DVRY

Schools - trade (DeVry Institutes), corporate training (Corporate Educational Services) & business (Keller School of Management)

 **See page 200 for a full profile of this company.**

DIETZGEN CORPORATION

250 Wille Rd.
Des Plaines, IL 60018
Phone: 847-635-5200
Fax: 847-635-5210

CEO: Larry Kujovich
CFO: Roger Drewes
HR: —
Employees: 310

1994 Est. Sales: $52.4 mil.
1-Yr. Sales Change: 2.7%
Ownership: Privately Held

Drafting, engineering & reproduction equipment & supplies

DOALL COMPANY

254 N. Laurel Ave.
Des Plaines , IL 60016
Phone: 847-824-1122
Fax: 847-699-7542

CEO: Michael L. Wilkie
CFO: David Wall
HR: Kevin Hennesy
Employees: 1,800

1994 Sales: $192 million
1-Yr. Sales Change: 25.5%
Ownership: Privately Held

Wholesale distribution - machine tools & industrial supplies

DOMINICK'S FINER FOODS INC.

505 Railroad Ave.
Northlake, IL 60164
Phone: 847-562-1000
Fax: 847-409-3955

CEO: Ronald W. Burkle
CFO: Darren Karst
HR: Edwina Erlemann
Employees: 18,000

1994 Est. Sales: $2,500 mil.
1-Yr. Sales Change: 16.3%
Ownership: Subsidiary

Retail - supermarkets; subsidiary of Yucaipa

DONLEN CORPORATION

2315 Sanders Rd.
Northbrook, IL 60062
Phone: 847-714-1400
Fax: 847-714-1500

CEO: Don Rappeport
CFO: Ron Prince
HR: Suzanne Gutowsky
Employees: 124

1994 Sales: $156 million
1-Yr. Sales Change: 19.1%
Ownership: Privately Held

Transportation - fleet management & vehicle leasing

DSC LOGISTICS

1750 S. Wolf Rd.
Des Plaines, IL 60018
Phone: 847-390-6800
Fax: 847-390-7276

CEO: Ann McIlrath Drake
CFO: Ed Carroll
HR: David Higgins
Employees: 2,200

1994 Sales: $162 million
1-Yr. Sales Change: 15.7%
Ownership: Privately Held

Transportation - 3rd-party logistics provider

DUCHOSSOIS INDUSTRIES, INC.

845 N. Larch Ave.	CEO: Craig Duchossois	1994 Est. Sales: $1,000 mil.
Elmhurst, IL 60126	CFO: James S. Yerbic	1-Yr. Sales Change: 0.0%
Phone: 708-279-3600	HR: Lyn Fleichhacker	Ownership: Privately Held
Fax: 708-530-6091	Employees: 8,000	

Diversified operations - transportation, entertainment, defense, consumer products

DUFF & PHELPS CREDIT RATING CO.

55 E. Monroe St., 35th Floor	CEO: Paul J. McCarthy	1994 Sales: $40.4 million
Chicago, IL 60603	CFO: Paul J. McCarthy	1-Yr. Sales Change: 23.9%
Phone: 312-368-3100	HR: Cynthia Tupak	Exchange: NYSE
Fax: 312-368-2060	Employees: 183	Symbol: DCR

Financial - credit rating service (spin-off of Duff & Phelps Corporation)

DUKANE CORPORATION

2900 Dukane Dr.	CEO: J. McWilliams Stone Jr.	1994 Sales: $80.4 million
St. Charles, IL 60174	CFO: Michael Ritschdorff	1-Yr. Sales Change: 5.5%
Phone: 708-584-2300	HR: Bob Scarlett	Ownership: Privately Held
Fax: 708-584-2308	Employees: 725	

Diversified operations - ultrasonic plastics assembly systems; audiovisual presentation products; advanced facility communications systems; underwater location devices; LCD panels

DUNKIN' DONUTS MIDWEST DISTRIBUTION CENTER, INC.

1479 Regency Court	CEO: Thomas L. Jensen	1994 Sales: $40.3 million
Calumet City, IL 60409	CFO: Ted Komp	1-Yr. Sales Change: 11.3%
Phone: 708-891-9110	HR: —	Ownership: Cooperative
Fax: 708-891-9238	Employees: 28	

Food - cooperative owned by & distributing to Dunkin' Donut franchisees

DUO-FAST CORPORATION

3702 River Rd.	CEO: Robert Torstenson	1994 Est. Sales: $236 mil.
Franklin Park, IL 60131	CFO: Robert Grimley	1-Yr. Sales Change: 9.8%
Phone: 847-678-0100	HR: —	Ownership: Privately Held
Fax: 847-678-6824	Employees: 2,800	

Metal products - industrial fasteners

DUPLEX PRODUCTS, INC.

1947 Bethany Rd.	CEO: Benjamin L. McSwiney	1994 Sales: $266.3 million
Sycamore, IL 60178	CFO: Andrew A. Campbell	1-Yr. Sales Change: 2.3%
Phone: 815-895-2101	HR: Sue DuChanois	Exchange: AMEX
Fax: 815-895-6173	Employees: 1,852	Symbol: DPX

Paper - business forms

DURACO PRODUCTS, INC.

1109 E. Lake St.	CEO: John Licht	1994 Sales: $69.1 million
Streamwood, IL 60107	CFO: John Licht	1-Yr. Sales Change: 37.9%
Phone: 708-837-6615	HR: Gwen Aller	Ownership: Privately Held
Fax: 708-837-7136	Employees: 292	

Housewares - decorative plastic planterware & accessories

DYNA GROUP INTERNATIONAL, INC.

1801 W. 16th St.	CEO: Roger R. Tuttle	1994 Sales: $10 million
Broadview, IL 60153	CFO: Tom Heslinga	1-Yr. Sales Change: -6.5%
Phone: 708-450-9200	HR: Kevin McCue	Exchange: Nasdaq (SC)
Fax: 708-450-9273	Employees: 360	Symbol: DGIX

Business services - promotional products including belt buckles, model miniatures, key chains & picture frames

EAGLE FINANCE CORP.

1509 N. Milwaukee Ave.	CEO: Charles F. Wonderlic	1994 Sales: $13.7 million
Libertyville, IL 60048-1380	CFO: Robert J. Braasch	1-Yr. Sales Change: 121.0%
Phone: 847-680-4555	HR: Charles F. Wonderlic Jr.	Exchange: Nasdaq
Fax: 847-680-9492	Employees: 131	Symbol: EFCW

Financial - auto sales contract servicing

E&D WEB, INC.

4633 W. 16th St.	CEO: Christopher Love	1994 Sales: $50 million
Cicero, IL 60650	CFO: Christopher Love	1-Yr. Sales Change: 2.0%
Phone: 708-656-6600	HR: —	Ownership: Privately Held
Fax: 708-656-8390	Employees: 145	

Printing - full-service, commercial web offset printer

EASTERN AMERICAN NATURAL GAS TRUST

311 W. Monroe St., 12th Fl.
Chicago, IL 60606
Phone: 312-461-6676
Fax: 312-765-8052

Oil & gas - US royalty trust

CEO: Daniel G. Donovan
CFO: Daniel G. Donovan
HR: —
Employees: —

1994 Sales: $12.2 million
1-Yr. Sales Change: 22.0%
Exchange: NYSE
Symbol: NGT

ED MINIAT, INC.

945 W. 38th St.
Chicago, IL 60609
Phone: 312-927-9200
Fax: 312-927-8839

Food - processed meats; cooking oils

CEO: Ronald M. Miniat
CFO: John Molton
HR: Danielle Gutelius
Employees: 213

1994 Sales: $138.4 million
1-Yr. Sales Change: 45.1%
Ownership: Privately Held

EDELMAN PUBLIC RELATIONS WORLDWIDE

200 E. Randolph
Chicago, IL 60601
Phone: 312-240-3000
Fax: 312-240-2900

Business services - public relations firm

CEO: Daniel J. Edelman
CFO: Darryl Salerno
HR: Sandy Harling
Employees: 800

1994 Sales: $74.1 million
1-Yr. Sales Change: 16.9%
Ownership: Privately Held

EDUCATIONAL PUBLISHING CORPORATION

5623 W. 115th St.
Alsip, IL 60482
Phone: 708-385-0400
Fax: 708-385-9733

Publishing - educational products

CEO: Tony Malak
CFO: Craig Adkins
HR: James Murphy
Employees: 260

1994 Sales: $42 million
1-Yr. Sales Change: 6.3%
Ownership: Privately Held

EDWARD DON & COMPANY

2500 S. Harlem Ave.
North Riverside, IL 60546
Phone: 708-442-9400
Fax: 708-442-0436

Food service equipment & supplies distribution

CEO: Robert E. Don
CFO: Leon Ellin
HR: Jim Walsh
Employees: 1,062

1994 Sales: $325 million
1-Yr. Sales Change: 10.2%
Ownership: Privately Held

EESCO INC.

3939 S. Karlov Ave.	CEO: Stanley C. Weiss	1994 Sales: $340 million
Chicago, IL 60632	CFO: Steve J. Riordan	1-Yr. Sales Change: 12.2%
Phone: 312-376-8750	HR: Mark R. Camus	Ownership: Privately Held
Fax: 312-376-0289	Employees: 785	

Electrical, electronic & communications products distribution

ELEK-TEK, INC.

7350 N. Linder Ave.	CEO: Cameron B. Estes Jr.	1994 Sales: $305.6 million
Skokie, IL 60077	CFO: John M. Lader	1-Yr. Sales Change: 37.5%
Phone: 847-677-7660	HR: Rory K. Zaks	Exchange: Nasdaq
Fax: 847-677-1081	Employees: 882	Symbol: ELEK

Computers - superstores, catalog & direct sales

 See page 201 for a full profile of this company.

ELKAY MANUFACTURING COMPANY

2222 Camden Ct.	CEO: Ronald C. Katz	1994 Sales: $264.2 million
Oak Brook, IL 60521	CFO: Clark G. Carpenter	1-Yr. Sales Change: 34.2%
Phone: 708-574-8484	HR: Walter E. Reilly	Ownership: Privately Held
Fax: 708-574-5012	Employees: 2,375	

Building products - stainless steel sinks, water coolers, faucets & wooden kitchen cabinets

EMKAY, INC.

805 W. Thorndale Ave.	CEO: Gary L. Tepas	1994 Sales: $69.5 million
Itasca, IL 60143	CFO: Tim Braida	1-Yr. Sales Change: 3.0%
Phone: 708-250-7400	HR: Michelle Murphy	Ownership: Privately Held
Fax: 708-250-9778	Employees: 110	

Leasing - commercial vehicles

EMPRESS RIVER CASINO CORPORATION

2300 Empress Dr.	CEO: Thomas J. Lambrecht	1994 Sales: $215.3 million
Joliet, IL 60434	CFO: John G. Costello	1-Yr. Sales Change: 14.9%
Phone: 815-744-9400	HR: John Potempa	Ownership: Privately Held
Fax: 815-744-9476	Employees: 1,900	

Gambling resorts & casinos - riverboat casinos on the Des Plaines River

ENCO MANUFACTURING COMPANY

5000 W. Bloomingdale Ave.
Chicago, IL 60639
Phone: 312-745-1500
Fax: 312-745-1118

Wholesale distribution - machine tools

CEO: Charles Usiskin
CFO: Jim McMahon
HR: Diana Pierce
Employees: 270

1994 Sales: $50.8 million
1-Yr. Sales Change: 37.7%
Ownership: Privately Held

ENCYCLOPÆDIA BRITANNICA INC.

310 S. Michigan Ave.
Chicago, IL 60604
Phone: 312-347-7000
Fax: 312-294-2176

Publishing - reference books (Encyclopædia Britannica & Merriam-Webster); educational services

CEO: Joseph J. Esposito
CFO: James Goulka
HR: Karl Steinberg
Employees: 2,350

1995 Sales: $405 million
1-Yr. Sales Change: -10.7%
Ownership: Privately Held

 See page 202 for a full profile of this company.

ENVIRODYNE INDUSTRIES, INC.

701 Harger Rd., Ste. 190
Oak Brook, IL 60521
Phone: 708-571-8800
Fax: 708-571-0959

Diversified operations - sausage casings; packaging films; plastic utensils

CEO: Donald P. Kelly
CFO: John S. Corcoran
HR: —
Employees: 4,900

1994 Sales: $599 million
1-Yr. Sales Change: 2.0%
Exchange: Nasdaq (SC)
Symbol: EDYN

 See page 203 for a full profile of this company.

ENVIRONETX

1351 Irving Park Blvd.
Itasca, IL 60143
Phone: 708-875-3700
Fax: 708-875-3701

Furniture - business furnishings

CEO: John T. Matthews
CFO: Jeff Warner
HR: Barbara Vaughn
Employees: 150

1994 Sales: $50 million
1-Yr. Sales Change: 8.7%
Ownership: Privately Held

ENVIROPUR WASTE REFINING & TECH INC.

7601 W. 47th St.
McCook, IL 60525
Phone: 708-442-6000
Fax: 312-229-0677

Oil refining & marketing

CEO: S. N. Rubin
CFO: Wade Dauner
HR: Wade Dauner
Employees: 57

1994 Sales: $17.3 million
1-Yr. Sales Change: 101.2%
Exchange: Nasdaq
Symbol: EPUR

EQUITY GROUP INVESTMENTS, INC.

2 N. Riverside Plaza	CEO: Sheli Z. Rosenberg	1994 Sales: —
Chicago, IL 60606	CFO: —	1-Yr. Sales Change: —
Phone: 312-454-1800	HR: —	Ownership: Privately held
Fax: 312-454-1063	Employees: —	

Financial - venture capital investment firm (owns Zell/Chillmark Fund, 45.9% of American Classic Voyages, 25.8% of Itel Corp., 13.3% of Equity Residential Properties Trust)

 See page 204 for a full profile of this company.

EQUITY RESIDENTIAL PROPERTIES TRUST

2 N. Riverside Plaza	CEO: Douglas Crocker II	1994 Sales: $231 million
Chicago, IL 60606	CFO: David J. Neithercut	1-Yr. Sales Change: 106.1%
Phone: 312-474-1300	HR: Beverley Petrunich	Exchange: NYSE
Fax: 312-454-0434	Employees: 1,635	Symbol: EQR

Real estate investment trust - multifamily residential properties

ERO, INC.

585 Slawin Ct.	CEO: D. Richard Ryan	1994 Sales: $126.7 million
Mount Prospect, IL 60056-2183	CFO: Ted Lueken	1-Yr. Sales Change: 32.7%
Phone: 847-803-9200	HR: Mary Ann Phelan	Exchange: Nasdaq
Fax: 847-803-9223	Employees: 499	Symbol: EROI

Leisure & recreational products - children's recreational products, including tents, sleeping bags, diving masks & flippers

EUROMARKET DESIGNS INC.

725 Landwehr Rd.	CEO: Gordon Segal	1995 Sales: $274 million
Northbrook, IL 60062	CFO: Bruce Schneidewind	1-Yr. Sales Change: 18.1%
Phone: 847-272-2888	HR: Susie Muellman	Ownership: Privately Held
Fax: 847-272-5276	Employees: 1,400	

Retail - housewares & home furniture (Crate and Barrel)

EVANS, INC.

36 S. State St.	CEO: Patrick J. Regan	1995 Sales: $86.8 million
Chicago, IL 60603	CFO: Bill Koziel	1-Yr. Sales Change: -10.3%
Phone: 312-855-2000	HR: Dean Obrecht	Exchange: Nasdaq
Fax: 312-855-2128	Employees: 825	Symbol: EVAN

Retail - apparel & furs

EVEREN SECURITIES, INC.

77 W. Wacker Dr.	CEO: James R. Boris	1994 Sales: $530 million
Chicago, IL 60601	CFO: Daniel D. Williams	1-Yr. Sales Change: -21.3%
Phone: 312-574-6000	HR: Jennifer DiBiase	Exchange: NYSE
Fax: 312-574-8966	Employees: 2,840	Symbol: EVR

Financial - brokers, securities & investment banking services to corporate & municipal clients (formerly Kemper Securities)

FALCON BUILDING PRODUCTS, INC.

2 N. Riverside Plaza, Ste. 1100	CEO: William K. Hall	1994 Sales: $440.7 million
Chicago, IL 60606	CFO: Sam A. Cottone	1-Yr. Sales Change: 18.4%
Phone: 312-906-9700	HR: —	Exchange: NYSE
Fax: 312-454-0614	Employees: 3,400	Symbol: FB

Building products - air distribution products, bathroom fixtures (Mansfield) & air compressors

F&B MANUFACTURING COMPANY

1375 Mt. Prospect Rd.	CEO: Milada Anderson	1994 Sales: $51.6 million
Des Plaines, IL 60018	CFO: Elizabeth Kepuraitis	1-Yr. Sales Change: -15.5%
Phone: 847-827-1200	HR: Dawn Winter	Ownership: Privately Held
Fax: 847-827-2851	Employees: 430	

Auto parts manufacturing & distribution

FANSTEEL INC.

Number One Tantalum Place	CEO: William D. Jarosz	1994 Sales: $89.3 million
North Chicago, IL 60064	CFO: R. M. McEntee	1-Yr. Sales Change: -0.1%
Phone: 847-689-4900	HR: M. J. Mocniak	Exchange: NYSE
Fax: 847-689-0307	Employees: 867	Symbol: FNL

Metal processing & fabrication

FARLEY FOODS USA

2945 W. 31st St.	CEO: William H. Ellis	1994 Sales: $285 million
Chicago, IL 60623	CFO: Gary Ricco	1-Yr. Sales Change: 23.9%
Phone: 312-254-0900	HR: Bernie Panocha	Ownership: Privately Held
Fax: 312-254-0795	Employees: 2,400	

Food - candy & snacks

FARLEY, INC.

233 S. Wacker Dr.
Chicago, IL 60606
Phone: 312-876-1724
Fax: 312-993-1749

CEO: William Farley
CFO: Larry Switzer
HR: Susan Vanderhorn
Employees: 1,800

1994 Sales: $176 million
1-Yr. Sales Change: -18.1%
Ownership: Privately Held

Metal products; Western boots (Dingo, Lucchese)

FAUL CHEVROLET & GEO

151 E. Lake-Cook Rd.
Palatine, IL 60074
Phone: 847-359-7700
Fax: 847-359-8471

CEO: Laurence Faul
CFO: Kris Pitt
HR: Kris Pitt
Employees: 265

1994 Est. Sales: $85.9 mil.
1-Yr. Sales Change: 0.0%
Ownership: Privately Held

Retail - new & used cars

FCL GRAPHICS, INC.

4600 N. Olcott Ave.
Harwood Heights, IL 60656
Phone: 708-867-5500
Fax: 312-867-7768

CEO: Fank C. Calabrese
CFO: Phil Bauman
HR: Russ Reeves
Employees: 140

1994 Sales: $48 million
1-Yr. Sales Change: 33.3%
Ownership: Privately Held

Printing - commercial

FEDERAL SIGNAL CORPORATION

1415 W. 22nd St., Ste. 1100
Oak Brook, IL 60521-9945
Phone: 708-954-2000
Fax: 708-954-2030

CEO: Joseph J. Ross
CFO: Henry L. Dykema
HR: —
Employees: 5,243

1994 Sales: $677.2 million
1-Yr. Sales Change: 19.8%
Exchange: NYSE
Symbol: FSS

Diversified operations - emergency vehicles; cutting tools; communications equipment; neon signs

FELLOWES MANUFACTURING COMPANY

1789 Norwood Ave.
Itasca, IL 60143
Phone: 708-893-1600
Fax: 708-893-9777

CEO: James Fellowes
CFO: Doug Elder
HR: D'Arcy Didier
Employees: 1,258

1995 Sales: $220 million
1-Yr. Sales Change: 15.5%
Ownership: Privately Held

Office equipment - file cabinets & other document storage products; portable paper shredders

FEL-PRO, INC.

7450 N. McCormick Blvd.
Skokie, IL 60076
Phone: 847-674-7700
Fax: 847-568-1905

CEO: Dave Weinberg
CFO: Pamela Lieberman
HR: Arliss McLean
Employees: 2,510

1994 Sales: $365 million
1-Yr. Sales Change: 9.0%
Ownership: Privately Held

Automotive & trucking - engine gaskets; industrial chemicals

FERALLOY CORPORATION

8755 W. Higgins Rd.
Chicago, IL 60631
Phone: 312-380-1500
Fax: 312-380-1535

CEO: Frank M. Walker
CFO: Donald C. Martensen
HR: Walter Burzynski
Employees: 560

1994 Sales: $378 million
1-Yr. Sales Change: 13.9%
Ownership: Privately Held

Steel - flat-rolled

FERRARA PAN CANDY COMPANY

7301 W. Harrison St.
Forest Park, IL 60130
Phone: 847-366-0500
Fax: 847-366-5921

CEO: Salvatore Ferrara II
CFO: James Bufardi
HR: Rose Rubio
Employees: 450

1994 Est. Sales: $125 mil.
1-Yr. Sales Change: 25.0%
Ownership: Privately Held

Food - confections & fruit snacks

FIDELITY BANCORP, INC.

5455 W. Belmont Ave.
Chicago, IL 60641
Phone: 312-736-4414
Fax: 312-736-6471

CEO: Raymond Stolarczyk
CFO: Jim Kinney
HR: Lindalee Hansen
Employees: 105

1994 Sales: $21.1 million
1-Yr. Sales Change: -10.6%
Exchange: Nasdaq
Symbol: FBCI

Financial - savings & loans (Fidelity Federal Savings)

FIELD CONTAINER COMPANY L. P.

1500 Nicholas Blvd.
Elk Grove Village, IL 60007
Phone: 847-437-1700
Fax: 847-956-3249

CEO: Larry Field
CFO: Tom Cox
HR: —
Employees: 2,232

1994 Sales: $425 million
1-Yr. Sales Change: 4.9%
Ownership: Privately Held

Containers - packaging & paperboard; ink; gift wrap

THE FIELD MUSEUM

1200 S. Lakeshore Dr.
Chicago, IL 60605-2496
Phone: 312-922-9410
Fax: 312-554-9630

Museum - natural history

CEO: Willard L. Boyd
CFO: Wayne E. Heiden
HR: Marilyn Martinson
Employees: 411

1994 Sales: $26.8 million
1-Yr. Sales Change: —
Ownership: Privately Held

FINANCIAL SECURITY CORPORATION

1209 N. Milwaukee Ave.
Chicago, IL 60622
Phone: 312-227-7020
Fax: 312-227-6689

Financial - savings & loans

CEO: Daniel K. Augustine
CFO: William C. Preissner
HR: Tim Bruess
Employees: 86

1994 Sales: $19.9 million
1-Yr. Sales Change: -2.5%
Exchange: Nasdaq
Symbol: FNSC

FIRST ALERT, INC.

780 McClure Rd.
Aurora, IL 60504-2495
Phone: 708-851-7330
Fax: 708-851-7538

CEO: Malcolm Candlish
CFO: Gary L. Lederer
HR: Lisa Reynolds
Employees: 2,095

1994 Sales: $248.4 million
1-Yr. Sales Change: 57.6%
Exchange: Nasdaq
Symbol: ALRT

Appliances - home-safety devices including smoke & carbon monoxide detectors

 See page 205 for a full profile of this company.

FIRST CHICAGO CORPORATION

One First National Plaza
Chicago, IL 60670
Phone: 312-732-4000
Fax: 312-732-5976

Banks - money center

CEO: Richard L. Thomas
CFO: Robert A. Rosholt
HR: Marvin James Alef Jr.
Employees: 17,630

1994 Sales: $5,094.6 million
1-Yr. Sales Change: 5.6%
Exchange: NYSE
Symbol: FNB

 See pages 84–85 for a full profile of this company.

FIRST COMMONWEALTH, INC.

444 N. Wells
Chicago, IL 60610
Phone: 312-644-1800
Fax: 312-644-1822

Insurance - dental benefits

CEO: Christopher Multhauf
CFO: Scott Sanders
HR: —
Employees: 100

1994 Sales: $22.1 million
1-Yr. Sales Change: 27.7%
Exchange: Nasdaq
Symbol: FCWI

FIRST INDUSTRIAL REALTY TRUST, INC.

150 N. Wacker Dr., Ste. 150	CEO: Michael T. Tomasz	1994 Sales: $69.4 million
Chicago, IL 60606	CFO: Michael J. Havala	1-Yr. Sales Change: 109.0%
Phone: 312-704-9000	HR: Peg Booth	Exchange: NYSE
Fax: 312-704-6606	Employees: 57	Symbol: FR

Real estate investment trust - industrial properties

FIRST MERCHANTS ACCEPTANCE CORPORATION

570 Lake Cook Rd., Ste. 126	CEO: Mitchell C. Kahn	1995 Sales: $22.6 million
Deerfield, IL 60015	CFO: Thomas R. Ehmann	1-Yr. Sales Change: 126.0%
Phone: 847-948-9300	HR: Brian Hausmann	Exchange: Nasdaq
Fax: 847-948-9303	Employees: 200	Symbol: FMAC

Financial - finances the purchase of used automobiles by acquiring dealer-originated retail installment contracts

FIRST MIDWEST BANCORP, INC.

300 Park Blvd., Ste. 405	CEO: Robert P. O'Meara	1994 Sales: $216.9 million
Itasca, IL 60143-0459	CFO: Donald J. Swistowicz	1-Yr. Sales Change: 9.0%
Phone: 708-875-7450	HR: Phillip E. Glotfelty	Exchange: Nasdaq
Fax: 708-778-4070	Employees: 1,293	Symbol: FMBI

Banks - Midwest

FIRST NATIONAL ENTERTAINMENT CORP.

125 S. Wacker Dr., Ste. 300	CEO: Eugene E. Denari Jr.	1994 Sales: $5.4 million
Chicago, IL 60606	CFO: Eugene E. Denari Jr.	1-Yr. Sales Change: 285.7%
Phone: 312-214-2525	HR: —	Exchange: Nasdaq (SC)
Fax: 312-214-7041	Employees: 14	Symbol: FNAT

Retail - video stores in California (Video Plus, Video Tyme, Speedy Video), Las Vegas (Video Tyme) & Des Moines, IA (Five Star Video)

FIRST OAK BROOK BANCSHARES, INC.

1400 16th St.	CEO: Eugene P. Heytow	1994 Sales: $45.3 million
Oak Brook, IL 60521	CFO: Rosemarie Burget	1-Yr. Sales Change: 7.9%
Phone: 708-571-1050	HR: Mary C. Campbell	Exchange: Nasdaq
Fax: 708-954-3877	Employees: 277	Symbol: FOBBA

Banks - Midwest

FIRSTFED BANCSHARES, INC.

749 Lee St.
Des Plaines, IL 60016-6471
Phone: 847-294-6500
Fax: 847-824-4402

Banks - Midwest

CEO: Larry G. Gillie
CFO: Paul Larsen
HR: Lynn Miller
Employees: 85

1994 Sales: $32 million
1-Yr. Sales Change: 9.2%
Exchange: Nasdaq
Symbol: FFDP

FITIGUES, INC.

700 N. Sangamon
Chicago, IL 60622
Phone: 312-455-8866
Fax: 312-455-8868

Apparel - casual clothing for men, women & children

CEO: Andrea Rosenstein
CFO: Carol Skolnik
HR: Eleanor Johnson
Employees: 50

1994 Sales: $13 million
1-Yr. Sales Change: —
Ownership: Privately Held

THE FLORSHEIM SHOE COMPANY

130 S. Canal St.
Chicago, IL 60606-3999
Phone: 312-559-2500
Fax: 312-559-7408

Men's shoes

CEO: Charles J. Campbell
CFO: Larry J. Svoboda
HR: John Diebold
Employees: 3,248

1994 Sales: $302 million
1-Yr. Sales Change: 0.8%
Exchange: Nasdaq
Symbol: FLSC

See pages 86–87 for a full profile of this company.

FLORSTAR SALES, INC.

1325 Mittel
Woodale, IL 60191
Phone: 708-595-7500
Fax: 708-616-6220

Wholesale distribution - floor coverings

CEO: Wade Cassidy
CFO: Wade Cassidy
HR: Mark Gwizdalski
Employees: 267

1994 Sales: $106.9 million
1-Yr. Sales Change: 7.4%
Ownership: Privately Held

FLUID MANAGEMENT L.P.

1023 Wheeling Rd.
Wheeling, IL 60690
Phone: 847-537-0880
Fax: 847-537-3221

Machinery - metering & mixing equipment for the ink, paint & coatings industries

CEO: Joseph Rigel
CFO: Thomas Carney
HR: Kathleen Nelis
Employees: 560

1994 Sales: $73.1 million
1-Yr. Sales Change: 22.4%
Ownership: Privately Held

FMC CORPORATION

200 E. Randolph Dr.
Chicago, IL 60601
Phone: 312-861-6000
Fax: 312-861-6176

CEO: Robert N. Burt
CFO: Michael J. Callahan
HR: William W. Murray
Employees: 21,344

1994 Sales: $4,010.8 million
1-Yr. Sales Change: 6.3%
Exchange: NYSE
Symbol: FMC

Diversified operations - chemicals, defense systems, machinery & equipment

See pages 88–89 for a full profile of this company.

FOLGER ADAM COMPANY

16300 W. 103rd Ave.
Lemont, IL 60439
Phone: 708-739-3900
Fax: 708-739-3958

CEO: Roger Greene
CFO: Scott Walters
HR: Fred Fike
Employees: 566

1994 Sales: $72 million
1-Yr. Sales Change: 8.3%
Ownership: Privately Held

Protection - detention equipment & systems; architectural security products

FOLLETT CORPORATION

2233 West St.
River Grove, IL 60171-1895
Phone: 708-583-2000
Fax: 708-452-9347

CEO: P. Richard Litzsinger
CFO: Kenneth J. Hull
HR: Richard Waichler
Employees: 7,200

1995 Sales: $712.8 million
1-Yr. Sales Change: 10.3%
Ownership: Privately Held

Diversified operations - college bookstores; software; publishing

See page 206 for a full profile of this company.

FORSYTHE MCARTHUR ASSOCIATES, INC.

7500 Frontage Rd.
Skokie, IL 60077
Phone: 847-675-8000
Fax: 847-675-2130

CEO: Richard A. Forsythe
CFO: Gordon Decker
HR: Jan Bonnuci
Employees: 139

1994 Sales: $160 million
1-Yr. Sales Change: 1.3%
Ownership: Privately Held

Leasing - computer & communications equipment

FORT DEARBORN LITHOGRAPH COMPANY

6035 W. Gross Point Rd.
Niles, IL 60714
Phone: 312-774-4321
Fax: 312-774-1091

CEO: Thomas W. Adler
CFO: Robert Dombro
HR: William Samuels
Employees: 550

1994 Sales: $98 million
1-Yr. Sales Change: 60.7%
Ownership: Privately Held

Paper - labels for the food, beverage, paint & chemical industries

FRANCISCAN SISTERS HEALTH CARE CORP.

9223 W. St. Francis Rd.
Frankfort, IL 60432
Phone: 815-469-4888
Fax: 815-469-4864

CEO: Jerry Pearson
CFO: John Naiden
HR: John Landstrom
Employees: 5,750

1994 Sales: $368.8 million
1-Yr. Sales Change: 3.9%

Hospitals - not-for-profit system comprised of 4 hospitals, 2 nursing homes, 25 clinics & a college of nursing

FRANK CONSOLIDATED ENTERPRISES

666 Garland Place
Des Plaines, IL 60016
Phone: 847-699-7000
Fax: 847-699-8075

CEO: James S. Frank
CFO: Ford Pearson
HR: Ruth Kurtz
Employees: 2,020

1994 Sales: $1,124 million
1-Yr. Sales Change: -32.2%
Ownership: Privately Held

Retail - new & used cars; fleet management

FRUIT OF THE LOOM, INC.

233 S. Wacker Dr.
Chicago, IL 60606
Phone: 312-876-1724
Fax: 312-993-1749

CEO: William Farley
CFO: Larry Switzer
HR: Burgess D. Ridge
Employees: 37,400

1994 Sales: $2,297.8 million
1-Yr. Sales Change: 21.9%
Exchange: AMEX
Symbol: FTL

Apparel - underwear, T-shirts, infant & toddler clothing, sweatshirts

🏭 **See pages 90–91 for a full profile of this company.**

FURNAS ELECTRIC COMPANY

1000 McKee St.
Batavia, IL 60510
Phone: 708-879-6000
Fax: 708-879-0867

CEO: Richard W. Hansen
CFO: Bill Lynch
HR: Tom Caughlin
Employees: 1,500

1994 Sales: $130 million
1-Yr. Sales Change: 10.2%
Ownership: Privately Held

Instruments - industrial motor controls

G. HEILEMAN BREWING COMPANY, INC.

9399 W. Higgins Rd., Ste. 700
Rosemont, IL 60018
Phone: 847-292-2100
Fax: 847-292-6870

CEO: M. Lou Lowenkron
CFO: Daniel J. Schmid Jr.
HR: Jeff Scheel
Employees: 2,200

1994 Sales: $636 million
1-Yr. Sales Change: -9.1%
Ownership: Privately Held

Beverages - beer (Colt 45, Old Style, Special Export)

🏭 **See pages 92–93 for a full profile of this company.**

GALILEO INTERNATIONAL PARTNERSHIP

9700 W. Higgins Rd., Ste. 400
Rosemont, IL 60018
Phone: 847-518-4000
Fax: 847-518-4085

CEO: Jim Barlett
CFO: Paul Bristow
HR: Willie Steiner
Employees: 2,000

1994 Sales: $801 million
1-Yr. Sales Change: —
Ownership: Privately Held

Transportation - travel reservation system (Galileo: 50%-owned by North American air carriers Air Canada, United Airlines & USAir & 50%-owned by European air carriers)

GARVEY INTERNATIONAL, INC.

One Foxfield Sq.
St. Charles, IL 60174
Phone: 708-377-9966
Fax: 703-377-9934

CEO: Bob M. White
CFO: Alita Jimenez
HR: —
Employees: 208

1994 Sales: $118.1 million
1-Yr. Sales Change: 26.6%
Ownership: Privately Held

Agricultural operations - grain & feed; transportation

GATX CORPORATION

500 W. Monroe St.
Chicago, IL 60661-3676
Phone: 312-621-6200
Fax: 312-621-6646

CEO: James J. Glasser
CFO: David M. Edwards
HR: William L. Chambers
Employees: 5,800

1994 Sales: $1,155 million
1-Yr. Sales Change: 6.3%
Exchange: NYSE
Symbol: GMT

Transportation - rail tank cars & bulk liquid storage; ships; warehouses; commercial aircraft

See pages 94–95 for a full profile of this company.

GAYLORD CONTAINER CORPORATION

500 Lake Cook Rd., Ste. 400
Deerfield, IL 60015-4921
Phone: 847-405-5500
Fax: 847-405-5585

CEO: Marvin A. Pomerantz
CFO: Daniel P. Casey
HR: Mike McDermott
Employees: 4,100

1995 Sales: $1,051.4 million
1-Yr. Sales Change: 34.0%
Exchange: AMEX
Symbol: GCR

Containers - brown corrugated containers & paper bags

GENERAL AMERICAN DOOR COMPANY

5050 Baseline Rd.
Montgomery, IL 60538
Phone: 708-859-3000
Fax: 708-859-8122

CEO: Joseph L. Kee
CFO: Ronald Brazener
HR: Renee Waugh
Employees: 300

1994 Sales: $30 million
1-Yr. Sales Change: 7.1%
Ownership: Privately Held

Building products - sectional overhead garage doors

GENERAL BINDING CORPORATION

One GBC Plaza	CEO: Govi Reddy	1994 Sales: $420.4 million
Northbrook, IL 60062-4195	CFO: Edward J. McNulty	1-Yr. Sales Change: 11.8%
Phone: 847-272-3700	HR: Gary Smith	Exchange: Nasdaq
Fax: 847-272-1389	Employees: 3,226	Symbol: GBND

Office equipment & supplies - binding, laminating & paper-shredding systems

 See page 207 for a full profile of this company.

GENERAL DRUG COMPANY

200 N. Fairfield Ave.	CEO: Seymour Stroller	1995 Sales: $341 million
Chicago, IL 60612	CFO: Michael Garvey	1-Yr. Sales Change: 150.7%
Phone: 312-826-4242	HR: Debra Smiley	Ownership: Privately Held
Fax: 312-826-6231	Employees: 180	

Drugs & sundries - wholesale

GENERAL EMPLOYMENT ENTERPRISES, INC.

One Tower Ln., Ste. 2100	CEO: Herbert F. Imhoff	1995 Sales: $16.7 million
Oakbrook Terrace, IL 60181-4600	CFO: Kent M. Yauch	1-Yr. Sales Change: 17.6%
Phone: 708-954-0400	HR: Sherry Hubacek	Exchange: AMEX
Fax: 708-954-0456	Employees: 300	Symbol: JOB

Personnel - employment services

GENERAL INSTRUMENT CORPORATION

181 W. Madison St.	CEO: Richard S. Friedland	1994 Sales: $2,036.3 million
Chicago, IL 60602	CFO: Charles T. Dickson	1-Yr. Sales Change: 46.2%
Phone: 312-541-5000	HR: Clark E. Tucker	Exchange: NYSE
Fax: 312-541-8038	Employees: 12,300	Symbol: GIC

Electrical components - semiconductors; broad-band communications equipment

 See pages 96–97 for a full profile of this company.

GEORGE S. MAY INTERNATIONAL COMPANY

303 S. Northwest Hwy.	CEO: Donald J. Fletcher	1994 Est. Sales: $72.6 mil.
Park Ridge , IL 60068	CFO: Roy Matthews	1-Yr. Sales Change: 10.0%
Phone: 847-825-8806	HR: Sandra Cronin	Ownership: Privately Held
Fax: 847-825-7937	Employees: 1,000	

Consulting - management consulting for small-to-medium-sized businesses

GERBER PLUMBING FIXTURES CORPORATION

4656 W. Touhy Ave.
Chicago, IL 60646
Phone: 708-675-6570
Fax: 708-675-8135

CEO: Alan Lewis
CFO: John Deiter
HR: Brian Fiala
Employees: 900

1994 Sales: $104 million
1-Yr. Sales Change: 15.6%
Ownership: Privately Held

Building products - plumbing fixtures, including faucets & fittings, for commercial & residential use

G. K. ENTERPRISES, INC.

15700 S. Lathrop Ave.
Harvey, IL 60426
Phone: 708-331-4000
Fax: 312-786-0755

CEO: Jeffrey L. Kahn
CFO: Tim Murphy
HR: Joe Masek
Employees: 370

1994 Sales: $65 million
1-Yr. Sales Change: 6.6%
Ownership: Privately Held

Machinery - cranes, chemical processing equipment & material handling products

GLOBE GLASS & MIRROR COMPANY

2 N. La Salle St.
Chicago, IL 60602
Phone: 312-278-6900
Fax: 312-578-7211

CEO: Joseph Kellman
CFO: Scott Pettit
HR: Mike Croll
Employees: 1,250

1994 Sales: $206.4 million
1-Yr. Sales Change: 12.4%
Ownership: Privately Held

Auto parts - glass repair & replacement

GLS CORPORATION

1750 N. Kingsbury St.
Chicago, IL 60614
Phone: 312-664-3500
Fax: 312-664-1301

CEO: Steven L. Dehmlow
CFO: John R. Walles
HR: Mickey McElroy
Employees: 229

1994 Sales: $165.5 million
1-Yr. Sales Change: 15.7%
Ownership: Privately Held

Chemicals - fiberglass composite materials

GONNELLA BAKING COMPANY

2006 W. Erie St.
Chicago, IL 60612
Phone: 312-733-2020
Fax: 312-733-7056

CEO: Robert Gonnella Sr.
CFO: Robert Gonnella Jr.
HR: —
Employees: 305

1994 Sales: $41 million
1-Yr. Sales Change: 6.2%
Ownership: Privately Held

Food - bakery goods

GRANT THORNTON

1 Prudential Plaza
Chicago, IL 60601
Phone: 312-856-0001
Fax: 312-565-4719

CEO: Robert Nason
CFO: Ted J. Thompson
HR: Sandra Knipp
Employees: 3,000

1994 Sales: $254 million
1-Yr. Sales Change: 1.6%
Ownership: Privately Held

Business services - accounting & technical consulting

GRAYCOR, INC.

One Graycor Dr.
Homewood, IL 60430
Phone: 708-206-0500
Fax: 708-206-0505

CEO: Melvin Gray
CFO: Mike Mizanin
HR: Bill O'Neil
Employees: 900

1994 Sales: $140 million
1-Yr. Sales Change: 34.6%
Ownership: Privately Held

Construction - heavy

GREAT AMERICAN MANAGEMENT AND INVESTMENT, INC.

2 N. Riverside Plaza
Chicago, IL 60606
Phone: 312-648-5656
Fax: 312-454-0614

CEO: Rod F. Dammeyer
CFO: Sam A. Cottone
HR: Gerald A. Spector
Employees: 7,000

1994 Sales: $1,010.3 million
1-Yr. Sales Change: -14.0%
Exchange: Nasdaq (SC)
Symbol: GAMI

Diversified operations - building, electrical, industrial, automotive & specialty products; investments

GROWTH ENVIRONMENTAL, INC.

2211 S. York Rd., Ste. 115
Oak Brook, IL 60521
Phone: 708-990-2751
Fax: 708-990-2763

CEO: Alvin K. Eaton
CFO: Timothy E. Meyer
HR: —
Employees: 275

1994 Sales: $19.9 million
1-Yr. Sales Change: 151.9%
Exchange: Nasdaq (SC)
Symbol: GCER

Consulting, engineering, remediation & analytical laboratory services to assist commercial, industrial & governmental clients in complying with environmental laws & regulations

HA-LO INDUSTRIES, INC.

5980 Touhy Ave.
Niles, IL 60714
Phone: 847-647-2300
Fax: 847-647-5999

CEO: Lou Weisbach
CFO: Richard A. Magid
HR: Barbara G. Berman
Employees: 202

1994 Sales: $68.6 million
1-Yr. Sales Change: 92.2%
Exchange: Nasdaq
Symbol: HALO

Business services - distributor of premium advertising products

 See page 208 for a full profile of this company.

HAMMACHER SCHLEMMER & COMPANY

303 W. Erie St.
Chicago, IL 60610
Phone: 312-664-8170
Fax: 312-664-8618

Specialty retail & mail order

CEO: John Semmelhack
CFO: Brian Hycy
HR: Tina Chapel
Employees: 250

1994 Sales: $89 million
1-Yr. Sales Change: 11.3%
Ownership: Privately Held

HARPO ENTERTAINMENT GROUP

110 N. Carpenter St.
Chicago, IL 60607
Phone: 312-633-1000
Fax: 312-633-1111

CEO: Oprah Winfrey
CFO: Doug Pattison
HR: —
Employees: 141

1994 Est. Sales: $120 mil.
1-Yr. Sales Change: 9.1%
Ownership: Privately Held

Film & TV production (The Oprah Winfrey Show); studio rental

 See page 209 for a full profile of this company.

HARTMARX CORPORATION

101 N. Wacker Dr.
Chicago, IL 60606
Phone: 312-372-6300
Fax: 312-444-2710

CEO: Elbert O. Hand
CFO: Glenn R. Morgan
HR: Lorraine Dickson
Employees: 11,000

1994 Sales: $725 million
1-Yr. Sales Change: -1.8%
Exchange: NYSE
Symbol: HMX

Men's clothing (#1 in US: Hickey Freeman, Hart Schaffner & Marx)

See pages 98–99 for a full profile of this company.

HARZA ENGINEERING COMPANY

233 S. Wacker Dr.
Chicago, IL 60606
Phone: 312-831-3000
Fax: 312-831-3999

CEO: Richard Meagher
CFO: E. R. Hoelterhoff
HR: Jennifer Kohl
Employees: 807

1994 Sales: $112.5 million
1-Yr. Sales Change: 2.3%
Ownership: Privately Held

Pollution control - engineering & environmental consulting firm

HEALTH TECH INDUSTRIES, INC.

117 W. 154th St.
South Holland, IL 60473
Phone: 708-339-5200
Fax: 708-339-1700

CEO: Ben Washington
CFO: Greg Meyers
HR: Sheryll Enlow
Employees: 35

1994 Sales: $19 million
1-Yr. Sales Change: —
Ownership: Privately Held

Medical products - pharmaceuticals & medical supplies distribution

HEALTHCARE COMPARE CORPORATION

3200 Highland Ave.
Downers Grove, IL 60515-1223
Phone: 708-241-7900
Fax: 708-719-0076

CEO: James C. Smith
CFO: Joseph E. Whitters
HR: Nancy Zambon
Employees: 1,600

1994 Sales: $186.6 million
1-Yr. Sales Change: 18.3%
Exchange: Nasdaq
Symbol: HCCC

Business services - medical cost management services for hospitals & doctors' practices

HEARTLAND PARTNERS, L.P.

547 W. Jackson Blvd.
Chicago, IL 60661
Phone: 312-294-0440
Fax: 312-663-9397

CEO: Edwin Jacobson
CFO: Leon F. Fiorentino
HR: —
Employees: 25

1994 Sales: $3.5 million
1-Yr. Sales Change: -52.1%
Exchange: AMEX
Symbol: HTL

Real estate operations - development & leasing of former railroad rights-of-way, station grounds, & rail yards

HEICO ACQUISITIONS INC.

70 W. Madison St., Ste. 5600
Chicago, IL 60602
Phone: 312-419-8220
Fax: 312-419-9417

CEO: Michael Heisley
CFO: Michael Heisley
HR: —
Employees: 5

1995 Sales:—
1-Yr. Sales Change: —
Ownership: Privately Held

Financial - venture capital investment firm (holdings in Andy Frain Services, David Wire, Newbury Industries, Nutri/System, Tom's Foods)

HEINEMANN'S BAKERIES, INC.

3925 W. 43rd St.
Chicago, IL 60632
Phone: 312-523-5000
Fax: 312-523-7985

CEO: Vincent J. Graham Jr.
CFO: Andrew Geryol
HR: —
Employees: 630

1994 Sales: $40.7 million
1-Yr. Sales Change: 2.8%
Ownership: Privately Held

Food - bakery goods distributed through supermarkets

HELENE CURTIS INDUSTRIES, INC.

325 N. Wells St.
Chicago, IL 60610
Phone: 312-661-0222
Fax: 312-836-0125

CEO: Ronald J. Gidwitz
CFO: Lawrence A. Gyenes
HR: Robert K. Niles
Employees: 3,400

1995 Sales: $1,265.6 million
1-Yr. Sales Change: 6.6%
Exchange: NYSE
Symbol: HC

Cosmetics & toiletries

 See pages 100–101 for a full profile of this company.

HELLER SEASONINGS & INGREDIENTS, INC.

6363 W. 73rd St.
Bedford Park, IL 60638
Phone: 312-581-6800
Fax: 708-594-2342

Food - seasonings

CEO: John Heller
CFO: John Heller
HR: John Schaefer
Employees: 168

1994 Sales: $34.3 million
1-Yr. Sales Change: 3.0%
Ownership: Privately Held

HENRY CROWN AND CO.

222 N. LaSalle St.
Chicago, IL 60601
Phone: 312-236-6300
Fax: 312-899-5039

CEO: Lester Crown
CFO: Paul Dwyer
HR: Patricia Slizewski
Employees: 1,500

1995 Sales: —
1-Yr. Sales Change: —
Ownership: Privately Held

Financial - investment firm with diversified industrial holdings (CC Industries, General Dynamics)

HENRY VALVE COMPANY

3215 North Ave.
Melrose Park, IL 60160
Phone: 708-344-1100
Fax: 708-344-0026

CEO: Lorraine T. Henry
CFO: Jerry Flynn
HR: Donna Russell
Employees: 500

1994 Sales: $43 million
1-Yr. Sales Change: 7.5%
Ownership: Privately Held

Building products - valves, accesssories for the air-conditioning & refrigeration industries

HERITAGE FINANCIAL SERVICES, INC.

17500 S. Oak Park Ave.
Tinley Park, IL 60477
Phone: 708-532-8000
Fax: 708-636-2183

Banks - Midwest

CEO: Richard T. Wojcik
CFO: Paul A. Eckroth
HR: Karen K. Myers
Employees: 440

1994 Sales: $66.6 million
1-Yr. Sales Change: 8.5%
Exchange: Nasdaq
Symbol: HERS

HEWITT ASSOCIATES LLC

100 Half Day Rd.
Lincolnshire, IL 60069
Phone: 847-295-5000
Fax: 847-295-7634

Consulting - specializing in human resources

CEO: Dale L. Gifford
CFO: Donald R. Hessler
HR: David Wille
Employees: 4,493

1994 Sales: $396 million
1-Yr. Sales Change: 11.1%
Ownership: Privately Held

HEXACOMB CORPORATION

75 Tri-State International
Lincolnshire, IL 60069
Phone: 847-317-1991
Fax: 847-317-0007

CEO: Douglas Walmsley
CFO: Frank ten Brink
HR: June Lewand
Employees: 500

1994 Sales: $60 million
1-Yr. Sales Change: 22.4%
Ownership: Privately Held

Paper - honeycomb paper products

HIGHLAND PARK LINCOLN MERCURY SALES, INC.

55 Skokie Hwy.
Highland Park, IL 60035
Phone: 847-831-5880
Fax: 847-831-4392

CEO: Alan Frisch
CFO: Marty Price
HR: Michele Beyer
Employees: 59

1994 Sales: $42.2 million
1-Yr. Sales Change: 6.6%
Ownership: Privately Held

Retail - new & used cars

HILL MECHANICAL GROUP

4241 N. Ravenswood Ave.
Chicago, IL 60613
Phone: 312-929-6600
Fax: 312-929-9549

CEO: Warren Hill
CFO: Emmanuel Lacson
HR: —
Employees: 431

1994 Sales: $77 million
1-Yr. Sales Change: 10.6%
Ownership: Privately Held

Building - heating, air conditioning & plumbing contractor; garbage handling systems

HINSDALE FINANCIAL CORPORATION

One Grant Sq.
Hinsdale, IL 60521
Phone: 708-323-1776
Fax: 708-323-0052

CEO: Kenne P. Bristol
CFO: Richard A. Hojnicki
HR: Peg Perfetto
Employees: 257

1994 Sales: $42.1 million
1-Yr. Sales Change: 5.8%
Exchange: Nasdaq
Symbol: HNFC

Banks - Midwest (Hinsdale Federal Bank for Savings)

HOFFER PLASTICS CORPORATION

500 Collins St.
South Elgin, IL 60177
Phone: 847-741-5740
Fax: 847-741-3086

CEO: Robert A. Hoffer
CFO: S. Schambach
HR: Leo Nelson
Employees: 675

1994 Sales: $78 million
1-Yr. Sales Change: 2.6%
Ownership: Privately Held

Chemicals - plastics

HOSTMARK MANAGEMENT GROUP, INC.

1600 Golf Rd., Ste. 800	CEO: C. A. Cataldo	1994 Sales: $188.3 million
Rolling Meadows, IL 60008	CFO: Charles Gavzer	1-Yr. Sales Change: 17.7%
Phone: 847-439-8500	HR: Christine Miller	Ownership: Privately Held
Fax: 847-439-8755	Employees: 6,100	

Real estate development - hotels & restaurants management & development

HOUSEHOLD INTERNATIONAL, INC.

2700 Sanders Rd.	CEO: W. F. Aldinger	1994 Sales: $4,603 million
Prospect Heights, IL 60070	CFO: David A. Schoenholz	1-Yr. Sales Change: 3.3%
Phone: 847-564-5000	HR: Colin P. Kelly	Exchange: NYSE
Fax: 847-205-7452	Employees: 15,500	Symbol: HI

Financial - consumer loans, credit cards, equity loans & life insurance

See pages 102–103 for a full profile of this company.

HOUSTON FOODS COMPANY

3501 Mount Prospect Rd.	CEO: Joseph Vasselli	1994 Sales: $91.5 million
Franklin Park, IL 60131	CFO: Gary D. Musick	1-Yr. Sales Change: 30.3%
Phone: 847-616-9191	HR: —	Ownership: Privately Held
Fax: 847-616-8883	Employees: 125	

Food - specialty gift packages & popcorn products

HUB GROUP DISTRIBUTION SERVICES

3250 N. Arlington Heights Rd.	CEO: Thomas Juedes	1994 Sales: $11.6 million
Arlington Heights, IL 60004	CFO: Shaunna Burhop	1-Yr. Sales Change: —
Phone: 847-253-6800	HR: —	Ownership: Privately Held
Fax: 847-253-5093	Employees: 28	

Transportation - logistics management services

THE HUB GROUP, INC.

377 E. Butterfield, Ste. 700	CEO: David P. Yeager	1994 Sales: $686.7 million
Lombard, IL 60148	CFO: William L. Crowder	1-Yr. Sales Change: 20.9%
Phone: 708-271-3600	HR: —	Ownership: Privately Held
Fax: 708-964-6475	Employees: 633	

Transportation - intermodal trucking

HUMPHREYS, INC.

2009 W. Hastings St.	CEO: Sheldon Young	1995 Sales: $135 million
Chicago, IL 60608	CFO: Lawrence Fleming	1-Yr. Sales Change: 17.4%
Phone: 312-997-2358	HR: Marilyn Bly	Ownership: Privately Held
Fax: 312-997-2147	Employees: 900	

Leather & related products - belts & other accessories

HYATT CORPORATION

200 W. Madison St.	CEO: Jay A. Pritzker	1994 Est. Sales: $2,600 mil.
Chicago, IL 60606	CFO: Ken Posner	1-Yr. Sales Change: 4.0%
Phone: 312-750-1234	HR: Larry Deans	Ownership: Privately Held
Fax: 312-750-8550	Employees: 52,275	

Hotels

 See pages 104–105 for a full profile of this company.

ICM INDUSTRIES, INC.

122 S. Michigan Ave.	CEO: Jack Rutherford	1994 Sales: $115 million
Chicago, IL 60603	CFO: Raymond Imp	1-Yr. Sales Change: 22.7%
Phone: 312-939-5008	HR: —	Ownership: Privately Held
Fax: 312-939-4985	Employees: 750	

Components for the automotive, farm & construction equipment industries

IDEX CORPORATION

630 Dundee Rd.	CEO: Donald N. Boyce	1994 Sales: $399.5 million
Northbrook, IL 60062	CFO: Wayne P. Sayatovic	1-Yr. Sales Change: 29.5%
Phone: 847-498-7070	HR: Jerry N. Derck	Exchange: NYSE
Fax: 847-498-3940	Employees: 3,000	Symbol: IEX

Machinery - fluid-handling and industrial products

 See page 210 for a full profile of this company.

IGA, INC.

8725 W. Higgins Rd.	CEO: Thomas S. Haggai	1994 Sales: $16,500 million
Chicago, IL 60631	CFO: Jim Anderson	1-Yr. Sales Change: —
Phone: 312-693-4520	HR: Jim Anderson	Ownership: Cooperative
Fax: 312-693-4533	Employees: 130,000	

Retail - alliance of 3,600 independent supermarkets with operations in 49 states, Australia, Canada, China, Japan, Korea, Papua New Guinea & the West Indies

 See pages 106–107 for a full profile of this company.

ILLINOIS AUTO ELECTRIC COMPANY

656 County Line Rd.
Elmhurst, IL 60126
Phone: 708-833-4300
Fax: 708-823-6104

CEO: H. Bruce Sirotek
CFO: Richard Johnson
HR: Sandra Hutchinson
Employees: 170

1994 Sales: $51.1 million
1-Yr. Sales Change: 21.7%
Ownership: Privately Held

Transportation - truck equipment service & distribution

ILLINOIS CENTRAL CORPORATION

455 N. Cityfront Plaza Dr.
Chicago, IL 60611-5504
Phone: 312-755-7500
Fax: 312-755-7839

CEO: E. Hunter Harrison
CFO: Dale W. Phillips
HR: James M. Harrell
Employees: 3,250

1994 Sales: $593.9 million
1-Yr. Sales Change: 5.2%
Exchange: NYSE
Symbol: IC

2,700 miles of main line rail between Chicago & the Gulf of Mexico (Illinois Central Railroad), primarily carrying chemicals, coal & paper to the North & coal, grain & milled grain products to the South

ILLINOIS SUPERCONDUCTOR CORPORATION

451 Kingston Ct.
Mount Prospect, IL 60010
Phone: 847-391-9400
Fax: 847-299-9609

CEO: Ora E. Smith
CFO: Stephen G. Wasko
HR: Beth Kubow
Employees: 12

1994 Sales: $0.2 million
1-Yr. Sales Change: 0.0%
Exchange: Nasdaq
Symbol: ISCO

Telecommunications equipment - wireless products, including cellular phone filters

ILLINOIS TOOL WORKS INC.

3600 W. Lake Ave.
Glenview, IL 60025-5811
Phone: 847-724-7500
Fax: 847-657-4261

CEO: W. James Farrell
CFO: Michael W. Gregg
HR: John Karpan
Employees: 19,500

1994 Sales: $3,461.3 million
1-Yr. Sales Change: 9.6%
Exchange: NYSE
Symbol: ITW

Metal products - fasteners; industrial fluids & adhesives

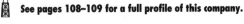 **See pages 108–109 for a full profile of this company.**

IMC GLOBAL INC.

2100 Sanders Rd.
Northbrook, IL 60062-6146
Phone: 847-272-9200
Fax: 847-205-4805

CEO: Wendell F. Bueche
CFO: Robert C. Brauneker
HR: Allen C. Miller
Employees: 6,800

1995 Sales: $1,924 million
1-Yr. Sales Change: 33.5%
Exchange: NYSE
Symbol: IGL

Fertilizers - crop nutrients for the international agricultural community; mining & processing of potash; phosphate crop nutrients marketing

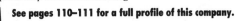 **See pages 110–111 for a full profile of this company.**

INDECK ENERGY SERVICES, INC.

1130 Lake Cook Rd., Ste. 300	CEO: Gerald R. Forsythe	1994 Sales: $132.2 million
Buffalo Grove, IL 60089	CFO: Lawrence Lagowski	1-Yr. Sales Change: 21.0%
Phone: 847-520-3212	HR: Kevin Yessian	Ownership: Privately Held
Fax: 847-520-9883	Employees: 171	

Energy - independent cogeneration plants

INDECK POWER EQUIPMENT COMPANY

1111 S. Willis Ave.	CEO: Gerald Forsythe	1994 Sales: $31 million
Wheeling, IL 60090	CFO: Gerald Forsythe	1-Yr. Sales Change: -13.9%
Phone: 847-541-8300	HR: Sandy Holm	Ownership: Privately Held
Fax: 847-541-9984	Employees: 94	

Machinery - steam boiler plants, water treatment systems & diesel generators

INDIANA FEDERAL CORPORATION

56 Washington St.	CEO: Peter R. Candela	1994 Sales: $48 million
Valparaiso, IN 46383	CFO: George J. Eberhardt	1-Yr. Sales Change: -6.4%
Phone: 219-462-4131	HR: Mark Zimmerman	Exchange: Nasdaq
Fax: 219-464-2041	Employees: 311	Symbol: IFSL

Banks - Midwest

INDUSTRIAL COATINGS GROUP, INC.

2141 S. Jefferson St.	CEO: John P. Clark	1994 Sales: $54.9 million
Chicago, IL 60616	CFO: Thomas Lavelle	1-Yr. Sales Change: 3.0%
Phone: 312-421-4030	HR: —	Ownership: Privately Held
Fax: 312-421-8422	Employees: 343	

Chemicals - coated fabrics, extruded plastic films

INFLO HOLDINGS CORPORATION

One Hollow Tree Ln.	CEO: Sam K. Reed	1994 Est. Sales: $1,700 mil.
Elmhurst, IL 60126	CFO: Jerry Baglien	1-Yr. Sales Change: —
Phone: 708-833-2900	HR: Dennis P. Christensen	Ownership: Privately Held
Fax: 708-530-8773	Employees: 9,000	

Food - cookies & crackers (Keebler); joint venture between Flowers Industries & Invus Group Ltd.

INFORMATION RESOURCES, INC.

150 N. Clinton St.
Chicago, IL 60661
Phone: 312-726-1221
Fax: 312-726-0360

CEO: Gian M. Fulgoni
CFO: Gary M. Hill
HR: Julie Chandler
Employees: 6,360

1994 Sales: $376.6 million
1-Yr. Sales Change: 12.6%
Exchange: Nasdaq
Symbol: IRIC

Business services - information services to the consumer packaged good industry

 See page 211 for a full profile of this company.

THE INLAND GROUP, INC.

2901 Butterfield Rd.
Oak Brook, IL 60521
Phone: 708-218-8000
Fax: 708-954-5693

CEO: Daniel L. Goodwin
CFO: Alan Kremin
HR: Norma Pearck
Employees: 800

1994 Est. Sales: $532 mil.
1-Yr. Sales Change: -4.3%
Ownership: Privately Held

Real estate development & brokerage

INLAND STEEL INDUSTRIES, INC.

30 W. Monroe St.
Chicago, IL 60603
Phone: 312-346-0300
Fax: 312-899-3197

CEO: Robert J. Darnall
CFO: Earl L. Mason
HR: Judd R. Cool
Employees: 15,500

1994 Sales: $4,497 million
1-Yr. Sales Change: 15.7%
Exchange: NYSE
Symbol: IAD

Steel - production & distribution

 See pages 112–113 for a full profile of this company.

INTERCARGO CORPORATION

1450 E. American Ln.
Schaumburg, IL 60173
Phone: 847-517-2990
Fax: 847-517-2996

CEO: James R. Zuhlke
CFO: Lawrence P. Goecking
HR: Sheila Lake
Employees: 287

1994 Sales: $80.9 million
1-Yr. Sales Change: 59.6%
Exchange: Nasdaq
Symbol: ICAR

Insurance - property & casualty

THE INTERLAKE CORPORATION

550 Warrenville Rd.
Lisle, IL 60532-4387
Phone: 708-852-8800
Fax: 708-719-7152

CEO: W. Robert Reum
CFO: Stephen Gregory
HR: Craig A. Grant
Employees: 4,536

1994 Sales: $752.6 million
1-Yr. Sales Change: 10.5%
Exchange: NYSE
Symbol: IK

Machinery - material handling

INTERMATIC, INCORPORATED

Intermatic Plaza
Spring Grove, IL 60081
Phone: 815-675-2321
Fax: 815-675-2112

CEO: Lee Vinyard
CFO: James R. Bohn
HR: Linnea Tenbruin
Employees: 965

1994 Sales: $154 million
1-Yr. Sales Change: 1.0%
Ownership: Privately Held

Electrical devices - timing devices & low-voltage lighting systems

INTERNATIONAL JENSEN INCORPORATED

25 Tri-State International Office Ctr.
Lincolnshire, IL 60069
Phone: 847-317-3700
Fax: 847-317-3842

CEO: Robert G. Shaw
CFO: Marc T. Tanenberg
HR: Kris Nelson
Employees: 1,800

1995 Sales: $252.8 million
1-Yr. Sales Change: 14.6%
Exchange: Nasdaq
Symbol: IJIN

Audio & video home products - loudspeakers & loudspeaker components for the domestic &
international automotive original equipment manufacturers & home audio markets

IVEX PACKAGING CORPORATION

100 Tri-State Dr.
Lincolnshire, IL 60069
Phone: 847-945-9100
Fax: 847-945-9184

CEO: George V. Bayly
CFO: Frank Tannura
HR: Jerry S. Lawrence
Employees: 2,500

1994 Sales: $418.5 million
1-Yr. Sales Change: 6.7%
Ownership: Privately Held

Paper & plastic specialty packaging

JACK CARL/312-FUTURES, INC.

200 W. Adams St., Ste. 1500
Chicago, IL 60606
Phone: 312-407-5700
Fax: 312-419-5868

CEO: Burton J. Meyer
CFO: Allyson D. Laackman
HR: Kaye Zenger
Employees: 251

1995 Sales: $41.7 million
1-Yr. Sales Change: 10.9%
Exchange: Nasdaq (SC)
Symbol: FUTR

Financial - investment management

JACOBS TWIN

6750 W. Grand Ave.
Chicago, IL 60635
Phone: 312-889-3030
Fax: 312-889-7758

CEO: Harold Jacobs
CFO: Jeff Jacobs
HR: Donna Janusz
Employees: 293

1994 Sales: $119.8 million
1-Yr. Sales Change: 19.3%
Ownership: Privately Held

Retail - new & used cars

JAKE'S PIZZA INTERNATIONAL, INC.

16 Official Rd.	CEO: James J. Banks	1994 Sales: $4 million
Addison, IL 60101	CFO: Glen Hjort	1-Yr. Sales Change: 33.3%
Phone: 708-543-0022	HR: Glen Hjort	Exchange: Nasdaq (SC)
Fax: 708-543-2220	Employees: 37	Symbol: JAKE

Retail - pizza restaurants in the Chicago area

JEL SERT COMPANY

PO Box 261	CEO: Charles T. Wegner	1994 Est. Sales: $105 mil.
West Chicago, IL 60186	CFO: Mark Benrus	1-Yr. Sales Change: 0.0%
Phone: 708-231-7590	HR: Jose Mendoza	Ownership: Privately Held
Fax: 708-231-3993	Employees: 450	

Beverages - juice drinks & powdered beverages (Fla-Vor-Aid, Wyler's, Mondo Fruit Squeezer)

JENNER & BLOCK

330 N. Wabash St., 43rd Fl.	CEO: Louis A. Strom	1994 Sales: $131.4 million
Chicago, IL 60611	CFO: Greg Goldsborough	1-Yr. Sales Change: 8.1%
Phone: 312-222-9350	HR: Sheryl Ross	Ownership: Privately Held
Fax: 312-527-0484	Employees: 945	

Law firm with offices in Chicago; Washington, DC; Lake Forest, IL & Miami

JERNBERG INDUSTRIES

328 W. 40th Place	CEO: M. Eldon Wheeler	1994 Sales: $87.2 million
Chicago, IL 60609	CFO: T. M. McDonald	1-Yr. Sales Change: -4.6%
Phone: 312-268-3004	HR: Michael Mills	Ownership: Privately Held
Fax: 312-268-3220	Employees: 428	

Metal products - ferrous forgings, primarily for the auto industry

JEWEL FOOD STORES, INC.

1955 W. North Ave.	CEO: Edward J. McManus	1994 Est. Sales: $2,950 mil.
Melrose Park, IL 60160	CFO: Eileen Kowalski	1-Yr. Sales Change: —
Phone: 708-531-6000	HR: Ed Buron	Ownership: Subsidiary
Fax: 708-531-6001	Employees: 29,000	

Retail - supermarkets; subsidiary of American Stores Company

JG INDUSTRIES, INC.

1615 W. Chicago Ave.	CEO: William Hellman	1995 Sales: $196.2 million
Chicago, IL 60622	CFO: William Guzik	1-Yr. Sales Change: 11.3%
Phone: 312-850-8000	HR: —	Exchange: Nasdaq
Fax: 312-421-1057	Employees: 1,597	Symbol: JGIN

Retail - regional department stores (Goldblatt's)

J. H. ROBERTS INDUSTRIES

3158 Des Plaines Ave.	CEO: John H. Roberts	1994 Sales: $148.9 million
Des Plaines, IL 60018	CFO: Laurence Collins	1-Yr. Sales Change: 22.6%
Phone: 847-699-0080	HR: Joyce Becella	Ownership: Privately Held
Fax: 847-699-0082	Employees: 730	

Steel - manufacturing & distribution

JMB REALTY CORPORATION

900 N. Michigan Ave.	CEO: Neil Bluhm	1994 Sales: $1,100 million
Chicago, IL 60611	CFO: Howard Kogen	1-Yr. Sales Change: 12.8%
Phone: 312-440-4800	HR: Gail Silvers	Ownership: Privately Held
Fax: 312-915-2310	Employees: 12,500	

Real estate operations & management; owns 40% of Urban Shopping Centers

JOE RIZZA ENTERPRISES INC.

7222 W. Cermak Rd.	CEO: Joseph R. Rizza	1994 Sales: $293 million
North Riverside, IL 60546	CFO: Joseph R. Rizza	1-Yr. Sales Change: 14.0%
Phone: 708-442-1140	HR: Valerie DiGiovanni	Ownership: Privately Held
Fax: 708-442-1707	Employees: 500	

Diversified operations - new & used car dealerships; real estate; insurance

JOHN B. SANFILIPPO & SON, INC.

2299 Busse Rd.	CEO: Jasper B. Sanfilippo	1994 Sales: $209 million
Elk Grove Village, IL 60007	CFO: Gary P. Jensen	1-Yr. Sales Change: 3.2%
Phone: 847-593-2300	HR: Dave Meyers	Exchange: Nasdaq
Fax: 847-593-3085	Employees: 1,274	Symbol: JBSS

Food - processor, packager, marketer & distributor of shelled & unshelled nuts sold under a variety of private labels & the company's (Evon's, Sunshine Country, Texas Pride) brand names

THE JOHN D. AND CATHERINE T. MACARTHUR FOUNDATION

140 S. Dearborn St., Ste. 1100
Chicago, IL 60603
Phone: 312-726-8000
Fax: 312-917-0200

Charitable foundation

CEO: Adele Simmons
CFO: Lawrence L. Landry
HR: William E. Lowry
Employees: 195

1994 Sales: $150.4 million
1-Yr. Sales Change: -36.4%
Ownership: Foundation

🏢 **See page 212 for a full profile of this company.**

JOHN G. SHEDD AQUARIUM

1200 S. Lake Shore Dr.
Chicago, IL 60605
Phone: 312-939-2438
Fax: 312-939-8069

Indoor aquarium (#1 worldwide)

CEO: Ted Beattie
CFO: Joyce Simon
HR: Nanette Schonberg
Employees: 250

1995 Sales: $19.3 million
1-Yr. Sales Change: —

THE JOHN NUVEEN COMPANY

333 W. Wacker Dr.
Chicago, IL 60606-1286
Phone: 312-917-7700
Fax: 312-917-8049

Financial - investment management

CEO: Richard J. Franke
CFO: Donald E. Sveen
HR: —
Employees: 537

1994 Sales: $220.3 million
1-Yr. Sales Change: -10.3%
Exchange: NYSE
Symbol: JNC

JOHNSON PUBLISHING COMPANY, INC.

820 S. Michigan Ave.
Chicago, IL 60605
Phone: 312-322-9200
Fax: 312-322-0918

CEO: John H. Johnson
CFO: Eunice W. Johnson
HR: La Doris Foster
Employees: 2,662

1994 Sales: $307 million
1-Yr. Sales Change: 4.4%
Ownership: Privately Held

Diversified - periodical publishing (Ebony, Jet), radio broadcasting, cosmetics & hair care

🏢 **See pages 114–115 for a full profile of this company.**

JOHNSTOWN AMERICA INDUSTRIES, INC.

980 N. Michigan Ave., Ste. 1000
Chicago, IL 60611
Phone: 312-280-8844
Fax: 312-280-4820

CEO: James D. Cirar
CFO: Andrew M. Weller
HR: —
Employees: 2,000

1994 Sales: $468.1 million
1-Yr. Sales Change: 42.2%
Exchange: Nasdaq
Symbol: JAII

Transportation - equipment & leasing, railroad freight cars

JORDAN INDUSTRIES, INC.

1751 Lake Cook Rd.	CEO: John W. "Jay" Jordan	1994 Sales: $424.4 million
Deerfield, IL 60015	CFO: Jonathan Boucher	1-Yr. Sales Change: 18.3%
Phone: 847-945-5591	HR: —	Ownership: Privately Held
Fax: 847-945-5698	Employees: 3,900	

Diversified operations - safety reflectors; torque converters, hydraulic pumps & other related products; missile ground handling products; specialty electric motors; precision gear & gear box products; home health care products

JUNO LIGHTING, INC.

2001 S. Mt. Prospect Rd., PO Box 5065	CEO: Robert S. Fremont	1994 Sales: $126.8 million
Des Plaines, IL 60017-5065	CFO: George J. Bilek	1-Yr. Sales Change: 16.2%
Phone: 847-827-9880	HR: Patricia Perez	Exchange: Nasdaq
Fax: 847-827-2925	Employees: 915	Symbol: JUNO

Building products - recessed & track lighting fixtures

JUPITER INDUSTRIES, INC.

919 North Michigan Ave.	CEO: Edward W. Ross	1995 Sales: —
Chicago, IL 60611	CFO: George Murphy	1-Yr. Sales Change: —
Phone: 312-642-6000	HR: —	Ownership: Privately Held
Fax: 312-642-2316	Employees: —	

Financial - venture capital investment firm with holdings in department stores (controlling interest in JG Industries, owner of Goldblatt's), real estate, natural gas & insurance

J. W. ALLEN & COMPANY

555 Allendale Dr.	CEO: J. William Allen	1994 Sales: $73 million
Wheeling, IL 60090	CFO: Al Foster	1-Yr. Sales Change: 7.4%
Phone: 847-459-5400	HR: Diane Baker	Ownership: Privately Held
Fax: 847-459-0314	Employees: 360	

Food - bakery products

K & R EXPRESS SYSTEMS, INC.

15 W. 460 Frontage Rd.	CEO: Lawrence Klong	1994 Sales: $40.6 million
Hinsdale, IL 60521	CFO: David Gerstein	1-Yr. Sales Change: 17.0%
Phone: 708-323-3230	HR: Jim Halloran	Ownership: Privately Held
Fax: 708-323-0159	Employees: 360	

Transportation - trucking services

KATTEN MUCHIN & ZAVIS

525 W. Monroe St., Ste. 1600
Chicago, IL 60661
Phone: 312-902-5200
Fax: 312-902-1061

Law firm

CEO: Michael R. Marget
CFO: Norman H. Steinberg
HR: —
Employees: 1,015

1994 Sales: $124 million
1-Yr. Sales Change: -0.8%
Ownership: Privately Held

KECK, MAHIN & CATE

77 W. Wacker Dr., 49th Fl.
Chicago, IL 60601-1693
Phone: 312-634-7700
Fax: 312-634-5000

Law firm

CEO: Clarence O. Redman
CFO: Thomas N. Kracowiak
HR: Lois C. Kuch
Employees: 600

1994 Sales: $87 million
1-Yr. Sales Change: -7.9%
Ownership: Privately Held

KELSO-BURNETT COMPANY

5200 Newport Dr.
Rolling Meadows, IL 60008
Phone: 847-259-0720
Fax: 847-259-0839

Building - electrical & data cabling contractor

CEO: Terry Butz
CFO: Jim Kostek
HR: —
Employees: 276

1994 Sales: $35.8 million
1-Yr. Sales Change: 1.7%
Ownership: Privately Held

KEMPER CORPORATION

One Kemper Dr.
Long Grove, IL 60049
Phone: 847-320-3435
Fax: 847-320-4535

Financial - asset management; life insurance

CEO: David B. Mathis
CFO: John H. Fitzpatrick
HR: Frederic C. McCullough
Employees: 8,530

1994 Sales: $1,601.8 million
1-Yr. Sales Change: 13.7%
Exchange: NYSE
Symbol: KEM

THE KEMPER NATIONAL INSURANCE COMPANIES

One Kemper Dr.
Long Grove, IL 60049
Phone: 847-320-2000
Fax: 847-320-2494

Insurance - property & casualty

CEO: Alfred K. Kenyon
CFO: Walter L. White
HR: Fred McCullough
Employees: 9,000

1994 Sales: $3,010 million
1-Yr. Sales Change: -4.9%
Ownership: Mutual

See pages 116–117 for a full profile of this company.

KIRKLAND & ELLIS

200 E. Randolph Dr.	CEO: Douglas McLemore	1994 Sales: $215 million
Chicago, IL 60601	CFO: Patricia Fitzpatrick	1-Yr. Sales Change: 13.2%
Phone: 312-861-2000	HR: Sally Howard	Ownership: Privately Held
Fax: 312-861-2200	Employees: 1,200	
Law firm		

KLEIN TOOLS, INC.

7200 McCormick Blvd.	CEO: Michael S. Klein	1994 Sales: $111.6 million
Skokie, IL 60659	CFO: Richard T. Klein Jr.	1-Yr. Sales Change: 9.6%
Phone: 847-677-9500	HR: Walter Maciag	Ownership: Privately Held
Fax: 847-677-4476	Employees: 923	

Tools - professional hand tools & personal protective equipment

KREHER STEEL COMPANY

1550 N. 25th Ave.	CEO: Thomas W. Kreher	1994 Sales: $95 million
Melrose Park, IL 60160	CFO: Ed Nemergut	1-Yr. Sales Change: 21.8%
Phone: 708-345-8180	HR: —	Ownership: Privately Held
Fax: 708-345-8293	Employees: 85	

Metal products distribution - steel service centers

KUKLA PRESS, INC.

855 Morse Ave.	CEO: Stanley J. Kukla	1994 Sales: $42 million
Elk Grove Village, IL 60007	CFO: Steve Funk	1-Yr. Sales Change: 5.0%
Phone: 847-593-1090	HR: Darlene McPhearson	Ownership: Privately Held
Fax: 847-593-0406	Employees: 200	

Printing - commercial web offset printing

LAKEWOOD ENGINEERING & MANUFACTURING COMPANY

501 N. Sacramento Blvd.	CEO: C.W. Kraus	1994 Sales: $80 million
Chicago, IL 60612	CFO: Beth Dunning	1-Yr. Sales Change: 21.2%
Phone: 312-722-4300	HR: Frank Castro	Ownership: Privately Held
Fax: 312-722-1541	Employees: 550	

Building products - electric fans & heaters

LANDAUER, INC.

2 Science Rd.	CEO: Thomas M. Fulton	1995 Sales: $34 million
Glenwood, IL 60425-1586	CFO: James M. O'Connell	1-Yr. Sales Change: 4.3%
Phone: 708-755-7000	HR: Lana Gowen	Exchange: AMEX
Fax: 708-755-7035	Employees: 260	Symbol: LDR

Engineering - R&D services

LANE INDUSTRIES, INC.

1200 Shermer Rd.	CEO: William N. Lane III	1994 Sales: $553 million
Northbrook, IL 60062	CFO: Forrest M. Schneider	1-Yr. Sales Change: 18.9%
Phone: 847-498-6789	HR: Linda Datz	Ownership: Privately Held
Fax: 847-498-2104	Employees: 7,000	

Diversified operations - business machines & supplies; ranching; lodging; broadcasting

LAWSON PRODUCTS, INC.

1666 E. Touhy Ave.	CEO: Bernard Kalish	1994 Sales: $213.1 million
Des Plaines, IL 60018	CFO: Jerome Shaffer	1-Yr. Sales Change: 8.9%
Phone: 847-827-9666	HR: James J. Smith	Exchange: Nasdaq
Fax: 847-827-8277	Employees: 810	Symbol: LAWS

Metal products - distribution

LAWTER INTERNATIONAL, INC.

990 Skokie Blvd.	CEO: Daniel J. Terra	1994 Sales: $191.1 million
Northbrook, IL 60062	CFO: William S. Russell	1-Yr. Sales Change: 11.0%
Phone: 847-498-4700	HR: Sue Vollmer	Exchange: NYSE
Fax: 847-498-0066	Employees: 577	Symbol: LAW

Chemicals - specialty

L. E. MYERS CO. GROUP

2550 W. Golf Rd., Ste. 200	CEO: Charles M. Brennan III	1994 Sales: $86.8 million
Rolling Meadows, IL 60008-4007	CFO: Elliott C. Robbins	1-Yr. Sales Change: -20.0%
Phone: 847-290-1891	HR: —	Exchange: NYSE
Fax: 847-290-1892	Employees: 1,000	Symbol: MYR

Construction - electrical power lines

LEO BURNETT COMPANY, INC.

35 W. Wacker Dr., Ste. 2200
Chicago, IL 60601
Phone: 312-220-5959
Fax: 312-220-6533

Advertising

CEO: William T. Lynch
CFO: Roger A. Haupt
HR: Michael Breslin
Employees: 6,308

1994 Sales: $675 million
1-Yr. Sales Change: 8.5%
Ownership: Privately Held

 **See pages 118–119 for a full profile of this company.**

LETTUCE ENTERTAIN YOU ENTERPRISES, INC.

5419 N. Sheridan Rd.
Chicago, IL 60640
Phone: 312-878-7340
Fax: 312-878-7667

CEO: Richard Melman
CFO: Jay Steiber
HR: Susan Southgate-Fox
Employees: 3,600

1994 Sales: $125 million
1-Yr. Sales Change: 11.6%
Ownership: Privately Held

Retail - theme restaurants (Ed Debevics, Shaw's Crab House, The Pump Room, R.J. Grunt's, Scoozi!, Hat Dance, Mity Nice Grill, Un Grand Cafe)

See page 213 for a full profile of this company.

LEVY RESTAURANTS

980 N. Michigan Ave., 4th Fl.
Chicago, IL 60611
Phone: 312-664-8200
Fax: 312-280-2739

CEO: Lawrence F. Levy
CFO: Bob Seissert
HR: Margie Mintz
Employees: 3,500

1994 Sales: $98.6 million
1-Yr. Sales Change: 9.1%
Ownership: Privately Held

Retail - restaurants (D.B. Kaplan's, Dos Hermanos) & food concessions (Arlington Park, Comiskey Park, Disney World, McCormick Place, Wrigley Field)

LIBERTY BANCORP, INC.

5700 N. Lincoln Ave.
Chicago, IL 60659
Phone: 312-334-1200
Fax: 312-334-6995

Financial - savings & loans

CEO: Fredric G. Novy
CFO: Joseph W. Stachnik
HR: Susan Schliep
Employees: 151

1994 Sales: $38 million
1-Yr. Sales Change: -4.8%
Exchange: Nasdaq
Symbol: LBCI

LIBERTYVILLE CLASSIC GROUP

941 S. Milwaukee Ave.
Libertyville, IL 60048
Phone: 847-367-1700
Fax: 847-367-6054

Retail - new & used cars

CEO: Julius Marks Jr.
CFO: Karen L. Casey
HR: Don Marks
Employees: 200

1994 Est. Sales: $143.2 mil.
1-Yr. Sales Change: 7.9%
Ownership: Privately Held

LIFEWAY FOODS, INC.

7625 N. Austin St.
Skokie, IL 60077
Phone: 847-967-1010
Fax: 847-967-6558

Food - fermented dairy beverage (kefir)

CEO: Michael Smolyansky
CFO: Michael Smolyansky
HR: —
Employees: 20

1994 Sales: $3.5 million
1-Yr. Sales Change: 16.7%
Exchange: Nasdaq (SC)
Symbol: LWAY

LINCOLN PARK ZOO

2200 N. Cannon Dr.
Chicago, IL 60614
Phone: 312-742-2000
Fax: 312-742-2226

Zoo

CEO: Kevin Bell
CFO: Troy Baresel
HR: Jessica Berger
Employees: 160

1995 Sales: $10 million
1-Yr. Sales Change: 40.8%

LINDBERG CORPORATION

6133 N. River Rd., Ste. 700
Rosemont, IL 60018
Phone: 847-823-2021
Fax: 847-823-0795

CEO: Leo G. Thompson
CFO: Stephen S. Penley
HR: Jerome R. Sullivan
Employees: 610

1994 Sales: $99.9 million
1-Yr. Sales Change: 43.5%
Exchange: Nasdaq
Symbol: LIND

Metal processing & fabrication - heat-treating processes to improve mechanical properties, durability & wear resistance

LIND-WALDOCK & COMPANY

1030 W. Van Buren St.
Chicago, IL 60607
Phone: 312-413-6000
Fax: 312-413-6129

Financial - discount commodity brokerage

CEO: Barry Lind
CFO: Thomas Anderson
HR: Lisa Gaglianese
Employees: 650

1994 Sales: $65.1 million
1-Yr. Sales Change: 18.8%
Ownership: Privately Held

LITTELFUSE, INC.

800 E. Northwest Hwy.
Des Plaines, IL 60016-3049
Phone: 847-824-1188
Fax: 847-824-3024

CEO: Howard B. Witt
CFO: James F. Brace
HR: Jon B. Anderson
Employees: 2,270

1994 Sales: $194.5 million
1-Yr. Sales Change: 21.0%
Exchange: Nasdaq
Symbol: LFUS

Electrical products - fuses for power equipment & circuit protection devices for the electronics & automotive industries

LLOYD CREATIVE TEMPORARIES

1001 E. Toughy Ave., Ste. 170
Des Plaines, IL 60618
Phone: 847-297-7030
Fax: 847-297-6561

CEO: Charles Graziani
CFO: Ron Loker
HR: —
Employees: 800

1994 Sales: $8.2 million
1-Yr. Sales Change: —
Ownership: Privately Held

Personnel - temporary-employment services

LOEBER MOTORS, INC.

1111 N. Clark St.
Chicago, IL 60610
Phone: 312-944-0500
Fax: 312-944-1075

CEO: George Loeber
CFO: George Loeber
HR: Kris Colelle
Employees: 210

1994 Sales: $111.3 million
1-Yr. Sales Change: 14.6%
Ownership: Privately Held

Retail - new & used cars

LOMBARD LINCOLN MERCURY, INC.

500 E. Roosevelt Rd.
Lombard, IL 60148
Phone: 708-495-2500
Fax: 708-495-2124

CEO: Larry Sherman
CFO: Gerry Klein
HR: Gerry Klein
Employees: 50

1994 Sales: $46.7 million
1-Yr. Sales Change: 17.9%
Ownership: Privately Held

Retail - new & used cars

LONG COMPANY

300 W. Washington St.
Chicago, IL 60606
Phone: 312-726-4606
Fax: 312-726-4625

CEO: Bernard Forrest
CFO: John Growcock
HR: Helen Mayberry
Employees: 33

1994 Sales: $45.7 million
1-Yr. Sales Change: 7.0%
Ownership: Cooperative

Food - bakery cooperative

LORD, BISSELL & BROOK

115 S. LaSalle St.
Chicago, IL 60603
Phone: 312-443-0700
Fax: 312-443-0336

CEO: Thomas Stevens
CFO: Thomas E. Young
HR: —
Employees: 560

1994 Sales: $87 million
1-Yr. Sales Change: 4.8%
Ownership: Privately Held

Law firm

LOREN BUICK, INC.

1620 Waukegan Rd.
Glenview, IL 60025
Phone: 847-729-8900
Fax: 847-724-8429

Retail - new & used cars

CEO: Irving N. Segal
CFO: Dennis Doerse
HR: Sharon Ritzler
Employees: 70

1994 Sales: $76.2 million
1-Yr. Sales Change: 62.8%
Ownership: Privately Held

LOYOLA UNIVERSITY OF CHICAGO

820 N. Michigan Ave.
Chicago, IL 60611
Phone: 312-915-6000
Fax: 312-915-6449

CEO: John J. Piderit
CFO: David J. Meagher
HR: Mimi Winter
Employees: 9,556

1995 Sales: $696.5 million
1-Yr. Sales Change: 4.5%

Jesuit-run Catholic university offering 50 undergraduate degree programs & 49 graduate degree programs

LYNCH GROUP

5333 W. Irving Park Rd.
Chicago, IL 60641
Phone: 312-283-1200
Fax: 312-794-7024

Retail - new & used cars

CEO: Rick Lynch
CFO: John Napoleon
HR: Doris Kulas
Employees: 175

1994 Est. Sales: $81 mil.
1-Yr. Sales Change: 7.1%
Ownership: Privately Held

LYON METAL PRODUCTS, INC.

PO Box 671
Aurora, IL 60507
Phone: 708-892-8941
Fax: 708-892-8966

CEO: R. Peter Washington
CFO: D.M. Harrison
HR: Carol Stathis
Employees: 800

1994 Sales: $95 million
1-Yr. Sales Change: 5.6%
Ownership: Privately Held

Steel shelving, shop equipment, racks & tool storage systems

LYRIC OPERA OF CHICAGO

20 N. Wacker Dr., Ste. 860
Chicago, IL 60606
Phone: 312-332-2244
Fax: 312-419-8345

Opera

CEO: James W. Kozad
CFO: Robert E. Allgyer
HR: Dana Herpe
Employees: 1,077

1995 Sales: $19 million
1-Yr. Sales Change: 9.2%

MACLEAN-FOGG COMPANY

1000 Allanson Rd.	CEO: Barry L. MacLean	1994 Sales: $175 million
Mundelein, IL 60060	CFO: Patrick O'Conner	1-Yr. Sales Change: 16.7%
Phone: 847-566-0010	HR: Vince Piat	Ownership: Privately Held
Fax: 847-566-0026	Employees: 1,200	

Metal processing & fabrication components for the automotive, power utility & telecommunications industries

MAF BANCORP, INC.

55th St. & Holmes Ave.	CEO: Allen M. Koranda	1995 Sales: $131.9 million
Clarendon Hills, IL 60514	CFO: Jerry A. Weberling	1-Yr. Sales Change: 20.2%
Phone: 708-325-7300	HR: David W. Kohlsaat	Exchange: Nasdaq
Fax: 708-325-1193	Employees: 509	Symbol: MAFB

Banks - Midwest

MAGNECO/METREL, INC.

223 Interstate Rd.	CEO: Chester L. Connors	1994 Sales: $39.2 million
Addison, IL 60101	CFO: Chester L. Connors	1-Yr. Sales Change: 13.6%
Phone: 708-543-6660	HR: —	Ownership: Privately Held
Fax: 708-543-1479	Employees: 260	

Ceramics - high-temperature refractory ceramics for the steel industry

MANUFACTURED HOME COMMUNITIES, INC.

2 N. Riverside Plaza	CEO: Samuel Zell	1994 Sales: $68.8 million
Chicago, IL 60606	CFO: Thomas P. Heneghan	1-Yr. Sales Change: 63.8%
Phone: 312-454-0100	HR: Ellen Kelleher	Exchange: NYSE
Fax: 312-474-0205	Employees: 4,600	Symbol: MHC

Real estate investment trust - manufactured-housing communities

MARKET FACTS, INC.

3040 W. Salt Creek Ln.	CEO: Verne B. Churchill	1994 Sales: $55.5 million
Arlington Heights, IL 60005	CFO: Timothy J. Sullivan	1-Yr. Sales Change: 21.7%
Phone: 847-590-7000	HR: Karen Duncan	Exchange: Nasdaq
Fax: 847-590-7325	Employees: 903	Symbol: MFAC

Business services - market research

THE MARMON GROUP

225 W. Washington St.
Chicago, IL 60606
Phone: 312-372-9500
Fax: 312-845-5305

CEO: Robert A. Pritzker
CFO: Robert C. Gluth
HR: George Frese
Employees: 28,000

1994 Sales: $5,301 million
1-Yr. Sales Change: 22.7%
Ownership: Privately Held

Diversified operations - industrial materials, automobile & medical products

See pages 120–121 for a full profile of this company.

MARTIN OIL MARKETING LTD.

4501 W. 127th St.
Alsip, IL 60658
Phone: 708-385-6500
Fax: 708-385-6598

CEO: Carl C. Greer
CFO: Thomas A. Floyd
HR: —
Employees: 150

1994 Sales: $461.5 million
1-Yr. Sales Change: 8.6%
Ownership: Privately Held

Oil & gas exploration & production

MATERIAL SCIENCES CORPORATION

2300 E. Pratt Blvd.
Elk Grove Village, IL 60007
Phone: 847-439-8270
Fax: 847-439-0737

CEO: G. Robert Evans
CFO: William H. Vrba
HR: Frank J. Lazowski Jr.
Employees: 925

1995 Sales: $227.7 million
1-Yr. Sales Change: 21.3%
Exchange: NYSE
Symbol: MSC

Steel - specialty alloys

MAY & SPEH, INC.

1501 Opus Place
Downers Grove, IL 60515
Phone: 708-964-1501
Fax: 708-719-0290

CEO: Larry Speh
CFO: Will Engel
HR: Mark Jeske
Employees: 300

1994 Sales: $52 million
1-Yr. Sales Change: 25.3%
Ownership: Privately Held

Data collection & systems - data processing & other services to direct marketers

MAYER, BROWN & PLATT

190 S. LaSalle St.
Chicago, IL 60603
Phone: 312-782-0600
Fax: 312-701-7711

CEO: Robert Helman
CFO: Steven R. Wells
HR: Lori Monthei
Employees: 533

1994 Sales: $263 million
1-Yr. Sales Change: 4.0%
Ownership: Privately Held

Law firm

MAZZETTA COMPANY

1990 St. Johns Ave.
Highland Park, IL 60035
Phone: 847-433-1150
Fax: 847-433-8973

Food - frozen seafood importing

CEO: Thomas Mazzetta
CFO: Thomas Mazzetta
HR: Thomas Mazzetta
Employees: 12

1994 Sales: $114 million
1-Yr. Sales Change: -1.7%
Ownership: Privately Held

MCCAIN MANUFACTURING CORPORATION

6200 W. 60th St.
Chicago, IL 60638
Phone: 312-586-6200
Fax: 312-586-6210

Machinery - bookbinding systems

CEO: Tom Carroll
CFO: David Harrell
HR: Denise Franco
Employees: 206

1994 Est. Sales: $120.1 mil.
1-Yr. Sales Change: 3.0%
Ownership: Privately Held

MCCLIER

401 E. Illinois St.
Chicago, IL 60611
Phone: 312-836-7700
Fax: 312-836-7710

Building - architecture, engineering, construction & consulting services

CEO: Grant G. McCullagh
CFO: Janeanne Upp
HR: —
Employees: 400

1995 Sales: $150 million
1-Yr. Sales Change: 74.4%
Ownership: Privately Held

MCDERMOTT, WILL & EMERY

227 W. Monroe St.
Chicago, IL 60606-5096
Phone: 312-372-2000
Fax: 312-984-7500

Law firm

CEO: Lawrence Gerber
CFO: Molly Condon
HR: Lori Cerone
Employees: 1,190

1994 Sales: $207 million
1-Yr. Sales Change: 15.0%
Ownership: Privately Held

MCDONALD'S CORPORATION

McDonald's Plaza
Oak Brook, IL 60521
Phone: 708-575-3000
Fax: 708-575-3392

Retail - food & restaurants

CEO: Michael R. Quinlan
CFO: Jack M. Greenberg
HR: Stanley R. Stein
Employees: 183,000

1994 Sales: $8,320.8 million
1-Yr. Sales Change: 12.3%
Exchange: NYSE
Symbol: MCD

See pages 122–123 for a full profile of this company.

MCWHORTER TECHNOLOGIES, INC.

400 E. Cottage Place
Carpentersville, IL 60110
Phone: 847-428-2657
Fax: 847-428-9440

CEO: John R. Stevenson
CFO: Jeffrey M. Nodland
HR: Mia Igyarto
Employees: 550

1994 Sales: $242.3 million
1-Yr. Sales Change: 128.8%
Exchange: NYSE
Symbol: MWT

Paints & allied products - resins

MEDICUS SYSTEMS CORPORATION

One Rotary Center, Ste. 400
Evanston, IL 60201
Phone: 847-570-7500
Fax: 847-570-7518

CEO: Richard C. Jelinek
CFO: Deborah R. Suckow
HR: Mary Stewart
Employees: 285

1995 Sales: $33.8 million
1-Yr. Sales Change: -2.0%
Exchange: Nasdaq
Symbol: MECS

Computers - decision-support software for the health care industry

MEDLINE INDUSTRIES, INC.

1200 Town Line Rd.
Mundelein, IL 60060
Phone: 847-949-5500
Fax: 847-949-2109

CEO: Jon Mills
CFO: Meredith Mendes
HR: Heidi Dinter
Employees: 2,000

1994 Sales: $475.8 million
1-Yr. Sales Change: 15.3%
Ownership: Privately Held

Medical supplies, including clothing & linens, shoe covers, surgical instruments, admission kits, catheters, irrigation trays, walkers, wheelchairs & furniture

MELSON TECHNOLOGIES, INC.

707 Skokie Blvd., Ste. 700
Northbrook, IL 60062-2842
Phone: 847-291-4000
Fax: 847-291-4022

CEO: Larry P. Roches
CFO: Michael O'Rourke
HR: Robert J. Forsberg
Employees: 140

1994 Est. Sales: $10 mil.
1-Yr. Sales Change: —
Ownership: Privately Held

Computers - systems & software for real estate portfolio & investment management (Skyline ReSource, ReCap Pro-Ject)

MERCHANTS BANCORP, INC.

34 S. Broadway
Aurora, IL 60507
Phone: 708-896-9000
Fax: 708-859-7599

CEO: Calvin R. Myers
CFO: J. Douglas Cheatham
HR: Susan Anderson
Employees: 265

1994 Sales: $39.8 million
1-Yr. Sales Change: 9.9%
Exchange: Nasdaq
Symbol: MBIA

Banks - Midwest

MERCURY FINANCE CO.

40 Skokie Blvd., Ste. 200
Northbrook, IL 60062
Phone: 847-564-3720
Fax: 847-564-3758

CEO: John N. Brincat
CFO: Charley A. Pond
HR: Robert Lutgen
Employees: 1,500

1994 Sales: $252.5 million
1-Yr. Sales Change: 29.9%
Exchange: NYSE
Symbol: MFN

Financial - auto & consumer loans & credit insurance

 See page 214 for a full profile of this company.

MESIROW FINANCIAL HOLDINGS INC.

350 N. Clark St.
Chicago, IL 60610
Phone: 312-595-6000
Fax: 312-595-7208

CEO: James C. Tyree
CFO: Eve Slusarczyk
HR: Dale Swanson
Employees: 505

1994 Sales: $83 million
1-Yr. Sales Change: 6.4%
Ownership: Privately Held

Financial services & venture capital firm

METAMOR TECHNOLOGIES LTD

One N. Franklin, Ste. 1500
Chicago, IL 60606
Phone: 312-638-2667
Fax: 312-251-2998

CEO: Irv Shapiro
CFO: Dan Shapiro
HR: Marcie Newman
Employees: 130

1994 Sales: $7.9 million
1-Yr. Sales Change: —
Ownership: Privately Held

Computers - consulting services

METHODE ELECTRONICS, INC.

7444 W. Wilson Ave.
Chicago, IL 60656
Phone: 708-867-9600
Fax: 708-867-9130

CEO: William T. Jensen
CFO: Kevin J. Hayes
HR: Louise Moyana
Employees: 3,000

1995 Sales: $274.5 million
1-Yr. Sales Change: 27.2%
Exchange: Nasdaq
Symbol: METHA

Electronic components - connectors, fiber optic & cable assemblies

METRA

547 W. Jackson
Chicago, IL 60661
Phone: 312-322-6900
Fax: 312-322-6765

CEO: Philip A. Pagano
CFO: Lowell E. Anderson
HR: Barbara Akins
Employees: 2,400

1995 Sales: $193.4 million
1-Yr. Sales Change: 5.1%
Ownership: Privately Held

Transportation - commuter rail system serving the 6 counties of northeastern Illinois

 See page 215 for a full profile of this company.

MFRI, INC.

7720 Lehigh Ave.	CEO: David Unger	1995 Sales: $75.5 million
Niles, IL 60714	CFO: Michael D. Bennett	1-Yr. Sales Change: 152.5%
Phone: 847-966-1000	HR: Debbie Foy	Exchange: Nasdaq
Fax: 847-966-8563	Employees: 442	Symbol: MFRI

Filtration products - industrial filter bags & leak detection systems

MIDDLEBY CORPORATION

1400 Postmaster Dr.	CEO: David P. Riley	1994 Sales: $130 million
Elgin, IL 60120-9272	CFO: John J. Hastings	1-Yr. Sales Change: 6.5%
Phone: 847-741-3300	HR: Beth Crater	Exchange: AMEX
Fax: 847-741-5363	Employees: 957	Symbol: MBY

Food service equipment - conveyor ovens, toasters & other cooking & warming equipment; heavy duty gas ranges, broilers, grills & convection ovens (Southbend); commercial refrigeration equipment

MIDLAND PAPER COMPANY

1825 Greenleaf Ave.	CEO: E. S. Hooker III	1994 Sales: $347 million
Elk Grove Village, IL 60007	CFO: William Carpenter	1-Yr. Sales Change: 122.4%
Phone: 847-981-7300	HR: Kim Baratta	Ownership: Privately Held
Fax: 847-981-0216	Employees: 205	

Wholesale distribution - printing paper

MILWAUKEE LAND COMPANY

547 W. Jackson Blvd.	CEO: Edwin Jacobson	1994 Sales: $1.1 million
Chicago, IL 60661	CFO: Leon F. Fiorentino	1-Yr. Sales Change: —
Phone: 312-294-0497	HR: —	Exchange: AMEX
Fax: 312-663-9397	Employees: 3	Symbol: MWK

Financial - closed-end investment company

MINER ENTERPRISES, INC.

1200 E. State St.	CEO: William E. Withall	1994 Sales: $84 million
Geneva, IL 60134	CFO: Kris Jurasek	1-Yr. Sales Change: 21.7%
Phone: 708-232-3000	HR: James M. Meyers	Ownership: Privately Held
Fax: 708-232-3123	Employees: 500	

Metal products - railroad car parts, container hardware & hydraulic lifting equipment

MINUTEMAN INTERNATIONAL, INC.

111 S. Rohlwing Rd.	CEO: Jerome E. Rau	1994 Sales: $41.5 million
Addison, IL 60101	CFO: Thomas J. Nolan	1-Yr. Sales Change: 8.6%
Phone: 708-627-6900	HR: Phyllis Gillam	Exchange: Nasdaq
Fax: 708-627-1130	Employees: 221	Symbol: MMAN

Appliances - vacuum cleaners & floor- & carpet-cleaning products for commercial & industrial use

MMI COMPANIES, INC.

540 Lake Cook Rd.	CEO: B. Frederick Becker	1994 Sales: $177.2 million
Deerfield, IL 60015-5290	CFO: Paul M. Orzech	1-Yr. Sales Change: 14.4%
Phone: 847-940-7550	HR: Merrilee Hepler	Exchange: NYSE
Fax: 847-374-1332	Employees: 400	Symbol: MMI

Insurance - medical malpractice insurance & specialized clinical risk management services

MOLEX INCORPORATED

2222 Wellington Ct.	CEO: Frederick A. Krehbiel	1995 Sales: $1,197.7 million
Lisle, IL 60532	CFO: John C. Psaltis	1-Yr. Sales Change: 24.2%
Phone: 708-969-4550	HR: Kathi M. Regas	Exchange: Nasdaq
Fax: 708-969-1352	Employees: 9,500	Symbol: MOLX

Electrical, electronic & fiber optic interconnectors & systems; switches & application tooling for the computer, business equipment, home enterainment, automotive & telecommunications industries

 See page 216 for a full profile of this company.

MONTGOMERY WARD HOLDING CORP.

One Montgomery Ward Plaza	CEO: Bernard F. Brennan	1994 Sales: $7,038 million
Chicago, IL 60671-0042	CFO: John L. Workman	1-Yr. Sales Change: 17.3%
Phone: 312-467-2000	HR: Robert A. Kasenter	Ownership: Privately Held
Fax: 312-467-3975	Employees: 58,600	

Retail - major department stores

 See pages 124–125 for a full profile of this company.

MORNINGSTAR INC.

225 W. Wacker Dr.	CEO: Joseph Mansueto	1995 Sales: $33.0 million
Chicago, IL 60606-1224	CFO: Patrick Geddes	1-Yr. Sales Change: 45.8%
Phone: 312-696-6000	HR: Liz Michaels	Ownership: Privately Held
Fax: 312-696-6001	Employees: 350	

Publishing - information on mutual funds, annuities & stocks, available in print, diskette, CD-ROM & online formats

 See page 217 for a full profile of this company.

MORTON INTERNATIONAL, INC.

100 N. Riverside Plaza
Chicago, IL 60606-1596
Phone: 312-807-2000
Fax: 312-807-2241

CEO: S. Jay Stewart
CFO: Thomas F. McDevitt
HR: Christopher K. Julsrud
Employees: 13,800

1995 Sales: $3,354.9 million
1-Yr. Sales Change: 16.6%
Exchange: NYSE
Symbol: MII

Chemicals - adhesives, coatings & specialty products; salt; automobile airbags

 See pages 126–127 for a full profile of this company.

MOTOR WORKS OF BARRINGTON, INC.

1475 Barrington Rd.
Barrington, IL 60010
Phone: 847-381-8900
Fax: 847-381-9396

CEO: Paul D. Tamraz
CFO: Tony Costabile
HR: Lynn Barr
Employees: 180

1994 Sales: $96 million
1-Yr. Sales Change: -17.2%
Ownership: Privately Held

Retail - new & used cars

MOTOROLA, INC.

1303 E. Algonquin Rd.
Schaumburg, IL 60196
Phone: 847-576-5000
Fax: 847-576-8003

CEO: Gary L. Tooker
CFO: Carl F. Koenemann
HR: James Donnelly
Employees: 132,000

1994 Sales: $22,245 million
1-Yr. Sales Change: 31.1%
Exchange: NYSE
Symbol: MOT

Electrical products - #1 world maker cellular telephones; networking equipment, semiconductors, switches, communications products, lighting ballasts, workstations & servers

 See pages 128–129 for a full profile of this company.

MUSEUM OF SCIENCE & INDUSTRY

57th & Lakeshore Dr.
Chicago, IL 60637
Phone: 312-684-1414
Fax: 312-684-2907

CEO: James S. Kahn
CFO: Frank W. Luerssen
HR: Elaine Vinson
Employees: 528

1994 Sales: $39.8 million
1-Yr. Sales Change: 3.1%

Museum

M-WAVE, INC.

216 Evergreen St.
Bensenville, IL 60106
Phone: 708-860-9542
Fax: 708-860-5350

CEO: Joseph A. Turek
CFO: Paul H. Schmitt
HR: —
Employees: 200

1994 Sales: $28 million
1-Yr. Sales Change: 42.9%
Exchange: Nasdaq
Symbol: MWAV

Electrical components - Teflon-coated printed circuit boards

NALCO CHEMICAL COMPANY

One Nalco Center
Naperville, IL 60563-1198
Phone: 708-305-1000
Fax: 708-305-2900

CEO: E. J. Mooney
CFO: William E. Buchholz
HR: James F. Lambe
Employees: 5,601

1994 Sales: $1,170.9 million
1-Yr. Sales Change: 3.9%
Exchange: NYSE
Symbol: NLC

Chemicals - specialty chemicals & services for water & industrial process treatment, pollution control, mining & mineral processing & other industrial processes

NATIONAL COUNCIL OF YOUNG MEN'S CHRISTIAN ASSOCIATIONS OF THE UNITED STATES OF AMERICA

101 N. Wacker Dr., Ste. 1400
Chicago, IL 60606
Phone: 312-977-0031
Fax: 312-977-9063

CEO: David Mercer
CFO: Michael Renehan
HR: Wyley Moore
Employees: 20,000

1994 Sales: $1,935 million
1-Yr. Sales Change: 9.8%

Leisure & recreational services - athletic facilities

NAVISTAR INTERNATIONAL CORPORATION

455 N. Cityfront Plaza Dr.
Chicago, IL 60611
Phone: 312-836-2000
Fax: 312-836-2192

CEO: John R. Horne
CFO: Robert C. Lannert
HR: John M. Sheahin
Employees: 14,910

1994 Sales: $5,337 million
1-Yr. Sales Change: 13.0%
Exchange: NYSE
Symbol: NAV

Trucks - medium & heavy

 See pages 130–131 for a full profile of this company.

NELSEN STEEL & WIRE COMPANY

9400 W. Belmont Ave.
Franklin Park, IL 60131
Phone: 847-671-9700
Fax: 847-671-6833

CEO: C. Davis Nelson II
CFO: Kevin Lamb
HR: Jack Stanley
Employees: 200

1994 Sales: $100 million
1-Yr. Sales Change: 17.6%
Ownership: Privately Held

Steel - cold-finished steel bars & cold heating wires

NELSON WESTERBERG, INC.

1500 Arthur Ave.
Elk Grove Village, IL 60007
Phone: 847-437-2080
Fax: 847-437-2199

CEO: John R. Westerberg
CFO: Ed Pionke
HR: Jeanne Madsen
Employees: 410

1994 Sales: $51.8 million
1-Yr. Sales Change: 15.4%
Ownership: Privately Held

Transportation - moving & storage

NEOPHARM, INC.

225 E. Deerpath, Ste. 250
Lake Forest, IL 60045
Phone: 847-295-8678
Fax: 847-295-8680

CEO: William C. Govier
CFO: Timothy R. Kelly
HR: —
Employees: 10

1994 Sales: $0 million
1-Yr. Sales Change: —
Ownership: Privately Held

Drugs - R&D of drugs for the diagnosis & treatment of cancer

NEWLY WEDS FOODS, INC.

4140 W. Fullerton Ave.
Chicago, IL 60639
Phone: 312-489-7000
Fax: 312-489-0530

CEO: Charles T. Angell
CFO: John Seely
HR: Bruce Nevers
Employees: 750

1994 Sales: $140.2 million
1-Yr. Sales Change: 8.0%
Ownership: Privately Held

Food - batter, breading, coating mixes, English muffins & spices

NICOR INC.

1844 Ferry Rd., PO Box 3014
Naperville, IL 60566-3014
Phone: 708-305-9500
Fax: 708-983-9328

CEO: Thomas L. Fisher
CFO: Donald W. Lohrentz
HR: John C. Flowers
Employees: 3,400

1994 Sales: $1,609.4 million
1-Yr. Sales Change: -3.9%
Exchange: NYSE
Symbol: GAS

Utility - gas distribution to upper third of Illinois (Northern Illinois Gas) & containerized shipping
between Palm Beach, FL & 22 ports in the Caribbean, Central America & Mexico (Tropical Shipping)

NIGHTINGALE-CONANT CORPORATION

7300 N. Lehigh Ave.
Niles, IL 60714
Phone: 847-647-0300
Fax: 847-647-7145

CEO: Vic Conant
CFO: Sid Lemer
HR: Michael Burgess
Employees: 250

1994 Sales: $64.1 million
1-Yr. Sales Change: 15.1%
Ownership: Privately Held

Publishing - motivational audio programs

NIPSCO INDUSTRIES, INC.

5265 Hohman Ave.
Hammond, IN 46320-1775
Phone: 219-853-5200
Fax: 219-647-6073

CEO: Gary L. Neale
CFO: Stephen P. Adik
HR: Owen C. Johnson Jr.
Employees: 4,391

1994 Sales: $1,676.4 million
1-Yr. Sales Change: 0.5%
Exchange: NYSE
Symbol: NI

Utility - electric power (Northern Indiana Public Service)

 See pages 132–133 for a full profile of this company.

NORTH AMERICAN PROCESSING COMPANY

1565 Ellinwood Ave.
Des Plaines, IL 60016
Phone: 847-803-1210
Fax: 847-803-1180

CEO: Robert N. Lenahan
CFO: Frank Lenahan
HR: Sue Arndt
Employees: 15

1994 Sales: $108.9 million
1-Yr. Sales Change: -27.8%
Ownership: Privately Held

Food - meat products importing & distribution

NORTH BANCSHARES, INC.

100 W. North Ave.
Chicago, IL 60610
Phone: 312-664-4320
Fax: 312-664-4289

CEO: Mary Ann Hass
CFO: Martin W. Trofimuk
HR: Vic Caputo
Employees: 35

1994 Sales: $6 million
1-Yr. Sales Change: —
Exchange: Nasdaq
Symbol: NBSI

Financial - savings & loans

NORTHEASTERN ILLINOIS UNIVERSITY

5500 N. St. Louis
Chicago, IL 60625
Phone: 312-583-4050
Fax: 312-794-2903

CEO: Salme H. Steinberg
CFO: Philip Weiss
HR: Gloria Carter
Employees: 2,004

1994 Sales: $68.4 million
1-Yr. Sales Change: 8.1%

Public university offering 35 undergraduate & 33 graduate degree programs

NORTHERN ILLINOIS UNIVERSITY

Normal Rd.
DeKalb, IL 60115
Phone: 815-753-1000
Fax: 815-753-0430

CEO: John E. La Tourette
CFO: Eddie R. Williams
HR: Steve Cunningham
Employees: 3,600

1994 Sales: $38.9 million
1-Yr. Sales Change: -4.0%

Public university offering over 50 undergraduate & more than 70 graduate degree programs

NORTHERN STATES FINANCIAL CORP.

1601 N. Lewis Ave.
Waukegan, IL 60085-1761
Phone: 847-244-6000
Fax: 847-244-6098

CEO: Fred Abdula
CFO: Howard A. Jaffe
HR: Colleen Cawaski
Employees: 163

1994 Sales: $30.1 million
1-Yr. Sales Change: -1.0%
Exchange: Nasdaq (SC)
Symbol: NSFC

Banks - Midwest

NORTHERN TRUST CORPORATION

50 S. La Salle St. Chicago, IL 60675 Phone: 312-630-6000 Fax: 312-630-1512	CEO: William A. Osborn CFO: Perry R. Pero HR: William Setterstrom Employees: 6,608	1994 Sales: $1,478.5 million 1-Yr. Sales Change: 17.5% Exchange: Nasdaq Symbol: NTRS

Banks - Midwest (The Northern Trust Company)

 See pages 134–135 for a full profile of this company.

NORTHFIELD LABORATORIES INC.

1560 Sherman Ave., Ste. 1000 Evanston, IL 60201-4422 Phone: 847-864-3500 Fax: 847-864-3577	CEO: Richard E. DeWoskin CFO: Jack J. Kogut HR: Jack J. Kogut Employees: 40	1995 Sales: $0 million 1-Yr. Sales Change: — Exchange: Nasdaq Symbol: NFLD

Biomedical & genetic products - blood transfusion alternatives development

NORTHWESTERN GOLF COMPANY

835 N. Church Court Elmhurst, IL 60126 Phone: 708-530-1425 Fax: 708-530-1610	CEO: Nat Rosasco CFO: Paul Runkel HR: — Employees: 500	1994 Sales: $95 million 1-Yr. Sales Change: 0.0% Ownership: Privately Held

Leisure & recreational products - golf clubs

NORTHWESTERN HEALTHCARE

980 N. Michigan Ave., Ste. 1500 Chicago, IL 60611 Phone: 312-335-6000 Fax: 312-335-6020	CEO: Bruce E. Spivey CFO: Tom Chan HR: — Employees: 16,427	1995 Sales: $1,680 million 1-Yr. Sales Change: 11.7% Ownership: Privately Held

Hospitals - system serving the Chicago area (member institutions include The Children's Memorial Medical Center, Evanston Hospital Corporation, Northwestern Memorial Hospital)

NORTHWESTERN UNIVERSITY

633 Clark St. Evanston, IL 60208-1117 Phone: 847-491-3741 Fax: 847-491-2376	CEO: Henry S. Bienen CFO: C. William Fischer HR: Guy E. Miller Employees: 5,650	1994 Sales: $676.3 million 1-Yr. Sales Change: 7.8%

Private, nondenominational university offering 95 undergraduate & 74 graduate degree programs

 See pages 136–137 for a full profile of this company.

NSBANCORP, INC.

2300 N. Western Ave.	CEO: Henry R. Smogolski	1994 Sales: $78.3 million
Chicago, IL 60647	CFO: Stephen G. Skiba	1-Yr. Sales Change: -19.3%
Phone: 312-489-2300	HR: Gary M. Smogolski	Exchange: Nasdaq
Fax: 312-489-7498	Employees: 402	Symbol: NSBI

Financial - savings & loans (Northwestern Savings Bank)

O'BRYAN BROTHERS, INC.

4220 W. Belmont Ave.	CEO: Michael L. O'Bryan	1994 Sales: $45 million
Chicago, IL 60641	CFO: Allan Bartina	1-Yr. Sales Change: 12.5%
Phone: 312-283-3000	HR: Carroll Brahm	Ownership: Privately Held
Fax: 312-283-7816	Employees: 480	

Apparel - lingerie

OFFICE ELECTRONICS INCORPORATED

865 W. Irving Park Rd.	CEO: David B. Sheshull	1994 Sales: $89.3 million
Itasca, IL 60143	CFO: Robert Houston	1-Yr. Sales Change: -5.2%
Phone: 708-285-9000	HR: Amy Schuett	Ownership: Privately Held
Fax: 708-285-9110	Employees: 423	

Paper - business forms (d/b/a OEI Business Forms)

OIL-DRI CORPORATION OF AMERICA

410 N. Michigan Ave., Ste. 400	CEO: Richard M. Jaffee	1995 Sales: $152.9 million
Chicago, IL 60611	CFO: Richard L. Pietrowski	1-Yr. Sales Change: 9.4%
Phone: 312-321-1515	HR: Karen Jaffe Cofsky	Exchange: NYSE
Fax: 312-321-1271	Employees: 665	Symbol: ODC

Chemicals - cat box absorbents; industrial & environmental absorbents

OLD REPUBLIC INTERNATIONAL CORPORATION

307 N. Michigan Ave.	CEO: A. C. Zucaro	1994 Sales: $1,679 million
Chicago, IL 60601	CFO: Paul D. Adams	1-Yr. Sales Change: -3.3%
Phone: 312-346-8100	HR: Charles Strizak	Exchange: NYSE
Fax: 312-726-0309	Employees: 5,400	Symbol: ORI

Insurance - specialty & general programs in property & liability, title, mortgage guaranty, life & disability

OLD SECOND BANCORP INC.

37 S. River St.
Aurora, IL 60507
Phone: 708-892-0202
Fax: 708-892-9630

Banks - Midwest

CEO: James Benson
CFO: Ronald J. Carlson
HR: Arvan Reese
Employees: 340

1994 Sales: $48.9 million
1-Yr. Sales Change: 4.5%
Exchange: Nasdaq
Symbol: OSBC

OLD WORLD INDUSTRIES, INC.

4065 Commercial Rd.
Northbrook, IL 60062-1851
Phone: 847-559-2000
Fax: 847-559-1329

CEO: Tom Hurvis
CFO: Rick Schweiger
HR: Nancy Sidner
Employees: 135

1994 Est. Sales: $1,000 mil.
1-Yr. Sales Change: —
Ownership: Privately Held

Diversified operations - antifreeze (Peak, Full Force); spark plugs (SplitFire); cotton exporting to the Far East & Europe; golf & T-shirts

OPTION CARE, INC.

100 Corporate North, Ste. 212
Bannockburn, IL 60015
Phone: 847-615-1690
Fax: 847-615-1794

Health care - outpatient & home

CEO: John N. Kapoor
CFO: J. Jeffrey Fox
HR: —
Employees: 379

1994 Sales: $59.4 million
1-Yr. Sales Change: 18.3%
Exchange: Nasdaq
Symbol: OPTN

THE ORCHESTRAL ASSOCIATION

220 S. Michigan Ave.
Chicago, IL 60604
Phone: 312-435-8122
Fax: 312-786-1207

CEO: Henry Fogel
CFO: Tom Hallett
HR: Ellen Romberg
Employees: 98

1995 Sales: $24.2 million
1-Yr. Sales Change: 2.1%

Foundation supporting the Chicago Symphony Orchestra

OUTBOARD MARINE CORPORATION

100 Sea-Horse Dr.
Waukegan, IL 60085
Phone: 847-689-6200
Fax: 847-689-5555

CEO: Harry W. Bowman
CFO: Jim Maurice
HR: Richard H. Medland
Employees: 8,500

1995 Sales: $1,078 million
1-Yr. Sales Change: 4.2%
Exchange: NYSE
Symbol: OM

Leisure & recreational products - powerboats (Chris-Craft) & marine motors (Johnson, Evinrude)

See pages 138–139 for a full profile of this company.

OXFORD INTERNATIONAL LTD.

4237 W. 42nd Place	CEO: Michael Oslac	1994 Sales: $60 million
Chicago, IL 60632	CFO: Richard Canman	1-Yr. Sales Change: 19.5%
Phone: 312-927-3715	HR: Anne Mueller	Ownership: Privately Held
Fax: 312-927-5308	Employees: 750	

Audio & video home products - audio systems to the automotive industry (Top Down Surround Sound)

PADDOCK PUBLICATIONS, INC.

217 W. Campbell St.	CEO: Stuart Paddock Jr.	1994 Sales: $71 million
Arlington Heights, IL 60006	CFO: Robert Donahue	1-Yr. Sales Change: 10.9%
Phone: 847-870-3600	HR: —	Ownership: Privately Held
Fax: 847-818-9187	Employees: 575	

Publishing - newspapers (Daily Herald)

PAMPERED CHEF LTD.

350 S. Rte. 53	CEO: Dorris Christopher	1995 Est. Sales: $200 mil.
Addison, IL 60101	CFO: Dorris Christopher	1-Yr. Sales Change: —
Phone: 708-261-8900	HR: Dorris Christopher	Ownership: Privately Held
Fax: 708-261-8586	Employees: 20,400	

Retail - direct sales of gourmet kitchen & cooking supplies

PARKVIEW METAL PRODUCTS, INC.

4931 W. Armitage Ave.	CEO: Nels Leutwiler	1994 Est. Sales: $50 mil.
Chicago, IL 60639	CFO: Bob Killelea	1-Yr. Sales Change: 5.9%
Phone: 312-622-8414	HR: John Kingma	Ownership: Privately Held
Fax: 312-622-8773	Employees: 383	

Metal products - hand-tooled precision metal stampings & assemblies

PATERNO IMPORTS LTD.

2701 S. Western Ave.	CEO: Anthony J. Terlato	1994 Sales: $115 million
Chicago, IL 60608	CFO: John Scribner	1-Yr. Sales Change: 4.5%
Phone: 312-247-8000	HR: Pat Dixon	Ownership: Privately Held
Fax: 312-247-8734	Employees: 357	

Beverages - wine marketing & distribution

PATRICK DEALER GROUP

526 Mall Dr.
Schaumburg, IL 60173
Phone: 847-605-4000
Fax: 847-619-4510

CEO: Hanley Dawson III
CFO: Marty Stilwell
HR: —
Employees: 275

1994 Sales: $173 million
1-Yr. Sales Change: 10.2%
Ownership: Privately Held

Retail - new & used cars

PAUL H. SCHWENDENER, INC.

400 N. State St.
Chicago, IL 60610
Phone: 312-321-6160
Fax: 312-321-0286

CEO: Michael S. Schwendener
CFO: James Arnold
HR: Joseph Zasky
Employees: 250

1994 Sales: $141 million
1-Yr. Sales Change: 6.8%
Ownership: Privately Held

Building - general contractor & construction management

PC QUOTE, INC.

300 S. Wacker Dr., Ste. 300
Chicago, IL 60606
Phone: 312-913-2800
Fax: 312-913-2900

CEO: Louis J. Morgan
CFO: Richard F. Chappetto
HR: Darlene E. Czaja
Employees: 76

1994 Sales: $12.9 million
1-Yr. Sales Change: 5.7%
Exchange: AMEX
Symbol: PQT

Financial - electronic stock quotation service

See page 218 for a full profile of this company.

PC WHOLESALE

444 Scott Dr.
Bloomingdale, IL 60108
Phone: 708-307-3636
Fax: 708-307-2450

CEO: Chuck Wolande
CFO: David Kielman
HR: Christine Schuver
Employees: 40

1994 Sales: $65 million
1-Yr. Sales Change: 66.7%
Ownership: Privately Held

Computers - PC product distribution

PEAPOD, INC.

1033 University Pl.
Evanston, IL 60201
Phone: 847-492-8900
Fax: 847-492-0172

CEO: Andrew Parkinson
CFO: Dave Beedie
HR: Toya Campbell
Employees: 450

1995 Est. Sales: $20 mil.
1-Yr. Sales Change: —
Ownership: Privately Held

Computers - online shopping service that delivers groceries in Chicago & San Francisco

PEOPLES ENERGY CORPORATION

122 S. Michigan Ave.	CEO: Richard E. Terry	1995 Sales: $1,033.4 million
Chicago, IL 60603	CFO: Kenneth S. Balaskovits	1-Yr. Sales Change: -19.2%
Phone: 312-431-4000	HR: John Ibach	Exchange: NYSE
Fax: 312-431-0112	Employees: 3,278	Symbol: PGL

Utility - gas distribution (People's Gas Light & Coke, North Shore Gas Company)

PEPPER COS. INC.

643 N. Orleans St.	CEO: Richard S. Pepper	1994 Sales: $485.4 million
Chicago, IL 60610	CFO: Thomas M. O'Leary	1-Yr. Sales Change: 19.9%
Phone: 312-266-4703	HR: John Beasley	Ownership: Privately Held
Fax: 312-266-2792	Employees: 921	

Building - general contracting

PERSONAL CREATIONS, INC.

530 Executive Dr.	CEO: Daniel Randolph	1994 Sales: $5.6 million
Willowbrook, IL 60521	CFO: Gene Wolf	1-Yr. Sales Change: 51.4%
Phone: 708-655-3200	HR: Kathy Meyer	Ownership: Privately Held
Fax: 708-655-3299	Employees: 70	

Retail - personalized gifts, including sweatshirts, bathrobes & decorations

PHOENIX DUFF & PHELPS CORPORATION

55 E. Monroe St., Ste. 3600	CEO: Francis E. Jeffries	1994 Sales: $65.9 million
Chicago, IL 60603	CFO: Lorrie P. Zogg	1-Yr. Sales Change: -18.8%
Phone: 312-263-2610	HR: Cynthia Tupak	Exchange: NYSE
Fax: 312-263-3149	Employees: 290	Symbol: DUF

Financial - investment management

PINNACLE BANC GROUP, INC.

2215 York Rd., Ste. 208	CEO: John J. Gleason	1994 Sales: $44 million
Oak Brook, IL 60521	CFO: Sara J. Mikuta	1-Yr. Sales Change: -20.1%
Phone: 708-574-3550	HR: Mary Kawas	Exchange: Nasdaq (SC)
Fax: 708-780-7342	Employees: 282	Symbol: PINN

Banks - Midwest

PIONEER FINANCIAL SERVICES, INC.

1750 E. Golf Rd.	CEO: Peter W. Nauert	1994 Sales: $774.2 million
Schaumburg, IL 60173	CFO: David L. Vickers	1-Yr. Sales Change: 10.7%
Phone: 847-995-0400	HR: Beverly Long	Exchange: NYSE
Fax: 847-413-7264	Employees: 1,570	Symbol: PFS

Insurance - accident & health

PITTWAY CORPORATION

200 S. Wacker Dr., Ste. 700	CEO: King Harris	1994 Sales: $778 million
Chicago, IL 60606-5802	CFO: Paul R. Gauvreau	1-Yr. Sales Change: 19.7%
Phone: 312-831-1070	HR: —	Exchange: AMEX
Fax: 312-831-0808	Employees: 5,400	Symbol: PRYA

Diversified operations - burglar & fire alarms (Ademco Security); trade magazine publishing (Penton); real estate

 See page 219 for a full profile of this company.

PLATINUM ENTERTAINMENT, INC.

2001 Butterfield Rd., Ste. 1400	CEO: Steve Devick	1994 Sales: $10.4 million
Downers Grove, IL 60515	CFO: Shannon Saegor	1-Yr. Sales Change: —
Phone: 708-769-0033	HR: —	Ownership: Privately Held
Fax: 708-769-0049	Employees: 87	

Leisure & recreational products - gospel music recordings

PLATINUM TECHNOLOGY, INC.

1815 S. Meyers Rd.	CEO: Andrew J. Filipowski	1994 Sales: $95.7 million
Oakbrook Terrace, IL 60181	CFO: Michael P. Cullinane	1-Yr. Sales Change: 53.9%
Phone: 708-620-5000	HR: Jennifer Werneke	Exchange: Nasdaq
Fax: 708-691-0710	Employees: 743	Symbol: PLAT

Computers - database management software for mainframes

 See page 220 for a full profile of this company.

PLAYBOY ENTERPRISES, INC.

680 N. Lake Shore Dr.	CEO: Christie Hefner	1995 Sales: $247.2 million
Chicago, IL 60611	CFO: David I. Chemerow	1-Yr. Sales Change: 12.9%
Phone: 312-751-8000	HR: Denise M. Bindelglass	Exchange: NYSE
Fax: 312-751-2818	Employees: 593	Symbol: PLA

Publishing - periodicals (Playboy magazine); cable channel; catalog & product marketing

 See page 221 for a full profile of this company.

PLUNKETT FURNITURE COMPANY

2500 W. Golf Rd.	CEO: Hugh Plunkett	1994 Sales: $42.5 million
Hoffman Estates, IL 60196	CFO: John Plunkett	1-Yr. Sales Change: 7.6%
Phone: 847-843-9000	HR: Bernice Bass	Ownership: Privately Held
Fax: 847-843-9096	Employees: 35	

Retail - home furnishings

PORTEC, INC.

One Hundred Field Dr., Ste. 120	CEO: Michael T. Yonker	1994 Sales: $97.6 million
Lake Forest, IL 60045	CFO: Nancy A. Kindl	1-Yr. Sales Change: 26.9%
Phone: 847-735-2800	HR: Patricia A. Riccio	Exchange: NYSE
Fax: 847-735-2828	Employees: 779	Symbol: POR

Diversified operations - construction & railroad equipment, materials handling

POWER CONTRACTING & ENGINEERING CORPORATION

1895 Rohlwing Rd.	CEO: Tom Settles	1994 Sales: $250 million
Rolling Meadows, IL 60008	CFO: Dave Anderskow	1-Yr. Sales Change: 4.2%
Phone: 847-259-1100	HR: Sharon Kaiser	Ownership: Privately Held
Fax: 847-259-3026	Employees: 125	

Building - commercial general contracting & construction management

PRECISION TWIST DRILL COMPANY

One Precision Plaza	CEO: Arthur R. Beck	1994 Sales: $86.2 million
Crystal Lake, IL 60014	CFO: Norm Margolin	1-Yr. Sales Change: 7.5%
Phone: 815-459-2040	HR: Dan McMullen	Ownership: Privately Held
Fax: 815-459-2804	Employees: 1,470	

Machine tolls - high-speed steel & carbide cutting tools

PREFERRED STAFFING

1600 Golf Rd., Ste. 110	CEO: Bill Cumming	1994 Sales: $10.9 million
Rolling Meadows, IL 60008	CFO: Glenda Pears	1-Yr. Sales Change: —
Phone: 847-981-8140	HR: —	Ownership: Privately Held
Fax: 847-290-1628	Employees: 1,061	

Personnel - temporary-employment services

PREMARK INTERNATIONAL, INC.

1717 Deerfield Rd.	CEO: Warren L. Batts	1994 Sales: $3,450.8 million
Deerfield, IL 60015	CFO: Lawrence B. Skatoff	1-Yr. Sales Change: 11.4%
Phone: 847-405-6000	HR: James C. Coleman	Exchange: NYSE
Fax: 847-405-6013	Employees: 24,000	Symbol: PMI

Diversified operations - plastic containers (Tupperware); electrical appliances (West Bend Co.); flooring (Florida Tile); food equipment

 See pages 140–141 for a full profile of this company.

PREMIER FINANCIAL SERVICES, INC.

27 W. Main St.	CEO: Richard L. Geach	1994 Sales: $43.2 million
Freeport, IL 60132	CFO: David L. Murray	1-Yr. Sales Change: 18.7%
Phone: 815-233-3671	HR: Jack Croffoot	Exchange: Nasdaq
Fax: 815-233-3697	Employees: 338	Symbol: PREM

Banks - Midwest (First Bank North, First Bank South, First National Bank of Northbrook, First Security Bank of Cary Grove)

PRIME RESIDENTIAL, INC.

77 W. Wacker Dr., 40th Fl.	CEO: David M. Glickman	1994 Sales: $35.1 million
Chicago, IL 60423	CFO: Adam D. Peterson	1-Yr. Sales Change: 75.5%
Phone: 312-917-1600	HR: Margaret Shontz	Exchange: Nasdaq
Fax: 312-782-5867	Employees: 240	Symbol: PRES

Real estate investment trust - apartment properties, primarily in Arizona, Illinois, & Texas

QST INDUSTRIES INC.

231 S. Jefferson St.	CEO: Ely Lionheart	1994 Sales: $250 million
Chicago, IL 60661	CFO: Jeffrey A. Carlevato	1-Yr. Sales Change: 19.0%
Phone: 312-930-9400	HR: Andrea Glavka	Ownership: Privately Held
Fax: 312-930-0118	Employees: 400	

Textiles - trim components, including pocketing, lining, interlining, waistbands & cut pockets for the apparel industry

THE QUAKER OATS COMPANY

321 N. Clark St., PO Box 049001	CEO: William D. Smithburg	1995 Sales: $6,365.2 million
Chicago, IL 60604-9001	CFO: Robert S. Thomason	1-Yr. Sales Change: 6.9%
Phone: 312-222-7111	HR: Douglas J. Ralston	Exchange: NYSE
Fax: 312-222-8304	Employees: 17,000	Symbol: OAT

Food - cereals, beverages (Ardmore Farms, Gatorade, Snapple), food (Aunt Jemima, Celeste, Rice-A-Roni)

 See pages 142–143 for a full profile of this company.

QUALITY SCREW & NUT COMPANY

101 Frontier Way	CEO: Art Wondrasek	1994 Sales: $31.8 million
Bensenville, IL 60106	CFO: Gary Mitchell	1-Yr. Sales Change: 22.3%
Phone: 708-595-0000	HR: Jackie Udell	Ownership: Privately Held
Fax: 708-595-1440	Employees: 202	

Metal products - cold-headed screws & nuts

QUILL CORPORATION

100 Schelter Rd.	CEO: Jack Miller	1994 Sales: $418 million
Lincolnshire, IL 60069-3621	CFO: Arnold Miller	1-Yr. Sales Change: 8.9%
Phone: 847-634-6650	HR: Philip Petrilli	Ownership: Privately Held
Fax: 847-634-5816	Employees: 1,248	

Business services - business-to-business direct marketing of office & warehouse supplies

 See page 222 for a full profile of this company.

QUIXOTE CORPORATION

One E. Wacker Dr.	CEO: Philip E. Rollhaus Jr.	1995 Sales: $185.4 million
Chicago, IL 60601	CFO: Myron R. Shain	1-Yr. Sales Change: 4.8%
Phone: 312-467-6755	HR: Dorothy French	Exchange: Nasdaq
Fax: 312-467-1356	Employees: 1,599	Symbol: QUIX

Diversified operations - highway safety devices; stenographic equipment; compact discs

 See page 223 for a full profile of this company.

RACING CHAMPIONS, INC.

800 Roosevelt Rd., Ste. C-320	CEO: Robert Dods	1994 Sales: $43.2 million
Glen Ellyn, IL 60137	CFO: Curt Stoelting	1-Yr. Sales Change: —
Phone: 708-790-3507	HR: Barb Gilbertsen	Ownership: Privately Held
Fax: 708-790-9474	Employees: 25	

Leisure & recreational products - die-cast motor sports car replicas

RAND MCNALLY & COMPANY

8255 N. Central Park Ave.	CEO: Andrew McNally IV	1994 Sales: $439 million
Skokie, IL 60076-2970	CFO: James J. Habschmidt	1-Yr. Sales Change: 11.1%
Phone: 847-329-8100	HR: Kurt D. Steele	Ownership: Privately Held
Fax: 847-673-0539	Employees: 4,200	

Publishing - maps, atlases & other geographic information, including travel guide CD-ROMs (TripMaker); airline & surface transportation tickets & baggage tags; specialty labels, tags & cards

 See page 224 for a full profile of this company.

RAULAND-BORG CORPORATION

3450 W. Oakton St.	CEO: William Krucks	1994 Sales: $44.1 million
Skokie, IL 60076	CFO: Rick Stockfleet	1-Yr. Sales Change: 7.6%
Phone: 847-679-0900	HR: Maria Anders	Ownership: Privately Held
Fax: 847-679-6219	Employees: 285	

Telecommunications equipment - professional sound & communications equipment

RESTAURANT CO.

One Pierce Place, Ste. 100E	CEO: Donald Smith	1994 Sales: $853.7 million
Itasca, IL 60143	CFO: Mike Donahoe	1-Yr. Sales Change: 3.0%
Phone: 708-250-0471	HR: Jeanne Scott	Ownership: Privately Held
Fax: 708-250-0382	Employees: 35,000	

Retail - restaurants (Perkins, Friendly's Ice Cream)

RESTONIC CORPORATION

9450 W. Brynmawr	CEO: Ed Scott	1994 Sales: $130 million
Rosemont, IL 60018	CFO: Cheryl Prindle	1-Yr. Sales Change: 1.6%
Phone: 312-346-9044	HR: Cheryl Prindle	Ownership: Privately Held
Fax: 312-671-1676	Employees: 1,115	

Furniture - mattresses (ErgoSleep)

REYNOLDS MACHINE & TOOL CORPORATION

2033 N. 17th Ave.	CEO: James P. Reynolds	1994 Sales: $33.5 million
Melrose Park, IL 60160	CFO: Don Lopotko	1-Yr. Sales Change: 9.8%
Phone: 708-344-3280	HR: Roseanna Rich	Ownership: Privately Held
Fax: 708-344-0723	Employees: 85	

Wholesale distribution - machine tools & industrial supplies

RHC/SPACEMASTER CORPORATION

1400 N. 25th Ave.	CEO: A. R. Umans	1994 Sales: $126.5 million
Melrose Park, IL 60160	CFO: Stanley Jewell	1-Yr. Sales Change: 18.8%
Phone: 708-345-2500	HR: Linda Atkinson	Ownership: Privately Held
Fax: 708-345-3823	Employees: 1,350	

Furniture - retail store fixtures

RICHARDSON ELECTRONICS, LTD.

40W267 Keslinger Rd.	CEO: Edward J. Richardson	1995 Sales: $208.1 million
LaFox, IL 60147-0393	CFO: William J. Garry	1-Yr. Sales Change: 20.9%
Phone: 708-208-2340	HR: Joseph C. Grill	Exchange: Nasdaq
Fax: 708-208-2550	Employees: 540	Symbol: RELL

Electronics - electron tubes & semiconductors distribution

RICHCO PLASTIC COMPANY

5825 N. Tripp Ave.	CEO: Craig Richardson	1994 Sales: $60.4 million
Chicago, IL 60646	CFO: Frank Bartman	1-Yr. Sales Change: 31.3%
Phone: 312-539-4060	HR: Sandra Varela	Ownership: Privately Held
Fax: 312-509-6683	Employees: 698	

Plastic fasteners

RIDGE PONTIAC

1533 River Rd.	CEO: Kevin Mize	1994 Sales: $37.8 million
Des Plaines, IL 60018	CFO: George Millios	1-Yr. Sales Change: -13.7%
Phone: 847-824-3141	HR: Sue Bursonia	Ownership: Privately Held
Fax: 847-824-7638	Employees: 70	

Retail - new & used cars

RITTENHOUSE, INC.

250 S. Northwest Hwy.	CEO: Simon Blattner	1994 Sales: $135 million
Park Ridge, IL 60068	CFO: John Peterka	1-Yr. Sales Change: 3.8%
Phone: 847-692-9130	HR: Diana Schultz	Ownership: Privately Held
Fax: 847-692-9820	Employees: 750	

Office equipment & supplies - paper & business machine supplies

RIVER FOREST BANCORP, INC.

3959 N. Lincoln Ave.	CEO: Robert J. Glickman	1994 Sales: $127.8 million
Chicago, IL 60613	CFO: David A. Dykstra	1-Yr. Sales Change: 12.2%
Phone: 312-549-7100	HR: Barbara J. Kessner	Exchange: Nasdaq
Fax: 312-989-5158	Employees: 581	Symbol: RFBC

Banks - Midwest

RODMAN & RENSHAW CAPITAL GROUP INC.

233 S. Wacker Dr., 45th Fl.	CEO: Charles W. Daggs III	1994 Sales: $77.3 million
Chicago, IL 60606	CFO: John T. Hague	1-Yr. Sales Change: -11.5%
Phone: 312-526-2000	HR: Charles Henry	Exchange: NYSE
Fax: 312-526-2798	Employees: 490	Symbol: RR

Financial - investment management

ROSE PACKING COMPANY

65 S. Barrington Rd.	CEO: William R. Rose	1994 Sales: $100 million
Barrington, IL 60010	CFO: Bob Bell	1-Yr. Sales Change: 0.0%
Phone: 847-381-5700	HR: Bob Bell	Ownership: Privately Held
Fax: 847-381-9424	Employees: 600	

Food - fresh & processed pork

ROTARY INTERNATIONAL

1560 Sherman Ave.	CEO: Geoffrey Large	1994 Sales: $59.0 million
Evanston, IL 60201	CFO: Mary Wolfenberger	1-Yr. Sales Change: 11.5%
Phone: 847-866-3243	HR: Calvin Henderson	
Fax: 847-328-8554	Employees: 450	

Membership organization - business & charitable activities

 See pages 144–145 for a full profile of this company.

R. R. DONNELLEY & SONS COMPANY

77 W. Wacker Dr.	CEO: John R. Walter	1994 Sales: $4,888.8 million
Chicago, IL 60601	CFO: Cheryl A. Francis	1-Yr. Sales Change: 11.4%
Phone: 312-326-8000	HR: Steven J. Baumgartner	Exchange: NYSE
Fax: 312-326-8543	Employees: 39,000	Symbol: DNY

Printing - telephone books, magazines, mail-order catalogs, computer manuals; disk duplication & other computer services

 See pages 146–147 for a full profile of this company.

RUSH-PRESBYTERIAN-ST. LUKE'S MEDICAL CENTER

1653 W. Congress Pkwy.	CEO: Leon M. Henikoff	1994 Sales: $745.5 million
Chicago, IL 60612	CFO: Kevin J. Necas	1-Yr. Sales Change: -17.8%
Phone: 312-942-5000	HR: —	
Fax: 312-942-5581	Employees: 8,511	

Hospitals - not-for-profit system comprised of 8 hospitals in the Chicago area

RYKOFF-SEXTON, INC.

1050 Warrenville Rd.	CEO: Mark Van Stekelenburg	1995 Sales: $1,569 million
Lisle, IL 60532	CFO: Richard J. Martin	1-Yr. Sales Change: 2.9%
Phone: 708-964-1414	HR: Robert J. Harter Jr.	Exchange: NYSE
Fax: 708-971-7900	Employees: 5,330	Symbol: RYK

Food - wholesale to restaurants, health care facilities, schools & colleges, hotels & airlines

RYMER FOODS INC.

4600 S. Packers Ave., Ste. 400	CEO: John L. Patten	1994 Sales: $166.7 million
Chicago, IL 60609	CFO: Ludwig A. Streck	1-Yr. Sales Change: 12.6%
Phone: 312-927-7777	HR: Ludwig A. Streck	Exchange: NYSE
Fax: 312-650-0500	Employees: 408	Symbol: RYR

Food - frozen meat & seafood entrees for restaurant chains & retail consumption

SAFETY-KLEEN CORP.

1000 N. Randall Rd.	CEO: John G. Johnson Jr.	1994 Sales: $791.3 million
Elgin, IL 60123	CFO: Robert W. Willmschen Jr.	1-Yr. Sales Change: -0.5%
Phone: 847-697-8460	HR: Robert J. Burian	Exchange: NYSE
Fax: 847-468-8560	Employees: 6,600	Symbol: SK

Pollution control equipment & services - contaminated fluid recycling

See pages 148–149 for a full profile of this company.

SAFEWAY INSURANCE COMPANY

790 Pasquinelli Dr.	CEO: William Parrillo	1994 Sales: $169.9 million
Westmont, IL 60559	CFO: Jack Ikenaga	1-Yr. Sales Change: 12.9%
Phone: 708-887-8300	HR: Mary Hels	Ownership: Privately Held
Fax: 708-887-9236	Employees: 392	

Insurance - property & casualty

SAGE ENTERPRISES INC.

999 E. Touhy Ave.	CEO: Gary Greenberg	1994 Est. Sales: $243 mil.
Des Plaines, IL 60018	CFO: Gary Greenberg	1-Yr. Sales Change: 0.0%
Phone: 847-827-0066	HR: Donna Gosciej	Ownership: Privately Held
Fax: 847-827-6420	Employees: 350	

Food - wholesale specialty foods to grocers

ST. PAUL BANCORP, INC.

6700 W. North Ave.
Chicago, IL 60635
Phone: 312-622-5000
Fax: 312-804-2285

Financial - savings & loans

CEO: Joseph C. Scully
CFO: Robert N. Parke
HR: Robert N. Pfeiffer
Employees: 1,103

1994 Sales: $283 million
1-Yr. Sales Change: -2.2%
Exchange: Nasdaq
Symbol: SPBC

SALTON/MAXIM HOUSEWARES, INC.

550 Business Center Dr.
Mount Prospect, IL 60056
Phone: 847-803-4600
Fax: 847-803-1186

Appliances - household

CEO: Leonhard Dreimann
CFO: William B. Rue
HR: Juanita Rusin
Employees: 72

1995 Sales: $77 million
1-Yr. Sales Change: 57.8%
Exchange: Nasdaq
Symbol: SALT

S&C ELECTRIC COMPANY

6601 N. Ridge Blvd.
Chicago, IL 60626
Phone: 312-338-1000
Fax: 312-338-8079

Electrical products - high-voltage switches

CEO: John R. Conrad
CFO: Stan Slabas
HR: Stan Slabas
Employees: 1,719

1994 Sales: $201.9 million
1-Yr. Sales Change: 1.5%
Ownership: Privately Held

SARA LEE CORPORATION

3 First National Plaza
Chicago, IL 60602-4260
Phone: 312-726-2600
Fax: 312-726-3712

Diversified operations - foods & coffee; hosiery (Hanes, L'eggs); shoe care (Kiwi) & leather goods (Coach)

CEO: John H. Bryan
CFO: Judith A. Sprieser
HR: Gary C. Grom
Employees: 149,100

1995 Sales: $17,719 million
1-Yr. Sales Change: 14.1%
Exchange: NYSE
Symbol: SLE

See pages 150–151 for a full profile of this company.

SAYERS COMPUTER SOURCE

1150 Feehanville Dr.
Mount Prospect, IL 60056
Phone: 847-391-4040
Fax: 847-294-0750

Computer - hardware & software distribution; systems integration services

CEO: Gale Sayers
CFO: Ann Chiodo
HR: Jeanette Kratz
Employees: 70

1994 Sales: $53 million
1-Yr. Sales Change: 32.5%
Ownership: Privately Held

SCHAWK, INC.

1695 River Rd.	CEO: David A. Schawk	1994 Sales: $186.1 million
Des Plaines, IL 60018	CFO: Marie M. Graul	1-Yr. Sales Change: 10.1%
Phone: 847-827-9494	HR: Robert E. Drew	Exchange: NYSE
Fax: 847-827-1264	Employees: 1,902	Symbol: SGK

Printing - prepress; injection-molded filtration devices for the automotive, health care, industrial & consumer markets

SCHUMACHER ELECTRIC CORPORATION

7474 N. Rogers Ave.	CEO: Donald A. Schumacher	1994 Sales: $57.3 million
Chicago, IL 60626	CFO: Ralph Cernohouz	1-Yr. Sales Change: 1.1%
Phone: 312-973-1600	HR: Shirley Wiet	Ownership: Privately Held
Fax: 312-973-7781	Employees: 790	

Electrical products - battery chargers & custom transformers

SCHWARZ PAPER COMPANY

8338 Austin Ave.	CEO: Andrew J. McKenna	1994 Sales: $208.5 million
Morton Grove, IL 60053	CFO: Thomas Reger	1-Yr. Sales Change: 18.8%
Phone: 847-966-2550	HR: Harold Chukerman	Ownership: Privately Held
Fax: 847-966-1271	Employees: 520	

Paper - packaging & promotional materials

SCOTSMAN INDUSTRIES, INC.

775 Corporate Woods Pkwy.	CEO: Richard C. Osborne	1994 Sales: $266.6 million
Vernon Hills, IL 60061	CFO: Donald D. Holmes	1-Yr. Sales Change: 62.6%
Phone: 847-215-4500	HR: Richard M. Holden	Exchange: NYSE
Fax: 847-913-9844	Employees: 2,182	Symbol: SCT

Commercial ice machines (Scotsman, Crystal Tips), food prep & storage equipment (Delfield, Shellyglas, Shellymatic), drink dispensing equipment (Booth) primarily for the food service industry

 See page 225 for a full profile of this company.

SEARS, ROEBUCK AND CO.

Sears Tower	CEO: Arthur C. Martinez	1994 Sales: $53,920 million
Chicago, IL 60684	CFO: James M. Denny	1-Yr. Sales Change: 6.1%
Phone: 312-875-2500	HR: Anthony J. Rucci	Exchange: NYSE
Fax: 312-875-8351	Employees: 360,570	Symbol: S

Retail - major department stores

 See pages 152–153 for a full profile of this company.

SEGERDAHL CORPORATION

1351 S. Wheeling Rd.
Wheeling, IL 60090
Phone: 847-541-1080
Fax: 847-419-3337

CEO: Earl E. Segerdahl
CFO: John Annel
HR: Eileen Weglarz
Employees: 235

1994 Sales: $75 million
1-Yr. Sales Change: 25.0%
Ownership: Privately Held

Printing - commercial; mailing & distribution

SEIGLE'S HOME & BUILDING CENTERS, INC.

1331 Davis Rd.
Elgin, IL 60123
Phone: 847-742-2000
Fax: 847-697-6521

CEO: Mark Seigle
CFO: D. Vahey
HR: Rick Motler
Employees: 760

1994 Sales: $151.1 million
1-Yr. Sales Change: 10.1%
Ownership: Privately Held

Building products - retail

SEKO-AIR FREIGHT, INC.

790 Busse Rd.
Elk Grove Village, IL 60007
Phone: 847-806-4800
Fax: 847-806-1270

CEO: Peter Baker
CFO: William Wascher
HR: Marilyn Satkiewicz
Employees: 800

1994 Sales: $92.8 million
1-Yr. Sales Change: 17.3%
Ownership: Privately Held

Transportation - domestic & international air freight forwarding

SELFIX, INC.

4501 W. 47th St.
Chicago, IL 60632
Phone: 312-890-1010
Fax: 312-890-0523

CEO: James R. Tennant
CFO: James E. Winslow
HR: Bob Anderson
Employees: 385

1994 Sales: $41 million
1-Yr. Sales Change: 3.3%
Exchange: Nasdaq
Symbol: SLFX

Housewares - plastic hangers & shelves

SENDAI MEDIA GROUP

1920 Highland Ave., 2nd Fl.
Lombard, IL 60148
Phone: 708-916-7222
Fax: 708-916-7227

CEO: Steve Harris
CFO: Lambert Smith
HR: Lori Gignac
Employees: 105

1994 Sales: $27.3 million
1-Yr. Sales Change: —
Ownership: Privately Held

Publishing - computer & video-game magazines (The Internet Underground, Electronic Gaming Monthly, Computer Game Review); online entertainment forum (NUKE Internet Interface)

SERTA INC.

2800 River Rd.
Des Plaines, IL 60018
Phone: 847-699-9300
Fax: 847-699-8380

Furniture - mattresses & box springs

CEO: Edward F. Lilly
CFO: Rich Domovic
HR: —
Employees: 2,000

1994 Sales: $470 million
1-Yr. Sales Change: 23.7%
Ownership: Privately Held

SERVICEMASTER LIMITED PARTNERSHIP

2300 Warrenville Rd.
Downers Grove, IL 60515
Phone: 708-271-1300
Fax: 708-271-5753

Building - maintenance & services

CEO: Carlos H. Cantu
CFO: Ernest J. Mrozek
HR: Debra Kass
Employees: 34,000

1994 Sales: $2,985.2 million
1-Yr. Sales Change: 8.2%
Exchange: NYSE
Symbol: SVM

See pages 154–155 for a full profile of this company.

SEYFARTH, SHAW, FAIRWEATHER & GERALDSON

55 E. Monroe St., Ste. 4200
Chicago, IL 60603
Phone: 312-346-8000
Fax: 312-269-8869

Law firm

CEO: Andrew R. Laidlaw
CFO: James J. McGowan
HR: Steffani Francis
Employees: 400

1994 Sales: $106 million
1-Yr. Sales Change: 8.2%
Ownership: Privately Held

SHURFINE INTERNATIONAL, INC.

2100 N. Mannheim Rd.
Northlake, IL 60164
Phone: 847-681-2000
Fax: 847-681-5862

Food - distribution of private-label groceries & sundries to supermarket chains

CEO: Paul T. Jasper
CFO: Eric Stuhlmann
HR: Carol Lemmer
Employees: 164

1995 Sales: $1,059.2 million
1-Yr. Sales Change: 8.3%
Ownership: Privately Held

SIDLEY & AUSTIN

One First National Plaza, Ste. 3940
Chicago, IL 60603
Phone: 312-853-7000
Fax: 312-853-7036

Law firm with offices in Chicago, London, Los Angeles, New York, Singapore, Tokyo & Washington, DC

CEO: R. Eden Martin
CFO: William B. White
HR: Sandy D. Boyer
Employees: 1,606

1994 Sales: $254.5 million
1-Yr. Sales Change: 1.2%
Ownership: Privately Held

SIGMATRON INTERNATIONAL, INC.

2201 Landmeier Rd.	CEO: Gary R. Fairhead	1995 Sales: $45.3 million
Elk Grove Village, IL 60007	CFO: Linda K. Blake	1-Yr. Sales Change: 23.4%
Phone: 847-956-8000	HR: Nancy Geiser	Exchange: Nasdaq
Fax: 847-956-8082	Employees: 703	Symbol: SGMA

Electrical components - contract manufacturer of printed circuit boards

SIPI METALS CORPORATION

1720 N. Elston Ave.	CEO: Leslie S. Pinsof	1994 Est. Sales: $76 mil.
Chicago, IL 60622	CFO: Marion A. Cameron	1-Yr. Sales Change: 3.4%
Phone: 312-276-0070	HR: —	Ownership: Privately Held
Fax: 312-276-7014	Employees: 150	

Metal processing & fabrication; computer & office machine sales

SKIDMORE, OWINGS & MERRILL

224 S. Michigan Ave., Ste. 1000	CEO: Adrian D. Smith	1994 Sales: $79 million
Chicago, IL 60604	CFO: Dan A. DeCanniere	1-Yr. Sales Change: 16.2%
Phone: 312-554-9090	HR: —	Ownership: Privately Held
Fax: 312-360-4545	Employees: 733	

Business services - architectural & engineering firm (#1 in the US)

SLEEPECK PRINTING COMPANY

815 25th Ave.	CEO: Michael W. Sleepeck	1994 Est. Sales: $56.6 mil.
Bellwood, IL 60104	CFO: Bob Gardner	1-Yr. Sales Change: 2.9%
Phone: 708-544-8900	HR: —	Ownership: Privately Held
Fax: 708-544-8928	Employees: 400	

Printing - card packs & packaged promotions for the direct-marketing industry

SOFT SHEEN PRODUCTS INC.

1000 E. 87th St.	CEO: Edward G. Gardner	1994 Est. Sales: $94 mil.
Chicago, IL 60619	CFO: Sharon Walker	1-Yr. Sales Change: -2.7%
Phone: 312-978-0700	HR: Robert Keller	Ownership: Privately Held
Fax: 312-978-2297	Employees: 419	

Cosmetics & toiletries - ethnic health & hair care products

SOFTNET SYSTEMS, INC.

One Overlook Place	CEO: John Jellinek	1995 Sales: $21.3 million
Lincolnshire, IL 60069	CFO: Martin A. Koehler	1-Yr. Sales Change: 121.9%
Phone: 847-793-2000	HR: Emily Harder	Exchange: AMEX
Fax: 847-821-6907	Employees: 15	Symbol: SOF

Computers - imaging processing systems for hospital documents

SOLAR PRESS, INC.

1120 Frontenac Rd.	CEO: Frank C. Hudetz	1994 Sales: $63.2 million
Naperville, IL 60563	CFO: Kelly Gilroy	1-Yr. Sales Change: 15.5%
Phone: 708-983-1400	HR: Paula Gustofson	Ownership: Privately Held
Fax: 708-983-1494	Employees: 853	

Printing - graphic design; offset & flexographic printing; specialty packaging services

SOMMER & MACA INDUSTRIES, INC.

5501 W. Ogden Ave.	CEO: Allan L. Maca	1994 Sales: $37.6 million
Chicago, IL 60650	CFO: Jeff Zielazinski	1-Yr. Sales Change: 11.6%
Phone: 312-242-2871	HR: Jeff Zielazinski	Ownership: Privately Held
Fax: 708-863-5462	Employees: 216	

Machinery - glass-processing equipment; glazing supplies & tools distribution

SONNENSCHEIN NATH & ROSENTHAL

233 S. Wacker Dr., Ste. 8000	CEO: Donald G. Lubin	1994 Sales: $118 million
Chicago, IL 60606	CFO: David Schadler	1-Yr. Sales Change: 14.6%
Phone: 312-876-8000	HR: —	Ownership: Privately Held
Fax: 312-876-7934	Employees: —	

Law firm

SOUTHSIDE FORD TRUCK SALES, INC.

810-850 W. Pershing Rd.	CEO: Carl E. Statham	1994 Sales: $48.7 million
Chicago, IL 60609	CFO: Sherman Baker	1-Yr. Sales Change: 3.8%
Phone: 312-247-4000	HR: Lillian Bybee	Ownership: Privately Held
Fax: 312-247-7152	Employees: 76	

Retail - new & used cars & trucks

SOUTHWEST BANCSHARES, INC.

4062 Southwest Hwy.
Hometown, IL 60456-1134
Phone: 708-636-2700
Fax: 708-422-9620

CEO: Richard E. Webber
CFO: Richard E. Webber
HR: —
Employees: 101

1994 Sales: $26.1 million
1-Yr. Sales Change: 0.8%
Exchange: Nasdaq
Symbol: SWBI

Banks - Midwest (Southwest Federal Savings & Loan Association of Chicago, Southwest Bancshares
Development Corporation)

SPECIALTY FOODS CORP.

520 Lake Cook Rd., Ste. 520
Deerfield, IL 60015
Phone: 847-267-3000
Fax: 847-267-0015

CEO: Thomas B. Herskovits
CFO: Andy Balbirer
HR: John D. Reisenberg
Employees: 13,900

1994 Sales: $1,979 million
1-Yr. Sales Change: -1.0%
Ownership: Privately Held

Food - cheese, baked goods, prepared meats, pickles & chips

 See pages 156–157 for a full profile of this company.

SPIEGEL, INC.

3500 Lacey Rd.
Downers Grove, IL 60515-5432
Phone: 708-986-8800
Fax: 708-769-3101

CEO: John J. Shea
CFO: James W. Sievers
HR: Harold S. Dahlstrand
Employees: 19,700

1994 Sales: $3,016 million
1-Yr. Sales Change: 16.2%
Exchange: Nasdaq
Symbol: SPGLA

Retail - mail order & outdoorwear stores (Eddie Bauer)

 See pages 158–159 for a full profile of this company.

SPORTMART INC.

1400 S. Wolf Rd., Ste. 200
Wheeling, IL 60090
Phone: 847-520-0100
Fax: 847-520-1570

CEO: Larry J. Hochberg
CFO: Thomas T. Hendrickson
HR: Joseph A. DeFalco Jr.
Employees: 4,512

1995 Sales: $424.2 million
1-Yr. Sales Change: 25.4%
Exchange: Nasdaq
Symbol: SPMT

Retail - sporting goods

 See page 226 for a full profile of this company.

SPRING AIR COMPANY

2980 River Rd.
Des Plaines, IL 60018
Phone: 847-297-5577
Fax: 847-299-0196

CEO: Jeff Holmes
CFO: Mike Rakauskas
HR: Pat DeMarco
Employees: 1,500

1994 Sales: $330 million
1-Yr. Sales Change: 20.0%
Ownership: Privately Held

Furniture - mattresses

SPS TRANSACTION SERVICES, INC.

2500 Lake Cook Rd.	CEO: Robert L. Wieseneck	1994 Sales: $245.8 million
Riverwoods, IL 60015	CFO: Thomas C. Schneider	1-Yr. Sales Change: 19.6%
Phone: 847-405-3700	HR: Stu Holman	Exchange: NYSE
Fax: 847-405-3854	Employees: 3,480	Symbol: PAY

Business services - point-of-sale transaction processing; developing & administering consumer & commercial private-label credit card programs

SPSS INC.

444 N. Michigan Ave.	CEO: Jack Noonan	1994 Sales: $51.8 million
Chicago, IL 60611	CFO: Edward Hamburg	1-Yr. Sales Change: 21.3%
Phone: 312-329-3500	HR: —	Exchange: Nasdaq
Fax: 312-329-3668	Employees: 410	Symbol: SPSS

Computers - software for statistical applications

SPYGLASS, INC.

1230 E. Diehl Rd.	CEO: Douglas P. Colbeth	1995 Sales: $10.4 million
Naperville, IL 60563	CFO: Thomas S. Lewicki	1-Yr. Sales Change: 188.9%
Phone: 708-505-1010	HR: Jan Shaffer	Exchange: Nasdaq
Fax: 708-505-4944	Employees: 73	Symbol: SPYG

Computers - software (Mosaic) for the World Wide Web

 See page 227 for a full profile of this company.

STANDARD FINANCIAL, INC.

4192 S. Archer Ave.	CEO: David Mackiewich	1994 Sales: $104.7 million
Chicago, IL 60632-1890	CFO: Thomas M. Ryan	1-Yr. Sales Change: 6.4%
Phone: 312-847-1140	HR: —	Exchange: Nasdaq
Fax: 708-986-7011	Employees: 575	Symbol: STND

Banks - Midwest (Standard Federal)

STEINER ELECTRIC COMPANY

1250 Touhy Ave.	CEO: Harold M. Kerman	1994 Sales: $105 million
Elk Grove Village, IL 60007	CFO: Barry Sanders	1-Yr. Sales Change: 22.1%
Phone: 847-228-0400	HR: —	Ownership: Privately Held
Fax: 847-228-1352	Employees: 320	

Wholesale distribution - electrical supplies, motors & drives; motor repair services

STEPAN COMPANY

22 W. Frontage Rd.
Northfield, IL 60093
Phone: 847-446-7500
Fax: 847-501-2443

CEO: F. Quinn Stepan
CFO: Walter J. Klein
HR: Craig Gardiner
Employees: 1,265

1994 Sales: $443.9 million
1-Yr. Sales Change: 1.2%
Exchange: AMEX
Symbol: SCL

Chemicals - surfactants, polymers & specialty products

STEVE FOLEY AUTO GROUP

100 Skokie Blvd.
Northbrook, IL 60062
Phone: 847-564-4090
Fax: 847-564-5787

CEO: Stephen X. Foley
CFO: John Shiels
HR: John Shiels
Employees: 238

1994 Sales: $126.5 million
1-Yr. Sales Change: 14.4%
Ownership: Privately Held

Retail - new & used cars

STIMSONITE CORPORATION

7524 N. Natchez Ave.
Niles, IL 60714-2110
Phone: 847-647-7717
Fax: 847-647-1205

CEO: Jay R. Taylor
CFO: Thomas C. Ratchford
HR: Michael A. Cherwin
Employees: 265

1994 Sales: $55.9 million
1-Yr. Sales Change: 21.8%
Exchange: Nasdaq
Symbol: STIM

Rubber & plastic products - reflective highway safety products

STOCK YARDS PACKING COMPANY

340 N. Oakley Blvd.
Chicago, IL 60612
Phone: 312-733-6050
Fax: 312-733-0738

CEO: Daniel Pollack
CFO: Stanley Katz
HR: —
Employees: 100

1994 Sales: $70 million
1-Yr. Sales Change: 11.1%
Ownership: Privately Held

Food - wholesale meats to restaurants & hotels; mail-order steaks

STONE CONTAINER CORPORATION

150 N. Michigan Ave.
Chicago, IL 60601-7568
Phone: 312-346-6600
Fax: 312-580-4919

CEO: Roger W. Stone
CFO: Arnold F. Brookstone
HR: Gayle M. Sparapani
Employees: 29,100

1994 Sales: $5,748.7 million
1-Yr. Sales Change: 13.6%
Exchange: NYSE
Symbol: STO

Paper & paper products - paperboard & paper packaging, white paper & pulp

 See pages 160–161 for a full profile of this company.

STROMBECKER CORPORATION

600 N. Pulaski Rd.
Chicago, IL 60624
Phone: 312-638-1000
Fax: 312-638-3679

CEO: Daniel B. Shure
CFO: Michael Glickman
HR: Jean Shaw
Employees: 450

1994 Sales: $54.1 million
1-Yr. Sales Change: 0.0%
Ownership: Privately Held

Toys - cap guns (#1 worldwide), model cars & cowboy-related toys

STS HOLDINGS, INC.

1415 Lake Cook
Deerfield, IL 60015
Phone: 847-272-6520
Fax: 847-498-2721

CEO: Thomas Wolf
CFO: Michael Russell
HR: Cheryl Smith
Employees: 450

1994 Est. Sales: $44.7 mil.
1-Yr. Sales Change: 0.4%
Ownership: Privately Held

Consulting - civil, hydropower & landfill engineering

SUBURBFED FINANCIAL CORP.

3301 W. Vollmer Rd.
Flossmoor, IL 60422
Phone: 708-333-2200
Fax: 708-333-9215

CEO: Daniel P. Ryan
CFO: Steven E. Stock
HR: Lester J. Wolf
Employees: 175

1994 Sales: $22.1 million
1-Yr. Sales Change: 5.7%
Exchange: Nasdaq (SC)
Symbol: SFSB

Financial - savings & loans

SUNDANCE HOMES, INC.

1375 E. Woodfield Rd.
Schaumburg, IL 60173
Phone: 847-255-5555
Fax: 847-413-4693

CEO: Maurice Sanderman
CFO: Daniel J. O'Brien
HR: Karen Chamberlain
Employees: 176

1994 Sales: $118.7 million
1-Yr. Sales Change: 52.6%
Exchange: Nasdaq
Symbol: SUNH

Building - development of land & construction of single-family homes for entry-level buyers in the Chicago metropolitan area

SUPERIOR GRAPHITE COMPANY

120 S. Riverside Plaza
Chicago, IL 60606
Phone: 312-559-2999
Fax: 312-559-9064

CEO: Peter R. Carney
CFO: Ron Pawelko
HR: —
Employees: 350

1994 Sales: $50 million
1-Yr. Sales Change: 16.3%
Ownership: Privately Held

Chemicals - natural & synthetic graphites

SWEETHEART HOLDINGS, INC.

7575 S. Kostner Ave.
Chicago, IL 60652
Phone: 312-767-3300
Fax: 312-838-2226

CEO: William F. McLaughlin
CFO: Roger A. Cregg
HR: James Mullen
Employees: 8,600

1994 Sales: $845.5 million
1-Yr. Sales Change: 1.9%
Ownership: Privately Held

Plastic & paper disposable food service & packaging products, including cups, plates & flatware

SYSTEM SOFTWARE ASSOCIATES, INC.

500 W. Madison St., 32nd Fl.
Chicago, IL 60661
Phone: 312-641-2900
Fax: 312-474-7500

CEO: Roger E. Covey
CFO: Joseph J. Skadra
HR: Marc Ugol
Employees: 1,790

1994 Sales: $334.4 million
1-Yr. Sales Change: 27.0%
Exchange: Nasdaq
Symbol: SSAX

Computers - business application software

 See page 228 for a full profile of this company.

TANG INDUSTRIES, INC.

1699 Wall St., Ste. 720
Mount Prospect, IL 60056-6213
Phone: 847-228-1860
Fax: 847-228-0456

CEO: Cyrus Tang
CFO: Kurt R. Swanson
HR: —
Employees: 3,500

1994 Sales: $1,100 million
1-Yr. Sales Change: 25.3%
Ownership: Privately Held

Metal products - fabrication & distribution

T. C. MANUFACTURING COMPANY

1527 Lyons St.
Evanston, IL 60201
Phone: 847-869-2320
Fax: 847-866-8596

CEO: Shiro F. Shigura
CFO: P. A. Clemmens
HR: Dorothy Maybrun
Employees: 520

1994 Sales: $78 million
1-Yr. Sales Change: -3.7%
Ownership: Privately Held

Chemicals - protective coatings; flexible packaging; generic drugs

TECHNOLOGY SOLUTIONS COMPANY

205 N. Michigan Ave., Ste. 1500
Chicago, IL 60601
Phone: 312-861-9600
Fax: 312-861-9601

CEO: John T. Kohler
CFO: Martin T. Johnson
HR: Debbie Steele
Employees: 423

1995 Sales: $65.8 million
1-Yr. Sales Change: 23.7%
Exchange: Nasdaq
Symbol: TSCC

Computers - consulting & systems integration services

 See page 229 for a full profile of this company.

TELEPHONE AND DATA SYSTEMS, INC.

30 N. LaSalle St., Ste. 4000	CEO: LeRoy T. Carlson Jr.	1994 Sales: $730.8 million
Chicago, IL 60602-2587	CFO: Murray L. Swanson	1-Yr. Sales Change: 23.7%
Phone: 312-630-1900	HR: C. Theodore Herbert	Exchange: AMEX
Fax: 312-630-1908	Employees: 5,322	Symbol: TDS

Utility - telephone; cellular telephone; radio paging

 See page 230 for a full profile of this company.

TELLABS, INC.

4951 Indiana Ave.	CEO: Michael J. Birck	1994 Sales: $494.2 million
Lisle, IL 60532	CFO: Peter A. Guglielmi	1-Yr. Sales Change: 54.2%
Phone: 708-969-8800	HR: Dave Southard	Exchange: Nasdaq
Fax: 708-852-7346	Employees: 2,585	Symbol: TLAB

Telecommunications equipment - advanced equipment for voice & data transport & access systems

 See page 231 for a full profile of this company.

TELTREND INC.

620 Stetson Ave.	CEO: Howard L. Kirby Jr.	1995 Sales: $62.1 million
St. Charles, IL 60174	CFO: Douglas P. Hoffmeyer	1-Yr. Sales Change: 25.5%
Phone: 708-377-1700	HR: Barb Genske	Exchange: Nasdaq
Fax: 708-377-0823	Employees: 293	Symbol: TLTN

Telecommunications equipment - transmission products, channel units, repeaters & termination units

TELULAR CORPORATION

920 Deerfield Pkwy.	CEO: Richard T. Gerstner	1995 Sales: $33 million
Buffalo Grove, IL 60089	CFO: Daniel O. Wagster	1-Yr. Sales Change: 86.4%
Phone: 847-465-4500	HR: Marci Feldman	Exchange: Nasdaq
Fax: 847-465-4502	Employees: 273	Symbol: WRLS

Telecommunications equipment - technology linking wireless & wireline systems

 See page 232 for a full profile of this company.

TEMPEL STEEL COMPANY

5215 Old Orchard Rd.	CEO: Vincent J. Buonanno	1994 Sales: $336 million
Skokie, IL 60077	CFO: Ron Bailitz	1-Yr. Sales Change: 17.1%
Phone: 847-581-9400	HR: —	Ownership: Privately Held
Fax: 847-581-9025	Employees: 1,500	

Steel - magnetic steel lamination for the electronic & electrical industries

TNT FREIGHTWAYS CORPORATION

9700 Higgins Rd., Ste. 570
Rosemont, IL 60018
Phone: 847-696-0200
Fax: 847-696-2080

CEO: J. Campbell Carruth
CFO: Christopher L. Ellis
HR: Rosemary Maziarka
Employees: 12,184

1994 Sales: $1,016.5 million
1-Yr. Sales Change: 13.1%
Exchange: Nasdaq
Symbol: TNTF

Transportation - truck

 See page 233 for a full profile of this company.

TOOTSIE ROLL INDUSTRIES, INC.

7401 S. Cicero Ave.
Chicago, IL 60629
Phone: 312-838-3400
Fax: 312-838-3564

CEO: Melvin J. Gordon
CFO: G. Howard Ember Jr.
HR: Maurice Buddemeier
Employees: 1,700

1994 Sales: $296.9 million
1-Yr. Sales Change: 14.4%
Exchange: NYSE
Symbol: TR

Food - confectionery (Tootsie Roll, Tootsie Pops, Sugar Babies)

 See page 234 for a full profile of this company.

TOPCO ASSOCIATES, INC.

7711 Gross Point Rd.
Skokie, IL 60077
Phone: 847-676-3030
Fax: 847-676-4949

CEO: W. Steven Rubow
CFO: Steven K. Lauer
HR: Ronald Ficks
Employees: 375

1995 Sales: $3,700 mil.
1-Yr. Sales Change: 19.6%
Ownership: Privately Held

Wholesale distribution - food, paper products & cosmetics to supermarkets

See pages 162–163 for a full profile of this company.

TORCO HOLDINGS, INC.

111 E. Wacker Dr., Ste. 1300
Chicago, IL 60601
Phone: 312-616-1700
Fax: 312-616-9388

CEO: Anthony M. Tortoriello
CFO: Michael Tassi
HR: Helen Kennedy
Employees: 90

1994 Sales: $82 million
1-Yr. Sales Change: 17.1%
Ownership: Privately Held

Diversified operations - industrial fuel oil marketing & natural gas distribution; new & used car dealerships

TOWN AND COUNTRY HOMES, INC.

1603 16th St.
Oak Brook, IL 60521
Phone: 708-617-5577
Fax: 708-617-5967

CEO: William J. Ryan
CFO: Michael Ryan
HR: —
Employees: 115

1995 Est. Sales: $225 mil.
1-Yr. Sales Change: —
Ownership: Privately Held

Building - single-family homes

TRANS LEASING INTERNATIONAL, INC.

3000 Dundee Rd.
Northbrook, IL 60062
Phone: 847-272-1000
Fax: 847-272-2174

CEO: Richard Grossman
CFO: Norman Smagley
HR: —
Employees: 109

1995 Sales: $30.5 million
1-Yr. Sales Change: 15.1%
Exchange: Nasdaq
Symbol: TLII

Leasing - general office & medical equipment to healthcare providers

TREASURE ISLAND FOODMART, INC.

3460 N. Broadway Ave.
Chicago, IL 60657
Phone: 312-327-4265
Fax: 312-327-6337

CEO: Christ Kamberos
CFO: Bob Johnson
HR: —
Employees: 650

1994 Est. Sales: $70.4 mil.
1-Yr. Sales Change: 5.1%
Ownership: Privately Held

Retail - grocery store

TRIANGLE TECHNOLOGIES, INC.

1441 Branding Ln.
Downers Grove, IL 60515
Phone: 708-969-8200
Fax: 708-969-8201

CEO: James Wolande
CFO: James Wolande
HR: Donna Cullen
Employees: 16

1994 Sales: $7 million
1-Yr. Sales Change: 45.8%
Ownership: Privately Held

Computers - local- & wide-area networks (LANs & WANs) & data communication services

TRIBUNE COMPANY

435 N. Michigan Ave.
Chicago, IL 60611
Phone: 312-222-9100
Fax: 312-222-0449

CEO: John W. Madigan
CFO: Donald C. Grenesko
HR: John T. Sloan
Employees: 9,900

1994 Sales: $2,154.9 million
1-Yr. Sales Change: 9.3%
Exchange: NYSE
Symbol: TRB

Publishing - newspapers; radio & TV broadcasting (WGN); newsprint operations; book publishing
(Contemporary); professional baseball team (Chicago Cubs)

 See pages 164–165 for a full profile of this company.

TRO LEARNING, INC.

1721 Moon Lake Blvd., Ste. 555
Hoffman Estates, IL 60194
Phone: 847-781-7800
Fax: 847-781-7835

CEO: William R. Roach
CFO: Sharon Fierro
HR: Jerry Duewel
Employees: 267

1994 Sales: $28.4 million
1-Yr. Sales Change: 7.2%
Exchange: Nasdaq
Symbol: TUTR

Computers - microcomputer-based interactive learning systems (PLATO) for education & instructional
use by schools, colleges, the military, airlines & correctional institutions

TRUE NORTH COMMUNICATIONS INC.

101 E. Erie St.
Chicago, IL 60611-2897
Phone: 312-751-7000
Fax: 312-751-3501

CEO: Bruce Mason
CFO: Terry M. Ashwill
HR: Doris Radcliffe
Employees: 3,929

1994 Sales: $403.7 million
1-Yr. Sales Change: 8.3%
Exchange: NYSE
Symbol: TNO

Advertising, direct marketing, public relations, sales promotions (formerly Foote, Cone & Belding)

 See page 235 for a full profile of this company.

TRUSTMARK INSURANCE COMPANY

400 Field Dr.
Lake Forest, IL 60048
Phone: 847-615-1500
Fax: 847-615-3910

CEO: Donald M. Peterson
CFO: Richard D. Batten
HR: Robert R. Worobow
Employees: 1,419

1994 Sales: $711 million
1-Yr. Sales Change: 7.4%
Ownership: Privately Held

Insurance - group & individual health & life

TTX COMPANY

101 N. Wacker Dr.
Chicago, IL 60606
Phone: 312-853-3223
Fax: 312-984-3865

CEO: R. C. Burton Jr.
CFO: Robert E. Zimmerman
HR: Andrew F. Reardon
Employees: 2,000

1994 Sales: $810 million
1-Yr. Sales Change: 11.0%
Ownership: Privately Held

Transportation - operation & leasing of national pool of intermodal, autorack & other flatcars & boxcars

TURTLE WAX, INC.

5655 W. 73rd St.
Chicago, IL 60638
Phone: 708-563-3600
Fax: 708-563-3359

CEO: Dennis J. Healy
CFO: Ray Kolodziej
HR: Randy Johnson
Employees: 850

1994 Est. Sales: $145 mil.
1-Yr. Sales Change: 9.8%
Ownership: Privately Held

Soap & cleaning preparations - car cleaning & polishing products

TUTHILL CORPORATION

908 N. Elm St.
Hinsdale, IL 60521
Phone: 708-655-2266
Fax: 708-655-2297

CEO: James Tuthill Jr.
CFO: James Tuthill Jr.
HR: —
Employees: 2,000

1994 Sales: $237 million
1-Yr. Sales Change: 17.9%
Ownership: Privately Held

Industrial processing - engineered industrial products & components

UAL CORPORATION

1200 E. Algonquin Rd.
Elk Grove Township, IL 60007-0666
Phone: 847-952-4000
Fax: 847-952-7578

CEO: Gerald Greenwald
CFO: Douglas A. Hacker
HR: Paul G. George
Employees: 77,900

1994 Sales: $13,950 million
1-Yr. Sales Change: -3.9%
Exchange: NYSE
Symbol: UAL

Transportation - United Airlines

 See pages 166–167 for a full profile of this company.

UNDERWRITERS LABORATORIES INC.

333 Pfingsten Rd.
Northbrook, IL 60062
Phone: 847-272-8800
Fax: 847-272-8129

CEO: Tom Castino
CFO: Larry Newman
HR: Howard Simon
Employees: 3,900

1994 Sales: $300 million
1-Yr. Sales Change: —
Ownership: Privately Held

Business services - product safety testing & certification

 See page 236 for a full profile of this company.

UNICOM CORPORATION

10 S. Dearborn St., PO Box 767
Chicago, IL 60690-0767
Phone: 312-394-4321
Fax: 312-394-3110

CEO: James J. O'Connor
CFO: John C. Bukovski
HR: J. Stanley Graves
Employees: 18,460

1994 Sales: $6,277.5 million
1-Yr. Sales Change: 19.3%
Exchange: NYSE
Symbol: UCM

Utility - electric power

 See pages 168–169 for a full profile of this company.

UNIFIED HEALTHCARE NETWORK

2160 S. First Ave., Bldg. 105
Maywood, IL 60153
Phone: 708-216-9190
Fax: 708-216-9181

CEO: Burton F. Vanderlaan
CFO: —
HR: —
Employees: —

1994 Est. Sales: $1,100 mil.
1-Yr. Sales Change: —
Ownership: Privately Held

Hospitals - not-for-profit affiliation of 7 independently owned hospitals serving the Chicago area (Loyola University Medical Center, Resurrection Medical Center, St. Bernard Hospital, St. Francis Hospital)

UNIMED PHARMACEUTICALS, INC.

2150 E. Lake Cook Rd.
Buffalo Grove, IL 60089
Phone: 847-541-2525
Fax: 847-541-2569

CEO: Stephen M. Simes
CFO: David E. Riggs
HR: Beverly Lascola
Employees: 20

1994 Sales: $8 million
1-Yr. Sales Change: 11.1%
Exchange: Nasdaq
Symbol: UMED

Drugs - therapeutic pharmaceuticals for people with AIDS & cancer chemotherapy patients & for recurrent vertigo associated with Meniere's disease

UNITED HOMES, INC.

2100 Golf Rd.
Rolling Meadows, IL 60008
Phone: 847-427-2450
Fax: 847-427-2480

Building - single-family homes

CEO: Edward F. Havlik
CFO: Mike Havlik
HR: Mike Havlik
Employees: 90

1994 Sales: $45.8 million
1-Yr. Sales Change: 32.4%
Ownership: Privately Held

UNITED STATES CELLULAR CORPORATION

8410 W. Bryn Mawr, Ste. 700
Chicago, IL 60631
Phone: 312-399-8900
Fax: 312-399-8936

Telecommunications services - cellular telephone services

CEO: H. Donald Nelson
CFO: Kenneth R. Meyers
HR: Douglas S. Arnold
Employees: 2,250

1994 Sales: $332.4 million
1-Yr. Sales Change: 34.4%
Exchange: AMEX
Symbol: USM

 See page 237 for a full profile of this company.

UNITED STATIONERS INC.

2200 E. Golf Rd.
Des Plaines, IL 60016-1267
Phone: 847-699-5000
Fax: 847-699-8046

CEO: Joel D. Spungin
CFO: Allen B. Kravis
HR: Robert H. Cornell
Employees: 3,600

1995 Sales: $980.6 million
1-Yr. Sales Change: —
Exchange: Nasdaq
Symbol: USTR

Office equipment & supplies - wholesale supplies, furniture, computer products, facilities management supplies & business presentation products

UNITRIN, INC.

One E. Wacker Dr.
Chicago, IL 60601
Phone: 312-661-4600
Fax: 312-661-4690

CEO: Richard C. Vie
CFO: Eric J. Draut
HR: Ken Oehler
Employees: 7,289

1994 Sales: $1,365.5 million
1-Yr. Sales Change: 0.2%
Exchange: Nasdaq
Symbol: UNIT

Insurance - life & health, property & casualty; consumer finance services

UNIVERSAL AUTOMOTIVE INDUSTRIES, INC.

3350 N. Kedzie
Chicago, IL 60618-5722
Phone: 312-478-2323
Fax: 312-478-9066

CEO: Yehuda Tzur
CFO: Dan Maeir
HR: Martha Cvkota
Employees: 110

1994 Sales: $39.7 million
1-Yr. Sales Change: 19.6%
Exchange: Nasdaq
Symbol: UVSL

Automotive - aftermarket replacement parts for domestic & imported cars, vans & light trucks; brake rotors (UBP Universal Brake Parts)

THE UNIVERSITY OF CHICAGO

5801 S. Ellis Ave.	CEO: Hugo F. Sonnenschein	1995 Sales: $1,313.3 million
Chicago, IL 60637	CFO: Lawrence J. Furnstahl	1-Yr. Sales Change: 7.9%
Phone: 312-702-1234	HR: JoAnn Shaw	
Fax: 312-702-0353	Employees: 10,954	

Private, nondenominational university offering 50 undergraduate degree programs & 91 graduate degree programs; hospitals

▉ **See pages 170–171 for a full profile of this company.**

THE UNO-VEN COMPANY

3850 N. Wilke Rd.	CEO: Daniel J. Tippeconnic	1994 Sales: $2,144 million
Arlington Heights, IL 60004	CFO: Richard J. Estlin	1-Yr. Sales Change: -5.0%
Phone: 847-818-1800	HR: Debra Ellis	Ownership: Joint Venture
Fax: 847-818-7155	Employees: 1,100	

Oil refining & marketing; joint venture between Unocal Corp. & PDVSA

UNR INDUSTRIES, INC.

332 S. Michigan Ave.	CEO: Thomas A. Gildehaus	1994 Sales: $372.4 million
Chicago, IL 60604-4385	CFO: Henry Grey	1-Yr. Sales Change: 19.0%
Phone: 312-341-1234	HR: —	Exchange: Nasdaq
Fax: 312-341-0349	Employees: 2,200	Symbol: UNRI

Steel - welded tubing, shopping carts & supermarket storage & display equipment; stainless steel & composite sinks, steel towers & equipment shelters

URBAN SHOPPING CENTERS, INC.

900 N. Michigan Ave., Ste. 1500	CEO: Matthew S. Dominski	1994 Sales: $77.7 million
Chicago, IL 60611	CFO: Adam S. Metz	1-Yr. Sales Change: 9.4%
Phone: 312-915-2000	HR: —	Exchange: NYSE
Fax: 312-915-3180	Employees: 2,455	Symbol: URB

Real estate investment trust - shopping centers (Water Tower Place, Oakbrook Center)

US 1 INDUSTRIES INC.

1000 Colfax	CEO: Michael E. Kibler	1994 Sales: $20.7 million
Gary, IN 46406	CFO: James C. Day	1-Yr. Sales Change: -42.5%
Phone: 219-944-6116	HR: —	Exchange: NYSE
Fax: 800-377-3715	Employees: 15	Symbol: USO

Transportation - interstate freight trucking; refrigerated trucking

U.S. CAN CORPORATION

900 Commerce Dr., Ste. 302
Oak Brook, IL 60521-1967
Phone: 708-571-2500
Fax: 708-573-0715

CEO: William J. Smith
CFO: Timothy W. Stonich
HR: Anthony F. Bonadonna
Employees: 3,500

1994 Sales: $563.2 million
1-Yr. Sales Change: 23.8%
Exchange: NYSE
Symbol: USC

Containers - metal containers for personal care, household, automotive & paint products (#1 in US)

U.S. PRECISION GLASS COMPANY

1900 Holmes Rd.
Elgin, IL 60123
Phone: 847-931-1200
Fax: 847-931-4144

CEO: W. Glenn Gies
CFO: Jacob Master
HR: Lynette Eeg
Employees: 590

1994 Sales: $46.5 million
1-Yr. Sales Change: 6.2%
Ownership: Privately Held

Custom-machined glass parts

U.S. ROBOTICS CORPORATION

8100 N. McCormick Blvd.
Skokie, IL 60076
Phone: 847-982-5010
Fax: 847-982-5235

CEO: Casey G. Cowell
CFO: Ross W. Manire
HR: Elizabeth S. Ryan
Employees: 1,451

1995 Sales: $889.3 million
1-Yr. Sales Change: 134.8%
Exchange: Nasdaq
Symbol: USRX

Computers - modems (#1 in US: Courier, Sportster, WorldPort), network hubs & ethernet adapters

 See page 238 for a full profile of this company.

USG CORPORATION

125 S. Franklin St.
Chicago, IL 60606-4678
Phone: 312-606-4000
Fax: 312-606-4093

CEO: Eugene B. Connolly
CFO: Richard H. Fleming
HR: S. Gary Snodgrass
Employees: 12,300

1994 Sales: $2,290 million
1-Yr. Sales Change: 19.5%
Exchange: NYSE
Symbol: USG

Building products - gypsum

See pages 172–173 for a full profile of this company.

VANCE PUBLISHING CORPORATION

400 Knightsbridge Pkwy.
Lincolnshire, IL 60069
Phone: 847-634-2600
Fax: 847-634-4379

CEO: James Staudt
CFO: Walter Kay
HR: Laura Christensen
Employees: 317

1994 Est. Sales: $40.1 mil.
1-Yr. Sales Change: 2.8%
Ownership: Privately Held

Publishing - trade magazines

VARLEN CORPORATION

55 Shuman Blvd., PO Box 3089	CEO: Richard L. Wellek	1995 Sales: $341.5 million
Naperville, IL 60566-7089	CFO: Richard A. Nunemaker	1-Yr. Sales Change: 17.0%
Phone: 708-420-0400	HR: —	Exchange: Nasdaq
Fax: —	Employees: 2,531	Symbol: VRLN

Transportation - railroad shock absorbers, truck & trailer hubs, fuel water separators & stamped metal components

VELSICOL CHEMICAL CORPORATION

10400 W. Higgins Rd., Ste. 600	CEO: Arthur R. Sigel	1994 Sales: $116 million
Rosemont, IL 60018	CFO: Lawrence Hartman	1-Yr. Sales Change: 16.0%
Phone: 847-298-9000	HR: Donna Jennings	Ownership: Privately Held
Fax: 847-298-9015	Employees: 600	

Chemicals - cyclic intermediates & plasticizers

VIENNA SAUSAGE MANUFACTURING COMPANY

2501 N. Damen Ave.	CEO: Jim Eisenberg	1994 Sales: $90.1 million
Chicago, IL 60647	CFO: George Sklenick	1-Yr. Sales Change: -2.7%
Phone: 312-278-7800	HR: Jamie Eisenberg	Ownership: Privately Held
Fax: 312-278-4759	Employees: 550	

Food - processed meats, desserts, pickles & pizza

THE VIGORO CORPORATION

225 N. Michigan Ave.	CEO: Robert E. Fowler Jr.	1994 Sales: $727.4 million
Chicago, IL 60601	CFO: James J. Patterson	1-Yr. Sales Change: 25.8%
Phone: 312-819-2020	HR: John Overbeck	Exchange: NYSE
Fax: 312-819-2027	Employees: 1,900	Symbol: VGR

Fertilizers - potash & nitrogen, primarily for corn growers

VISIONTEK INC.

1175 Lakeside Dr.	CEO: Mark Polinsky	1994 Sales: $302 million
Gurnee, IL 60031	CFO: Craig Gutmann	1-Yr. Sales Change: 63.2%
Phone: 800-360-7102	HR: Michele Feldman	Ownership: Privately Held
Fax: 708-360-7401	Employees: 180	

Computers - PC & printer memory upgrades

VITALINK PHARMACY SERVICES, INC.

1250 E. Diehl Rd., Ste. 208
Naperville, IL 60563
Phone: 708-505-1320
Fax: 708-505-1319

CEO: Donald C. Tomasso
CFO: Scott T. Macomber
HR: Stephen A. Thompson
Employees: 775

1995 Sales: $112.3 million
1-Yr. Sales Change: 13.9%
Exchange: Nasdaq
Symbol: VTLK

Medical services - institutional pharmacy services to nursing facilities

See page 239 for a full profile of this company.

VOLVO SALES & SERVICE CENTER, INC.

4375 Lincoln Ave.
Lisle, IL 60532
Phone: 708-852-6000
Fax: 708-852-0464

CEO: Horst Korallus
CFO: Tom Taylor
HR: Susette Nordstrom
Employees: 350

1994 Sales: $110 million
1-Yr. Sales Change: 10.0%
Ownership: Privately Held

Retail - new & used cars

WALGREEN CO.

200 Wilmot Rd.
Deerfield, IL 60015
Phone: 847-940-2500
Fax: 847-940-2804

CEO: Charles R. Walgreen III
CFO: Roger Polark
HR: John A. Rubino
Employees: 61,900

1995 Sales: $10,395.1 mil.
1-Yr. Sales Change: 12.6%
Exchange: NYSE
Symbol: WAG

Retail - drugstores

See pages 174–175 for a full profile of this company.

WALLACE COMPUTER SERVICES, INC.

4600 W. Roosevelt Rd.
Hillside, IL 60162
Phone: 312-626-2000
Fax: 708-449-1161

CEO: Robert J. Cronin
CFO: Michael J. Halloran
HR: Barry L. White
Employees: 3,765

1995 Sales: $712.8 million
1-Yr. Sales Change: 21.2%
Exchange: NYSE
Symbol: WCS

Paper - business forms, industrial & consumer catalogs, direction & price lists, pressure-sensitive labels & other office supplies

WALSH GROUP

929 W. Adams St.
Chicago, IL 60607
Phone: 312-563-5400
Fax: 312-563-5467

CEO: Daniel Walsh
CFO: Matt Walsh
HR: Marilyn Honkisz
Employees: 4,000

1994 Sales: $450 million
1-Yr. Sales Change: 30.4%
Ownership: Privately Held

Building - general contracting, construction management & development services

WARRIOR INSURANCE GROUP INC.

6640 S. Cicero Ave.
Bedford Park, IL 60638
Phone: 708-233-7000
Fax: 708-233-7007

CEO: Jim Halberg
CFO: Michael Rosenstein
HR: Johanna Ryan
Employees: 609

1994 Sales: $118.3 million
1-Yr. Sales Change: 18.5%
Ownership: Privately Held

Insurance - multiline

WASHINGTON NATIONAL CORPORATION

300 Tower Pkwy.
Lincolnshire, IL 60069
Phone: 847-793-3000
Fax: 847-570-5566

CEO: Robert W. Patin
CFO: Thomas C. Scott
HR: Tom Fahy
Employees: 1,088

1994 Sales: $656.9 million
1-Yr. Sales Change: 4.5%
Exchange: NYSE
Symbol: WNT

Insurance - life

WEBER-STEPHEN PRODUCTS COMPANY

200 E. Daniels Rd.
Palatine, IL 60067
Phone: 847-934-5700
Fax: 847-934-0291

CEO: James Stephen
CFO: Leonard Gryn
HR: Joseph Moore
Employees: 500

1994 Est. Sales: $130 mil.
1-Yr. Sales Change: 4.3%
Ownership: Privately Held

Leisure & recreational products - barbecue grills (Weber); restaurants

WELLS-GARDNER ELECTRONICS CORPORATION

2701 N. Kildare Ave.
Chicago, IL 60639
Phone: 312-252-8220
Fax: 312-252-8072

CEO: Anthony Spier
CFO: Richard L. Conquest
HR: Eugene C. Ahner
Employees: 176

1994 Sales: $33.4 million
1-Yr. Sales Change: -7.2%
Exchange: AMEX
Symbol: WGA

Color & monochrome video monitors & open-frame monitor touch sensors for coin-operated electronic video games, point-of-purchase & interactive video terminals, automotive diagnostic equipment

WESTCO BANCORP, INC.

2121 S. Mannheim Rd.
Westchester, IL 60154-4363
Phone: 708-865-1100
Fax: 708-865-1135

CEO: David C. Burba
CFO: Richard A. Brechlin
HR: —
Employees: 60

1994 Sales: $21.7 million
1-Yr. Sales Change: -4.4%
Exchange: Nasdaq
Symbol: WCBI

Banks - Midwest (First Federal Savings & Loan Association of Westchester)

WHITE HEN PANTRY INC.

660 Industrial Dr.
Elmhurst, IL 60126-1580
Phone: 708-833-3100
Fax: 708-833-7034

Retail - convenience food stores

CEO: R. G. Robertson
CFO: Robert B. Knight
HR: Kathy Zuodar
Employees: 276

1995 Sales: $306.6 million
1-Yr. Sales Change: 2.5%
Ownership: Privately Held

WHITMAN CORPORATION

3501 Algonquin Rd.
Rolling Meadows, IL 60008
Phone: 847-818-5000
Fax: 847-818-5045

Diversified operations - soft drink bottling (Pepsi General); auto service (Midas); refrigeration equipment

CEO: Bruce S. Chelberg
CFO: Thomas L. Bindley
HR: Lawrence J. Pilon
Employees: 15,271

1994 Sales: $2,658.8 million
1-Yr. Sales Change: 5.1%
Exchange: NYSE
Symbol: WH

 See pages 176–177 for a full profile of this company.

WICKES LUMBER COMPANY

706 N. Deer Path Dr.
Vernon Hills, IL 60061
Phone: 847-367-3400
Fax: 847-367-3750

Building products - retail & wholesale lumber

CEO: J. Steven Wilson
CFO: George A. Bajalia
HR: E. Trevor Dignall
Employees: 4,523

1994 Sales: $986.9 million
1-Yr. Sales Change: 16.5%
Exchange: Nasdaq
Symbol: WIKS

 See pages 178–179 for a full profile of this company.

WILLIAM BLAIR & COMPANY

222 W. Adams St.
Chicago, IL 60606
Phone: 312-236-1600
Fax: 312-368-9418

Financial - venture capital investment firm, securities brokerage & investment management

CEO: E. David Coolidge III
CFO: John Kayser
HR: Tony Zimmer
Employees: 555

1994 Sales: $150 million
1-Yr. Sales Change: 0.0%
Ownership: Privately Held

WM. WRIGLEY JR. COMPANY

410 N. Michigan Ave.
Chicago, IL 60611
Phone: 312-644-2121
Fax: 312-644-0097

Food - gum (Big Red, Doublemint, Extra, Freedent, Juicy Fruit, Spearmint, Winterfresh)

CEO: William Wrigley
CFO: John F. Bard
HR: David E. Boxell
Employees: 7,000

1994 Sales: $1,661.3 million
1-Yr. Sales Change: 15.3%
Exchange: NYSE
Symbol: WWY

 See pages 180–181 for a full profile of this company.

WILTON INDUSTRIES, INC.

2240 W. 75th St.
Woodridge, IL 60517
Phone: 708-963-7100
Fax: 708-963-6791
Housewares & home accessories

CEO: Vincent A. Naccarato
CFO: R. P. Zenner
HR: Ruth Ann Miller
Employees: 530

1994 Sales: $118.3 million
1-Yr. Sales Change: 6.6%
Ownership: Privately Held

WINSTON & STRAWN

35 W. Wacker Dr.
Chicago, IL 60601-9703
Phone: 312-558-5600
Fax: 312-558-5700

CEO: James M. Neis
CFO: J. Scott Hall
HR: Julie L. Stafford
Employees: 926

1995 Sales: $145.9 million
1-Yr. Sales Change: 1.6%
Ownership: Privately Held

Law firm with offices in Chicago; Washington, DC; New York; Paris; Geneva & Riyadh, Saudi Arabia

WIRTZ CORPORATION

680 N. Lakeshore Dr., 16th Fl.
Chicago, IL 60611
Phone: 312-943-7000
Fax: 312-943-9017

CEO: William Wirtz
CFO: Max Mohler
HR: Cindy Krch
Employees: 1,780

1994 Sales: $410 million
1-Yr. Sales Change: —
Ownership: Privately Held

Beverages - wine & liquor distribution (Judge & Dolph, Griggs, Copper & Company, Edison Liquor Corp., DeLuca Liquor & Wine, Longhorn Liquors); professional hockey team (Chicago Blackhawks)

WISCONSIN CENTRAL TRANSPORTATION CORPORATION

6250 N. River Rd., PO Box 5062
Rosemont, IL 60017-5062
Phone: 847-318-4600
Fax: 847-318-4618

CEO: Edward A. Burkhardt
CFO: Thomas F. Power Jr.
HR: David French
Employees: 1,704

1994 Sales: $211.1 million
1-Yr. Sales Change: 39.2%
Exchange: Nasdaq
Symbol: WCLX

Transportation - regional railroad (#1 in US: Wisconsin Central Ltd.; Fox Valley & Western Ltd.; WCL Railcars, Inc.; Sault Ste. Marie Bridge Company & Wisconsin Central International, Inc.)

 **See page 240 for a full profile of this company.**

WMS INDUSTRIES INC.

3401 N. California Ave.
Chicago, IL 60618
Phone: 312-961-1111
Fax: 312-961-1099

CEO: Neil D. Nicastro
CFO: Harold H. Bach Jr.
HR: Michael Sirchio
Employees: 3,381

1995 Sales: $385.4 million
1-Yr. Sales Change: 7.6%
Exchange: NYSE
Symbol: WMS

Leisure & recreational products - pinball & video games (Mortal Kombat); gambling equipment; hotels & casinos

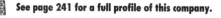 **See page 241 for a full profile of this company.**

WMX TECHNOLOGIES, INC.

3003 Butterfield Rd.	CEO: Dean L. Buntrock	1994 Sales: $10,097.3 mil.
Oak Brook, IL 60521	CFO: James E. Koenig	1-Yr. Sales Change: 10.5%
Phone: 708-572-8800	HR: Edward Kalebich	Exchange: NYSE
Fax: 708-572-3094	Employees: 74,400	Symbol: WMX

Pollution control equipment & services - waste collection, disposal & recycling, air pollution control, industrial remediation

 See pages 182–183 for a full profile of this company.

WOODFIELD FORD SALES, INC.

815 E. Golf Rd.	CEO: Charles F. Latimer	1994 Sales: $74.4 million
Schaumburg, IL 60173	CFO: Frank Grimmbacher	1-Yr. Sales Change: -4.0%
Phone: 847-605-0800	HR: Bea Roden	Ownership: Privately Held
Fax: 847-605-8908	Employees: 168	

Retail - new & used cars

WOODHEAD INDUSTRIES, INC.

2150 E. Lake Cook Rd., Ste. 400	CEO: C. Mark DeWinter	1995 Sales: $120 million
Buffalo Grove, IL 60089	CFO: Robert G. Jennings	1-Yr. Sales Change: 13.5%
Phone: 847-465-8300	HR: Robert A. Moulton	Exchange: Nasdaq
Fax: 847-465-8310	Employees: 1,079	Symbol: WDHD

Electrical products - control & power distribution devices for industrial uses

WORLD'S FINEST CHOCOLATE, INC.

4801 S. Lawndale Ave.	CEO: Edmond Opler Jr.	1994 Est. Sales: $137.7 mil.
Chicago, IL 60632	CFO: Karl Hows	1-Yr. Sales Change: 8.0%
Phone: 312-847-4600	HR: Greg Serratore	Ownership: Privately Held
Fax: 312-847-7804	Employees: 850	

Food - chocolate & confectioneries

WOZNIAK INDUSTRIES, INC.

2 Mid America Plaza, Ste. 706	CEO: Edward F. Wozniak	1994 Sales: $70 million
Oakbrook Terrace, IL 60181	CFO: Anthony G. Vastardis	1-Yr. Sales Change: 0.0%
Phone: 708-954-3400	HR: Anson Cranmer	Ownership: Privately Held
Fax: 708-954-3605	Employees: 500	

Metal & plastic components

W.W. GRAINGER, INC.

5500 W. Howard St.	CEO: Richard L. Keyser	1994 Sales: $3,023.1 million
Skokie, IL 60077-2699	CFO: Jere D. Fluno	1-Yr. Sales Change: 15.0%
Phone: 847-982-9000	HR: Gary J. Goberville	Exchange: NYSE
Fax: 847-982-3489	Employees: 11,343	Symbol: GWW

Machinery - electrical

 See pages 184–185 for a full profile of this company.

ZEBRA TECHNOLOGIES CORPORATION

333 Corporate Woods Pkwy.	CEO: Edward L. Kaplan	1994 Sales: $107.1 million
Vernon Hills, IL 60061-3109	CFO: Charles R. Whitchurch	1-Yr. Sales Change: 22.4%
Phone: 847-634-6700	HR: Ellen Barnes	Exchange: Nasdaq
Fax: 847-634-1830	Employees: 501	Symbol: ZBRA

Optical character recognition - bar code printers & related equipment

 See page 242 for a full profile of this company.

ZENITH CONTROLS, INC.

830 W. 40th St.	CEO: Arthur Coren	1994 Sales: $30.2 million
Chicago, IL 60609	CFO: Bob Doherty	1-Yr. Sales Change: -1.6%
Phone: 312-247-6400	HR: Pat Schopper	Ownership: Privately Held
Fax: 312-247-7805	Employees: 251	

Electrical components - power switching systems & control equipment

ZENITH ELECTRONICS CORPORATION

1000 Milwaukee Ave.	CEO: Albin F. Moschner	1994 Sales: $1,469 million
Glenview, IL 60025-2493	CFO: Kell B. Benson	1-Yr. Sales Change: 19.6%
Phone: 847-391-7000	HR: Michael J. Kaplan	Exchange: NYSE
Fax: 847-391-8334	Employees: 22,500	Symbol: ZE

Audio & video home products - TVs, including high-definition, large-screen & projection models; VCRs; remote controls

 See pages 186–187 for a full profile of this company.

ZOLL FOODS CORPORATION

15600 S. Wentworth Ave.	CEO: Steve Zoll	1994 Sales: $64.8 million
South Holland, IL 60473	CFO: Gerald Stankus	1-Yr. Sales Change: 17.6%
Phone: 708-333-3900	HR: Vidalia Coleman	Ownership: Privately Held
Fax: 708-333-5300	Employees: 180	

Food - premium pork ribs; food-service menu research & development

CHICAGO The Indexes

INTRODUCING
HOOVER'S COMPANY
PROFILES ON DEMAND

A new fax delivery service that puts detailed company profiles from the

Hoover's Company Database
at your fingertips

WHY WAIT? Get invaluable information immediately on more than 1,000 public and private companies.

The information is arranged in the same easy-to-use format as the company profiles found in *Hoover's Handbooks* and includes company overviews and histories, up to 10 years of key financial and employment data, lists of products and key competitors, names of key officers, addresses, and phone and fax numbers.

IT'S SIMPLE.

1. Choose any number of companies from the index on the following pages.

2. Then call **415-598-4335**, 24 hours a day, 7 days a week, to receive a detailed profile for only $2.95* for each company you choose. Have your fax number and the five-digit company code number ready.

3. A voice-automated system will guide you through your order, and you'll receive your company profiles via fax within minutes.

*American Express, MasterCard, and Visa accepted.

Company	Number
3Com Corporation	12475
AAON, Inc.	16562
AB Volvo	41854
ABB Asea Brown Boveri Ltd	40615
Acclaim Entertainment, Inc.	10544
Accor SA	40552
Acordia, Inc.	12336
ACT Manufacturing, Inc.	43463
Active Voice Corporation	16684
Adaptec, Inc.	12515
Adobe Systems Incorporated	12518
ADTRAN, Inc.	40558
Advance Ross Corporation	12522
Advanta Corp.	12489
Airbus Industrie	40566
Akzo Nobel N.V.	41855
Alcan Aluminum Limited	42408
Alcatel Alsthom Compagnie Generale d'Electricite	41751
All Nippon Airways Co., Ltd.	41752
Alliance Semiconductor Corporation	16807
Allianz AG Holding	40572
Allied Domecq PLC	50001
Altera Corporation	12568
Alternative Resources Corporation	20015
America Online, Inc.	15558
American Business Information, Inc.	15513
American Classic Voyages Co.	15544
American Freightways Corporation	12657
American HomePatient, Inc.	13121
American Homestar Corporation	20161
American Medical Response, Inc.	15818
American Medical Security Group, Inc.	40587
American Power Conversion Corporation	12609
American United Global, Inc.	15518
AmeriData Technologies, Inc.	16433
Anglo American Corporation of South Africa Limited	41809
Apple South, Inc.	15463
Applebee's International, Inc.	13585
Arctco, Inc.	13346
Argosy Gaming Company	14601
Ascend Communications, Inc.	41997
Aspect Telecommunications Corporation	14113
Atmel Corporation	14420
Authentic Fitness Corporation	15727
Avid Technology, Inc.	15999
Baby Superstore, Inc.	42110
Banco Espirito Santo e Comercial de Lisboa, S.A.	42907
Bank of Montreal	42380
Barclays PLC	41754
Barefoot Inc.	15449
BASF Group	41755
Bass PLC	41788
B.A.T. Industries	41762
Bayer AG	41808
Bayerische Motoren Werke AG	41758
BCE, Inc.	43059
Beazer Homes USA, Inc.	16951
Bed Bath & Beyond, Inc.	14933
Bell Microproducts Inc.	16410
Benchmark Electronics, Inc.	13094
Benetton Group S.p.A.	41756
Benson Eyecare Corporation	11905
Bertelsmann AG	40661
BET Holdings, Inc.	10916
Biogen, Inc.	12776
The BISYS Group, Inc.	14874
Bloomberg L.P.	40671
The Body Shop International PLC	41856
Bombardier Inc.	42381
Books-A-Million, Inc.	14665
The Boots Company PLC	42397
The Boston Beer Company, Inc.	40674
Boston Chicken, Inc.	16244
Boston Technology, Inc.	14031
Breed Technologies, Inc.	11296
Bridgestone Corporation	41861
Brinker International, Inc.	10330
Brite Voice Systems, Inc.	12584
British Aerospace Public Limited Company	40681
British Airways PLC	41761
The British Petroleum Company PLC	41759
British Telecommunications PLC	41763
The Broken Hill Proprietary Company Limited	41757
BTR PLC	42398
Buffets, Inc.	12815
Cable and Wireless Public Limited Company	41766
Cabletron Systems, Inc.	10276
Cadbury Schweppes PLC	41767
Callaway Golf Company	15521
Cambridge Technology Partners, Inc.	13621
Cameron Ashley Inc.	17198
Canadian Imperial Bank of Commerce	40707
Canadian Pacific Limited	41851
Canal +	41802
Canandaigua Wine Company, Inc.	11800
Canon Inc.	41862
Carlsberg A/S	40715
Carmike Cinemas, Inc.	12900
Carrefour SA	40719
Cascade Communications Corp.	42090
Casio Computer Co., Ltd.	41863
Catalina Marketing Corporation	15571
CDW Computer Centers, Inc.	16199
CellStar Corporation	41895
Checkpoint Systems, Inc.	12955
The Cheesecake Factory Incorporated	15835
Cheyenne Software, Inc.	12967
Chiron Corporation	12972
Ciba-Geigy Limited	41771
CIDCO Incorporated	17123
Cifra, S.A. de C.V.	42411
Cirrus Logic, Inc.	12986
Clear Channel Communications, Inc.	11824
Club Mediterranee S.A.	42391
Cognex Corporation	13017
Coles Myer Ltd.	42412
CommNet Cellular Inc.	15401
CONMED Corporation	12850
The Continuum Company, Inc.	11847
Cornerstone Imaging, Inc.	16506
Cracker Barrel Old Country Store, Inc.	13128
Credit Acceptance Corporation	15713
Credit Lyonnais	40792
CS Holding	40794
Daewoo Group	40802
The Dai-Ichi Kangyo Bank, Limited	41864
The Daiei, Inc.	50022
Daimler-Benz Aktiengesellschaft	41231
DAKA International, Inc.	13165
Del Webb Corporation	10445
Dentsu Inc.	40829
Deutsche Bank AG	40833
Deutsche Lufthansa AG	41803
Dial-A-Mattress Franchise Corporation	42092
Dialogic Corporation	42073
Digi International Inc.	14110
DOVatron International Inc.	11577
Dreyer's Grand Ice Cream, Inc.	13233
DSC Communications Corporation	13159
EIS International, Inc.	15796
Aktiebolaget Electrolux	41778
Electronics for Imaging, Inc.	15872
Elf Aquitaine	41775
Ente Nazionale Idrocarburi S.p.A.	40875
Evergreen Marine Corporation, Ltd.	42001
Express Scripts, Inc.	15773
Fair, Isaac and Company, Incorporated	13357
Ferolito, Vultaggio & Sons	42106
Fiat S.p.A.	41777
First Alert, Inc.	17196
First USA, Inc.	15687
Fletcher Challenge Limited	42413
FORE Systems, Inc.	42045
Formosa Plastics Corporation	40934
Forschner Group, Inc.	13503
Fossil, Inc.	16093
Foster's Brewing Group Ltd.	42414
Fried. Krupp AG Hoesch-Krupp	41144
FTP Software, Inc.	16553
Fuji Photo Film Co., Ltd.	41760
Fujitsu Limited	41865
The General Electric Company P.L.C.	41750
General Nutrition Companies, Inc.	15942
George Weston Limited	41280
Glaxo Wellcome PLC	41781
Glenayre Technologies, Inc.	14179
Global Village Communication, Inc.	16980
The Good Guys, Inc.	14910
Grand Casinos, Inc.	15382
Grand Metropolitan PLC	41782
Green Tree Financial Corporation	10679
Groupe Danone	41774
Guinness PLC	41783
The Gymboree Corporation	16057
HA-LO Industries, Inc.	10660
Hanson PLC	41784
Havas S.A.	42387
Healthsource, Inc.	13876
Healthwise of America, Inc.	16990
Heartland Express, Inc.	13665
Heilig-Meyers Co.	10717
Heineken N.V.	41852
Henkel KGaA	41028
Herbalife International, Inc.	15594
HFS Inc.	10003
Hirsch International Corporation	16992